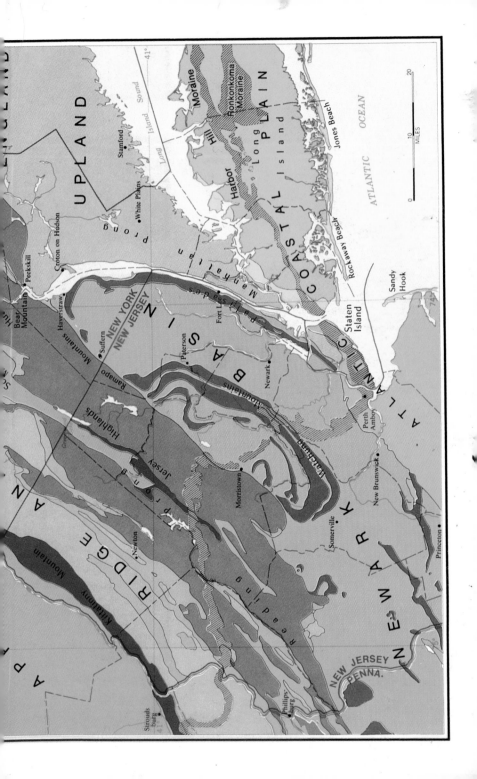

NEW JERSEY WALK BOOK

SECOND EDITION

NEW JERSEY
WALK BOOK

A COMPANION TO THE NEW YORK WALK BOOK

Edited by Daniel D. Chazin

Illustrated by Jack Fagan

NEW YORK–NEW JERSEY TRAIL CONFERENCE
2004

Published by
New York-New Jersey Trail Conference
156 Ramapo Valley Road
Mahwah, New Jersey 07430

Library of Congress Cataloging-in-Publication Data

New Jersey walk book : a companion to the New York walk book / edited by
Daniel D. Chazin ; illustrated by Jack Fagan.— 2nd ed.
    p. cm.
    Includes bibliographical references and index.
    ISBN 1-880775-33-6
    1. Hiking—New Jersey—Guidebooks. 2. Trails—New Jersey—Guidebooks.
3. New Jersey—Guidebooks. I. Chazin, Daniel D. II. New York-New Jersey Trail
Conference.
    GV199.42.N5N494 2004
    917.4904'44—dc22

                                                    2004000954

Cover design by Nora Porter
Cover photo: Delaware Water Gap, by Nick Zungoli
Book design, layout, and typesetting by Nora Porter

Although the editor and publisher have attempted to make the information as accurate as possible, they accept no responsibility for any loss, injury, or inconvenience sustained by any person using this book.

CONTENTS

MAPS

GEOLOGIC MAP *(frontis)*

TRAIL MAPS
(back of book)

PREFACE

This second edition of the *New Jersey Walk Book* is a complete revision of the first edition, published in 1998. The coverage of the book builds upon the basic organization devised by Jane Daniels, editor of the first edition, but the trail descriptions have been greatly expanded, and new features have been added. For this edition, some important changes have been made. The material previously covered in the two chapters "East Jersey Highlands" and "Greenwood Lake Area" now appears in three chapters: "The Ramapo Mountains," "The Wyanokies," and "Bearfort Ridge and Wawayanda." The "Northwestern Jersey" chapter in the 1998 edition has been combined with "The Kittatinnies" chapter. In addition, the description of the Long Path along the Palisades is now included in "The Palisades" chapter, and the sections of the Appalachian Trail in Wawayanda State Park and along the Kittatinny Ridge are described in the chapters that cover these areas. A new index entry, "Public Transportation," indicates which trails can be accessed by those without cars.

This edition has been greatly enhanced by the valuable contributions of Dr. Jack Fagan and Dr. Joan Ehrenfeld. Jack, a skilled artist and illustrator, provided all of the sketches for this edition of the *New Jersey Walk Book,* nearly all of which were drawn especially for this book. Moreover, using his talents as a retired professor of geology, Jack wrote chapter 4, "Geology," as well as the various sections on geology interspersed throughout the work. The author of *Scenes and Walks in the Northern Shawangunks*, Jack also contributed over 100 sketches to the seventh edition of the *New York Walk Book* and wrote the geologic sections of that book. We are all grateful for Jack's willingness to share his extraordinary talents.

Dr. Joan Ehrenfeld, professor of ecology at Rutgers University, added an important component to this edition by writing chapter 3, "Ecology," as well as most of the other material on ecology that appears throughout the book. Thanks are also due to Nancy Slowik, of the Palisades Nature Association, who prepared the Ecology section for chapter 5, "The Palisades," and to Edwin McGowan, Science Director of the Trail Conference, who contributed the Ecology section at the beginning of chapter 11, "The Kittatinnies."

Two Trail Conference volunteers—John J. Moran and Martin Cohen—deserve special mention for their devoted efforts. Both of these volunteers spent

many hours measuring trails with a wheel and then writing drafts of the trail descriptions. John measured and described nearly all of the trails described in chapter 6, "The Ramapo Mountains," and chapter 7, "The Wyanokies," while Marty did the same for those in chapter 8, "Bearfort Ridge and Wawayanda." Other volunteers also made important contributions. John Jurasek coordinated the revisions for chapter 5, "The Palisades." Bob Jonas reviewed the material in chapter 7, "The Wyanokies," as did Alan Abramowitz for chapter 8, "Bearfort Ridge and Wawayanda." Fred Hafele rewrote descriptions for the Lenape Trail in chapter 9, "The Watchungs." Bob Isley and Don Steig contributed trail descriptions for the Morristown National Historical Park in chapter 10, "Morris County." Bob Boysen shared drafts of his forthcoming book on the Kittatinnies, which was invaluable in the preparation of chapter 11, and made many helpful comments. Ken Lewaine, Cass and Ruth Lewart, and Ken Sieben contributed and reviewed trail descriptions for chapter 13, "The Jersey Shore." Others who prepared and/or reviewed descriptions include Sue Deeks, Bob Fuller, Dave Kientzler, H. Max Lopp II, Bob Sickley, and Brian Sniatkowski.

Many state, county, and local park officials provided valuable information on the parks covered in this book. The contributions of several park officials— who devoted special time and effort to improve the quality of material on their parks—deserve special recognition. They include Eric Nelsen and Jim Hall of the Palisades Interstate Park Commission, Janet McMillan and Al Kent of the Morris County Park Commission, Rocky Gott of Kittatinny Valley State Park, Doug Kiovsky of the Hunterdon County Department of Parks and Recreation, James Faczak of Cheesequake State Park, and Tony Petrongolo and Laurie Pettigrew of the New Jersey DEP, Division of Fish and Wildlife.

The selection of "Further Reading" was updated and expanded thanks to the efforts of Loren Mendelsohn, Chief of the Science/Engineering Library of the City College of New York. John Jurasek coordinated the revision of the maps, with cartography by Robert L. Murray. Barbara Erdsneker and Geraldine Ryan assisted with the proofreading. I would also like to thank my friends Tom Balcerski, Kenny Harcsztark, Jon Hutt, Mike Kirschenbaum, Dennis Puzak, and Keith Scherer, who accompanied me on hikes to scout out the trails.

Finally, the book could not have been produced without the dedicated efforts of Nora Porter, who so aptly fit the illustrations to the text and designed the beautiful cover.

Daniel D. Chazin, Editor
New Jersey Walk Book, 2nd edition

ONE

TRAILS AND TRAIL DEVELOPMENT

rails were the first paths in America. The routes of the early Native Americans[1] led from villages and campsites to hunting and fishing grounds, often following streams and crossing mountain ranges through the notches and divides of the rugged terrain. The white settlers adopted these routes for hunting, trading, and military expeditions. But unlike the footpaths of Europe, these American paths were marked by ax blazes on trees. Because these early paths often followed the easiest grades, they were natural routes for the highways and railroads to come.

Early Trails and the Search for Open Space

By the early part of the twentieth century, few of the original Native Americans' paths remained. With the advent of railroads, rural areas became more accessible for the city dweller, and people with leisure time sought out the woods and streams for recreation. However, farmers found these fun-seekers to be a nuisance, and so they often posted their property against trespassing. In response, "clubs" of wealthy businessmen from the cities purchased lakes, ponds, and natural areas, and then closed them off to public use.

Barred from access to open space, those who sought exercise and a chance to enjoy nature followed rural roads. Up to about 1900, these roads provided pleasant walking, to be shared with only an occasional slow-moving

[1]The term "Native American" is used throughout this book when a specific nation is not known.

horse-drawn vehicle. In the first decade of the twentieth century, with the invasion of the automobile, highway surfaces were improved to meet the demands of auto traffic. Secondary routes were asphalted to extend state and county road systems. Walkers began searching for safer, more pleasurable routes. With the state park system making publicly owned land more available, walkers retreated to long-abandoned paths and eighteenth century woods roads, which offered delightful strolls through second-growth forest. However, because these routes were originally meant to take people someplace, they often missed the scenic areas. So hiking clubs and individuals began to build their own trails over routes that the Native Americans and settlers would never have thought of using. These routes were selected because they offered a vista, a stroll through a stand of silver beech, or access to a place that had previously been inaccessible or unknown. Deer paths often proved useful because they followed natural terrain and were frequently the easiest routes up a mountain or across a valley.

The New York-New Jersey Trail Conference

As trails began to spread throughout the Hudson Highlands and the Wyanokies, it became evident that planned trail systems would be necessary if hiking areas were to be properly utilized and protected. In 1920, Major William A. Welch, general manager of the Palisades Interstate Park, called together representatives of hiking organizations in New York. Their goal was to plan a network of marked trails that would make the Bear Mountain-Harriman State Parks more accessible to the public. The meeting resulted in an informal federation known as the Palisades Interstate Park Trail Conference. Raymond Torrey, Will Monroe, Meade Dobson, Frank Place, J. Ashton Allis and their friends planned, cut, and marked what are now the major park trails. The first one to be completed was the 20-mile Ramapo-Dunderberg Trail from Jones Point on the Hudson River to Tuxedo. In 1923, the first section of the Appalachian Trail to be finished was constructed in Bear Mountain Park. That same year, the organization changed its name to the New York-New Jersey Trail Conference, unit-

Figure 1-1. Dickinson, Torrey, and Place (sketch by Robert L. Dickinson, from the first edition of New York Walk Book, 1923)

ing under one banner a number of hiking organizations throughout the metropolitan area.

From its founding, the Trail Conference has been an organization of volunteers. In 2003, this not-for-profit federation of over 85 hiking and outdoors clubs and nearly 10,000 individuals maintained a network of over 1,500 miles of marked trails from the Connecticut border to the Delaware Water Gap. With few exceptions, the trails are for foot traffic only. The Trail Conference's veritable corps of trained volunteers has been both repairing eroded and overused trails and building new trails to standards designed to prevent deteriorating conditions. In 2002, over 1,000 volunteers and 66 clubs devoted nearly 30,000 hours to trail maintenance. But in spite of the Conference's massive efforts, it is estimated that only 2 to 3 percent of the hiking public knows who takes care of the trails.

The Trail Conference also serves as a unified voice for trail concerns and land protection in New York and New Jersey. Over many years, the Trail Conference has been involved in saving open space. When an issue affects trails, the volunteers and staff of the Trail Conference bring their concerns to the attention of organizations that are geared financially and legally to pursue the task. In other instances, the Trail Conference forms a coalition with its affiliated hiking clubs, governmental and law enforcement agencies, other nonprofit groups, and interested citizens to resolve an issue. Partners on various projects have included the Adirondack Mountain Club, Catskill Center, Highlands Coalition, Mohonk Preserve, National Park Service (NPS), New Jersey Department of Environmental Protection (Division of Parks and Forestry), New York-New Jersey Highlands Regional Study, New York Office of Parks, Recreation and Historic Preservation, New York Department of Environmental Conservation, Open Space Institute, Palisades Interstate Park Commission, Scenic Hudson, United States Forest Service (USFS), and the Sterling Forest Coalition. The Trail Conference's advocacy work also includes generating position papers and conducting public education activities.

Since its founding, Trail Conference volunteers and its member clubs have worked to extend hiking opportunities to the public and to build trails opening new areas. Although much of the land upon which they have built trails is publicly owned, about 20 percent is not. Hikers have enjoyed some areas only through the kindness of landowners on whose property the trails traverse. As the population grew, public access to some trails was limited when commercial developers and landowners closed trails due to occasional abuses.

Open Space Preservation

In the 1960s, federal, state, and county governments began acquiring land for public use. About the same time, but on a much smaller scale, The Nature Conservancy, the Audubon Society, and numerous local land trusts and conservancies began preserving open space. These acquisitions increased opportunities for outdoor recreation.

Since its start in 1961, New Jersey's Green Acres program has funded the purchase of over 470,000 acres of open space and the development of hundreds of recreational facilities throughout the state. Nine Green Acres Bond Acts have authorized the expenditure of over $1.4 billion for open space preservation (not including farmland preservation).

In 1997, the New Jersey legislature authorized counties and municipalities to dedicate funds from local property tax levies towards open space preservation, recreation, and historic preservation. By 2002, such dedicated funds had been established by 20 counties and 207 municipalities. These funds generate approximately $156 million annually.

In 1999, in order to create a more stable and predictable source of funding for open space preservation, the legislature proposed an amendment to the New Jersey constitution establishing the Garden State Preservation Trust. This amendment, which was overwhelmingly approved by the voters, authorizes the dedication of $98 million annually for a ten-year period towards open space preservation, recreation, and historic preservation. It also authorizes the bonding of another $1 billion during this same ten-year period, with the debt service being paid from the dedicated $98 million annually.

Minnewaska

Just before the stunning Storm King victory over Con Edison in 1980 (see *New York Walk Book*, chapter 15, "Storm King"), the Trail Conference helped organize yet another massive grass-roots effort, this time to preserve the Shawangunk Ridge. The fight to save Minnewaska, as it became known, was to prevent the Marriott Corporation from constructing a hotel, condominium complex, and championship golf course. In the process, many miles of trails would be destroyed and Lake Minnewaska would be polluted (see *New York Walk Book*, chapter 13, "The Shawangunks").

In 1980, the Marriott Corporation submitted a draft of its environmental impact statement. Testimony at public hearings pointed out the recreational

Figure 1-2. Lake Minnewaska

value of the area and questioned the adequacy of the proposed water supply. The New York State Department of Environmental Conservation (DEC) gave conditional approval to the environmental impact statement. However, DEC was taken to court, with the case eventually reaching the New York Court of Appeals. By 1985, the Marriott Corporation, exhausted by seven lawsuits, and having spent over a million dollars without ever having broken ground, gave up on their plan. Environmental groups pushed for permanent protection, and the property was absorbed into Minnewaska State Park Preserve.

Sterling Forest

The fight to save Minnewaska was barely over when the next threat reared its ugly head—the proposed development of Sterling Forest. This 20,000-acre parcel connects New York's Harriman Park with the New Jersey Highlands.

As early as 1930, Raymond Torrey recognized the importance of preserving Sterling Forest, with its spectacular views and its accessibility for urban residents in search of nature and open space. His vision was not to be fulfilled in his lifetime. When the Harriman family offered the land to New York State as a park in the 1940s, the state declined the acquisition. At that time, state officials believed that the land had too many wetlands, that there were insufficient funds for management, and that New York had sufficient parklands for the future. Instead, in 1947, City Investing Company purchased the property, and immediately announced plans for development. Fortunately, the several small communities that sprang up in the valley did not impinge on the forests, which stayed intact.

By 1980, Sterling Forest had become the largest single tract of undeveloped forested private land remaining in the New York metropolitan area and had been sold several times. In the late 1980s, the Sterling Forest Corporation, owner of the property, proposed a massive development, with homes for 35,000 residents and 8,000,000 square feet of office space.

Spearheaded by the efforts of JoAnn Dolan, former Executive Director of the Trail Conference, and her husband Paul, an executive with ABC News, the Trail Conference and the Appalachian Mountain Club co-founded the Sterling Forest Coalition in 1988. Strengthening the resolve to protect the forest, a Public-Private Partnership to Save Sterling Forest was formed, pooling the skills and resources within the environmental community. Over 30 groups—including the Palisades Interstate Park Commission, New York-New Jersey Trail Conference, Passaic River Coalition, Environmental Defense Fund, Adirondack Mountain Club, The Nature Conservancy, Regional Plan Association, Scenic Hudson, Appalachian Mountain Club, Sierra Club, Appalachian Trail Conference and other regional/national organizations—participated in the most coordinated effort that had ever been made to protect land in this region.

In 1990, Passaic County—with the help of the New Jersey Green Acres program—took the first bold step and paid $9.2 million to condemn the entire 2,100-acre New Jersey section of Sterling Forest. In 1994, New Jersey Governor Christine Whitman signed a bill authorizing $10 million to purchase Sterling Forest land in New York, but only if New York also funded the purchase. Subsequently, New York Governor George Pataki matched New Jersey's support with $16 million, and Congress appropriated $17.5 million. The Open Space Institute and Scenic Hudson each contributed $2.5 million from the Lila Acheson and DeWitt Wallace Fund for the Hudson Highlands, and the Victoria

Foundation contributed $1 million. Smaller donations from the private sector, including gifts from school children, totaled $500,000. The sale was assured when the Doris Duke Charitable Foundation donated the remaining $5 million in December 1997 to create the Doris Duke Wildlife Preserve, for which the Trail Conference currently holds the easement. Much of the private funding was sought by the negotiating land trust leaders of the Trust for Public Land and the Open Space Institute.

Finally, in February 1998, the Palisades Interstate Park Commission (PIPC) purchased approximately 15,280 acres of Sterling Forest for $55 million, forming the nucleus of Sterling Forest State Park. In December 2000, an additional 2,000 acres were acquired from Sterling Forest Corporation, expanding Sterling Forest State Park to over 17,000 acres.

Trail Development

Interest in trail development is more than a local issue. A nationwide project, Trails for All Americans, seeks to have trail opportunities within 15 minutes of most Americans' homes or places of work. In 1988, the President's Commission on Americans Outdoors called for the creation of a vast network of hiking and jogging trails, bikeways, and bridle paths. The commission envisioned a nationwide system of trails that would tie this country together with threads of green, linking communities and providing access to the natural world.

The New York metropolitan area already has an extensive hiking trail system in place. A perusal of the tables of contents of earlier editions of the *New York Walk Book* attests to the long-term availability of trails in this area. What was not always evident was the need for linkages between areas, although two major linkages have existed for years. The Long Path begins on the New Jersey Palisades and extends for over 300 miles northward past the Catskills toward the Adirondacks, linking Harriman with smaller parks and the Catskills. On its way from Georgia to Maine, the Appalachian Trail links the Kittatinnies, the Jersey Highlands, Harriman-Bear Mountain, the East Hudson Highlands, Fahnestock, and the South Taconics.

Many counties, cities, and towns are connecting their parks with greenways. Existing linkages include the Patriots' Path in New Jersey and the Paumanok Path on Long Island. More linkages are possible as the Highlands Trail wends its way between the Delaware and Hudson Rivers.

Assistance in Developing Trails

The expertise gained in the 1980s when the Appalachian Trail was moved onto protected woodlands helped fuel interest in other trail projects. Although Trail Conference volunteers work with park officials to build new trails, trails connecting protected open space need another type of assistance. The National Park Service Rivers and Trails Assistance Program (later renamed the NPS Rivers, Trails and Conservation Assistance Program) funded portions of the project to extend the Long Path north to the Adirondacks. The Trail Conference's volunteer corps grew to meet the challenge of building 100 miles of trail, and the Trail Conference began building relationships with local residents, municipalities, and private landowners. The 28-mile Shawangunk Ridge Trail also forged similar relationships on a smaller scale.

Another multi-partner trail project—the Highlands Trail—highlights the natural beauty of the New Jersey and the New York Highlands region. Begun in 1992 and funded through grants from the NPS Rivers, Trails and Conservation Assistance Program, this trail will run for about 160 miles along the Highlands Ridge from the Delaware River to the Hudson River. When complete, the Highlands Trail will be a greenway in New York and New Jersey linking the publicly owned open spaces. The threat of development in some areas along the route has spurred the project forward. By the spring of 2003, over 120 miles of trail were built and open to the public.

Permanent Protection for Trail Corridors

In 2003, the Trail Conference is implementing a program to permanently protect trail corridors for the Long Path, Highlands Trail, and Shawangunk Ridge Trail. The Trail Conference's long-term goal is to assemble various parcels to create these linear corridors and then transfer them to public ownership. In 1998, pursuant to this plan, the Trail Conference negotiated the purchase of five parcels, totaling 400 acres, needed to protect five miles of the Long Path on the Ginseng Ridge, north of the Catskills. These parcels were acquired by the New York State Department of Environmental Conservation in 2001.

The 28-mile Shawangunk Ridge Trail, which connects Minnewaska State Park Preserve in New York with High Point State Park in New Jersey, has been threatened by several proposals for commercial development on the top of the ridge. Together with other non-profit organizations and the New York State Department of Environmental Conservation, the Trail Conference is actively

working to close the remaining gaps at Roosa Gap, in the Basha Kill area, and north of High Point State Park.

Threats to Trails and Trail Lands

Even with increased interest in protecting open space and providing more trails, threats that were never before envisioned now endanger both trails and trail lands. Interaction with other special interest or non-traditional user groups has become critical to solving problems.

Fiscal Threats

By the end of the 1980s, increased demands for reduced taxes resulted in massive cuts in state budgets. Moneys were no longer available for land purchases, and funds for park management or maintenance were severely curtailed. As a result, not-for-profit organizations have formed partnerships with the state to ensure open space protection and management. For example, since its origin in 1920, the Trail Conference has supplied volunteer trail maintainers. With the budget cuts, state partners have come to rely on these maintainers even more. In New York, Scenic Hudson Land Trust and the Open Space Institute own land that, by agreement, the state will manage until it has funds to purchase it. Fishkill Ridge Conservation Area and Hubbard-Perkins Conservation Area are two examples of land managed in this way. These close relationships allow each partner to specialize in what its staff and volunteers do best and to stretch ever-shrinking budgets.

Children's camps have also suffered from the recession. They require open space, but the cost of upkeep is sometimes too great for a not-for-profit organization to justify holding on to the property. In 1994, the Open Space Institute succeeded in protecting Clear Lake, a Boy Scout property adjacent to Fahnestock State Park. A portion of the property is open to the public for hiking.

Physical Threats

Without proper education, well-meaning outdoor enthusiasts can love a particular trail or scenic place to death. For example, on a holiday weekend in 1994, a nature sanctuary was overrun with visitors because a newspaper article recommended the place. Even when an area can tolerate many visitors, it cannot accommodate the six-pack of beer and the bonfire that some folks consider a necessary part of their outdoor experience.

Non-hiking user groups instinctively use the vast trail network that exists

in the New York-New Jersey region, often not realizing that hikers maintain the trails for other hikers. Bicycles, horses, and motorized vehicles cause damage because the soil and trail design are not suited for anything other than foot traffic. Education and signage are important to ensure that correct users are on the trail and to prevent user conflicts.

The illegal use of motorized and other vehicles on park lands destroys trails that volunteers have labored hard to build. Users of all-terrain vehicles (ATVs) often run through sensitive areas, destroying vegetation and damaging the trails by causing siltation, creating potholes, and widening the narrow path that has been built to respect and fit into the natural environment. Their noise further degrades the outdoor experience by destroying the natural tranquility that hikers seek.

Public Education

As part of its effort to promote public interest in hiking and to educate people about available resources and the safe, proper use of the trail system, the Trail Conference publishes maps and guidebooks. The maps cover trails in the Catskills, Bear Mountain-Harriman State Parks, Sterling Forest State Park, North Jersey, West Hudson, East Hudson, Shawangunks, South Taconics, Hudson Palisades, and the Kittatinnies. Besides the *New Jersey Walk Book* and its companion volume the *New York Walk Book*, the Trail Conference's publications include *Circuit Hikes in Northern New Jersey, Day Walker, Guide to the Long Path, Harriman Trails: A Guide and History, Health Hints for Hikers, Hiking Long Island, Iron Mine Trails, Scenes and Walks in the Northern Shawangunks,* and others. These books complement the *Walk Books,* providing more detailed information.

To join the New York-New Jersey Trail Conference, order publications, or receive more information, contact the New York-New Jersey Trail Conference, 156 Ramapo Valley Road, Mahwah, NJ 07430; (201) 512-9348; visit the Conference's web site, www.nynjtc.org; or send e-mail to info@nynjtc.org.

TWO

SUGGESTIONS FOR HIKERS

f you can walk, you can hike; age is no obstacle. Sometimes, you don't even have to be able to walk to enjoy a trail, as a few trails are now accessible to the handicapped. Whatever your goals, the suggestions presented here should provide enough information to help you start hiking.

A good way to become familiar with hiking trails is to meet and learn from experienced hikers, something easily accomplished by hiking with a club, an organized group, or friends who hike regularly. Hiking clubs abound in the New York area. For a list of them, send your request, with a self-addressed, stamped envelope, to the New York-New Jersey Trail Conference, 156 Ramapo Valley Road, Mahwah, NJ 07430.

Whether you hike with a club or with friends, you will need a knowledge of the area in which you plan to hike if you want to have a safe and enjoyable outing. Trail maps, guidebooks, park offices, and experienced hikers can give you valuable information. Guidebooks and trail maps are available for purchase from the New York-New Jersey Trail Conference. Most camping and outdoors stores, as well as many bookstores, carry trail maps and guides. Trail maps for state, county, and local parks are sometimes available at park entrances, but often lack important details.

Planning Your Hike

Planning a hike is easy if you hike with a club. Most hiking clubs publish a

regular schedule of hikes. Read the description in the club literature or talk to a member, and pick a hike that suits your abilities and interests. If you cannot or prefer not to hike with a club, and you are a beginning hiker, go with several friends. Choose your route from the trails described in this book or in the books listed in "Further Reading," and bring a trail map along.

Level of Hiking Difficulty
Be realistic about your physical condition and any limitations you might have; neither you nor your fellow hikers will enjoy the outing if you are frequently stopping to catch your breath. Once on the trail, start slowly and pace yourself. If you are in doubt, consult with your doctor before going on a hike.

On smooth, level ground, your pace may be two to three miles an hour. It takes longer to pick your way over a rocky path or to hike uphill. You should allow at least 30 minutes per mile, not including rest stops. Measure all the ascents and add five minutes for every 100 feet of elevation gain.

Types of Hikes
The simplest type of hike is *out and back*, which starts at a trailhead, follows the trail (or a network of trails), and returns by the same route. Often, more than one trail begins at a trailhead, so it is possible to go out on one trail and return on another trail, forming a *loop hike.*

Safety and Comfort
You can do many things to make sure that your hike proceeds without incident. Begin by making sure that your maps and guidebooks are up to date and your equipment is in good condition.

Hiking Alone
Hiking alone is generally discouraged, especially for those who have not had any trail experience. A group of at least four hikers is advisable, because in case of injury, one person can stay with the injured hiker while two people go for help. Whether you are hiking alone or with someone else, always let someone know where you will be hiking and when you plan to return.

First Aid
For a one-day hike, carry Band-Aids®, an antiseptic for cuts and scratches, moleskin for blisters, and tweezers to remove splinters and ticks. Put the moleskin on irritated spots before a blister forms. Other useful items are an Ace®

bandage with clips, gauze pads, antibiotic ointment, adhesive tape, and safety pins. Carry these items, plus a pencil and paper, in a lightweight metal box or waterproof case, in your pack.

Learn to recognize the symptoms of hypothermia and heat stroke, which often sneak up on their victims and can be fatal. Hypothermia occurs when the body loses more heat than it can generate, and the body temperature drops. The symptoms of hypothermia include shivering, difficulty using hands, stumbling, losing articles of clothing, speech deficiency, blurred thinking, and amnesia. In heat stroke, the body temperature rises to over 105 degrees Fahrenheit, and the pulse rate can soar to over 160, possibly followed by convulsions and vomiting. For more details on hypothermia, heat stroke, and other medical emergencies on the trail, refer to books listed in "Further Reading."

Waste Disposal and Sanitation
Carry toilet paper in a plastic bag. If no toilet facilities are available, bury waste six inches deep, at least 200 feet away from any stream or lake, and at least 50 feet from the trail.

Hunting Season
Many area parks have a hunting season in the late fall. Park offices can give you hunting schedules, and the *Trail Walker*, published by the New York-New Jersey Trail Conference, prints a hunting schedule in its September/October issue. If you want to hike during hunting season, it is best to hike in areas where hunting is prohibited. Be sure to wear some item of blaze orange if you hike in areas where hunting is permitted.

Inclement Weather
Inclement weather can be any weather from severe cold to excessive heat, with or without rain or snow, and with or without a thunderstorm—which is dangerous primarily because of lightning. If you are on an exposed ledge or on a mountain peak during a thunderstorm, go to lower, covered ground quickly. If you are on the trail, avoid taking shelter under a lone tree, which may attract lightning.

Wet weather is dangerous to hikers even during the summer, because it can cause hypothermia in the event of exposure. The best way to avoid hypothermia is by carrying the proper clothing in your pack: waterproof rain gear (including a jacket or parka with a hood and rain pants), a wool or pile sweater or shirt, and a polypropylene undergarment for warmth.

Winter Hiking
Hiking in winter requires special equipment, such as crampons and snowshoes, to enable you to safely traverse the snow and ice you are likely to encounter. The first time you try a winter hike, make sure you are properly equipped, and go with an experienced group of four or more.

Wild Fruits and Mushrooms
Do not eat any wild plants without positively identifying them. Learn to recognize the common edible berries by hiking with someone who has experience, and by reading some of the publications listed under "Further Reading."

Poison Ivy
Poison ivy grows aggressively in all kinds of conditions. In the woods, it either acts as a ground cover or becomes a climbing vine. It is identified by a group of

three green, asymmetrical leaves, which include a short-stemmed middle leaf; often, one edge of a poison ivy leaf is smooth and curved, while the other edge might have one or more serrations. It may bear white or green berries. Avoid contact with all parts of the plant, including the bare vines.

Contact with poison ivy causes a rash which appears from 12 to 48 hours after exposure. The rash is accompanied by intense itching. Neither your own nor someone else's rash can transmit poison ivy's toxic oil; only exposure to the oil itself will. Over-the-counter medications help control the itching.

Figure 2-1. Poison ivy

If you suspect you have come in contact with poison ivy, wash the affected areas as soon as possible with strong soap or laundry detergent.

Insects
Insect repellent, long sleeves, long pants tucked into your socks, and a hat are the best guards against insects. While DEET (*diethyl M toulamide*) is an effective insect repellent, it can be toxic, especially to infants and children, so it should be used sparingly (30 percent DEET maximum) and only when absolutely necessary.

Ticks are a problem in New Jersey—especially deer ticks, which carry Lyme disease. Deer ticks are no bigger than a pin-head, making them difficult to spot. But the prevalence of ticks should not deter you from hiking as long as you take

the proper precautions. Wear long sleeves, and tuck long pants into socks. As soon as you return home, examine your body thoroughly for ticks, especially in the groin area and armpits. If you are bitten by a tick, take care to remove it slowly with tweezers, so that its mouth part does not remain embedded in the skin.

If you suspect that you have Lyme disease, contact your doctor. Lyme disease symptoms include flu-like symptoms, joint and muscle pain, fatigue, or a bulls-eye rash. Lyme disease can be treated with antibiotics, but if not treated, it can become a disabling chronic condition.

Some people are strongly allergic to bee or wasp stings. If you have had a strong reaction in the past, ask your doctor for instructions.

Snakes

The region's two poisonous snakes, the eastern timber rattlesnake and the copperhead, are rarely encountered. When confronted, these snakes will generally attempt to escape rather than attack.

A rattlesnake is recognized by the rattle on its tail. Its markings are not uniform, varying in coloration from yellow or tan to nearly black. When suddenly disturbed, a rattlesnake will rattle.

The copperhead is pale brown with reddish blotches on its body and a coppery tinge on its head. It is slow-moving and quiet, which increases the chance of an unexpected encounter.

When hiking during the snake season (spring to late fall), be alert, particularly when climbing rock ledges and over logs. Look before placing your hand on an overhead ledge for support. If you are bitten, do not panic; note the size and distinguishing marks of the snake. Wrap the bite tightly with a bandage, but not so tightly that you cut off circulation. Proceed at a moderate pace and, once out of the woods, promptly seek medical assistance.

Rabies

In the New York metro area since 1990, rabies has become endemic to wild animals, particularly skunks and raccoons. Do not attempt to feed any wild animal. Stay well clear of any animal acting strangely or a nocturnal animal that is out prowling around in broad daylight. Do not touch any dead animals, as you can contract rabies from a dead animal. Rabies is fatal if not treated promptly. If bitten by any animal, leave the trail immediately and seek medical assistance.

Bears

While brown bears (grizzlies) are not found in New Jersey's hiking areas, their smaller relative—black bears—have become very prevalent in northern New Jersey. They are more dangerous to your food than to you, and hence are more of a problem for backpackers than for day-hikers. Do not make any attempt to feed them. If you are lucky enough to see one, do not approach the bear. Instead, make lots of noise and move slowly but deliberately in the opposite direction.

Equipment

If you are a new hiker, try using your existing gear and equipment as much as possible until you see what other hikers use, hear their opinion, and decide what will suit you best. You might also wish to rent or borrow equipment to help you better determine what you should buy.

Necessary equipment for a day hike includes adequate footwear, clothing, a hat, rain gear, a first-aid kit, insect repellent (in season), food (or at least a snack), and at least two quarts of water. Some hikers find that a hiking stick gives them added stability. You will also need a pack to carry your gear comfortably.

Footwear

A good pair of boots is of vital importance for hiking. At a minimum, hiking boots should provide water resistance, ankle support, and a non-slip sole. For protection against blisters, wear a pair of heavy socks (such as wool) over light liner socks that can wick away moisture. Make sure your boots fit properly; your feet should have enough room, but they should not slide forward in the boot, which can bruise the toes, nor should they have too much heel lift. Remember that if boots are uncomfortable in the store, they will be even more uncomfortable on the trail.

Make sure to break in your boots before wearing them for a full day of hiking. Wear them for short intervals at home and then on a few short hikes, making sure they are completely comfortable before you wear them on a longer hike.

Clothing

What you wear depends, of course, on the weather and the time of year. In summer, you can wear a tee-shirt and shorts, or you may prefer to wear a lightweight pair of pants and a long-sleeved shirt to protect yourself against

insects, sun, or scratches from vegetation. A hat with a brim provides protection from the sun.

Be prepared for wet weather, whatever the season. Wool and some synthetics such as polypropylene provide warmth when wet. Cotton is a poor choice because it retains moisture and takes hours to dry once it becomes wet. Down is also a poor choice, as it also loses its ability to insulate when wet. If there is any chance of rain or very strong winds, you will want a highly water-resistant, wind-resistant parka.

In cold weather, layering is especially important. Wear your hiking clothes in several thin (rather than fewer heavy) layers. Begin with a light polypropylene garment next to your skin, and add a long-sleeved wool or synthetic shirt and/ or sweater, depending on the conditions in which you will be hiking. Colder weather may warrant wool pants or long underwear. Your outer garment should be a waterproof and windproof parka. A head covering (preferably, a wool cap) is essential in cold weather, since you lose most of your body heat through your head. Other clothing to take in cold weather are wool or synthetic gloves or mittens (mittens retain heat better) and spare dry socks in a waterproof plastic bag.

As soon as you feel yourself beginning to perspire, remove a layer (or layers, if needed) of clothing. Put the layer(s) back on when you stop to rest.

Safety Gear
When hiking with a group, share the weight, as not everyone needs everything. Everyone should have a first-aid kit, flashlight, map, and compass. Additional safety items might include cigarette lighter, pocket knife, personal medications, safety pins, duct tape (wrapped around your water bottle), and a space blanket—an emergency blanket made from aluminized Mylar film, available in camping and outdoor stores.

Food
Hiking is not the time to skip breakfast or scrimp on lunch. A good lunch might include one or two sandwiches, chips or pretzels, an apple or orange, and a candy bar. Many people fare better snacking continually through the day, rather than having one large meal. Fresh and dried fruit, raw vegetables, trail mix, granola bars, nuts, chocolate, and hard candy are all good snacks. Small children, in particular, often run out of energy while hiking and need frequent snacks.

Water

The importance of taking sufficient water on a hike cannot be overemphasized. Most people need at least two quarts of water, more in hot weather or on a very long hike. Do not wait until you are thirsty to drink. To prevent dehydration, make sure you take frequent drinks of water as you hike.

For day hikes, fill a plastic bottle with tap water from home. A Nalgene® bottle (available from camping supply stores) is a good choice, but an empty soda bottle will also suffice. Unless you purify the water by means of tablets or a filter, do not drink from springs, streams, or ponds, as they may be polluted with *Giardia* or coliform bacteria. Do not depend upon finding a reliable water supply at shelters or along the trails.

Pack (Knapsack)

A pack should be large enough to carry your extra garments, lunch, water bottles, safety gear, and insect repellent comfortably. A pack that is jammed tight will not be comfortable to carry, and may feel heavier than it actually is.

On the Trail

Hiking is just like walking—you put one foot in front of the other. Your speed will vary as the terrain varies. In rocky areas, be careful about your foot placement. Do not trust a rock or a log to remain still when you put your weight on it, particularly going downhill. A log can easily roll, and lichen or moss on rocks can be deceptively slippery. Hiking downhill is harder on your knees because of the additional weight dropped on the joint.

Stop and rest periodically. At lunchtime, take off your boots and air out your feet if it is not too cold. Stop at trail junctions if you are traveling in a group and let everyone catch up before proceeding.

Blazes and Cairns

Members of the New York-New Jersey Trail Conference volunteer to be responsible for marking and maintaining over 1,500 miles of trails in the New York-New Jersey metropolitan area. The trails are marked with either painted blazes or plastic or metal tags.

These blazes communicate various messages. Two blazes, with one painted higher than the other, indicate a change in direction; the top blaze indicates the direction of the turn. Three blazes painted as the three points of a triangle indicate a trail's end or beginning. Each trail is blazed in its own individual color

or shape to distinguish it from other trails that it crosses. The trail descriptions in this book indicate the color or shape of each trail's blaze. Where a paint blaze is not practical (for example, above treeline), watch instead for a pile of stones—called a *cairn*—purposely placed to lead you to the next step on the trail.

Unless the route of the trail is very clearly defined, you should normally be able to see the next blaze in front of you.

Lost—You or the Trail?
If you can't find a blaze in front of you, turn around and see if you can spot one going the other way. If you can, use its placement and direction to try and find the next blaze in front of you. If you can't, you should stop, look around, then go back to the last blaze or cairn that you saw. If no blaze or cairn is in sight, look at the ground for a trace of the path. If no trail is visible, stop and relax. Think about where you have been. Look at your map. Do not wander. Three of

Figure 2-2. Cairn

anything—a shout, whistle, or flash of light—is a call for help. If you are with a group or have recently seen other hikers, signal every few minutes while you wait for your absence to be noted, and for someone to come to your aid.

While waiting for help, begin planning what you will do next. With your map, choose the most direct route out to the nearest road or known trail, based on your best estimation of where you are. Note where north is on the map and correct your bearing for magnetic declination—generally about 12 degrees west of true north in New Jersey. Use your compass to follow the route that you select. In most places, following any stream downhill is a good route. If darkness falls, stay put and keep warm with those extra garments in your pack and possibly with a fire, *but note the following precautions:* build the fire in front of a rock, because its heat will be increased by reflection, having first made sure that you have cleared the ground down to mineral soil. Be careful not to let the fire spread.

Taking Care of the Trails and Woodlands

Hiker Etiquette
Do not pick flowers or collect rocks or artifacts—leave them there for other hikers to enjoy. Hike quietly! Use existing trails, and try to stay in the middle of the path. Do not shortcut switchbacks. Not everyone likes dogs, so if you hike with them, keep them under control on a leash. If your dog defecates on or near the trail, bury the waste farther away or pack it out. When hiking with a group, walk single-file except on wide woods roads. If you encounter a wet or muddy spot, walk through it, getting your boots wet, rather than widening the trail at the edges.

Litter
The conscientious hiker's motto is "Leave nothing but footprints." Whatever you carry into the woods, you can carry it out. Help keep the trails the way you would like to find them by picking up litter left by inconsiderate trail users.

Smoking
Leave your cigarettes home when you go hiking, but if you must smoke, do it only when you stop for a break—never when you are moving along the trail. Carry a plastic bag or small metal container to carry out used matches and cigarette butts, and always make sure they are completely out.

Multi-Use Trails
Some trails mentioned in this book are multi-use trails, which means they may also be open to other users, such as bicyclists, horseback riders, in-line skaters, and, in season, cross-country skiers or snowshoers. People in wheelchairs, even motorized ones, are considered to be on foot. No other type of motorized vehicle, however, should be on a trail. If you encounter an ATV on the trail, take down the license number and report it to the park police.

On trails used by horseback riders, bicyclists, and pedestrians, the common practice is for bicycles to yield to pedestrians, and both bicycles and pedestrians to yield to horses. On ski trails, hikers should stay out of the ski tracks.

Fires
On day hikes, you should have no need for a fire at all. The only good reason for building a fire is for warmth in the event you become lost and cold and find yourself in emergency bivouac conditions.

Trail Problems

Report trail problems, such as permanent wet spots, missing blazes, and trees blocking the trail, to the New York-New Jersey Trail Conference. Their volunteers maintain most of the trails in the area, and the Trail Conference knows who maintains the remainder of the trails. If you hike often, obtain a supply of trail report cards from the Trail Conference, which you can use to keep a record of trail problems. The sooner you report problems, the sooner they will be fixed.

Do not be a phantom maintainer—that is, do not do the maintainer's work of clearing and blazing the trail. The assigned maintainer will not mind if you pick up small amounts of litter or throw an occasional small branch off the trail, but for more serious problems, be sure to contact the Trail Conference. If you want to maintain a trail, become a Trail Conference member, and let them know of your interest in trail work. A volunteer will assign you to maintain a trail or have a trail crew contact you. Trail crews are made up of Trail Conference members who go out regularly to repair trails in a specific area. By maintaining trails with other hikers, you will learn the correct trail maintenance skills.

Private Property

Hiking trails are not always on public land. They sometimes cross private land, with the owner's permission. When hiking on private property, stay on the trail, leave no litter, and build no fires, so that the landowner will continue to allow the public access.

Park Closings

When the woods are dangerously dry from lack of rain, parks and public areas may be closed to hikers. The New York-New Jersey Trail Conference urges complete cooperation with the public authorities who make these decisions. When the parklands are closed, stay out of the woods, and request others to do likewise.

Overnight Backpacking Trips

Some parks permit overnight backpacking. However, before you go, check with the park concerning their regulations. Adhere to the group size restrictions. Many areas restrict group sizes to ten or fewer, a good rule even if there is no official restriction. If your group is larger, consider staying at two or more distinct campsites in order to lessen the impact on the environment.

THREE

ECOLOGY

 ew Jersey has an amazing diversity of natural ecosystems.

In the popular imagination, New Jersey is the land of intersecting highways and shopping malls. But tucked between the highways—and in the regions more distant from the maze of pavement—there are forests, fields, and wetlands which encompass a wide range of natural communities. This diversity comes in part from the extraordinary geological diversity of this small state (see chapter 4, "Geology")—which results in many different kinds of soil and topography—and in part from the fact that species from both northern and southern regions intermingle here. In addition, the long history of human habitation and use of the land has modified and shaped the vegetation in diverse ways. Thus, hikers in New Jersey have an opportunity to see more different kinds of natural community than they would probably see in a comparable amount of walking in any other state.

Plant communities are described by ecologists in terms of the dominant types of plants (trees, shrubs, grasses, forbs (broad-leaved herbaceous plants), mosses, etc.), the prominent features of their life histories (deciduous vs. evergreen leaves, annual vs. perennial), and the most common species of the dominant forms. Based on these criteria, New Jersey's vegetation can be placed into three major groups (or "biomes"). In addition, a distinctive set of plant communities which does not belong to any of the major biomes is found along the Jersey shore.

The northwestern area of the state is part of the *mixed hardwood biome*.

The forests in this area contain a mixture of broad-leaved tree species, including maples, birches, ashes, hickories, and oaks. This biome grades, further north, into the northern hardwoods biome, which is found at lower elevations throughout New England. A diagonal zone extending from the northeast corner of the state to the southwest is part of the *oak-hickory biome*. Here, the forests primarily contain oaks and hickories, with smaller numbers of other species. This biome is found throughout the mid-Atlantic region and into the south. It is generally associated with conditions warmer and drier than those found in the more northern areas. Particularly in the Highlands, these two biomes coexist, with mixed hardwoods at lower elevations—in moister, cooler places—and oak-hickory forests taking over at higher elevations, as the environment becomes warmer and drier. The southeastern region of the state is the northern tip of the southern *pine-oak biome*, which includes a large region extending southward from New Jersey along the Atlantic Coast to Georgia and northern Florida. As its name indicates, the major species found in this biome are pines and oaks.

THE MIXED HARDWOOD BIOME

Northwestern New Jersey—which includes the Highlands, the Kittatinnies, and the intervening Great Valley (the areas described in the Ramapo Mountains, Wyanokies, Bearfort Ridge and Wawayanda, Morris County, and Kittatinnies chapters)—contains steeper slopes and higher elevations than found elsewhere in the state. This topography produces strong contrasts between north- and south-facing slopes, which—when combined with the variety of soil conditions in this section of the state—give rise to pronounced variations in the types of plant communities seen in the course of a hike.

At the lower elevations, where the soils are thicker and richer, diverse forests of many species are often found—oaks (red, white, and black), maples (sugar and red), hickories (pignut, bitternut, mockernut, and shagbark), beech, elm, birches (black and yellow), white ash, yellow poplar (tulip tree)—and a number of less common species are mixed together. As a trail wends its way up, down, across, and around slopes, differences in the composition of the forest can be readily observed.

The ground-level plants of these low-elevation stands are equally diverse. They usually contain a mixture of shrubs, including maple-leaved viburnum,

Figure 3-1. Four trees typical of the mixed hardwood biome

several kinds of lowbush blueberry, huckleberries, spicebush, and witchhazel. These shrubs are often mixed with grass-like sedges and true grasses, or with a dense bed of hay-scented fern. Mountain laurel is another shrub that may be abundant and even form thickets, its evergreen leaves and delicate spring flowers giving a unique "feel" to the woods. In other areas, a dense rhododendron thicket may develop, usually on the moister, cooler northern and western slopes. The twisting, intertwined stems of this large shrub form an almost impenetrable maze, and the trail may run through a tunnel of stems.

In these low-lying areas, saplings of the canopy tree species often mingle with several species of small trees that never become part of the canopy. The most noticeable of these subcanopy trees is hornbeam (also called ironwood or musclewood, because the wavy surface of the trunk is reminiscent of a bodybuilder's arm). Another subcanopy tree prominent in the spring is flowering dogwood (although its abundance has been greatly reduced in the recent past by an introduced disease, the dogwood anthracnose).

In the intermediate elevations, the diversity of vegetation depends on the kind of rock that forms the soil. Few herbaceous plants are found on soils formed from acidic, sandy bedrock, whereas limestones and other nutrient-rich rocks allow a great diversity of such plants to thrive.

On north- and west-facing slopes—most often in narrow ravines—hemlocks may form a dense evergreen canopy. Because hemlock casts a heavy shade, these forests often have few or no shrubs or herbs. Instead, a thick, soft forest floor of dead and partially decayed needles covers the ground. Unfortunately, many hemlocks are now dead or dying because of the introduction from Asia of the woolly adelgid. These insects form white masses on the undersides of the needles, and literally suck the plant dry. The hemlock groves often change

gradually into the hardwood forests as one climbs a ridge, becoming less frequent as the grade steepens, and the soils become thinner and drier.

As one climbs and approaches a summit or ridgetop, the forests change notably in character. The trees become shorter and less numerous, and there may be much larger gaps between tree crowns than in the lower elevation forests. The tree crowns often spread out from twisted branches emanating from a short trunk. These differences in shape reflect the harsh conditions of ridges and summits—ice-crystal-laden winds in the winter, desiccating winds in the summer, and very thin, dry soils all year.

Trees found along the ridges differ from those found at lower elevations. Scarlet, black, and especially chestnut oak are most common near the summits, and red maple, black birch, and hickories may also be found. Juneberry (also known as serviceberry) is a common species of small tree, its white flowers providing a spectacular, if brief, display early in the spring, with the berries (sought eagerly by wildlife as well as hikers) present—again briefly—in June.

On the highest, most exposed summits and ridges, a community reminiscent of the Pinelands to the south is encountered. Pitch pines—sometimes dwarfed and twisted like bonsai—are found scattered among rock outcrops, occasionally growing from seemingly soil-less clefts in the rock. Around them may be found short scrub oaks, abundant lowbush blueberries and huckleberries, and a variety of herbaceous plants and grasses tolerant of the very thin, dry acidic soils and the exposed, severe conditions of the ridges. Among the most prominent of these plants are pale corydalis, with delicate yellow-and-pink slipper-shaped flowers, bunches of panic grass and hairgrass, and several goldenrods. Lichens plaster the rocks, and mosses grow in any interstices not colonized by vascular plants.

THE OAK-HICKORY BIOME

The region included in this biome (the Watchungs, Central Jersey, and a band extending south along the western edge of state) is, without doubt, the region most profoundly affected by the history of intense human settlement and use. Farms and towns were well established throughout the area by the late 1600s (English and Dutch in the north, Swedes in the south), with much of the native forest having been cleared for fields, and the remaining woods being maintained as woodlots for firewood and construction timber. The woods that

remain and those that have replaced the farm fields reflect this intensive history of use.

Upland forests are mostly dominated by oaks (red, white, and black) and hickories (pignut, mockernut, and shagbark). Smaller numbers of a variety of other species may be present, including yellow poplar, red maple, beech, white ash, black cherry, and sassafras. The most common shrub in the understory is maple-leaved viburnum. Other understory plants include such shrub species as lowbush blueberry, witchhazel, and spicebush, and several vines—including Virginia creeper, wild grapes, catbriars, and the ubiquitous poison ivy. Unfortunately, a number of non-native invasive species—such as multiflora rose and Japanese honeysuckle—are also common. These forests also support a variety of herbaceous plants on the forest floor, many of which flower in the early spring before the trees leaf out.

As one proceeds southward, several species may be observed that are not found in more northern areas. These include American holly, apparent as a striking evergreen in the otherwise deciduous forests, sweetgum, which drops abundant prickly ball-shaped fruits on the forest floor, and southern red oak. In addition, stands of Virginia pine are found along southwestern edge of the state. A dense and diverse shrub layer combines the shrubs found in north Jersey with those found in the Pinelands and areas to the south. Most prominent in many of these forests are catbriar vines: the tangle of sharp-thorned, green stems is painfully obvious in the winter.

There are also many small pockets of wetland left in the region. Some of these wetlands are remnants of the large lakes—Glacial Lakes Passaic and Hackensack—formed when glaciers dammed the rivers that carried their meltwater, about 10,000 years ago. Over the course of the next several thousand years, these lakes accumulated thick layers of fine clayey sediments slowly settling from the lake waters. Later, colonists and developers found these clays too wet and difficult to drain, leaving them for use as wet meadows for grazing, or simply as swamps for timber. Today, these hardwood swamps provide welcome bits of open space, habitat for wildlife, and opportunities for walking in a largely suburban landscape. Among the trees, red maple is most abundant; other species to be found include pin oak, swamp white oak, black gum, white and green ash, American and red elm, black cherry, and sweetgum. The swamps also typically have a dense understory of shrubs—spicebush, blackhaw viburnum, catbriars, and abundant poison ivy vines. Wetter sites will have a diversity of herbs, and many types of sedges (genus *Carex* and its relatives). The most

prominent sedge, seen in wetter sites, is tussock sedge: as it grows, it forms prominent raised mounds, each crowned by a graceful cascade of grasslike stems and leaves.

The history of human use and human presence is often seen in the forests of this area in the form of multiple-trunked trees, abundant exotic species (in some cases, forming the majority of the plants seen in the understory), and physical evidence of past human activity in the form of ditches, walls, excavations, and unnatural-looking mounds of soil.

THE PINE-OAK BIOME

The pine-oak biome, which extends from New Jersey to northern Florida, is characterized by forests of pines, oaks, and mixtures of oaks and pines. In most of this biome, taller pines—such as loblolly pine, slash pine, and shortleaf pine—predominate. These species are extensively harvested for pulp (used to make paper) and lumber.

Figure 3-2. Pitch pine

The Pinelands of New Jersey, however, differ significantly from the vast areas of pines in the more southerly states. In New Jersey, the predominant species is the pitch pine—a species noted for its remarkable resistance to forest fire. Pitch pine grows in very sandy soils and on exposed, harsh ridgetops throughout the Appalachian Mountains, from Maine to Georgia, but only in the New Jersey Pinelands is it the dominant species of tree over a large region. Pitch pines thrive in the dry, sandy soils of the Pinelands, to which many other species cannot adapt.

For a more extensive discussion of the unique and unusual veg-

etation of the Pinelands, see the Ecology section of chapter 14, "The Pinelands."

PLANT ADAPTATION

An observant hiker will quickly become aware of subtle and not-so-subtle changes in the plant community, apparent over the course of even a short hike. These changes result, in part, from the differing environmental requirements of the various species. Just as individual people vary in their likes, dislikes, abilities, and tolerances for stress, different species of plants vary in their responses to the environment. Among the physical factors affecting plants, the most important are the nature of the soil, the position of a site on a slope, and the compass direction toward which it faces. The depth, texture, and mineral origins of a soil determine both its nutrient-supplying capacity and its moisture-holding characteristics. Soils can range from dense, wet clays that give rise to wetlands, to rapidly draining coarse, sandy soils on which only drought-tolerant plants can grow. They also range from very nutrient-rich to very nutrient-poor, depending on the type of rock from which the soil developed.

Aspect (the compass direction in which a slope faces) affects how much direct sunlight the site receives, and at what time of day. North- and northwest-facing slopes receive little or no direct sunlight; thus, they stay cooler and moister than south-facing slopes which are exposed to direct sunlight. Southeast-facing slopes get sun in the morning, while the air is still cool, while southwest-facing slopes get sun in the afternoon, in the heat of the day. Coves and ravines harbor cool air currents, while exposed ridgetops are subject to extremes of wind, ice, and temperature.

EVER-CHANGING PLANT COMMUNITIES

Ecologists have long known that plant communities tend to change over time, in response to changes in the environment resulting from the growth of the plants themselves. This process, called "succession," is useful in interpreting the history of a site from the quality of the plant community currently growing there. The earliest colonizers of a bare site—whether it is a new dune or an abandoned farm field—require high light levels and cannot grow in the shade. Plants that are tolerant of some shade and do not grow in direct sunlight will become established beneath these early colonizers. They, in turn, are replaced

by others tolerant of heavy shade. Eventually, the highly shade-tolerant plants replace all others. Beech, sugar maple, and hemlock are good examples of such highly shade-tolerant species.

However, this sequence assumes that nothing disrupts the sequential replacement of species. This assumption rarely holds, because disturbances large and small are as integral to the forest as the shade-driven successional replacement of species. Windstorms, outbreaks of insect pests and pathogens, fire, and mortality resulting from combinations of these events create small and large gaps in the canopy. Within these gaps, a light-based mini-succession may occur within the matrix of an intact forest, allowing light-demanding herbaceous plants to flower, albeit briefly. At the same time, the standing dead trunks and the fallen trunks provide home to a large number of animals. Gap-phase reproduction, as ecologists term it, can account for much of the diversity of a forest. Dead and windthrown trees are truly as vital to the life of the forest as are the living trees.

Humans also modify the natural dynamics of forests, both intentionally and unintentionally. Native Americans sometimes used fire to drive game and manage the vegetation that supported the game. The European colonists cleared large areas for agriculture, selectively harvested timber, managed vegetation to promote desirable species, and cut wood extensively and frequently to provide wood products and fuel for the iron industry. Today, almost all forests in New Jersey are the result of succession on former agricultural land or land that was repeatedly logged. Few forests in New Jersey are more than about 100 years old, and even fewer can claim to be "virgin" forest, uncut since the days of the first European colonists.

People have also profoundly modified the forests by introducing species not previously known in New Jersey. Some species were purposely introduced for their useful qualities. Black locust was introduced from the midwest during the Colonial period because its exceptionally hard, rot-resistant wood and thorny branches formed excellent hedges for fields; this tree is now a common part of the forest throughout the state (except in the Pinelands). Others were inadvertently introduced, with disastrous results. The most prominent examples of these are the chestnut blight, Dutch elm disease, and the gypsy moth.

Exotic (non-native) plant species are now part of every plant community. It has recently been estimated that about one-third of the 3,000 plant species found in New Jersey were introduced after the European colonists arrived. In many places, these introduced species have taken over the forest. Thus, thickets

of Japanese barberry and multiflora rose and carpets of Japanese honeysuckle can be seen in almost every patch of woods and field. The forests are also continuously threatened by newly arrived pests and pathogens. In 2003, forest scientists are anxiously watching for signs of the spread of a damaging insect, the Asian longhorn beetle, and a new fungal disease, sudden oak death, which is spreading from California.

READING THE FOREST

With a little bit of knowledge, the history of a landscape can be discerned from clues in the vegetation, and a hiker can reconstruct ecological and human history while striding along. The sequence of tree species that are typical of forest succession is one good clue: the earliest trees to colonize former agricultural fields are red cedars and gray birch. Finding dead or dying trees of these short-lived, light-demanding species within the forest matrix is a sure indication that the site was farmed within the past 40 to 50 years. The size of the trees is another obvious indicator—uniformly small trees suggest a forest that is at most 60 to 80 years old. Another useful clue is the appearance of the forest floor. The ground in a mature forest (over 150 years old) is uneven, due to the mounds of soil brought up by windthrown trees, and is littered by large numbers of dead trunks and large branches from trees that have reached the normal end of their lives. In contrast, a young forest developed from former agricultural land has a flat forest floor, with little dead timber. Similarly, a forest with some dead trees and light-filled gaps is probably fairly

Figure 3-3. Dead trees in Wawayanda State Park

old and represents a site maintained as forest (perhaps used as a woodlot or a game reserve) throughout the 1800s; in a forest without such features, the canopy trees are not yet old enough to begin dying. The density of the trees is another clue: in young forests, small trees grow densely together, but as the forest matures, the smaller, less vigorous trees die and the surviving stronger canopy trees become larger, more widely spaced, and more variable in size.

In many parts of the region, cattle were grazed in forests on land that was too stony or steep to plow. Evidence of this practice can be seen in grassy understories, where shrubs have not yet recolonized, and from bits of very old barbed wire embedded in trees whose trunks have grown around the wire strands. Stone walls also provide evidence that the fields were cleared for agriculture (either plowed fields, livestock pastures, or both), probably early in Colonial history (late 1600s to late 1700s).

Other evidence comes from the form of the trees. One will occasionally see large trees, in the interior of the forest, with spreading branches emerging low on the trunk. This growth form occurs only on trees that originally grew in the open—in the middle of a pasture, for instance. These "wolf" trees (as they are termed by foresters) are evidence that the forest has grown up around this prior inhabitant of an open area. Trees with multiple trunks emerging from one base indicate that the tree originated from some kind of disturbance—such as grazing, fire, or logging—as a set of sprouts from a root base.

In sum, there is much to learn from reading the woods, and this knowledge can only enhance the experience of hiking.

FOUR

GEOLOGY

orthern New Jersey is a region especially well-endowed with a variety of landforms. Looking at a satellite image of this area is a good way to obtain an overview of the various features of our landscape that are a result of underlying geology. Figure 4-1 shows the principal areas of contrasting physiography—the ups and downs—of northern New Jersey. Note the contrast between the relief of the area known as the Highlands and that of the regions just to their northwest and southeast. Observe the differences in height of the ridges in the Highlands and the adjoining areas of gentler relief. Ridges are formed by differing resistance to erosion of the adjacent layers of underlying bedrock that have been tilted to varying angles and otherwise disturbed.

Almost all of the bedrock of northern New Jersey is made up layers that are no longer flat lying, having been bent and tilted during the various episodes of uplift in Earth's history. The weathering and partial erosion of tilted layers have produced the linear relief of roughly parallel high and low topographic elements. The difference in heights of these layers reflects the different resistance to erosion of the various rock layers and their mineral content (Figure 4-2).

Broadly speaking, all of northern New Jersey is part of the Appalachian Fold Belt, an elongate zone of the earth's crust extending from Alabama to Newfoundland. Long ago, this region underwent compression, mountain building, and various episodes of general uplift (each followed by an erosional interval). The overall term for such events is *orogeny*. Geologists now believe that the orogenies of the Appalachian Belt were the result of the slow interaction of separate sections or *plates* of the earth's crust. The outer surface of our planet

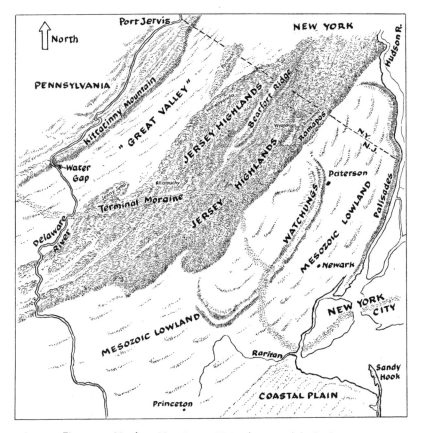

Figure 4-1. Northern New Jersey: Major features of the landscape.

appears to be composed of more than a dozen of these great crustal plates. Over billions of years, these plates have slowly migrated across the earth's surface in various directions, driven by forces operating from the zone below the crust, which is called the *mantle*. At various times, plates have gradually moved apart, slowly collided, or slid past one another. The collision of plates appears to have caused the orogenies that resulted in the formation of great mountain ranges, while the drifting apart of plates has allowed the development of ocean basins.

The early North American plate seems to have collided at least three separate times with crustal plates now located across the Atlantic. These collisions

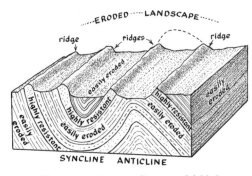

Figure 4-2. *Cutaway diagram of folded strata and ridges.*

caused three episodes of orogenic folding during the Paleozoic Era, known as the Taconian, the Acadian, and the Alleghenian. They are noted in Figure 4-3, which shows the standard subdivisions of geologic time. The time values assigned to these periods are based on the study of fossils and the analysis of radioactive minerals found in rocks. The color Geologic Map, which forms the endpapers at the beginning of this book, shows the approximate distribution of rocks of various ages found in northern New Jersey and southern New York.

Some layered rocks found in northern New Jersey within the Appalachian Belt are not folded. These strata were formed in the Mesozoic Era, subsequent to the last Paleozoic orogeny (folding episode), and they now *overlie* the folded terrain (Figure 4-4).

OUR OLDEST ROCKS

The very oldest rocks found on the surface of the earth are over four billion years old. They are called *Precambrian*, which simply means that they were formed before the Cambrian Period (*i.e.*, over 600 million years ago). In most of the

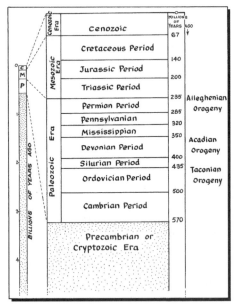

Figure 4-3. *Geologic time scale.*

Figure 4-4. Simplified cross-section of the bedrock geology of northern New Jersey.

United States, the majority of surface rocks were formed during the Paleozoic, Mesozoic, or Cenozoic eras. However, these upper strata are covering an underlying "basement" of Precambrian rock.

In many areas of northern New Jersey, younger rocks have been eroded away so that the once-underlying Precambrian rocks are exposed at the surface. In northern New Jersey, the most extensive area of Precambrian outcrop is the Jersey Highlands. These Highlands may be thought of as an upraised block of Precambrian basement rock. Part of this uplift must have taken place along the great Ramapo Fault that runs along a line drawn from Suffern (at the New York border) southwestward to Morristown. This fault line marks the dramatic contrast between the high rampart of the ancient, upraised Highlands rocks to the northwest, and the Mesozoic Lowland of slightly dipping sandstones and shales to the southeast (Figure 4-4).

The Jersey Highlands are a generally mountainous region, with ridgetops reaching 1,300 feet above sea level in some places. Their topography makes the Highlands an ideal location for hiking trails. Indeed, many regions described in this book are part of the Precambrian Highlands, including the Ramapos, the Wyanokies, and Wawayanda State Park—areas which present the hiker with scenic landscapes of glacially-smoothed mountaintops and valleys with scattered lakes.

The bedrock of the Highlands consists largely of relatively hard and weather-resistant minerals that erode very slowly. As a result, these rocks—despite their age—have attained higher elevations than adjacent younger, softer rocks which have been more easily eroded down. The dominant rock type is *granite gneiss*—a metamorphosed, coarsely-crystalline rock characterized by light bands of feldspar and quartz, alternating with thin, darker bands of biotite and hornblende (Figure 4-5). Almost all the ridges of the Highlands have gneiss out-

crops, usually with conspicuous, steeply-dipping mineral
bands. It is the northeast-
southwest orientation of this
gneissic layering, easily seen on
the summits of the Ramapos
and elsewhere, that accounts
for the direction of most Highland ridges.

The Highland gneisses
(as well as other Precambrian
rocks in New Jersey) were
originally formed under conditions of extreme heat and
pressure, miles below the surface of the earth. Subsequently,
they were exposed to a combination of uplift and erosion.
Several varieties of gneiss may

Figure 4-5. Precambrian gneiss.

be found in the Jersey Highlands, differing in their variety of feldspar and
percentages of other minerals.

Other types of Highland rocks contain high percentages of magnetite. This
uncommon but valuable mineral is an oxide of iron which occurs in relatively
thin layers, or "veins." The presence of magnetite gave rise to the iron mining
industry, important during Colonial times and in the nineteenth century. Ore
from the Jersey Highlands was processed in a number of furnaces located near
Greenwood and Wawayanda lakes. Obtaining fuel for these furnaces required
the cutting of vast expanses of woodland over many decades.

PALEOZOIC LOWLANDS AND RIDGES

West of the Jersey Highlands lies a belt underlain by folded Ordovician and
Cambrian age rocks. This region is sometimes called the Great Valley, in contrast to the Highlands and the still higher Kittatinnies located further west.
Despite its low elevation, this expanse is part of the Appalachian Fold Belt and
has experienced several episodes of folding. Made up of relatively weak shales
and limestones, most of the folds have long ago been worn down to elevations

Figure 4-6. Outcrop showing anticlinal folding in Paleozoic strata in the Appalachian Fold Belt of northern New Jersey.

of only a few hundred feet above sea level (Figure 4-6). Much of the Great Valley is old farmland, steadily being converted to housing tracts. Trail development in this lowland region has been limited to the Appalachian Trail corridor and a few former railroad grades.

On the western end of the Great Valley rises Kittatinny Mountain—a topographic and geologic continuation of the Shawangunks of New York State. The crest of the ridge consists of Silurian-aged quartzite conglomerates and sandstones called the Shawangunk Formation. The outcropping of this extremely erosion-resistant unit (which dips to the northwest) has resulted in ridgetop elevations averaging about 1,500 feet above sea level, with the highest elevation being 1,803 feet, at the base of the High Point Monument (this is the highest point in the state of New Jersey). The Appalachian Trail follows a route along the Kittatinny crest.

The northwestern slopes of Kittatinny Mountain are underlain by a sequence of tilted Late Silurian red sandstones and shales which form the prominent outcrops encountered on trails that climb Mount Tammany at the Delaware Water Gap. (The crest of Mount Tammany is Shawangunk Formation.) Late Silurian red strata outcrop along the west slopes of Kittatinny Mountain from Worthington to Stokes State Forest and into High Point State Park. Downslope from Stokes State Forest, about halfway to the Delaware River Water Gap National Recreation Area, Lower Devonian strata begin to appear, dipping westward toward the Pocono Mountains of Pennsylvania.

On the color Geologic Map used as the endpapers at the front of this book, the Kittatinny region is shown as a purple band (Silurian) with a blue band (Devonian) next to the Delaware River. Note that the only other outcrops of Devonian and Silurian (blue and purple) in New Jersey form an elongate belt trending southwestward from Greenwood Lake that is surrounded on both

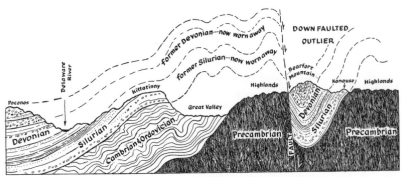

Figure 4-7. Cross-section: Kittatinny to Bearfort Mountain.

sides by the brown-colored Precambrian of the Jersey Highlands. (See also Figure 4-4.) This Siluro-Devonian outcrop, sometimes called the Green Pond Outlier, includes the high, narrow ridge of Bearfort Mountain and an even narrower ridge of the Kanouse.

The Bearfort-Kanouse belt is called a down-faulted *outlier*, based on the probability that these Siluro-Devonian layers were once continuous, at higher elevations, with the same aged strata of the Kittatinny-Delaware River region. Having been lowered along a break, or fault, in the earth's crust some 250 million years ago, the outlier strata were then isolated from the Kittatinny area by long-term erosion of the once-connecting layers (Figure 4-7).

Bearfort Mountain is composed of the very hard and durable Schunemunk Conglomerate, formed in the Devonian era. Sometimes called "puddingstone," this conglomerate contains many well-rounded pebbles of white quartz and pinkish sandstone in a reddish-purple matrix (Figure 4-8). The largest pebbles are over seven inches in diameter, but most are only an inch or two across. The Kanouse ridge is upheld by the Green Pond Conglomerate—a formation of similar appearance but of Silurian age. This reddish-matrix conglomerate has pebbles that are mostly quartz and, on average, are somewhat smaller than those of the Schunemunk Conglomerate.

Figure 4-8. Typical specimen of the Devonian Schunemunk Conglomerate.

The structure of the Siluro-Devonian outlier is basically synclinal. In the north, near Greenwood Lake, this synclinal structure is especially well-devel-

oped, with Terrace Pond filling the very center of the downfold at the crest of Bearfort Mountain (see Figure 8-1). West Pond, further north, also lies near the center of the synclinal structure. Near the south end of the Siluro-Devonian outlier, part of the synclinal structure of the Schunemunk Conglomerate has been truncated by the west border fault. Additional faults have resulted in a mix of the Silurian terrain with the Green Pond Conglomerate on several ridgetops.

MESOZOIC LOWLANDS

The folded structure of Bearfort Mountain reflects the last of the plate collisions that produced the orogenic folding in eastern North America toward the end of the Paleozoic era (Alleghenian Orogeny). Subsequently, the interaction was reversed: the two plates began to move apart and an intervening oceanic crust began to form and widen. The tensional movement (or rifting) also caused a number of breaks to develop, roughly parallel to our eastern coastline. These became the major faults that are found along the eastern United States from Virginia to Massachusetts. Strips of crust adjacent to these faults began to subside about 200 million years ago, forming basins (or rift valleys) similar to those today in East Africa. In our region, the Ramapo Fault is the northwestern boundary of an ancient rift valley labeled Mesozoic Lowland in Figure 4-4.

Beginning late in the Triassic Period, much sediment was deposited in this broad lowland. Under pressure, these sediments were transformed into shales and reddish-brown sandstones. (The latter is a stone used in many eighteenth

Figure 4-9. Columnar jointing: Palisades cliffs.

and nineteenth century dwellings and churches still to be found in New York and New Jersey and considered historic treasures.) Both crustal sinking east of the Ramapo Fault and sediment deposition continued into the Jurassic Period. They were followed by intrusions of magma that rose through cracks and followed bedding planes of the sedimentary layers. Fed by these intrusions and spreading out onto the earth's surface, three basalt flows hardened to form the Watchung ridges. At about the same time, an even thicker mass of magma pushed its way farther eastward. Cooling and hardening underground, this intrusive layer has been exposed by subsequent erosion to become the Palisades cliffs along the west side of the Hudson River. The cliffs were given the name "palisades" because of their resemblance to the vertical log walls that protected early settlements in the area (Figure 4-9).

The Palisades are made up of a rock called diabase. It has essentially the same composition as the volcanic basalt of the Watchungs but with a coarser texture that reflects slower cooling underground than at the Watchungs, where the molten material extruded out onto the earth's surface and cooled rapidly. The igneous layers of the Palisades and Watchungs have been tilted gently to the west and now stand out as ridges above the adjacent, more easily eroded sedimentary layers of the Mesozoic Lowland (Figure 4-4). In the Geologic Map at the front of this book, the Palisades and the several Watchung ridges are shown in red, cutting across the dark green of the Mesozoic Lowland. Also shown on the map—in a light yellow-green—is the adjacent Atlantic Coastal Plain.

THE COASTAL PLAIN

The Atlantic Coastal Plain extends southward from Perth Amboy. With gentle surface relief, it ranges from sea level to about 340 feet in elevation. The Coastal Plain is underlain by beds of sand, clay, and marl which dip at a very slight angle toward the sea. The sediments were carried out to sea and deposited on the former continental shelf during the Late Cretaceous Period and the Cenozoic Era. The relatively young sediments are still unconsolidated for the most part. Along Poricy Brook, a few miles inland from the Atlantic Highlands coast, marine fossils about 75 million years old may be pulled from the still-soft enclosing clays.

Most of the Coastal Plain sedimentary layers represent material eroded from Highland areas of northern New Jersey and Pennsylvania, carried out to the former continental shelf, to be uplifted in comparatively recent times. In

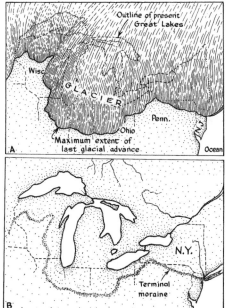

Figure 4-10. A: Maximum extent of Ice Age glaciers in eastern United States. B: Terminal moraine after melting away of the glaciers.

effect, the inner part of the Atlantic shelf has now become the Coastal Plain. The Pinelands of New Jersey is largely underlain by Cenozoic-aged, sandy strata which show their marine origin in the seashells, shark's teeth, and other fossils that are found occasionally in these layers that outcrop along the banks of streams (see Figure 13-10).

THE ICE AGE

In most of the hiking areas of northern New Jersey, whatever the age of the bedrock underfoot, there is also likely to be evidence of a much more recent geologic phenomenon: the glaciers of the Ice Age. During the last two million years, great ice sheets (similar to those of modern Antarctica) spread southward from northern Canada into the United States (Figure 4-10). There were at least four distinct periods of ice advance, each advance being separated by hundreds of thousands of years from the others. Between the periods, the ice sheets melted away. Each sheet left a deposit of debris—a *terminal moraine*—marking its maximum advance. The last of these major ice advances, known as the Wisconsin Glaciation, left the terminal moraine that runs from Staten Island

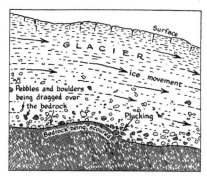

Figure 4-11. Erosion of bedrock takes place when embedded rock fragments are dragged over it.

across the Mesozoic Lowland, the Highlands, and the Great Valley (see color Geologic Map and Figure 4-1).

The glaciers that passed over northern New Jersey during the Ice Age were, on average, some 1,000 feet thick. At their maximum thickness, they covered almost every part of the landscape. With embedded rock debris, the glacial ice acted as a massive grindstone, eroding hills and valleys (Figure 4-11). The overall effect was

Figure 4-12. Bedrock overridden by Ice Age glaciers may show striations (scratches), chattermarks, and grooves, and is often topped by erratic boulders.

the smoothing of the bedrock surfaces. Where large rock fragments, carried from upglacier, were dragged over the bedrock, deep grooves, striations (scratches), and crescent-shaped chattermarks were produced (Figure 4-12). Where only fine rock fragments scoured the bedrock, a gleaming polish often resulted. Glacially-smoothed bedrock is found throughout the Jersey Highlands; especially well-preserved striations and polish may be encountered on the Kittatinny and Bearfort ridges and in Jenny Jump State Forest.

Bedrock knobs overridden by ice typically develop an asymmetrical profile. Smoothed by abrasion on the side from which the glacier advanced, they are steepened on the opposite or leeward side by a process of "plucking," which involves ice freezing into cracks and pulling out rock fragments. Such outcrops are called *roches moutonées* (Figure 4-13) and are to be seen in the Wyanokies, on Bearfort Mountain, and along other hiking routes.

Perhaps the most widespread evidence of the great Ice Age glaciers are the *erratics*—boulders transported by ice and laid down as the ice melted away approximately 10,000 years ago. Erratics can most easily be recognized when they are of a rock

Figure 4-13. Roche moutonée: glaciated outcrops.

type different from the bedrock on which they rest. They are widespread in northern New Jersey and absent in the southern half of the state.

LOOKING BACKWARD

Most bedrock outcrops in northern New Jersey have been overridden by glaciers; some were only lightly scoured, others dramatically sculpted. Ice Age glaciation, however, was just the latest event in the geologic history of a particular rock outcrop.

Different types of bedrock tell different stories. Let us take as an example the purple-red rock that borders Terrace Pond on Bearfort Ridge. Geologists have determined that these layers represent sediment that was laid down in a shallow sea, during the Devonian Period. At that time, a high mountain range—that dated back to still earlier times, probably the Ordovician—was being rapidly eroded. Fragments of its ancient bedrock, including pieces of quartz, were carried downhill by rushing rivers. Tumbling over and over in the rivers, the rocks were worn down to pebbles. On reaching the mouths of these rivers, the pebbles were deposited in shallow, tidal water, where they were further wave-rounded and mixed with finer sand and iron-rich silt. The worn pebbles of white quartz remained embedded in the silts. The iron in the silts eventually oxidized into hematite particles that give the rocks the purple-red color seen today.

By about 350 million years ago, the great accumulation of these pebbly, reddish layers of sediment had become compacted and chemically altered into the very hard rock strata we see today—the Schunemunk Conglomerate. At that time, however, this great thickness of redbeds was still as flat-lying as it had been when laid down near sea level. The next vital occurrence in geologic history was the uplift and folding of the layers. This event—the Alleghenian Orogeny—took place approximately 250 million years ago, when, as most geologists believe, the African crustal plate moved against our American plate. The result was that the Paleozoic rocks of northern New Jersey were warped upward, thousands of feet high in places, and buckled into a number of synclines and anticlines. This orogeny produced the tight Bearfort-Schunemunk Syncline which left some strata steeply dipping, almost vertical in places.

Subsequent movements of the crust along faults, probably about 180 million years ago, together with later erosion, produced the present isolation of

the Bearfort rocks from the similar aged strata to the west in the Kittatinny-Delaware region (Figure 4-7).

In summary, the rocks around Terrace Pond were formed long before the Ice Age came along to sculpt and scratch their surfaces. The pebbles themselves originated in the Ordovician Period or earlier, the beds were laid down flat in the Devonian, folded and uplifted by the close of the Permian, isolated by faulting near the end of the Triassic and by major erosion of rivers during subsequent periods of time. Finally, the Ice Age glaciers put the finishing touches on Bearfort Mountain.

For the curious walker, rocks encountered along any trail have a story to tell. The rocks of northern New Jersey have their own unique histories. The bedrock may be a reddish conglomerate like Bearfort Mountain's, formed in an ocean; the once-molten diabase of the Palisades cliffs; the ancient granite gneiss of the Wyanokies, crystallized thousands of feet below ground; or the basalts of the Watchungs that poured out as hot lava onto the surface. Regardless of the type of rock one may encounter, knowing the geologic history of the area can make any hike more interesting.

FIVE

THE PALISADES

ome unknown early voyager up the Hudson River named the cliffs of the lower river the Palisades, probably because the giant pillars of traprock bore a likeness to the palisaded villages of the Native Americans. In fact, the Lenni Lenape called the cliffs "we-aw-ken," the middle syllable of which means "rocks that look like rows of trees." This unique geological formation begins at the Rahway River in New Jersey, crosses the western edge of Staten Island, continues north along the Hudson River into Rockland County, New York, turns inland at Haverstraw Bay, and then ends abruptly at Mount Ivy. The cliffs are most prominent from Edgewater, New Jersey to Haverstraw, New York, with a brief detour inland at Nyack. The Long Path traverses most of the ridgetop. When combined with other intersecting trails, it offers many opportunities for circular routes encompassing not only woods and meadows but also history and interesting architecture. See the *New York Walk Book,* chapter 17, "Rockland County," for information about the New York Palisades.

History

Native Americans were known to have visited the Palisades, probably just after the last Ice Age. There is evidence of Native American habitation dating back to 5000 B.C.E. in the form of Clovis projectile points found in clam heaps along the Hudson River. They fished and gathered shellfish while living in small villages consisting of groups of barked wigwams. The Native Americans retained their presence along the Palisades until well after the arrival of the first Europeans.

There is some debate as to the identity of the first European to view the Palisades. It was either the Italian explorer Giovanni da Verrazano in 1524 or the Portuguese explorer Estavan Gomez in 1525. Well-documented Palisades events began on September 13, 1609, when Henry Hudson, sailing on the *Half Moon,* made his second anchorage of the day opposite the present location of Fort Lee, New Jersey. Searching for the Northwest Passage, Hudson sailed north on the river that now bears his name as far as the present site of Albany, but he returned when he failed to find an outlet up the river.

The narrow strip of land between the river and the cliffs from Fort Lee to Alpine was known as "Under the Mountain." It had many inhabitants spread up and down the river. Within this large community of terraced farms, there were densely settled areas with names such as "Pear Tree," "Pickletown," and "Undercliff." At the beginning of the twentieth century, descendants of the original settlers were still tilling the ground and gathering French pears from tall and ancient trees. The river swarmed with shad in season. Many families became rich, thanks to the shallows of the river and the rocks on the shore. The swamp-edged island of Manhattan required docks and bulkheads, and the Palisades offered the needed building materials—hard blocks of stone for erecting walls, as well as softer stone for constructing houses.

In the days when river steamers burned wood, it was cut on top of the Palisades and pitched down where the water was deep along the shore—such as High Gutter Point at the state line. When fireplaces heated houses, wealthy New Yorkers bought sections of land on top of the plateau, each with a convenient spot for throwing down wood. These "pitching points" had to have a smooth or small-stone slope, with a fair landing place below, or a cliff edge overhanging the river. If there were huge rocks, logs would wedge or smash; consequently, a wooden chute was built to slide the timbers to shore.

The Palisades played an important role during the American Revolution. In 1776, General Hugh Mercer of the Continental Army built Fort Lee in order to retain control of the river. On top of the cliff, a redoubt guarded the sunken ships and chained logs which stretched across to Jeffries Hook on the Manhattan side, where the little red lighthouse now stands under the George Washington Bridge. In November 1776, after General George Washington retreated from the Battle of White Plains, he watched from Fort Lee the British attack on Fort Washington in Manhattan and its subsequent surrender. As General Charles Cornwallis crossed the Hudson River to Alpine with six thousand men, Washington ordered his troops to abandon Fort Lee in such haste that the

British found kettles on the fires when they arrived. Washington thereupon made his famous retreat to the Delaware River.

Geology

The contrast between the red sandstones and shales, found as horizontal strata at the bottom of the cliffs, and the gray-brown vertical columns above it, may intrigue the hiker in the Palisades. The bedrock of the New Jersey section of the Palisades Interstate Park is of two kinds: sedimentary strata and igneous intrusive rocks. Both were formed during the late Triassic and early Jurassic periods. During the Triassic period, as dinosaurs began to dominate the land mass, the Atlantic Ocean basin started to open. Down-dropped fault blocks formed. For millions of years, sand and mud washed down from surrounding highlands and spread out over wide areas in sedimentary layers, piling up to thousands of feet in thickness. Consolidated by pressure and by the deposition of mineral matter that penetrated the porous mass and cemented particles together, these deposits are today the reddish-brown sandstones and black shales known to geologists as the Newark Series.

After these strata were laid down, molten rock was forced upward, at first through rifts and then between sedimentary layers, to form a single, prominent sill—the Palisades—about

Figure 5-1. The Palisades at Alpine

1,000 feet thick at places for some 40 miles along the Hudson. As the molten mass cooled underground, contraction fissures broke the sheet into crude vertical columns, often hexagonal or pentagonal in outline. Eventually, this rock was exposed by erosion; repeated freezing and thawing caused huge blocks to fall off, creating the talus slopes at the base of the cliffs.

Newark sandstone forms the walls of most of the old Dutch farmhouses in northern New Jersey and Rockland County, as well as the brownstone fronts of many older homes in Manhattan. Reddish-brown ledges of Newark sandstone are exposed in many places along the Shore Trail. The rock occurs near the river level but is often hidden behind the talus.

Ecology

Along the narrow strip of land known as the New Jersey Palisades, there are a surprising variety of plants and animals, forming several distinct habitats. The ridgetop habitat, located along the cliff edge, is dominated by chestnut oaks and red oaks, with a lower canopy layer of black birch, shadbush, and hickory. Exposed outcrops of diabase rock are often covered with lichens and surrounded by plants tolerant of drier conditions, such as grasses, mosses, and certain shrubs (lowbush blueberry, for example). Further away from the cliffs, a mixed-oak forest (characterized by red, white, and black oaks) predominates. Until the early 1900s, when it was decimated by the chestnut blight, the forest was dominated by the American chestnut. Today, chestnut sprouts from old stumps may still be seen along the trails. Migratory birds—such as the scarlet tanager, Baltimore oriole, wood thrush, and indigo bunting—nest along the Palisades in late spring and summer. In the fall, migrating hawks and vultures may be observed from several vantage points along the cliff edge. White-tailed deer, red fox, Eastern coyote, southern flying squirrel, and raccoon also frequent this habitat, but these animals are generally nocturnal and thus rarely seen.

A very different plant and animal community is found along the talus slopes between the cliffs and the Hudson River. Here, native plant species include the paper birch, red-berried elder, and bladdernut, although these have been displaced in some areas by non-native, invasive species—such as the ailanthus, royal pawlonia, and Asiatic bittersweet—which thrive in open or disturbed sites. (These invasive species are also found in the ridgetop habitat.) Along the river, plants characteristic of salt marsh vegetation—such as the groundsel tree, saltmarsh cordgrass, and seaside goldenrod—may be seen. Another species prevalent along the talus slopes is poison ivy, which is actually native to the area. Reptiles found here include the northern copperhead, black rat snake, and five-lined skink. The Palisades is also the only refuge in New Jersey for the Allegheny woodrat, an endangered species.

History of the Palisades Interstate Park

The beginning of the Palisades Interstate Park dates from the time when the residents of New York City were slowly aroused to the devastations of the quarrymen blasting along the cliffs for traprock. Around the middle of the nineteenth century, much of the loose and easily accessible talus was removed to be used as ships' ballast. The real menace to the Palisades came with the demand for more concrete to build skyscrapers and roads. Quarries were opened from Weehawken to Hook Mountain. To stop this activity, New York and New Jersey jointly created the Palisades Interstate Park Commission (PIPC) in 1900. Enabling legislation in New Jersey was advanced by the New Jersey Federation of Women's Clubs. In New York, Andrew H. Green, founder of the American Scenic and Historic Preservation Society, worked for the necessary legislation with the support of Governor Theodore Roosevelt and other conservation-minded officials. Land was acquired and developed as parks, with the appropriate facilities.

In the early days, most of this development was accomplished through gifts of money donated by the commissioners and other interested individuals, with most of the early protection occurring in New Jersey. Eventually, it was the two states which provided funds for development projects. Of the many individuals who contributed generously of their time, talents, and money to create the park system, special recognition must be given to George W. Perkins, Sr., who was the Commission's first president and the organizing genius of its development. With the story of his leadership should be coupled the generosity of J. Pierpont Morgan at a critical time, and other notable gifts of land and funds, both private and public. As a result, quarrying of the river faces of much of the Palisades in Bergen and Rockland counties was stopped. Subsequently, the PIPC was also charged with preserving the natural beauty of the lands lying in New York State on the west side of the Hudson, including the Ramapo Mountains as well as other state park lands in Rockland and Orange counties and those in Sullivan and Ulster counties outside the Catskill Forest Preserve.

In 1933, John D. Rockefeller, Jr. offered to the PIPC certain parcels of land on top of the Palisades that he had been assembling for some time. He wanted to preserve these Palisades ridgetop lands from uses that were inconsistent with PIPC's ownership and to protect the Palisades themselves. This was largely in response to the building of the George Washington Bridge and the realization that this would likely bring vast development to the top of the Palisades. He

also hoped that an adequately wide strip of the land might ultimately be developed as a parkway. At the time, there seemed little likelihood of finding funds for a parkway, but various options were explored. In 1935, legislation was passed that enabled the Commission to accept deeds to the land offered. Additional properties were donated by the Twombleys and by the trustees of the estate of W.O. Allison. The parkway, completed to Bear Mountain in 1958, is a tree-lined, limited-access drive for noncommercial traffic only. Since 1937, both the New York and New Jersey sections of the Palisades Interstate Park have been administered by PIPC under a compact that legally cemented a uniquely successful tradition of cooperation between the two states.

PALISADES STATE PARK

The New Jersey section of the Palisades Interstate Park, officially known as the Palisades State Park, encompasses about 2,500 acres along the Hudson River from Fort Lee to the New York-New Jersey state line. It is a long narrow park, averaging less than an eighth of a mile wide. Those arriving by car have several access points from US 9W and the Palisades Interstate Parkway, with parking available at the Fort Lee Historic Park, Alpine Administration Building, and State Line Lookout. Roads lead down the cliffs to Ross Dock, Englewood Boat Basin, and Alpine Boat Basin, where parking is available. The park is also readily accessible by public transportation. Red and Tan Lines buses #9A and #9W run hourly along US 9W to and from the George Washington Bridge Bus Station and the Port Authority Bus Terminal at 41st Street. For information on bus service, contact the Red and Tan Lines (Rockland Coaches) at (201) 263-1254; www.redandtanlines.com.

For general information about the park, contact Palisades Interstate Park, New Jersey Section, P.O. Box 155, Alpine, NJ 07620; (201) 768-1360; www.njpalisades.org.

Trails in Palisades State Park

Two main trails traverse the length of the Jersey Palisades: the Long Path, which runs along the top of the cliffs, and the Shore Trail, which runs along their base. In addition, several trails climb the Palisades, linking the Long Path with the Shore Trail and making loop hikes possible.

At State Line Lookout, there are several old bridle paths, built in the 1930s, that crisscross the area between the cliffs and the Parkway. These paths are now used for walking and, given the proper snow conditions, cross-country skiing. The old US 9W roadbed, now closed to vehicular traffic, which extends north from the State Line Lookout to the state line, is another option for those who want an easy walk.

Long Path   *Length: 13.0 miles Blaze: aqua*

Extending north from the George Washington Bridge, the Long Path follows the level cliff-top of the Palisades. For most of the way to the State Line Lookout, it runs along a narrow strip of land between the Parkway and the cliff edge. As a result, the sounds of traffic on the Parkway can be heard along the trail. North of State Line Lookout, the parkway curves further inland, so hikers along this section of the Long Path can escape the sounds of the automotive traffic.

For those coming from New York City, the most scenic approach to the Long Path is on foot across the George Washington Bridge. Frequent bus service is available from the George Washington Bridge Bus Station to the Bridge Plaza in Fort Lee. For those arriving by car, parking is available at the Fort Lee Historic Park.

The Long Path begins at the Fort Lee Historic Park, just off Hudson Terrace in Fort Lee. It follows a macadam path down to Hudson Terrace, then turns right and continues north along the paved sidewalk. After crossing under the George Washington Bridge at 0.3 mile, the trail turns right at the foot of the stairs leading up to the north side pedestrian walkway of the bridge. It crosses a pedestrian bridge over the ramp leading from the bridge to the Palisades Interstate Parkway and follows a wide path which swings towards the edge of the cliff. As the trail turns left to parallel the cliff edge, a side trail continues ahead to a broad viewpoint over the Hudson River, with the George Washington Bridge to the south and Ross Dock to the north.

At 0.8 mile, the Carpenters Trail (blue) descends to the right, leading to the Shore Trail. The Carpenters Trail runs jointly with the Long Path for 300 feet, and then leaves to the left, towards a footbridge over the Palisades Interstate Parkway. Here, a short unmarked trail to the right leads to a viewpoint over the river, with Ross Dock directly below to the north. The Long Path continues ahead, parallel to and just below the level of the Parkway, with views through the trees over the river to the right.

Figure 5-2. View from the Long Path above Englewood Boat Basin

After passing a concrete base to the right—the former site of a mounted cannon from the Spanish-American War—the Long Path passes several stone walls. At 1.4 miles, the trail passes to the right of a gas station along the Parkway, where water, restrooms, and snacks are available. Just north of the gas station, the Long Path crosses a concrete slab which spans a stream.

Reaching the iron fence surrounding Allison Park at 1.6 miles, the Long Path turns left, then turns right and follows the paved access road leading to the park. Although the Long Path skirts it, the park (maintained by the Palisades Interstate Park Commission) is open to the public for most of the year (pets not permitted). Restrooms and water are available seasonally, and it offers views over the Hudson River.

Just beyond the next intersection, the Long Path bears left and heads uphill. It continues north along a parapet which overlooks the grounds of St. Peter's College to the right. This parcel—the former site of the Palisades Mountain House, built in 1871 and destroyed by fire in 1884—is the only one along the Palisades that remains in private ownership. After passing St. Michael's Villa, the Long Path follows the shoulder of the Parkway, then bears right and reenters the woods. It soon turns left and follows an abandoned paved road—a remnant of a "tourist camp" operated by the Palisades Interstate Park Commission in the 1920s and 1930s. As the trail once again approaches the Park-

way, the pavement ends, and the Long Path continues ahead on a footpath below the level of the Parkway.

At 2.4 miles, the Long Path crosses a bridge over a wide stream and descends stone steps to reach Palisade Avenue. Here, the Dyckman Hill Trail (yellow) descends to the Englewood Boat Basin. The Long Path bears right, turns left at the next intersection and climbs steps to the right, then turns left to closely parallel the cliff edge. It soon traverses the former Dana Estate, with an exotic Austrian pine near the Parkway. Then, at 3.1 miles, as the Long Path turns left, an unmarked trail leads ahead to the High Tom promontory—once used for pitching logs to the river below—with expansive views over the river.

The Long Path passes through the Rockefeller Lookout at 3.5 miles, with views across the river of the Henry Hudson Bridge, spanning the Harlem River, and Manhattan's Inwood Park. The medieval-looking monastery is the Cloisters of the Metropolitan Museum of Art. Reentering the woods at the northern end of the lookout, the Long Path passes the stone ruins of the former Cagdene Estate. After passing a depressed meadow known as Devil's Hole, a short side trail to the right leads to Clinton Point—a striking viewpoint, with the cliff edge appearing to overhang the water below. Soon, the Long Path crosses a stream on a stone-faced bridge and, just beyond, the trail begins to run along the fence of the Greenbrook Sanctuary, to the right.

At 5.4 miles, the Long Path crosses the entrance road to the Greenbrook Sanctuary, a nature preserve with several miles of trails and an interpretive center, open to members only (except for special events). The Long Path continues north along the fence, descending below the grade of the Parkway to cross two streams. Just beyond the end of the fence, at 6.3 miles, the Huyler's Landing Trail (red), which connects to the Shore Trail, leaves to the right.

The Long Path reaches the Alpine Lookout at 6.8 miles. The lookout is built on the site of Manuel Rionda's "Rio Vista" estate—the largest of the cliff-top estates along the Palisades. The best viewpoint is from a pinnacle just south of the parking area. At the end of the lookout, the trail reenters the woods. It goes by a series of old stone walls and foundations, with views to the right of the Alpine Boat Basin far below. At 8.2 miles, an underpass to the left leads to US 9W and Closter Dock Road.

At 8.4 miles, the Long Path goes through a tunnel beneath the Alpine Approach Road. On the north side of the tunnel, it reaches a T intersection. To the right, the Closter Dock Trail (orange) descends to the Alpine Boat Basin and the Shore Trail. The Long Path turns left and continues along the paved road,

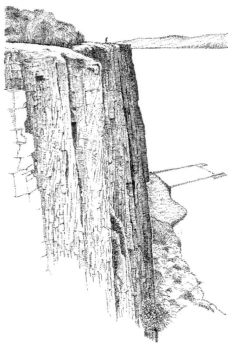

Figure 5-3. Ruckman Point

passing the Administration Building for the New Jersey section of the Palisades Interstate Park (the former Oltman House). Restrooms and water are available at the Administration Building (which also serves as the park police headquarters), and hikers may park in a parking lot just north of the building. At the northern end of the parking lot, the Long Path reenters the woods on a wide path. Soon, the Armstrong Radio Tower—the first FM radio tower in the world, built in the 1920s—is visible to the left, west of the parkway.

The Long Path continues through the woods, with views over the Hudson River to the right. In winter, 300-foot-high ice columns often form where the water plunges over the cliff edge. The trail passes Bombay Hook and continues over broad, flat rocks to reach the end of abandoned and overgrown Ruckman Road at 10.3 miles. Here, a short distance to the right of the trail, there are fine views from Ruckman Point (just south of a concrete-block wall), 520 feet above the river. The abandoned pilings in the river to the north are the remains of the former Forest View marina.

In another 75 feet, the Long Path continues straight ahead as a wide path to the right—a dead-end route—leads for 0.2 mile over a section of cliff that has split from the main face of the Palisades, with excellent views. The Long Path now proceeds through the former Burnet Estate, passing some exotic plants that were planted by the estate's former owners. At 10.7 miles, the trail bears right at a Y intersection and, in another 500 feet, a wide woods road joins from the left. To the left, the road is the route of the Forest View Trail (blue/white), which leads to a footbridge over the Parkway and to US 9W (where limited

parking is available). The entrance to Camp Alpine of the Boy Scouts of America, where Red and Tan Lines buses #9A and #9W stop, is a short distance to the north along US 9W.

The Long Path continues straight ahead (joining the Forest View Trail) and, at 10.9 miles, reaches the Women's Federation Monument, a watchtower built to commemorate the efforts of the New Jersey Federation of Women's Clubs at the beginning of the twentieth century to preserve the Palisades. The trail proceeds north from the clearing for the monument and descends rather steeply on rock steps. At the base of the descent, the Forest View Trail leaves to the right, descending very steeply to reach the Shore Trail near Forest View. The Long Path continues ahead, crossing a stream, and begins to climb on rock steps.

At the top of the climb, the Long Path turns right and runs along the access road to the State Line Lookout. This paved road was originally built as part of New Jersey State Highway Route 1 (later designated as US 9W), but the road was cut off when the Palisades Interstate Parkway was constructed in the 1950s. A short distance ahead, the road is blocked off with large rocks (vehicles bear left here to reach a parking area). Then, at 11.6 miles, the Long Path passes the State Line Lookout. To the left, the Lookout Inn offers snacks, souvenirs, water, restrooms, and a phone. Several cross-country ski trails, which follow woods roads formerly used as bridle paths, begin here. To the right, Point Lookout, which offers a panoramic view over the river, is the highest point in the New Jersey section of the Palisades Interstate Park (532 feet).

In another 750 feet, the Long Path bears right, leaving the paved road (which turns inland), and begins to follow a woods road that runs parallel to the cliffs. This woods road is also designated as Ski Trail E. At 12.2 miles, Ski Trail E leaves sharply to the left. Just ahead, the Long Path turns right onto a narrower path, then again turns right at a chain-link fence which marks the New Jersey-New York state line. It descends on stone steps along the fence, passing a stone boundary monument erected in 1882, then turns left and goes through a gate in the fence, entering New York. Continuing close to the edge of the cliffs, the trail passes High Gutter Point, whose name recalls the early wood-burning river steamboats that docked at a wooden chute along the riverbank to obtain fuel. Hook Mountain, the mile-long pier at Piermont and the Tappan Zee Bridge may be seen to the north.

After descending, sometimes steeply, on stone steps, the Long Path enters Skunk Hollow, with hemlocks and waterfalls, at 12.5 miles. (Unfortunately, the

Figure 5-4. George Washington Bridge from the Shore Trail

hemlocks have been greatly diminished due to infestation by the woolly adelgid.) It bears left and descends more gradually, entering the Lamont Sanctuary (the site of a former African-American community). After crossing a stream on wooden bridges, the Shore Trail (white) leaves to the right. The Long Path turns left and follows the stream, ascending gradually. At 13.0 miles, it reaches US 9W at the entrance to the Lamont-Doherty Earth Observatory, just north of the New Jersey-New York state line. Red and Tan buses #9A and #9W stop here.

For information on the route of the Long Path to the north, consult the *Long Path Guide,* published by the Trail Conference.

Shore Trail *Length: 12.2 miles Blaze: white*

The Shore Trail runs along the Hudson River from Fort Lee to the New Jersey-New York state line. For most of its route, it follows a nearly-level path that closely hugs the shoreline, but north of Forest View, about 10.5 miles from the start, its character becomes rugged as it weaves up and down among the talus, and it then climbs rather steeply to its end at the state line.

The trail can be reached via foot or bus across the George Washington Bridge to Bridge Plaza in Fort Lee. From the bus stop, walk south to the first cross street and turn left, toward the river. At the base of the incline, turn right onto Hudson Terrace, which leads to the entrance to Fort Lee Historic Park. For those arriving by car, parking is available here. The historic park offers views over the Hudson River and Manhattan. The redoubt of 1776 on the

southern tip (Bluff Point)—which guarded the barriers placed in the river to prevent passage by the British—has been recreated. Exhibits at the visitor center explain the events which took place here during the Revolutionary War.

Returning to the street, the hiker should turn left and follow Hudson Terrace downhill to the park entrance and the beginning of the Shore Trail. At first, the trail follows a gravel path parallel to the Henry Hudson Drive, but it soon descends to the river on stone steps. The trail heads north, reaching the Hazzards' boat launching ramp, just south of the George Washington Bridge, at 0.6 mile. From here north to Ross Dock, the Shore Trail follows along the paved access road to Hazzard's Ramp. The absence of talus at the base of the cliffs in this area is the result of the quarrying once done here.

At 1.1 miles, the Carpenters Trail (blue) leaves to the left. The first of five connector trails between the Shore Trail and the Long Path, the Carpenters Trail climbs on switchbacks to the top of the cliffs, passing panoramic views over the river on the way. A short distance beyond, the Shore Trail goes through a pedestrian tunnel beneath the Ross Dock access road and enters the Ross Dock picnic and recreation area, renovated by the park in 2000. Restrooms are available seasonally here.

In several locations along the trail north of Ross Dock, steps lead into the river—remnants of swimming beaches that once lined the river in this area. Then, at 2.5 miles, the Shore Trail reaches a refreshment stand at the southern end of the Englewood Boat Basin, where parking is available. A short distance beyond, the Dyckman Hill Trail (yellow)—the second connector trail to the top of the cliffs, which follows a cascading stream for part of the way—leaves to the left.

The Shore Trail continues north through the boat basin. After going through the Bloomers picnic area at the northern end of the boat basin, it passes the stone ruins of a bathhouse above to the left. A short distance beyond, a high tide detour trail leaves to the left (it rejoins the Shore Trail in 0.3 mile). The Shore Trail goes around Franks Rock—a huge boulder hanging between the trail and the shoreline—with the High Tom promontory towering above. At 3.2 miles, the trail briefly runs adjacent to the Henry Hudson Drive, which descends to the river level here. This area was part of the settlement known as "Under the Mountain" in the days before the park was established. Scattered between the small farms were quarries, fishing shacks, and manure and bone factories. A small cemetery—a relic of this settlement—is located just west of the Henry Hudson Drive here. A short distance beyond, the trail passes

the ruins of the Undercliff bathhouse, built in 1922.

At the Canoe Beach—about half a mile north of the Undercliff bathhouse—the trail passes some old stone picnic tables, fashioned from rocks fallen from the cliffs. Then, at 4.5 miles, the remnants of Powder Dock may be seen jutting into the river on the right, with Clinton Point looming above between the trees. After crossing Lost Brook at 4.9 miles, with a small waterfall, the trail passes a curved wall to the left. Just beyond, the trail goes through the overgrown Lambier's picnic area, with a beautiful view upriver to the north.

At 5.8 miles, the trail reaches Greenbrook Falls—a large waterfall over a rock face to the left. The falls may be only a trickle in August and an ice mass in January, and are most impressive after spring rains. The trail crosses just below the falls on large boulders. Half a mile beyond Greenbrook Falls, the trail passes the ruins of Huyler's Dock—a stone jetty to the right. This was an important transfer point for goods and passengers between the interior of New Jersey and New York City in the nineteenth century. Just beyond, at 6.3 miles, a woods road departs to the left by a picnic table. This is the Huyler's Landing Trail (red)—the third connector between the Shore Trail and the Long Path—which follows the old road (said to be used by the British under Cornwallis to ascend the cliffs in 1776) to the top of the cliffs.

For the remaining mile to the Alpine Boat Basin, the path wanders up and down the washouts along the river's edge. Beyond a fine growth of laurel is a big boulder called *Hay-Kee-Pook* (his body). Legend has it that a lovelorn Native American committed suicide here. When the trail reaches the grassy level, the slender pinnacle of Bombay Hook is visible to the north. This highest, most isolated, and most conspicuous pillar of rock along the Palisades curves up 70 feet between two mighty slides.

At 7.6 miles, the Shore Trail reaches the Alpine Boat Basin, with parking and picnic facilities. Just beyond is the Kearney House. Originally it was a farm house, then a nineteenth-century homestead and tavern, and eventually a park police station. In the summer, it is open as a museum. Behind the Kearney House is the start of the Closter Dock Trail (orange), which climbs on switchbacks to join the Long Path near the present park Administration Building.

Figure 5-5. Kearney House

About half a mile north of the Al-

Figure 5-6. Giant Stairs

pine Boat Basin, the Shore Trail passes Cape Flyaway, a fishermen's village in the nineteenth century. A short distance beyond, the trail arrives at a fork. The path to the left traverses a former picnic ground before rejoining the Shore Trail in about half a mile, just south of Bombay Hook. The Shore Trail follows the right fork, which leads to Excelsior Dock and continues to the grassy expanse at Twombley's Landing, named for the former owner who donated his land to the park. Half a mile farther—beyond the point at which the upland trail rejoins the Shore Trail and near a stand of white birch—hikers have a view of two big points protruding from the cliff face.

At 10.0 miles, near the former Forest View landing (once a park picnic area), the Forest View Trail (blue/white)—the most northerly connector path—ascends steeply on stone steps to the top of the cliffs. About half a mile north of Forest View, the Shore Trail goes by the 500-foot-high cliffs of Indian Head, a rock formation thought to resemble the face of a Native American.

A short distance beyond Indian Head, the trail becomes much rougher as it traverses the talus of the Giant Stairs—immense blocks of stone shed from the cliffs. This stretch of rock scrambling is slow and difficult for even the agile hiker. The trail climbs over the caves and cavities created by these rock masses—homes for raccoons, foxes, rodents, and snakes—with traverses over mixed scree and talus alternating with wooded segments. In this area, the trail is often marked with white crescent blazes.

After descending the "stairs" to the shore, the Shore Trail passes a swampy section that marks the state line. The trail continues ahead along the shore until

it reaches an "Italian Garden," with ruins of colonnades (once part of the Lawrence-Tonetti Estate) at the foot of the Peanut Leap Cascade. Here, the trail leaves the shoreline just beyond a small patio on the north side of the cascade, and it begins to climb, paralleling the stream. At 12.2 miles, at the top of the climb, the Shore Trail ends at a junction with the Long Path (aqua). To the left, the Long Path leads to State Line Lookout in 1.1 miles. Continuing straight leads to US 9W at the state line in 0.4 mile.

OTHER AREAS NEAR THE PALISADES

Two nature sanctuaries adjacent to the Palisades cliffs provide opportunities for short walks through pleasant surroundings. The nearby Teaneck Greenway enables pedestrians to explore the banks of the Hackensack River.

Flat Rock Brook Nature Center

The 150-acre Flat Rock Brook Nature Center, nestled in a suburban area, was founded in 1973 to protect open space in Englewood and provide environmental education for both children and adults. The 3.5 miles of marked trails take visitors along streams, past ponds and wetlands, through wildflower meadows and woodlands, and along the base of quarry cliffs. An 800-foot boardwalk loop trail is accessible to the handicapped.

A suggested 1.7-mile loop hike begins at the sign for the "Children's Garden" at the rear entrance to the nature center building. Continue on the White Trail, which climbs gently to a meadow where the Yellow Trail intersects, and continue ahead on the White Trail to a T intersection. Turn left here and follow both white and blue blazes along a wide path. At the next Y intersection, bear left onto the White Trail, as the Blue Trail continues straight ahead, then turn left at the next junction. Just ahead is an overlook to the southwest. The tall building in the foreground is the Marriott at Glenpointe in Teaneck. On a clear day, the First Watchung Mountain is visible in the distance.

Return to the junction and continue straight ahead on the Red Trail. Proceed ahead, following the red blazes, as the White Trail leaves to the left and the Blue Trail leaves to the right. (At the latter intersection, follow the signs to the "bridge"). The Red Trail now begins a gentle descent. At the next Y intersection, bear right onto the Yellow Trail, which continues to descend a little more steeply, then levels off.

Be alert for a sharp right turn in the Yellow Trail, adjacent to a yellow "B.C.U.A." sign. Continue on the Yellow Trail as it crosses Flat Rock Brook on large boulders, then immediately turn left onto the Orange Trail. Follow the Orange Trail as it parallels the brook, with private residences beyond a fence to the right. Soon the brook widens into MacFadden's Pond, named for the physical culturist Bernarr MacFadden (1868-1955), who lived nearby in the early 1900s. At the end of the pond, cross a wooden bridge over its outlet. On the opposite side of the bridge, turn right onto the Red Trail. Follow the Red Trail as it descends along an attractive stream, with wooden steps provided along the steeper sections, and turn left at a T intersection at the bottom of the hill, following the sign pointing to the "nature center." (Straight ahead, the trail leads in a short distance to a picnic area with a children's nature playground and restrooms.) The Red Trail now ascends steadily. At the top of the climb, turn right onto a wide path, again following the sign to the "nature center," continue ahead on the wide path where the Red Trail leaves to the left, then turn left at the paved road to return to the parking area.

To reach the Flat Rock Brook Nature Center, take NJ 4 to the Jones Road exit in Englewood. Turn right at the top of the ramp, and continue to the first stop sign, which is Van Nostrand Avenue. Turn right onto Van Nostrand Avenue and continue past the "dead end" sign to the nature center at the top of the hill. For more information, contact Flat Rock Brook Nature Center, 445 Van Nostrand Avenue, Englewood, NJ 07631; (201) 567-1265; www.flatrockbrook.org.

Tenafly Nature Center

The Tenafly Nature Center, founded in 1961, manages a 52-acre parcel of land leased from the Borough of Tenafly as well as the adjacent 330-acre Lost Brook Preserve, also owned by the Borough of Tenafly. The preserve includes second-growth woodland and wetlands, with the attractive three-acre Pfister's Pond in the northwest corner, near the nature center building. There are about seven miles of trails.

A suggested four-mile hike starts from the parking area at the end of Hudson Avenue, adjacent to the visitor center, and proceeds ahead on the Main Trail, a wide dirt road which is the continuation of Hudson Avenue. After about 200 feet, turn right on the Red Trail, which proceeds south. Soon, the trail bears left and begins to follow a stream. Be alert for a trail junction at two

large tulip trees, where the Purple Trail begins. Turn right and follow the Purple Trail across the stream on a footbridge, then continue along the Purple Trail to a T intersection where the Blue Trail, which leads to an adjacent residential street, comes in from the right. Turn left here, continuing to follow the Purple Trail. After crossing a brook, the Purple Trail ends at a T intersection with the Allison Trail (yellow). Turn right and follow the Allison Trail to a Y intersection, then bear right onto the Haring Rock Trail (orange).

Near the southern boundary of the nature center propery, a huge glacial erratic may be seen to the left of the trail. This is the Haring Rock, after which the trail is named. Just beyond, turn left onto the Seely Trail (yellow/orange), which proceeds southeast, parallel to East Clinton Avenue (visible through the trees on the right). After crossing the Green Brook, turn left onto the Allison Trail (yellow) and follow it northward. As the trail approaches the Green Brook, it makes a slight detour to the left to cross the brook on a footbridge, then turns left, rejoining the main trail route. Continue ahead on the yellow-blazed Allison Trail, passing several junctions with other trails, until the Allison Trail ends at the Main Trail, a wide dirt road.

Turn left and follow the Main Trail past the historic Lambier House, a private residence which dates back to the 1870s. A short distance beyond, turn right onto the White Trail, and follow it around Pfister's Pond, using boardwalks to cross several wet areas. After passing a wooden shelter, the White Trail ends at a junction with the Main Trail. Turn right and follow the Main Trail back to the parking area.

To reach the Tenafly Nature Center from US 9W in Tenafly, proceed west on East Clinton Avenue. In 1.7 miles, turn right at the traffic light onto Engle Street, then turn right at the next T intersection and follow Hudson Avenue uphill to its end at the nature center. Public transportation is available via Red and Tan Lines buses #9A and #9W from the George Washington Bridge Bus Station and the Port Authority Bus Terminal at 41st Street. The nearest bus stops are on US 9W, at the entrance to the Greenbrook Sanctuary and at Montammy Drive. A short connecting trail leads into the nature center property opposite the entrance to the Greenbrook Sanctuary, but hikers unfamiliar with the trails may wish to get off at Montammy Drive, follow US 9W south to Hudson Avenue (a gravel woods road), and proceed west on Hudson Avenue to the nature center building, where a map may be obtained.

For more information, contact the Tenafly Nature Center, 313 Hudson Avenue, Tenafly, NJ 07670, (201) 568-6093; www.tenaflynaturecenter.org.

Teaneck Greenway

The Teaneck Greenway, when completed, will extend along the Hackensack River from Terhune Park north to Historic New Bridge Landing, a distance of 3.5 miles, creating a green buffer between the developed area of Teaneck and the river. It will include a pedestrian walkway for walkers and joggers. As of 2003, only three small segments have been completed. However, it is anticipated that a longer section of the greenway through Fairleigh Dickinson University will be opened in the summer of 2004.

For more information, contact Friends of the Hackensack River Greenway through Teaneck, Inc., P.O. Box 3028, Teaneck, NJ 07666; www.teaneckgreenway.org.

SIX

THE RAMAPO MOUNTAINS

The Ramapo Mountains—the east-
ernmost part of the New Jersey Highlands—form a striking escarpment along
the northwest corner of Bergen County. Although their elevations exceed 1,000
feet in only a few locations, the gain in elevation from the Ramapo River below
is quite substantial. The proximity of these mountains—which are traversed by
a dense network of trails—to the highly-developed areas of Bergen and Passaic
counties makes them a favorite destination of hikers. Most of the land in the
Ramapos is now in public ownership, although it is divided between several
state and county parks.

History

Like the rest of the Highlands, the Ramapo Mountains are formed of Precambrian metamorphic rocks. The ancient bedrock is composed primarily of granite gneiss, but other rock types also occur. Some of the rocks are rich in iron-
bearing minerals—most commonly, magnetite.

Iron mining and smelting began in the Ringwood area in 1740, when
Cornelius Board, a surveyor and prospector, established an ironworks along
the Topomopack River (now known as the Ringwood River). Two years later,
he sold the operation to members of the Ogden family of Newark, who built a
blast furnace and formed the Ringwood Iron Company, named after a town in
the New Forest of England. In 1764, the ironworks were sold to the American
Company, a syndicate of British investors headed by Peter Hasenclever, a German with iron-mining and smelting experience. Hasenclever came to America to

run the operation, becoming one of the foremost ironmasters in this country. He brought hundreds of iron miners, charcoal burners, and other specialists from Germany, and his operations extended to Long Pond as well as into the Hudson Highlands and the Mohawk Valley.

Hasenclever introduced the newest English and German ironmaking methods and greatly improved the output at Ringwood. He built a dam on Long Pond (known today as Greenwood Lake) to supply power to the nearby blast furnaces, which remained in operation from 1766 to 1882. He also dammed Tuxedo Lake so that its outlet, Summit Brook, could flow into the Ringwood River to increase the supply of water power for the furnaces at Ringwood Manor. Difficulties caused by overextension of his business, failure to receive payment from England for his iron, and the general disturbance of international trade as unrest grew in the colonies led Hasenclever to suffer one of the biggest economic crashes of the time. In 1767, he was dismissed by his English employers, whom he then sued—but by the time a judgment was obtained against them, he had died.

In 1771, the American Company sent Robert Erskine, a Scottish engineer, to straighten out the iron business at Ringwood and elsewhere. Erskine sided with his adopted country when the colonies revolted, and the Ringwood and Long Pond ironworks became important suppliers of munitions to the Continental Army. Much of George Washington's maneuvering in northern New Jersey after the fall of New York was designed to defend Ringwood—a strategically placed supply depot, located midway between Morristown and Newburgh, New York. The second of the great iron chains across the Hudson, at West Point, was made of metal from the Long Mine near Sterling Lake.

In 1777, Erskine was appointed Surveyor General to the Continental Army by General Washington and made the first good maps of the Highlands of northern New Jersey and southern New York. Erskine died in 1780, and his remains were placed in a stone vault on the Ringwood Manor property in a graveyard where more than 150 soldiers of the Revolution are reported to have been buried. Washington, who is believed to have been present at the Manor the day Erskine died, returned in 1782 to plant a tree at Erskine's grave. The grave may still be seen on the west shore of Sally's Pond, but the tree was destroyed by lightning in 1912.

Following the Revolution, the Ringwood Ironworks were inactive until 1807, when Martin Ryerson purchased them and began successful operations. Because the mines contained such a high grade of ore, they were purchased in

1853 by Peter Cooper, owner of the Trenton Ironworks, inventor, philanthropist, and founder of the Cooper Union for the Advancement of Science in New York City. Peter Cooper's son Edward and Abram Stevens Hewitt, who would become Peter Cooper's son-in-law, managed the business. Hewitt eventually became one of nineteenth-century America's foremost ironmasters.

During the Civil War years, the Trenton Ironworks, using iron ore mined in Ringwood and smelted at Long Pond, supplied the Union Army. The ironworks helped build the beds that supported mortars for General Grant, and they produced the armor plate for the ironclad ship *Monitor*. Following the war, as Cooper, Hewitt & Company, Edward Cooper and Abram Hewitt expanded their business interests and, by 1870, had purchased many other ironworks. Hewitt was also involved in politics, serving in Congress for several terms. Both he and Edward Cooper served terms as mayor of New York City.

Peter Cooper became one of the largest single landowners in New Jersey, with the Ringwood properties consisting of nearly 100,000 acres. Upon Cooper's death in 1884, title to Ringwood Manor passed to Abram Hewitt. The Ringwood Company was reformed in 1905 by Hewitt's wife, Sarah Amelia Hewitt, following her husband's death. It was this firm that worked the Ringwood Mines during World War I.

The Peter's Mine, the largest mine in the area, was worked on and off from 1740 until 1931, and the two furnaces at the Ringwood Ironworks relied upon this mine for ore. By 1931, there were 17 levels below the mine entrance, and the shaft went down 1,800 feet below the ground. The mine reopened briefly during World War II, but work was stopped by the war's end, and the mine shafts were subsequently filled in. Many of the other mines in the Ringwood group were Keeler, Blue, Cannon, and Hope. All of these mines are on private property, and some have been completely obliterated. For a detailed history of these mines, refer to Edward Lenik's *Iron Mine Trails*, published by the Trail Conference.

History of the Parks

In 1936, Abram Hewitt's son Erskine deeded the Ringwood Manor House and 95 surrounding acres to the State of New Jersey. His nephew, Norvin Hewitt Green, gave additional property, bringing the total to 579 acres. Green also donated 1,000 acres in the Wyanokies which became the Norvin Green State Forest. Abram S. Hewitt State Forest, another gift, is west of Greenwood Lake

and south of the New York state line.

State, federal, and Bergen County funding has allowed numerous additions to be made to the publicly owned acreage in the Ramapos. In 1964, a 541-acre tract that includes Shepherd Lake was added. In 1966, a 1,000-acre tract containing Skylands Manor was purchased from Shelton College, and in 1972 the Bear Swamp Lake section was acquired from a vacation home club. In 1976, the estate of the late Clifford F. MacEvoy became Ramapo Mountain State Forest. Next, in 1978, came the purchase of the Green Engineering Camp of Cooper Union, which contained several trails laid out by the former Cooper Union Hiking Club. The 1981 acquisition of the 540-acre Muscarelle Tract closed the gap between Ringwood State Park and Ramapo Mountain State Forest.

Public enjoyment of the Ramapos was further broadened by state- and county-funded expansion of the Ramapo Valley County Reservation, whose trails provide access to the Ramapos from the east. The 1993 purchase of the Ramapo Land Company property created an almost solid expanse of public land in the Ramapos along the New York border. Bergen County has acquired the former Boy Scout camps Tamarack and Glen Gray, and Camp Yaw Paw, still owned by a Boy Scout foundation, is also protected open space.

Ecology

The forests of the Ramapos are divided between the northern hardwoods biome, mostly encountered in the valleys and bottomlands, and the oak-hickory biome, encountered on the upper slopes and dry ridges. The lower slopes and valleys—which have a cooler, moister climate than the upper slopes—support a forest of sugar maples, beech, hemlock, and yellow and black birches. White pines are also occasionally found in these low-lying areas. This species, which is characteristic of forests throughout New England, is rarely found in the rest of New Jersey. Its presence here identifies the Ramapos as a transitional zone between the forests of the mid-Atlantic region and those of New England. The striped maple—a small understory tree with large paired leaves and green-striped bark—is another species more typical of New England that may be found in the Ramapos.

As one heads upslope, the climate warms and the soils thin, with the vegetation gradually transformed into a typical oak-hickory forest. Red, white, black, and chestnut oaks, a variety of hickories, and black birch predominate,

with an understory of lowbush blueberries and huckleberries (rather than the viburnum and other taller shrubs found at lower elevations). Red cedar and pitch pine occupy the exposed rocky outcrops at the highest elevations, since few other tree species can survive in this harsh environment.

While most of the Ramapo forests are healthy and composed of native species, disturbances caused by human activity have resulted in the proliferation of exotic species in some areas. Thus, dense thickets of Japanese barberry may be seen along various trails, including the Yellow-Silver Trail in Ramapo Valley County Reservation. In other areas (such as the section of the Schuber Trail along the Ramapo River in Ramapo Valley County Reservation), an open, disturbed canopy allows exotic vines and other weeds to proliferate.

The forests of the Ramapos also support a great diversity of wildlife. Deer and bear are common, but beavers, porcupines, and mink may also be found. Copperheads, racers, and rat snakes inhabit the area, and the rugged, rocky sections house one of the last strongholds of the timber rattlesnake in New Jersey. They are rarely encountered by hikers and need not be feared, if left alone.

Figure 6-1. Beaver

Ruffed grouse, broad-winged hawks, great horned owls, pileated woodpeckers, brown creepers, hooded warblers, ovenbirds, scarlet tanagers, and towhees are just a few of the birds that nest in the forests of the Ramapos. Over two hundred other species may be found in these woods throughout the year.

CAMPGAW MOUNTAIN COUNTY RESERVATION

Located in Mahwah, the 1,300-acre Campgaw Mountain County Reservation offers hiking, downhill skiing, horseback riding, picnicking, archery, and camping (by permit only). Horses are not permitted on hiking trails, and bicycles are not permitted on any trails in the reservation. A Nike missile base once occupied parts of Campgaw Mountain, including the Saddle Ridge stable area. Although hiking access is free, fees may be charged for other activities. The reservation is bounded on the east by Campgaw Road and I-287, and on the

west by Ramapo Valley Road (US 202).

To reach the reservation, take Ramapo Valley Road (US 202) to Darlington Avenue (County 2). Proceed east on Darlington Avenue for 0.3 mile, then turn right onto Campgaw Road (County 3) and continue to the park entrance road, which is on the right. The reservation can also be reached from NJ 208. Take the Summit Avenue exit in Franklin Lakes, and turn left at the end of the ramp. At the next traffic light, turn left onto Franklin Avenue. Continue to the following traffic light, and turn right onto Pulis Avenue (County 3). Follow Pulis Avenue for 1.4 miles, then turn left onto Campgaw Road. In 1.6 miles, after passing the entrance road to the Darlington Golf Course on the right, turn left onto the park entrance road. The main parking lot for hikers is at a maintenance area on the left, 0.6 mile from Campgaw Road.

For more information, contact the Bergen County Parks Department, One Bergen County Plaza, Hackensack, NJ 07601; (201) 336-7275, www.co.bergen.nj.us/parks.

Trails in Campgaw Mountain County Reservation

Campgaw Mountain County Reservation offers a complex network of marked trails in a rather compact area. The flat trails at the base of Campgaw Mountain are ideal for those who are looking for a short, easy hike, and they can be combined with those that lead to the viewpoint at the summit of the mountain for a longer, more challenging hike.

Beeches Trail   *Length: 0.5 mile Blaze: green*

The Beeches Trail starts just south of the ski concession building at the base of the ski slope. It proceeds south on a broad path, then turns left at 0.1 mile onto the Indian Trail (yellow). The two trails descend for about 150 feet along an old woods road, after which the Beeches Trail turns right and continues south on a generally level path. It crosses an unmarked woods road at 0.2 mile and the Rocky Ridge Trail (blue) at 0.3 mile. Gradually descending, the Beeches Trail ends at 0.5 mile, where the Old Cedar Trail (red) comes in from the right and continues ahead.

Dogwood Lane Trail   *Length: 0.3 mile Blaze: white*

Starting in the woods at an intersection with the Gray Birch Trail (pink), the

Dogwood Lane Trail at first parallels a stone wall on the right, then turns left in about 100 feet to cross puncheons over a wet area. At 0.1 mile, the Old Cedar Trail (red) starts to the right. After paralleling a stone wall to the left, the Dogwood Lane Trail crosses the paved ski area access road at 0.2 mile. It follows a wide path parallel to the park entrance road, with a pond visible through the trees on the right. At 0.3 mile, the trail ends at a four-way intersection. The Indian Trail (yellow) begins here and proceeds straight ahead. To the left, a spur of the Hemlock Trail (orange) comes in from the main parking area. To the right, the Hemlock Trail begins its counterclockwise loop around the pond, while the clockwise direction of the loop continues ahead, running concurrently with the Indian Trail.

Gray Birch Trail   *Length: 0.8 mile Blaze: pink*

The Gray Birch Trail is a level trail that follows woods roads through overgrown farmland. Starting at a utility pole at the south end of the main parking area, the trail proceeds east for 300 feet along a paved road (a remnant of Fyke Road, cut off by I-287), then turns left (north) to join a woods road that skirts to the right of a park building. Beyond a grassy power line swath, the trail winds through beech and oak woods. At 0.4 mile, it bears to the right of an old stone wall and crosses the paved park entrance road to reenter the woods. At 0.5 mile, the Dogwood Lane Trail (white) continues ahead as the Gray Birch Trail turns sharply right through a gap in a stone wall, which it then parallels. Passing through another gap in a stone wall, the trail follows along an archery range on the left, then loops to the right, ending at the park road at 0.8 mile.

Hemlock Trail   *Length: 0.7 mile Blaze: orange*

The Hemlock Trail makes a loop around an attractive pond. It begins across the paved entrance road from the center entrance to the main parking area and proceeds west for 300 feet. Here, it reaches a complex trail intersection. The Dogwood Lane Trail (white) begins here and leaves to the right, while the Indian Trail (yellow), which also starts at this intersection, leaves to the left. The Hemlock Trail begins its loop here, as it proceeds to the left (clockwise) and runs jointly with the Indian Trail. In 250 feet, another intersection is reached. Here, the Old Cedar Trail (red) approaches from the left and turns to continue straight ahead, while the Indian and Hemlock trails turn right on a wide dirt road. Soon, the Indian Trail leaves to the left as the Hemlock Trail continues ahead on the dirt road, passing the ruin of a stone building to the left. At 0.3 mile, the trail

bears right, leaving the dirt road, and descends to the west shoreline of the pond. Beyond a pumphouse, the trail joins a dirt road. After turning right to cross the pond's dam on a dirt path alongside a paved road, it descends into the woods, following the pond's east shore. Stumps visible in the water indicate that the area covered by the lake was forested before the dam was built. Ascending to a dirt road, the trail completes its loop at 0.7 mile.

Indian Trail   *Length: 0.6 mile Blaze: yellow*

To reach the trailhead for the Indian Trail—which offers the most direct route to the top of the ski slope—from the main parking area, follow the Hemlock Trail (orange) west for 300 feet to a four-way intersection, where the Indian Trail begins to the left. After running concurrently with the Hemlock Trail for 250 feet, another intersection is reached. Here, the Old Cedar Trail (red) approaches from the left and turns to continue straight ahead, while the Indian and Hemlock trails turn right on a wide dirt road. Soon, the Hemlock Trail continues ahead on the dirt road as the Indian Trail leaves to the left. At 0.3 mile, the Beeches Trail (green) joins from the left. The two trails run concurrently for 150 feet, after which the Beeches Trail leaves to the right. Soon, the Indian Trail bears right and begins a gradual ascent of Campgaw Mountain. The Indian Trail joins the Rocky Ridge Trail (blue) at 0.6 mile, where it crosses a water pipe. Both trails continue ahead for another 250 feet to end at a utility pole at the top of the ski slope, where a white-blazed trail which connects with the Old Cedar Trail (red) leaves to the left. The top of the ski slope affords expansive views to the east. To the left are the hills of Harriman Park, and in the center is northern Bergen County, with Mahwah in the foreground. The Palisades can be seen on the horizon, and the Manhattan skyline is visible to the right on a clear day. The Rocky Ridge Trail can be used as an alternative return route.

Old Cedar Trail   *Length: 2.8 miles Blaze: red*

This trail, the longest in the reservation, makes a nearly circular loop around Campgaw Mountain. Although the first half mile of the trail goes through a more developed area of the park, the remainder of the trail traverses less-used areas.

The Old Cedar Trail begins at a chain barrier to a gravel road across from the south entrance to the main parking area. The Rocky Ridge Trail (blue) also starts here, and both trails head west along a gravel road, arriving at high-

voltage power lines in 100 feet. Here, the Rocky Ridge Trail departs to the left, while the Old Cedar Trail continues straight ahead, past a yellow steel gate.

At a four-way intersection, reached about 500 feet from the start, the Indian Trail (yellow) and the Hemlock Trail (orange) come in from the right and turn to continue straight ahead, while the Old Cedar Trail turns left, leaving the gravel road. Proceeding through an oak-beech forest, the trail passes a park building to the left, crosses the Rocky Ridge Trail, continues through a low area with abundant surface roots, and recrosses under the power lines through oak saplings at 0.2 mile. The Old Cedar Trail soon crosses the park entrance road diagonally to the right and follows a rocky path, with the park entrance road on the right and I-287 in the distance on the left. It bears sharply right and soon begins to parallel an old stone wall to the left. At 0.5 mile, just before a cul-de-sac parking area on the left (where the Silver Trail begins), the Old Cedar Trail recrosses the paved road and goes over an intermittent stream on a wooden footbridge. After a short climb, it bears right, then turns left and again passes under the power lines. At 0.7 mile, the Beeches Trail (green) proceeds straight ahead as the Old Cedar Trail turns sharply left.

Leaving the developed portion of the park, the Old Cedar Trail now begins a steady, gradual ascent. It bears right to cross a stream and then parallels it. Soon, it bears right, away from the stream, and continues its winding, gentle ascent. At 1.2 miles, near the crest of the ridge, the Rocky Ridge Trail joins from the right, and the two trails run jointly for 25 feet. The Rocky Ridge Trail then continues straight ahead, while the Old Cedar Trail turns sharply left and begins to descend. After leveling off and winding along the backslope of Campgaw Mountain, it again climbs to the summit ridge.

At 1.8 miles, as it nears the crest of the ridge, the Old Cedar Trail crosses two stone walls. Just beyond, a building at the top of the ski area may be visible through the trees on the right, and there are seasonal views to the left (west) over Ramapo Valley County Reservation. Here, a white-blazed trail to the right leads in 500 feet to an east-facing viewpoint over Bergen County from atop the ski slope, and connects to the Indian and Rocky Ridge trails.

Continuing ahead, the Old Cedar Trail curves to the east and descends gradually. At 2.4 miles, it bears left to follow a berm which skirts the north end of the large parking lot for the ski area. At the end of the berm, the trail bears left and reenters the woods. After descending along a hillside, it turns left and, at 2.6 miles, crosses Fyke Brook on a wooden bridge. The Old Cedar Trail then curves to the right and gradually ascends, ending in woods at 2.8 miles, where

it intersects the Dogwood Lane Trail (white). To complete the loop back to the starting point, turn left on the Dogwood Lane Trail. When the Dogwood Lane Trail ends in 0.1 mile, bear right and continue ahead on the Gray Birch Trail (pink), which leads back to the main parking area in another 0.5 mile.

Rocky Ridge Trail   *Length: 0.9 mile Blaze: blue*
The Rocky Ridge Trail, which leads to the top of the ski slope, begins at a chain barrier to a gravel road across from the south entrance to the main parking area. The Old Cedar Trail (red) also starts here, and both trails head west, arriving at power lines in 100 feet. Here, the Old Cedar Trail continues straight ahead, while the Rocky Ridge Trail turns left and continues under the power lines. At a yellow gate, reached at 0.1 mile, the Rocky Ridge Trail turns right and descends to cross the Old Cedar Trail. After passing a swampy area to the left, it ascends along the wide route of an abandoned bobsled run, crossing the Beeches Trail (green) on the way. An old shack to the right once housed machinery used to make snow for the bobsled run. At 0.5 mile, as it approaches the ridge, the trail bears right and climbs steeply on a winding footpath. At the crest of the ridge, the Rocky Ridge Trail turns right to join the Old Cedar Trail, which leaves to the left in 25 feet. The Rocky Ridge Trail continues ahead along the ridgeline on a rocky footpath. After passing through an area with many cedar trees, the Indian Trail (yellow) joins from the right, and both trails cross a water pipe. The two trails continue ahead for another 250 feet to an expansive east-facing viewpoint at the top of the ski slope, where the Rocky Ridge Trail ends at a utility pole at 0.9 mile. Here, a white-blazed trail which connects with the Old Cedar Trail (red) leaves to the left.

Silver Trail   *Length: 0.7 mile Blaze: silver*
The Silver Trail begins at a utility pole barrier in the cul-de-sac parking area at the south end of the paved park entrance road. Continuing south across a picnic area, the trail crosses an unmarked woods road and passes around a second pole barrier. At a Y intersection in 0.1 mile, the trail bears right for 60 feet, then turns left and descends gradually. After ascending on an eroded woods road, it levels off and turns left onto a rocky path at 0.3 mile, passing a huge oak tree. The trail climbs to cross a stone wall at 0.5 mile, and it ends at the park boundary at 0.7 mile, just before reaching Rockridge Court, a private residential street.

RAMAPO VALLEY COUNTY RESERVATION

European immigrants first settled what is now Ramapo Valley County Reservation around 1720. Rock walls are still present from the farms that sprang up, and the area that now makes up the reservation once boasted gristmills and sawmills, as well as a bronze foundry. The land was ultimately purchased by A.B. Darling, whose country estate gave the name Darlington to the area. The foundation of his manor house, near the entrance to the park, is still visible. The Darling gravesite is located about a mile north of the park entrance, west of US 202, and just south of an old stone farmhouse.

In 1972, funds from the state Green Acres program and the federal government enabled the County of Bergen to acquire the 2,145-acre Ramapo Valley County Reservation, which has expanded considerably since then. Left in its natural wild state, the reservation is mostly hilly, forming part of the eastern tier of the Ramapos. No open fires are permitted in the park without a permit. Tent camping, which also requires a permit, is allowed only in designated areas near Scarlet Oak Pond and the Ramapo River. The reservation has a carry-in, carry-out policy for trash. Bicycles and horses are not permitted on any trails in the reservation.

The entrance to the reservation is on Ramapo Valley Road (US 202), about two miles south of NJ 17 in Mahwah. There is access for the disabled. For more information, contact the Bergen County Parks Department, One Bergen County Plaza, Hackensack, NJ 07601; (201) 336-7275; www.co.bergen.nj.us/parks.

Trails in Ramapo Valley County Reservation

Ramapo Valley County Reservation is a favorite location for pleasant afternoon strolls. But the reservation's trails also connect with those in Ringwood State Park to the west, Ramapo Mountain State Forest to the southwest, and Camp Glen Gray to the south, making possible a wide variety of rugged day-long hikes. Features of interest include the Ramapo River, Scarlet Oak Pond, MacMillan Reservoir, and Hawk Rock.

Halifax Trail   *Length: 3.1 miles Blaze: green on white*
The Halifax Trail connects Ramapo Valley County Reservation with the Skylands

Manor section of Ringwood State Park. It is the northernmost marked trail in the reservation, and can easily be combined with other trails to make a loop hike.

The Halifax Trail begins at a junction with the Schuber Trail, 0.5 mile from the start of the Schuber Trail at the Ramapo Reservation parking lot on Ramapo Valley Road (US 202). It proceeds east on a wide gravel road and, in 0.2 mile, crosses the Silver Trail diagonally to the left at the western end of Scarlet Oak Pond. It continues ahead on a wide path for 0.1 mile, then turns left, immediately crossing a wooden bridge over a stream, and enters the woods on a footpath. The Halifax Trail soon begins to climb Monroe Ridge, first gradually, then more steeply. After a short rocky section, it reaches Hawk Rock at 0.6 mile. This east-facing ledge offers an expansive view over much of Bergen County, with Ramapo College in the foreground to the left. On clear days, the Manhattan skyline is visible in the distance.

The Halifax Trail now bends to the left and continues to ascend. After reaching the crest of the ridge, the trail crosses the route of a gas pipeline at 1.0 mile and begins to descend. It briefly joins an eroded woods road, then turns left on a footpath, reaching a woods road which traverses Havemeyer Hollow at 1.3 miles. The Halifax Trail turns left and follows this relatively level road up the valley. (To the right, the woods road leads in 0.2 mile to the picturesque Havemeyer Reservoir.) At 1.5 miles, the Havemeyer Trail (blue on white) leaves to the left. Just beyond, the Halifax Trail crosses a stream and continues along the woods road, with the stream to the left.

At 1.8 miles, the Halifax Trail turns left, leaving the woods road, and passes through a rocky, wet area. It once again crosses the stream and turns right onto a narrower woods road, continuing to ascend. At 2.4 miles, the White Trail (which can be used as an alternate return route) begins to the left. Just beyond, the Halifax Trail crosses the route of another pipeline. At 2.7 miles, after passing two woods roads which depart to the right and once more crossing a gas pipeline route, the Halifax Trail joins Bear Swamp Road, which comes in from the left. It follows the road (sections of which are paved) for 750 feet, then turns right and descends on an eroded woods road, soon crossing Bear Swamp Brook on a wooden bridge at 3.1 miles. Just beyond the brook, at a Y intersection, the Hoeferlin Memorial Trail (yellow) starts to the left. Here, the Halifax Trail bears right and heads north for another three miles, entering the Skylands Manor section of Ringwood State Park. For a description of this section of the trail, see pp. 108-09.

Havemeyer Trail   *Length: 0.8 mile Blaze: blue on white*
The Havemeyer Trail connects the Halifax Trail with the Ridge Trail. Starting from the Halifax Trail (green on white), the Havemeyer Trail heads southwest, soon passing an excavation to the left. The ascent steepens and, at 0.4 mile, the trail turns right on a woods road which comes up from the left. Then, at 0.5 mile, the Havemeyer Trail bears sharply left onto another woods road, the route of the White Trail, and levels off. The two trails run jointly for about 500 feet, after which the Havemeyer Trail turns sharply right, leaving the White Trail. It climbs to the summit of Monroe Ridge, where it crosses a gas pipeline, and descends to end, at 0.8 mile, at a junction with the Ridge Trail (blue).

Marsh Loop Trail   *Length: 0.3 mile Blaze: red*
The Marsh Loop Trail connects the Schuber Trail with the Yellow-Silver Trail. It can be combined with these two trails to make a one-mile loop around the marsh for which the trail is named.

Beginning at the Schuber Trail (orange), 1.4 miles from the parking lot on Ramapo Valley Road (US 202), the Marsh Loop Trail heads south and soon begins to parallel the stone-lined walls of an old mill race channel. After crossing this channel, it reaches the northern end of a *Phragmites* marsh (a remnant of a millpond that once served a bronze foundry) at 0.1 mile, and it runs parallel to the marsh for about 700 feet. The Marsh Loop Trail curves to the left beyond the southern edge of the marsh, and it ends at 0.3 mile at the Yellow-Silver Trail. To complete the loop around the marsh, hikers should turn left at this junction.

Red-Silver Trail   *Length: 0.7 mile Blaze: red/silver*
The Red-Silver Trail skirts the northeast shoulder of Rocky Mountain as it connects the Schuber Trail with the Shore Trail at Bear Swamp Lake. It begins at the Schuber Trail (orange), 1.5 miles from the parking lot on Ramapo Valley Road (US 202), and proceeds north. It crosses a stream, ascends gently, and gradually curves to the west. After traversing a rocky section at 0.4 mile, the trail begins to descend, soon turning left on a woods road. It crosses the right-of-way of a gas pipeline at 0.6 mile, and it ends 300 feet later at Bear Swamp Lake, at a junction with the Shore Trail (blue).

Ridge Trail   *Length: 1.9 miles Blaze: blue*
Starting from the Silver Trail, 0.7 mile from the parking lot on Ramapo Valley

Road (US 202), the Ridge Trail climbs moderately on a wide, rocky path with several railroad-tie steps. It briefly joins a woods road, then bears left, leaving the road, and continues uphill on a narrower path. At 0.3 mile, the Ridge Trail rejoins the woods road, which comes in from the right. In another 60 feet, a trail to the left, blazed blue with red triangles, leads 375 feet to a lookout over the Ramapo Valley from a rock ledge, with the Manhattan skyline visible in the distance on a clear day. The trail now proceeds through an area with a thick understory of young maple trees. At 0.4 mile, the Ridge Trail turns left onto a footpath, as the White Trail (which begins here) continues ahead on the woods road. The Ridge Trail ascends briefly and soon begins to follow a stone wall to the right. It descends gradually and then climbs over three minor ridges. After bearing right at an exposed rock ledge, the trail turns left at 1.0 mile onto a woods road, which it follows for the remainder of the route. To the right, the woods road is the route of the Havemeyer Trail (blue on white). The remains of the Nickel Mine are near this junction, about 275 feet west of the Ridge Trail. At 1.2 miles, the Ridge Trail makes a sharp bend to the left and begins to head in a southwest direction, descending steadily to cross a seasonal stream. It crosses another stream at 1.7 miles and climbs to end, 1.9 miles from its start, at the Schuber Trail (orange).

The Ridge Trail may be combined with the Silver and Schuber trails to make a 4.1-mile loop hike from the parking area on Ramapo Valley Road (US 202).

Schuber Trail   *Length: 6.5 miles Blaze: orange*
The Schuber Trail, dedicated in a National Trails Day ceremony on June 1, 2002, celebrates the acquisition by Bergen County of several Scout properties in the Ramapo Mountains. It links Ramapo Valley County Reservation with Camp Glen Gray and the former Camp Tamarack, passing through county property for almost its entire length.

The Schuber Trail begins at a kiosk in the southwest corner of the parking lot for the reservation along Ramapo Valley Road (US 202). The Silver Trail also begins here, and both trails descend on a wide path. After briefly joining a paved road, the trails continue ahead to cross the Ramapo River on a steel truss bridge. In another 250 feet, the Schuber Trail turns left at an open grassy area, leaving the wide Silver Trail, and following a narrower path through an area of tangled vines. A short distance beyond, at a Y intersection, the Schuber Trail bears left and continues along a shoreline footpath in the floodplain of the

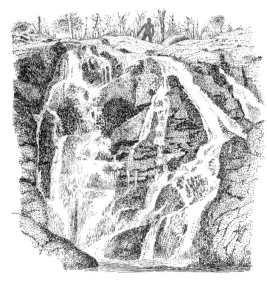

Figure 6-2. Waterfall on the Schuber Trail

Ramapo River. (If the trail is flooded, return to the Silver Trail, turn left, follow it for 0.1 mile to its intersection with the Halifax Trail (green on white), and turn left onto the Halifax Trail for 0.2 mile to rejoin the Schuber Trail.)

At 0.5 mile, after turning right, away from the river, the Schuber Trail turns left onto an intersecting path. Just beyond, the Halifax Trail (green on white) begins to the right, leading in 0.2 mile back to the Silver Trail and continuing up Havemeyer Hollow to Ringwood State Park. After crossing a wooden bridge over a stream, the Schuber Trail turns right at an abandoned stone cabin and begins a rocky ascent along the stream. The trail briefly levels off at 0.7 mile, with attractive cascades and pools in the stream to the right.

After curving to the right, the Schuber Trail reaches a junction with the wide park road leading to the MacMillan Reservoir. Here, at 0.9 mile, the Schuber Trail turns left and begins to follow a paved section of the park road. (To the right, the Silver Trail follows the park road eastward, reaching the parking lot on Ramapo Valley Road (US 202) in 0.8 mile.) After crossing a bridge over a stream, the Schuber Trail curves to the left where an unmarked trail, which leads to the eastern shore of the MacMillan Reservoir, continues ahead. Just beyond, at 1.1 miles, the trail passes to the left of the dam of the reservoir.

The Schuber Trail now becomes rockier and continues to climb. In 500 feet, by an old stone wall, the Yellow-Silver Trail leaves to the left. The Schuber Trail now passes under a canopy of *Corkbark euonymus*, quite showy during late autumn. At 1.4 miles, as the Schuber Trail begins to descend, the Marsh Loop Trail (red) goes off to the left. Then, in 650 feet, the Schuber Trail contin-

ues ahead on a narrower path as the main woods road curves to the right and becomes the Ridge Trail (blue) (this is the western end of that trail). At 1.8 miles, just before reaching an intermittent stream, the Red-Silver Trail continues ahead as the Schuber Trail turns sharply left.

The Schuber Trail now ascends a rocky hillside and follows the southeastern shoulder of Rocky Mountain. After passing through a rocky area, it crosses a stream on rocks at 2.1 miles. Staying to the left of a prominent rocky ridge, the trail climbs steadily, then goes through a cleft in the ridge at 2.4 miles. It descends a grassy slope to reach Bear Swamp Road at 2.8 miles. Here, the Schuber Trail turns right and follows the paved road.

In another 500 feet, the Schuber Trail turns left and crosses a wooden bridge over Bear Swamp Brook. About 150 feet beyond the bridge, the trail turns left again, leaving the paved road, and re-enters the woods. It soon approaches a particularly wild and beautiful section of the brook, featuring cascades, pools, and a deep rock cut.

A short distance beyond, the brook curves to the left as the trail continues ahead, climbing over a rocky area. After crossing a stream on rocks, the trail passes to the right of an abandoned cabin (once part of the adjacent Camp Yaw Paw). The Schuber Trail now crosses a second stream and, at 3.3 miles, turns left onto a woods road, joining the Yellow Trail, which comes in from the right. The Schuber Trail soon turns right, leaving the woods road, then bears left and begins a steep and rocky ascent. Reaching the crest of the ridge, the trail bears right and continues along the ridge, entering Camp Glen Gray, now owned by Bergen County. Soon, the Old Guard Trail (green tulip tree leaf on white) leaves to the right.

The Schuber Trail reaches the height of the ridge (996 feet) at 3.8 miles, with a broad viewpoint to the east from a rock ledge to the left of the trail. The view to the left looks back toward the hills of Ramapo Valley County Reservation. In the center lies suburban Bergen County, with the Manhattan skyline visible on the horizon to the right. Here, the Schuber Trail leaves the Yellow Trail, which continues ahead along the ridge. The Schuber Trail turns sharply right and descends, soon joining a grassy woods road.

At 4.2 miles, the Schuber Trail turns right onto another woods road. (To the left, this woods road is the route of the Yellow-Silver Trail, which begins here.) The Schuber Trail skirts a cable barrier and crosses a wooden bridge over the outlet of Sanders Pond, to the right of the trail. After climbing over a knoll, it descends to a T intersection with Cannonball Road at 4.6 miles. Here, the

Schuber Trail continues straight ahead on a footpath, descending to a tributary of North Brook, where it turns left and joins the Old Guard Trail.

After climbing to a rock outcrop overlooking North Brook, the trails cross an old woods road and reach the Tindall Cabin. Here, the Old Guard Trail leaves to the left, while the Schuber Trail continues ahead to cross the brook on a wooden footbridge. It bears left, passing stone foundations of the former Sanders Farm. After skirting an archery range to the left, the Schuber Trail joins Mary Post Road. It crosses a plank bridge, passes a rifle range to the right, and gradually curves to the left, going past more cabins and campsites. At a sign for the Ramapo Campsite, the Matapan Rock Trail (red on white) leaves to the right, reaching the joint Hoeferlin Memorial (yellow) and Cannonball (white C on red) trails in 0.7 mile and continuing to the Matapan Rock viewpoint, a short distance beyond.

At 5.3 miles, the trail reaches the shore of Lake Vreeland. After crossing a culvert over South Brook, with the lake to the left and a swamp to the right, the Schuber Trail turns right, leaving the lake shore. The Millstone Trail (white) joins, and both trails continue past the Explorer Cabin to a fork. Here, the Millstone Trail takes the right fork, while the Schuber Trail bears left, following the route of the former Bottle Cap Trail, marked by red-painted bottle caps nailed to the trees. It continues to ascend over a rocky trailway.

The Millstone Trail crosses at 5.6 miles. Soon afterwards, the Schuber Trail leaves Camp Glen Gray and enters the former Camp Tamarack, another Scout property that has been acquired by Bergen County. It crosses a stream in a rocky area at 5.8 miles and continues over rolling terrain.

At 6.1 miles, the Schuber Trail crosses another stream and passes the site of an abandoned archery range. The trail now begins to ascend, heading southwest on a winding footpath. After briefly joining the gated entrance road to Camp Tamarack, the Schuber Trail ends at Skyline Drive at 6.5 miles, opposite the large upper parking area at the crest of the hill. Here, the Hoeferlin Memorial Trail (yellow) crosses Skyline Drive, and the Todd Trail (white) begins.

Shore Trail   *Length: 2.0 miles Blaze: blue*
The Shore Trail loops around Bear Swamp Lake, serving as an important connector to several other trails. It is actually in Ringwood State Park, but is included in this section because it adjoins Ramapo Valley County Reservation and is mostly used by hikers coming from the reservation.

Described here in a clockwise direction, the Shore Trail starts at a wooden

bridge that crosses the dam at the south end of the lake, just west of Bear Swamp Road. In 100 feet, the northern end of the Cannonball Trail (white C on red) is passed to the left. The Shore Trail bears right and proceeds north along the western shore of the lake, soon passing a rock outcrop overlooking the lake and several stone chimneys and cellar holes—remnants of former cottages of the Bear Lake Club, a private summer-home community. After ascending to an overlook, the trail descends to cross a small stream and continues through a rocky area. At 0.7 mile, just past another stream crossing, the Shore Trail continues straight ahead as a woods road forks left. Soon, the Hoeferlin Memorial Trail (yellow) joins from the left. The two trails run jointly for 500 feet, after which the Hoeferlin Memorial Trail bears left and continues for 0.1 mile to its terminus at the Halifax Trail (green on white).

The Shore Trail takes the right fork, descending on a footpath around the north end of the lake to cross a wooden bridge over Bear Swamp Brook, the main inlet of the lake, at 1.1 miles. It turns right (south) and continues along the eastern shore of the lake, passing below the bouldery slope of Drag Hill. At 1.4 miles, the Shore Trail emerges onto a clearing and turns right onto Bear Swamp Road, portions of which are paved. It follows this road for the remainder of its route. The Red-Silver Trail, which leads into Ramapo Valley County Reservation and connects with the Schuber Trail (orange), leaves to the left at 1.6 miles. Continuing along Bear Swamp Road, the Shore Trail passes more ruins of summer cottages. At 2.0 miles, it turns right and reaches the dam, completing the loop.

Silver Trail   *Length: 0.8 mile Blaze: silver*

The Silver Trail begins at a kiosk in the southwest corner of the parking lot for Ramapo Valley County Reservation along Ramapo Valley Road (US 202). The Schuber Trail also begins here, and both trails descend on a wide path. After briefly joining a paved road, the trails continue ahead to cross the Ramapo River on a steel truss bridge. Just beyond the bridge, a wide unmarked trail leaves to the right and makes an 0.6-mile horseshoe loop around Scarlet Oak Pond, rejoining the Silver Trail at the western end of the pond. In another 250 feet, the Schuber Trail (orange) leaves to the left. Just ahead, the Silver Trail begins to follow the southwest shore of the pond.

At the west end of the pond, reached at 0.4 mile, the Halifax Trail (green on white) crosses diagonally. (To the left, it connects in 0.2 mile with the Schuber Trail.) The Silver Trail now bears left and begins a steady climb through an oak-

maple forest, following the park service road up toward the
MacMillan Reservoir. At 0.7
mile, the Ridge Trail (blue)
goes off to the right. Then, at
0.8 mile, just beyond a
stream crossing, the Silver
Trail ends at a junction with
the Schuber Trail, which comes
in from the left and continues
ahead along the park road, leading to the MacMillan Reservoir
and beyond.

Figure 6-3. Bridge on park road below
MacMillan Reservoir

White Trail   *Length: 1.0 mile Blaze: white*

The White Trail diverges from the Ridge Trail (blue) 0.4 mile from its start on
the Silver Trail (1.1 miles from the parking lot on Ramapo Valley Road (US
202)). It climbs to the top of Monroe Ridge and then descends to cross the
route of a gas pipeline at 0.2 mile. At 0.4 mile, the Havemeyer Trail (blue on
white) joins from the left, runs concurrently with the White Trail for 500 feet,
and then leaves to the right. At 0.6 mile, the White Trail begins to descend and,
at 0.9 mile, it approaches another pipeline. (To the left, up Drag Hill, the pipeline can be followed for about 400 feet to a tower at the junction of two
pipelines, from where there are views of the surrounding countryside.) Just
before the pipeline, the White Trail bears right into the woods and continues to
descend until it ends, 1.0 mile from the start, at a junction with the Halifax Trail
(green on white), which can be used as an alternate return route.

Yellow-Silver Trail   *Length: 2.6 miles Blaze: yellow/silver*

The Yellow-Silver Trail traverses the southern portion of the reservation. It
begins at an intersection with the Schuber Trail (orange), 500 feet beyond the
dam of the MacMillan Reservoir (1.1 miles from the parking lot on Ramapo
Valley Road (US 202)). At first, it ascends rather steeply, passing through a
recently-disturbed area with a thick understory. The Yellow-Silver Trail soon
loops around to head in a westerly direction, skirting Matty Price Hill. At 0.5
mile, the western end of the Marsh Loop Trail (red) is passed to the right as the
Yellow-Silver Trail curves to the left. The Yellow-Silver Trail soon begins a gentle

but steady descent, passing the ruins of a former goat farm and reaching Bear Swamp Road at 1.2 miles. Here, it briefly joins the road to cross Bear Swamp Brook on a wooden bridge, then leaves to the right and continues south, ascending on a woods road. At 2.1 miles, it turns right onto a footpath, then turns right onto another woods road and climbs on switchbacks to cross the Yellow Trail at 2.4 miles. It continues ahead to end, 2.6 miles from its start, at another junction with the Schuber Trail.

CAMP GLEN GRAY

Located in Mahwah, between Ramapo Valley County Reservation and Ramapo Mountain State Forest, Camp Glen Gray was opened by the Eagle Rock Council of the Boy Scouts of America in 1917 and served as a Boy Scout camp until 2002, when it was acquired by Bergen County. The more remote portions of the 750-acre camp are managed by the Bergen County Parks Department as part of Ramapo Valley County Reservation, but the "core area" of the camp— which includes cabins, lean-tos, and campsites—is operated by the Friends of Glen Gray. These rustic overnight facilities are available for rental by groups, families, or individuals.

Camp Glen Gray is traversed by a network of hiking trails, including the Schuber Trail (described in the Ramapo Valley County Reservation section, pp. 80-83) and the Yellow Trail (described in the Ramapo Mountain State Forest section, pp. 101-02), which extend beyond the camp boundaries. In 2003, many of these trails are being reconditioned and realigned. One of the most interesting trails, the Millstone Trail, is described below. Although the hiking trails that traverse the camp are open to the public during daylight hours, parking at the camp is limited to overnight guests. The closest access for day hikers where parking is available is the upper parking area on Skyline Drive, the southern terminus of the Schuber Trail.

For more information about Camp Glen Gray, or to reserve overnight accommodations, contact Friends of Glen Gray, 200 Midvale Mountain Road, Mahwah, NJ 07430; (201) 327-7234; www.glengray.org.

Millstone Trail   *Length: 2.0 miles Blaze: white*
The Millstone Trail is a two-mile loop trail which passes various features of interest, including several millstones once quarried in the area. The trail is de-

scribed here in a counterclockwise direction.

Beginning just west of the Camp Glen Gray office, on the main camp road, the trail bears left on a woods road that climbs above the camp parking area and continues past the Rotary Cabin and the dam and along the south shore of Lake Vreeland. At 0.2 mile, just before reaching the Mothers Pavilion, the Millstone Trail turns left onto a woods road, joining the Schuber Trail (orange), which comes in from the west. Both trails pass the Explorer Cabin and then split at a fork in the road. The Millstone Trail takes the right fork, while the Schuber Trail leaves to the left. After climbing rather steeply, the Millstone Trail bears left, leaving the woods road, and continues on a rocky footpath through dense thickets, passing the Azalea Swamp to the right.

Ascending to the east, the Millstone Trail crosses the Schuber Trail at 0.6 mile and approaches the Rocky Slide Gulch, with a small pile of iron-ore tailings visible to the right just before the trail descends into the shallow gulch. After turning right and briefly following the gulch, the Millstone Trail turns left and ascends Millstone Hill on a rocky footpath. Reaching the crest of the ridge, it descends slightly and then makes a short, steep climb, passing to the right of a glacial erratic called "Sitting Hen Rock." The trail bears right and resumes its ascent. At 0.9 mile, just beyond the crest of the hill, it reaches the Southwest Lookout. After descending gradually, the trail climbs to pass another erratic, labeled "Balancing Rock and Rattlesnake Cave," in an open area at 1.2 miles. A patch of prickly pear cactus, which blooms in early July, may be seen nearby.

The Millstone Trail now bears left and begins a gradual descent. Just after the Yellow Trail joins from the right at 1.3 miles, several abandoned millstones in various stages of completion may be seen to the left of the trail. Continuing to descend along an old woods road, the two trails pass a millstone in nearly perfect condition 25 feet to the right. At a T intersection, reached at 1.5 miles, the trails turn left at an old stone wall, which marks the camp boundary.

Continuing to descend, the trails cross paved Midvale Mountain Road at 1.6 miles. They bear left and head west, parallel to Fox Brook, then turn right to cross two branches of the brook on rocks at 1.7 miles. The trails now begin to climb, reaching a junction in a level area at 1.8 miles. Here, the Yellow Trail turns right, while the Millstone Trail turns left and climbs to a seasonal viewpoint from a rock outcrop. The Millstone Trail descends, crosses a tributary stream, and skirts to the left of the Gray Cabin. After recrossing Fox Brook on a plank bridge, the Millstone Trail ends at the camp entrance road (just before the office) at 2.0 miles, completing the loop.

RAMAPO MOUNTAIN STATE FOREST

A rugged 2,264-acre area, Ramapo Mountain State Forest has elevations ranging from about 200 to 1,100 feet. It includes wild lands in the municipalities of Oakland, Pompton Lakes, Ringwood, and Wanaque. The centerpiece of the forest is Ramapo Lake, formerly called Lake LeGrande. Even earlier, it was called Rotten Pond, a name more than likely derived from Dutch settlers who called it Rote (Rat) Pond, after the muskrats that they trapped there. Fishing is permitted, but swimming is not allowed. Several private inholdings at the southern end of the forest are served by one-lane access roads, with public access only on foot. Portions of other estate roads, no longer maintained for vehicles, are marked as hiking trails. Hunting (in season) is permitted in the wild northern part of the forest. No fires or camping are permitted.

Hikers arriving by car have four main access points. Two can be reached by taking I-287 to Exit 57 and continuing north on Skyline Drive. The first access point, known as the lower parking area, is a short distance north of the I-287 interchange, on the left side of Skyline Drive, and is signed "Ramapo Mountain State Forest." The second access point, known as the upper parking area, is one mile further north on the left. The other two access points are reached by proceeding south on West Oakland Avenue from Exit 57. To reach the third access point, continue south along West Oakland Avenue for about 1.1 miles, then turn right onto Pool Hollow Road and park on the right, just before the railroad tracks. The fourth access point is about another mile further south along West Oakland Avenue, which becomes Colfax Avenue in Pompton Lakes. Turn right onto Schuyler Avenue, and then right again onto Barbara Drive, where parking for several cars is available near the end of the road.

Public transportation to the area from the Port Authority Bus Terminal in New York City is available via NJ Transit buses #194 and #197. The nearest stop is at the intersection of Wanaque Avenue and Cannonball Road, adjacent to the former Pompton Lakes railroad station. To reach the trailhead of the Cannonball Trail, follow Cannonball Road east for 0.3 mile to DuPont Place. Turn right onto DuPont Place, which becomes Walnut Street and curves to the left, then turn right onto Barbara Drive and continue to the cul-de-sac at the end of the street, where the Cannonball Trail begins.

For more information, contact Ringwood State Park, 1304 Sloatsburg Road, Ringwood, NJ 07456; (973) 962-7031; www.njparksandforests.org.

Trails in Ramapo Mountain State Forest

More than 20 miles of trails have been laid out since the state acquired Ramapo Mountain State Forest. The late Frank Oliver of the New York-New Jersey Trail Conference laid out most of the trail routes, and units of the Youth Conservation Corps cleared them in 1977 and 1978. The trails provide gradual ascents to several viewpoints from rock ledges. Two thru-trails traverse the forest: the Hoeferlin Memorial Trail, honoring William Hoeferlin, a noted trailblazer and map-maker, and the Cannonball Trail, which follows portions of the historic Cannonball Road, a Revolutionary War route which originated in Pompton Lakes, formerly the site of a furnace used to produce cannon. All trails east of Skyline Drive are hiking-only, as is the Hoeferlin Memorial Trail west of Skyline Drive to its trailhead on Pool Hollow Road.

Cannonball Trail *Length: 7.7 miles Blaze: white* C *on red*

In his 1966 book, *Vanishing Ironworks of the Ramapos*, James M. Ransom defined the Cannonball Road, after which this trail is named, as part historic, part legendary. His historical evidence about the Pompton Furnace reveals that cannonballs were cast there in great quantity during the American Revolution. The furnace was located adjacent to the northern end of the natural basalt dam of Pompton Lake. Today, only a portion of the support for the charging bridge from the hillside to the top of the furnace remains.

From here, the obvious valley route to the Hudson would have followed the Ramapo River towards Stony Point, the present route of US 202. Because the Loyalists might have warned the British, it seems reasonable to believe that a hidden route was laid out through the Ramapos. The route had to have easy grades over the ridge for heavily laden oxen-drawn wagons. In the 1970s, the old route was uncovered, using old maps and Ransom's book. Today's Cannonball Trail follows portions of the historic Cannonball Road.

To reach the southern trailhead in Pompton Lakes, hikers should take I-287 to Exit 57 (Skyline Drive) and proceed south on West Oakland Avenue, which becomes Colfax Avenue. In 2.1 miles, turn right onto Schuyler Avenue, cross the railroad tracks, and turn right onto Barbara Drive. Parking is available on the left side of the street just before it ends in a cul-de-sac.

The trail begins at the left side of the cul-de-sac, by a boulder barrier. It

Figure 6-4. Cannonball Trail in winter

immediately turns right and crosses a railroad siding leading into the former duPont plant. After continuing across the left side of a ballfield, the trail bears left, climbing steeply into the woods and entering Ramapo Mountain State Forest. Near the top of the rise, the South Ridge Trail (white) starts to the right. Here, the Cannonball Trail bears left and descends along the shoulder of a ridge on a rocky footpath. The trail soon levels off and begins to parallel a fence to the left.

The Cannonball Trail proceeds north between low ridges along an eroded woods road. As the trail approaches I-287, the sound of traffic gradually increases. At 0.8 mile, the Hoeferlin Memorial Trail (yellow) joins from the right, and both trails cross I-287 on a pedestrian bridge. On the north side of the bridge, they follow a woods road until, at 1.1 miles, the Hoeferlin Memorial Trail leaves to the right. A large glacial erratic is perched on a ledge to the right of the trail just before the trail junction.

The Cannonball Trail continues ahead on the woods road. After crossing a stream, the trail begins to ascend a rocky, eroded stretch of the road. At 1.5 miles, at a Y intersection, it turns right onto a level gravel road for 400 feet, then turns left at the next intersection to join another gravel road that runs along the

western shore of Ramapo Lake. This level, well-graded road is a welcome contrast to the rocky, eroded roads that the trail has followed up to this point. After passing a building on the hillside to the left of the trail that was formerly used as a ranger station, the trail reaches a rock ledge to the right that offers a pleasant view of the lake.

At 2.2 miles, another gravel road joins from the left, and the trail follows the road over a stone causeway that isolates a quiet pond on the left from the main body of the lake. A short distance beyond the causeway, the Cannonball Trail turns left onto an intersecting gravel road. It continues on this road for 450 feet and then turns right onto a footpath, along with the MacEvoy Trail (blue) that joins from the road ahead.

The footpath reaches another gravel road at 2.6 miles. Here, the MacEvoy Trail turns right, while the Cannonball Trail turns left, following the gravel road uphill around a sharp curve. In 150 feet, the Castle Point Trail (white) leaves to the left, leading uphill to the ruins of a former mansion. At the top of the hill, where the road curves sharply to the left, the Cannonball Trail leaves the road and enters the woods on a footpath to the right. It crosses a stream and begins to ascend, steeply in places, to reach a paved road at 3.0 miles.

The trail briefly turns left on the road, detours to the right on a footpath, then rejoins the road, passing a private house on the right. Just beyond the house, the trail bears right and reenters the woods, until it once again rejoins the road at 3.5 miles. After passing the northern trailhead of the Castle Point Trail to the left, the Cannonball Trail crosses Skyline Drive (just east of the Bergen/Passaic county line) and continues north on a wide woods road, parallel to and just east of Skyline Drive. At 3.7 miles, the Hoeferlin Memorial Trail rejoins from the right, and the two trails stay together for the next 1.6 miles.

After crossing a stream in a wet area at 4.2 miles, the trails emerge to cross a pipeline alongside Skyline Drive. The trails continue along the shoulder of Skyline Drive for 350 feet, then bear right and reenter the woods on a footpath blocked off by boulders. At 4.6 miles, the Matapan Rock Trail (red on white) crosses. (To the left, this trail leads in 500 feet to Matapan Rock, which offers a view to the west, with Skyline Drive directly below, and the Wanaque Reservoir in the distance. To the right, it leads 0.7 mile to Camp Glen Gray, where it connects with the Schuber Trail (orange).) Just beyond, the joint Cannonball/Hoeferlin Memorial trails turn left onto an access road leading to a radio tower, then in 50 feet turn right and continue north on a footpath. After passing abandoned cars off to the right, the Hoeferlin Memorial and Cannonball trails

bear left and ascend to the ridgeline, passing a large glacial erratic on the way. At the crest of the ridge, they bear right onto an old woods road.

At 5.2 miles, the Cannonball Trail forks to the right and begins to descend, while the Hoeferlin Memorial Trail continues ahead along the ridge. The Cannonball Trail crosses a stream and passes through a boulder field at 5.7 miles, and at 6.1 miles, it turns left and joins a woods road, another segment of the original Cannonball Road. The Old Guard Trail (green tulip tree leaf on white) briefly joins the Cannonball Trail here and then crosses it at 6.4 miles.

The Cannonball Trail passes the ruin of a concrete swimming pool to the right at 6.5 miles and enters Camp Yaw Paw, a Boy Scout camp operated by the Northern New Jersey Council, BSA. This area was a charcoal production site in the 1850s. At 6.7 miles, the Yellow Trail leaves to the right and, a short distance beyond, the Cannonball Trail goes by a small lean-to on the right. Just past the camp Nature Center on the left, the Green Trail (green on white) departs to the left, leading in 0.4 mile to the Erskine Lookout. The Cannonball Trail continues ahead past Cannonball Lake, which is visible through the trees on the right. Near the north end of Cannonball Lake, at 7.0 miles, the Blue Trail (which connects with the Hoeferlin Memorial Trail) begins to the left.

Just beyond, the Cannonball Trail bears right and crosses the outlet of Iaoapogh Lake, then turns left, passes the Coyle Cabin, and continues along rock ledges on the east side of the lake. At the end of the lake, the trail bears left and enters Ringwood State Park. After crossing some old stone walls, the Cannonball Trail passes the southern trailhead of the Crossover Trail (white) to the left at 7.4 miles. Continuing its descent to the east along a winding woods road, the Cannonball Trail ends at the southern end of Bear Swamp Lake at 7.7 miles. Here, the Shore Trail (blue) starts its 2.0-mile loop around the lake.

Castle Point Trail   *Length: 1.0 mile Blaze: white*

This trail, which leads to the ruins of a castle-like fieldstone mansion, begins on a paved road leading south from Skyline Drive, about 0.3 mile northwest of the upper parking area. This road is also the route of the Cannonball Trail (white C on red). After 25 feet along the paved road, the Castle Point Trail turns right, into the woods. In another 250 feet, the trail reaches a rock outcrop with a westward view across a valley. Descending rather steeply from the outcrop, the trail follows a rocky footpath through mountain laurel, crossing a stream at 0.2 mile. After turning left on the route of a gas pipeline for 350 feet, the trail turns left again to join an ascending woods road, using a footpath to shortcut

Figure 6-5. Stone tower on the Castle Point Trail

a bend in the road. The trail turns left at 0.4 mile, briefly joins a utility line, then bears right to ascend to the ridgeline over smooth rock exposures.

At 0.5 mile, after passing a west-facing view over the Wanaque Reservoir and the Wyanokies, the trail reaches a stone tower. This structure once held a water cistern, used to supply water to the mansion (note the rusted pipes adjacent to the tower). Descending to the west side of the ridge, the trail passes the ruins of a concrete swimming pool at 0.7 mile.

Soon, the Castle Point Trail reaches the ruins of the mansion. Known as Foxcroft, it was built around 1910 by William Porter, a stockbroker. He died soon after, but his widow occupied it until her death in 1940. It fell into ruin in the late 1950s and was set afire by vandals. Today, only the stone walls remain. Just beyond, there is an expansive south-facing view over Ramapo Lake and its surrounding mountains. On a clear day, the New York City skyline may be visible to the east. Climbing over a rock wall, the trail now descends the steep, rocky south-facing slope of the ridge. It ends at 1.0 mile at an estate road, the route of the Cannonball Trail. (To the left, the Cannonball Trail can be used as an alternate return route.)

Hoeferlin Memorial Trail   *Length: 9.6 miles Blaze: yellow*
The Hoeferlin Memorial Trail is named for William Hoeferlin, a dedicated hiker, trailblazer, and mapmaker. (It should not be confused with the Hoeferlin Trail (blue) in Wawayanda State Park, which is named after the same person but is a separate and distinct trail.) The Hoeferlin Memorial Trail runs along the ridge of the Ramapo Mountains from Pompton Lakes to north of Bear Swamp Lake. To reach the southern trailhead from I-287, take Exit 57 (Skyline Drive), proceed south on West Oakland Avenue for 1.1 miles, and turn right onto Pool

Hollow Road, where there is room to park several cars on the north side of the road, just west of the intersection, and before reaching the railroad tracks.

To reach the trailhead, proceed west on Pool Hollow Road for 200 feet, crossing the active New York, Susquehanna and Western Railroad. Here, a triple blaze marks the start of the trail. The trail continues along the road, passing through a residential area, with a pond on the right. It bears right, leaving the road, and passes a corral on the left. Soon, it rejoins the road, which begins to ascend through a ravine.

At 0.3 mile, the South Ridge Trail (white) leaves to the left. The Hoeferlin Memorial Trail continues ahead, then descends along a rocky stretch of road. At 0.6 mile, it turns right and joins the Cannonball Trail (white C on red). Both trails now cross I-287 on a pedestrian bridge. On the north side of the bridge, they follow a woods road until, at 0.8 mile, the Hoeferlin Memorial Trail leaves to the right. A large glacial erratic is perched on a ledge to the right of the trail just before the trail junction.

The Hoeferlin Memorial Trail now ascends on a winding footpath, first gradually and then more steeply. At 1.1 miles, it turns right onto an old estate road, then bears left onto an intersecting woods road. After bearing left at a Y intersection, the trail descends on a footpath, crossing a stream in a ravine at 1.3 miles. It ascends to a south-facing viewpoint from a rock outcrop, with High Mountain in the background and industrial buildings in the valley below. Continuing to climb, the trail crosses smooth rock ledges and, after a steep climb, reaches a west-facing viewpoint over the Wyanokies through pines at 1.7 miles. Just beyond, the Lookout Trail (red) joins from the right.

The joint Hoeferlin Memorial/Lookout trails continue ahead, reaching a rock ledge with a limited view over Ramapo Lake to the northwest at 1.8 miles. They descend through laurel thickets to cross a seasonal stream, then climb to another rock outcrop with an expansive view of Ramapo Lake directly below, and the Wyanokies beyond. The trails now descend steadily, reaching the gravel road around the shore of Ramapo Lake at 2.3 miles. Here, the Lookout Trail ends, while the Hoeferlin Memorial Trail turns right and follows the gravel road along the lake shore, passing the start of the Lookout Trail in another 350 feet. The Hoeferlin Memorial Trail continues over a dam and, at the northern end of the dam, is briefly joined by the MacEvoy Trail (blue), which soon leaves to the right (reaching the lower parking area on Skyline Drive in 0.6 mile).

Just beyond, at 2.5 miles, the Hoeferlin Memorial Trail bears right and ascends on a paved estate road. At a bend in the road, the trail leaves to the right

and reenters the woods on a footpath. It descends gradually to a ravine, joins a woods road, and crosses a stream at 3.1 miles. Now ascending, it approaches the estate road that it previously followed, but bears right and continues on the woods road. After passing a pond to the left, the trail rejoins the estate road and emerges, at 3.6 miles, at the upper parking area on Skyline Drive.

The Hoeferlin Memorial Trail crosses the road and turns left, briefly joining the Todd Trail (white). In 75 feet, it reaches a junction—just before the entrance road to Camp Tamarack—where the Todd Trail ends and the Schuber Trail (orange) begins. Passing through a boulder barrier along the road, the Hoeferlin Memorial Trail turns right, ascends a rock outcrop to level off on a ridge, then descends along a rocky footpath. At 4.1 miles, it turns right onto a woods road and rejoins the Cannonball Trail, which comes in from the left. The two trails run jointly for the next 1.6 miles.

After crossing a stream in a wet area at 4.7 miles, the trails emerge to cross a pipeline alongside Skyline Drive. The trails continue along the shoulder of Skyline Drive for 350 feet, then bear right and reenter the woods on a footpath blocked off by boulders. At 5.0 miles, the Matapan Rock Trail (red on white) crosses. (To the left, this trail leads in 500 feet to Matapan Rock, which offers a view to the west, with Skyline Drive directly below, and the Wanaque Reservoir in the distance. To the right, it leads 0.7 mile to Camp Glen Gray, where it connects with the Schuber Trail (orange).) Just beyond, the joint Cannonball/Hoeferlin Memorial trails turn left onto an access road leading to a radio tower, then in 50 feet turn right and continue north on a footpath. After passing abandoned cars off to the right, the Hoeferlin Memorial and Cannonball trails bear left and ascend to the ridgeline, passing a large glacial erratic on the way. At the crest of the ridge, they bear right onto an old woods road.

At 5.7 miles, the Cannonball Trail forks to the right and begins to descend, while the Hoeferlin Memorial Trail continues ahead along the ridge, descending gradually on a winding footpath, and reaching a junction with the Ringwood-Ramapo Trail (red), which departs to the left at 6.1 miles. The Hoeferlin Memorial Trail now turns slightly eastward, away from the edge of the west-facing ridge, leaving Ramapo Mountain State Forest and entering Ramapo Valley County Reservation. After a relatively level stretch, in which it twice crosses the Old Guard Trail (green tulip tree leaf on white), the Hoeferlin Memorial Trail dips to cross a seasonal stream in a ravine at 6.9 miles. It then climbs to reach the Erskine Lookout at 7.3 miles. The Wyanokies are visible in the distance to the west, with the Wanaque Reservoir in the foreground. Here, the Green Trail

(green on white) heads east, connecting in 0.4 mile with the Cannonball Trail at Camp Yaw Paw.

Now in Ringwood State Park, the Hoeferlin Memorial Trail descends to the northeast on an old woods road, reaching a particularly rocky section of the road at 7.5 miles, where Iaoapogh Lake may be visible through the trees when the leaves are down. Then, at 7.8 miles, the Blue Trail, which connects with the Cannonball Trail just south of Iaoapogh Lake, leaves to the right. After crossing a stream at 7.9 miles, the Hoeferlin Memorial Trail climbs a rocky footpath to reach a panoramic view from Ilgenstein Rock at 8.2 miles. Bear Swamp Lake is directly below, with Drag Hill and Rocky Mountain in the background. On clear days, the Manhattan skyline is visible on the horizon to the right. Here, the Crossover Trail (white) joins from the right.

From the lookout, the Hoeferlin Memorial/Crossover trails proceed north on a rocky footpath along the eastern face of the ridge. At 8.6 miles, the Crossover Trail departs to the left. Just beyond, the trenches and tailings of the Butler Mine may be seen to the left. The Hoeferlin Memorial Trail soon curves to the east and descends rather steeply on switchbacks to cross a stream on rocks at 9.0 miles. It continues to descend on a more gentle grade, reaching the western shore of Bear Swamp Lake at 9.4 miles. Here, it joins the Shore Trail (blue), and both trails continue north along the lake shore. In 500 feet, the Shore Trail leaves to the right, while the Hoeferlin Memorial Trail continues ahead, descending on a woods road. At 9.6 miles, the Hoeferlin Memorial Trail ends at a junction with the Halifax Trail (green on white).

Lookout Trail
Length: 1.9 miles Blaze: red

The Lookout Trail is a loop trail that leads to an east-facing lookout over Oakland and continues to several other overlooks that offer views to the west. To reach the trailhead from the lower parking area on Skyline Drive, follow the MacEvoy Trail (blue) for 0.6 mile to its junction with the Hoeferlin Memorial Trail (yellow) near the dam of Ramapo Lake, then turn left and follow the Hoeferlin Memorial Trail across the dam. The Lookout Trail begins on the left, about 75 feet beyond the southern end of the dam.

After a brief climb, the Lookout Trail descends to parallel a stream, then bears right, away from the stream, and ascends steadily. At 0.5 mile, it levels off, passes a large rock ledge to the left, and descends slightly, soon reaching a fork in the trail, where the blazed trail bears right. To the left, an unmarked trail leads

in 350 feet to an expansive viewpoint over Oakland, with High Mountain in Wayne visible beyond. On a clear day, the New York City skyline can be seen in the distance. I-287 is visible to the left and, unfortunately, the sounds of traffic on this busy highway can be heard.

From the fork in the trail, the Lookout Trail proceeds in a generally westward direction, with several short but steep ups and downs. At 1.1 miles, it approaches a large rock formation. The trail bears left to climb this imposing feature, then bears right at the top. Just beyond, at 1.2 miles, the Hoeferlin Memorial Trail (yellow) joins from the left. A few feet to the left along the Hoeferlin Memorial Trail is a west-facing viewpoint through pines, with the Wyanokies visible in the distance.

The joint Hoeferlin Memorial/Lookout trails turn right, reaching a rock ledge with a limited view over Ramapo Lake to the northwest at 1.4 miles. They descend through laurel thickets to cross a seasonal stream, then climb to another rock outcrop. This outcrop, reached at 1.6 miles, offers an expansive view of Ramapo Lake directly below, with the Wyanokies beyond. The trails now descend steadily, reaching the gravel road around the shore of Ramapo Lake at 1.9 miles. Here, the Lookout Trail ends. To return to the beginning of the loop, turn right and follow the Hoeferlin Memorial Trail along the lakeshore road for 350 feet.

Together with the portions of the MacEvoy and Hoeferlin Memorial trails used for access, the Lookout Trail makes a 3.5-mile "lollipop"-loop round-trip hike from the lower parking area on Skyline Drive.

MacEvoy Trail   Length: 2.3 miles Blaze: blue

The MacEvoy Trail is named for Clifford MacEvoy, a public works contractor, whose estate became Ramapo Mountain State Forest. It begins at the south end of the lower parking area on Skyline Drive and heads southwest, immediately passing stone wall ruins. In 100 feet, it turns right onto a woods road and begins to parallel a stream to the left with attractive cascades, especially after heavy rains. The trail climbs over a low but rather steep rock formation at 0.1 mile and continues to ascend more gradually, crossing a tributary stream at 0.4 mile. Here, the Todd Trail (white) leaves to the right.

Soon, Ramapo Lake comes into view, and the MacEvoy Trail descends to reach a paved estate road at 0.6 mile. It turns left onto this road, joining the Hoeferlin Memorial Trail (yellow), which comes in from the right. The two

Figure 6-6. Ramapo Lake

trails run together for only 70 feet, after which the Hoeferlin Memorial Trail bears left and crosses a wide dam, while the MacEvoy Trail turns right and continues west along the gravel lakeshore road, soon passing below a private residence on a ledge to the right.

At 1.0 mile, the MacEvoy Trail continues straight ahead, as the lakeshore road bends to the left. The MacEvoy Trail passes between two gateposts and ascends on a gravel estate road. Just before an S curve in the road, the MacEvoy Trail turns left, leaving the road, and enters the woods on a footpath together with the Cannonball Trail (white C on red), which joins from the right. Both trails continue along a winding footpath until they reach another woods road at 1.3 miles. Here, the Cannonball Trail leaves to the left, while the MacEvoy Trail turns right onto the road.

Reaching the route of a gas pipeline at 1.6 miles, the MacEvoy Trail turns right, follows the pipeline for 300 feet, then turns left onto another woods road. It continues north along the road until, at 2.1 miles, it turns right, leaving the road, and begins a steady descent, ending at the cul-de-sac of Wolfe Drive, where limited parking is available.

Ramapo Lake Lakeshore Path   *Length: 2.6 miles Blaze: various*
Although not a formal blazed trail, the wide estate road that encircles Ramapo

Lake is a popular walk. Ramapo Lake is the hub of the trail system in the area, and the loop hike around the lake is accessible from several other trails. This hike is described here in a clockwise direction.

The Ramapo Lake Lakeshore Path is most easily approached via the MacEvoy Trail (blue) from the lower parking area on Skyline Drive. Upon reaching a paved estate road, 0.6 mile from Skyline Drive, the MacEvoy Trail turns left, joining the Hoeferlin Memorial Trail (yellow), and follows the road downhill for 70 feet. The MacEvoy Trail turns right here, but to follow the Lakeshore Path in a clockwise direction, the hiker should continue straight ahead, crossing the dam. Just beyond the dam, the eastern leg of the Lookout Trail (red) leaves to the left. Then, in another 350 feet, the Hoeferlin Memorial Trail leaves to the left, along with the western leg of the Lookout Trail. The Lakeshore Path, now unmarked, continues ahead on the wide estate road, running close to the eastern shore of Ramapo Lake, with views across the lake. It proceeds through dense laurel thickets, crosses a causeway over an arm of the lake, and passes a swamp to the left. Here, the Lakeshore Path follows an inland route past some rock outcrops. It soon resumes running parallel to the lake shore, but some distance from the lake, with dense vegetation blocking most views over the lake.

Just past the southern end of the lake, 1.0 mile from the north end of the dam, a T intersection is reached. To follow the Lakeshore Path, turn right. (The left branch leads in 0.3 mile to the Hoeferlin Memorial Trail.) Then, in another 300 feet, at a Y intersection, the Lakeshore Path bears right and is joined by the Cannonball Trail (white C on red). The Lakeshore Path now proceeds north, paralleling the western shore of Ramapo Lake, but some distance from the water. At 1.6 miles, after passing a building on the hillside to the left that was formerly used as a ranger station, the trail reaches a rock ledge to the right that offers a pleasant view of the lake.

Another gravel road joins from the left at 1.7 miles, and the Lakeshore Path follows the road over a stone causeway that isolates a quiet pond on the left from the main body of the lake. Then, at 1.9 miles, at a Y intersection, the Cannonball Trail turns left onto an intersecting gravel road, while the Lakeshore Path (now once again unmarked) bears right and continues along a winding section of road. After passing a small, abandoned stone building along the lake shore to the right, the Lakeshore Path bears right at the next intersection at 2.1 miles. Now joined by the MacEvoy Trail (blue), the Lakeshore Path continues along the northern end of the lake, passing a private residence on a ledge to the

left at 2.4 miles. The beginning of the loop at the northern end of the dam is reached at 2.6 miles.

South Ridge Trail   *Length: 0.7 mile Blaze: white*
The South Ridge Trail provides an alternative route which bypasses a wide, eroded section of the Cannonball Trail. It begins at a Y intersection with the Cannonball Trail (white C on red) on a hillside just north of a ballfield, about 750 feet from the trailhead for the Cannonball Trail on Barbara Drive. Here, the Cannonball Trail bears left and levels off, while the South Ridge Trail bears right and ascends, briefly joining a woods road. It soon descends into a shallow valley, then continues its gradual ascent, reaching the crest of the ridge at 0.5 mile, with some views through the trees when the leaves are down. The trail now descends to end, at 0.7 mile, at an old estate road, the route of the Hoeferlin Memorial Trail (yellow). To the left, the Hoeferlin Memorial Trail leads in 0.3 mile to the Cannonball Trail.

A 1.8-mile loop hike from Barbara Drive is possible, using the South Ridge, Hoeferlin Memorial, and Cannonball trails.

Todd Trail   *Length: 2.0 miles Blaze: white*
The Todd Trail begins on the east side of Skyline Drive, adjacent to the Camp Tamarack entrance road, opposite the upper parking area at milepost 1.4. The Schuber Trail (orange) also begins here, and the Hoeferlin Memorial Trail (yellow) intersects. The Todd Trail proceeds south along Skyline Drive for 75 feet to the next utility pole. Here, the Hoeferlin Memorial Trail turns right and crosses Skyline Drive, while the Todd Trail turns left into the woods and descends to the east along a winding, rocky footpath, with several switchbacks. After ascending from a shallow ravine, it descends and turns right onto a woods road at 0.5 mile, then immediately turns left onto an intersecting road. In another 200 feet, the Yellow Trail starts to the left. With abandoned buildings of the former Camp Todd visible ahead, the Todd Trail turns sharply right, leaving the woods road, and ascends to a grassy knoll atop Todd Hill. It then descends slightly and bears right to reach, at 0.8 mile, a viewpoint to the southeast, with Crystal Lake along the Ramapo River directly below, the town of Oakland behind it, and High Mountain in the distance.

From the viewpoint, the trail makes a short, steep descent and continues along the side of a hill. After crossing a woods road, the trail turns left on a grassy woods road. It follows a series of woods roads and climbs on a footpath

to cross Skyline Drive at 1.5 miles. The trail now ascends a knoll and descends through a mountain laurel thicket. It bears left to parallel a stream, which it follows south, ending at a junction with the MacEvoy Trail (blue) at 2.0 miles. Ramapo Lake is 0.2 mile to the right.

Yellow Trail   *Length: 3.9 miles Blaze: yellow*
The Yellow Trail (not to be confused with the Hoeferlin Memorial Trail, also blazed yellow) runs along the eastern ridge of the Ramapo Mountains from Todd Lake to Camp Yaw Paw. To reach the southern trailhead of the Yellow Trail from the upper parking area on Skyline Drive, proceed east on the Todd Trail (white). After 0.5 mile, the Todd Trail turns right on a woods road, then immediately turns left onto another woods road. The Yellow Trail begins on the left side of the road, about 200 feet beyond the second turn.

From the trailhead, the Yellow Trail proceeds north, reaching Todd Lake in 0.1 mile. Here, the trail bears left and follows along the west shore of the lake, passing a rock ledge at lake level with a view over the water. After climbing steeply to a rock outcrop near the north end of the lake (from which a water tower for the Ramapo Reserve development is visible to the right), the Yellow Trail begins a steady, rather steep descent to a valley. The trail passes a small waterfall to the left, then crosses a stream at 0.8 mile. Beyond the stream, the trail joins an old woods road and begins to ascend. Turning left at 0.9 mile, the trail leaves the woods road and ascends the hillside to the west, with a stone wall to the right. It soon bears right and heads north, continuing to climb steadily. At 1.2 miles, the trail levels off on a shoulder of the ridge, with views through the trees of Campgaw Mountain to the east.

At 1.3 miles, the Yellow Trail turns right and joins the Millstone Trail (white). Just beyond the junction, several abandoned millstones in various stages of completion may be seen to the left of the trail. Descending along an old woods road, the two trails pass a millstone in nearly perfect condition 25 feet to the right. At a T intersection, reached at 1.5 miles, the trails turn left at an old stone wall, which marks the camp boundary.

Continuing to descend, the trails cross paved Midvale Mountain Road at 1.6 miles. They bear left and head west, parallel to Fox Brook, then turn right to cross two branches of the brook on rocks at 1.7 miles. The trails now begin to climb, reaching a junction in a level area at 1.8 miles. Here, the Millstone Trail leaves to the left, while the Yellow Trail turns right, briefly follows an old woods road, then turns left and heads north, climbing steadily through a wooded

valley. At 2.2 miles, the trail reaches the crest of the rise and, after a brief descent, continues along a level woods road. It crosses a stream on rocks at 2.5 miles and, just beyond, passes some old stone foundations. Just ahead, it turns right onto a wide woods road—the route of the Yellow-Silver Trail—and, in 100 feet, reaches the rusted frame of an old fire tower. Here, the Yellow Trail turns left and begins to ascend, soon passing a stone foundation on a ledge.

At the high point of the ridge (996 feet), the Schuber Trail (orange) joins from the left. Here, at 2.8 miles, there is an expansive viewpoint over northern Bergen County from a rock outcrop to the right of the trail, with the Manhattan skyline visible on the horizon to the right. On a clear day, the Verrazano-Narrows Bridge may be seen to the extreme right. The Yellow Trail and the Schuber Trail continue ahead along the ridge, descending gradually. Soon, the Old Guard Trail (green tulip tree leaf on white) leaves to the left. At 3.0 miles, the Yellow Trail, along with the Schuber Trail, bears left and begins a rather steep, rocky descent, joining a narrow woods road about halfway down. At the base of the descent, at 3.3 miles, the two trails turn left onto a wide woods road. A short distance beyond, the Schuber Trail leaves to the right, while the Yellow Trail continues ahead along the woods road, crossing a stream on rocks and then proceeding across a clearing for a gas pipeline. It crosses a wet area on puncheons at 3.6 miles and ascends into Camp Yaw Paw. After passing the Dogwood Cabin (used as a Scoutcraft center) to the right, the Yellow Trail ends at 3.9 miles, at a junction with the Cannonball Trail (white C on red).

The Yellow Trail may be combined with the Todd Trail and the Schuber Trail to make a 6.0-mile loop hike from the upper parking area on Skyline Drive. Alternatively, it can be combined with the Todd, Cannonball, and Hoeferlin Memorial trails for an 8.0-mile loop hike.

RINGWOOD STATE PARK

Bordering New York State, Ringwood State Park features both wild lands and landscaped gardens. The park is named for Ringwood Manor, a large mansion containing a priceless collection of relics from the iron-making days, as well as the furnishings of the Ryerson, Cooper, and Hewitt families from about 1810 to 1930. Tours of the manor house are available between 10:00 a.m. and 3:00 p.m., Wednesday to Sunday. For more information, contact Ringwood Manor at (973) 962-7031. (For historical information about Ringwood Manor, see

the History section, pp. 67-69 above.) Also contained within the park is Shepherd Lake, with swimming, picnicking, boating, and trapshooting facilities.

Figure 6-7. *Ringwood Manor*

Skylands Manor is another notable feature of the park. Clarence McKenzie Lewis, who purchased the land from the estate of Francis Lynde Stetson, completed this 44-room Tudor mansion of native granite in 1929. Stetson, who acquired the property in 1891, had hired Samuel Parsons, Jr., founder of the American Society of Landscape Architects, protégé of Frederick Law Olmsted and at one time New York City Parks Commissioner, to design the grounds. Lewis, like Stetson, was a trustee of the New York Botanical Garden. Today, volunteers help maintain the Skylands plantings, managed as the New Jersey State Botanical Gardens. Skylands Manor is open for tours on the first Sunday of each month from March to December. For more information, contact Skylands Manor at (973) 962-7527.

Access to the Ringwood area from the northeast is from NY 17 just south of Sloatsburg, New York, via Sterling Mine Road (County 72), which becomes Sloatsburg Road where it crosses into New Jersey. There are three main parking areas, with fees charged in season. The Ringwood Manor entrance on the right includes a main parking area near the Manor House and a picnic parking area near several trailheads. The Skylands Manor area is another half-mile south, on the left via Morris Avenue. Skylands, in turn, provides access to Shepherd Lake, with additional ample parking. These areas can also be approached from the south via Skyline Drive and Greenwood Lake Turnpike (County 511). Hikers may also reach the area via New Jersey Transit bus #197 from the Port Authority Bus Terminal in New York City. Hunting is permitted in designated areas of the park. For more information, contact Ringwood State Park, 1304 Sloatsburg Road, Ringwood, NJ 07456; (973) 962-7031; www.njparksandforests.org.

Figure 6-8. Wanaque Reservoir from Governor Mountain on the Cooper Union Trail

Cooper Union Trail   *Length: 4.7 miles Blaze: yellow*

The Cooper Union Trail is a "lollipop"-loop trail which begins on the east side of Sloatsburg Road, just south of the New Jersey-New York state line. Limited parking may be available along the shoulder of the road, just north of the state line. The trail begins by following a woods road. At 0.1 mile, it bears right at a Y junction and starts to climb through maple and beech woods. A short distance beyond, the Cupsaw Brook Trail (blue) leaves to the left. The Cooper Union Trail soon reaches the ridgeline of Cupsaw Mountain and begins to descend. It reaches a junction with the Ringwood-Ramapo Trail (red) at 0.5 mile. Here, the Cooper Union Trail turns right, leaving the woods road, and ascends on a footpath together with the Ringwood-Ramapo Trail. (A trail shelter is 200 feet ahead on the woods road, the southbound route of the Ringwood-Ramapo Trail.) After running jointly for about 200 feet, the Cooper Union Trail turns left, while the Ringwood-Ramapo Trail continues ahead (leading in 0.4 mile to the picnic parking area at Ringwood Manor).

The Cooper Union Trail soon regains the ridgetop and continues along the ridge, with limited views to the left, through the trees. After passing a broader viewpoint from an open rock, the trail begins to descend and reaches the southern end of the Cupsaw Brook Trail, which leaves sharply to the left at 1.1 miles. In another 250 feet, the Crossover Trail (white) joins from the left. The two trails run together for 250 feet until, at a Y intersection, the Crossover Trail leaves to the right, while the Cooper Union Trail bears left. It soon turns left

again at a T intersection and, in another 100 feet, crosses Morris Avenue, 1.2 miles from the start.

The trail now continues through a thick understory of young beech trees. It crosses the route of a gas pipeline at 1.6 miles. After crossing a woods road and then a stream, it proceeds through a swampy area. For the next mile, the Cooper Union Trail winds through a generally low-lying area, crossing several woods roads, until it reaches Carletondale Avenue at 2.7 miles.

Crossing the paved road, the Cooper Union Trail bears left and skirts privately-owned church property. It crosses a stream on a small wooden bridge, ascends on a woods road through hemlocks, and, at 3.0 miles, reaches the start of the loop. Proceeding straight ahead (to follow the loop in a counterclockwise direction), the trail begins a gradual ascent, leveling off and passing two large glacial erratics to the left at 3.2 miles. After a sharp left turn, the ascent steepens until the crest of Governor Mountain is reached at 3.5 miles. The trail now passes through a cedar forest dotted with glacial erratics. Soon, there are limited views through the trees to the right, but the best views are from an open rock ledge, known as Suicide Ledge, reached at 3.8 miles, after a short descent. From here, there are expansive views over the Wanaque Reservoir to the west and south, with Sterling Forest visible to the northwest.

After a brief climb and then another short descent, the trail follows the eastern ridge of Governor Mountain, encountering many exposed granite surfaces and passing several limited viewpoints. At 4.5 miles, it bears sharply left and descends on a switchback, reaching the beginning of the loop at 4.7 miles.

Crossover Trail   *Length: 5.6 miles Blaze: white*

The Crossover Trail connects the Ringwood Manor and Skylands Manor areas of Ringwood State Park with Bear Swamp Lake and Ramapo Valley County Reservation. Except for a short 0.2-mile section at its southern end, it features gentle and moderate grades, following woods roads and old carriage roads for most of its length.

To reach the northwestern trailhead, park at the northerly parking area at Ringwood Manor (follow signs to the picnic area) and take the Ringwood-Ramapo Trail (red) east, crossing the Ringwood River on wooden bridges and then the busy Sloatsburg Road. The Crossover Trail begins to the right just beyond the road crossing. It ascends gradually along a shoulder of Cupsaw Mountain, following a woods road. At 0.5 mile, it turns left, briefly joining the Cooper Union Trail (yellow), then departs to the right as the Cooper Union

Trail continues straight ahead. After passing an old stone foundation to the left, the Crossover Trail turns left on paved Morris Avenue to cross Cupsaw Brook on a stone-walled bridge at 0.9 mile. A dam and pond are visible to the left, and a gravel parking area is on the left side of the road just beyond the bridge.

In another 500 feet, the Crossover Trail turns right and briefly follows the route of a gas pipeline. A short distance beyond the end of the fence, it turns left, leaving the pipeline, and re-enters the woods. At 1.3 miles, it bears left and begins a steady ascent. It emerges, at 1.6 miles, at the entrance to Skylands Manor, and passes between two stone eagles (which formerly adorned New York City's Pennsylvania Station). Continuing ahead along the paved access road, it passes Parking Area A to the left and then bears left at a fork in the road. Now proceeding through the manor grounds, the trail goes by a number of interesting trees (planted as part of the estate) and passes to the right of a greenhouse and an English Tudor guest house with a sundial clock on its chimney.

Figure 6-9. Swan Pond

At 1.8 miles, the Crossover Trail turns left onto an unpaved carriage road which follows the western base of Mount Defiance. For the next 2.6 miles, the trail follows a series of carriage roads with gentle grades. At 2.0 miles, just before the trail crosses a stream and passes between two concrete gateposts, an unmarked woods road to the right leads to quiet Swan Pond, which is soon visible through the trees to the right. In another 60 feet, the Halifax Trail (green on white), which can be used as an alternate return route, begins to the left.

The Crossover Trail turns left at 2.4 miles and begins a gradual ascent. It passes a road to the right that leads back to Parking Area C at Skylands Manor and continues ahead as a branch of the road switches back to the left. At 2.8 miles, it curves left and reaches the crest of the ridge, where it crosses the Ringwood-Ramapo Trail (red). The Crossover Trail now begins a gradual

descent, crosses a wide woods road, and then ascends gently. It turns left at 3.3 miles, leaving the carriage road, ascends into the woods on a footpath, then turns left onto a woods road.

At 3.5 miles, the Crossover Trail leaves the road and ascends on a short footpath to Gatum Pond, where it rejoins the carriage road. Stone steps lead down to the water's edge. This tranquil, pleasant setting is a good spot for a lunch break. Continuing ahead on the level road, the trail passes an old cable fence to the right, with Brushwood Pond visible in the distance. The Crossover Trail now makes several sharp turns, switchbacking up the ridge on carriage roads, until—at 4.4 miles—it turns right, leaving the road, and ascends on a footpath. Upon reaching a shoulder of the ridge, it turns right and continues to ascend on a woods road. Here, the Pierson Ridge Trail (blue) begins to the left and leads north 1.0 mile to the Halifax Trail.

The woods road followed by the Crossover Trail soon reaches the crest of the ridge, where it narrows to a footpath. At 4.9 miles, in an area of stunted ridge growth, the Crossover Trail reaches a junction with the Hoeferlin Memorial Trail (yellow). The Butler Mine is 0.1 mile to the left along the Hoeferlin Memorial Trail, but the Crossover Trail turns right at the junction and proceeds south. The joint Crossover and Hoeferlin Memorial trails follow a rocky, winding footpath along the eastern face of the ridge, reaching Ilgenstein Rock at 5.4 miles. This rock outcrop affords a panoramic view, with Bear Swamp Lake below, and Rocky Mountain and Drag Hill in the background. The Manhattan skyline is visible in the distance to the right. Just beyond, the Hoeferlin Memorial Trail leaves to the right, while the Crossover Trail bears left and descends steeply through a rock hollow. The Crossover Trail ends at 5.6 miles at a junction with the Cannonball Trail (white C on red). To the left, the Cannonball Trail leads in 0.4 mile to Bear Swamp Lake.

Cupsaw Brook Trail   *Length: 1.4 miles Blaze: blue*
Both ends of the Cupsaw Brook Trail connect to the Cooper Union Trail, enabling hikers to make a 2.7-mile loop hike from Sloatsburg Road or to avoid a climb over Cupsaw Mountain.

To reach the northern trailhead, follow the Cooper Union Trail (yellow) east from its trailhead on Sloatsburg Road. About 250 feet after the Cooper Union Trail bears right at a Y intersection, 0.1 mile from its start, the Cupsaw Brook Trail leaves to the left. It ascends gradually through the woods on a footpath, climbing a shoulder of Cupsaw Mountain. At 0.2 mile, it steeply

descends a rocky slope to a woods road in a valley. It turns right and follows the relatively level road, soon beginning to parallel Cupsaw Brook to the left. After passing through a rocky area, it crosses a seasonal tributary stream and bears right on a footpath, away from Cupsaw Brook.

At 1.0 mile, the Cupsaw Brook Trail turns right onto a woods road, joining the Ringwood-Ramapo Trail (red). In 100 feet, after crossing a tributary stream on rocks, the Ringwood-Ramapo Trail leaves to the right, while the Cupsaw Brook Trail continues ahead on the woods road. It climbs a small hill, descends steadily, and then ascends briefly to end at the Cooper Union Trail at 1.4 miles. To the right, the Cooper Union Trail leads north 1.1 miles to the northern trailhead of the Cupsaw Brook Trail.

Halifax Trail   *Length: 3.0 miles Blaze: green on white*

The western trailhead of the Halifax Trail is on the east side of the Crossover Trail (white), 0.3 mile southeast of Parking Lot A at Skylands Manor, and 60 feet beyond an unmarked woods road which leads west to Swan Pond. The Halifax Trail heads east on an old carriage road, ascending Mount Defiance on a long series of switchbacks. Near the top, at 0.4 mile, a short side trail leads left to a viewpoint. The New Jersey State Botanical Gardens at Skylands Manor may be seen in the foreground, with the Wyanokies in the distance. Continuing eastward, the trail skirts a rock formation on the left and descends into a hollow on the crest of Mount Defiance. Here, at 0.5 mile, the Halifax Trail briefly joins the Ringwood-Ramapo Trail (red).

The Halifax Trail now descends on another series of switchbacks, leveling off at 0.9 mile to turn left onto a woods road. Almost immediately, it turns right onto another woods road and passes between the two Glasmere Ponds. Veering left into the woods at 1.0 mile, the trail gradually ascends on a footpath to a third woods road and cuts across a hairpin turn in that road. After crossing yet another woods road and then a gas pipeline at 1.5 miles, the trail ascends more steeply to the top of the Pierson Ridge, then descends on a winding footpath.

At 1.7 miles, the Halifax Trail crosses a woods road. Here, the Pierson Ridge Trail (blue) leaves to the right, connecting in 1.0 mile with the Crossover Trail (white). The Halifax Trail now ascends, keeping Spruce Swamp to the right, and crosses a maintenance road for a gas pipeline at 1.9 miles. Soon, the trail swings to the south, and it joins the maintenance road to recross the pipeline at 2.3 miles. It continues south on a woods road, beginning a steady

descent at 2.8 miles, with Bear Swamp below to the left. At 3.0 miles, just before a wooden bridge over Bear Swamp Brook, the Hoeferlin Memorial Trail (yellow) leaves to the right. The Halifax Trail continues ahead for another 3.1 miles, entering Ramapo Valley County Reservation. For a description of this section of the trail, see pp. 77-78.

Manor Trail *Length: 3.0 miles Blaze: blue*

The Manor Trail is a relatively easy loop trail through the woods west of Ringwood Manor. To reach the trailhead from the parking area adjacent to the manor house, follow the footpath that leads along the rear of the manor house. Near the end of the house, turn right and climb the stone steps. At the top of the steps, turn left on a dirt road which leads, in about 200 feet, to a T intersection with another woods road.

To follow the trail in a counter-clockwise direction, turn right and proceed along the woods road for 0.3 mile to a Y intersection. The White Trail, which begins here, leaves to the right, while the Manor Trail bears left onto a grassy woods road. After passing through an area where the thick understory forms a canopy overhead, the Manor Trail bears right, leaving the road, and proceeds into the woods on a footpath. The trail continues through a rocky, wet area, crossing several small tributary streams. After crossing the main stream at 0.7 mile, a flooded 30-foot-wide excavation may be seen to the right of the trail. At 0.9 mile, after a short climb, the trail joins an old woods road. Then, at 1.2 miles, the trail descends to cross another wide stream. (Both streams feed Sally's Pond, which will be encountered near the end of the hike.) The trail briefly parallels the stream on a rocky footpath and then ascends gradually, eventually joining another old woods road.

At 1.5 miles, the trail crosses the route of a gas pipeline, with views to the west. The hills across the valley are part of the section of Sterling Forest purchased by Passaic County in 1990 and now administered by the Palisades Interstate Park Commission. The valley is the site of several abandoned iron mines, including the Hope and Peter's mines. Just beyond the pipeline crossing, the Manor Trail joins a wide woods road and begins a gradual descent. At 1.9 miles, long strands of one-inch-thick twisted-strand wrought iron cables are embedded in the trail. These iron cables are remnants of mining activity during the nineteenth century at the nearby Hope and Peter's mines. It is possible that they were intended for use in a gravity conveyor system for the iron ore, constructed in 1858 but apparently never put into successful operation.

Just beyond, as the trail approaches Margaret King Avenue, it swings to the left, as a side road, blocked off with boulders, leads down to the paved, heavily-trafficked road. Following a wider woods road, the trail goes by an occupied residence on the right at 2.1 miles. After passing tennis courts on the right, a dirt road to the right leads out to the Ringwood Municipal Building, as the trail bears left, continuing ahead on a wide woods road.

At 2.5 miles, the trail passes an open area to the right, with Sally's Pond beyond. This pond, created in 1895 to provide a scenic body of water in the landscape, was named after one of Abram Hewitt's three daughters. A short distance ahead, a cemetery comes into view on the right. The two large graves nearest the trail are those of Robert Erskine and his assistant. Near the pond are the graves of members of the Hewitt family, while an iron gate adjacent to the trail marks the graves of the Morris family. Continuing ahead, the trail crosses two bridges over streams that lead to Sally's Pond. At the next fork in the road, marked by two abandoned farm buildings on the left, the trail curves to the right, reaching the start of the loop at 3.0 miles.

Ringwood-Ramapo Trail   *Length: 7.3 miles Blaze: red*
The northern trailhead of the Ringwood-Ramapo Trail is at the picnic area at the north end of Ringwood Manor, where parking is available. The Ringwood-Ramapo Trail proceeds east, crossing two wooden bridges over the Ringwood River and then crossing the heavily-traveled Sloatsburg Road. At 0.1 mile, about 100 feet beyond Sloatsburg Road, the Crossover Trail (white) leaves to the right. The Ringwood-Ramapo Trail now ascends Cupsaw Mountain, winding through a mixed forest. As it nears the crest of the ridge, the climb steepens.

At 0.4 mile, on the ridgetop, the Cooper Union Trail (yellow) joins from the right, and both trails run jointly for 200 feet, descending to a woods road. Here, the Cooper Union Trail leaves to the left, while the Ringwood-Ramapo Trail turns right, reaching a shelter (built by "The Hiking, Eating, Arguing and Puzzle-Solving Club of the Cooper Union") in another 200 feet. The trail now descends into a rocky valley where, at 0.7 mile, it turns left onto a woods road, joining the Cupsaw Brook Trail (blue) for 100 feet. After crossing a tributary stream on rocks, the Cupsaw Brook Trail leaves to the left. A short distance beyond, the Ringwood-Ramapo Trail also turns left, leaving the woods road, which continues ahead to cross Cupsaw Brook (the woods road ahead is the route of a bike path). The Ringwood-Ramapo Trail soon turns right to cross the brook and then parallels it, continuing through several wet areas. After a

steady ascent, the trail turns left onto a woods road at 1.3 miles, soon reaching a paved road at a traffic circle near Shepherd Lake.

The trail turns right on the paved road, then immediately left, following the sign in the middle of the traffic circle for the boat launch. It continues straight ahead along a gravel road which follows the south shore of the lake, soon passing the boathouse and reentering the woods. At 1.8 miles, the Ringwood-Ramapo Trail turns right, leaving the road, and begins to head uphill. It crosses a woods road, reaches the top of a rise, and descends, crossing a bike trail and then, at 2.4 miles, the route of a gas pipeline.

Figure 6-10. Building at Skylands Manor

The Ringwood-Ramapo Trail now begins to climb the northern shoulder of Mount Defiance, first gradually, then more steeply. At 2.6 miles, before reaching the 1,040-foot summit, there is a view to the west over Ringwood Manor and the Cupsaw Lake area. The trail descends steeply from the summit and follows along the crest of the ridge, paralleling impressive cliffs on the right. The Halifax Trail (green on white) joins briefly at 2.9 miles and soon leaves to the left. In another 350 feet along the Ringwood-Ramapo Trail, there is a viewpoint from a rock outcrop to the right of the trail. The New Jersey State Botanical Gardens at Skylands Manor may be seen in the foreground, with the Wyanokies in the distance and the Wanaque Reservoir to the left. The trail continues south along the ridge until, at 3.2 miles, it turns left onto a gravel carriage road. Ascending gradually, the trail crosses to the east side of the ridge and then descends to intersect the Crossover Trail (white) at 3.9 miles.

The Ringwood-Ramapo Trail continues ahead on a grassy woods road, with many exposed rocks, soon reaching a graffiti-scarred rock ledge known as Warm Puppy Rock, with views to the west. Here, it turns left and descends on a footpath, passing another rock ledge to the left with east-facing views. Just beyond, the trail descends steeply over rocks, then continues to descend more gradually. At 4.2 miles, it turns right onto a carriage road, then immediately turns left and renters the woods, crossing a stream on a flat rock and passing a swampy area to the right. Just beyond, at a T intersection, the trail turns left on a wide fire road, which it follows for 0.2 mile.

At 4.5 miles, the Ringwood-Ramapo Trail turns right, leaving the fire road, and ascends on a footpath. After crossing a stream on a single-plank bridge, it reaches a T intersection and turns left, continuing to ascend on a woods road. Then, at another T intersection, it bears left and continues to climb. At 4.8 miles, the trail turns left onto a footpath and climbs gently to reach the crest of the ridge at 5.1 miles. From the ridgetop, it descends to cross a stream on a wooden bridge at 5.3 miles. It then crosses a woods road and continues ahead into the woods on a footpath, which soon curves to the right.

After climbing to a seasonal viewpoint over a valley to the east from a rock ledge to the left of the trail, the Ringwood-Ramapo Trail turns left and descends into the valley. At 5.7 miles, it turns right onto a woods road, then immediately turns left, leaving the road, and begins to parallel High Mountain Brook to the left. At 5.9 miles, it turns left, crosses the brook on rocks, then begins to climb the ridge to the east, first passing through several rocky areas and then continuing on switchbacks. Leveling off on a shoulder of the ridge, the trail passes a cliff and boulder slope to the left and crosses a stream at 6.3 miles.

After climbing a rocky slope and crossing another stream on the way, the Ringwood-Ramapo Trail approaches the crest of the ridge at 6.7 miles. To the west, there are views through the trees over the Erskine Lakes, with the Wanaque Reservoir and the dam of the Monksville Reservoir in the background. Here, the Old Guard Trail (green tulip tree leaf on white) joins for 0.1 mile. The Ringwood-Ramapo Trail now descends slightly, continuing along the shoulder of the ridge, then turns left, regaining the crest. At 7.3 miles, it ends at a junction with the Hoeferlin Memorial Trail (yellow). To the right, the Hoeferlin Memorial Trail leads to the upper parking area on Skyline Drive in 2.5 miles.

White Trail   *Length: 1.0 mile Blaze: white*

The White Trail connects the Ringwood Manor picnic area with the Manor Trail. Beginning at the picnic parking area, about 200 feet north of the trailhead of the Ringwood-Ramapo Trail (red), the White Trail heads west, ascending on a woods road. After leveling off, the trail turns left opposite a massive rock outcrop at 0.3 mile and ascends on a winding footpath. At 0.5 mile, it turns left onto a woods road and begins a steady descent. Then, at 0.7 mile, it bears left and continues to descend on a footpath. After turning left to rejoin the woods road at 0.9 mile, the White Trail ends at the Manor Trail (blue), 1.0 mile from the start. Ringwood Manor is 0.3 mile ahead.

SEVEN

THE WYANOKIES

he name "Wyanokie" is a variant of the Native American word "Winaki," commonly rendered *Wanaque*, meaning "place of sassafras." The Wyanokies range in elevation from 400 to 1,300 feet, and although within sight of the New York skyline, the hiker can find peace and beauty aplenty in the area's streams, waterfalls, and scenic vistas.

Most trails in the Wyanokies are in Norvin Green State Forest, but some extend into watershed property owned by the North Jersey District Water Supply Commission. Also included in this chapter are the lands immediately to the north, which border the Monksville Reservoir and Greenwood Lake—Long Pond Ironworks State Park, Tranquility Ridge Park (the New Jersey section of Sterling Forest, owned by Passaic County and managed by the New Jersey office of the Palisades Interstate Park Commission), and the Wanaque Wildlife Management Area. As of 2003, all trails in this area are hiking-only.

Norvin Green State Forest

The 4,210-acre Norvin Green State Forest has one of the largest concentrations of trails in the state. Most of this land was donated to the State of New Jersey in 1946 by Norvin Hewitt Green, nephew of Ringwood Manor owner Abram S. Hewitt.

Primary access to the area is from a parking area adjacent to the Weis Ecology Center, a private, non-profit environmental education center, affiliated with the New Jersey Audubon Society, which offers programs for Scout and school groups and family programs on weekends (preregistration required).The

center is located on Snake Den Road (East), uphill from West Brook Road. To reach the Weis Ecology Center, take Skyline Drive to its northwestern end at Greenwood Lake Turnpike (County 511), then turn left and proceed south for 1.6 miles to West Brook Road. Turn right onto West Brook Road and cross the Wanaque Reservoir on a narrow causeway. At the next T intersection, turn left, then take the second left onto Snake Den Road, following signs to the Weis Ecology Center. Continue for 0.6 mile to a large dirt parking area on the right side of the road, just before the entrance to the center. Large groups who wish to hike in the area should call the center in advance. For more information, or to preregister for programs, contact the Weis Ecology Center, 150 Snake Den Road, Ringwood, NJ 07456; (973) 835-2160; www.njaudubon.org.

Access is also available from the Otter Hole parking area on Glenwild Avenue, where the Hewitt-Butler Trail crosses. To reach this parking area, take take I-287 to Exit 53. At the bottom of the ramp, turn left onto Hamburg Turnpike. Upon entering Bloomingdale, the name of the road changes to Main Street. After 1.3 miles (from Route 287), bear right at a fork in the road (following the sign to West Milford), and in another 0.1 mile, turn right (uphill) onto Glenwild Avenue. Continue ahead for 3.2 miles to the parking area on the right side of the road, identified by a "Welcome to Bloomingdale" sign at its eastern end.

Norvin Green State Forest borders watershed lands adjoining the Wanaque Reservoir, which is patrolled by uniformed guards of the North Jersey District Water Supply Commission. Hikers who enter watershed property are advised to remain on the marked hiking trails. As of 2003, the privately-owned Saddle Mountain area, south of West Brook Road, is closed to hikers. For more information on Norvin Green State Forest, contact Ringwood State Park, 1304 Sloatsburg Road, Ringwood, NJ 07456; (973) 962-7031; www.njparksandforests.org.

Trails in Norvin Green State Forest

The original trails in Norvin Green State Forest were laid out in the early 1920s by Professor Will S. Monroe of Montclair and his co-workers in the Green Mountain Club. When he retired, the property and trail maintenance were taken over by the Nature Friends, who named the area Camp Midvale. Their former camp is now the Weis Ecology Center. Several trails in the area traverse

private lands. Hikers are asked to respect the property owners and stay on the trails. Failure to do so could jeopardize the generosity of the owners in allowing the public to hike.

The largest concentration of trails in Norvin Green State Forest is in the area south of West Brook Road. Several trails run through the northern section of the forest, north of West Brook Road. These trails are described in the next section of this chapter, the Monksville/Stonetown Area.

Camp Wyanokie Trail   *Length: 1.2 miles Blaze: yellow on white*
The Camp Wyanokie Trail (formerly the northern section of the Mine Trail) begins in Camp Wyanokie at a chain barrier on the east side of Snake Den Road (West), about 1.0 mile south of West Brook Road. This point is also the northern terminus of the Wyanokie Circular Trail (red on white). Limited parking is available along Snake Den Road (West) at Camp Wyanokie.

The Camp Wyanokie Trail proceeds east and descends to Boy Scout Lake. It follows a camp road along the north shore of the lake and crosses a dam over its outlet. At the eastern side of the dam, the trail turns left and descends to the north through the valley between Cobb Hill and Saddle Mountain, following along the east side of the outlet stream. At 0.7 mile, a wide dirt road descends from the right to ford the stream. The outlet stream joins the wider West Brook, which approaches from the left, at 0.9 mile. Here, the trail curves eastward, proceeding through a residential area to end, at 1.2 miles, at West Brook Road, just east of the highway bridge over West Brook. Limited parking is available 0.2 mile to the east, on the south side of West Brook Road, just west of the southern terminus of the northern section of the Hewitt-Butler Trail (blue).

Carris Hill Trail
        Length: 0.9 mile Blaze: yellow
The Carris Hill Trail connects the Lower Trail with the Hewitt-Butler Trail at the summit of Carris Hill, offering several expansive views along the way. It begins at the Lower Trail (white), 0.1 mile

Figure 7-1. Glacial boulder atop lichen-encrusted surface on the Carris Hill Trail

from the start of that trail at the Posts Brook Trail (white). After traversing a level but rocky area, the Carris Hill Trail crosses a stream and begins a rather steep climb. The grade soon moderates, but at 0.3 mile, the trail again climbs steeply over rocks, coming out at a viewpoint to the southeast from a rock outcrop. It continues to climb to another rock outcrop, with a somewhat broader view. Here, the trail bears right and ascends to the left of a 40-foot-high massive rock face. At the top of the ascent, at 0.5 mile, a short detour to the right leads to an expansive viewpoint to the east. The Wanaque Reservoir, contained by the Raymond, Wolf Den, and Green Swamp dams, is in the foreground, with a long viaduct of I-287 clearly visible in the distance.

The Carris Hill Trail now climbs more gradually, soon reaching another viewpoint, where a ten-foot-high balanced glacial erratic is silhouetted against the sky. The trail curves to the right and, at 0.7 mile, reaches a fifth viewpoint—this one to the south, and also featuring a large glacial erratic. Continuing ahead through laurel, the Carris Hill Trail ends, at 0.9 mile, at a junction with the joint Hewitt-Butler (blue) and Highlands (teal diamond) trails on the summit of Carris Hill. There are views to the north and west from a rock outcrop at the summit.

Hewitt-Butler Trail   *Length: 6.4 miles Blaze: blue*

This southern section of the Hewitt-Butler Trail connects Norvin Green State Forest with Camp Vacamas, just north of Butler. Parking for the northern trailhead is at the Weis Ecology Center parking area on Snake Den Road (East). Parking near the midpoint of the trail is available on Glenwild Avenue, and Camp Vacamas provides parking at the southern trailhead.

To reach the northern trailhead from the Weis Ecology Center parking area, proceed west along paved Snake Den Road, following the Otter Hole Trail (green). In 0.3 mile, the pavement ends, and the Otter Hole Trail continues ahead on a dirt road. In another 0.1 mile, the Hewitt-Butler Trail begins to the left. The Mine Trail (yellow on white) also starts here, and both trails run jointly, ascending steeply through laurel. In 300 feet, the Mine Trail continues straight ahead as the Hewitt-Butler Trail turns sharply right and continues to climb, first gradually and then more steeply. At 0.4 mile, the trail levels off, with a rock outcrop to the right—surrounded by pitch pines—offering a view of Assiniwikam Mountain to the northwest. In another 100 feet, the Macopin Trail (white), which leads back to the Otter Hole Trail, leaves to the right. The Hewitt-Butler Trail continues through a mountain laurel thicket and climbs to

a rock ledge with a balanced boulder.

After a slight descent, the Hewitt-Butler Trail reaches a T intersection at 0.6 mile. Here, the Hewitt-Butler Trail turns right, joining the Wyanokie Circular Trail (red on white), which comes in from the left, and the Highlands Trail (teal diamond). (The Highlands Trail runs jointly with the Hewitt-Butler Trail for the next 2.5 miles.) All three trails continue south to cross a seasonal stream on rocks. Then, at 0.8 mile, the Wyanokie Circular Trail departs to the right. The Hewitt-Butler Trail continues ahead, ascending to a rock outcrop with several erratics at 1.0 mile. This spot—with Wyanokie High Point visible back along the trail to the left—is known as Yoo-Hoo Point. The trail continues ahead, heading south along the ridge. At 1.5 miles, after a steep, winding ascent past granite outcrops, the trail arrives at the open summit of Carris Hill, with a 360° view over the Wanaque Reservoir to the east and the surrounding Wyanokies to the south, west, and north. Here, the Carris Hill Trail (yellow) leaves to the left, descending to the southeast.

After traversing another rocky high point, the Hewitt-Butler Trail begins a steady descent along the southwest side of Carris Hill. It levels off in a flat area and briefly joins a woods road—the route of the world's first oil pipeline, constructed in 1880 and abandoned in 1927, that extended 315 miles from Olean, New York to Bayonne, New Jersey. After crossing a rocky area, the Hewitt-Butler Trail arrives, at 2.2 miles, at a T junction with a woods road. Here, the Posts Brook Trail (white) leaves to the left, while the Hewitt-Butler Trail turns right and immediately crosses a tributary stream to Posts Brook, which parallels the trail to the left. At 2.6 miles, the Wyanokie Crest Trail (yellow) joins from the right for 75 feet, then leaves to the left. The Hewitt-Butler Trail now begins a gradual ascent, soon joining a broad woods road that comes in from the left.

At 3.1 miles, the Hewitt-Butler Trail bears left and descends on a rocky woods road. In another 250 feet, the Otter Hole Trail (green), together with the Highlands Trail, leaves to the right. The Hewitt-Butler Trail proceeds ahead to cross the wide Posts Brook on large boulders. This spot, which features attractive cascades and a waterfall, is known as the Otter Hole. (The stream crossing may be a little difficult when the water is high.) After passing to the right of a large erratic, the trail ascends to a parking area on the north side of paved Glenwild Avenue at 3.2 miles.

Crossing to the south side of the road, the trail reenters the woods and ascends steeply through laurel, then turns right and heads west, parallel to the

Figure 7-2. Osio Rock from Torne Mountain on the Hewitt-Butler Trail

road. It soon descends and, at 3.4 miles—with the road visible on the right—reaches a junction with the Torne Trail (red), which leaves to the left. (The Torne Trail, which rejoins the Hewitt-Butler Trail in 0.4 mile, can be used to bypass the rugged climb of Torne Mountain.) The Hewitt-Butler Trail now begins a rather steep climb of Torne Mountain, reaching the summit at 3.6 miles, with a view over Buck Mountain to the north and the Pequannock Watershed to the west. The trail continues south along the ridgeline, with more views from bare rock outcrops, and soon begins a gradual descent, with views to the southeast over Osio Rock. After a steep section, the Hewitt-Butler Trail reaches the south end of the Torne Trail at 4.1 miles, in a gully filled with large boulders.

The Hewitt-Butler Trail now begins to climb Osio Rock, passing several large glacial erratics to the right at 4.3 miles, with views of the bare rock slopes of Torne Mountain to the northwest. Then, at 4.4 miles, the trail reaches the summit of Osio Rock, with 360° views. The Wanaque Reservoir is visible to the northeast, with the Ramapos—scarred by the cut for I-287—beyond. High Mountain may be seen to the southeast, with the New York City skyline in the background on a clear day.

From the summit, the trail begins a winding descent, with views across the valley to the northwest. At 4.8 miles, as the descent moderates, the trail parallels a feeder stream of Kampfe Lake for about 500 feet, then turns left, crosses the stream, and ascends along a rocky, steep path through a valley. It then descends gradually, passing a rock promontory to the left at 5.4 miles.

At 5.8 miles, the Hewitt-Butler Trail bears left at a fork and enters the property of Camp Vacamas. It crosses a stream on logs, crosses a woods road diagonally to the right, and climbs to a rock outcrop below a lone cedar. After descending and then climbing another rock outcrop, the trail descends steeply

over rocks to a fork, at 6.2 miles, where it bears right. Lake Larriwein (also known as Henion Pond) comes into view just before a steep descent into the parking area of Camp Vacamas, where the Hewitt-Butler Trail ends at 6.4 miles.

The small parking area at the southern trailhead is made available to hikers through the courtesy of the directors of this privately-owned camp. Hikers are asked to leave spaces for camp vehicles, and if necessary, to park outside the camp's property. Lake Larriwein is not open to the public for swimming or fishing.

To reach the parking area at Camp Vacamas, take I-287 to Exit 53. At the bottom of the ramp, turn left onto Hamburg Turnpike. Upon entering Bloomingdale, the name of the road changes to Main Street. After 1.3 miles (from I-287), bear right at a fork in the road, following the signs to West Milford. The road name now changes back to Hamburg Turnpike. Continue ahead for another 1.3 miles to Macopin Road, and turn right. Camp Vacamas is on the right in 1.3 miles.

Lower Trail   *Length: 1.4 miles Blaze: white*
The Lower Trail, which connects the Wyanokie Circular and Posts Brook Trails, can be used to bypass the steep climbs of Wyanokie High Point and Carris Hill, or as part of a loop hike. The northern trailhead of the Lower Trail is on the Wyanokie Circular Trail (red on white), about 500 feet west of its junction with the Mine Trail (yellow on white), and just beyond a stream crossing. The Lower Trail heads south along an east-facing shoulder of the Wyanokie High Point-Carris Hill ridge, crossing a number of small streams and passing through several rocky areas along the way. At 0.7 mile, it descends to the valley floor at the foot of the ridge, soon passing several rock outcrops. The trail now runs close to the boundary of the watershed lands of the Wanaque Reservoir. The Carris Hill Trail (yellow) leaves to the right at 1.3 miles, and the Lower Trail continues south, parallel to a chain-link fence marking the boundary of the watershed lands. The Lower Trail ends, at 1.4 miles, at a large boulder on the Posts Brook Trail (white), just north of Posts Brook.

Macopin Trail   *Length: 0.6 mile Blaze: white*
The Macopin Trail connects the Otter Hole Trail with the Hewitt-Butler Trail. Its western trailhead is on the east side of the Otter Hole Trail (green), 1.5 miles northeast of Otter Hole and 1.2 miles southwest of the Snake Den Road (East)

parking area. (The trailhead is just south of the Otter Hole Trail's crossing of Blue Mine Brook.) The Macopin Trail proceeds eastward, crossing two streams in a rocky area. It alternates several steep climbs with level sections, and ends, at 0.6 mile, at a junction with the Hewitt-Butler Trail (blue).

Mine Trail   *Length: 2.6 miles Blaze: yellow on white*
The eastern trailhead of the Mine Trail is on the south side of Snake Den Road, about 200 feet east of the large parking area for the Weis Ecology Center. Here, the Mine Trail and the Wyanokie Circular Trail (red on white) begin. They proceed south jointly, following a narrow corridor through private property. After going through a stand of spruce trees, the trails continue into a deciduous forest of maple and oak and enter a valley. At 0.2 mile, the Wyanokie Circular Trail continues ahead as the Mine Trail turns right and begins to ascend, crossing Blue Mine Brook at 0.3 mile. Now ascending steeply, the trail winds south along a ridge through mixed hardwoods and evergreens. It then turns left and descends to recross the brook above Wyanokie Falls. The Mine Trail continues to descend, crossing the Wyanokie Circular Trail at 0.7 mile.

Figure 7-3. Entrance to Roomy Mine

Curving to the north, the Mine Trail begins a steady climb of Ball Mountain, reaching its western ridge at 0.8 mile, with a view of Wyanokie High Point to the west. After descending slightly and climbing to the eastern ridge, the trail turns southward, passing to the left of an open pit of the Roomy Mine, with adjacent tailings, at 1.0 mile. The trail ascends past a quartz outcrop to a summit, and then drops down steeply over ledges and mine tailings to reach an old mining road at 1.2 miles. Here, the Roomy Mine Trail (orange) begins to the right. The Roomy Mine

Trail passes the main opening of the Roomy Mine to the right and connects in 0.1 mile with the Wyanokie Circular Trail (red on white).

The Roomy Mine, named after Benjamin Roome, a nineteenth century surveyor, was opened shortly after 1840 and was worked until about 1857. The ore vein was about four feet thick and dipped sharply to the southeast. The main horizontal mine shaft, which can be entered, extends about 100 feet into the hillside. A flashlight is needed to explore this mine, and a hard hat is also recommended.

The Mine Trail turns left on the mining road and soon reaches a junction, where it turns left to rejoin the Wyanokie Circular Trail. Proceeding along the valley floor, the trail again comes to Blue Mine Brook at 1.6 miles. Before crossing, continue ahead for 100 feet to see the flooded Blue Mine. This mine—named for the dark blue color of its magnetite ore—was discovered by Peter Hasenclever about 1765. The shaft went down 250 feet, with a drift of over 50 feet at the bottom. The Blue Mine was worked on and off from 1867 to 1905. During the 1890s, it produced about 300 tons of ore a month. A concrete pad—which once served as a base for steam-operated equipment—is in front of the mine, and tailings are piled above and to the rear of the entrance.

The Mine/Wyanokie Circular trails cross Blue Mine Brook on a wooden bridge, built in 2002 as an Eagle Scout project. Beyond the brook, both trails gradually ascend past another mine pit and more tailings to the left. A short distance beyond, the trails pass by an old stone shelter with a corrugated metal roof in a clearing to the right. This shelter was constructed in the 1930s by the Green Mountain Club. At 1.8 miles, the Wyanokie Circular Trail bears left, while the Mine Trail turns right and continues to ascend on a woods road. After leveling off in a wet area and crossing two streams at 2.1 miles, the trail begins to ascend, at first gradually, then more steeply through laurel. At 2.5 miles, the Hewitt-Butler Trail (blue) joins from the left, and the Mine Trail begins to descend, ending at 2.6 miles at a junction with the Otter Hole Trail (green) on Snake Den Road, here a dirt road. To the right, the Otter Hole Trail leads in 0.4 mile to the parking area on Snake Den Road (East), near the Weis Ecology Center, and can be used to complete the loop.

Otter Hole Trail   *Length: 2.7 miles Blaze: green*
The Otter Hole Trail, which follows woods roads for nearly its entire route, connects the large parking area on Snake Den Road (East), just east of the Weis

Ecology Center, with the parking area on Glenwild Avenue, near the Otter Hole. It intersects many of the trails in Norvin Green State Forest and is often used in combination with other trails to form loop hikes.

The eastern terminus of the Otter Hole Trail is on Snake Den Road (East), about 200 feet east of the large parking area for the Weis Ecology Center. This point is also the start of the joint Mine Trail (yellow on white)/ Wyanokie Circular Trail (red on white), which

Figure 7-4. Pool at Otter Hole

heads south, entering the woods on a footpath. The Otter Hole Trail proceeds west along paved Snake Den Road, passing through a residential area. It crosses a bridge over Blue Mine Brook and goes past a large swimming pool on the right. The pavement ends at 0.3 mile, and at 0.4 mile, the joint Hewitt-Butler Trail (blue)/Mine Trail (yellow on white) leaves to the left (this is the western terminus of the Mine Trail). The Otter Hole Trail continues ahead on the dirt road, soon crossing Blue Mine Brook on rocks (with the stone abutments of the former bridge still remaining).

On the west side of the brook, the W Trail (green W on white) joins from the right. In another 150 feet, the W Trail begins a loop. One branch of the loop goes off to the left, while the other branch continues ahead along the road, running concurrently with the Otter Hole Trail. At 0.6 mile, a stone wall runs along the right side of the road for about 100 feet. At the end of the stone wall, the W Trail departs to the left. The Otter Hole Trail continues ahead along the road, passing through the former Winfield Farm. Remnants of the farm, in-

cluding cellar holes, stone foundations and a restored well, may be seen along the road.

An unmarked woods road leaves to the right at 0.7 mile. This road (formerly the route of the Mine Trail) leads into the privately-owned Saddle Mountain area, which is closed to the public. The Otter Hole Trail now leaves the road it has been following and ascends to the right, following a rocky hillside footpath, to avoid a muddy and frequently flooded section of the road. It rejoins the road (now marked as the "Glenwild Fire Road") at 1.0 mile. Then, at 1.2 miles, another woods road (which leads in 0.2 mile to the Wyanokie Circular Trail) leaves to the right. Just beyond, the Otter Hole Trail again crosses Blue Mine Brook on rocks, and the Macopin Trail (white) leaves to the left.

The Otter Hole Trail now begins to ascend. At 1.3 miles, an unmarked woods road leaves to the left, and a short distance beyond, the Wyanokie Circular Trail (red on white) crosses. A rock outcrop to the right of the trail at 2.1 miles provides a view across a valley to Buck Mountain. Then, at 2.3 miles, the Wyanokie Crest Trail (yellow) crosses. Here, the Highlands Trail (teal diamond) joins from the right and begins to run concurrently with the Otter Hole Trail. After a short climb, the Otter Hole Trail descends steeply to reach its southwestern terminus, 2.7 miles from its eastern trailhead, at a junction with the Hewitt-Butler Trail (blue). To the right, the Hewitt-Butler Trail leads in 0.1 mile to the parking area on Glenwild Avenue, on the way crossing Posts Brook at the Otter Hole, a beautiful area of cascades and pools.

Posts Brook Trail
Length: 2.8 miles Blaze: white

The southern trailhead of the Posts Brook Trail is at the intersection of Doty Road and Ringwood Avenue (County 511) in Haskell, where parking is available at a municipal parking lot at the northwest corner of the intersection. Public transportation to the trailhead from the Port Authority Bus Terminal in New York City is available via NJ Transit bus #197. The trail proceeds west along paved Doty Road in a residential area, passing to the left of Lake Washington (also known as Rainbow Valley Lake).

At 1.0 mile, the trail passes several historic buildings. A private home on the left side of the road, constructed of stone, dates back to the 1700s. Just beyond, a barn with a sign "Camp Thomas Brooks" was built in 1916 and once was used by a Girl Scout camp. On the right side of the road, a brown building served as a barracks for airplane spotters during World War II.

A short distance beyond, at the crest of the hill (just beyond a PLEASE DRIVE SLOWLY sign), the trail turns right and enters the woods, heading in a northwest direction. Here, 1.1 miles from the start, the trail enters the private property of the Lake Iosco Association. It goes through a ravine and enters a wet area with mountain laurel. After crossing log bridges over two streams, the trail passes through thick rhododendrons before turning right along paved East Shore Drive for 300 feet. As the road curves left at 1.5 miles, the trail bears right and ascends a grassy woods road, soon entering watershed lands of the Wanaque Reservoir, where the trail narrows to a footpath. After going over several low ridges, the trail crosses an ATV track (with metal markers) and then crosses a woods road diagonally to the right. An old mine pit with tailings may be seen on the right side of the road, adjacent to the trail crossing.

Figure 7-5. Chikahoki Falls

The trail continues through a low area, crossing another old woods road. To the right, the Green Swamp Dam of the Wanaque Reservoir is visible through the trees. After proceeding through a rocky area at 2.0 miles, the trail begins to parallel Posts Brook to the left, passing an attractive cascade and pool. It climbs rather steeply and continues through the gorge of the brook. Many of the hemlocks that formerly shaded this gorge have fallen victim to the woolly adelgid, but the gorge is still a place of spectacular beauty. At 2.2 miles, the trail turns sharply right and climbs over some huge boulders. It continues through a level area and then climbs to run high above the gorge to the left.

At 2.3 miles, the trail passes to the left of a fenced-off stone dam, which diverts the main flow of Posts Brook into the Wanaque Reservoir. Above the dam, the trail crosses the now-wider brook on rocks (this crossing can be very difficult if the water is high) and ascends to reach a junction at 2.4 miles. Here, at a large boulder, the Lower Trail (white) leaves to the right. (Be careful at this intersection, as both the Posts Brook Trail and the Lower Trail are blazed white.)

The Posts Brook Trail proceeds ahead, passing between large rock outcrops. It crosses a seasonal stream in a wet area and begins to run alongside Posts Brook. At 2.7 miles, it passes Chikahoki Falls and continues along the brook, which features attractive cascades. The Posts Brook Trail ends at 2.8 miles at a junction with the joint Hewitt-Butler (blue)/Highlands (teal diamond) trails, which come in from the right and continue ahead on the same woods road.

Torne Trail
Length: 0.4 mile Blaze: red

The Torne Trail bypasses a rugged climb of Torne Mountain on the Hewitt-Butler Trail. It can be combined with the Hewitt-Butler Trail to make a 1.5-mile loop hike over Torne Mountain, starting from the Otter Hole parking area on Glenwild Avenue at the Bloomingdale/West Milford boundary.

The northern trailhead of the Torne Trail is on the Hewitt-Butler Trail (blue), 0.2 mile west of the Otter Hole parking area on Glenwild Avenue. The Hewitt-Butler Trail runs close to Glenwild Avenue here, and a short unmarked trail leads north from the trail to the road. From the trailhead, the Torne Trail proceeds south. It climbs briefly, levels off, and then descends through a valley, which soon becomes a very rocky and boulder-filled gully. At 0.4 mile, the Torne Trail ends at a second junction with the Hewitt-Butler Trail, which crosses the gully amid large boulders.

W Trail
Length: 0.7 mile Blaze: green W on white

The W Trail is a short "lollipop"-loop trail which is entirely on the property of the Weis Ecology Center. It can be used for a short nature walk, and it also provides an alternative, more pleasant route to the Hewitt-Butler and Otter Hole trails, bypassing the paved residential areas along Snake Den Road (East).

To reach the eastern trailhead of the W Trail, proceed west from the western end of the large parking area on Snake Den Road (East), crossing the Nature

Center field of the Weis Ecology Center. At the western end of the field, a red signboard marks the start of the trail. The trail crosses four wooden bridges and passes above a large stream-fed swimming pool. At 0.4 mile, it reaches Snake Den Road—the route of the Otter Hole Trail (green)—at the site of a former bridge over Blue Mine Brook. (The southern section of the Hewitt-Butler Trail (blue) begins 0.1 mile to the left along the Otter Hole Trail.) Here, the W Trail turns right and runs along Snake Den Road, jointly with the Otter Hole Trail.

In another 150 feet, the beginning of the loop is reached. Followed in a clockwise direction, the W Trail turns left, leaving the road, and continues along a stream. At 0.5 mile, it turns right, away from the stream, and passes through the former Winfield Farm. It then turns right again and returns to the Otter Hole Trail. (A short detour to the left along the Otter Hole Trail leads to interesting remnants of the Winfield Farm, including cellar holes, stone foundations and a restored well.) The W Trail now turns right and runs concurrently with the Otter Hole Trail for 650 feet, rejoining the "tail" of the loop at 0.7 mile.

Will Monroe Loop
Length: 1.0 mile Blaze: pink

Named for Professor Will S. Monroe of the Montclair State Normal School (now Montclair State University), who laid out most of the trails in the Wyanokies during the 1920s, this loop trail leads to several expansive viewpoints on Assiniwikam Mountain. The Will Monroe Loop begins at the junction of the Wyanokie Circular Trail (red on white) and the Wyanokie Crest Trail (yellow), 0.6 mile south of the northwestern terminus of the Wyanokie Circular Trail at Boy Scout Lake. After climbing to an open area where the trees have been killed by drought and gypsy moth infestations, the trail descends to a shady glen, then continues to climb through mountain laurel thickets.

At 0.3 mile, the trail climbs up a crevice in the bedrock and emerges at a north-facing viewpoint from a rock outcrop. After a short descent, it reaches a viewpoint to the south. In the spring, this area is frequented by migratory birds, including the indigo bunting. Then, at 0.5 mile, the trail turns sharply left and reaches a broad viewpoint over the Ramapo Mountains to the east. Just beyond, it arrives at the summit of Assiniwikam Mountain (1,200 feet). Hikers should remain on the trail, as the private property to the east has been closed to hiking. The trail continues along rounded rock outcrops, with views to the northeast over Windbeam, Bear, Board, and Horse Pond mountains.

Turning left at 0.7 mile, the trail re-enters the woods, passing some interest-

ing rock formations. After a short climb, the trail heads downhill to end, 1.0 mile from the start, at a junction with the Wyanokie Circular Trail. To return to Boy Scout Lake, turn right and follow the Wyanokie Circular Trail for 0.3 mile.

Wyanokie Circular Trail *Length: 4.4 miles Blaze: red on white*

The Wyanokie Circular Trail extends from the Weis Ecology Center parking area on Snake Den Road (East) to Boy Scout Lake at Camp Wyanokie, where it connects with the Camp Wyanokie Trail, which continues to West Brook Road. Despite its name, the Wyanokie Circular Trail is no longer "circular," as a portion of the trail which formerly traversed private property in the Saddle Mountain area has been closed by the landowner. However, it can be combined with other trails to create loop hikes.

The eastern trailhead of the Wyanokie Circular Trail is on the south side of Snake Den Road (East), about 200 feet east of the large parking area for the Weis Ecology Center. Here, the Wyanokie Circular Trail and the Mine Trail (yellow on white) begin. They proceed south jointly, following a narrow corridor through private property. After going through a stand of spruce trees, the trails continue into a deciduous forest of maple and oak and enter a valley. At 0.2 mile, the Mine Trail leaves to the right. The Wyanokie Circular Trail continues ahead on a woods road and starts to descend. The Mine Trail crosses at 0.3 mile, and at 0.4 mile, the Roomy Mine Trail (orange) leaves to the left, leading in about 500 feet to the Roomy Mine.

The Mine Trail rejoins from the left at 0.5 mile. Proceeding along the valley floor, the Mine/Wyanokie Circular trails reach Blue Mine Brook at 0.8 mile. Before crossing the brook on a wooden bridge, built in 2002 as an Eagle Scout project, continue ahead for 100 feet to see the flooded Blue Mine. (For a description of this mine, see the entry for the Mine Trail, p. 121.) Beyond the brook, both trails gradually ascend past another mine pit and more tailings to the left. A short distance beyond, the trails pass by an old stone shelter with a corrugated metal roof in a clearing to the right. This shelter was constructed in the 1930s by the Green Mountain Club. At 1.0 mile, the Wyanokie Circular Trail bears left, while the Mine Trail leaves to the right. Then, at 1.1 miles, just beyond a stream crossing, the Lower Trail (white) departs to the left.

The Wyanokie Circular Trail now begins a steady ascent, climbing about 500 feet in elevation to the summit of Wyanokie High Point. The first part of the ascent is gradual, but the climb steepens as the summit is approached. The last part of the climb is over bare rock, with the trail marked by blazes painted

Figure 7-6. Wanaque Reservoir from Wyanokie High Point

on the rock. Just before the summit is reached at 1.8 miles, there is an expansive view to the southeast over the Wanaque Reservoir. But the best views are from the summit itself, marked by a bolt drilled into the rock. To the east, beyond the reservoir, a long bridge carrying I-287 over a low area is clearly visible. Beyond that, the New York City skyline may be seen on a clear day. Saddle, Assiniwikam, and Buck mountains are visible to the north and west.

From the summit, the Wyanokie Circular Trail descends very steeply over bare rock. Extreme care is required here in wet weather. The trail continues to descend through a mountain laurel thicket and, at 1.9 miles, the Hewitt-Butler Trail (blue) joins from the right, along with the Highlands Trail (teal diamond). All three trails continue south to cross a stream on rocks. Then, at 2.1 miles, the Hewitt-Butler/Highlands trails continue ahead, while the Wyanokie Circular Trail turns right, ascending gradually over open rocks. At 2.3 miles, at the end of a laurel thicket, the trail crosses an intermittent stream and ascends to a south-facing ridgeline. It continues over several rock outcrops and descends to cross a woods road at 2.8 miles. After proceeding through another dense laurel thicket, the Outlaw Trail (orange) leaves to the left at a large boulder, connecting

in 0.2 mile with the Wyanokie Crest Trail (yellow). The Wyanokie Circular Trail now descends, reaching the Glenwild Fire Road—the route of the Otter Hole Trail (green)—at 3.2 miles.

The Wyanokie Circular Trail crosses the road and heads north. After a brief climb, it descends steadily, passing through an area with many large glacial erratics. It crosses a rocky woods road at 3.6 miles and starts its ascent of Assiniwikam Mountain, climbing over several rock outcrops. After passing a viewpoint, the Wyanokie Circular Trail reaches a junction at 3.8 miles. The Wyanokie Crest Trail (yellow) leaves to the left, while the Will Monroe Loop (pink) begins to the right. The Wyanokie Circular Trail now descends steeply over rocks. At 4.1 miles, the Will Monroe Loop rejoins from the right, and the Wyanokie Circular Trail crosses a swampy valley floor amid boulders and exposed tree roots. Turning left after crossing a stream, the trail reaches a T intersection, where it turns right onto unpaved Snake Den Road (West) at 4.3 miles. After passing through a residential area, the trail enters Camp Wyanokie, with Boy Scout Lake on the right. The Wyanokie Circular Trail ends, 4.4 miles from the start, at a chain barrier on the right side of the road, beyond a dirt parking area to the left. To the right is the trailhead of the Camp Wyanokie Trail (yellow on white), which heads north to West Brook Road.

Wyanokie Crest Trail   *Length: 4.4 miles Blaze: yellow*

The Wyanokie Crest Trail traverses a remote part of Norvin Green State Forest and reaches Buck Mountain, the highest summit in the Wyanokies, with outstanding views. Its southern terminus is on Glenwild Avenue, 0.7 mile south of the Otter Hole parking area and 0.1 mile north of Kampfe Lake. Limited parking is available at the trailhead.

The trail heads north, following a stream that feeds into Kampfe Lake, crossing it twice as it meanders through a glacial wetland. At 0.3 mile, it bears right, leaving the stream, crosses a woods road, and continues along rolling terrain. After a short descent, it crosses the braided streambed of Posts Brook on rocks and logs, then turns right onto the joint Hewitt-Butler/Highlands Trail (blue/teal diamond) at 0.6 mile. In 75 feet, the Wyanokie Crest Trail leaves to the left, heading north, and gently descends to a feeder stream of Posts Brook, which it reaches at 0.9 mile. The next mile of the trail goes through one of the wildest areas in all of Norvin Green State Forest. The trail closely follows the stream, heading uphill, with occasional rough footing, particularly at the two places where it crosses the stream. There are several cascades along the

Figure 7-7. Viewpoint at Buck Mountain

stream, which is most scenic during periods of high water.

Bearing left and leaving the stream at 1.4 miles, the trail skirts a swampy area before ascending steeply to a rock outcrop, with seasonal views. After a short descent, the trail continues to ascend to an open area at the high point of the ridge. Here, at 1.8 miles, the short Outlaw Trail (orange), which connects to the Wyanokie Circular Trail, leaves to the right. After a gentle descent, the Wyanokie Crest Trail continues south along the ridge, emerging, at 2.1 miles, at a viewpoint to the west which overlooks Buck Mountain. The trail now descends steadily, tunneling through laurel. It crosses a brook and then the Otter Hole Trail (green) at 2.3 miles. Here, the Highlands Trail (teal diamond) joins from the left.

The Wyanokie Crest Trail continues to descend to a hollow, where it crosses a wider stream on rocks. It then climbs steeply, gaining 200 vertical feet in only 0.1 mile, and reaches a viewpoint from the ledges of Buck Mountain at 2.5 miles. This east-facing viewpoint offers a broad panorama, with I-287 visible in the distance. Just past the viewpoint, the trail turns left onto a woods road, and crosses over to the western side of the mountain. It soon reaches a second

viewpoint, marked by a single pine tree wedged into the bedrock. This expansive viewpoint overlooks the south and west, with Torne Mountain visible directly ahead.

From the viewpoint, the Wyanokie Crest Trail heads north through laurel, passing several huge boulders on either side of the trail. At 2.8 miles, the Highlands Trail departs to the left, and then the Wyanokie Crest Trail joins a woods road that comes in from the right. The trail soon turns right at a T intersection, then bears left at a Y intersection and climbs gently to level off along the ridge of Buck Mountain. This section of the trail has been abused by ATV's, and hikers should carefully follow the yellow trail blazes, which often depart from the ATV tracks. Along the ridge, the trail reaches the highest elevation in the Wyanokies (1,290 feet), but there are no views from this wooded spot.

At 3.4 miles, the Wyanokie Crest Trail comes out at another east-facing viewpoint over Assiniwikam Mountain, with the view partially obscured by vegetation. It now begins a gradual descent into a broad valley, where it parallels a brook, crossing it several times. The last brook crossing, at 3.8 miles, is marked by an unusual split boulder. The trail then ascends briefly and continues along undulating terrain, crossing several woods roads. After crossing the third woods road, the Wyanokie Crest Trail ascends to end, at 4.4 miles, at a junction with the Wyanokie Circular Trail (red on white) on a shoulder of Assiniwikam Mountain. Straight ahead, the Will Monroe Loop (pink) leads to a series of viewpoints on Assiniwikam Mountain.

Monksville/Stonetown Area

Part of Norvin Green State Forest extends north of West Brook Road, and the North Jersey District Water Supply Commission also has watershed lands in this area. Although the trail network in this area is not as extensive as in the area south of West Brook Road, several trails traverse the area, offering rugged climbs and expansive views.

Burnt Meadow Trail   *Length: 1.2 miles Blaze: yellow*
The eastern trailhead of the Burnt Meadow Trail is on the Horse Pond Mountain Trail (white), 1.1 miles south of the parking area at the intersection of East Shore Road and Greenwood Lake Turnpike (County 511) (via the Hewitt-Butler and Horse Pond Mountain trails). From a large boulder at the crest of Horse Pond Mountain, the Burnt Meadow Trail descends steeply to the west

over rock ledges, but the descent soon moderates as the trail begins to follow several old woods roads. After crossing a stream at 0.3 mile, the trail ascends briefly and then descends to reach paved Burnt Meadow Road (the paving ends just south of the trail crossing) at 0.4 mile, where limited parking is available. The trail turns right and follows the paved road for 250 feet, then turns left onto a wide dirt road. It follows several woods roads until, at 1.0 mile, it crosses Hewitt Brook on rocks and begins to climb Long Hill. The climb soon steepens, and at 1.1 miles, the trail reaches a viewpoint over Horse Pond Mountain from a rock outcrop. After crossing a flat, grassy area, the Burnt Meadow Trail ends at 1.2 miles, at a junction with the Hewitt-Butler Trail (blue).

Together with portions of the Hewitt-Butler and Horse Pond Mountain trails, the Burnt Meadow Trail can be used to make a 5.8-mile "lollipop"-loop hike, beginning at the parking area at the junction of East Shore Road and Greenwood Lake Turnpike (County 511).

Hewitt-Butler Trail   *Length: 7.2 miles Blaze: blue*
This northern section of the Hewitt-Butler Trail extends south from the intersection of Greenwood Lake Turnpike (County 511) and East Shore Road in Hewitt to West Brook Road, near the Ringwood/West Milford boundary. A large parking area is located at the northern trailhead, on the south side of Greenwood Lake Turnpike at its intersection with East Shore Road. This parking area also serves the Sterling Ridge Trail (blue on white), which begins beyond a guardrail at the northeast quadrant of the intersection of Greenwood Lake Turnpike and East Shore Road. The northern trailhead of the Hewitt-Butler Trail can also be reached via NJ Transit bus #197 from the Port Authority Bus Terminal in New York. Although the trail is officially blazed blue, blue-on-white blazes are used in several sections.

The Hewitt-Butler Trail begins just east of the parking area, beyond the highway bridge over Hewitt Brook. For the first 0.9 mile, it runs concurrently with the Highlands Trail (teal diamond). The trail heads uphill, briefly joins a woods road, then turns left and continues on a footpath. After descending to cross a stream, the trail climbs a rocky embankment and joins an old railbed – the route of the former New York and Greenwood Lake Railway, later part of the Erie Railroad. It continues along the railbed for 0.2 mile, dipping down at one point to cross a gas pipeline right-of-way, where the fill for the embankment has been removed.

At 0.6 mile, the trail turns right, leaving the railbed, and soon begins to

ascend on an old woods road. Then, at 0.9 mile, the Horse Pond Mountain Trail (white), together with the Highlands Trail, continues ahead, as the Hewitt-Butler Trail turns right. The Hewitt-Butler Trail ascends through oaks and pines, with views through the trees to the right, then continues through undulating terrain. At 1.2 miles, the Hewitt-Butler Trail turns right and rejoins the Horse Pond Mountain/Highlands trails (which follow a shorter but steeper route to reach this point). All three trails now continue south, ascending to an open ridgetop and then descending steeply to reach a clearing for a power line at 1.4 miles, with views to the east over the Monksville Reservoir.

The Horse Pond Mountain/Highlands trails continue ahead, while the Hewitt-Butler Trail turns sharply right and descends along the power lines, crossing paved Burnt Meadow Road (where limited parking is available) at 1.6 miles. Continuing to descend, the trail crosses Hewitt Brook on rocks at 1.7 miles. It ascends from the brook, crosses a woods road and, at 2.0 miles, turns left, away from the power lines, and heads south on another woods road. It soon turns left onto a footpath, leaving the woods road. After a brief descent, the Hewitt-Butler Trail climbs towards the ridge of Long Hill.

At 2.6 miles, the Burnt Meadow Trail (yellow) leaves to the left. The Hewitt-Butler Trail continues to climb, first gradually and then more steeply, until it reaches an expansive east-facing viewpoint from the crest of Long Hill at 3.2 miles. The view includes Horse Pond, Harrison, and Windbeam mountains, with the Ramapo Mountains behind in the distance. Continuing south along the ridge, the trail turns right and joins a power-line maintenance road at 3.8 miles. The trail runs along or adjacent to this road for the next mile. Then, at 4.8 miles, as the power lines turn right to descend the mountain, the trail reaches a west-facing viewpoint from open rocks, with the view dominated by the ridges of Kanouse and Bearfort mountains.

The Hewitt-Butler Trail now bears left and descends on a woods road along the south-facing slope of West Brook Mountain. Soon, another woods road joins from the right and, at 5.1 miles, the trail briefly joins a woods road that runs north-south. After ascending a rocky slope, the trail arrives at a viewpoint to the south and west at 5.8 miles. The trail turns left at 6.2 miles and makes a short, steep ascent. (Some of the blazes in this section are blue-on-white, rather than solid blue.) After passing below a hilltop residence, the trail reaches Manaticut Point at 6.7 miles. Windbeam Mountain is visible directly to the east, with the Watchungs and Ramapos beyond to the southeast. The Manhattan skyline may be seen in the distance on a clear day. To the south are the

Figure 7-8. Monksville Reservoir from Horse Pond Mountain

Wyanokies, with a large quarry in the foreground.

The trail now descends steeply over ledges. At 7.0 miles, after a descent on switchbacks, the trail levels off and follows a woods road into a hemlock ravine. It soon turns sharply right, leaving the woods road, and descends steeply to cross the West Brook on rocks. Just beyond, at 7.2 miles, the northern section of the Hewitt-Butler Trail ends at paved West Brook Road. Limited parking is available at a turnout on the south side of the road, just west of the trailhead.

Horse Pond Mountain Trail   *Length: 2.1 miles Blaze: white*
The Horse Pond Mountain Trail connects the northern section of the Hewitt-Butler Trail on Horse Pond Mountain with the Stonetown Circular Trail on Harrison Mountain. Its northern trailhead is on the Hewitt-Butler Trail, 0.9 mile south of Greenwood Lake Turnpike. Here, the Hewitt-Butler Trail (blue) heads west, while the Horse Pond Mountain Trail proceeds south, ascending steadily, first on a woods road, then over rock outcrops. After a brief descent, the Hewitt-Butler Trail rejoins from the right, having followed a longer but more gradual route to this point. Both trails ascend to an open ridgetop and then descend steeply to reach a clearing for power lines at 0.3 mile, with views to the east over the Monksville Reservoir.

Here, the Hewitt-Butler Trail turns sharply right and descends along the

power lines, while the Horse Pond Mountain Trail continues ahead along the rocky ridgeline. The trail is crossed by many ATV tracks, so hikers should take care to remain on the blazed trail. At 0.6 mile, a horse farm is visible below on the right. After a steep ascent, the trail reaches a viewpoint to the east from open rocks at 1.0 mile. The entire Monksville Reservoir is visible, with Monks Mountain in the background. Beyond the viewpoint, the trail briefly continues to climb and then descends to the left of a stone wall, reaching a junction at 1.1 miles with the Burnt Meadow Trail (yellow), which departs to the right at a large boulder.

After climbing to another rise, the Horse Pond Mountain Trail descends, mostly along woods roads, to cross a stream in a valley at 1.7 miles. It now begins a steep ascent of Harrison Mountain, reaching a limited viewpoint along the ridge before ending, at 2.1 miles, at the Stonetown Circular Trail (red triangle on white). A parking area at the end of Lake Rickonda Road is 0.6 mile to the east along the Stonetown Circular Trail.

The Horse Pond Mountain Trail is co-aligned, for its entire length, with the Highlands Trail (teal diamond).

Stonetown Circular Trail   *Length: 9.4 miles Blaze: red triangle on white*
The Stonetown Circular Trail is a loop trail which climbs over Signal Rock, Tory Rocks, and Harrison Mountain on the west side of Stonetown Road, and Board, Bear, and Windbeam mountains east of the road. The entire 9.4-mile loop makes for a very strenuous hike, and many hikers choose to cover only half of the trail at a time. At the southern end, limited parking is available at a gate to watershed property on Stonetown Road, with ample parking at an athletic field along Mary Roth Drive, 0.5 mile to the north. At the northern end, there is limited parking at the northern end of Lake Rickonda Road and at the southern end of White Road.

The trailhead for the Stonetown Circular Trail is at a stone road marker on the right side of Stonetown Road, just north of West Brook Road and about 50 feet south of Wanaque Reservoir Gate #17. Limited parking is available adjacent to the trailhead (please do not block the gate). Proceeding in a clockwise direction, the trail heads north along the paved road. At 0.5 mile, Mary Roth Drive leaves to the left, with ample parking available down the road at an athletic field. At 0.6 mile, just beyond a firehouse, the trail turns left (west) to follow paved Magee Road across a bridge over Burnt Meadow Brook. In an-

other 200 feet, the trail turns sharply right and heads north along a woods road.

At 0.8 mile, the trail continues straight ahead as unmarked woods roads depart left and right. The trail soon leaves the woods road it has been following and turns left onto a footpath. After a short ascent, it descends into a swampy area and then climbs to briefly rejoin the woods road. At 1.0 mile, the trail climbs over rocks and continues to ascend along a grassy footpath, reaching a viewpoint at 1.1 miles, with limited views to the east over Board, Bear, and Windbeam mountains. Then, at 1.3 miles, the trail ascends to Signal Rock's higher but more limited viewpoint. The trail descends steeply over rocks, then continues to descend more moderately on a footpath. It continues along several woods roads, crossing a stream on rocks at 1.6 miles, and then bears right and proceeds ahead on a footpath.

After descending through a rocky area, the trail ascends steeply over ledges to reach Tory Rocks at 1.9 miles, where spaces between the tumbled boulders are reputed to have been hideouts of Tory supporters during the American Revolution. The summit offers views over the surrounding Norvin Green State Forest, with Windbeam Mountain prominent to the east. Descending from Tory Rocks, the trail twice turns left onto woods roads, then bears right onto another road. It reaches a boulder barrier at 2.4 miles and turns right onto unpaved Burnt Meadow Road, which is open to vehicular traffic.

Figure 7-9. Tory Rocks

At 2.8 miles, the Stonetown Circular Trail crosses a bridge over Burnt Meadow Brook and then turns right, leaving Burnt Meadow Road. For the next 0.4 mile, the trail follows a series of woods roads, crossing a stream at 3.0 miles. At 3.2 miles, the trail turns left on dirt Harrison Mountain Lake Road (open to vehicular traffic), then leaves to the right in 300 feet. The trail now ascends the southwest slope of Harrison Mountain, first gradually, then more steeply as it approaches the crest of the ridge, where it runs along rock ledges. Harrison Mountain Lake is visible through the trees at 3.6 miles. The trail passes beneath power lines at 3.9 miles and, at 4.0 miles, it turns right, leaving a woods road, and ascends steeply along a rocky footpath.

At 4.1 miles, the Horse Pond Mountain Trail (white) leaves to the left. Here, the Highlands Trail (teal diamond) joins the Stonetown Circular Trail and runs concurrently with it for the next 5.3 miles. The Stonetown Circular Trail ascends a rock outcrop to again pass beneath power lines at 4.2 miles, with a 270° view over the Monksville Reservoir, the Ramapos, and the Wyanokies. To the southeast are Board, Bear, and Windbeam mountains, which the Stonetown Circular Trail will traverse to complete its loop. After descending steadily, first steeply, then more gradually, the trail continues through a swampy area to reach paved Lake Rickonda Road at 4.7 miles. Limited parking is available here.

The trail proceeds south along this residential road, turning left (north) at 4.9 miles to rejoin Stonetown Road. Then, at 5.2 miles, it turns right onto paved White Road. The pavement ends at 5.6 miles, with limited parking. Here, the trail turns sharply left onto a dirt road. After a woods road leaves to the right, the trail turns right at 5.7 miles and ascends on a footpath. Entering the lands of the North Jersey District Water Supply Commission, the trail descends over a long rock slab, with a view across the valley. The trail then bears right and continues to descend through a rocky area. After turning right onto a woods road, the trail passes a swampy area to the left at 5.9 miles and crosses a stream at 6.1 miles. Soon, it crosses a woods road and begins a steady ascent of Board Mountain. The summit, reached at 6.3 miles, is marked by open rock ledges with a view to the north over the Monksville Dam, which separates the Monksville and Wanaque reservoirs.

The trail passes a small cedar grove as it descends the southern slope of Board Mountain, steeply in places. Leveling off at 6.8 miles, the trail crosses a woods road and begins to ascend Bear Mountain, first gradually, then more steeply. After passing through a pitch pine grove, the trail descends into a

saddle and ascends to reach the cone-shaped summit of Bear Mountain at 7.3 miles. The summit offers 360° views, with Norvin Green State Forest to the south and west. The trail now begins to descend, steeply at first, with views to the southeast. It crosses a stream at 7.7 miles and a woods road at 7.9 miles. To the right, this road leads to paved Windbeam Lane (which, in turn, continues to Stonetown Road).

After crossing a stream in a swampy area at 8.0 miles, the Stonetown Circular Trail begins to climb Windbeam Mountain, first through hemlock and mixed hardwoods, then over more open terrain. At 8.5 miles, a grove of white birch conceals the concrete piers of an old tower. Here, the trail turns left, joining a woods road. Then, at 8.7 miles, it turns right, leaving the road, and descends steeply over rocks to reach a saddle. The trail now ascends to reach a viewpoint at 8.8 miles, amid pitch pine and cedar. Saddle Mountain, with its quarry, is prominent to the southwest. Turning right, the trail descends steeply over rocks, reaching the base of a hollow, then ascends to reach the summit of Windbeam Mountain at 8.9 miles. A broad panorama is afforded from this peak—the highest in the immediate area. The Wanaque Reservoir is directly below to the east, with the Ramapo Mountains beyond, and other peaks of the Wyanokies may be seen to the north, west, and south.

The trail now descends to the southwest, with views over the Wanaque Reservoir to the east. After a steep section with wooden steps at 9.1 miles, the trail levels off in a rocky area. At 9.4 miles, the Stonetown Circular Trail reaches Stonetown Road, completing its loop.

Long Pond Ironworks State Park

Long Pond Ironworks State Park is dominated by the Monksville Reservoir, completed in 1987, and formed by damming the Wanaque River north of the Wanaque Reservoir. Access to the reservoir and the Monks Trail is via two boat launch areas south of Greenwood Lake Turnpike (County 511). Public transportation to the area is available via NJ Transit bus #197 from the Port Authority Bus Terminal in New York.

Historically, Long Pond, later called Greenwood Lake, gained prominence when Peter Hasenclever directed the construction of a dam, 200 feet long and five feet high, across the southern end of Long Pond, to provide water power for his ironworks downstream in the Hewitt area. Long Pond Ironworks was built in 1766 on Long Pond River, now known as the Wanaque, 3½ miles west

of Ringwood. The original furnace used ore from the Hope
Mine at Ringwood. Later, just
before the Civil War, Abram
Hewitt built two furnaces at
Long Pond, along with two
waterwheels. The ironworks,
which once supported a thriving community, were in operation until 1882.

The complex contains the
ruins of three furnaces, the oldest of which was built by Peter
Hasenclever in 1766. The ru-

Figure 7-10. Furnace at Long Pond Ironworks

ins of this furnace were discovered in a mound covered with leaves in 1956 and
were excavated in 1957. A stone arch survives from a second furnace, built in
1862 by Peter Cooper and Abram S. Hewitt. The two original 25-foot
waterwheels burned in 1957. One has been stabilized in its ruined condition;
the other was reconstructed on its original hub in 1994 with a grant from the
New Jersey Historic Trust and Green Acres funds.

The ironworks site, including several relocated historic frame buildings
(currently under restoration) and ruins of furnaces and waterwheels, is now
contained within Long Pond Ironworks State Park. The site was protected
when the Monksville Reservoir was filled; however, the shoreline of the reservoir is fairly close by, and much adjacent land was submerged. The Friends of
the Long Pond Ironworks provide tours of the site. For further information,
call (973) 657-1688. Long Pond Ironworks State Park is administered by
Ringwood State Park, 1304 Sloatsburg Road, Ringwood, NJ 07456; (973)
962-7031; www.njparksandforests.org.

Trails in Long Pond Ironworks State Park

Three trails in Long Pond Ironworks State Park lead to remnants of the historic
mines and ironworks. The Sterling Ridge Trail, the longest of the three, goes
past the site of the Long Pond Ironworks on the Wanaque River and extends

through adjacent parkland into New York State. The Monks Trail passes several open pits of the Winston Mine, opened shortly after the Civil War and abandoned by 1880. The Whritenour Mine Trail, a short loop trail, accesses the site of the Whritenour Mine, worked around 1880. In addition, the northern end of the Hewitt-Butler Trail (described in the Stonetown/Monksville section, above) passes through a portion of Long Pond Ironworks State Park west of the Monksville Reservoir.

Monks Trail
Length: 1.7 miles Blaze: white

The Monks Trail is a loop trail that offers hikers a pleasant jaunt through varied terrain, passes several openings of the Winston Mine, and climbs to a view over the Monksville Reservoir. To reach the northern trailhead, turn into the access road leading to the northern boat launch area for the Monksville Reservoir in Long Pond Ironworks State Park, which leaves from the south side of Greenwood Lake Turnpike (County 511), 0.3 mile west of its intersection with Margaret King Avenue. Proceed to the parking area, then walk back along the road towards the entrance. The trailhead is 0.1 mile from the northeast end of the parking area, on the south side of the road.

The Monks Trail begins by climbing a flight of wooden steps and continues along the hillside, parallel to the entrance road. At 0.1 mile, it turns right onto a woods road and climbs to a wider woods road, where it turns right again and continues to ascend gradually. After passing a rock outcrop to the right at 0.3 mile, the trail levels off. It goes under a power line at 0.4 mile and then crosses a gas pipeline. Just beyond the gas pipeline crossing, as the trail begins to descend, two open pits of the Winston Mine are about 100 feet to the left of the trail.

At 0.5 mile, as the woods road curves to the left, the trail turns right, leaving the road, and continues on a footpath through the woods. After crossing a stream, the trail proceeds along a narrow ridge and continues through a rocky area. At the base of a descent, two small mine openings are visible to the left—one filled with water, the other containing discarded tires. As the trail continues ahead, the Monksville Reservoir is visible through the trees.

At 0.8 mile, the trail turns right at a T intersection. Just beyond a wet area, a side trail leads left to the southern boat launch area, where parking is available. The Monks Trail now bears right and begins a steady ascent of Monks Mountain on a winding footpath, climbing about 300 vertical feet in the next

quarter of a mile. As the trail levels off at 1.1 miles, a side trail, also blazed white, departs to the left, passing a rocky cedar-studded high point and descending slightly to reach a viewpoint over the Monksville Reservoir in 300 feet. The Monksville Dam is visible to the left, with Harrison Mountain in the background.

The Monks Trail continues ahead, passing to the left of the rocky summit of Monks Mountain at 1.3 miles. It begins to descend, first rather steeply on rocks, then more gradually. After passing a large lichen-covered rock outcrop on the right, it bears left and descends steeply, leveling off in a broad valley at 1.5 miles. The trail now bears right and continues to descend gradually. Upon reaching overhead power lines at 1.7 miles, the trail turns left and continues under the power lines to its terminus at a woods road. To the right, the woods road, which runs parallel to the shore of the reservoir, leads back to the northern boat launch parking area in 0.5 mile.

Including the walk along the road parallel to the reservoir and the side trip to the viewpoint at the top of the mountain, the full loop is 2.5 miles long.

Sterling Ridge Trail   *Length: 8.6 miles Blaze: blue on white*
The Sterling Ridge Trail traverses the Tuxedo Mountains between Hewitt, New Jersey and NY 17A, east of the village of Greenwood Lake, New York. The New Jersey section of the trail traverses Long Pond Ironworks State Park, the Wanaque Wildlife Management Area, and Tranquility Ridge (a Passaic County park, administered by the New Jersey office of the Palisades Interstate Park Commission), while the New York section goes through Sterling Forest State Park, administered by the Sterling Forest office of the Palisades Interstate Park Commission.

The southern trailhead is at the junction of Greenwood Lake Turnpike (County 511) and East Shore Road. Parking is available on the south side of Greenwood Lake Turnpike, opposite the trailhead. Public transportation to the trailhead is available via NJ Transit bus #197. From the trailhead, the Sterling Ridge Trail proceeds northeast on a woods road, the former main street of the village of Hewitt. After intersecting another old road at the ruins of a building, formerly the company store, the trail bears left, then turns right and crosses the Wanaque River on a wooden footbridge at 0.4 mile. Before crossing the bridge, continue straight ahead to see the ruins of the Long Pond Ironworks complex.

After crossing the bridge, the Sterling Ridge Trail bears left and follows an old road that soon veers away from the river to follow a tributary. At 1.1 miles,

the Jennings Hollow Trail (yellow) leaves to the left. Soon, the Sterling Ridge Trail curves to the left as the woods road continues ahead, leading to the Patterson Mine. The Sterling Ridge Trail now ascends Big Beech Mountain, leveling off, at 2.0 miles, at a false summit which offers views to the south. Ascending more steeply, the trail reaches the actual summit at 2.2 miles, with views of Bearfort Mountain and the Wyanokies. After a steep descent, the trail reaches the New York-New Jersey state line at 2.6 miles.

The Sterling Ridge Trail now crosses several woods roads, including the Lake-to-Lake Trail (white), at 2.7 miles. The Sterling Ridge Trail then ascends and, at 3.1 miles, it reaches a high point with views to the south. Descending from this viewpoint, the trail reaches a west-facing viewpoint at 3.4 miles. At 3.9 miles, the trail makes a right turn, followed by a steep ascent and then level ridge walking. The Fire Tower Trail (red) joins from the west at 4.4 miles, in a hemlock grove.

At 5.0 miles, the Sterling Ridge Trail makes a sharp left turn and ascends to reach the Sterling Forest Fire Tower, built in 1922. The tower offers spectacular 360° views of Sterling Forest. Here, the Fire Tower Trail leaves to the right, descending to the east on a woods road. The Sterling Ridge Trail continues ahead, with many ups and downs over the next two miles. An orange-blazed trail crosses at 5.5 miles, and a granite gneiss outcrop at 5.9 miles provides views to the east, with Sterling Lake visible in the foreground and the mountains of Harriman State Park in the distance.

The Sterling Ridge Trail crosses a power line at 7.5 miles and reenters the woods. At 8.5 miles, the Sterling Valley Trail (yellow) comes in from the right on a woods road. Both trails continue ahead, passing a cable barrier across the road to reach a parking area. Here, the Sterling Valley Trail leaves to the right, while the Sterling Ridge Trail continues ahead to end at 8.6 miles at NY 17A, 1.8 miles east of the junction of NY 210 and NY 17A in the village of Greenwood Lake.

The Highlands Trail (teal diamond) is co-aligned with the Sterling Ridge Trail for its entire length.

Whritenour Mine Trail   *Length: 0.4 mile Blaze: yellow*

The Whritenour Mine Trail is a short loop trail that passes by several open pits of the Whritenour Mine. It begins on the south side of Greenwood Lake Turnpike (County 511), 0.1 mile west of the bridge over the Monksville Reservoir.

Parking is available at the headquarters of Long Pond Ironworks State Park on the opposite side of the road.

From the trailhead, the trail heads south on a footpath. In 150 feet, with stone foundations visible on the right, the trail turns left and joins a woods road. It climbs through a valley and then begins to descend rather steeply towards the reservoir. At 0.2 mile, about 150 feet before reaching the shore of the reservoir, the first open pit of the Whritenour Mine may be seen on the right, about 20 feet from the trail. Just beyond, a second mine pit is visible on the right. The third pit is at the bottom of the descent, along the shore of the reservoir. This pit is now flooded by the waters of the reservoir.

The trail now turns left and proceeds along the shore of the reservoir, passing a fourth pit to the left. It continues close to the edge of the reservoir until it reaches Greenwood Lake Turnpike at 0.4 mile. The blazed trail ends here, but hikers should follow the paved road for 0.1 mile to return to the starting point, completing the loop.

Wanaque Wildlife Management Area

The 2,319-acre Wanaque Wildlife Management Area is located adjacent to and just east of Greenwood Lake. Hunting is permitted, and the area is home to a wide variety of animals, including deer, turkey and grouse. Various species of cold- and warm-water fish found in the area include trout in the Wanaque River and largemouth bass and chain pickerel in Green Turtle Pond. Although there are few marked hiking trails, there is a network of unmarked woods roads, with access from adjoining paved roads. For more information, contact the New Jersey Department of Environmental Protection, Division of Fish and Wildlife, 501 East State Street, P.O. Box 400, Trenton, NJ 08625; (609) 984-0547; www.njfishandwildlife.org.

Jennings Hollow Trail   *Length: 3.0 miles Blaze: yellow*

The Jennings Hollow Trail is a "lollipop"-shaped loop trail which follows woods roads through bottomland with numerous stream crossings, including Jennings Creek and several of its tributaries. A highlight of the trail is a view across an extensive wetland along the return segment of the loop.

The Jennings Hollow Trail starts from the Sterling Ridge Trail (blue on white), 1.1 miles from its southern trailhead at the intersection of East Shore Road and Greenwood Lake Turnpike (County 511). Proceeding northwest, it

*Figure 7-11. Wetland along the
Jennings Hollow Trail*

reaches the start of the loop at 0.7 mile, just beyond a plank bridge over a stream. Taking the right-hand branch of the loop, the trail passes a stone wall, keeping to the right of Jennings Creek. Then, at 1.7 miles, the trail swings west through a hemlock ravine to cross the creek at a cascade.

Now on the return portion of the loop, the trail follows uneven terrain and crosses several feeder streams before turning south. At 2.0 miles, the trail joins a woods road that comes in from the right, and it descends to skirt the edge of a broad wetland, with an extensive stand of drowned trees. The Jennings Hollow Trail then crosses the outlet of the wetland and rejoins the woods road before turning left to recross Jennings Creek at 2.6 miles. (The woods road, now unblazed, continues ahead for another 0.3 mile to a gate opposite a parking area on East Shore Road, 1.7 miles north of County 511.) The Jennings Hollow Trail returns to the start of the loop at 3.0 miles.

Sterling Forest

Sterling Forest was extensively involved in the early history of the mining and smelting industries in America. Iron mines in Sterling Forest helped supply the

Continental Army of the American Revolution and the Union Army during the Civil War. Ore from Sterling and Long mines, smelted at Sterling Furnace, was used to make a great chain that spanned the Hudson at West Point, with the intention of obstructing the British fleet.

By 1980, Sterling Forest had become the largest undeveloped, forested property remaining in the New York-New Jersey metropolitan area. The preservation of this unique and biologically rich property became the focus of many conservation organizations and public agencies, which formed the Sterling Forest Coalition and the Public-Private Partnership to Save Sterling Forest. In 1990, Passaic County, with assistance from the New Jersey Green Acres program, took the first bold step and condemned the 2,100-acre New Jersey section of Sterling Forest. This land, known as Tranquility Ridge, was dedicated as parkland open for public use. In the spring of 1996, Sterling Forest Corporation agreed to sell 15,280 acres of the New York section of the forest to public agencies for $55 million. Funds were raised from a variety of public and private sources over the next two years and finally, in February 1998, the property was purchased, forming the nucleus of Sterling Forest State Park. In December 2000, an additional 2,000 acres were acquired from Sterling Forest Corporation, expanding the New York park to over 17,000 acres.

The New Jersey section of Sterling Forest, owned by Passaic County, is managed by the New Jersey office of the Palisades Interstate Park Commission. Other than a portion of the Sterling Ridge Trail (see the Long Pond Ironworks section, above), there are, as of 2003, no marked trails in the New Jersey section of Sterling Forest, but hiking is permitted on woods roads and unmarked trails during daylight hours. Access is from a parking area on Beech Road, which leads north from Greenwood Lake Turnpike (County 511), 0.3 mile west of its intersection with Margaret King Avenue. The parking area, which primarily serves a boat rental concession for the Monksville Reservoir, is on the west side of the road, 0.4 mile north of Greenwood Lake Turnpike. For more information, contact the New Jersey office of the Palisades Interstate Park Commission, Box 155, Alpine, NJ 07620; (201) 768-1360; www.njpalisades.org.

EIGHT

BEARFORT RIDGE AND WAWAYANDA

earfort Ridge, formed of the unusual Schunemunk conglomerate, is an anomaly in the midst of the Highlands. With its many overlooks, colorful bedrock, and stunted pitch pines, it is one of the most picturesque mountain ridges in all of New Jersey. Wawayanda State Park, just to the west, includes much former farmland, with many of the trails following old woods roads, but it also contains the fascinating Cedar Swamp. Wawayanda Mountain, at the western end of the park, features expansive overlooks and a rugged section of the Appalachian Trail that climbs a vertical distance of 800 feet in less than a mile. Although quite different from each other, these two areas combine to create a spectacular area for hiking in northwest Passaic County and northeast Sussex County.

BEARFORT RIDGE

Bearfort Ridge—which extends from the New York-New Jersey state line, just west of Greenwood Lake, to the Clinton Reservoir, a short distance north of NJ 23—is a southward extension of Schunemunk Mountain in New York. It is composed of Schunemunk conglomerate, often referred to as "puddingstone." This type of rock is quite different from that found elsewhere in the Highlands. Bearfort Ridge reaches an elevation of nearly 1,500 feet above sea level, and the higher elevations are often characterized by pitch pines growing out of the bedrock.

Bearfort Ridge may be divided into three sections. The most northerly

section, north of Warwick Turnpike, is in the Abram S. Hewitt State Forest. South of Warwick Turnpike, the ridge is part of Wawayanda State Park. Terrace Pond is the most distinctive feature on this portion of the ridge, which is separated from the remainder of the park by Clinton Road. The most southerly portion of the ridge is in the Pequannock Watershed, owned by the City of Newark.

Scenic hiking trails traverse the entire length of the ridge, and one may walk from the Clinton Reservoir all the way to the New York state line—a hiking distance of over 13 miles. The unusual geology of the ridge makes for very interesting hikes, and loop hikes are possible in all three sections of the ridge.

Geology

The "puddingstone" Schunemunk conglomerate which is characteristic of Bearfort Ridge is studded with pebbles of pink sandstone and white quartz, some of which reach a diameter of seven inches, although most are an inch or two across. This rock is highly resistant to erosion, which accounts for the ridge standing well above the surrounding region.

Bearfort Ridge has the same basic synclinal structure as Schunemunk Mountain. The syncline has a central axis that passes under Terrace Pond and West Pond. Terrace Pond is an especially good place to observe the conglomerate beds as they dip downward from either side toward the center of the pond.

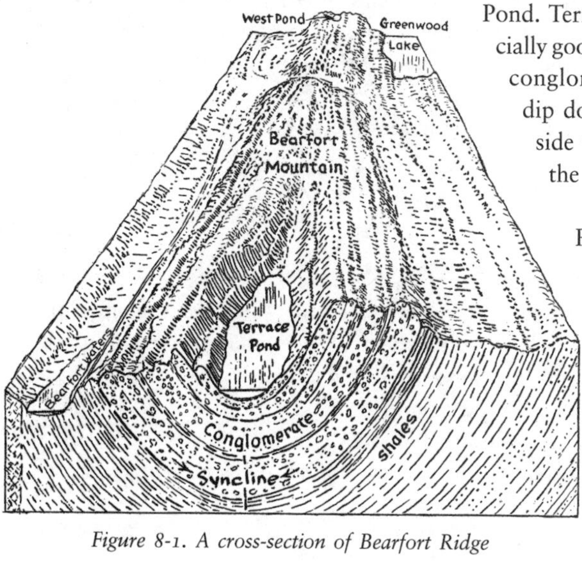

Figure 8-1. A cross-section of Bearfort Ridge

East of Bearfort Ridge is a long shale-and-limestone valley which includes Greenwood Lake. Together, the ridge and the valley comprise a down-faulted Paleozoic section which is sandwiched be-

tween the Wawayanda and Wyanokie areas of the Precambrian Highlands. This elongate wedge of Devonian and Silurian strata can be traced as a long blue-and-purple band on the color Geologic Map used as the endpapers at the front of this book.

For a more detailed discussion of the geology of Bearfort Ridge, see chapter 4, "Geology," pp. 38-40, 44-45.

Abram S. Hewitt State Forest

The 2,000-acre Abram S. Hewitt State Forest encompasses the section of Bearfort Ridge between Greenwood Lake and Upper Greenwood Lake, north of Warwick Turnpike. The forest is isolated and accessible only on foot. It has four major trails: Bearfort Ridge, Ernest Walter, Quail, and State Line. In addition, the Appalachian Trail traverses the northwest corner of the forest and extends west to Long House Road and Warwick Turnpike. These trails are often combined to create interesting and scenic loop hikes.

Starting at the southern terminus of the Bearfort Ridge Trail on Warwick Turnpike, a popular 6.0-mile loop hike utilizes the Bearfort Ridge, Ernest Walter, and Quail trails. For a longer hike, one may combine the Bearfort Ridge, Ernest Walter, Appalachian, State Line, and Quail trails into a rugged 7.7-mile loop. A 4.1-mile "lollipop"-loop hike, starting from the trailhead of the State Line Trail on Lakeside Road (County 511), is also possible.

Abram S. Hewitt State Forest is administered by Wawayanda State Park. For more information, contact Wawayanda State Park, 885 Warwick Turnpike, Hewitt, NJ 07421; (973) 853-4462; www.njparksandforests.org.

Bearfort Ridge Trail   *Length: 3.0 miles Blaze: white*
The Bearfort Ridge Trail traverses the ridge of Bearfort Mountain, following ridges of deep-red Devonian puddingstone (Schunemunk conglomerate) through a summit forest of pitch pine, hemlock, and mountain laurel. The southern trailhead is on Warwick Turnpike, 0.3 mile west of the junction of Warwick Turnpike and Union Valley Road, and just east of a concrete bridge over a stream. There is a small parking area on the north side of the road, immediately west of the bridge, and just east of the intersection of Warwick Turnpike with White Road. Public transportation is available via NJ Transit bus #197 to Warwick Turnpike and Union Valley Road, 0.3 mile east of the trailhead.

From the trailhead, the trail proceeds uphill through rhododendrons and hemlocks. At 0.1 mile, it joins a woods road that comes in from the right. Just beyond, the Bearfort Ridge Trail turns left, leaving the road, as the Quail Trail (orange) continues ahead on the road. The Bearfort Ridge Trail continues to ascend on a wide footpath. It crosses a seasonal stream at 0.4 mile and levels off through mountain laurel. After descending briefly to cross a wider stream at 0.6 mile, the trail continues through a rhododendron grove. Then, at 0.7 mile, a blue-blazed trail which leads 0.2 mile back to Warwick Turnpike leaves to the left.

The Bearfort Ridge Trail now begins a steady, rather steep climb. At 0.9 mile, it passes a large, lichen-covered outcrop to the right, and it continues to climb until it reaches the crest of the ridge—marked by pitch pines—at 1.0 mile. Here, a large conglomerate rock outcrop to the left offers an expansive view to the south. Upper Greenwood Lake is visible to the west and, on a clear day, the New York City skyline may be seen in the distance to the east.

The trail now bears right and proceeds north along the puddingstone conglomerate ridge, through pitch pines. After a brief but steep climb, the vegetation changes to hemlocks and laurels. The trail continues at an elevation of about 1,300 feet, having climbed about 600 feet from the trailhead. At 1.5 miles, the trail crosses an open rock outcrop, with several large glacial erratics, and passes more pitch pines. After a short descent to cross a wet area, the trail climbs to reach, at 2.1 miles, a rock ledge overlooking a swamp to the west. Here, a narrow wedge of the bedrock has split away from the main ledge, forming a deep crevice.

After a short climb, the Bearfort Ridge Trail reaches a rock outcrop with a huge boulder at 2.4 miles. It continues along a whaleback rock, through pitch pines, and reaches a limited viewpoint to the east. The trail now descends steeply, through hemlocks and laurels, to cross a stream amid jumbled rocks, and it climbs to a viewpoint from a rock outcrop with pitch pines at 2.7 miles. After a gentle descent, the trail levels off. It then climbs to a rock outcrop marked by several cedar trees, with an expansive view. Surprise Lake is visible to the north, and Sterling Forest and the Wyanokies may be seen to the east, with an arm of the Monksville Reservoir visible in the distance. Here, at 3.0 miles, the Bearfort Ridge Trail ends at a junction with the Ernest Walter Trail (yellow).

Ernest Walter Trail   *Length: 1.9 miles Blaze: yellow*
The Ernest Walter Trail, named for a dedicated hiker and trail maintainer,

Figure 8-2. Greenwood Lake from the Ernest Walter Trail

makes a loop around West Pond and Surprise Lake in the northern section of Abram S. Hewitt State Forest. It offers expansive views over Greenwood Lake and traverses rugged terrain south and west of West Pond.

The eastern terminus of the Ernest Walter Trail is on the State Line Trail (blue on white), 0.7 mile west of Lakeside Road (County 511). The Ernest Walter Trail heads south, climbing steadily along a rocky footpath to reach—at 0.1 mile—a large, glacially-smoothed outcrop of puddingstone conglomerate rock at the top of a rise. From here, there is an expansive view to the east over the six-mile-long Greenwood Lake, 600 vertical feet below, with the Sterling Ridge in the background. The trail continues along the ridge, reaching another viewpoint to the east from a long rock outcrop, with pitch pines, at 0.3 mile.

The trail now bears right and descends to cross the outlet of a swamp to the right of the trail. At 0.5 mile, it reaches the eastern shore of pristine, spring-fed Surprise Lake. Just beyond, the Quail Trail (orange) begins to the left. The Ernest Walter Trail bears right and soon begins to pass through a dense rhododendron grove, with the thick rhododendrons forming a canopy over the trail in places. After crossing a stream, the outlet of Surprise Lake, the trail climbs to reach a viewpoint at the northern terminus of the Bearfort Ridge Trail (white). Here, 1.0 mile from the start of the Ernest Walter Trail, Surprise Lake is visible through the trees to the north, and Sterling Forest and the Wyanokies may be

seen to the east, with an arm of the Monksville Reservoir in the distance.

From this junction, the Ernest Walter Trail heads west over rugged, rocky terrain. At 1.1 miles, after a short, steep descent, a side trail to the right leads to a viewpoint overlooking West Pond. Just beyond, the trail descends very steeply to cross the outlet stream of West Pond, then climbs to wind through a mixed forest of hemlocks and deciduous trees. West Pond again comes into view to the right, through the trees, at 1.5 miles. Just beyond, the trail crosses a small stream, the outlet of a swamp to the left. It proceeds through pitch pines, follows a long, smooth rock, and continues over more level terrain through a largely deciduous forest. At 1.9 miles, the Ernest Walter Trail turns right and descends to end at a junction with the Appalachian Trail (white). To return to the start of the loop, turn right and follow the Appalachian Trail for 0.3 mile, then turn right onto the State Line Trail for 0.5 mile.

Quail Trail   *Length: 2.4 miles Blaze: orange*

The Quail Trail is a woods road which roughly parallels the Bearfort Ridge Trail from Warwick Turnpike to Surprise Lake. It is an easier route than the Bearfort Ridge Trail and is often combined with that trail to form a loop hike.

To reach the start of the Quail Trail, follow the Bearfort Ridge Trail (white) north from its southern terminus on Warwick Turnpike. After 0.1 mile, the Bearfort Ridge Trail turns left onto a woods road, then turns left again in 100 feet, leaving the woods road. The Quail Trail begins here and continues ahead on the woods road through a dense forest of hemlocks and deciduous trees. At 0.2 mile, the trail bears left as another woods road leaves to the right. The Quail Trail ascends gradually, with a few steeper sections. It crosses a stream at 0.5 mile and then parallels it to the right. Soon, an old woods road (blocked by fallen trees) goes off to the right as the Quail Trail proceeds ahead on the main woods road. The trail climbs rather steeply around a large rock outcrop to the right at 0.9 mile and continues through mountain laurel.

After a short descent, the Quail Trail crosses another stream at 1.6 miles and climbs slightly to cross Cooley Brook on rocks at 1.7 miles. It continues to ascend, reaching a high point at 2.2 miles, and then descends to end at 2.4 miles at a junction with the Ernest Walter Trail (yellow). To the left, the Ernest Walter Trail leads in 0.5 mile to the northern terminus of the Bearfort Ridge Trail (white). Surprise Lake is 100 feet to the right along the Ernest Walter Trail.

Figure 8-3. Overlook at West Pond

State Line Trail — Length: *1.2 miles Blaze: blue on white*
The eastern trailhead of the State Line Trail is on Lakeside Road (County 511), opposite the Greenwood Lake Marina, and just south of the New York-New Jersey state line. It is accessible by public transportation from the Port Authority Bus Terminal in New York via NJ Transit bus #197. Trailhead parking is available on the west side of Lakeside Road, on the south side of the dirt driveway that leads uphill from the road. (Do not park at the Greenwood Lake Marina or on the north side of the driveway.)

From the trailhead, the State Line Trail climbs the eastern slope of Bearfort Mountain, rather steeply in places. At 0.7 mile, after a climb of about 550 vertical feet, the Ernest Walter Trail (yellow) leaves to the left. Soon, the State Line Trail levels off and then descends slightly. It continues generally uphill, with some short descents, to its terminus at the Appalachian Trail (white), 1.2 miles from the trailhead on Lakeside Road. The New York-New Jersey state line, marked by paint on the rocks, is 0.1 mile to the right along the Appalachian Trail. The western end of the Ernest Walter Trail is 0.3 mile to the left.

Terrace Pond

Terrace Pond—an aquatic gem that lies at an altitude of 1,380 feet—is surrounded by high cliffs of puddingstone conglomerate, with nearby blueberry swamps and impressive stands of rhododenron. Although formally part of Wawayanda State Park, it is separated from the rest of the park by Clinton Road, and its features are visually and geologically distinct from those of the remainder of the park. Accordingly, the trails in the Terrace Pond area are described here, in the Bearfort Ridge section. The Terrace Pond area was designated a natural area in 1978.

For more information, contact Wawayanda State Park, 885 Warwick Turnpike, Hewitt, NJ 07421; (973) 853-4462; www.njparksandforests.org.

Trails in the Terrace Pond Area

Terrace Pond, a favorite destination of hikers since the 1930s, is surrounded by a network of trails. Access to the pond is available from several trailheads.

The most popular trailhead, which offers the option of a loop hike around the pond, is on the east side of Clinton Road, 7.5 miles north of NJ 23 and 1.7 miles south of Warwick Turnpike. A large parking area is on the west side of the road, opposite the trailhead. If coming from the south, the parking area is just north of the Wildcat Mountain Wilderness Center (Project U.S.E.); if coming from the north, it is 0.2 mile south of the gas line cut. The Terrace Pond North Trail (blue) and the Terrace Pond South Trail (yellow) both begin here, and the two trails can be combined (along with a portion of the Terrace Pond Circular Trail (white)) to make a 5.2-mile loop hike around the pond. Variations are possible by using the Yellow Dot Trail or a portion of the Terrace Pond Red Trail for part of the route.

Access from Stephens Road to the south is available via the Terrace Pond Red Trail (red) and the Spring North Trail (blue), and from Warwick Turnpike to the north, the pond may be accessed via the Terrace Pond North Trail (blue).

Spring North Trail
Length: 2.0 miles Blaze: blue

The Spring North Trail begins at a parking area on Stephens Road, 0.5 mile northwest of Union Valley Road (County 513). It follows a grassy woods road through a deciduous forest for most of its length, soon passing an old furnace site to the left of the trail. At 1.7 miles, it turns left and descends along the steep,

rocky route of a gas pipeline. Just before reaching a very wet area at the base of the descent, at 1.9 miles, it bears sharply left, leaving the gas pipeline, and heads southwest. It ends at 2.0 miles at a junction with the Terrace Pond Red Trail (red). Together with the Terrace Pond Red Trail, the Spring North Trail can be used as part of a loop hike to Terrace Pond from Stephens Road.

Terrace Pond Circular Trail   *Length: 1.1 miles Blaze: white*
The Terrace Pond Circular Trail circles Terrace Pond, connecting with the Terrace Pond North, Terrace Pond South, Terrace Pond Red, and Yellow Dot trails. Proceeding clockwise from its start at an intersection with the Terrace Pond North Trail (blue) at the northwest corner of the pond, the Terrace Pond Circular Trail (running concurrently with the Terrace Pond North Trail) soon reaches an unmarked trail to the right, which leads to a rock outcrop overlooking the pond. The trails descend to cross the outlet of the pond on a log bridge at 0.1 mile (this crossing may be extremely difficult if the water level is high), then climb very steeply to a junction. Here, the Terrace Pond North Trail continues straight ahead, while the Terrace Pond Circular Trail turns right and proceeds south.

In another 250 feet, as the trail turns left, an unmarked path continues ahead to a viewpoint over the pond from a high rock ledge. The trail now climbs steeply to reach another rock ledge with a view, passes an enormous glacial erratic to the right, and continues atop a long rock outcrop, with some pitch pines. Towards the end of the outcrop, at 0.5 mile, the Yellow Dot Trail (yellow on white) leaves to the left. The Terrace Pond Circular Trail now turns sharply right and descends. After climbing a rock outcrop with a large hemlock growing out of a crevice, the trail continues to climb through laurels. At 0.7 mile, the Terrace Pond Circular Trail descends and bears right, reaching the terminus of the Terrace Pond South Trail (yellow), which departs to the left. The Terrace Pond Circular Trail now heads north through rhododendrons and laurels, with a rock escarpment to the left and a swampy area to the right. The Terrace Pond Red Trail (red) leaves to the left at 0.9 mile. After a scramble over rocks, the Terrace Pond Circular Trail arrives at an open area looking over the pond. It continues north, passing more views of the pond, to reach the Terrace Pond North Trail at 1.1 miles, completing the loop.

Terrace Pond North Trail   *Length: 3.8 miles Blaze: blue*
The Terrace Pond North Trail begins on the east side of Clinton Road, 7.5 miles

north of NJ 23 and 1.7 miles south of Warwick Turnpike. This trailhead is also the start of the Terrace Pond South Trail (yellow). The two trails run jointly for 25 feet to a Y intersection, where the Terrace Pond North Trail departs to the left. Beginning at 0.2 mile, it crosses several wet areas on puncheons. (During periods of wet weather, portions of the trail may be flooded.) The Terrace Pond North Trail reaches a wide cut for a gas pipeline at 0.4 mile. It turns right and follows the pipeline cut uphill for about 500 feet, then again turns right and reenters the woods. The trail continues to ascend, with several steep climbs separated by relatively flat sections. After passing an underground stream to the left, the trail climbs a rounded rock outcrop at 1.2 miles. The top of this outcrop, just to the right of the trail, offers expansive views to the west over the Wawayanda Plateau.

Descending from the rock outcrop, the Terrace Pond North Trail proceeds through several wet areas, crossed on puncheons and logs. At 1.4 miles, at the northwest corner of the pond, the Terrace Pond Circular Trail (white) joins from the right. After a steep climb, an unmarked trail to the right leads to a rock outcrop overlooking the pond. The trails descend to cross the outlet of the pond on a log bridge, then climb very steeply to a junction at 1.6 miles. Here, the Terrace Pond Circular Trail leaves to the right, while the Terrace Pond North Trail continues straight ahead.

The Terrace Pond North Trail passes a series of rock outcrops, some with views to the left over an interior valley, and goes through an area with thick mountain laurel. At 2.1 miles, the Terrace Pond North Trail again reaches the gas pipeline route and turns right. It follows the wide cleared swath of the gas line for about 0.6 mile, with several ups and downs and some steep sections. At 2.7 miles, it bears left at a lichen-covered rock, leaving the pipeline, and briefly follows a woods road. When the woods road curves to the right, the trail continues ahead on a footpath.

At 3.0 miles, the trail reaches an expansive viewpoint to the east from an exposed rock outcrop, with Greenwood Lake visible to the northeast. After passing another viewpoint, the trail turns right, heads downhill, and bears left to join a woods road. It follows the woods road to its end at Warwick Turnpike, 3.8 miles from the southern trailhead. Limited parking is available at a turnout on the north side of the road just west of the trailhead on Warwick Turnpike.

In 2003, a relocation is planned that will move the trail away from the gas pipeline swath and onto a more attractive woodland footpath. For information on the status of this proposed relocation, contact the Trail Conference office at

Figure 8-4. Terrace Pond

(201) 512-9348, or check the Trail Conference's website, www.nynjtc.org/trails.

Terrace Pond Red Trail
Length: 2.6 miles Blaze: red

The Terrace Pond Red Trail, which provides access to Terrace Pond from the south, begins at parking area P8 on Stephens Road, 0.8 mile northwest of Union Valley Road (County 513). It proceeds north along an old woods road through a deep forest, pleasantly dark in some sections. At 1.4 miles, the Spring North Trail (blue) leaves to the right. Then, at 1.6 miles, the Terrace Pond Red Trail turns left and joins the Yellow Dot Trail (yellow on white). The two trails run jointly for 100 feet, after which the Terrace Pond Red Trail turns right and begins a more rugged section. It climbs steeply up a ridge which it follows to the north, continuing to ascend gradually. It then descends to a valley, crosses a stream, and continues across several low ridges. A huge rock outcrop soon comes into view. The trail turns right, parallels the outcrop, then climbs to its top and continues along it. The outcrop is composed of reddish-purple

puddingstone conglomerate rock, with quartz pebbles embedded in the rock.

After following the outcrop for some distance, the trail descends to the right and, at 2.2 miles, reaches a junction with the Terrace Pond South Trail (yellow). The two trails run together for a short distance, with the Terrace Pond Red Trail soon leaving to the left. The Terrace Pond Red Trail climbs along another rock outcrop, then steeply ascends over rocks to reach a limited viewpoint to the east through the trees. Just beyond, Terrace Pond may be seen below to the right. Continuing along its rugged, rocky route, the trail passes to the left of a huge boulder with some interesting crevices. It then descends steeply over rocks to end at a junction with the Terrace Pond Circular Trail (white) at 2.6 miles.

Terrace Pond South Trail
Length: 3.2 miles Blaze: yellow

The Terrace Pond South Trail begins on the east side of Clinton Road, 7.5 miles north of NJ 23 and 1.7 miles south of Warwick Turnpike. This trailhead is also the start of the Terrace Pond North Trail (blue). The two trails run jointly for 25 feet to a Y intersection, where the Terrace Pond South Trail departs to the right. It proceeds through mountain laurel and white pines, crossing several wet areas on puncheons. (During periods of wet weather, portions of the trail may be flooded.) At 0.6 mile, the trail enters a thick rhododendron grove, with the large rhododendron bushes forming a canopy over the trail in places. After crossing a low stone wall at 1.1 miles, the Terrace Pond South Trail turns left onto a woods road. It soon turns left onto another woods road.

At 1.6 miles, the trail bears sharply left at a junction of woods roads. After passing a swamp to the left, the trail bears right, bypassing a flooded section of the woods road, and crosses the outlet of the swamp on rocks. In wet seasons, there is an attractive cascade to the right. The trail then goes over two concrete pipes and, just beyond, at 2.1 miles, reaches a fork. Here, the Yellow Dot Trail (yellow on white) continues straight ahead, while the Terrace Pond South Trail turns left, descending to a wet area.

The trail continues across undulating terrain. After crossing an area with many large boulders, it climbs an outcrop of puddingstone conglomerate rock at 2.7 miles, with views through the trees to the west and south. It descends through a gully and joins the Terrace Pond Red Trail (red), which comes in from the right, at 3.0 miles. The two trails run together for a short distance, with the Terrace Pond Red Trail soon leaving to the left. The Terrace Pond South Trail

continues ahead through another gully to end at the Terrace Pond Circular Trail (white) at 3.2 miles.

Yellow Dot Trail   *Length: 1.0 mile Blaze: yellow on white*
Beginning at a sharp turn in the Terrace Pond South Trail (yellow), 2.1 miles from its trailhead on Clinton Road, the Yellow Dot Trail proceeds northeast on a level woods road. At 0.2 mile, the Terrace Pond Red Trail (red) joins from the left, and both trails run together for 100 feet to a T intersection. Here, the Terrace Pond Red Trail turns right, while the Yellow Dot Trail turns left, continuing to follow the woods road. After descending through a valley, the woods road ends at 0.8 mile, and the Yellow Dot Trail heads steeply uphill on a footpath, leveling off on a rock outcrop, with several glacial erratics. To the left of the trail, there is a broad viewpoint to the east, with the New York City skyline visible on a clear day. After another steep climb, the Yellow Dot Trail ends at 1.0 mile, at a junction with the Terrace Pond Circular Trail (white).

Pequannock Watershed

The City of Newark's Pequannock Watershed property adjoins the southern boundary of Wawayanda State Park. Encompassing 15,000 acres in Morris, Passaic, and Sussex counties, it is traversed southeast to northwest by NJ 23. The watershed contains five major reservoirs, totaling almost 2,000 acres, which provide a substantial portion of the water supply for the City of Newark and also serve portions of Pequannock, Wayne, Belleville, and Bloomfield townships. The clear lakes, streams, and ponds, the mountains with their dramatic rock outcroppings, the forests, and the varied vegetation of the watershed all combine to make it one of the most scenic areas in New Jersey.

The area of the Pequannock Watershed was of economic importance during the height of the iron industry in the eighteenth and nineteenth centuries. Its forests supplied wood for charcoal used at furnaces and ironworks located along the rivers. The area also produced iron ore, and several shafts and surface sites are still in existence. Later, the affluent built summer homes. In April 1900, the City of Newark acquired the property.

In 1974, the Newark Watershed Conservation and Development Corporation (NWCDC), a non-profit corporation, was assigned responsibility for managing the property on behalf of the City of Newark. As part of a major policy shift in land use, the NWCDC subscribed to the multiple-use concept

and opened the property for recreational use by the general public through a controlled access-by-permit program. At the same time, the NWCDC invited an all-volunteer trails development group to create and maintain a hiking trail system for the Clinton, Buckabear, Bearfort, Hanks Pond, and Echo Lake sections. This trails group completed, measured, and mapped a 25-mile trail system in these areas. The NWCDC subsequently entered into a Memorandum of Understanding with the New York-New Jersey Trail Conference to have their volunteer maintainers assist with the marking and maintenance of the watershed trail system. Acquisitions through New Jersey's Green Acres program have made it possible to connect trails in the watershed with those in Wawayanda State Park, thus permitting more extensive hikes in this beautiful area.

Hiking in the Pequannock Watershed is by permit only. For more information, or to obtain a hiking permit, contact the NWCDC, by mail at P.O. Box 319, Newfoundland, NJ 07435; or in person at their office at 223 Echo Lake Road, West Milford, NJ 07480; (973) 697-2850.

Trails in the Pequannock Watershed

Most of the trails in the Pequannock Watershed are concentrated in the area around the Clinton Reservoir and Hanks Pond, north of NJ 23. These trails run primarily in a southwest-northeast direction, following the rocky ridges of Bearfort Mountain. Connections between the various northeast-southwest trails are provided by the Highlands Trail, the Twin Brooks Trail, and several short blue-blazed trails, thus facilitating a variety of loop hikes.

The primary access to trails in this area is from Clinton Road, which extends north from NJ 23. The watershed has assigned numbers to the trailhead parking areas, with parking area P1 being located at the intersection of Clinton Road and Van Orden Road, 1.7 miles north of NJ 23. Parking areas P2 to P5, all on Clinton Road, are located, respectively, 2.9, 3.9, 4.5, and 6.1 miles north of NJ 23. Parking area P8 is on Stephens Road, about one mile west of Union Valley Road (County 513). Parking area P9 is on Paradise Road, 0.1 mile north of its intersection with Schoolhouse Cove Road. To reach this parking area from NJ 23, take Clinton Road north for 1.2 miles, turn left (opposite the Clinton Furnace) onto Schoolhouse Cove Road, continue for 1.0 mile to Paradise Road, and turn right onto Paradise Road. Public transportation to the area is available via NJ Transit buses #194 and #195, which run along NJ 23.

Trails are also located on Pequannock Watershed lands south of NJ 23. For descriptions of these trails, see the Farny Highlands section of chapter 10, "Morris County," pp. 221-30.

Bearfort Waters/Clinton Trail   *Length: 4.6 miles Blaze: yellow*

The Bearfort Waters/Clinton Trail is a major north–south trail that connects the main section of Wawayanda State Park with the Pequannock Watershed. It runs parallel to and west of Clinton Road, and it is accessible from several parking areas along the road.

The northern trailhead of the Bearfort Waters/Clinton Trail is on the Old Coal Trail (red), 0.4 mile from the southern terminus of the Old Coal Trail on Clinton Road. The Bearfort Waters/Clinton Trail heads southwest, leaving Wawayanda State Park and entering the Pequannock Watershed. At 1.0 mile, it crosses Mossmans Brook on stepping stones (which may be underwater during times of high water). To the left, there is an interesting beaver swamp.

The Bearfort Waters/Clinton Trail reaches a junction with a woods road, known as Delazier Road, at 1.2 miles. To the left, the woods road leads in 0.1 mile to parking area P5 on Clinton Road. The Bearfort Waters/Clinton Trail turns right, joining the woods road, and follows the road across Mossmans Brook. At 1.7 miles, it turns left, leaving the road, and heads southwest, crossing another brook at 1.8 miles and continuing over grassy slopes and through patches of laurels.

At 2.9 miles, the trail joins an old gas pipeline route that comes in from the right. It turns right, leaving the pipeline route, at 3.1 miles. (A blue-blazed connecting trail continues ahead along the old pipeline route, reaching the Clinton West Trail at 0.1 mile, with parking area P4 on Clinton Road another 0.3 mile further along the Clinton West Trail.) The Bearfort Waters/Clinton Trail now begins to descend, reaching the north end of Buckabear Pond at 3.6 miles.

After climbing to a high point overlooking the pond, the trail descends to the shoreline and heads south along the western shore of the pond. In 2003, beaver activity has raised the level of the pond, and portions of the trail may be flooded during wet periods. A relocation, which will route the trail further inland, has been planned, but until the relocation is completed, hikers may have to bushwhack around flooded trail sections. At 4.0 miles, a woods road reaches the shore of the pond in a flat area. The Bearfort Waters/Clinton Trail crosses

the inlet stream of the pond at 4.2 miles, and it ends, 4.6 miles from its start, at a junction with the Clinton West Trail (white).

Buckabear Pond Trail   *Length: 0.7 mile Blaze: red triangle on white*
Starting from parking area P3 on Clinton Road, 3.9 miles north of NJ 23, the Buckabear Pond Trail heads southwest, following an old woods road along the west side of Clinton Reservoir. At 0.2 mile, the trail turns right and goes steeply up the ridge to cross the Clinton West Trail (white) at 0.4 mile. Just beyond, the Buckabear Pond Trail turns left, leaving the woods road, and descends to end at a junction with the Clinton West Trail at 0.7 mile, at a dam which divides an arm of the Clinton Reservoir from Buckabear Pond. The southern end of the Bearfort Waters/Clinton Trail (yellow) is 250 feet ahead, across the dam.

Clinton West Trail   *Length: 4.5 miles Blaze: white*
The eastern trailhead of the Clinton West Trail is on the west side of Clinton Road, 400 feet south of parking area P4, which is 4.5 miles north of NJ 23. After briefly following a woods road, the trail turns right and follows a footpath through a hemlock grove. At 0.1 mile, it turns sharply left and steeply ascends Bearfort Mountain on a rocky footpath, following the route of an old gas pipeline. It reaches the crest of the ridge at 0.3 mile. Here, the Clinton West Trail turns left and proceeds south along the ridge, while a blue-blazed connecting trail continues ahead, reaching the Bearfort Waters/Clinton Trail in 0.1 mile. The Clinton West Trail follows an undulating path along the ridge through an open, deciduous forest, with blueberry bushes and mountain laurel, reaching the highest point on the ridge, with limited views of the Clinton Reservoir, at 1.1 miles. After passing a line of cliffs to the right at 1.3 miles, the trail climbs to a expansive viewpoint over the Clinton Reservoir from open rocks.

The Buckabear Pond Trail (red triangle on white) crosses at 1.5 miles. (To the left, this trail leads in 0.4 mile to parking area P3 on Clinton Road; to the right, it shortcuts a long loop of the Clinton West Trail, reaching the Buckabear Pond dam in 0.3 mile.) Continuing south along the ridge, the Clinton West Trail climbs to reach a high point at 2.1 miles, with an unmarked side trail to the left leading to another viewpoint over the reservoir. The trail now begins a steady descent, curving to the west and then to the north, and follows an old woods road through a dense stand of mountain laurel. It reaches the level of the reservoir at 2.7 miles and continues heading north, closely following the eastern shore of an arm of the reservoir.

At 2.9 miles, the Clinton West Trail reaches a dam that regulates the water flow from Buckabear Pond (to the north) to an arm of Clinton Reservoir (to the south). Here, the Buckabear Pond Trail (red triangle on white) leaves to the right. The Clinton West Trail turns left and crosses the dam. In 2003, beaver activity in the area has raised the level of Buckabear Pond, and the dam crossing may be flooded in high-water periods (in the winter, it may be icy).

At the west side of the dam, the Bearfort Waters/Clinton Trail (yellow) begins to the right. Here, the Clinton West Trail turns left and heads south, following the west shore of the Clinton Reservoir. At 3.1 miles, it passes bronze plaques commemorating three individuals who were instrumental in creating the Pequannock Watershed trail system. Continuing along the shore of the reservoir, the trail follows the route of a horse trail built by the Civilian Conservation Corps in the 1930s.

The Highlands Trail (teal diamond) leaves to the right at 3.8 miles. A short distance beyond, the Clinton West Trail turns left, leaving the woods road that it has been following. After rejoining the woods road, the trail continues heading in a southwest direction to end, 4.5 miles from its start, at parking area P9 on Paradise Road, just north of its intersection with Schoolhouse Cove Road.

All but the southern 0.7 mile of the Clinton West Trail is coaligned with the Highlands Trail (teal diamond).

Echo Lake East Trail *Length: 2.1 miles Blaze: white*
The Echo Lake East Trail follows a relatively level route along the east shore of Echo Lake. It begins on Echo Lake Road, just north of a culvert, 0.4 mile northeast of the NWCDC office. Parking is available at the trailhead. After passing the dam of Echo Lake, the Echo Lake East Trail begins to run north along the east shore of the lake, with cliffs to the right. For the first mile, the Highlands Trail (teal diamond) runs concurrently with the Echo Lake East Trail. At 1.0 mile, the Highlands Trail leaves to the right, while the Echo Lake East Trail continues north along the lake shore. At 1.7 miles, near the northern tip of Echo Lake, the trail turns right, leaving the lakeshore. It heads uphill to end on Gould Road, just west of Macopin Road, 2.1 miles from the start.

Fire Tower Ridge Trail *Length: 2.5 miles Blaze: red/white*
From its trailhead on Clinton Road, 0.4 mile north of parking area P1 at the intersection of Clinton and Van Orden roads, the Fire Tower Ridge Trail climbs gently along a well-graded, wide woods road. At 0.1 mile, a blue-blazed con-

necting trail leaves to the right, leading in 0.3 mile to the Hanks East Trail (white). A short distance ahead, the Fire Tower Ridge Trail reaches a stone foundation at the intersection of woods roads. Here, the Hanks West Trail (blue/white) begins to the right. Another blue-blazed connecting trail leaves to the left at 0.4 mile, leading in 0.4 mile to the Fire Tower West Trail (yellow) and parking area P2.

At 0.5 mile, the Fire Tower Ridge Trail curves sharply right and reaches the site of Cross Castle. Built in 1907 as the home of Richard F. Cross, the three-story stone mansion was sold to the City of Newark in 1919 and soon abandoned. The stone walls were finally demolished in 1988, and only part of one wall and portions of the foundation remain.

The trail curves left and continues along a narrower woods road, with views of Hanks Pond through the trees to the right. At 0.6 mile, a dirt road to the left leads to a circular stone water tower built to supply water to Cross Castle (the water tower can also be seen from the trail). The trail continues to climb on the woods road along the ridge of Bearfort

Figure 8-5. Bearfort Fire Tower

Mountain until, at 1.3 miles, the woods road ends at a rock outcrop. The trail bears right and continues on a footpath along the rocky ridge. It passes a blueberry swamp to the left at 1.4 miles, and descends to a rock cleft with an underground stream at 1.6 miles. Here, it reaches a junction with the Newark Connector Trail (blue). To the right, the connector trail leads to the Hanks West (blue/white) and Hanks East (white) trails. The Fire Tower Ridge Trail continues ahead, now running concurrently with the Newark Connector Trail, and passes another swamp to the left.

After crossing a small stream at 1.8 miles, the trail reaches a fork. Here, the Newark Connector Trail leaves to the left, leading to the Fire Tower West Trail, while the Fire Tower Ridge Trail bears right and continues to head north along

the ridge. It emerges onto a clearing at 2.4 miles, with the Bearfort Fire Tower (manned seasonally) visible directly ahead. The Fire Tower Ridge Trail turns sharply left and ends a short distance ahead at a junction with the Fire Tower West Trail (yellow).

Fire Tower West Trail *Length: 2.6 miles Blaze: yellow*
The Fire Tower West Trail begins at parking area P2 on Clinton Road, 2.9 miles north of NJ 23. At 0.1 mile, a blue-blazed connecting trail leaves to the right, leading in 0.4 mile to the Fire Tower Ridge Trail (red/white). The Fire Tower West Trail continues ahead through thick mountain laurel, climbing gradually and running parallel to a rocky ridge on the right. At 1.0 mile, it briefly joins a woods road. Then, at 1.3 miles, after passing dramatic cliffs to the right, the Twin Brooks Trail (white) leaves to the left. The Fire Tower West Trail continues ahead, now joined by the Highlands Trail (teal diamond). The Newark Connector Trail (blue), which crosses the ridge to the Fire Tower Ridge Trail (red/white), the Hanks West Trail (blue/white), and the Hanks East Trail (white) leaves to the right at 1.4 miles.

After passing a rock outcrop with good views over pristine Cedar Pond to the northwest at 1.9 miles, the Fire Tower West Trail joins a woods road at 2.1 miles. Here, the Fire Tower Ridge Trail leaves to the right. Just beyond, the Highlands Trail departs to the right, reaching the Bearfort Fire Tower in 200 feet. The Fire Tower West Trail continues ahead, descending to end at parking area P8 on Stephens Road at 2.6 miles.

Hanks East Trail *Length: 3.3 miles Blaze: white*
The Hanks East Trail begins at parking area P1 at the intersection of Clinton and Van Orden roads. It follows a wide woods road for 0.2 mile, then leaves to the right and begins to follow a narrower woods road. (At this junction, a blue-blazed connecting trail leaves to the left and leads in 0.2 mile to the Fire Tower Ridge Trail (red/white).) The Hanks East Trail heads in a northeasterly direction along the woods road through dense mountain laurel, with Hanks Pond visible through the trees on the left (the trail does not approach the shore of the pond). At 1.0 mile, near the northern end of the pond, the trail narrows to a footpath. Then, at 1.6 miles, the Newark Connector Trail (blue) leads left to the Hanks West (blue/white), Fire Tower Ridge (red/white), and Fire Tower West (yellow) trails.

Figure 8-6. Hanks West Trail

At 1.8 miles, the Hanks East Trail turns left onto a wide rock outcrop that resembles a causeway. The trail now takes on a more rugged character. It soon bears right and follows a rocky ridge, reaching a viewpoint over a blueberry swamp to the left from a wide rock ledge studded with pitch pines at 2.2 miles.

A junction with the Highlands Trail (teal diamond) at a large rock outcrop is reached at 2.5 miles, with views over Union Valley and Kanouse Mountain to the east. To the right, the Highlands Trail leads down to Union Valley Road. The westbound Highlands Trail joins the Hanks East Trail, and the two trails run jointly for 250 feet. The Highlands Trail then leaves to the left, while the Hanks East Trail continues ahead. The Hanks East Trail crosses the power line to the fire tower (visible to the left) at 2.8 miles, crosses a small stream at 3.2 miles, and ends at Stephens Road, 3.3 miles from the start.

Hanks West Trail *Length: 2.8 miles Blaze: blue/white*

The Hanks West Trail begins at a junction with the Fire Tower Ridge Trail (red/white), 0.2 mile north of the southern trailhead of the Fire Tower Ridge Trail on Clinton Road. The junction is marked by the stone foundation of an old building. The Hanks West Trail heads east to the shore of Hanks Pond, turns left, and follows a woods road along the pond. Remaining mostly level for the first mile, it continues through a hardwood forest. At 1.4 miles, the Hanks West

Trail crosses the Newark Connector Trail (blue). (To the right, this trail leads to the Hanks East Trail (white); to the left, it leads to the Fire Tower Ridge Trail.) Just beyond, the Hanks West Trail crosses a small stream.

At 2.1 miles, the Highlands Trail (teal diamond) joins from the left. (To the left, the Highlands Trail climbs steeply to a junction with the Fire Tower Ridge Trail and the Fire Tower West Trail (yellow) at the Bearfort Fire Tower.) After running concurrently with the Hanks West Trail for only 100 feet, the Highlands Trail leaves to the right, reaching the Hanks East Trail and descending to Union Valley Road. The Hanks West Trail continues ahead, crossing the power line that leads to the Bearfort Fire Tower at 2.3 miles and descending to end at Stephens Road, 2.8 miles from its start.

Twin Brooks Trail   *Length: 1.0 mile Blaze: white*
The picturesque Twin Brooks Trail connects the eastern end of the Clinton West Trail (white) with the midpoint of the Fire Tower West Trail (yellow). Running against the grain of the ridgeline, it crosses two ridges and two brooks on the way.

From its western trailhead at parking area P4 on the east side of Clinton Road, 4.5 miles north of NJ 23, the Twin Brooks Trail proceeds south through a hemlock grove along Mossmans Brook. At 0.2 mile, it bears left, leaving the brook, and climbs a low ridge through laurels and pines. The trail descends to reach Cedar Brook at 0.5 mile. It turns right, follows the brook for a short distance, then turns left and crosses the brook on a one-log bridge. After climbing over a second ridge, it descends to cross Clinton Brook on another one-log bridge at 0.9 mile. The Twin Brooks Trail now climbs to end, 1.0 mile from its start, at the Fire Tower West Trail (yellow). For its entire length, the Twin Brooks Trail is co-aligned with the Highlands Trail (teal diamond).

WAWAYANDA STATE PARK

Wawayanda State Park embraces over 17,500 acres of forests and waters in the rough, hilly country of the New Jersey Highlands. The name, pronounced *Wa-wa-yanda,* is the phonetic rendition of the Lenape name, said to mean "winding, winding water," or "water on the mountain." The name was first applied around 1700 to the meadowlands in the valley below.

Wawayanda Lake, one of the focal points of the park, is 1½ miles long, has

5½ miles of wooded shoreline, and covers 255 acres. Laurel Pond, east of Wawayanda Lake, is about ten acres in area, and is mostly spring-fed. At the southeastern end of the pond, on a steep slope, is a stand of hemlock that is probably the only virgin timber in the area.

Toward the eastern part of the Wawayanda "Plateau" (it is not a plateau in the geological sense), on which most of the park is situated, various old woods roads and paths lead southward through one of the finest forests of its kind in New Jersey. A swamp containing an extensive stand of Atlantic white cedar is noteworthy for being so far from its usual haunts along the seacoast marshes. The rhododendron, whose great glossy leaves are attractive in any season, is enhanced in July by its beautiful flowers.

Wawayanda State Park includes the Barrett Farm Historic Site. Located on Barrett Road, the 160-acre farm is one of the last intact nineteenth-century farmsteads in the North Jersey Highlands. Owned by the Barrett family from 1860 to 1983, it was acquired by the state's Department of Environmental Protection (DEP) to buffer the Appalachian Trail. The farm was declared a National Historic District in 1989, and the DEP intends to develop it as a living history museum. An adjacent building leased by the Vernon Township Historical Society is a museum, open to the public on weekends.

Wawayanda State Park also includes the Terrace Pond Natural Area, east of Clinton Road. The trails in this section of the park, which is geologically part of the Bearfort Ridge, are described in the Bearfort Ridge section of this chapter, pp. 154-59. All of the trails in Wawayanda State Park west of Clinton Road, with the exception of the Appalachian Trail and the Cedar Swamp Trail, are multi-use trails on which mountain bikes and horses are permitted. The Appalachian Trail and the Cedar Swamp Trail (as well as all of the trails in the Terrace Pond Natural Area) are hiking-only trails.

The main entrance to the park is off Warwick Turnpike, about two miles north of Upper Greenwood Lake. There is also parking on Clinton Road, 1.7 miles from its northern terminus at Warwick Turnpike, or 7.5 miles from its southern terminus at NJ 23. For further information, contact Wawayanda State Park, 885 Warwick Turnpike, Hewitt, NJ 07421; (973) 853-4462; www.njparksandforests.org.

History

Wawayanda Lake, once called Double Pond, was originally two bodies of water separated by a narrow strip of land that still shows, in part, as Barker Island

near the center of the present lake. During the middle of the nineteenth century, the Thomas Iron Company built the earthen dam at the northeastern end of the lake. In addition, a wingdam was constructed on the eastern shore, over which spill waters that help feed Laurel Pond. These dams raised the level of the lake by about 7½ feet.

Near the northeastern end of Wawayanda Lake are the ruins of the Wawayanda Furnace, a charcoal blast furnace where iron was produced. Oliver Ames and his sons, William, Oakes, and Oliver, Jr., constructed it in 1845-46. William supervised the work, and his initials, W.L.A., and the date "1846" are still visible on a lintel in the main arch of the old furnace. Wheels for railroad cars were produced here and, during the Civil War, the Ames factories filled government orders for shovels and swords.

The Wawayanda Mine is 2½ miles northeast of the iron furnace along the east side of Wawayanda Road and consists of five openings or shafts. The largest was 100 feet deep and traveled along a vein of ore 12 to 15 feet wide. Men and mules worked in shifts in the mines, hauling the ore and tailings to the surface. The Mule Barn, whose foundation still exists, was directly opposite the most southeasterly shaft, across a small creek on the west side of Wawayanda Road. A story told by old-timers of the area relates that several men and one or more mules were buried in a tunnel cave-in.

Recognized as a recreational resource since the 1850s, Wawayanda Lake and its environs were not secured for permanent public use until 1963. A developer was eyeing the property then owned by the New Jersey Zinc Company, which was in financial distress, with the intent of turning it into a subdivision. The Green Acres bond program made the acquisition of Wawayanda Lake one of its top priorities, and the purchase of the first 4,000 acres took place in 1963. Eleven adjacent tracts, totaling 3,200 acres, were added in 1966, with subsequent purchases bringing it up to its present size.

The first YMCA camp in the United States was at Wawayanda Lake. Camp Wawayanda operated here first in 1886, and continuously from 1903 to 1917, when it moved to Lake Aeroflex, as it is known today, in Andover (now Kittatinny Valley State Park). In 1958, the camp moved to its current location at Frost Valley in the Catskills.

Trails in Wawayanda State Park

The trail system in Wawayanda State Park is composed primarily of woods roads, marked with colored blazes and designated by signs at each end. They are, for the most part, fairly level and are excellent for seasonal cross-country skiing. For a variety of reasons, snow cover accumulates faster and lasts longer here than in other nearby areas. Many of the trails pass through low-lying areas, and portions of the trails may be flooded during wet seasons. The Appalachian Trail, which crosses the park from east to west, offers a more rugged experience, climbing rather steeply from NJ 94 to the crest of Wawayanda Mountain. Another trail of particular interest is the Cedar Swamp Trail, which follows a footpath through the dense Cedar Swamp. Portions of different trails may be combined to create loop hikes of varying lengths.

Appalachian Trail (Warwick Turnpike to NJ 94) *Length: 5.7 miles Blaze: white*
From Warwick Turnpike, about 0.3 mile north of the park entrance road, the Appalachian Trail (A.T.) proceeds west, crossing a plank bridge over the outlet of Parker Lake at 0.2 mile. The A.T. joins a woods road at 0.3 mile. To the left, the woods road is the route of the Hoeferlin Trail (blue) that leads in 0.2 mile to the park office, where parking is available. The A.T. takes the right fork and soon reaches a blue-blazed side trail to the left that goes up a small rise to the Wawayanda Shelter, where overnight camping is permitted for A.T. hikers.

At 0.7 mile, the A.T. turns left onto dirt Wawayanda Road. It follows the road for 0.2 mile, then turns right onto a woods road. It climbs to the crest of a rise and descends, passing a long-abandoned, overgrown field to the left. Then, at 1.3 miles, the A.T. turns left onto dirt Iron Mountain Road, passing a driveway to the left that leads to the stone foundations of the former Kazmar home. The trail crosses an 1890s-era iron bridge over the Double Kill at 1.5 miles. Just beyond, the A.T. bears right at a fork onto a woods road. The left fork is the route of the Iron Mountain Trail (blue), which leads south to Wawayanda Lake.

After crossing an intermittent stream and a wet area (on puncheons), the A.T. turns left onto an old woods road. A short distance beyond, at 2.3 miles, the trail turns left again and follows a wide woods road between stone walls. It soon passes an open field, the former High Breeze Farm, to the right, with views of Mounts Adam and Eve, the Shawangunks, and the Catskills.

Figure 8-7. Parker Lake

The A.T. crosses paved Barrett Road diagonally to the right at 2.6 miles. It enters a field and climbs to Luthers Rock, a glacial erratic, with a limited view to the west through the trees, at 3.0 miles. It descends to cross a stream on a wooden footbridge and gradually ascends to reach a high point (1,350 feet) at the crest of Wawayanda Mountain at 4.3 miles. Here, the Wawayanda Ridge Trail (blue) starts to the left, leading 0.8 mile to a viewpoint over Vernon Valley and Pochuck Mountain. Just ahead, at 4.4 miles, a blue-blazed side trail to the right leads 500 feet to Pinwheel's Vista, with views over the Shawangunks and Catskills to the north and Vernon Valley, Pochuck Mountain, and the Kittatinny Ridge to the west and south.

The A.T. now begins a steep descent along the western face of Wawayanda Mountain, following a long series of stone steps and switchbacks constructed by trail crews from the New York-New Jersey Trail Conference and the Appalachian Trail Conference in the early 1990s. At 4.7 miles, the A.T. reaches its southernmost point along Wawayanda Mountain and begins to head north, reaching the base of the descent at 5.2 miles. It bears left, crosses a stone wall,

and continues through a field. After crossing a gravel quarry road, the A.T. reaches NJ 94, where parking is available, 5.7 miles from Warwick Turnpike.

Banker Trail   *Length: 1.7 miles Blaze: yellow*
The Banker Trail runs in a generally north-south direction, connecting Banker Road with Double Pond Road. Beginning at the end of Banker Road, 0.6 mile west of Warwick Turnpike (parking is not permitted here), the Banker Trail proceeds south, crossing a stream and continuing through a dense rhododendron grove. The trail climbs slightly through mixed deciduous and hemlock woods. At 1.3 miles, the Cedar Swamp Trail (blue) leaves to the right, and the Banker Trail ends at 1.7 miles on Cherry Ridge Road. Parking is available here at a vehicle turnaround.

Black Eagle Trail

Length: 0.8 mile
Blaze: green on white
A generally level trail, with a few minor ascents and descents, the Black Eagle Trail connects the Hoeferlin Trail with Wawayanda Road. The southeastern terminus of the Black Eagle Trail is on the Hoeferlin Trail (blue), 0.6 mile south of the park office. The Black Eagle Trail first proceeds through a deciduous forest and then continues through a pine forest. It crosses the park entrance road at 0.7 mile and ends at 0.8 mile at unpaved Wawayanda Road.

Cedar Swamp Trail

Length: 1.5 miles Blaze: blue
The Cedar Swamp Trail is one of the few cut trails in Wawayanda State Park. It features some of the most outstanding foliage in the park, crossing the Cedar Swamp, with its unusual stand of tall inland Atlantic white cedar grow-

Figure 8-8. Cedar Swamp Trail

ing in a very wet environment. Portions of the trail may be quite wet in rainy seasons.

The northern end of the Cedar Swamp Trail is on the Double Pond Trail (yellow), 0.9 mile from the western end of the Double Pond Trail near Wawayanda Lake. The Cedar Swamp Trail proceeds south on a woods road through a deciduous forest. At 0.3 mile, it descends slightly to cross the Cedar Swamp on a 750-foot-long boardwalk. It continues on a footpath through dense rhododendron thickets, with the trail tunneling through the rhododendron in places. Continuing through a drier area, with mixed hardwoods and evergreens, the Cedar Swamp Trail ends at 1.5 miles at the Banker Trail (yellow).

Cherry Ridge Road (Banker Trail to Pumphouse Trail)

Length: 2.3 miles Blaze: none

Although not a blazed trail, this unpaved section of Cherry Ridge Road is often combined with other marked trails to form loop hikes. Beginning at the intersection of Cherry Ridge Road with the Banker Trail (yellow), 1.0 mile west of Clinton Road (parking is available at a vehicular turnaround at the trail intersection), Cherry Ridge Road proceeds northwest through dense rhododendron thickets. After descending to cross a stream, it climbs to pass a swamp on the left, then crosses another stream on a wooden bridge. At 0.8 mile, the Red Dot Trail (red) leaves to the right. Then, at 1.0 mile, a T intersection is reached. Here, the Old Coal Trail (red) begins to the left, while Cherry Ridge Road takes the right fork. It crosses a stream on a wooden bridge and ascends steadily to reach a junction with the Laurel Pond Trail (yellow), which leaves to the right at 1.4 miles. The Lookout Trail (white) begins to the left at 1.5 miles. Now heading in a southwest direction, Cherry Ridge Road continues ahead to reach the northern end of the unblazed Cabin Trail (marked by a park sign) at 2.2 miles. After bending to the northwest, Cherry Ridge Road reaches a junction with the Pumphouse Trail (orange), which leaves to the right at 2.3 miles.

Double Pond Trail

Length: 1.6 miles Blaze: yellow

The Double Pond Trail, a woods road, extends from the Wawayanda Furnace, at the northeast end of Wawayanda Lake, to the west end of Banker Road. Parking is available at the boating-and-fishing parking area at Wawayanda Lake. From the parking area, proceed east (left, when facing the lake) on a

woods road which runs along the north shore of the lake to the dam, then continue straight ahead, away from the lake. Upon reaching the Wawayanda Furnace, bear right and continue ahead to a junction, with restrooms to your left. Turn left here and cross a bridge. The signpost marking the start of the Double Pond Trail is just ahead.

The Double Pond Trail bears right and passes a group campsite. At 0.4 mile, it crosses a swamp on a boardwalk and a wooden bridge. Just beyond, the Red Dot Trail (red) leaves to the right. The next section of trail, which proceeds past highbush blueberry bushes and rhododendrons, may be flooded in wet weather. The trail continues through an area with mixed hemlocks and deciduous trees, reaching a Y intersection at 0.9 mile. Here, the Cedar Swamp Trail (blue) leaves to the right, while the Double Pond Trail continues ahead to the left, passing through a very dense rhododendron thicket. At 1.4 miles, the Hoeferlin Trail (blue) begins to the left. The Double Pond Trail continues ahead to its terminus, 1.6 miles from the start, at the end of Banker Road (parking here is not permitted).

Hoeferlin Trail *Length: 1.9 miles Blaze: blue*
The Hoeferlin Trail connects the Appalachian Trail with the Double Pond Trail. Parking is available at the park office, 0.2 mile from the northern end of the trail. Though also named for William Hoeferlin, this trail bears no other relation to the Hoeferlin Memorial Trail in Ramapo Mountain State Forest.

From its start on the Appalachian Trail (white), the Hoeferlin Trail proceeds south along a woods road. At 0.2 mile, it reaches the park entrance road. Here, the trail bears right, skirting the park office, then turns left, crosses the park entrance road, and reenters the woods. It climbs gently on a woods road through a dense hemlock forest, passing close to the park boundary to the east. As the Hoeferlin Trail levels off, the Black Eagle Trail (green on white) leaves to the right at 0.8 mile. The Hoeferlin Trail now begins to descend, narrowing in places to a footpath. Rhododendrons are interspersed with the hemlocks, and the trail becomes quite rocky in spots. After passing through a dense rhododendron thicket, with the trail tunneling through the rhododendrons overhead, the Hoeferlin Trail ends at 1.9 miles at a junction with the Double Pond Trail (yellow).

Iron Mountain Trail

Length: 1.4 miles Blaze: blue

The Iron Mountain Trail connects the Appalachian Trail with the boating-and-fishing parking area at Wawayanda Lake, following a woods road for its entire length. From its start on the Appalachian Trail (white), just west of the Iron Mountain Road bridge over the Double Kill, the Iron Mountain Trail proceeds south, crossing the main park road at 1.2 miles and ending at the boating-and-fishing parking area at Wawayanda Lake at 1.4 miles.

Laurel Pond Trail

Length: 1.5 miles Blaze: yellow

The Laurel Pond Trail follows a woods road that was surveyed as a public road in 1811 and remained open to traffic until the mid-1920s. It begins near the Wawayanda Furnace, at the northeast end of Wawayanda Lake. Parking is available at the boating-and-fishing parking area at Wawayanda Lake. From the parking area, proceed east (left, when facing the lake) on a woods road which runs along the north shore of the lake to the dam, then continue straight ahead, away from the lake. Upon reaching the Wawayanda Furnace, bear right. The trailhead of the Laurel Pond Trail is just ahead.

The trail crosses a wide wooden bridge and proceeds south along a woods road through rhododendrons. At 0.3 mile, Laurel Pond is visible through the trees to the right. Just beyond, an unmarked trail on the right leads through tunnels of rhododendron and hemlock thickets to a rocky outcrop overlooking the pond and continues down to the water level. The Laurel Pond Trail now climbs gradually to a high point, with a view over the Wawayanda Plateau from a rock ledge to the left of the trail. Here, at 0.7 mile, the Wingdam Trail (blue) leaves to the right. The Laurel Pond Trail continues gradually downhill, between massive rock outcrops. After a short climb, it ends at Cherry Ridge Road, 1.5 miles from its northern trailhead at the Wawayanda Furnace.

Lookout Trail

Length: 1.0 mile Blaze: white

The Lookout Trail connects the Old Coal Trail with Cherry Ridge Road, passing secluded Lake Lookout on the way. It begins on the Old Coal Trail (red), 0.4 mile from its northern terminus on Cherry Ridge Road, and descends along a woods road to Lake Lookout, reaching a grassy area at the north end of the lake. Here, at 0.4 mile, the trail diverges from the woods road and begins to follow a footpath. It climbs steadily, then turns sharply right and descends gently through maples, with an understory of ferns. After turning left and

Figure 8-9. Lake Lookout

leveling off, the trail descends through a thick hemlock forest to end, 1.0 mile from its start, at Cherry Ridge Road.

Old Coal Trail *Length: 2.8 miles Blaze: red*
The Old Coal Trail extends from Clinton Road to Cherry Ridge Road, connecting the main section of Wawayanda State Park with the Pequannock Watershed (via the Bearfort Waters/Clinton Trail) and with the Terrace Pond area. For its entire length, it follows woods roads.

The southern trailhead of the Old Coal Trail is at a gated road leading west from Clinton Road, 7.5 miles north of NJ 23 and 1.7 miles south of Warwick Turnpike. The trailhead is marked by signs for the Wildcat Mountain Wilderness Center (Project U.S.E.). There is a large parking area on the west side of Clinton Road, just north of the trailhead. The Terrace Pond North Trail (blue) and the Terrace Pond South Trail (yellow), both of which lead to Terrace Pond, begin on the east side of Clinton Road, opposite the parking area.

The Old Coal Trail proceeds west on the dirt road. It soon bears left and begins to parallel the southern end of the Bearfort Waters. At the end of this body of water, it curves right and passes to the left of the Ferber Cabin, a wooden building of the Wildcat Mountain Wilderness Center. The trail now bears left and heads south through a valley, with a swampy area to the left.

At 0.4 mile, the trail reaches a Y intersection. Here, the Bearfort Waters/Clinton Trail (yellow) takes the left fork and continues ahead, while the Old Coal Trail takes the right fork. The Old Coal Trail continues straight ahead at 0.5 mile as another woods road leaves to the right. Continuing on a winding woods road, the Old Coal Trail passes old stone walls at 0.8 mile and then descends gradually through a mountain laurel thicket to cross a swampy area. At 1.2 miles, the trail begins a rather steep ascent. After passing a large rock outcrop to the left, the trail reaches the crest of the rise at 1.4 miles and begins a steady descent through dense mountain laurel thickets.

At 1.8 miles, the trail passes to the left of an eroded gully—the result of a flash flood from a rainstorm in the late 1980s. It crosses the route of a gas pipeline at 1.9 miles and continues to descend, with a stone wall on the right. At the base of the descent, at 2.2 miles, the trail crosses a swamp on a dirt causeway. It bears left at the end of the swamp and ascends, passing a woods road that leaves to the left. Then, at 2.4 miles, the Lookout Trail (white) begins to the left. The Old Coal Trail continues ahead, crossing two small rises, to end at Cherry Ridge Road, 2.8 miles from its start on Clinton Road.

Pumphouse Trail *Length: 2.8 miles Blaze: orange*

The Pumphouse Trail connects the beach parking area at Wawayanda Lake with Cherry Ridge Road. From its start at the beach parking area, it proceeds south through a deciduous forest, following a rocky path around a swamp to the right at 0.7 mile. A woods road that leaves to the left at 2.0 miles leads to the ruins of an old pumphouse on the shore of Wawayanda Lake. The Pumphouse Trail continues south along a woods road to end, 2.8 miles from its start, at Cherry Ridge Road.

Red Dot Trail *Length: 2.8 miles (including both legs of loop) Blaze: red*

The Red Dot Trail connects the Double Pond Trail with Cherry Ridge Road. In the central section of the trail, there are two alternative, parallel routes. The hiker can choose either route or can combine both routes to make a "lollipop"-

loop hike, starting at either end of the Red Dot Trail.

The northern end of the Red Dot Trail is on the Double Pond Trail (yellow), 0.3 mile from the western end of the Double Pond Trail near the Wawayanda Furnace. The Red Dot Trail proceeds south on a woods road through mixed hemlocks and deciduous trees and soon crosses a stream on a wooden bridge. At 0.4 mile, the hemlocks end, and the trail continues through a deciduous forest. Just beyond, the trail divides at a Y intersection. Taking the left (easterly) fork, the trail ascends steadily on a woods road to the top of a rise and then descends on a winding footpath. At 1.4 miles, the trail reaches a T intersection, where the other branch of the trail joins from the right. To continue ahead towards Cherry Ridge Road, turn left here. The trail continues across relatively level terrain and crosses the outlet of a swamp to the left at 1.6 miles. The crossing on rocks can be difficult if the water is high. After a gradual climb through hemlocks and a descent through tangled vines, the Red Dot Trail ends at 2.0 miles at Cherry Ridge Road.

The westerly route of the trail is 0.2 mile shorter than the easterly route and is not as steep. The two alternative routes can be combined to create a 2.5-mile "lollipop"-loop hike, starting at the Double Pond Trail.

Wingdam Trail

Length: 1.2 miles Blaze: blue

The Wingdam Trail extends from a dam at the northeast corner of Wawayanda Lake to the Laurel Pond Trail. Parking is available at the boating-and-fishing parking area at Wawayanda Lake. From the parking area, proceed east (left, when facing the lake) on a woods road which runs along the north shore of the lake to a stone dam. Turn right here, crossing the dam, and bear right through a barrier of large boulders. The Wingdam Trail continues ahead on a wide gravel woods road. At 0.4 mile, the trail crosses a wooden bridge over an outlet of Wawayanda Lake, with the wingdam to the right. The water cascading over the wingdam feeds Laurel Pond, which may be seen through the trees on the left just beyond the bridge. After passing several woods roads, the trail narrows and climbs steeply to reach a rocky, grassy area at the top of a hill at 0.9 mile. The Wingdam Trail now descends slightly and ends, at 1.2 miles, at a junction with the Laurel Pond Trail (yellow).

NINE

THE WATCHUNGS

epicted with bright red shading on the color Geologic Map which forms the front endpapers of this book, the Watchungs consist of three narrow, curved ridges that extend from Bound Brook north to Oakland. The three ridges roughly parallel each other, with only a mile or two between them. The westernmost ridge, known as the Third Watchung, is lower and less prominent than the eastern two ridges, known as the First and Second Watchungs. Highways and railroads pass through gaps in the ridges at Paterson, Great Notch, Summit, and Plainfield. The extension of the Watchungs north of Paterson is also known as the Preakness Range.

The first edition of the *New York Walk Book*, published in 1923, stated that "[c]ontinuous trips with hardly any interruption by towns or farms are possible for many miles together along the crests" of the Watchung ridges, which featured "almost continuous woodland along their crests and slopes" (p. 114). In 1951, though, the third edition of the *Walk Book* warned hikers that "[r]eal estate developments have blocked passage in so many places" between Garret Mountain in Paterson and Eagle Rock Reservation in Montclair that the walk between these two parks "is no longer recommended" (p. 247). Today, suburban developments have covered all but isolated sections of the Watchungs, with areas for hiking limited to several parks and reservations. Most of these are extensively developed with park drives open to vehicular traffic, wide bridle paths and stables for horses, picnic areas, and other recreational facilities. Those who are seeking pristine wilderness will not find it here. But the parks are readily accessible by public transportation, and they contain networks of foot trails which traverse some remote and little-used areas.

The most northerly area of the Watchungs is the Preakness Range north of Paterson, where the High Mountain Park Preserve has protected a large section of the Second Watchung. Between Paterson and Great Notch, parts of the First Watchung ridge lie within Garret Mountain Reservation. Eagle Rock Reservation includes a portion of the First Watchung, and South Mountain Reservation—between Millburn and West Orange—covers both the First and Second Watchungs, as does Watchung Reservation, to the southwest.

History

Because of their height, the Watchungs played an important part in the American Revolution. Their walls form natural ramparts that could have been designed by a military engineer for General Washington's needs. The fronts of the ridges were steep and easy to protect, and they afforded many places for American scouts to watch the movements of the British Redcoats across the New Jersey flatlands to the east.

After Washington captured the Hessian garrison at Trenton and fought the British at Princeton, he eluded the superior forces that soon gathered, and escaped via the northern branch of the Raritan into his hill fortress around Morristown, where the enemy was afraid to pursue him. The only occasion when the British penetrated the Watchung barrier was in December 1776, when a small cavalry patrol surprised General Charles Lee and his aides in a tavern at Basking Ridge. After that, no British or Hessian soldier ever passed these ridges. Every month, Washington strengthened his main camp at Morristown and its outposts, which served as a rallying place and source of supplies for the rest of the war.

After the American Revolution, a series of events taking place within the Watchungs had far-reaching effects on the United States. In 1791, the federal government gave Alexander Hamilton the authority to create the Society for Useful Manufactures (S.U.M.). The society was to promote the formation of American industries and to establish a planned industrial city to be named Paterson. After considering other sites, a location on the Passaic River was chosen because of the power from a large waterfall and the close proximity of natural resources.

As the Industrial Revolution developed and a variety of industries emerged, Paterson's population soared, and it became a major industrial city. The first cotton mill opened in 1794 and the first silk mill in 1839. After 1837, Paterson

became noted for its steam locomotives, producing nearly half of America's locomotives. In 1858, the Dundee Manufacturing Company built a 450-foot dam across the Passaic River to produce power, and by 1873, 15 mills were situated along the Dundee water power canal. Paterson's reputation as a silk manufacturing center was established, such that by the late 1880s, it was known as Silk City. The first Colt revolver was made in Paterson, as well as the first submarine, and the engine in Charles Lindbergh's plane, *The Spirit of St. Louis*.

With such a concentration of industry, it is not surprising that Paterson was the birthplace of a strong and effective reform movement in the early 1900s. A series of welfare acts providing workmen's compensation and protection for laborers were among the social reforms associated with Woodrow Wilson, the governor of New Jersey. His efforts with the progressive movements brought him to national attention, and eventually led to his election to the presidency of the United States.

Geology

Formed of basaltic lava extruded early in the Jurassic Period, the Watchungs are similar in age to the Palisades and geologically distinct from the Ramapo Mountains, which are composed of Precambrian granite gneiss. Each of the three Watchung ridges is made up of a number of successive lava flows that poured out onto the early Jurassic landscape and hardened into basalt. By contrast, the Palisades are formed of diabase—an igneous rock with a coarser

Figure 9-1. Cutaway section of northeastern New Jersey

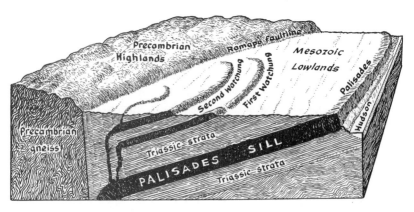

texture, resulting from slower underground cooling.

The igneous diabase of the Palisades and the basalts of the Watchungs both resulted from a great upwelling of magma (molten rock) along a fault line (or nearby cracks) in late Triassic sandstone-and-shale strata (known to geologists as the Newark Series). The Watchung basalts and the Palisades diabase were both interlayered with these tilted strata; thus, they are now themselves tilted westward about 15 degrees. The relationship of these several igneous units is shown in Figure 9-1.

HIGH MOUNTAIN PARK PRESERVE

Although much of the Preakness Range is occupied by William Paterson University, a golf course, and private homes, its northern end contains some 1,700 acres of protected open space, including High Mountain, which features an unobstructed view in all directions. Located north of Paterson, the Preakness Range is a continuation of the Second Watchung. Thanks to unremitting efforts by conservationists, Wayne Township, The Nature Conservancy, and the State of New Jersey acquired 1,057 acres on High Mountain in August 1993.

Access to High Mountain from the south is from Parking Lot #6 of William Paterson University. To reach this parking lot from the west, follow Hamburg Turnpike (County 504) east for 1.1 miles from Valley Road, turn left at College Entry #5, and follow College Road for 1.1 miles to Parking Lot #6. From the east, take Pompton Road to College Entry #1. Turn right and proceed straight ahead for 1.0 mile to Parking Lot #6. Cars should be parked in the uppermost tier of the parking lot, which is closest to the trailhead (on the opposite side of the road). During the holiday period (end of December and beginning of January), the university campus is normally closed, and the parking lot is not accessible. Public transportation to the campus is available via NJ Transit bus #748 from Paterson and #744 from Passaic and Paterson.

From the north, access is available from two points along Reservoir Drive and from Indian Trail Drive in Franklin Lakes. To reach Reservoir Drive, take NJ 208 to the Ewing Avenue exit in Franklin Lakes. Proceed south on Ewing Avenue for 1.8 miles to its end at High Mountain Road. Turn left onto High Mountain Road, follow it for 0.2 mile, then turn right onto Reservoir Drive. The northern trailhead of the Red Trail is 0.3 mile from High Mountain Road, opposite the intersection of Reservoir Drive with Navaho Trail Drive. Another

access point is the circle at the end of Reservoir Drive, 0.7 mile from High Mountain Road, from where a short side trail leads south to the Yellow Trail. To reach Indian Trail Drive from NJ 208, follow Ewing Avenue south for 0.9 mile to Franklin Lake Road (County 502). Turn right and continue on Franklin Lake Road for 1.5 miles to Indian Trail Drive, which is on the left. The northern trailhead of the Yellow Trail is at the circle at the southern end of Indian Trail Drive, 0.9 mile from Franklin Lake Road, at its intersection with Dakota Trail (a paved road).

For more information, contact Wayne Township, Department of Parks and Recreation, 475 Valley Road, Wayne, NJ 07470; (973) 694-1800 x3258; www.waynetownship.com.

Trails in High Mountain Park Preserve

There are over ten miles of trails in High Mountain Park Preserve, many of which follow woods roads. These trails may be combined to form various loop hikes. The best known feature of the park—for which it is named—is High Mountain, whose summit offers a panoramic view, which includes the New York City skyline and even the Atlantic Ocean.

Pancake Hollow Trail *Length: 2.8 miles Blaze: blue*

The Pancake Hollow Trail is a "lollipop"-loop trail that traverses the north-western portion of the Preakness Range. To reach the trailhead from Hamburg Turnpike (County 504), proceed north 1.3 miles on Valley Road and turn right onto Point View Parkway, then turn right onto Chicopee Drive. The trailhead is on the right near a large rock, 0.3 mile from Point View Parkway. In 150 feet, a short white-blazed trail that leads in 0.2 mile to the Yellow Trail leaves to the right. The Pancake Hollow Trail reaches a rocky ridge at 0.6 mile. Beech Mountain is to the east, Franklin Lake to the northeast, and Franklin Clove directly below. Passing a housing development, the trail heads uphill. At 0.9 mile, the Point View Reservoir comes into view on the left. At 1.3 miles, the trail turns left, with a woods road coming in on the right. In 100 feet, the trail reaches a Y junction, which marks the start of the loop. To hike the trail in a clockwise direction, take the left fork. After descending and crossing two brooks, the Pancake Hollow Trail passes a large glacial erratic on the left at 1.9 miles. Approaching Berdan Avenue at 2.4 miles, the Pancake Hollow Trail turns to go

through a stand of red cedar. It skirts a wet area and reaches the end of the loop at 2.8 miles.

Red Trail   *Length: 1.7 miles Blaze: red*

The Red Trail begins at a wooden sign across College Drive from the entrance to William Paterson University Parking Lot #6. It bears right and climbs along a woods road, passing the southern end of the Yellow Trail on the right at 0.5 mile and the White Trail on the left at 0.6 mile. After traversing an eroded section of the road, where the trail has been worn down to the bedrock, the Red Trail reaches the crest of the rise at 0.9 mile and begins to descend. It bears left at a fork at 1.2 miles and crosses the Yellow Trail at 1.3 miles. A short distance beyond, the Red Trail begins to parallel a stream to the right. At 1.6 miles, the trail turns right, leaving the woods road. It bears left, crosses an old stone wall, and continues through a rocky area to end, 1.7 miles from its start, on Reservoir Drive in Franklin Lakes, opposite its intersection with Navaho Trail Drive. Curbside parking is available at the northern trailhead.

Waterfall Trail   *Length: 0.2 mile Blaze: orange*

The Waterfall Trail begins on the Yellow Trail, 0.3 mile from the northern trailhead of the Yellow Trail on Indian Trail Drive in Franklin Lakes. It leads north along a wide woods road to the seasonal waterfall of Buttermilk Falls, which flows over fractured basalt rock. At the falls, it bears sharply right and loops back to the woods road.

White Trail   *Length: 1.6 miles Blaze: white*

The White Trail begins on the Red Trail, 0.6 mile from the southern trailhead of the Red Trail at Parking Lot #6 of William Paterson University. The White Trail heads west, descending steadily on a woods road through a mixed forest of deciduous trees and cedars. After a steep descent along a deeply eroded stretch of the road, the trail turns left, crosses a stream, then bears right to cross another stream. Just beyond, at 0.4 mile, it reaches a T intersection. Here, the trail turns right onto another woods road. At 0.6 mile, it begins to parallel the fairways of the North Jersey Country Club, which is to the left. The trail runs close to the golf course for about 0.1 mile, then bears right and heads into the woods, following a winding route over undulating terrain.

The White Trail approaches the reservoir of the golf course at 0.8 mile, with a side trail leading left to its concrete dam. Then, at 1.0 mile, the trail

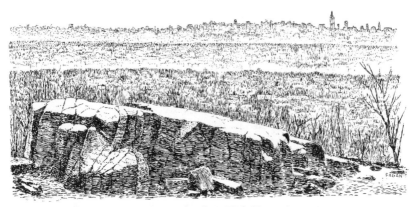

Figure 9-2. View from High Mountain

crosses a stream and turns right to parallel it. A short distance beyond, the trail
has been relocated onto a footpath to the left to bypass a very wet and eroded
section of the road. Upon rejoining the road, the trail begins to climb, now
following a rocky treadway through a valley, with talus slopes on either side. At
the crest of the rise, reached at 1.5 miles, another woods road leaves to the left.
The White Trail now descends gradually and, after a short climb, it ends at a
junction with the Yellow Trail at 1.6 miles.

Yellow Trail
Length: 4.9 miles Blaze: yellow

Featuring both views from High Mountain and interesting geological formations, the Yellow Trail is the longest one in the High Mountain Park Preserve. It
starts on the Red Trail, 0.5 mile north of its trailhead at William Paterson
University Parking Lot #6. The Yellow Trail proceeds east, climbs a small rise,
and heads downhill to cross a stream and wet area. It then curves north, passing just west of the ridge of Mount Cecchino. At 0.7 mile, the trail crosses a
small stream and begins a steady climb on a woods road to the summit of High
Mountain. Halfway up, the trail bears left, bypassing a very eroded section of
the road, and soon rejoins the road.

The grassy summit of High Mountain, reached at 1.0 mile, rewards the
hiker with a 360° view. Northwest and north lie the Ramapo Mountains, with
Suffern and the gap of the Ramapo River slightly east of north. To the east, the
horizon is bounded by the Palisades, with Hook Mountain at the northeast.

Southeast, the skyscrapers of Manhattan are visible, with the towers of the George Washington Bridge north of them. Nearer is the suburban sprawl of Bergen County, including the towns of Wyckoff and Ridgewood (northeast), and Fair Lawn (east), with Paterson lying in the bowl of the valley. Directly opposite is the slope of the First Watchung. The eastern cliff is almost vertical, as is the eastern side of the Second Watchung, of which High Mountain is the highest summit at 885 feet. To the near south is Veterans Memorial Point, at the northern end of the steep-sided Garret Mountain.

The Yellow Trail heads northwest across the broad summit, with the trail marked by paint blazes on the rocks. It descends to a col, crosses a secondary summit, then descends for about 200 vertical feet on an eroded woods road. At 1.5 miles, the Yellow Trail turns left, leaving the woods road it has been following, and enters the woods on a footpath. It descends gradually and begins to parallel a stream. After crossing the stream, the Yellow Trail crosses the Red Trail at 1.7 miles. Just beyond, it bears right and soon begins to head north on a woods road.

At 2.1 miles, the Yellow Trail bears left at a fork and leaves the woods road. It soon begins to descend on a footpath, with views through the trees to the left of Beech Mountain. Then, at 2.4 miles, the trail approaches Reservoir Drive, with a short side trail leading right to the circle at the end of the paved road. Here, the trail bends very sharply to the left, making a U-turn, and begins to head south through a hemlock grove. Most of the hemlocks are dying from the ravages of the woolly adelgid (see pp. 308-09). After passing through a rocky, wet area, the trail ascends and turns left onto a woods road.

At a fork, reached at 2.5 miles, the Yellow Trail turns right, while the White Trail begins to the left. The Yellow Trail now begins a steady climb of Beech Mountain, following just below the ridge line, and reaching two sweeping views of Point View Reservoir, Wayne, and the Pompton Hills. From the second viewpoint, reached at 3.2 miles, the trail heads north and descends on switchbacks, with some steep sections. After passing close to an office building on the left, the trail becomes a footpath for a short distance, then joins another woods road and descends to the south end of Franklin Clove. Here, at 4.2 miles, a white-blazed trail to the left leads 0.2 to the Pancake Hollow Trail (blue), near its trailhead.

The Yellow Trail now heads north, following a rocky treadway through Franklin Clove, with talus slopes on both sides of the trail. Franklin Clove was formed by glacial action late in the Ice Age. Glacial erosion was concentrated

here, creating a deep shady pass (with counterparts in Long Clove and Short Clove below Haverstraw in New York). At the north end of the clove, the Yellow Trail reaches a Y intersection at 4.6 miles. Here, the Waterfall Trail (orange) begins to the right, while the Yellow Trail takes the left fork. After traversing an earthen berm, the Yellow Trail ends, 4.9 miles from its start, at Indian Trail Drive in Franklin Lakes, where curbside parking is available.

GARRET MOUNTAIN RESERVATION

Garret Mountain Reservation is located in Paterson and West Paterson. It is administered by the Passaic County Parks Department and consists of 569 acres divided into two parks—Garret Mountain Park and Rifle Camp Park.

Garret Mountain Park includes Lambert Castle, built in 1893 by Catholina Lambert, a wealthy silk manufacturer. It houses a combined museum and library and is the headquarters of the Passaic County Historical Society. The main portion of the park—on the ridgetop above the castle—is encircled by a paved drive and has a variety of developed recreational facilities, but it also features two trails that traverse lesser-used areas and offer several panoramic overlooks. To reach the castle, take I-80 to Exit 57A and proceed south on NJ 19 to the Valley Road exit. Turn right onto Valley Road, then make the next right, which leads uphill to the castle, where parking is available. An admission fee is charged to enter the castle, but there is no charge for parking. The trailhead of the Garret Mountain Trail is at the southern end of the parking area. Public transportation to the intersection of Valley Road and Fenner Avenue, 0.3 mile west of the entrance to the castle, is available via NJ Transit's #192 bus from the Port Authority Bus Terminal in New York and the #702 bus from Paterson and Elmwood Park. For more information, contact the Passaic County Parks Department, 311 Pennsylvania Avenue, Paterson, NJ 07503; (973) 881-4832; www.passaiccountynj.org.

Rifle Camp Park consists of 225 acres and features an amphitheater, toboggan run, nature trail, and astronomical observatory. The John Crowley Nature Center sponsors songbird and hawk watches during migration and houses the observatory's seismograph. Entry is on the east side of Rifle Camp Road, 1.4 miles north of US 46 in West Paterson. For more information, contact Rifle Camp Park, Rifle Camp Road, West Paterson, NJ 07424; (973) 523-0024; www.passaiccountynj.org.

Trails in Garret Mountain Reservation

Garret Mountain Trail   *Length: 3.1 miles Blaze: yellow*

From the southern end of the parking area for Lambert Castle, the Garret Mountain Trail proceeds uphill on a macadam path and stone steps, then turns right onto a wide, paved path, which switchbacks up to the top of the mountain. At 0.2 mile, after passing through an opening in a stone wall, a junction is reached with the main loop of the trail. To follow the trail in a counter-clockwise direction, turn sharply right, briefly following the stone wall, then turn right again and proceed north. The trail soon begins to descend on a rocky path and stone steps.

After paralleling the paved park road (which runs to the left) for a short distance, a well-worn side trail to the right at 0.4 mile leads to an expansive east-facing viewpoint from the edge of a cliff. (A police firing range is located directly below, so gunshots may be heard.) Paterson may be seen directly below, with much of southern Bergen County beyond, and the Manhattan skyline is visible in the distance on a clear day. The Verrazano-Narrows Bridge is at the extreme right of this broad panorama.

The Garret Mountain Trail soon passes a small gravel parking area to the left and, about 300 feet beyond, follows along the right side of a grassy field. At the end of the field, at 0.6 mile, the Garret Mountain Trail descends on a footpath to reach an intersection with the White Trail, which leaves to the right at the entrance to an overlook. (The view from this overlook, which is accessible by car, is more limited to the south, but High Mountain in Wayne is visible to the north.) The Garret Mountain Trail crosses the road leading into the overlook and continues straight ahead, passing a plaque which honors a founder of the Passaic County park system.

At the next intersection, the trail bears right and follows a paved road that climbs to Veterans Memorial Point, the site of a communications tower. At 0.8 mile, just beyond a guardrail barrier at the end of the paved road, the trail bears left and descends into the woods. Then, at 1.0 mile, the White Trail crosses. Here, the Garret Mountain Trail turns sharply left, climbs over a small rise, and descends on switchbacks. At the base of the descent, the trail turns right onto a wide path, then bears left and crosses a park entrance road at 1.2 miles.

The Garret Mountain Trail passes through an opening in a guardrail and

begins to parallel Mountain Avenue. After crossing its outlet stream on a wooden footbridge, the trail runs along the west side of Barbour's Pond. At 1.7 miles, just beyond the end of the pond, the trail bears right at a fork and then left at the next fork. Soon, the trail crosses a stream, and turns right, paralleling the stream. It then turns left, away from the stream, and begins to climb. At the abandoned Weasel Drift picnic area, reached at 2.0 miles, the Rifle Camp Connector Trail (yellow) proceeds straight ahead, as the Garret Mountain Trail (also blazed yellow) bears left. The Garret Mountain Trail goes over a rise, then bears left and descends to cross a paved park road at 2.2 miles. In another 300 feet, it turns right onto a dirt bridle path and passes the southern end of the White Trail.

Just ahead, as the dirt path bears left, the Garret Mountain Trail continues straight ahead, climbing an embankment and again crossing the paved road. The trail turns right and runs along the grassy shoulder of the road, bearing left at two road intersections. (Do not follow the paved road leading ahead to the park stables.) At 2.4 miles, near the park boundary, the trail turns left, leaving the road, and ascends into the woods on a footpath. Just before reaching the access road to the stables, the trail bears right and passes between several concrete tank supports. It then curves to the left and begins to run along the ridge of Garret Mountain, with the stables to the left. At the end of the stables, the trail bears left, makes a short but steep descent, and then turns right, continuing along the ridge.

At 2.8 miles, the Garret Mountain Trail reaches an unobstructed viewpoint from the edge of the ridge, with a broad east-facing view. The trail continues north along the ridge, passing several more viewpoints. At 3.0 miles, it arrives at a stone observation tower, built in the 1890s as part of Lambert Castle. The tower is presently closed to the public (although there are plans to restore it). The trail skirts the tower to the left

Figure 9-3. Observation tower

189

and reaches the start of the loop, marked by a stone wall at the end of a grassy area, at 3.1 miles. To return to the parking lot at Lambert Castle, continue straight ahead on the descending macadam path.

Rifle Camp Trail   *Length: 2.0 miles Blaze: yellow*

The Rifle Camp Trail circles Rifle Camp Park, passing several panoramic viewpoints over the New York City skyline. It can be accessed from several points and is described here in a counter-clockwise direction, starting at the first parking lot on the right from the park entrance (designated for senior citizens/handicapped and par course).

From the south end of the parking lot, proceed ahead and turn left, downhill, onto the yellow-blazed trail. The trail descends steeply on a paved path, curves right at the base of the descent, and soon continues on a gravel path. At 0.1 mile, with the Great Notch Reservoir visible ahead, the trail bends left and crosses a stone culvert. It bears right at the next fork, bears left at a fitness station, and climbs to reach the park road at 0.3 mile. The trail turns right, parallel to the road, reenters the woods, then curves left and again approaches the road at a fitness station. Here, it turns right and heads south. After passing through a rock cut, the trail turns right at a T intersection at 0.5 mile.

Just ahead, the trail passes a small pond to the left. Here, a gullied road leaves to the right. (The road leads up to a viewpoint overlooking an active quarry, continues to another panoramic viewpoint over the New York City skyline, and descends to rejoin the Rifle Camp Trail.) In another 500 feet, after looping around the pond, the trail turns right, leaving the paved path that it has been following, and climbs into the woods. It bears left and continues through a rock cut, then descends to come out at a paved parking circle at 0.9 mile.

The trail crosses the circle, then bears right and follows a paved path uphill, passing the park's Nature Center on the right. At 1.0 mile, it reaches an expansive overlook to the east and south, with much of Paterson and Bergen County visible directly below, and the entire New York City skyline in the distance. The trail continues along the paved path for another 400 feet, then bears right at a fitness station, leaving the paved path, and follows a dirt path parallel to the fence that marks the cliff line. After bearing left, away from the fence, the trail crosses a seasonal stream and turns right onto a gravel road.

At 1.2 miles, the trail begins to run along a black metal fence, with a large red-roofed building beyond the fence. In 200 feet, it bears left, away from the

fence, crosses a stream, and passes an octagonal concrete foundation to the right. With a parking area visible ahead, the trail turns right at a T junction onto a wide path and crosses two stone culverts. It turns right at another T junction at 1.6 miles, then curves left at a fitness station, with a large apartment building visible beyond a fence to the right.

At 1.7 miles, the trail crosses the paved park entrance road diagonally to the left and reenters the woods on a footpath. After passing a grassy amphitheater and a small building to the left, the trail descends to a valley, where it begins to parallel a 500-foot-long concrete toboggan slide. At the top of the slide, the trail curves left and climbs rather steeply. In another 200 feet, the trail turns right onto a paved road in a picnic area. It passes a picnic shelter to the left and reaches the start of the loop, adjacent to the parking area, at 2.0 miles.

Rifle Camp Connector Trail   *Length: 0.7 mile Blaze: yellow*
This short trail, which follows paved roads for nearly its entire length, connects the Garret Mountain Trail with the Rifle Camp Trail, making it possible to combine these two trails into a longer walk. It begins at a junction with the Garret Mountain Trail (yellow) at the abandoned Weasel Drift picnic area in Garret Mountain Park, and proceeds through the parking area. The trail follows Weasel Drift and Rifle Camp roads past a firehouse and entrance to a bank office building on the left before reaching Rifle Camp Park and the Rifle Park Camp Trail (yellow).

White Trail   *Length: 1.5 miles Blaze: white*
The White Trail offers an alternative north-south route along the ridge of Garret Mountain. It connects with the Garret Mountain Trail at each end and crosses it midway, making possible a variety of loop hikes.

The White Trail begins at a junction with the Garret Mountain Trail (yellow), at the south end of the parking lot for the northern viewpoint on Garret Mountain (from where downtown Paterson is visible below, with High Mountain in the distance to the north). It follows a paved path along the right side of the viewpoint, turns right and descends stairs, then turns left and follows the stone wall. At the end of the wall, it descends into the woods, crosses a wooden bridge over a ditch, and follows along the right edge of an open area, with a radio tower visible to the left. The trail then continues to descend, soon bearing left. At the base of the descent, reached at 0.3 mile, the trail parallels an intermit-

tent stream to the right, then turns left and ascends, soon joining a woods road. At a huge boulder, the trail turns left, leaving the woods road, and climbs on a footpath.

After leveling off, the White Trail reaches a junction with the Garret Mountain Trail at 0.5 mile. Here, the White Trail bears left. It comes out at a gravel parking area, bears right, then turns left to cross the paved park drive and continues ahead on a chained-off gravel road. In 200 feet, it bears left at a fork and follows a bridle path for 250 feet, then turns right, crosses a small stream, and immediately turns right to follow along the base of a line of unusual flat-sided boulders. At 0.8 mile, the trail turns left onto another bridle path. In 250 feet, it bears right at a fork and continues along the bridle path. At a fork in another 800 feet, it bears left onto a footpath, then rejoins the bridle path.

At 1.1 miles, the trail turns sharply right, leaving the bridle path, and descends on a footpath into the woods, entering a little-used area of the park. It turns left at 1.4 miles, climbs a rocky ledge, and immediately turns right to cross a stream. The White Trail soon turns right onto a bridle path and ends, 1.5 miles from the start, at a junction with the Garret Mountain Trail, which may be followed in either direction to return to the start of the White Trail.

LENAPE TRAIL

A joint undertaking of the Sierra Club and the Essex County Department of Parks, Recreation, and Cultural Affairs, the Lenape Trail links a dozen county and municipal parks, a rail trail, the Patriots' Path, historic areas, and other landmarks along a 34-mile route. As of 2003, there is only one gap in the route—from Mayapple Hill, at the northern end of South Mountain Reservation, to Mt. Pleasant Avenue in West Orange. Due to the dense development of much of Essex County, much of the trail is routed along power lines and residential streets. Those portions of the trail that pass through parkland are open to foot travel only.

Glen Avenue (Millburn) to Mayapple Hill (West Orange)

Length: 6.0 miles Blaze: yellow

For a description of this section of the Lenape Trail, see the South Mountain Reservation section of this chapter, pp. 198-200.

Mt. Pleasant Avenue (West Orange) to Upper Mountain Avenue (Montclair)

Length: 12.7 miles Blaze: yellow

This section of the Lenape Trail begins at the intersection of Ellison Avenue and Mt. Pleasant Avenue in West Orange, at the crest of the Second Watchung. Public transportation is available via NJ Transit bus #71 from Newark.

The trail heads north on Ellison Avenue, passes through O'Connor Memorial Park, and reaches a power line. Here, the trail divides into two branches. The western branch—which provides a connection with the Patriots' Path in Morris County, but which, in 2003, does not connect to the rest of the Lenape Trail—turns left and heads west under the power line. (For a description of this branch of the trail, see below.)

The eastern branch of the Lenape Trail turns right at the power line and follows the power line downhill, soon beginning to parallel I-280. At the jughandle at the intersection of I-280 and Pleasant Valley Way, reached 0.9 mile from the start of this section, the trail turns left and proceeds north along Pleasant Valley Way. It follows Pleasant Valley Way for 0.4 mile, then turns right onto Hooper Avenue, which it follows to Lake Vincent Park, where it turns left. After proceeding through this small park, the trail turns left onto Carteret Street, crosses Conforti Avenue, and follows FitzRandolph Avenue. After a bend to the left, the trail turns right onto Hartshorn Terrace, then left onto Robertson Road. It follows Robertson Road uphill to its intersection with Eagle Rock Avenue, where it turns right.

After crossing the busy intersection of Eagle Rock Avenue and Prospect Avenue at 2.4 miles, the Lenape Trail enters Eagle Rock Reservation. At first, the trail closely parallels Eagle Rock Avenue, but it soon bears left and heads through the interior of the park, reaching a parking area at 3.0 miles. The trail turns left here, but proceeding straight ahead leads to an overlook adjacent to the Highlawn Pavilion, which offers a panoramic view of the New York City skyline and an impressive memorial to the September 11, 2001 World Trade Center tragedy. The Lenape Trail proceeds north, parallel to the park drive, crossing it at a hairpin turn in the road at 3.5 miles. Continuing to head north, the trail approaches the cliff edge, with views to the right. It then turns left, away from the cliff, and follows a series of woods roads. At 4.5 miles, it leaves Eagle Rock Reservation and turns right onto Afterglow Avenue.

The Lenape Trail now follows a series of quiet residential streets. It turns left onto Gordon Place, right onto Glen Road, and left onto Sunset Avenue, which crosses Mt. Prospect Avenue at a traffic light. At the end of Sunset

Avenue, the trail turns left onto Park Avenue, then right onto Manor Road, which it follows to Verona Park, reached at 5.5 miles.

The trail proceeds through Verona Park, crossing a stone bridge over a narrow point of Verona Lake. It exits the park, 6.2 miles from the start of the section, at the intersection of Lakeside Avenue and Bloomfield Avenue, where NJ Transit bus #29 from Newark stops. Again following local streets, the Lenape Trail turns left onto Bloomfield Avenue and right onto Gould Street. At the end of Gould Street, it turns left onto Personette Avenue, then right onto Grove Avenue and left onto Linden Avenue. After a right turn onto Fairview Avenue and a left onto Arnold Way, the trail reaches the West Essex Trail—a rail trail that follows the former Caldwell Branch of the Erie-Lackawanna Railroad—at 7.0 miles.

The Lenape Trail turns right and follows the West Essex Trail for the next 2.3 miles. At 8.6 miles, it crosses a bridge over Pompton Avenue (NJ 23), which can be reached via NJ Transit bus #11 from Newark and bus #195 from New York. Just beyond, the trail crosses the Peckman River on a high trestle. Then, at 8.8 miles, a branch trail leads left to Community Park and the Morgan Farm.

After crossing Bowden Road, the Lenape Trail turns right at 9.3 miles, leaving the West Essex Trail, and winds through the woods, soon approaching Ridge Road. The trail turns left, parallels the road for about 0.2 mile, then climbs to reach the paved road at 9.9 miles. It turns left and heads north along the road, following the western shore of the Cedar Grove Reservoir. At the northern end of the reservoir, reached at 10.3 miles, it turns right and reenters the woods. The trail skirts the north and east sides of the reservoir. After crossing Normal Avenue at 11.0 miles, it enters the 157-acre Mills Reservation and winds through the park on footpaths and woods roads.

Approaching the southern end of the park, the Lenape Trail swings east, emerging on the ridge of the First Watchung. It heads north, reaching a broad viewpoint to the south and east at 12.0 miles. The Manhattan skyline may be seen to the left, with the Verrazano-Narrows Bridge visible in the distance.

At 12.3 miles, the Lenape Trail turns sharply right, leaving the ridge, and descends into Mountainside Park in Montclair. It emerges onto Warfield Place, turns left onto Windsor Place, then left again onto Highland Avenue. The trail soon turns right, downhill, and continues along Laurel Place to reach Upper Mountain Avenue, 12.7 miles from the start of the section. Here, the Mountain Avenue station of NJ Transit's Montclair/Boonton Line offers hourly service to Penn Station in New York on weekdays.

Upper Mountain Avenue (Montclair) to Military Park (Newark)

Length: 13.3 miles Blaze: yellow

From the intersection of Laurel Place and Upper Mountain Avenue at the Mountain Avenue station of NJ Transit's Montclair/Boonton Line (where hourly service to Penn Station in New York is available on weekdays), the Lenape Trail proceeds east on Laurel Place. It turns left on Valley Road and right on Wellesley Road. After crossing Norwood Avenue, the trail continues along Overlook Road, turns right onto Grove Street, then turns left onto Windermere Road. At the end of the street, 0.9 mile from the start of the section, the trail enters Yanticaw Brook Park, and then continues to Brookdale Park in Bloomfield.

Going through town streets and past a schoolyard, the trail crosses the Garden State Parkway on a footbridge. Passing along streets in Nutley, the Lenape Trail enters Yanticaw Park and turns south. After running along 1.5 miles of quiet streets, the trail enters Belleville Park. Across Mill Street is the north end of Branch Brook Park, a John Charles Olmsted design. A festival every April at the Japanese cherry blossom area celebrates the flowering of hundreds of trees and draws thousands of visitors.

Wending its way south through Branch Brook Park for three miles, the trail passes Sacred Heart Cathedral, leaves the park, and crosses Clifton Avenue to follow Nesbit and James streets. In this historic area, nineteenth-century brownstones struggle against urban blight on the west and downtown commercial activity on the east. Passing the restored Ballantine House and Newark Museum, both of which are open to the public, the Lenape Trail crosses Washington Park before reaching Trinity Episcopal Cathedral, which served as a hospital during the Revolution. The trail terminates at the south end of Military Park near the Wars of America Monument by Gutzon Borglum. The Broad Street Station of the Newark City Subway may be taken to Newark Penn Station, from where NJ Transit and PATH trains run to New York.

Western Branch of Lenape Trail (O'Connor Memorial Park to Bloomfield Avenue)

Length: 7.0 miles Blaze: yellow

From a junction with the main branch of the Lenape Trail at a power line just north of O'Connor Memorial Park, the western branch of the trail proceeds west along the power line. After crossing and following several streets, it goes through the undeveloped Becker Tract, formerly the Henry Becker Dairy Farm. The Lenape Trail then enters undeveloped West Essex Park, a largely wooded wetland along the Passaic River.

At the northwest corner of Eisenhower Parkway and Eagle Rock Avenue, yellow blazes with a green dot mark a connecting link to Morris County's Patriots' Path. This link goes westward along Eagle Rock Avenue for several hundred feet, follows a power line to Foulerton's Brook, and continues west to Charm Acres. It crosses Eagle Rock Avenue again to the Center for Environmental Studies and connects with the Patriots' Path (white), which leads across the Passaic River one mile through swampy Lurker Park to a temporary end at Ridgedale Avenue in East Hanover.

From the Eisenhower Parkway-Eagle Rock Avenue intersection, the western branch of the Lenape Trail continues north along the west side of Eisenhower Parkway to cross Foulerton's Brook. It winds its way westerly and goes under I-280 near the Passaic River. The area in the vicinity of Foulerton's Brook and I-280 may be impassible at times of high water in the Passaic River. North of the underpass, the trail heads back east, paralleling I-280 to the power line, and then follows the power line north for two miles, ending at Bloomfield Avenue, near the Essex Mall at the intersection of Passaic Avenue. Public transportation to the Essex Mall is available via NJ Transit bus #71 from West Orange and bus #29 from Montclair and Newark.

SOUTH MOUNTAIN RESERVATION

Wooded hiking trails, picnic areas, and views are the main reasons for South Mountain Reservation's popularity. The park's 2,047 acres contain five marked hiking trails, many miles of carriage roads and bridle paths, and views of falls, millponds, and—off in the distance—Manhattan. Two year-round skating rinks, Turtle Back Zoo, and horseback riding also draw people to the reservation. Turtle Back Rock, located on the Turtle Back Trail in the northeastern section of the reservation, is an interesting rock formation, and the Turtle Back Zoo is the home of animals from many parts of the world. Picnic

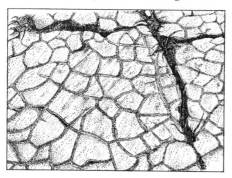

Figure 9-4. Turtle Back Rock

areas, some with views, are scattered throughout the reservation. Mountain bikes are not allowed on any of the trails in the reservation, although they are permitted on the paved roads (including Crest Drive and Valley View Drive, which are closed to vehicular traffic).

Essex County was one of the first in the nation to establish a network of open-space parks. Efforts here set the standard for county and state parks elsewhere. The South Mountain area had been environmentally damaged since the 1750s, when lumber crews chopped its hemlock groves to provide timber for New York City and Philadelphia. Lumberjacks were later replaced by foul-smelling paper mills. Then, in the 1890s, Essex County cried "Enough!" and began a program of buying and restoring land. A century later, the benefits of that decision are still there for people to enjoy. The Friends of South Mountain Reservation, Inc. and the Essex County Department of Parks, Recreation, and Cultural Affairs strive to preserve and restore the reservation's beauty.

The reservation is directly accessible by rail. The Millburn station on NJ Transit's Morristown Line is across Glen Avenue from the southern trailheads of the Lenape and Rahway trails at the Locust Grove parking area. Hourly service is provided on this line from Hoboken and Penn Station in Manhattan. NJ Transit bus #73 to Newark runs along Northfield Avenue, at the northern end of the reservation.

By car, the reservation is most easily reached by taking I-280 to Exit 7 and proceeding south on Pleasant Valley Way. After crossing Northfield Avenue, the road name changes to Cherry Lane, and south of South Orange Avenue, it is known as Brookfield Drive. The Mayapple Hill picnic area—the northern terminus of the Lenape Trail section in South Mountain Reservation—can be reached by turning right onto Cedar Avenue about 0.3 mile north of Northfield Avenue. The Oakdale picnic area is on the right side of Cherry Lane, just south of Northfield Avenue, and the Tulip Springs parking area is on the left, 0.9 mile south of Northfield Avenue. To reach the Locust Grove parking area, turn left at the intersection of Brookside Drive and Glen Avenue and proceed for 0.4 mile to the parking area, on the left side of the road, opposite Lackawanna Place.

For more information, contact the Essex County Department of Parks, Recreation, and Cultural Affairs, 115 Clifton Avenue, Newark, NJ 07104; (973) 268-3500; www.co.essex.nj.us.

Trails in South Mountain Reservation

South Mountain Reservation has five marked trails totaling over 15 miles, besides an extensive network of bridle paths and carriage roads. The trails may be combined into loop hikes, and the bridle paths and carriage roads offer additional opportunities for exploration.

Elmdale Trail   *Length: 2.0 miles Blaze: blue*
The Elmdale Trail is a "lollipop"-loop trail that follows the ridge of the Second Watchung from Glen Avenue to just south of South Orange Avenue. Beginning at the northwest corner of the intersection of Glen Avenue and Brookside Drive, 0.4 mile west of the Locust Grove parking area opposite the Millburn railroad station, the trail climbs on a footpath. It continues along the side of the hill close to the western edge of the reservation, with homes visible through the trees to the left, and then rises to the crest of the ridge. At 1.7 miles, a short 0.3-mile loop begins. Just beyond, both branches of the trail cross a carriage road. To the left (west), the road leads in 0.5 mile to South Orange Avenue. To the right (east), it leads in 0.2 mile to Brookside Drive.

Lenape Trail   *Length: 6.0 miles Blaze: yellow*
The longest trail in South Mountain Reservation, the Lenape Trail begins at the intersection of Glen Avenue and Lackawanna Place, opposite the Millburn railroad station. It follows the paved park entrance road to the Locust Grove parking area, passing the trailhead for the Rahway Trail (white) on the left. At the end of the parking area, the trail bears right onto a gravel road and follows it to a picnic area. It continues through the picnic area, then bears left and begins to climb the First Watchung on a wide path. It bears right at a fork, then turns left at a T intersection onto a woods road, continuing to climb. At the top of the ascent, it turns left, leaving the road, and follows a footpath to the paved Crest Drive (closed to vehicular traffic), where it turns left.

As the road curves to the right at 0.7 mile, the New York City skyline may be seen to the left through the trees, with the towers of the Verrazano-Narrows Bridge visible in the distance to the right. Just ahead—before reaching a plaque on a boulder commemorating a Revolutionary War battle that took place near here—the trail turns left, leaving the road, and descends to an observation platform with stone pillars at the site of Washington Rock, from which George

Washington sur-
veyed the country-
side during the
American Revolu-
tion. The view from
here is to the south-
west, with Millburn
and the NJ Transit
railroad tracks vis-
ible below, and
Watchung Reserva-
tion—the continua-
tion of the Watchung
range beyond the
Millburn-Springfield
gap—ahead in the
distance.

The Lenape Trail
now descends on a foot-
path. At 1.0 mile, an un-
marked side trail to the left
leads to an overlook over an
abandoned quarry. A short distance beyond, the Lenape Trail
crosses a bridle path and enters a remote, less-used area of the reservation. After a short descent, it crosses a
small stream at 1.3 miles, with the
Maple Falls Cascade—where the stream
plunges down a 25-foot sluiceway of exposed basalt—to the left, downstream.

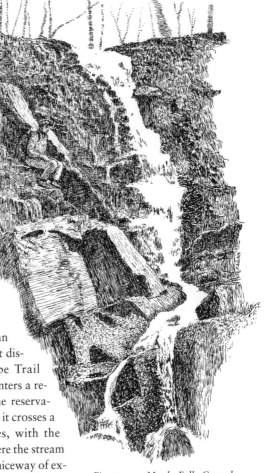

Figure 9-5. Maple Falls Cascade

The trail now follows a relatively level footpath, reaching Beech Brook
Cascades—where two brooks converge—at 1.9 miles. Beyond the cascade, the
trail begins a gradual climb, paralleling a brook in a shallow ravine to the right.
After bearing left and crossing a bridle path, the trail climbs to reach Mines
Point—named for exploratory pits dug by copper prospectors circa 1800—at
2.2 miles. Here, the trail bears right and heads north on a generally level foot-

path. At 2.7 miles, it reaches Ball's Bluff where, to the left of the trail, old stone pillars are remnants of a picnic shelter built in 1908.

Now descending steadily, the Lenape Trail crosses a bridle path and soon begins to parallel a stream. After crossing the stream, it turns right and proceeds uphill on a wide woods road. In another 500 feet, the trail turns left and descends a steep slope, soon reaching the base of Hemlock Falls, a scenic waterfall, at 3.0 miles. The trail now crosses a footbridge over the stream, turns left, and continues along a woods road to reach a junction at 3.2 miles. The northern trailhead of the Rahway Trail (white), which can be used as an alternate return route to Millburn, is straight ahead. Here, the Lenape Trail turns right onto a wide gravel road.

At a fork marked by a huge oak tree, the Lenape Trail bears left and follows a dirt road to cross a bridge over South Orange Avenue at 3.4 miles. A short distance beyond the bridge, it turns left, leaving the road, and proceeds through a pine grove. After descending through a mixed pine-deciduous forest, it crosses a paved park road at 3.6 miles and passes the Tulip Springs parking area (accessed from Cherry Lane to the west). It crosses the Rahway River on a footbridge and climbs to a picnic area, where it turns left. After passing through a dirt parking area, the trail bears left across a grassy field, crosses a row of trees, turns right to parallel the treeline, then bears left to reach the busy intersection of South Orange Avenue and Cherry Lane, where there is a traffic light.

Here, at 4.0 miles, the Lenape Trail crosses Cherry Lane and continues ahead, parallel to South Orange Avenue. At a signpost that marks the start of the Oakdale Trail (red), the Lenape Trail bears right. Just beyond, at a fork, the Oakdale Trail leaves to the right, while the Lenape Trail continues ahead, continuing to parallel South Orange Avenue. At 4.2 miles, the trail turns right and begins to head north along the crest of the Second Watchung, following a footpath through dense woods.

After passing through a dense tunnel of vegetation, the Lenape Trail reaches The Crag—a stone overlook to the right—at 5.2 miles. The Orange Reservoir may be seen below through the trees. The trail continues ahead, with homes visible through the trees to the left. At 5.4 miles, after intersecting a carriage road that leads downhill to the right to the Oakdale Trail and Cherry Lane, the Lenape Trail crosses a bridge over Northfield Avenue. For the next 0.2 mile, the trail closely parallels homes to the left. It then bears right at a fork, and after bearing right at a second fork, it reaches the Mayapple Hill parking area. Here, 6.0 miles from Millburn, this section of the Lenape Trail ends.

Oakdale Trail   *Length: 1.2 miles Blaze: red*

The Oakdale Trail extends along the side of the Second Watchung from Northfield Avenue to South Orange Avenue. The northern trailhead is on a carriage road that extends from the Lenape Trail downhill to the Oakdale picnic area (on Cherry Lane, just south of Northfield Avenue). From the trailhead, the Oakdale Trail proceeds south on a footpath, closely paralleling paved Valley View Drive (which is closed to vehicular traffic) for most of the way. The Oakdale Trail ends, 1.2 miles from its start, at a junction with the Lenape Trail (yellow), about 300 feet west of the intersection of South Orange Avenue and Cherry Lane.

The Oakdale Trail may be combined with the Lenape Trail and a short section of the carriage road to form a 2.7-mile loop hike.

Rahway Trail   *Length: 2.4 miles Blaze: white*

Running close to the Rahway River for most of its length, the Rahway Trail extends from just south of South Orange Avenue to the Locust Grove parking area. It may be combined with the Lenape Trail to form a 5.6-mile loop hike.

The northern trailhead of the Rahway Trail is on the Lenape Trail (yellow), 0.2 mile south of the bridge over South Orange Avenue. The Rahway Trail heads west and, at 0.1 mile crosses the Rahway River on rocks. In 2003, many of the rocks had been washed away, and the crossing was very difficult, except during periods of low water. For an alternative crossing of the river, backtrack to a fork in the trail (reached in about 200 feet) and turn left, following the blacked-out blazes of the former trail route to South Orange Avenue. Turn left and cross the road bridge over the river (take care, as the sidewalk is narrow and the road is heavily trafficked), then turn left at the end of the guardrail and follow the path along the river to rejoin the blazed trail.

The Rahway Trail follows along the river for a short distance and then climbs to continue along the side of a hill, with the river below to the left. This section of the trail is particularly scenic. At 0.6 mile, the trail turns left onto a gravel road, crosses a bridge back to the east bank of the river, then immediately turns right onto a footpath and begins to closely parallel the river. It crosses another gravel road at 0.9 mile and continues ahead along the riverbank.

At 1.3 miles, the trail passes an old dam in the river, with Brookside Drive now visible to the west, across the river. Just beyond, the trail joins a bridle path and passes through a rhododendron grove. The trail follows the bridle path uphill, then bears left and continues on a footpath, some distance away from

the river. It descends towards the river at 1.7 miles and crosses a stone-faced bridge over a tributary stream. Then, at 1.8 miles, it turns left onto a wide dirt road, follows the road for 200 feet, and turns right onto a footpath, soon passing Diamond Hill Pond on the right. At 2.2 miles, the trail bears left, away from the river, and it ends, 2.4 miles from its start, at a junction with the Lenape Trail (yellow) at the Locust

Figure 9-6. Diamond Hill Pond

Grove parking area, just north of the intersection of Glen Avenue and Lackawanna Place in Millburn.

Turtle Back Trail

Length: 3.0 miles Blaze: orange

Forming a loop in the northeastern section of the reservation, the Turtle Back Trail begins at a junction with the Lenape Trail (yellow) just north of the trail bridge over South Orange Avenue. Followed in a counter-clockwise direction, the trail proceeds east, descending to cross a carriage road. At 0.2 mile, it turns left onto another carriage road and begins to climb. Then, at 0.4 mile, it turns left, leaving the carriage road, and continues to climb. Soon, the trail begins to parallel the Longwood Carriage Road, which is to the right, along the ridge of the First Watchung.

At 1.5 miles, the trail passes to the left of Turtle Back Rock—an unusual rock formation, with striations resembling the back of a turtle. Just beyond, the trail turns sharply left and makes a U-turn. The trail now heads south along the side of the ridge, following two ravines. When the leaves are down, there are views of the Orange Reservoir to the right. The trail then curves to the right and descends to a junction with the Reservoir Carriage Road at 2.7 miles. Here, the

trail turns left, and it follows the road back to the trailhead, reached at 3.0 miles, completing the loop.

WATCHUNG RESERVATION

Watchung Reservation, managed by the Union County Division of Parks and Recreation, is a 2,000-acre wooded tract where animal and plant life are protected. Highlights of the park include Surprise Lake, the Deserted Village of Feltville/Glenside Park, the Trailside Nature and Science Center, Seeley's Pond, and the Watchung Stables. In May and early June, the dogwood and rhododendron near Surprise Lake are outstanding. Although I-78 traverses its northwestern flank, most of the reservation remains in a natural, wild state, and sound barriers muffle the road noise.

Opened in 1941, the Trailside Museum was New Jersey's first nature museum. It has a large collection of bird eggs, as well as exhibits featuring many native animals and birds. The Visitor Center and museum are open daily, except on holidays, from the end of March to Thanksgiving, from 1:00 p.m. to 5:00 p.m. There are four short nature trails: green (0.2 mile), orange (0.5 mile), blue (0.9 mile), and red (0.5 mile). Some of the reservation's trails are open to horses.

To reach Watchung Reservation, take US 22 to New Providence Road in Mountainside. Proceed north (uphill) on New Providence Road for 0.7 mile and make the fifth right-hand turn onto Ackerman Avenue. At the end of Ackerman Avenue, turn right onto Coles Avenue. The Trailside Nature and Science Center is reached in 0.3 mile, where the road makes a sharp right turn. Public transportation to the intersection of US 22 and New Providence Road in Mountainside is available via NJ Transit bus #114 from the Port Authority Bus Terminal in New York City, but hikers must walk uphill for 1.4 miles to reach the reservation. Access by rail is available via NJ Transit's Gladstone Line, which offers hourly service from Hoboken and Penn Station in New York. From the Murray Hill station, proceed east on Floral Avenue to South Street. Turn right and follow South Street for 1.2 miles to the I-78 overpass (after crossing Mountain Avenue, the name changes to Glenside Road). After crossing under I-78, turn right onto Glenside Avenue, then turn left in 250 feet onto Cataract Hollow Road, which enters the park. In about 800 feet, the Sierra Trail leaves to the left (at mile 6.0 of the trail description below).

For more information, contact the Trailside Nature and Science Center, Watchung Reservation, 452 New Providence Road, Mountainside, NJ 07092; (908) 789-3670; www.unioncountynj.org.

Sierra Trail   *Length: 10.8 miles Blaze: white square*

The Sierra Trail forms a loop that encircles the reservation, passing many points of interest along the way. Various connecting trails can be used to fashion a shorter loop. Before starting the hike, hikers should stop at the Trailside Nature and Science Center to obtain a free trail map, which shows the Sierra Trail as well as several short nature trails and other unmarked trails and bridle paths. The trail is described below in a clockwise direction.

From the Trailside Nature and Science Center, the trail proceeds west (downhill) along the extension of New Providence Road. At a large sign that reads "Nature Trail," the trail turns left, crosses a brook, and continues downhill alongside a small glen, running concurrently with the Green Trail. Just before a wide wooden bridge, the Sierra Trail turns left, leaving the Green Trail, and briefly joins the Yellow Trail. At the next intersection, the Sierra Trail turns right and begins to parallel a scenic gorge to the left. The Blue Trail soon joins, and the trails begin to descend.

At the end of the gorge, the trails approach Blue Brook. Here, the Blue Trail leaves to the right, while the Sierra Trail turns left and briefly follows the brook. The Sierra Trail soon bears left and climbs away from the brook, bears left again at the next intersection, then turns right at the next junction. At 0.8 mile, the trail crosses a small brook and bears left, uphill. After passing some houses to the left, it crosses a dirt road at 1.4 miles and soon begins a gradual descent.

At 2.0 miles, the Sierra Trail turns left onto a dirt road. It follows the dirt road for only 300 feet and then turns left, leaving the road and continuing on a footpath. The trail ascends through a beautiful pine forest, planted by the CCC in the 1930s, and soon reaches an open grassy area, with a picnic pavilion ahead. Here, the trail bears right and follows a cinder road out to the paved Sky Top Drive. It crosses the road at 2.4 miles and re-enters the woods, then makes a sharp right turn onto a wide woods road parallel to Sky Top Drive (which often may be seen to the right). At 3.3 miles, the trail begins to descend. As the trail bends to the left, a short path to the right leads to an overlook above an abandoned quarry, with I-78 visible in the distance.

After descending more steeply, the Sierra Trail makes a sharp right in sight of NJ 22 at 3.5 miles and follows an eroded gully (with a number of blowdowns)

down to Green Brook. It now runs along the brook, with New Providence Road on the other side. At 4.0 miles, it goes by the site of an old mill, with many brick and concrete ruins still visible. After passing the ruins of the dam that supplied power to the mill, the trail bears right and climbs steeply to an over-look, then descends and, at 4.6 miles, once again reaches Sky Top Drive.

The Sierra Trail turns left and follows the road, using the highway bridge to cross Blue Brook, with Seeley's Pond to the left. After crossing the bridge, the trail immediately turns right, goes through a grassy area, and re-enters the woods. It follows a footpath through some fairly dense vegetation and crosses several small brooks on a wooden boardwalk. Just beyond, the trail turns left onto Drake Farm Road, then turns right, leaving the road, and continues on a footpath. At 5.3 miles, it turns left on a wide dirt road and emerges, at 5.6 miles, on a paved road at the Deserted Village of Feltville. Named for David Felt, a New York City businessman who founded the village in 1845 to house the workers at his nearby paper mill, it was abandoned about thirty years later. In 2003, some of the buildings in the area are being restored.

The Sierra Trail follows the paved road through the village. After passing the general store and an adjacent home, the Sierra Trail turns right on a bridle path at 6.0 miles. In 200 feet, it turns right again onto another dirt road, and soon passes a small cemetery which contains the grave markers of the Willcocks and Badgley families, who first settled the area about 1736. The road soon narrows to a footpath. At 6.3 miles, the Sierra Trail turns right, descends on a dirt road for 400 feet, then turns left, leaving the road, and immediately bears right onto a footpath. Then, at 6.6 miles, the trail reaches the dam of Surprise Lake, built in 1845 to provide power for David Felt's paper mill. The trail continues along the northwestern shore of this long but narrow lake. At 7.4 miles, it turns right at paved W.R. Tracy Drive, crossing the lake on a bridge. On the other side of the bridge, it turns left and crosses the road.

The Sierra Trail now heads northeast on a bridle path. It turns right at 7.6 miles, briefly joining another bridle path, then turns left and continues heading northeast. After another right turn, the trail reaches a junction at 8.0 miles where it turns right and begins to head southwest. At 8.3 miles, it turns left, leaving the bridle path, and continues on a footpath, passing the Watchung Stables. Then, at 8.7 miles, it turns left, rejoining a bridle path.

At 9.2 miles, the Sierra Trail reaches a traffic circle at the junction of W.R. Tracy Drive and Summit Lane. It turns left, proceeds around the circle in a clockwise direction, crosses Summit Lane, then continues ahead on a footpath.

After climbing to the ridge of the First Watchung, the trail turns left onto a bridle path at 9.4 miles and follows it to a water tank. Here, at 9.7 miles, the trail makes a sharp bend to the right and begins to head southwest on a dirt road, crossing W.R. Tracy Drive at 10.1 miles. The trail bends to the right and re-crosses Summit Lane. Just beyond, it turns left on a footpath. After joining the Red Trail, the Sierra Trail passes the Trailside Nature and Science Center and reaches New Providence Road at 10.8 miles, completing the loop.

OTHER AREAS NEAR THE WATCHUNGS

Geologically, the Hackensack Meadowlands are part of the Mesozoic Lowland area between the Watchungs and the Palisades. Very different from the rugged Watchungs, they feature a small network of trails that offer the opportunity to explore a wetland teeming with wildlife.

Hackensack Meadowlands

When first settled in the mid-1600s, the Hackensack Meadowlands consisted of a mixture of freshwater marsh, salt marsh, and Atlantic white cedar swamp. Until the late 1800s, botanists flocked to the area to observe the unusual plants that grew there. A long history of ditching, diking, and exploitation altered and degraded the natural vegetation. In the early twentieth century, the Hackensack River was dammed to create the Oradell Reservoir. Much of the fresh water of the Hackensack River was diverted to satisfy the needs of the burgeoning population of North Jersey, thus starving the marsh and allowing it to become salty. As a result, the original plant communities disappeared, and the Meadowlands were invaded by a thick growth of phragmites. Even today, though, the logs and stumps of a once-magnificent forest of 500-year-old trees can be seen at low tide in the pools of water that border the New Jersey Turnpike. Later in the twentieth century, the wetlands and tidal marshes of the Hackensack River and the adjacent area were threatened with haphazard zoning, unregulated waste disposal, and lack of planning.

In 1969, the State of New Jersey enacted legislation which established the Hackensack Meadowlands Development Commission to preserve, enhance, and develop 32 square miles of the Hackensack Meadowlands. In 2001, the Hackensack Meadowlands Development Commission, which promoted development in the region, was transformed into the New Jersey Meadowlands

Figure 9-7. Canada geese

Commission, which emphasizes the protection and restoration of the remaining natural environment of the Meadowlands.

Much of the Meadowlands is vegetated by the common reed *Phragmites australis*, a tall grass with large seed plumes, which is visible from the New Jersey Turnpike. Originally, the area was thought to be incapable of supporting much wildlife. However, research has demonstrated that a remarkable diversity of birds, fish, and other wildlife characteristic of coastal marshes can be found in the Meadowlands—in the shadow of New York City.

Although the area is often thought of as a landfill, a visit to the Meadowlands is definitely not a trip to the dump. The 2,000-acre Richard W. DeKorte Park features a landscaped capped landfill and trails that take visitors out into observation areas and bird blinds. It also includes the Meadowlands Environment Center, which contains informative exhibits on the Meadowlands and its ecology. Adjacent to the park, and reachable from it, is the 3.5-acre Lyndhurst Nature Reserve.

A suggested 1.1-mile loop hike begins at a sign for the Marsh Discovery Trail, on the east side of the access road, near the security booth at the entrance to the parking lot. It proceeds along a boardwalk constructed of modular plastic panels which links a series of dredge-spoil islands—formed by dumping sediment from dredging operations—along Kingsland Creek. The park is situated along the Atlantic Flyway, and many species of birds and waterfowl can be observed along the trail. Benches and wildlife observation blinds provide op-

portunities to linger for a while and observe the natural surroundings. Marsh reeds line the trail, and the New York City skyline is visible in the distance.

In 0.5 mile, the Marsh Discovery Trail ends at a junction with the Transco Trail. Turn right and follow the Transco Trail along a dike constructed in the 1950s for a buried gas pipeline. The dike separates the waters of the Kingsland Tidal Impoundment—to the right—from the Saw Mill Creek Wildlife Management Area—to the left. Many native species have been planted along the trail, and several former truck turnarounds to the right of the trail have been converted to scenic overlooks.

Just past a gate at the end of the Transco Trail is a four-way junction. Turn right, cross a wooden deck that memorializes the World Trade Center tragedy of September 11, 2001, and continue on a brick-paved path in front of the Administration Building of the New Jersey Meadowlands Commission. In 400 feet—near the end of the building—turn left at a marked crosswalk, cross the paved road, and continue on the Kingsland Overlook Trail, a gravel path that leads up a low hill.

The Kingsland Overlook Trail climbs an artificial mound created by a landfill for household waste. This former eyesore has been capped by a waterproof membrane, covered with topsoil, and planted with attractive shrubs and trees. Walking along this beautiful trail, it is hard to imagine that it was once the site of a garbage dump! The trail provides views of the Kingsland Tidal Impoundment below, and the New York City skyline may be seen in the distance. The Kingsland Overlook Trail ends opposite the start of the Marsh Discovery Trail, completing the loop.

To reach Richard W. DeKorte Park, take the New Jersey Turnpike to Exit 16W. Follow NJ 3 west to the exit for NJ 17 south. Follow the ramp to Polito Avenue and turn left. At the end of Polito Avenue, turn left on Valley Brook Avenue and continue to the parking area for DeKorte Park, on the left just beyond the crossing of NJ Transit railroad tracks. Signs along the route direct you to the park. During the week, public transportation to the office buildings on Valley Brook Avenue is available via NJ Transit buses #76L and #76T. A walking lane on Valley Brook Avenue is called Meadows Path and leads to the park. For more information, contact Richard W. DeKorte Park, 2 DeKorte Park Plaza, Lyndhurst, NJ 07071; (201) 406-8300; www.meadowlands.state.nj.us.

TEN

MORRIS COUNTY

ntil the 1730s, when surveyors found iron in the hills, few people settled in the Jersey Highlands because it offered poorer farming than land to the south. The iron-rich hills, more than any other factor, shaped the development of the area and gave birth to an industry that forged a nation. With mines supplying the iron used for weaponry, New Jersey played an important role in the fight for independence. Establishment of routes through the Ramapo Mountains allowed munitions and supplies to reach the fighting forces in the Hudson Valley. As the iron industry developed in our new nation, an effective means of transportation was needed to bring coal from Pennsylvania and take iron out of the area. Thus, in the early nineteenth century, the Morris Canal was built. But the canal provided slow transportation and could not operate in the winter, and the arrival of railroads in the 1850s sounded its death knell.

The decline of the Morris Canal did not harm the area. Boatmen and canal workers found other employment. Small villages had already become towns. Farming and mining continued. By the time railroads crisscrossed the county, Morris County had become an industrial and agricultural area. Soon after high grade iron ore was discovered in the Mesabi Range of Minnesota in the 1890s, the iron industry faded. The railroads continued to bring coal to metropolitan New York for heating and industry until just after World War II.

At the start of the twenty-first century, with two major interstate highways crossing the area, development and suburban sprawl have begun to consume open space in Morris County. Although much of the area has been taken up by

single-family housing, Morris County has an extensive system of county parks, as well as state parks, wildlife management areas, watershed property, and a national historical park. These open spaces enhance the quality of life by preserving wildlife habitat, protecting aquifers and watersheds, and offering people places to hike, bird, hunt, or fish.

Two through trails are being developed across Morris County—the Highlands Trail and the Patriots' Path. As of 2003, about 50 miles of these trails have been completed. Linking larger parks with local trail systems, they create opportunities for longer hikes. When the linkages cross private lands, hikers should stay on the trails to respect the privacy of the landowners and to help ensure the continued existence of the trails in the future.

Geology

Most of Morris County is part of the Precambrian Jersey Highlands, which extends from Wawayanda State Park in the north through the Pequannock Watershed to Phillipsburg on the Delaware River. The ridges have rounded-to-flat tops, with frequent outcroppings of granite gneiss. There are also long, narrow sections of Paleozoic strata which have been downfolded or downfaulted into the predominately Precambrian terrain.

Evidence of glaciation may be seen throughout the Highlands. As the Wisconsin Glacier moved across the region, it cut scratches in bedrock, smoothed out rock outcrops, and left erratics perched on ridges. Its terminal moraine, almost one mile wide and 25 to 100 feet high, is a heterogeneous mixture of rocks and gravel. It stretches between Hackettstown and Morristown and then turns southeast, terminating in what is now Perth Amboy. Sand and gravel left as glacial lake or outwash deposits are sometimes as thick as 250 feet. They have been quarried in the past, and they are likely to be in the future.

Picatinny Arsenal

The 6,500-acre Picatinny Arsenal has long figured in the history of the region. In 1749, at the base of Picatinny Peak, an iron forge was constructed on a site that had water from a brook and iron from nearby mines. Known as the Middle Forge, it produced bar iron, some of which was used to manufacture munitions for the Continental Army during the American Revolution. In 1880, a powder depot was built on the site. Named for Picatinny Peak (Picatinny is thought to mean "rugged cliff by the water" in the language of the Lenape), the

site was chosen because the steep sides of the ten-mile-long valley could protect the surrounding area from the site's hazardous activities, and it was readily accessible to east coast fortifications. In 1907, a smokeless powder factory was established on the site, and the facility became known as Picatinny Arsenal. During World War II, the arsenal developed and manufactured munitions that were vital to the war effort, including artillery shells, mines, and grenades, and it continued developing and manufacturing munitions during the Korean and Vietnam wars. In 1977, the arsenal ended its munitions manufacturing operations, but it continued developing munitions and added the development of armaments (such as weapons delivery systems) to its mission. At the beginning of the twenty-first century, the arsenal not only contributes to military research, but also has about seven square miles of undeveloped land serving as wildlife habitat. The arsenal is not open to the public.

For more information, contact the Public Affairs Officer, Picatinny Arsenal, Picatinny Arsenal, NJ 07806; (973) 724-6365; www.pica.army.mil/public.

BERKSHIRE VALLEY WILDLIFE MANAGEMENT AREA

Located north of I-80 and west of NJ 15, the Berkshire Valley Wildlife Management Area encompasses approximately 1,850 acres of wetlands and upland mixed hardwood forest. Notable wildlife native to the area includes wild turkeys, deer, grouse, rabbits, black ducks, mallards, and wood ducks.

There are several access points to the Berkshire Valley WMA. To reach the first access point, take Exit 34B (NJ 15) from I-80. Proceed north on NJ 15 for 2.0 miles to Berkshire Valley Road, turn right at the jughandle, then turn left and proceed west on Berkshire Valley Road for 0.9 mile. The parking area is on the left, opposite Minnisink Road. A woods road leads from the parking area to an old gravel pit. This piece is cut off from the main portion of the management area by the river and an adjacent housing development. It is a good birding spot for warblers.

To reach the second access point, follow the directions above, but from the jughandle, make a U-turn and go south on NJ 15. In about 300 feet, at the crest of the hill, turn right at a sign for the Berkshire Valley WMA. The dirt road leads into a former gravel pit, with wetlands extending along the Rockaway River. Hikers heading away from the river go uphill into an upland mixed

hardwood forest.

The third access point is reached by taking Exit 30 from I-80 and heading north on Howard Boulevard. The parking area is on the right as the road climbs uphill. There are no obvious trails out of the parking area. However, after scrambling up the side of the parking area opposite the entrance, hikers cross a berm leading to a woods road which goes into the interior of the wildlife management area.

Another access point is reached by heading west on Berkshire Valley Road from NJ 15 and continuing for 2.2 miles to Gordon Road (just before a white firehouse). Turn right onto Gordon Road and continue for 0.3 mile. Just beyond Country Lane, the second right leads to a small parking area. Extending north from this parking area is the right-of-way of the former Lake Hopatcong Railroad, built in 1882 to connect with the Ogden Mine Railroad and abandoned in 1935. This right-of-way may be followed north for 2.1 miles to Minnisink Road.

Users of the Berkshire Valley Wildlife Management Area may wish to obtain the Stanhope and Dover USGS topographic quadrangle maps. For more information, contact New Jersey DEP, Division of Fish and Wildlife, 501 East State Street, P.O. Box 400, Trenton, NJ 08625; (609) 984-0547; www.njfishandwildlife.org.

BLACK RIVER

Also known as the Lamington River, the Black River flows into the Raritan River near Burnt Mills in Somerset County. Its route is protected in the area near Chester. Along its course, the Black River passes through the Black River Wildlife Management Area and sustains a freshwater marsh. Just beyond, it powers the historic Cooper Mill. Then, in both Black River County Park and Hacklebarney State Park, the river tumbles over rocks as it passes through a gorge.

Black River Wildlife Management Area

Located along the Black River, this 3,000-acre wildlife management area encompasses river bottom, swampy woodland, freshwater marsh, fields, and upland deciduous woods. Woods roads cross the mixed hardwood forest with a heavy understory and an occasional pine plantation. Some of the fields are

filled with wildflowers and grasses, while others are still cultivated. They provide habitat for grasslands species. The wildlife management area is well known for good birding, as more than 200 species have been found here, with about 100 nesting species. During spring migration, the area attracts a wide variety of waterfowl.

The Patriots' Path (white) follows four miles of the abandoned Chester Branch of the Delaware, Lackawanna & Western Railroad, which closely parallels the Black River through the wildlife management area between Pleasant Hill Road, near Chester, and Hugg Road in Ironia. Built in 1868 to serve the needs of the local iron industry, it carried iron ore from area mines and ingots from the Chester Furnace to Wharton and Dover, but freight traffic dropped precipitously when the iron boom in the area ended in 1892. In early 1933, passenger service ended, and the tracks were removed later in the year. The railbed with its gentle grade offers hikers easy walking and views of the freshwater marsh. Horses require an annual permit.

The Black River Wildlife Management Area is located near Chester, which is at the intersection of US 206 and County 513. There are five access points. To reach the two parking areas on Pleasant Hill Road, follow County 513 east to Hillside Road and turn left. At the Y junction, bear right onto Pleasant Hill Road. The first parking area is immediately south of the bridge over the Black River, where the Patriots' Path crosses the road. To reach the second parking area, continue on Pleasant Hill Road 1.7 miles past the Black River parking area. At a dirt road marked with a sign, turn and follow the road to a large parking area. To reach the third parking area, continue on Pleasant Hill Road, turning right at 1.8 miles, at the Y junction with

Figure 10-1. Chester Branch of the Delaware, Lackawanna & Western Railroad

Ironia Road. The parking area is 1.3 miles beyond the junction. The other two parking areas are off County 513, 1.7 and 2.6 miles from the junction of County 510 with County 513, east of Chester. The headquarters for the wildlife management area is located at the first of the two parking areas off County 513.

Users of the Black River Wildlife Management Area may wish to obtain the Chester USGS topographic quadrangle map. For more information, contact New Jersey DEP, Division of Fish and Wildlife, 501 East State Street, P.O. Box 400, Trenton, NJ 08625; (609) 984-0547; www.njfishandwildlife.org.

Black River County Park

Black River County Park, part of the Morris County Park System, consists of 510 acres located west of US 206 near Chester. It includes four important cultural sites—Cooper Mill, Kay Environmental Center, Bamboo Brook Outdoor Education Center, and Willowwood Arboretum—each of which not only is worth visiting in its own right, but also provides access to trails in the area.

A highlight of the park is the scenic Black River. The Black River Trail (blue) and the Bamboo Brook Trail (blue), spurs of the Patriots' Path, traverse the park. The Conifer Pass Trail (red), which closely parallels a wild section of the Black River for much of its route, connects at both ends with the Black River and Bamboo Brook trails, and may be combined with them to form a loop hike. A portion of the Conifer Pass Trail traverses a natural area, and a free permit (which may be obtained at the Kay Environmental Center) is required to hike this trail.

Cooper Mill—a restored grist mill that was built in 1826 by Nathan Cooper, utilizing then state-of-the-art technology—is located on County 513 at the northern end of the park. Purchased by the Morris County Park Commission in 1963, the mill was opened to the public in 1978. The mill is operated on weekends in the summer, when visitors may observe the stone grinding of whole wheat flour and corn meal. To reach Cooper Mill, take I-80 west to Exit 27A and continue south on US 206 for 8.0 miles. Turn right onto County 513 (formerly designated as NJ 24) and follow it for 1.2 miles to the entrance to Cooper Mill Park, on the left side of the road.

Much of the northern portion of Black River County Park was formerly the summer home of the Kay family. Elizabeth Donnell Kay was the driving force behind the Great Swamp Outdoor Education Center in Chatham. The

former Kay house is now the Kay Environmental Center and the New Jersey Field Office of The Nature Conservancy, which helps provide public programming for the park.

To reach the Kay Environmental Center from the north, take I-80 west to Exit 27A and continue south on US 206 for 9.5 miles. Turn right onto Pottersville Road and follow it for 0.9 mile to the entrance to the Kay Environmental Center, on the right side of the road (just past a brown barn). From the south, take I-287 to Exit 22 and proceed north on US 206 for 5.2 miles to Pottersville Road (County 512), where there is a traffic light. Continue ahead on US 206 for another 3.4 miles to a second intersection with Pottersville Road. Turn left here and proceed for 0.9 mile to the park entrance.

At the southern end of Black River County Park, two large estates—Bamboo Brook Outdoor Education Center and Willowwood Arboretum—feature landscaped gardens with thousands of native and exotic plants. Known originally as Merchiston Farm, Bamboo Brook Outdoor Education Center was the home of William and Martha Brookes Hutcheson from 1911 to 1959. The Center's 100 acres include fields, forest, and a formal garden designed by Mrs. Hutcheson, one of the first women to be trained as a landscape architect in the United States.

Willowwood Arboretum comprises 130 acres of rolling farmland and a shallow valley with 3,500 varieties of plants. Henry and Robert Tubbs bought the property in 1908 and developed the garden for half a century, with many of the specimens dating from their initial plantings. The Willowwood Farm became a private arboretum in 1950 and a part of the Morris County Park System in 1980. Lilacs, magnolias, hollies, lady-slipper, and ferns decorate the area.

To reach Bamboo Brook Outdoor Education Center and Willowwood Arboretum, take I-287 to Exit 22, go north on US 206 for 5.2 miles, and turn left onto Pottersville Road (County 512). In 0.5 mile, turn right onto Lisk Hill Road, and then at the T junction turn right onto Union Grove Road. At the next Y junction, turn left onto Longview Road. The entrance to Willowwood Arboretum is on the left, half a mile from the Y junction. The entrance to the Bamboo Brook Outdoor Education Center is half a mile further along Longview Road. For more information, contact the Morris County Park Commission, 53 East Hanover Avenue, P.O. Box 1295, Morristown, NJ 07962-1295; (973) 326-7600; www.morrisparks.com.

Black River Trail

Length: 1.9 miles Blaze: blue
The Black River Trail connects Cooper Mill with the Kay Environmental Center, following a former railbed for much of the way through attractive wetlands. From Cooper Mill on County 513, 1.2 miles west of US 206, the trail descends the stairs alongside the mill, continues through a grassy area, and turns left, briefly paralleling the river. The trail bears left, crosses several tributary streams on wooden bridges, and soon begins to parallel an abandoned railroad grade to the right. At 0.3 mile, it turns left onto the grade—the former route of the Hacklebarney Branch of the Central Railroad of New Jersey, built in 1873 to carry iron ore from mines along the river and abandoned in 1900. The railbed traverses an extensive wetland, with skunk cabbage the predominant vegetation.

At 0.5 mile, the trail passes Kay Pond (formerly known as Hacklebarney Pond) to the right. Here, the railroad had to be blasted through a rock cut, and the drill marks from the blasting may still be seen in the rock. The small building at the south end of Kay Pond

Figure 10-2. Cooper Mill

was once used to store ice cut from the pond in the winter.

Soon after passing the stone dam at the end of the pond, the trail goes by a fenced-in area to the left. This is the site of the former Hacklebarney Mine,

where a considerable amount of iron ore was mined in the last quarter of the nineteenth century. Just beyond, the trail reaches a bridge over the river and turns left, continuing to follow along the river. At 1.0 mile, the railroad grade ends and the trail continues on a slightly rougher footpath parallel to the river.

The trail reaches abandoned concrete abutments in the river—the remnants of a former bridge—at 1.2 miles. Here, the trail bears left and begins to head uphill. It bears left at the next fork and soon begins to parallel a tributary stream. The trail then curves right and continues to climb, passing a stone wall to the right and continuing through former fields, now overgrown with dense vegetation.

At 1.7 miles, the trail reaches a junction in a clearing, marked by a signpost. Here, the Conifer Pass Trail (red) joins from the right. The Black River Trail turns left, then turns left again at the next intersection. It ends, 1.9 miles from the start, at a parking area, with the Kay Environmental Center to the right. The Bamboo Brook Trail (blue), which continues ahead to the Bamboo Brook Outdoor Education Center and the Willowwood Arboretum, begins to the right, just east of the Kay Environmental Center.

Bamboo Brook Trail   *Length: 4.5 miles Blaze: blue*

Beginning at the parking area for the Kay Environmental Center, just east of the center, the Bamboo Brook Trail follows a wide path through overgrown fields, turns left onto a dirt road, and joins the paved entrance road. It follows the paved road for 0.2 mile to Pottersville Road, turns right, and follows Pottersville Road for 750 feet. At 0.5 mile, opposite a sign for "Devereux Deerhaven," the trail turns left and reenters the woods.

The trail bears right at a fork at 0.7 mile and begins to climb the rocky hillside, first rather steeply, then more gradually. After reaching the top of the hill, the trail descends to reach a junction, at 1.2 miles, with the Conifer Pass Trail (red), which leaves to the right. The Bamboo Brook Trail continues ahead, descending gradually. It reaches Bamboo Brook, just below a cascade in the brook, at 1.7 miles. Here, the trail turns sharply right and begins to parallel the brook. It turns right, away from the brook, at 2.0 miles and climbs gradually to cross paved Lamerson Road at 2.2 miles.

The Bamboo Brook Trail ascends on a woods road, bears left at a fork, then bears right onto a footpath. It turns left onto a woods road at 2.5 miles, immediately bears left at a T intersection, then turns sharply right, leaving the road. After passing through a second-growth forest in former fields, the trail

crosses paved Longview Road at 3.0 miles.

The trail continues through the woods and emerges, at 3.1 miles, onto a cultivated field. It turns right and proceeds along the edge of the field, then turns left at the end of the field and continues to skirt the field. At 3.4 miles, it turns right and soon begins to skirt a second field. At the end of the second field, the trail bears right onto a woods road, then immediately turns right and proceeds through a pine plantation, soon beginning to descend. At 3.7 miles, it joins a woods road. In another 500 feet, it turns left, continues on a footpath, then turns right onto another woods road.

Leaving the woods road at 4.0 miles, the trail begins to parallel a stream to the left. It crosses the stream at 4.2 miles and climbs to a field. It follows along the left side of the field, reenters the woods, and continues along the left side of another field until, at 4.5 miles, it crosses the entrance road to the Bamboo Brook Outdoor Education Center. The trail descends on a path and ends in front of the Hutcheson House. The Willowwood Trail (blue), which leads to the Willowwood Arboretum, continues ahead.

Willowwood Trail   *Length: 0.9 mile Blaze: blue*
The Willowwood Trail connects the Bamboo Brook Outdoor Education Center with the Willowwood Arboretum. It begins across from the Hutcheson House at the Bamboo Brook Outdoor Education Center and follows a dirt road past several barns. It descends to parallel a field and continues to descend through woods, reaching Bamboo Brook at 0.3 mile. It briefly turns left and

Figure 10-3. Willowwood Trail at the Bamboo Brook Outdoor Education Center

parallels the brook, then turns right and crosses the brook on a wide wooden bridge.

The trail climbs to a field, continues across the field, and passes through a gate in a fence at 0.6 mile. It bears left and skirts another field, crossing the entrance road to the Willowwood Arboretum at 0.8 mile. Just beyond, the trail reaches a fork. To the left, a branch of the trail follows a portion of the railbed of the abandoned Rockaway Valley Railroad. In 2003, this branch of the trail ends at Daly Road. The right branch leads to the Willowwood Arboretum, where it terminates at 0.9 mile.

Conifer Pass Trail   *Length: 1.9 miles Blaze: red*

The Conifer Pass Trail traverses a natural area along the Black River. It passes through attractive stands of conifers and runs along a wild river gorge. A free permit, which may be obtained at the Kay Environmental Center, is required to hike this trail.

Beginning at the west end of the parking area for the Kay Environmental Center, the Conifer Pass Trail heads west along a field, running jointly with the Black River Trail (blue). It turns right at a T intersection and reaches another junction at 0.2 mile. Here, the Black River Trail leaves to the right, while the Conifer Pass Trail continues straight ahead on a woods road which soon bends to the left and heads south. At 0.4 mile, the road turns sharply right and begins to head northwest.

Another junction is reached at 0.6 mile. Here, a green-blazed trail continues ahead on the woods road, continuing across the Black River and leading in 0.5 mile to the ruins of the Kay family summer home. The Conifer Pass Trail turns sharply left, leaving the road, and heads south on a footpath high above the river, with the river visible below through the trees to the right. At 1.0 mile, the trail joins a grassy woods road which turns sharply right and begins to descend. Just beyond the sharp turn, the trail turns left, leaving the road, and starts to descend to the river level.

The next section of the trail is especially picturesque, with the trail following closely along the Black River as it proceeds through a rocky gorge. After turning slightly away from the river to bypass rapids, the trail reaches a more placid section of the river at 1.3 miles. It now bears left, leaving the river gorge, and begins a rather steep climb. After passing two mine pits to the left, the grade moderates. The trail reaches a rocky area at the crest of a rise at 1.5 miles and descends on switchbacks through firs to cross Cedar Brook in an open area. It

then climbs gradually through a spruce-and-pine forest, with an understory of ferns, and crosses paved Pottersville Road at 1.7 miles. It turns right at a cairn and ends, 1.9 miles from the start of the trail, at a junction with the Bamboo Brook Trail (blue). To the

Figure 10-4. Rapids on the Black River

left, the Bamboo Brook Trail leads back to the Kay Environmental Center and can be used to complete a loop hike. Straight ahead, the Bamboo Brook Trail leads to the Bamboo Brook Outdoor Education Center and the Willowwood Arboretum.

Hacklebarney State Park

Situated about three miles southwest of Chester, Hacklebarney State Park includes a section of the deep hemlock-and-boulder-lined glacial gorge of the Black River. The park is traversed by a system of footpaths, but the trails are not marked. Its topography, with its ridges of gneiss, is rugged. The highest elevation on the west side of the Black River is 804 feet. Wildlife in the park includes bear, bobcat, deer, and coyote. Of the 893 acres in the park, 273 acres are dedicated to hiking and the remainder to hunting. The Lamington Natural Area portion of the park protects the gorge and endangered plant species.

One story about the origin of the park's name states that a quick-tempered iron ore foreman in the vicinity was persistently heckled, and soon *Heckle Barney*, as he was called, became Hacklebarney. Another theory is that the name is of Lenni Lenape derivation, meaning "to put wood on a fire on the ground," that is, a bonfire.

A suggested 2.8-mile loop hike begins at the parking area. Backtrack along the park entrance road to a gated gravel road that heads uphill at a "Smoky the Bear" sign. Turn sharply left onto this gravel road, and bear left at a fork in 350

feet. After passing a side trail to an overlook, the road reaches a clearing at a playground. At the end of the clearing, turn right in front of a park bench onto a wide dirt road (do not follow the paved path behind the bench). After a brief climb, the trail descends gradually along the side of a hill. It curves sharply left, descends stone steps, and soon begins to parallel Rhinehart Brook.

At the next junction, turn right and cross a wooden bridge over the brook, then bear left and follow the trail uphill, with the brook to the left. Turn left at the following intersection and descend to the Black River. After crossing two footbridges over tributary streams, the graded trail ends. Continue along the river for another half mile, following a narrow, rocky footpath, which may be indistinct in places, keeping the river to the right. The trail briefly joins a gravel road, but continues ahead on a footpath where the road ends. After passing a restroom building to the left in a picnic area, the trail joins a gravel road which curves left. Continue for about 100 feet beyond a footbridge over a stream and turn right onto a footpath that soon crosses the stream on another footbridge. Ahead, to the right, follow a rocky path which curves to the left and soon becomes wider and smoother.

After passing through a hemlock forest high above the Black River, the trail reaches a junction with a gravel fire road. Turn left and follow this road to a bridge over Trout Brook. Turn left, cross the bridge, then turn right and continue along the river to the parking area, bearing right at the next intersection.

To reach Hacklebarney State Park, take County 513 west for 1.3 miles from its intersection with US 206 in Chester, passing the entrance to Cooper Mill Park on the left. Immediately after crossing the bridge over the Black River, turn left, then turn sharply left onto State Park Road. Follow this road, with the Black River on the left, for 1.8 miles, then bear right where the road continues straight ahead unpaved. Continue for another 0.6 mile to the park entrance on the left.

For more information, contact Hacklebarney State Park, RD 2, Long Valley, NJ 07853; (908) 879-5677; www.njparksandforests.org.

THE FARNY HIGHLANDS

Nestled between I-80 and NJ 23 in north central New Jersey lie 35,000 acres of rugged land known as the Farny Highlands. Headwater streams flow through the area to reach, ultimately, the Passaic, Delaware, and Hudson river basins. In

the process, they not only supply clean drinking water to one-third of New Jersey residents, but also make the region a waterscape and a forested, mountainous landscape. About two-thirds of the area is public open space, including Farny State Park, Mahlon Dickerson Reservation, Wildcat Ridge and Weldon Brook wildlife management areas, Pyramid Mountain Natural Historical Area, watershed lands, and reservoirs.

Ecologically, this area supports a vast array of wildlife: bobcat, black bear, otter, mink, porcupine, native brook trout, timber rattlesnake, coyote, wood turtle, and wood rat. Birders can find 21 varieties of warblers, along with vireos, flycatchers, and owls. Seven species of hawks breed in the area. In the spring and summer, whip-poor-wills can be heard calling from the tops of the dry wooded ridges.

Bedrock in the region dates back to Precambrian times. Glacial erratics and extensive boulder fields are common. They are a result of the Wisconsin Glaciation, which receded from this area between 10,000 and 15,000 years ago. Some of the erratics are puddingstone—a conglomerate containing white quartzite pebbles in a purple matrix. Since magnetic iron ore is common in the region, anyone using a compass should question its accuracy.

Relics of the iron mining and smelting industry in the nineteenth century—mine shafts, charcoal pits, forges, tailings, and machinery—dot the area. Forge remnants and cast-off machinery can still be found near old stone walls and cellar holes. Extensive acreage was clear-cut to provide wood for the production of charcoal used to fuel the iron forges.

This section of the chapter describes the trail system adjacent to Green Pond Road (County 513) and the Split Rock Reservoir. Trails in Mahlon Dickerson Reservation and in the Pyramid Mountain Natural Historical Area are described elsewhere in this chapter.

Trails in the Farny Highlands

In 1995, the Morris Land Conservancy conceived the idea of a hiking trail to link the public open spaces in the Farny Highlands and asked the New York-New Jersey Trail Conference for assistance. With support from both the public and private sectors, the Trail Conference began securing public access to private lands and to the Newark and Jersey City watersheds. By 1997, Trail Confer-

ence volunteers had constructed three trails—the Beaver Brook Trail, the Four Birds Trail, and the Split Rock Loop Trail—totaling 32 miles. The Four Birds Trail and the Split Rock Trail are described below; the Beaver Brook Trail is described under Mahlon Dickerson Reservation.

Four Birds Trail   *Length: 19.4 miles Blaze: white*

The 19-mile Four Birds Trail crosses only one paved roadway throughout its course. Views are abundant along the trail year round; however, during the leaf-off seasons, there are views along over half of the trail. Although elevation gains and losses are a maximum of 400 feet, hikers will have plenty of exercise, as the trail ascends and descends over rock outcrops and through boulder fields numerous times along its challenging route.

The trail traverses four principal habitats—mature deciduous forests, lake shore, wetlands, and cliff/rock outcrops. The Four Birds Trail is so named to symbolize the biological diversity encountered along the trail. Wild turkeys, ospreys, great blue herons, and red-tailed hawks are regularly spotted in these four habitats, respectively. Black bear, river otter, white-tailed deer, beaver, and raccoon were also spotted during trail construction. Timber rattlesnakes are known to exist in the area, so caution should be exercised when hiking through the rockier regions of this trail.

The Newark Watershed Conservation and Development Corporation (NWCDC) regulates the use of the northern half of this trail (from Riley's Rise to NJ 23). Hiking and parking permits must be obtained before hiking this stretch of trail. For permits or more information, contact NWCDC by mail at P.O. Box 319, Newfoundland, NJ 07435, or at their office at 223 Echo Lake Road, West Milford, NJ 07480; (973) 697-2850.

There are five access points to the trail. To reach the southern trailhead, take Exit 37 (Hibernia/Rockaway) from I-80. Continue north on Green Pond Road (County 513) for 2.7 miles and turn right onto Lower Hibernia Road. The trailhead is at the end of a signed parking area on the left side of the road, just beyond the intersection. A second access point is at the trail crossing of Split Rock Road. To reach this point from Exit 37 of I-80, take Green Pond Road north for 6.5 miles and turn right onto Upper Hibernia Road. In 1.2 miles, turn left onto Split Rock Road and follow it for 0.7 mile to the trail crossing. Parking is not permitted on Split Rock Road at the trail crossing; however, cars may be parked at a boat launch area, 0.5 mile further east along Split Rock Road.

A third access point is at the trail crossing of Green Pond Road (County 513), 7.4 miles north of Lower Hibernia Road (10.1 miles north of I-80). A gravel parking turnout is on the left, 100 feet north of the trail crossing. (A parking permit is required from NWCDC.) The northern trailhead is located on Green Pond Road, 11.5 miles north of I-80 (and 0.1 mile south of NJ 23). Just before crossing the railroad tracks (heading north on Green Pond Road), turn left onto Bigelow Road. Park in the ballfield parking lot on the left and walk 0.2 mile to the road's end. The trail begins about 100 feet up the dirt road extension on the left. (A parking permit is required from NWCDC.)

Access to the Four Birds Trail is also available from a parking area at the end of the paved section of Upper Hibernia Road via the Flyway Spur Trail and the Beaver Pond Trail, which intersect the Four Birds Trail 2.6 and 3.3 miles, respectively, from its southern trailhead. For descriptions of these trails, see the Wildcat Ridge Wildlife Management Area section, pp. 230-31.

From the southern trailhead, the trail heads north into the woods, passing the ruins of old mine buildings. In 300 feet, it turns left onto a woods road. In another 125 feet, it bears left onto a footpath, then again turns left in 250 feet. (Straight ahead, a side trail leads to the barricaded entrance of the Hibernia Mine—the home of an estimated 26,000 little brown bats—which extends 2,500 feet below ground.) At 0.4 mile, the trail straddles a mining berm, merges with a woods road, and bears left. The ditch alongside the berm once contained the water pipes to Marcella Mine, used to operate the steam-powered machinery. The abandoned Hibernia Cemetery is 360 feet to the right down the woods road. Many immigrant workers in the mines are buried here; the headstones date back to the mid-nineteenth century.

At 1.1 miles, the trail crosses a mine road and begins a moderate descent down to an intermittent stream crossing. After heavy rainfalls, a cascade develops just to the right of the stream crossing. Dreamer's Rock is at 1.5 miles where the trail begins its ascent to the ridge. At 1.8 miles, a yellow-blazed spur trail to the right (south) leads 0.5 mile to Graffiti Cliffs, with views to the west of the Hibernia Valley. The main trail climbs to the ridge, where it crosses a heavily used woods road. Hikers need to stay alert in this area as extensive, illegal use by dirt bikes and ATVs has obscured parts of the trailway.

At 2.6 miles, the Flyway Spur Trail (orange) crosses. To the right, this trail leads 0.1 mile to an observation platform, with a panoramic view of the Rockaway Valley. To the left, it leads in 0.8 mile to a parking area at the end of Upper Hibernia Road. Just beyond, the Four Birds Trail crosses a gravel road.

To the right, this road leads to a television transmission tower. The Four Birds Trail now begins a steady descent. At the base of the descent, at 3.1 miles, the trail crosses a stream on rocks and begins a steady climb.

The Beaver Pond Trail (red), which leads in 0.5 mile to a parking area at the end of Upper Hibernia Road, leaves to the left at 3.3 miles. After crossing a woods road, the Four Birds Trail crosses a stream and begins a steep climb. At the top of the climb, at 3.7 miles, a rock outcrop to the right of the trail provides a limited view to the southeast. The trail now descends gently, then climbs briefly to reach, at 4.0 miles, the southern terminus of the Split Rock Loop Trail (blue), which leaves to the right.

The Four Birds Trail now descends, passing on the way a huge glacial erratic to the right of the trail. At the base of the descent, at 4.1 miles, the trail crosses a woods road and a stream. The trail now climbs, crosses under power lines, then turns left and parallels the power lines. After turning right, away from the power lines, the trail reaches dirt Split Rock Road at 4.6 miles. Parking is not permitted along Split Rock Road at the trail crossing, but cars may be parked at a boat launch parking area 0.5 mile to the right.

After crossing the road, the Four Birds Trail makes a short, steep climb up a rock outcrop, then descends gradually, with views of Split Rock Reservoir to the right. The trail crosses a woods road, then crosses a stream on rocks at 5.0 miles to enter a region locally known as the Bumps. The trail now steeply climbs a rock outcrop and continues along a rocky escarpment overlooking a gorge to the right. Soon, views open up over the reservoir to the right. The trail bears left and again climbs a rock outcrop, then continues along another rocky escarpment overlooking the reservoir.

At 5.5 miles, the trail bears left, away from the reservoir. It levels off and soon crosses a woods road. Then, at 5.9 miles, the trail begins a steep climb of a large rock outcrop—the highest point in the Bumps. The summit, reached at 6.1 miles, provides a view to the south. The trail now descends, recrossing the woods road. After another level stretch, the trail climbs a switchback to regain the ridge above the reservoir. It passes a small granite monument to the left at 7.1 miles. Just beyond, it goes through an area where some trees have grown to an impressive size. The largest specimen, Sentinel Oak, is a majestic red oak nearly four feet in diameter.

The Four Birds Trail comes down to reach the shore of the reservoir at 7.3 miles. Here, the trail bears left and begins to parallel the reservoir, crossing its inlet stream at 7.5 miles. The trail now continues parallel to the reservoir, but

further away from the water. At 8.1 miles, the trail again approaches the reservoir. It bears left at 8.4 miles, with a panoramic view of the reservoir from a rocky point to the right of the trail.

After crossing a rocky area at 8.8 miles, the trail reaches a woods road that leads down to the reservoir. Soon afterwards, it bears left, away from the reservoir. It begins to climb at 9.5 miles, reaching the top of Riley's Rise at 9.7 miles. As the trail descends, Tom-Tom Lookout, at 9.8 miles, offers a view east across the valley to Indian Cliffs, over which the Split Rock Loop Trail runs.

At 9.9 miles, the Four Birds Trail crosses a red-blazed woods road. Then, at 10.0 miles, it reaches the northern terminus of the Split Rock Loop Trail, which leaves to the right. After crossing a woods road at 10.3 miles, the Four Birds Trail begins a gradual climb of Big Bear Peak, reaching its high point—marked by a cairn—at 10.6 miles. The trail now descends to cross a stream at 11.0 miles. It continues along undulating terrain, passing through gaps in several stone walls and then paralleling another stone wall. After crossing a rocky area, it bears left to continue along a long rock outcrop, then proceeds through dense mountain laurel thickets.

The Four Birds Trail crosses dirt Timberbrook Road at 11.6 miles. (A left turn on Timberbrook Road leads, in 0.8 mile, to the main entrance of the Winnebago Scout Reservation.) The trail heads southwest and descends to reach Timber Brook Lake at 12.0 miles. This feature may appear as either a lake or a swamp, depending upon current beaver activity. (In the summer of 2003, the southern end of the lake resembled a swamp, with many dead trees, while the water level was higher at the northern end.) Here, a yellow-blazed trail leaves to the left. The Four Birds Trail turns right and follows a rocky footpath parallel to, but some distance away from, the lake shore.

After crossing two stone walls, the Four Birds Trail emerges onto a dirt road near the north end of the lake. It continues along the lake shore until it reaches a beaver dam at the outlet of the lake at 12.5 miles. The Four Birds Trail crosses the outlet stream on rocks just below the dam. It soon bears right, away from the lake, and crosses a wide woods road—the abandoned right-of-way of the Wharton and Northern Railroad. The trail reenters the woods, crosses another woods road, and crosses a stream on a split-log bridge.

At 13.1 miles, after crossing a gravel road, the Four Birds Trail bears left and begins to climb Copperas Mountain. The ascent is gradual at first, but steepens at 13.5 miles. After a short level stretch, the trail ascends very steeply to reach the crest of the ridge on Copperas Mountain at 13.8 miles. Here, there is

Figure 10-5. Charlotteburg Reservoir from the Four Birds Trail

a panoramic viewpoint over the Charlotteburg Reservoir from a rock ledge to the right of the trail, with NJ 23 visible in the distance to the north.

The Four Birds Trail turns right onto a grassy woods road at 13.9 miles. It follows this road along the ridge of Copperas Mountain for about half a mile, bearing right at a fork at 14.0 miles. At 14.4 miles, a short side trail leads to another east-facing viewpoint over the Charlotteburg Reservoir. Then, at 14.5 miles, the trail turns left, leaving the woods road, and descends along the western face of the mountain on a wide footpath. After crossing a woods road at 15.0 miles, the footpath narrows.

At 15.6 miles, the trail emerges onto paved Green Pond Road (County 513), where parking is available in a small turnout on the west side of the road, just north of the trail crossing. The Four Birds Trail crosses the road, enters a small tamarack/spruce forest, and follows a berm. It crosses several streams as it winds its way to the foot of Green Pond Mountain at 16.2 miles. After climbing, the trail reaches Notch Road at 16.6 miles and turns right. It follows this road for 900 feet and then turns right onto a narrower woods road. At 17.2 miles, the trail makes a sharp left off the road, re-entering the forest. The trail descends and, at 17.5 miles, crosses another woods road. After crossing a small stream, the trail reaches the base of cliffs at 17.7 miles. The trail bears

right and begins a moderately steep ascent, reaching, at 18.1 miles, the ridge with views from White Pine Bluff. The trail follows the ledges and turns away from the edge of the escarpment to weave

Figure 10-6. Four Birds Trail along the ridge of Green Pond Mountain

its way through an old upland pasture delineated by a series of stone walls. The Four Birds Trail descends to its northern terminus near NJ 23 in Newfoundland at 19.4 miles, where parking is available.

Split Rock Loop Trail   Length: 7.8 miles Blaze: blue

Passing through the high country to the south and east of Split Rock Reservoir, the Split Rock Loop Trail completes a loop with the Four Birds Trail. The terrain along this route is rockier and more abrupt than that found on the western side of the reservoir, and the grades of the hiking trails tend to be steeper. The views afforded the hiker on this trail far surpass those from the western shore. The Split Rock Loop Trail may be combined with a section of the Four Birds Trail to form a challenging 13.4-mile loop hike.

To reach the Split Rock Loop Trail from Exit 37 of I-80, take Green Pond Road (County 513) north for 6.5 miles and turn right onto Upper Hibernia Road. In 1.2 miles, turn left onto Split Rock Road. The crossing of the Four Birds Trail (which leads south 0.6 mile to the southern trailhead of the Split Rock Loop Trail) is reached at 0.7 mile, and the Split Rock Loop Trail crossing is at 1.5 miles. Parking is not permitted along Split Rock Road at either trail crossing; however, cars may be parked at a boat launch area, 0.5 mile east of the Four Birds Trail crossing and 0.3 mile west of the crossing of the Split Rock Loop Trail.

The southern trailhead of the Split Rock Loop Trail is on the Four Birds Trail (white), 0.6 mile south of Split Rock Road. The Split Rock Loop Trail heads east, winding its way through a scrub oak and hickory forest to reach, at 0.2 mile, a seasonal viewpoint. The trail descends through a more mature forest along an outcrop to a boulder-strewn glen at 0.5 mile. Entering the Maze at 0.7

mile, the trail snakes its way through large glacially deposited boulders, some of which are only several feet apart. After crossing an abandoned mine road, the trail passes over a massive finger of mine tailings and enters a mixed hardwood forest. The trail descends to cross a stream at 1.0 mile. Care should be taken in crossing the stream, particularly during periods of high water. If the marked route is impassable, other crossings can be found upstream.

At 1.2 miles, the Split Rock Loop Trail passes Cedar Point, with unobstructed views down the river valley, and crosses a rocky slope where, at the height of land, there are abundant views to the south. The trail continues through typical Highlands terrain, climbing rock outcrops and descending into small ravines with seasonal streams. After the next high point at 2.1 miles, the trail gently descends through a young forest before going under power lines.

The Split Rock Trail crosses dirt Split Rock Road at 2.3 miles. Parking is not permitted along Split Rock Road; however, cars may be parked at a boat launch area 0.3 mile to the west. The Split Rock Loop Trail heads north, meandering through a hardwood forest and remaining in sight of the reservoir. After reaching a shoreline vista over the reservoir, the trail heads uphill. At 3.3 miles, it crosses Charlotteburg Road, climbs a hill, and turns sharply to the left. The stone walls, cedars, and trees with broad full crowns suggest that this area was once open pasture.

At 3.8 miles, the trail reaches a balanced glacial erratic and passes a mine pit with scattered tailings. Continuing along the ridge, at a left turn in the trail, a short side trail leads right to a rock outcrop with a limited view of Buck Mountain. After climbing a small boulder-strewn ridge and descending slightly through a grassy understory, the trail reaches another side trail to the right at 4.3 miles. This side trail descends steeply, then climbs steeply to the open crest of Double D Peak, with 360° views. The Split Rock Loop Trail turns left shortly after the junction with the second side trail and descends through a mixed hardwood forest. At 4.9 miles, the trail crosses a stream on stepping stones and, over the course of a mile, passes over three ridges, with west-facing views from the last two ridges. The trail crosses Charlotteburg Road at 6.4 miles and closely parallels the shoreline, with views of the small wooded islands in the reservoir. It crosses Charlotteburg Road again and ascends Indian Cliffs. The trail briefly merges with a woods road at 6.8 miles and climbs along ledges to reach the pinnacle of Indian Cliffs, with the best views of the reservoir.

After descending steeply, at 7.3 miles, the Split Rock Trail follows the base of the cliffs past several huge boulders before turning right. It crosses

Charlotteburg Road for the last time and enters a small tama-rack (larch) forest. Commonly referred to as a deciduous evergreen, the larch loses its needles in the fall after turn-ing a beautiful shade of yellow. The trail reaches Misty Pond, formed and maintained by beavers. Care should be taken in this area, as occasionally beaver stop gnaw-ing through a tree, leaving it precariously balanced on a thin spindle of wood. The trail leaves Misty Pond and be-gins a moderate climb, ending at the Four Birds Trail at 7.8 miles.

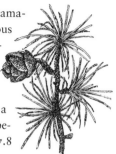

Figure 10-7. Larch

Wildcat Ridge Wildlife Management Area

The 2,994-acre Wildcat Ridge Wildlife Management Area features a multitude of wildlife. At the southern end, the abandoned and barricaded Hibernia Mine—on the Four Birds Trail, just east of Green Pond Road (County 513)—is the home of an estimated 26,000 little brown bats. The Beaver Pond Trail passes beaver-created wetlands, the focal point for many other wildlife species, includ-ing muskrats, otters, raccoons, and waterfowl. An observation platform at the end of the Flyway Spur Trail offers the opportunity to observe migrating hawks in the spring and fall. Three short trails traverse the area, and they can be combined with an 0.7-mile section of the Four Birds Trail (white) to form a 2.2-mile loop hike.

To reach the Wildcat Ridge Wildlife Management Area, take I-80 to Exit 37 (Hibernia/Rockaway). Continue north on Green Pond Road (County 513) for 6.5 miles and turn right onto Upper Hibernia Road. Continue on Upper Hibernia Road for 2.5 miles to the end of the paved section of the road. For the trailheads of the Beaver Pond Trail and the Connector Trail, turn left just beyond Brunache Road and park in a wide gravel area. For the trailhead of the Flyway Spur Trail, continue on the gravel extension of Upper Hibernia Road for another 0.2 mile to a signed parking area on the right side of the road.

For more information, contact New Jersey DEP, Division of Fish and Wildlife, 501 East State Street, P.O. Box 400, Trenton, NJ 08625; (609) 984-0547; www.njfishandwildlife.org.

Beaver Pond Trail   *Length: 0.5 mile Blaze: red*
The Beaver Pond Trail offers the shortest route from the parking area to the

Four Birds Trail on the ridge. Its trailhead is at the northeast corner of the wide gravel parking area just beyond the end of the paved section of Upper Hibernia Road. The trail enters the woods at a large glacial erratic and proceeds ahead on a gravel road, with an abandoned building of the Marcella Mine to the left. After passing Beaver Pond to the left at 0.1 mile, the trail bears right and climbs on a footpath to reach a south-facing viewpoint from a split rock to the right at 0.3 mile. The Beaver Pond Trail now descends to end, 0.5 mile from its start, at a junction with the Four Birds Trail (white). To the right, the Four Birds Trail leads in 0.7 mile to the Flyway Spur Trail (orange), which may be used as an alternate return route.

Connector Trail   *Length: 0.2 mile Blaze: yellow*
A short trail that links the Beaver Pond Trail (red) with the Flyway Spur Trail, the Connector Trail begins near the southwest corner of the wide gravel parking area just beyond the end of the paved section of Upper Hibernia Road. It heads south on a relatively level footpath, running parallel to and just east of the gravel extension of Upper Hibernia Road. At 0.1 mile, it turns right and begins to run along a berm that parallels a ditch—once used to carry a wooden conduit that supplied water to the Marcella Mine complex. The Connector Trail ends at 0.2 mile on a gravel road. Across the road, just to the left, is the trailhead of the Flyway Spur Trail (orange).

Flyway Spur Trail   *Length: 0.9 mile Blaze: orange*
Beginning on the south side of a gravel road that heads uphill from the southern end of the signed parking area on the west side of the gravel extension of Upper Hibernia Road, the Flyway Spur Trail heads south on a woods road. At 0.2 mile, it begins to climb. After traversing an exposed bedrock slab with glacial striations, the trail begins to descend, passing a rail with a pointed tip embedded in the ground alongside the trail (an old boundary marker). The trail goes through a valley, climbs rather steeply, crosses a woods road at 0.5 mile, and levels off.

At 0.8 mile, the Flyway Spur Trail crosses the Four Birds Trail (white). To the left, the Four Birds Trail leads 0.7 mile to the Beaver Pond Trail (red), which can be used as an alternate return route. The Flyway Spur Trail continues to end, 0.9 mile from its start, at the Hawk Watch Overlook, where an observation platform affords a panoramic view over the Rockaway Valley. On a clear day, the New York City skyline is visible in the distance to the left.

FRELINGHUYSEN ARBORETUM

In the late nineteenth century, Morristown was a fashionable summer address for prominent families. In 1891, George and Sarah Frelinghuysen built a Colonial Revival-style summer home and carriage house, naming it Whippany Farm. Their daughter, Matilda, inherited the property, turned it into a public arboretum and, in 1969, bequeathed the estate to Morris County. The 127-acre tract is known for its rose garden and other floral displays. The Frelinghuysen Mansion, an official historic site, houses the administrative headquarters of the Morris County Park Commission. The site includes several self-guiding nature trails which can be combined to form loop hikes. A section of the Patriots' Path (white) also traverses the property.

To reach the Arboretum from I-287 north, take Exit 36A. Proceed east in the center lane of Morris Avenue, and turn left onto Whippany Road. Continue to the second light, and make a left turn onto East Hanover Avenue. The entrance to the arboretum is on the left, opposite the Morris County Library. From I-287 south, take Exit 36 and follow signs for Ridgedale Avenue. Bear right on the exit ramp, and turn right at the traffic light onto Ridgedale Avenue. At the first traffic light, make a right turn onto East Hanover Avenue. The entrance to the Arboretum is on the right, opposite the Morris County Library. For more information, contact the Morris County Park Commission, 53 East Hanover Avenue, P.O. Box 1295, Morristown, NJ 07962-1295; (973) 326-7600; www.morrisparks.com.

THE GREAT SWAMP

The Great Swamp was created about 10,000 years ago when the melting waters of the Wisconsin Glacier poured into the Passaic Valley, forming the Glacial Lake Passaic. As the lake drained northward, it formed the Passaic River, leaving the Great Swamp behind.

In 1708, members of the Delaware Nation exchanged a 30,000-acre tract, including the Great Swamp, for a barrel of rum, 15 kettles, four pistols, four cutlasses, plus other goods, and 30 pounds cash. Settlements began to dot the area and, by 1844, farms appeared on the cleared uplands. As the small farms became uneconomical, they disappeared. Gradually, much of the cleared uplands reverted to woodlands, and the lower flat areas again became wet.

In 1959, the Great Swamp was proposed as the site for a New York metropolitan area airport. An alliance of concerned citizens and local and national conservation groups waged an extended battle and halted the construction. Their efforts raised more than a million dollars to purchase 3,000 acres which were donated to the U.S. Department of the Interior to establish the Great Swamp National Wildlife Refuge. Subsequently, more acreage has been added to the original tract. In 1968, under the Wilderness Act of 1964, Congress designated the eastern portion as a wilderness area. Today, the Great Swamp includes over 8,000 acres of protected public land.

Despite its name, the Great Swamp is not entirely swampland, but rather a mixture of marshes, meadows, dry woodlands, and brush-covered swamps. It is the intermingling of these four habitats that gives the Great Swamp its unique character. A difference of only one foot in elevation can result in dry woodlands instead of marshland. This diversity of terrain and habitat allows the Great Swamp to support a wide variety of plant and animal life.

Plants varying in size from tiny duckweed to the towering red oak are visible from the trails and boardwalks. Here, one will find some 300 species of birds, mammals, reptiles, amphibians, and fish. There are approximately 600 species of plants, including 215 species of wildflowers. The yellow marsh marigold in early April, the blue iris in May, and the pink-and-white mountain laurel in June are great attractions. The 26 threatened or endangered species include the bog turtle, wood turtle, and blue-spotted salamander. Of the more than 200 species of birds that are found in the Great Swamp, over 90 nest there.

Great Swamp National Wildlife Refuge

Over nine miles of trails meander through the federally administered 7,500-acre portion of the Great Swamp. The refuge's mission is to provide migrating, nesting, and feeding habitat for migratory birds. It also provides environmental education and compatible recreation opportunities. The Wildlife Observation Center provides wetland vistas and offers opportunities for wildlife observation and photography. The refuge also offers interpretive displays, an information kiosk, and two handicapped-accessible boardwalks that lead into the Great Swamp.

To reach the Great Swamp National Wildlife Refuge, take I-287 to Exit 30A and continue on North Maple Avenue to the traffic light at Madisonville Road. Turn left at the traffic light and follow the signs for the refuge. Maps are available at the refuge headquarters. For more information, contact the Great

Swamp National Wildlife Refuge, 152 Pleasant Plains Road, Basking Ridge, NJ 07920; (973) 425-1222; http://greatswamp.fws.gov.

Great Swamp Outdoor Education Center

Dedicated in 1963, the Great Swamp Outdoor Education Center is administered by the Morris County Park Commission. The 42-acre park is on the eastern edge of the Great Swamp, off Southern Boulevard in Chatham Township. Four short loop trails, each of which includes sections of boardwalk traversing wet areas, enable visitors to explore the various habitats. A handicapped-accessible boardwalk leads to a wildlife observation blind overlooking a pond. Environmental programs are offered at the Outdoor Education Center.

To reach the Great Swamp Outdoor Education Center, proceed west on NJ 124 from Chatham and turn left onto Fairmount Avenue. Turn right on Southern Boulevard and continue for about one mile to a sign that marks the road leading to the Outdoor Education Center. For more information, contact the Morris County Park Com-

Figure 10-8. Boardwalk through the Great Swamp

mission, 53 East Hanover Avenue, P.O. Box 1295, Morristown, NJ 07962-1295; (973) 326-7600; www.morrisparks.com.

Lord Stirling Park

The Somerset County Park Commission administers 900 acres on the western border of the Great Swamp National Wildlife Refuge. It was originally the location of the estate of William Alexander, the so-called Lord Stirling (whose title was legitimate but was never recognized by Parliament). Alexander served with distinction as an officer in the Revolutionary War. His estate was one of the grandest in the middle colonies. Alexander also owned vast tracts of moun-

tain land, including one on the New York-New Jersey border, which still bears his name: Sterling Forest.

In addition to an environmental education center, over eight miles of hiking trails loop their way around and through 450 acres, providing visitors with opportunities to visit a variety of habitats. A short boardwalk trail is handicapped accessible. The remaining acres are for equestrian use only. For more information, contact the Somerset County Park Commission, 190 Lord Stirling Road, Basking Ridge, NJ 07920; (908) 766-2489; www.park.co.somerset.nj.us.

HEDDEN COUNTY PARK

The original 40 acres of Hedden County Park were donated by the Hedden family of Dover in 1963, and in the ensuing years, its size has been increased to 380 acres. Five blazed footpaths traverse the park, including the Hedden Circular Trail (white), which loops around the central portion of the park, and the Indian Falls Trail (green), which passes an attractive waterfall.

To reach the park, take US 46 West in Dover. After the hospital, make a left onto Hurd Street. Turn left on Oak Street, and continue a short distance to Ford Street and the park entrance. For more information, contact the Morris County Park Commission, 53 East Hanover Avenue, P.O. Box 1295, Morristown, NJ 07962-1295; (973) 326-7600; www.morrisparks.com.

JOCKEY HOLLOW

It was to Jockey Hollow in January 1777 that George Washington brought his troops after their successful campaign against the Hessians at Trenton and the British at Princeton. The natural fortifications of the hills and ready source of supplies gave the army a chance to rest and regroup before the summer's campaign. The troops returned to Jockey Hollow during the winter of 1779-80, during which time 28 storms blasted the area, keeping critical supply routes closed. The bitter cold weather added more hardships to a commander already plagued with the inability to pay for supplies. In May 1780, the Marquis de Lafayette arrived with the news that 6,000 French troops were en route to Rhode Island. Washington began to rebuild his starved and threadbare army.

Connected by a hiking-only branch of the Patriots' Path, each of the three adjacent parks offers something different. Sitting on the southern edge of a

terminal moraine, Morristown National Historical Park offers an extensive network of well-graded trails that pass features of historical significance. Lewis Morris County Park has recreational facilities and trails for hikers, bikers, and horses. Birders will find a haven at the New Jersey Audubon Society's Scherman-Hoffman Sanctuaries, which also has a small network of hiking trails.

Morristown National Historical Park

Jockey Hollow, Fort Nonsense, and the Jacob Ford Mansion were of importance during the American Revolution. Today, they are part of the Morristown National Historical Park, created in 1935 as the nation's first national historical park. The 1,200-acre Jockey Hollow Encampment Area housed 10,000 soldiers of the Continental Army during the winter of 1779-80. The ample forests in the area provided wood to construct soldiers' huts and heat them, and the summit of Mount Kemble afforded a lookout point from which scouts could watch over the lowlands to the east to detect the movement of British troops. The reconstructed log huts are typical of hundreds once used as quarters for officers and men. The restored Wick House, built about 1750, served as military quarters for Major General Arthur St. Clair during the encampment of 1779–80.

Figure 10-9. Wick House

A 1937 reconstruction of Fort Nonsense is located north of the encampment area. Just why the place is called Fort Nonsense has been forgotten. One story says that the soldiers building it felt the project was merely labor meant to keep them busy, and as such was "Nonsense." The Jacob Ford Mansion, which served as Washington's headquarters during the 1779–80 encampment, is located just off I-287 in Morristown and includes an historical museum.

The Cross Estate Gardens, located at the New Jersey Brigade Encampment Area on Old Jockey Hollow Road, has parking for larger groups. The house, built in 1905, is not open to the public. The estate includes a carriage house, a five-story water tower, and a gatehouse. In 1929, Julia Cross made extensive improvements to the gardens, which included a formal walled garden and a native plant area. Volunteers of the New Jersey Historical Garden Federation maintain the gardens, which are open daily. The gardens also serve as an access point to the Patriots' Path.

To reach the Jockey Hollow section of Morristown National Historical Park, take I-287 to Exit 30B. At the first traffic light, turn right onto US 202 and proceed north for 1.8 miles. Turn left at the traffic light onto Tempe Wick Road, and continue for 1.4 miles to the park entrance on the right. The Visitor Center parking area is just ahead, and the Trail Center parking area, where most of the trails begin, can be reached by following the Tour Road past the Wick House and the soldiers' huts, and then turning right onto Jockey Hollow Road at a circular restroom building. NJ Transit trains from Hoboken and from Penn Station in New York City run to Morristown and Bernardsville, from where a taxi can be taken to Jockey Hollow. It is also possible to walk to the trailheads of the Patriots' Path from these railroad stations. An admission fee is payable at the Visitor Center, where maps and brochures are available.

For more information, contact Morristown National Historical Park, 30 Washington Place, Morristown, NJ 07960; (973) 539-2085; www.nps.gov/morr, or call the Jockey Hollow Visitor Center at (973) 543-4030.

Natural History

The 1779-80 encampment of the Continental Army at Jockey Hollow had a profound effect on the vegetation in the area. The forests were cut down for wood to build the soldiers' huts and to heat them over the harsh winter. In the intervening 200 years—and especially since the creation of the park in 1935—the forests have grown back. Today, two distinct types of forest may be seen within the park.

On Mount Kemble, on the eastern side of Jockey Hollow Road, forests that regenerated after the army left are now mature mixed hardwood forests, with a diversity of tree species. However, on the western side of Jockey Hollow Road, much of the land was kept cleared for agriculture by the families that had settled the land just prior to the Revolution. This land was slowly abandoned and started back on the path to forest in the late 1800s and early 1900s. Today, much of this forest is dominated by fast-growing trees that are more characteristic of young forests—ashes, tulip poplar, sassafras, and black locust (a species not native to New Jersey, but widely introduced by colonists for its superior qualities). These forests have also been heavily invaded by several exotic species; indeed, virtually all the plants growing in the understory of these forests are not native to New Jersey or the United States, and would not have been part of the forests that the soldiers encountered.

The historical forest—the resource that General Washington sought for his troops—can be reconstructed by examining the deeds for the farms in the area written just before the Revolution. At that time, large trees were used to identify property boundaries, and the names and locations of these boundary trees were recorded as part of the land descriptions in deeds. By tabulating all the trees named in these deeds, an idea of the composition of the original (pre-settlement) forest can be developed. A study of the deeds to the farms in Jockey Hollow shows that oaks (red, white, and black), chestnuts, and hickories were the common large trees in the 1740s. Unfortunately, chestnuts are now gone from our forests, a victim of the chestnut blight. But the other species are still dominant in parts of the area, and can give us an inkling of what the soldiers saw when they arrived—in two feet of snow in December 1777—to set up camp for the winter.

Trails in Morristown National Historical Park

There are over 15 miles of trails in the national historical park, most of which follow gentle grades along woods roads. Many trails have names which commemorate historical events that took place in the area (such as the New York Brigade Trail) or designate geographic features (such as the Mount Kemble Loop Trail). In addition, five loop trails, of varying length and difficulty, have been marked with colored blazes. Four of these trails begin at the Trail Center parking area, while one is more easily accessed from the Visitor Center parking area. A hiking-only branch of the Patriots' Path, which extends from the New

Jersey Audubon Society's Scherman-Hoffman Sanctuaries on Hardscrabble Road in Bernardsville to Lewis Morris County Park on Mendham Road, also passes through the park. Most of the blazed trails are co-aligned with the named trails for all or part of their route.

Small park maps are displayed on numbered signposts at all trail intersections, with each map including an arrow that indicates the hiker's current location. These numbered signposts are referred to in the trail descriptions that follow.

Aqueduct Trail   *Length: 1.5 miles Blaze: green*

The Aqueduct Trail, which closely parallels Primrose Brook for most of its length, is a self-guided interpretive loop trail that starts and ends at the Trail Center parking area. Copies of a trail map and guide are available at the bulletin board in the parking area, and lettered posts along the trail correspond to the descriptions contained in the guide. The trail highlights the features of the Morris Aqueduct Water System that was built in 1890 to supply the Town of Morristown with a dependable supply of pure water. It is blazed only in the clockwise direction, following the alphabetical order of the lettered posts.

To reach the start of the Aqueduct Trail from the Trail Center parking area, proceed south from signpost #35 on a gravel path, the route of the Yellow Trail. In 225 feet, after crossing a wooden bridge over Primrose Brook, the Aqueduct Trail begins to the right (signpost #36). It follows a woods road that parallels Primrose Brook, passing signpost #54 and reaching signpost #53 at 0.4 mile. Here, the trail bears left and immediately crosses the route of the 1890 aqueduct (signpost "F"). It soon begins a gentle climb and reaches a complex junction (signpost #50) at 0.7 mile. The Aqueduct Trail turns sharply right, descends log steps, crosses a wooden bridge over Primrose Brook, and turns right to follow a narrow path, with the brook on the right.

At 0.8 mile, the trail passes a huge tulip tree to the left and crosses the brook on a wooden bridge. In the next 0.3 mile, the trail crosses the brook four more times and utilizes puncheons to cross several wet areas. The Aqueduct Trail again reaches signpost #53 at 1.1 miles. Here, it turns left, following the sign "To Aqueduct Stop N." After crossing the brook once more, the Aqueduct Trail turns right at signpost #37 (also signpost "P") onto the route of the Patriots' Path (blue path-and-tree logo on white). It twice more crosses Primrose Brook on wooden bridges and ends, at 1.5 miles, at the Trail Center parking area (signpost #36).

Blue Trail   *Length: 2.7 miles Blaze: blue*

Combining portions of several named trails, the Blue Trail offers an attractive loop hike from the Trail Center parking area, passing the only expansive viewpoint in the park.

The Blue Trail begins at signpost #26, about 100 feet north of the parking area, just west of a stream that parallels Jockey Hollow Road. It crosses the stream on a wooden footbridge, turns left, and follows a narrow dirt path that heads north, with the stream to the left and the paved road to the right. Soon, the trail bears right and climbs above the stream, continuing to parallel the road to the right.

At 0.3 mile (signpost #24), the trail turns left and follows the paved road for about 200 feet, then turns right just before a circular restroom building, passing signpost #23 by a locked gate. It continues ahead on a rocky woods road, designated the New York Brigade Trail, and descends gradually. After crossing a bridge over a stream, it reaches signpost #22, where it joins the Grand Loop Trail (white), which comes in from the right. The joint white/blue trail follows a wide dirt road and passes a small pond on the right. A bench has been placed here, making it an attractive spot for a break.

The trail reaches a T intersection, marked by signpost #10, at 0.8 mile. Here, the Grand Loop Trail leaves to the left, while the Blue Trail turns right, crosses a bridge over a stream, and begins a gradual ascent. It bears right at the next Y intersection (signpost #11) and continues to climb. Then, at signpost #12, it bears left, joining the Mount Kemble Loop Trail. At 1.2 miles, the Blue Trail passes a locked gate (signpost #14) and reaches a T intersection.

The Blue Trail turns right, passing a private house to the left (here, the trail follows the park boundary). Just ahead, the Blue Trail first bears left at a Y intersection, then proceeds straight ahead, passing another locked gate and signpost #15 (do not follow the road that descends to the left). At 1.5 miles, it passes a stone monument and an interpretive sign which commemorate Stark's Brigade. Just beyond, the trail reaches an expansive east-facing viewpoint, accompanied by an interpretive sign, on the left side of the trail. The Watchung Mountains may be seen in the distance.

The Blue Trail now begins to descend. It continues ahead at signpost #16, where an unmarked path goes off to the left, but turns sharply left at signpost #17, following a sign for the Camp Road Trail. It reaches the next intersection, marked by signpost #19, at 2.2 miles. Here, the Blue Trail turns sharply right, joining the Camp Road Trail (shown on the park map as the Old Camp Road

Trail). After descending some more, the Blue Trail reaches signpost #20, where the Grand Loop Trail and the Patriots' Path join from the left.

All three trails continue ahead, crossing a stream on a wooden bridge. Just beyond, the Grand Loop Trail leaves to the right at signpost #21. The Blue Trail, together with the Patriots' Path, continues ahead, reaching a locked gate (signpost #27) at paved Jockey Hollow Road at 2.7 miles. The Trail Center parking area is just to the left.

Grand Loop Trail   *Length: 5.3 miles Blaze: white*

The Grand Loop Trail is the longest of the park's marked trails. It circles the core area of the park, passing through hardwood forests and over rolling hills.

To reach the start of the Grand Loop Trail from the Visitor Center parking area, walk through the Visitor Center, exiting the back door, and continue ahead to a T junction, opposite the Wick Farm. Turn left here, following a wide grassy road and passing the Wick House. Continue ahead downhill, cross a paved road, and proceed straight ahead along another paved road. Near the bottom of the hill, before reaching Tempe Wick Road, turn right at a sign to the Grand Loop Trail. (It is 0.3 mile from the Visitor Center to the start of the Grand Loop Trail.)

Upon reaching the white-blazed Grand Loop Trail, turn right and proceed uphill for 0.2 mile. This is the steepest climb on the trail and is not typical of the terrain on the remainder of the trail. The trail levels off and descends to reach a junction (signpost #3) at 0.4 mile. Here, the trail bears left, passes a wire enclosure, and climbs to the top of a hill, where it proceeds through thick barberry bushes and begins to closely parallel the park boundary (Lewis Morris County Park is to the left). After a descent into a valley, it climbs to reach a junction (signpost #4) at 1.2 miles. Here, the Patriots' Path (blue path-and-tree logo on white) joins from the right. A sign to the right points the way to the reconstructed soldiers' huts, which are worth a short side trip.

The Grand Loop Trail continues ahead, now running concurrently with the Patriots' Path, until the Patriots' Path leaves to the left at 1.4 miles (signpost #5). The Grand Loop Trail bears right and descends, passing signpost #6 and continuing across an open field. After crossing paved Sugarloaf Road, it reenters the woods at signpost #7. The trail ascends gradually, levels off, then bears right and descends across the side of a hill, with views through the trees to the left. At signpost #8, 2.0 miles from the start, it turns left and soon levels off. Then, at 2.3 miles, it crosses paved Jockey Hollow Road, passes signpost #9,

and reenters the woods. The trail now runs close to the park boundary, with private homes visible just to the left.

The Grand Loop Trail descends gradually and bends sharply to the left. Then, at signpost #10, reached at 2.8 miles, it turns right, joining the Blue Trail (which also continues straight ahead). The joint white/blue trail follows a wide dirt road and passes a small pond on the left. A bench has been placed here, making it an attractive spot for a break.

At 2.9 miles, a Y intersection is reached (signpost #22). Here, the Blue Trail leaves to the right, while the Grand Loop Trail takes the left fork. It descends gradually and begins to parallel a stream on the left. Then, at 3.2 miles, the Grand Loop Trail arrives at a T intersection (signpost #21), where it turns left. It is now once again joined by the Patriots' Path and the Blue Trail, both of which come in from the right. The joint trails cross a wooden bridge over a stream and soon arrive at signpost #20, where the Grand Loop Trail and the Patriots' Path turn sharply right, while the Blue Trail continues straight ahead.

The joint Grand Loop Trail/Patriots' Path descends to cross the Primrose Brook Trail (red) at signpost #30. Just beyond, it crosses Primrose Brook and then a feeder brook on wooden bridges and again crosses the Primrose Brook Trail at signpost #31. As the trail continues ahead, Mount Kemble is visible through the trees on the left. After a gradual ascent, the trail bears left and passes an interpretive sign with the story of the Connecticut Line. Then, just ahead, the Grand Loop Trail/Patriots' Path crosses the wide, unblazed Mendham Road Trail at 4.2 miles (signpost #55). (To the right, the Mendham Road Trail leads back to the Visitor Center in 0.4 mile and can be used to shorten the hike.)

Just before reaching paved Tempe Wick Road, the trail bears left and descends to cross the road at 4.3 miles (signpost #56). After descending to cross a stream on a wooden bridge (signpost #57), the trail climbs to a junction (signpost #58) at 4.5 miles. Here, the Patriots' Path (following the route of the New Jersey Brigade Trail) continues ahead, leading towards the Cross Estate and the Scherman-Hoffman Sanctuaries, while the Grand Loop Trail turns right, heading first west and then north, roughly parallel to Tempe Wick Road. At signpost #59, a dirt road joins from the left, and the Grand Loop Trail descends to end at Tempe Wick Road at 5.3 miles. To return to the Visitor Center parking area, turn right onto the road marked with a DO NOT ENTER sign (intended to regulate vehicular traffic) and proceed ahead past the Wick Farm to the Visitor Center.

Patriots' Path   *Length: 5.9 miles Blaze: blue path-and-tree logo on white*
This hiking-only branch of the Patriots' Path follows a varied route through
the rolling, wooded hills of Morristown National Historical Park and Lewis
Morris County Park. For much of its route, it is co-aligned with other trails, so
it is important to look carefully for blazes at each intersection. Parking is available at the southern end at the New Jersey Audubon Society's Scherman-Hoffman
Sanctuaries on Hardscrabble Road, and at the northern end, there is a parking
area at the trail crossing of Mendham Road (County 510). In addition, cars
may be parked at the Cross Estate on Old Jockey Hollow Road, at the Trail
Center of the Morristown National Historical Park on Jockey Hollow Road,
and at the Soldiers' Huts area.

From the parking area on Hardscrabble Road, about 0.2 mile east of its
intersection with Chestnut Avenue, the Patriots' Path goes uphill, together with
the Dogwood Trail (red). At 0.2 mile, the Dogwood Trail leaves to the right,
while the Patriots' Path descends to a Y intersection (signpost #64), where it
enters the Morristown National Historical Park. Here, the Patriots' Path bears

Figure 10-10. Patriots' Path

left (the right fork leads to the Brigade Huts and loops back to rejoin
the main trail). Just ahead, at 0.4 mile,
it turns right at a T intersection (signpost #63). The Patriots' Path, following the route of the New Jersey Brigade Trail, climbs steadily, passing a
white-blazed trail on the right that
leads back to the Dogwood Trail. At
0.9 mile (signpost #62), a side trail
leads left to the Public Gardens of the
Cross Estate. The Patriots' Path passes
another side trail to the Cross Estate
parking area at 1.2 miles and descends
to cross the Passaic River (which, at
this point, is a rocky brook) at 1.5
miles. It then climbs out of the river
valley and descends to join the Grand
Loop Trail (white) at 2.2 miles (signpost #58). Both trails now cross a
stream on a wooden bridge (signpost

#57) and then proceed across paved Tempe Wick Road (signpost #56). At 2.5 miles, they cross the wide, unmarked Mendham Road Trail (signpost #55). (To the left, the Mendham Road Trail leads in 0.4 mile to the Visitor Center and Wick House.)

After passing an interpretive sign with the story of the Connecticut Line, the trails bear right and begin a gradual descent. Ahead, Mount Kemble is visible through the trees on the right. After crossing the Primrose Brook Trail (red) (signpost #31), the trails cross a feeder brook and then Primrose Brook on wooden bridges, and recross the Primrose Brook Trail (signpost #30). After a short climb, the Patriots' Path and Grand Loop Trail turn left at signpost #20 onto the Old Camp Road Trail, the route of the Blue Trail. The trails cross a wooden bridge over a stream and soon arrive at the next intersection (signpost #21). Here, the Grand Loop Trail leaves to the right, while the Patriots' Path and the Blue Trail continue straight ahead along the Old Camp Road Trail, reaching Jockey Hollow Road just north of the Trail Center parking area at 3.8 miles (signpost #27).

The Blue Trail now leaves to the right, while the Patriots' Path turns left, goes through the parking area, and turns right onto the Aqueduct Trail (green) at signpost #36. It twice crosses Primrose Brook on wooden footbridges, then continues ahead on the unmarked Soldier Hut Trail at signpost #37, where the Aqueduct Trail leaves to the left. The Patriots' Path follows a footpath to an open field at the intersection of Grand Parade, Cemetery, and Sugarloaf roads (signpost #38), where the soldiers' huts are visible on a hill to the right. It crosses the paved road, passes signpost #40, and climbs to a T intersection with the Grand Loop Trail (signpost #4). Here, the Patriots' Path turns right, briefly rejoining the Grand Loop Trail. At the next intersection (signpost #5), it turns left, leaving the Grand Loop Trail. Just ahead, at 4.8 miles, the Patriots' Path leaves Morristown National Historical Park and enters Lewis Morris County Park.

In addition to the path-and-tree logos, the Patriots' Path through the county park is marked with blue blazes. For part of the route, it is coaligned with a yellow-blazed trail. The Patriots' Path descends to a Y intersection, where it bears right. After turning right and crossing a stream on a wooden bridge, it passes a small water impoundment and reaches a covered pavilion with picnic tables, a good place to stop for a break. Here, the trail turns left and continues along Sunrise Lake. The Patriots' Path turns right at a Y intersection to reach a gate at Mendham Road (County 510). It crosses the highway, goes through a

parking area on the opposite side, and continues ahead, crossing a wooden bridge over the Whippany River to join the main part of the Patriots' Path, on which bicycles are permitted, 5.9 miles from Hardscrabble Road.

Primrose Brook Trail   *Length: 1.1 miles Blaze: red*

The Primrose Brook Trail is a short but enjoyable loop hike from the Trail Center parking area which follows a footpath for its entire route. It begins at signpost #33, on the east side of Jockey Hollow Road, just beyond the road bridge over Primrose Brook south of the parking area. At first, it runs along the south side of the brook, soon passing several tall red cedar trees. After crossing a footbridge over a tributary stream, the trail briefly runs directly along the brook. It bears right, crosses a wet area on puncheons, and climbs away from the brook. The trail continues along the side of a hill, overlooking the brook below.

At 0.3 mile, the trail reaches signpost #32. Here, a sign "Short Trail" indicates that those who desire a shorter 0.6-mile hike should turn left onto a short cut that leads back to the return route. The main Primrose Brook Trail (indicated by a sign "Long Trail") continues ahead, soon beginning to descend as the terrain becomes less steep. The trail crosses a tributary stream, briefly parallels the stream, then turns off to the left.

After crossing the wide Grand Loop Trail (white) and Patriots' Path at 0.6 mile (signpost #31), the Primrose Brook Trail descends log steps and begins to follow Primrose Brook back to the starting point of the hike. It briefly runs close to the brook, bears left and crosses a tributary stream, then continues parallel to the main brook. At 0.7 mile, it descends stone steps and crosses Primrose Brook on a wooden bridge. Just ahead, it again crosses the Grand Loop Trail and the Patriots' Path (signpost #30).

The Primrose Brook Trail now crosses and recrosses the brook on rocks. It once again crosses to the south side of the brook, where it meets the end of the "short-cut" trail at 0.8 mile (signpost #29). Just beyond, it crosses the brook—for the fifth and last time—on a footbridge and continues along the north side of the brook to end, 1.1 miles from the start, at Jockey Hollow Road, opposite the Trail Center parking area.

Yellow Trail   *Length: 2.3 miles Blaze: yellow*

The Yellow Trail utilizes the Grand Parade and Soldier Hut trails to form a loop that passes two of the most interesting features of the park—the Wick House

Figure 10-11. Soldiers' huts

and the soldiers' huts.

Beginning from signpost #35 at the southwest corner of the Trail Center parking area, the Yellow Trail (following the route of the Grand Parade Trail) heads south, jointly with the Aqueduct Trail (green), and crosses a wooden bridge over Primrose Brook. It reaches a T intersection at signpost #34. Here, the Aqueduct Trail leaves to the right, while the Yellow Trail turns left. At signpost #46, the Yellow Trail turns right and begins to follow a rocky footpath that parallels paved Jockey Hollow Road to the left.

At 0.4 mile (signpost #47), the trail turns right and runs along the northern edge of a field, part of the Wick Farm. Then, at 0.6 mile, the Grand Parade Trail ends at the paved Cemetery Road, near an old red shack (signpost #48). (The historic Wick House is a short distance to the left.) Here, the Yellow Trail turns right and follows the paved road for 250 feet to signpost #49, where the Soldier Hut Trail begins. The Yellow Trail turns right and follows the Soldier Hut Trail, which bends left and parallels the road.

A complex intersection is reached at 1.0 mile (signpost #50), where the Yellow Trail intersects a woods road. The woods road to the right and a path that proceeds straight ahead are the route of the Aqueduct Trail. The Yellow Trail crosses the road, bears left, and continues to parallel the Cemetery Road. After passing signpost #39 at 1.5 miles, the trail enters an open field with some cedar trees. The reconstructed soldiers' huts are visible on a hill directly ahead across the road.

The Yellow Trail crosses the road and proceeds up the hill, passing to the

right of the soldiers' huts. Near the top of the hill, it bears right at signpost #41 and descends to reach a T intersection (signpost #42) at 1.9 miles. Here, the Yellow Trail turns right, joining the route of the Grand Parade Trail. It continues to descend, soon reaching the paved Grand Parade Road (signpost #43). The trail turns left and follows the road for 200 feet, passing several historical markers which commemorate the Grand Parade. It then turns right, crosses the paved road, and reenters the woods, passing signpost #44. The trail continues ahead to reach the Trail Center parking area (signpost #45) at 2.3 miles.

Scherman-Hoffman Sanctuaries

Owned by the New Jersey Audubon Society and encompassing 275 acres of land donated by the Scherman and Hoffman families, the Scherman-Hoffman Sanctuaries include woodland, field, and floodplain habitat supporting over 200 species of wildlife. Birds are the primary focus of the sanctuaries, as is evident when visiting the gift shop, but there are also several hiking trails, including a branch of the Patriots' Path (for a description of this trail, see the Morristown National Historical Park section, pp. 243-45). The trails in the sanctuaries can be combined with those in the Morristown National Historical Park to form a longer hike.

To reach the Scherman-Hoffman Sanctuaries, take Exit 30B of I-287. At the first traffic light (US 202), continue ahead onto Childs Road. Proceed along Childs Road for 0.2 mile, bear right at the next fork onto Hardscrabble Road, and follow this winding road for 0.9 mile to the entrance road to the sanctuaries. The trails may be accessed either by following the entrance road uphill to the visitor center, or by continuing along Hardscrabble Road for another 300 feet to a parking area on the right. For more information, contact the Scherman-Hoffman Sanctuaries, 11 Hardscrabble Road, Bernardsville, NJ 07924; (908) 766-5787; www.njaudubon.org.

Dogwood Trail   *Length: 1.3 miles Blaze: red*
The Dogwood Trail, which forms a loop around the sanctuaries, begins at the northeast corner of the parking area on Hardscrabble Road. It is described here in a clockwise direction. The Dogwood Trail ascends from the parking area, running concurrently with the Patriots' Path (blue path-and-tree logo on white). At 0.2 mile, it turns right, leaving the Patriots' Path, climbs to the highest point in the sanctuaries (600 feet), and descends, joining a woods road at 0.6 mile. (To the left, a white-blazed trail follows the road for 0.2 mile to the Patri-

ots' Path.) The Dogwood Trail continues to descend along the road until, at 0.8 mile, the River Trail (yellow) begins to the left. Leveling off, the Dogwood Trail crosses the Field Loop Trail (green) at 0.9 mile and continues past a field to reach another junction with the Field Loop Trail at 1.1 miles. Here, the Dogwood Trail turns right onto a gravel road. It follows the gravel road for 125 feet, then crosses the paved entrance road and climbs into the woods on a footpath. The trail descends gradually and reaches the start of the loop at 1.3 miles.

Field Loop Trail
Length: 0.7 mile Blaze: green

The Field Loop Trail begins at the north end of the visitor center parking area. It descends on a wide path, with a meadow to the right, crossing the Dogwood Trail (red) at 0.1 mile. The Field Loop Trail continues along the left side of a field, then bears left at a fork. It passes the south end of the River Trail (yellow) at 0.3 mile and continues ahead through a successional field, parallel to the Passaic River. It soon bears right, away from the river, crosses several wet areas on puncheons, and bears right at a Y intersection, reaching a gravel road and the Dogwood Trail (red) at 0.5 mile. The Field Loop Trail continues along the gravel road for 125 feet, then turns right and follows the entrance road uphill to end at the visitor center at 0.7 mile.

River Trail
Length: 0.3 mile Blaze: yellow

Considered by many to be the most interesting trail in the sanctuaries, this short trail connects the Dogwood Trail with the Field Loop Trail, running along the Passaic River for most of the way. The River Trail begins on the Dogwood Trail (red), 0.8 mile from its start at the parking area on Hardscrabble Road. At 0.1 mile, the River Trail bears right and begins to parallel the scenic Passaic River. It passes a huge four-foot-diameter tulip tree—one of the largest trees in the area—at 0.2 mile. After going through a narrow passage between two tulip trees, the trail bears right, away from the river, crosses a wooden bridge over a tributary stream, and ends, 0.3 mile from its start, at a junction with the Field Loop Trail (green).

The River Trail may be combined with the Dogwood Trail and the Field Loop Trail to form a 1.5-mile loop around the sanctuaries.

Lewis Morris County Park

This 1,154-acre county park, which borders the Jockey Hollow area of the Morristown National Historical Park on the northeast, is named for New Jersey's first governor. It offers hiking, camping, picnicking, lake swimming, ballfields, sledding, and ski touring. The Sunrise Lake area is the center of water recreation.

The park has over 11 miles of trails. Most of these are multiple-use trails, open to hikers, horses, and mountain bikers. A six-mile-long, yellow-blazed trail circles the perimeter of the park, and several connecting trails facilitate shorter loop hikes. The park is also traversed by the Patriots' Path, which extends southeast into the Morristown National Historical Park. As of 2003, the trail system in the park is being reblazed, with some of the trails being rerouted.

To reach Lewis Morris County Park, take Exit 35 (Morristown) of I-287. Continue to the Morristown Green in the center of Morristown and turn right onto Washington Street (County 510). Continue on County 510 (which becomes Mendham Road) for about three miles to the park. Hikers may wish to park at the Patriots' Path parking area, on the north side of Mendham Road. Access to the southern end of the park is available from Tempe Wick Road, a short distance west of the entrance to the Morristown National Historical Park. NJ Transit trains from Hoboken and from Penn Station in New York City run to Morristown, from which a taxi can be taken to the park. For more information, contact the Morris County Park Commission, 53 East Hanover Avenue, P.O. Box 1295, Morristown, NJ 07962-1295; (973) 326-7600; www.morrisparks.com.

LOANTAKA BROOK RESERVATION

Situated between Morristown and Madison, Loantaka Brook Reservation stretches along Loantaka Brook. Loantaka is a combination of two Native American words which mean "the place of cold water." The reference is to Loantaka Brook, which flows into the Great Swamp. The park contains nearly five miles of marked paved trails, which are open to bicyclists as well as hikers. The 1.1-mile Yellow Trail extends from South Street to Woodland Avenue. The 1.5-mile Blue Trail connects Kitchell Road with Loantaka Way. The 2.0-mile Red Trail leads from Woodland Avenue to Green Village Road. The three trails

may be combined to form a 3.6-mile continuous route from South Street to Green Village Road. Most of this route is paralleled by an unpaved bridle path. Included in the reservation is the Helen Hartley Jenkins Woods, with a rich variety of wildflowers and bird life.

To reach Loantaka Brook Reservation, take Exit 35 from I-287 and turn east onto NJ 124. At the traffic light at South Street, turn left, and proceed for 0.5 mile to the park entrance, on the left. For more information, contact the Morris County Park Commission, 53 East Hanover Avenue, P.O. Box 1295, Morristown, NJ 07962-1295; (973) 326-7600; www.morrisparks.com.

MAHLON DICKERSON RESERVATION

Mahlon Dickerson Reservation, named after a former New Jersey governor and United States senator active during the early nineteenth century, is the largest Morris County park (3,042 acres). The reservation, which offers year-round trailer, tent, and lean-to camping, is located on Weldon Road in Jefferson Township, east of NJ 15 near Lake Hopatcong. It adjoins the Weldon Brook Wildlife Management Area, with the Beaver Brook Trail continuing south through the wildlife management area to Berkshire Valley Road.

Many trails in the reservation follow old logging roads, especially well-suited for cross-country skiing when conditions are favorable. An attractive hike is the Pine Swamp Loop Trail—a 3.8-mile trail that goes to the edge of the Pine Swamp, a wet area densely covered with spruce, rhododendron, and native azalea. The Pine Swamp area is very remote; a plane that crashed here in May 1974 was not found until December of that year.

Within the park are 2.5 miles of an abandoned rail line. It was originally built in 1864 as the Ogden Mine Railroad to serve the iron mines in the area. At the time of its abandonment, it was part of the Edison Branch of the Central Railroad of New Jersey. The Saffin Pond parking area on Weldon Road, 3.0 miles north of NJ 15, provides access to the rail trail.

To reach the reservation, take I-80 to Exit 34B and proceed north on NJ 15 for 5.0 miles. Take the Weldon Road (Milton/Oak Ridge) exit, and follow Weldon Road north. The Saffin Pond parking area, on the right side of the road, 3.0 miles north of NJ 15, provides access to the Highlands Trail and the Ogden Mine Railroad. The Pine Swamp Loop Trail and the Highlands Trail may be accessed from a picnic parking area 1.3 miles north of Saffin Pond, on

the left side of the road. For more information, contact the Morris County Park Commission, 53 East Hanover Avenue, P.O. Box 1295, Morristown, NJ 07962-1295; (973) 326-7600; www.morrisparks.com.

Beaver Brook Trail
Length: 4.9 miles Blaze: white

The Beaver Brook Trail begins in Mahlon Dickerson County Reservation and continues south through the 2,700-acre Weldon Brook Wildlife Management Area. It is most easily hiked from north to south.

To reach either end of the trail, take I-80 to Exit 34B (NJ 15 North, Jefferson/Sparta). For the southern trailhead, follow NJ 15 north for 2.0 miles, then turn right onto Berkshire Valley Road. Follow Berkshire Valley Road for 2.0 miles, until the road crosses a truss bridge over a brook and intersects Taylor Road. The trailhead is in a clearing on the left, where parking is available. Access to the northern end is via the Highlands Trail (teal diamond) in Mahlon Dickerson Reservation. Follow NJ 15 north for 5.0 miles and take the Weldon Road (Milton/Oak Ridge) exit. Proceed north on Weldon Road for 3.0 miles and turn right into the Saffin Pond parking area. Hikers should follow a connector trail to the Highlands Trail (black diamond on teal diamond) from the southeast side of the parking area and turn left onto the Highlands Trail (teal diamond) at the dam at the end of the lake. The junction with the Beaver Brook Trail is on the right, 1.7 miles from the parking area, at the top of a hill, about 100 feet beyond a large boulder.

From the junction with the Highlands Trail, the Beaver Brook Trail gently climbs through a rocky hardwood forest, reaching a rock ledge with a view

Figure 10-12. Saffin Pond

through the trees of the ridge to the west. At 0.5 mile, the trail crosses a yellow-blazed woods road, with a signboard to the right. Here, the trail leaves Mahlon Dickerson Reservation and enters the Weldon Brook Wildlife Management Area. The trail levels off and crosses another woods road at 0.8 mile. It then descends gently and soon passes a small pit adjacent to the trail. The presence of these pits suggests that the area was once stripped of trees, which were used to manufacture charcoal for iron ore smelting furnaces.

Just beyond, at 1.1 miles, the trail switchbacks down to a boulder-and-log-strewn valley, then climbs through a dense laurel thicket. After crossing another woods road, the trail turns south and proceeds along the hillside on the western side of Lost Lake. Much beaver activity is evident in the area; indeed, the "lake" is actually a meadow flooded by a beaver dam. At the end of the lake, the trail passes through a split rock, turns left, crosses a small stream, and begins to parallel the southern side of the lake. It reaches the lake shore by a large fir tree near the beaver dam, then turns right and begins to parallel Beaver Brook, the outlet of the lake, passing several iron ore test pits. At 2.0 miles, the trail goes under power lines and crosses Beaver Brook on a wooden footbridge.

After crossing a woods road at 2.2 miles, the trail briefly follows a mining road, then descends to cross a tributary stream. Old stone walls in the area are evidence of prior settlement. After passing several mine pits and adjacent tailings piles, the trail bears left, turning away from the brook. At 2.7 miles, the trail runs along the edge of a 50-foot-high escarpment. After descending to cross a seasonal stream, the trail turns left at a rock ledge and continues to descend into a valley, then ascends to a hilltop, with several cedars.

The Beaver Brook Trail descends to reach, at 3.3 miles, an overlook from a long rock ledge, with views south down the Berkshire Valley. The trail now becomes somewhat more rugged. It bears right, descends steeply, then turns right onto a woods road and continues to descend through laurel. Soon, the trail turns right, leaving the road, and descends to cross a stream at 3.8 miles.

On the opposite side, the trail bears left and begins to climb the rocky slope. After crossing a tributary stream, it briefly joins an old woods road, then runs along a sharp line of demarcation between the steep hemlock-covered slopes to the left and a mixed hardwood forest to the right. It climbs steeply and continues along the side of the hill, with views of the Berkshire Valley below to the left. In early spring, this hillside is covered with wildflowers.

After a more gradual ascent, the Beaver Brook Trail reaches the crest of Mase Mountain at 4.4 miles and begins to descend over rock ledges, with views

to the left across the valley towards Green Pond Mountain and the roof of a guard tower at the Picatinny Arsenal. Continuing to descend, the trail turns left onto a woods road that parallels a stream and follows the road downhill, gradually leveling off. The Beaver Brook Trail ends at the trailhead parking area on Berkshire Valley Road at 4.9 miles.

Highlands Trail (Saffin Pond to picnic parking area)

Length: 3.2 miles Blaze: teal diamond

From the southeast side of the Saffin Pond parking area, follow a connecting trail, marked with black-diamond-on-teal-diamond blazes, which crosses a footbridge over a stream and proceeds south along the eastern shore of Saffin Pond, passing a number of trees that have been felled by recent beaver activity in the area.

At the southeast corner of the pond, by several picnic tables, a junction is reached with the Highlands Trail (teal diamond). Turn left and follow the Highlands Trail, which ascends gradually along a woods road. At 0.5 mile (from the parking area), the trail turns right at a T intersection and descends along an eroded woods road. At the base of the descent, the trail bears left and levels off, paralleling Weldon Brook—the outlet of Saffin Pond—on the right. It bears left at a Y intersection, where the trail narrows to a footpath.

At 1.4 miles, the trail crosses a stream on rocks (the crossing may be difficult if the water is high). It bears left and climbs to reach a high point, marked by a large boulder, at 1.7 miles. Just beyond, it reaches a T junction. Here, the Highlands Trail turns left, while the Beaver Brook Trail (white) begins to the right. The Highlands Trail bears left again and descends to cross a tributary stream. After climbing over a knoll, it descends to cross the main stream on a wooden bridge at 1.9 miles. Once more, the trail climbs through a rocky area and descends to cross the stream—for the third and final time—at 2.2 miles.

The Highlands Trail now begins to climb—steeply in places—passing by some sheer rock faces. After crossing a yellow-blazed woods road at 2.5 miles, the grade moderates. Soon, the trail passes a broad overlook to the right (southeast). No civilization is visible from here; only forested hillsides may be seen, with Lake Hopatcong in the distance to the right. After a slight dip, the trail climbs through mountain laurel to reach the Headley Overlook at 2.9 miles. This viewpoint is more popular because it is nearer the road, but the first overlook provides a less obstructed view.

The Highlands Trail now descends on a woods road, bearing right at a T

intersection. As the trail approaches the paved Weldon Road, it bears right at a fork, then crosses the road and soon emerges onto the picnic parking area at 3.2 miles. Ahead, the Highlands Trail descends for 0.2 mile to join the Pine Swamp Loop Trail (white), which it follows for 1.3 miles to Sparta Mountain Road.

Pine Swamp Loop Trail
Length: 3.8 miles
Blaze: white

To reach the start of the Pine Swamp Loop Trail, take Weldon Road to the picnic parking area on the northwest side of the road, 4.3 miles north of NJ 15. From the parking area,

Figure 10-13. Overlook on the Highlands Trail with Lake Hopatcong in the distance

proceed ahead for 0.2 mile on a service road, the route of the Highlands Trail (teal diamond), passing a fitness center and a water pump. The Pine Swamp Loop Trail begins at a T junction at the base of a descent.

Followed in a counterclockwise direction, the Pine Swamp Loop Trail (together with the Highlands Trail) continues heading downhill, crosses a stream, and turns left. It continues ahead at 0.3 mile as an unmarked woods road leaves to the left. The trail turns right at 0.6 mile and soon crosses another stream on a wooden footbridge. Then, at 0.8 mile, the trail bears left at a fork and begins to pass through an area with dense mountain laurel. It crosses a wet area on puncheons and, at 0.9 mile, joins a woods road that comes in from the right.

At 1.0 mile, the Pine Swamp Loop Trail turns right (straight ahead, a yellow-blazed trail is a shortcut route that soon rejoins the main trail). After crossing a bridge over a stream, the Pine Swamp Loop Trail reaches a junction

near paved Sparta Mountain Road at 1.2 miles. Here, the Highlands Trail leaves to the right, while the Pine Swamp Loop Trail turns sharply left.

The yellow-blazed trail rejoins from the left at 1.5 miles. Just beyond, a rocky ledge to the left of the trail affords a view of the unusual Pine Swamp, with its tall spruce, hemlock, rhododendron, and mountain laurel. The Pine Swamp Loop Trail continues through the swamp, crosses a stream, and ascends slightly to another junction at 1.9 miles, where the trail bears left and begins a steady climb. It reaches the highest point in Morris County (1,395 feet), marked by a sign, at 2.3 miles. Just beyond, the trail bears sharply left as a footpath joins from the right.

The Pine Swamp Loop Trail now descends steadily, reaching a complex junction at 2.8 miles. Here, the Pine Swamp Loop Trail turns left for 75 feet, then turns left again, joining the Boulder Trail (green), which starts here. The route of this trail is marked by a number of huge boulders on both sides of the trail. At 3.3 miles, the Pine Swamp Loop Trail turns right, leaving the Boulder Trail, and continues on a footpath. It turns right at 3.5 miles, joining a woods road for 100 feet, then turns left onto another woods road. After turning left at a T junction at 3.7 miles, the Pine Swamp Loop Trail ends at 3.8 miles, completing the loop.

MORRIS CANAL

Completed in 1831, the Morris Canal was built to transport coal from Pennsylvania and, hopefully, revitalize the New Jersey iron industry. Its main line stretched 102 miles from Phillipsburg on the Delaware River to Jersey City. After 1870, the canal ceased being profitable, but it continued to operate. It was not until 1918 that legal issues concerning water rights to the major bodies of water in northern New Jersey were finally settled, and the canal ceased operations in 1924.

Morris Canal boats were towed by a team of two mules connected to the boat by a 100-foot-long rope. The boat crew included at least a driver, walking along the towpath to lead the mules, and a captain, steering the boat constantly to prevent it from being pulled into the towpath embankment. To bypass rapids, locks and inclined planes were constructed to raise or lower canal boats, sometimes with 70-ton loads of cargo.

In 2003, much of the Morris Canal is gone, and those who seek long

Figure 10-14. Morris Canal lock at Saxton Falls

stretches of canal filled with water and a towpath alongside for walking will be disappointed. Modern development has obliterated much of the canal, and private property owners have restricted access. The county has placed markers at sites where the canal crossed what is now a major road. Remains of the canal can be seen at Hopatcong State Park and at Saxton Falls, one mile north of Stephens State Park. The remains of one of the twenty-eight locks of the canal are at the falls, while a section of the canal filled with water still exists in Hugh Force Park in Wharton. For those who accept the challenge of discovering where the canal was, the rewards are there—finding one's way, learning local history, and investigating the environment.

Joseph J. Macasek's book *Guide to the Morris Canal in Morris County* is a walking guide to the remains of the canal. Published by the Morris County Heritage Commission, it is available from him at 19 Budd Street, Morristown, NJ 07960. The Canal Society of New Jersey has an exhibit at Waterloo Village. For more information on the canal, contact the Canal Society of New Jersey, P.O. Box 737, Morristown, NJ 07963; (908) 722-9556; www.canalsocietynj.org.

Hugh Force Park
Length: 0.3 mile Blaze: none

Within Hugh Force Park is one of the best preserved sections of the canal, which appears much as it would have during its period of operation. The 0.6-mile round trip is suitable for families with young children, as it is along the level towpath and provides an ideal opportunity for experiencing the historic canal. To reach Hugh Force Park from US 46 in Wharton, proceed north for one mile on South Main Street and turn left onto Pine Street. Continue for 0.3 mile and turn left onto West Central Avenue. In 0.1 mile, turn right onto a driveway that leads to a parking area. The hike begins at the end of the parking area furthest from West Central Avenue and continues westward along the towpath beside the watered stretch of the Morris Canal.

When the canal was constructed in this location, its channel was excavated

by hand into the toe of the adjacent steep hillside. Supporting the canal and its towpath, a 10-to-12-foot-high man-made embankment separates the waterway from the adjacent Stephens Brook and Rockaway River. The High Bridge Branch of the Central Railroad of New Jersey was constructed along the hillside next to the canal in 1881, with a stone embankment supporting the right-of-way. It is easy to imagine a mule team walking along the towpath in this well-preserved section of canal.

In 0.3 mile, the water-filled section ends at the site of Lock 2 East. A flat grassy area at the end of the watered section marks the location of the former lock. Careful inspection in the grass reveals several large, flat stones which show the outline of the lock's buried walls.

Lock 2 East allowed the canal boats to overcome an eight-foot elevation change. This 90-foot-long by 11-foot-wide chamber had timber doors or gates at each end. By opening and closing the lock gates and operating small valves in the bottom of these gates, the water level—and hence a boat in the lock—could be raised or lowered. This process enabled boats to change elevation and continue on their journey. After the canal was abandoned in 1924 and dismantled, the locks were filled in with dirt.

Stone ruins of the lock tender's house are just south of the filled-in Lock 2 East. Lock tenders had to reside next to their locks so they would be readily available to service passing boats. Note the apple trees adjacent to the house site. The lock tender's family would often supplement their income by selling pies and bread to passing boatmen. Hikers should turn around at this point, as private property is past the locks.

MOUNT HOPE HISTORICAL PARK

Known locally as the Richard Mine, Mount Hope Historical Park was once a booming iron mining and processing site. It forms a part of the original Mount Hope Tract, first developed by John Jacob Faesch in 1772. Over the course of the years, three separate veins of ore—each of which runs in a southwesterly-to-northeasterly direction—were mined on the property. The property was divided into three ownerships, which operated the Teabo, Allen, and Richard mines, respectively. During World War II, the eastern end of the site was developed as the New Leonard Mining Complex—a state-of-the-art mining and ore-processing complex that produced 5,600,000 tons of ore by 1950. Mining

operations in the area ended in 1958, and the park was opened in 1997. Second-growth woodlands have reforested the areas that once were cleared for mining operations.

Four trails, all of which begin from the trailhead at the parking area, lead hikers through the former mining operations on woods roads. The Allen and Teabo operations are visible from the Red Trail. The Orange Trail leads to the Richard Mine. The short White and Blue trails lead hikers to the Old Teabo and Brennan mines, respectively. For personal safety, hikers are requested to stay on the marked trails.

A suggested 2.7-mile "lollipop"-loop hike combines the Red and Orange trails. From the trailhead at the east end of the parking area, follow the trail up a switchback to a trail junction under power lines at 0.1 mile. Turn left, now following the Red Trail. After crossing a seasonal stream, the mine pits of the Teabo #2 Mine—opened in the 1850s and abandoned by 1883—may be seen to the left at 0.3 mile. At 0.4 mile, turn right onto a diverging route of the Red Trail and begin to follow the loop in a counter-clockwise direction through second-growth woodlands, with an understory of blueberry bushes. This section of the trail departs from the main ore vein, so few mine pits may be seen until the next trail junction is reached at 0.9 mile. Turn right at this junction onto the Orange Trail, which passes several small mine pits.

At 1.1 miles, the Orange Trail turns right onto a narrower woods road. With a stream directly ahead, the trail turns left at 1.2 miles and begins a steady descent, reaching a T intersection—where the trail turns left—at 1.5 miles. Just beyond, the trail passes the remnants of the Richard #6 Mine, opened in 1897. Several mine pits and timbers may be seen to the left of the trail. At 1.7 miles, a rail across the trail marks the site of the Richard #2 Mine—one of New Jersey's most productive mines in the 1880s. Cables from the mining operations may be seen to the left of the trail.

After crossing under power lines, the Orange Trail bears left, leaving the wide woods road it has been following. The trail soon widens to a woods road and passes the stone ruins of several homes at 1.8 miles. Just beyond, the trail turns right under the power lines, then turns left onto an intersecting road. After a short climb, the trail passes six shafts of the Allen Mine, first opened in the 1830s. The mine shafts are behind a low ridge to the north and are not visible from the trail.

The Orange Trail ends at a junction at 2.0 miles. Bear right onto the Red Trail, which passes several trenches and mine pits of the Allen Mine to the left of

the trail. One of these pits, known as the Smoke Stack Shaft, was excavated in the 1850s to provide ventilation for the Allen Tunnel, which extended south to Teabo Road. (The tunnel itself is no longer visible.) At 2.2 miles, a huge pit of the Allen Mine may be seen to the right of the trail.

The trail returns to the start of the loop at 2.3 miles. Continue ahead, following the Red Trail back to the trail junction under the power lines, then turn right and continue to the parking area.

To reach Mount Hope Historical Park, take I-80 to Exit 35 (eastbound) or Exit 35B (westbound) and proceed north on Mt. Hope Avenue. In 0.5 mile, turn left onto Richard Mine Road. Continue for 0.7 mile and turn right onto Coburn Road (which becomes Teabo Road). The park entrance is 0.7 mile ahead on the left. For more information, contact the Morris County Park Commission, 53 East Hanover Avenue, P.O. Box 1295, Morristown, NJ 07962-1295; (973) 326-7600; www.morrisparks.com.

PATRIOTS' PATH

The Patriots' Path is a trail-and-greenway system in southern Morris County which links federal, state, county, and municipal parks, watershed lands, historic sites, and other points of interest. It was created as a joint effort of several groups, including the Morris County Park Commission and the New Jersey Conservation Foundation (which initiated the project). The Patriots' Path aims to protect and maintain the environment and aesthetics of stream valleys and uplands, while providing a network of hiking, biking, and horse trails, most of which lie along the along the corridors of the Whippany, Black, and Raritan rivers. In 1980, a completed portion of the path was designated as a National Recreation Trail. For more information, contact the Morris County Park Commission, 53 East Hanover Avenue, P.O. Box 1295, Morristown, NJ 07962-1295; (973) 326-7600; www.morrisparks.com.

Trails in the Patriots' Path System

In 2003, over 35 miles of the Patriots' Path have been established, with some 30 additional miles of trail projected for future development, when permission from landowners has been obtained. The Patriots' Path consists of a main trunk route, blazed white, and several side trails, blazed blue. Most of the main

trunk of the Patriots' Path is open to bicycles, and portions of the route are paved. Many of the side trails are for hiking only.

The main trunk of the Patriots' Path and the blue-blazed side trail that continues west along the Whippany River are described below. A 5.9-mile hiking-only branch of the Patriots' Path which links the Scherman-Hoffman Sanctuaries, Morristown National Historical Park, and Lewis Morris County Park with the main trunk of the Patriots' Path is described in the Jockey Hollow section of this chapter, pp. 243-45. The Black River, Bamboo Brook, and Willowwood trails—which together form a 7.3-mile trail through the Black River County Park—are described in the Black River section of this chapter, pp. 216-19. Another four-mile section of the Patriots' Path traverses the Black River Wildlife Management Area (see p. 213). Shorter, disconnected sections of the Patriots' Path traverse the Frelinghuysen Arboretum and Schooley's Mountain County Park.

Speedwell Lake to Woodland Road   *Length: 6.9 miles Blaze: white*
Over most of its length, this section of the Patriots' Path roughly parallels the Whippany River. There are numerous access points, most of which have parking. To reach the eastern end from The Green in Morristown, take Speedwell Avenue north to Speedwell Lake. The western end is near Clyde Potts Reservoir. Only about a mile of the route is paved, with the remainder either gravel or dirt. Mountain bikes are permitted on the portion between Speedwell Avenue in Morristown and East Main Street in Mendham Township.

Beginning at the parking lot at Speedwell Lake, the Patriots' Path heads west, following a gravel road along the south shore of the lake. At the end of the lake, it turns right onto Lake Road, crosses the Whippany River, then turns left, crosses the road, and continues on a gravel path parallel to the road. After crossing Watnong Brook on the highway bridge, it turns left onto a paved walkway and passes an historical marker commemorating the Rockaway Valley Railroad. Built in 1888 and abandoned in 1913, it was dubbed the "Rock-a-Bye Baby" because of its rough railbed. Portions of this section of the Patriots' Path follows its right-of-way.

The trail curves to the right and goes by a water treatment plant. It then bears left and begins to follow the railroad right-of-way, crossing Lake Valley Road (where parking for several cars is available) at 1.0 mile. Continuing upstream along the banks of the Whippany River, the Patriots' Path crosses Sussex Avenue at 1.8 miles. Cars may also be parked at this road crossing. To the

left, across the Whippany River and then right, a blue-blazed paved section of the Patriots' Path continues 0.8 mile to Washington Valley Road.

The main route of the Patriots' Path continues ahead, directly across Sussex Avenue, on a wide gravel path through wooded wetlands, which are often flooded after heavy rains. At 2.6 miles, the Patriots' Path crosses Washington Valley Road. To the left, a blue-blazed trail leads to the paved spur of the Patriots' Path mentioned above. The main route continues ahead along the railbed, but leaves it before reaching Whitehead Road at 3.1 miles. Here, the Patriots' Path turns left, crosses the highway bridge over a tributary stream, then turns right at a small parking area and passes through a wet region.

The Patriots' Path now begins a steady climb, joining a dirt road at the crest of the rise. After descending on a winding dirt road, it bears left and continues through an area overgrown with wild rose and honeysuckle thickets. Soon, the trail begins to follow a gravel road high above the Whippany River. It then descends to the river level, reaching a bridge over the river at 4.7 miles.

The Patriots' Path turns left and crosses the river, reaching a junction with the 5.9-mile branch of the Patriots' Path that leads into Lewis Morris County Park and the Morristown National Historical Park (see pp. 243-45 for a description of this branch of the trail). The blue-blazed branch trail continues ahead, while the main white-blazed route of the Patriots' Path turns right and follows the southern bank of the river, crossing Tingley Road at 5.0 miles.

At 5.6 miles, where Dismal Brook joins the Whippany River, another junction is reached. Here, the main white-blazed route of the Patriots' Path turns right, while a blue-blazed branch of the trail (described below) continues straight ahead. The main route crosses a footbridge over the Whippany River and reaches East Main Street (where parking is available) at 5.7 miles. The trail turns right, follows the paved road for 200 feet, then turns left to enter the Dismal-Harmony Natural Area. It follows Dismal Brook upstream through a hilly forested area and then turns left up a steep sidehill. As of 2003, the trail temporarily ends, 6.9 miles from Speedwell Avenue in Morristown, at Woodland Road near the Clyde Potts Reservoir (no parking is available here).

With the assistance of the Morris Land Conservancy, the Morris County Park Commission has acquired an easement that will permit a five-mile extension of the Patriots' Path through watershed lands in Mendham and Randolph.

Dismal Brook to Ralston Corners *Length: 4.6 miles Blaze: blue*
Beginning just south of East Main Street in Mendham, where Dismal Brook

joins the Whippany River, this branch of the Patriots' Path heads west, parallel to the Whippany River. Continuing to follow the abandoned right-of-way of the Rockaway Valley Railroad, the trail crosses Cherry Lane at 0.5 mile and Cold Hill Road at 1.5 miles. On the west side of Cold Hill Road, it follows a narrow corridor past a residence for senior citizens, then bends left to skirt a development. Soon, the trail begins to parallel the North Branch of the Raritan River. After passing a pond to the right of the trail, it crosses Mountain Avenue, where parking is available. Just beyond, the trail crosses to the north bank of the river. It briefly follows a paved road that leads to Ironia Road, crossed at 4.0 miles. The next section of the trail—from Ironia Road to Ralston Corners—is restricted to foot traffic only. At 4.6 miles, the trail reaches West Main Street in Mendham at Ralston Corners. Parking is available adjacent to the firehouse.

PYRAMID MOUNTAIN
NATURAL HISTORICAL AREA

The 1,280-acre Pyramid Mountain Natural Historical Area encompasses Pyramid and Turkey mountains in Kinnelon, Boonton, and Montville. Its features include unusual glacial erratics, dramatic rock outcrops, extensive wetlands, and waterfalls. The area, which had been threatened with development in the 1990s, was preserved thanks to the dedicated efforts of a coalition of citizen groups, conservation organizations, corporations, and government agencies.

Composed largely of Precambrian gneiss, Pyramid Mountain is adjacent to the Ramapo Fault, which runs along the western edge of the Newark Basin. One of the largest and most active faults in the region, the Ramapo Fault is the boundary between the Precambrian rocks of the Highlands region and the Mesozoic rocks of the Newark Basin. Many glacial erratics, including several truck-sized boulders, are found along the ridge of Pyramid Mountain. The two most remarkable erratics in the area are Bear Rock, one of the largest glacial erratics in the state, and Tripod Rock, which is perched atop three smaller boulders.

Chestnut oaks are plentiful on the high ridges. Witch hazel, maple leaf viburnum, and winterberry lend seasonal color to the hardwood understory. The area provides habitat for over 100 species of birds, 30 species of mammals, and over 400 species of plants. Seasonal birds include scarlet tanagers, yellow

and prairie warblers, rose-breasted grosbeaks, and indigo buntings. Black-capped chickadees and red-bellied woodpeckers are year-round residents. In season, fringed and bottle gentians, cardinal flowers, and wood lilies can be seen.

The area is administered by the Morris County Park Commission, with a visitors center on Boonton Avenue in Montville. It sponsors various programs and guided walks. To reach Pyramid Mountain Natural Historical Area, take I-287 to Exit 44 (Main Street, Boonton), and bear right onto Lathrop Avenue. Turn right at the stop sign onto Main Street (County 511), proceed along Main Street for 0.3 mile, then turn right onto Boonton Avenue. Continue on Boonton Avenue, still designated County 511, for 3.3 miles to the parking area for the Pyramid Mountain Visitors Center, on the left side of the road (the Visitors Center is opposite Mars Court, about 0.8 mile north of the intersection of County 511 and Taylortown Road). For more information, call the Visitors Center at (973) 334-3130 or contact the Morris

Figure 10-15. Rose-breasted grosbeak and prairie warbler

County Park Commission, 53 East Hanover Avenue, P.O. Box 1295, Morristown, NJ 07962-1295; (973) 326-7600; www.morrisparks.com.

Trails in the Pyramid Mountain Natural Historical Area

Pyramid Mountain Natural Historical Area is a popular place for families to hike. The over 20 miles of marked trails provide opportunities to visit glacial erratics, enjoy expansive views, see waterfalls, and observe wetlands. The Visitors Center on Boonton Avenue in Montville is a starting point for loop hikes over either Pyramid Mountain or Turkey Mountain. Since each area has its own distinct trail system, the trails on Pyramid Mountain are described separately from those on Turkey Mountain.

Pyramid Mountain Trails

Pyramid Mountain, located on the west side of Boonton Avenue, features a

network of trails that lead to Tripod Rock and Bear Rock—two unusual glacial erratics—passing several viewpoints on the way. Longer loop hikes are possible by combining the Butler-Montville Trail and the Kinnelon-Boonton Trail, which lead north from the Visitors Center to Kinnelon and Butler.

Butler-Montville Trail (Pyramid Mountain section)

Length: 5.8 miles Blaze: blue

The Butler-Montville Trail extends from Butler to the Visitors Center on Boonton Avenue in Montville, following the shore of the Butler Reservoir for part of its route. Parking is available on streets near the trailhead in Butler and at the Visitors Center on Boonton Avenue. Public transportation is available via NJ Transit bus #194 to the Meadtown Shopping Center, at the intersection of NJ 23 and Kinnelon Road in Butler. To reach the trailhead from this intersection, proceed south for 0.1 mile on Kinnelon Road, then continue on Kakeout Road for 0.6 mile to Bubbling Brook Road.

The northern trailhead of the Butler-Montville Trail is at a gate across Bubbling Brook Road, about 800 feet west of the intersection of Kakeout Road and Bubbling Brook Road. The trail follows a paved road along a stream, passing a dirt parking area to the left. Just beyond, it goes by an abandoned brick building, with an old concrete spillway across the stream. (This crumbling spillway is dangerous and should not be crossed under any circumstances.) The pavement ends at 0.4 mile, where the Butler Connecting Trail (blue on white) goes off to the left across a dam/causeway. Becoming a narrow trail, the Butler-Montville Trail continues close to the shore of Butler Reservoir, which is dotted with white pines. It crosses a wooden footbridge over Stonehouse Brook at 1.5 miles, continues across several wet areas on puncheons, and crosses Fayson Lakes Road at 1.8 miles.

After descending to cross a small stream, the trail goes through a meadow, where it bears left and continues along a woods road. It takes the left fork at two Y intersections and climbs to reach Miller Road, opposite Our Lady of the Magnificat School, at 2.5 miles. The trail turns right and runs along the paved road for about 500 feet, then turns right at a gate and descends on a woods road. Soon, it bears left, leaving the woods road, and continues along the side of a hill.

At 3.0 miles, the trail crosses Miller Road diagonally to the right, passes between two houses, and continues into the woods on a dirt road. After descending to cross a wet area on a long wooden bridge, it meanders along the

valley floor and eventually heads south on a woods road, paralleling a brook to the left, until it reaches the terminus of the Red-on-White Trail, which leaves to the left at 3.7 miles.

The Butler-Montville Trail continues along the side of the hill, with the brook below, then descends to the level of the brook, which widens to form Bear Swamp. At 4.1 miles, the trail reaches Bear Rock, a huge glacial erratic with an uncanny resemblance to a giant bear. Here, the Kinnelon-Boonton Trail (white) joins from the right. After turning left and crossing the brook on a wooden bridge, the joint trails reach a junction with the Yellow Trail, which leaves to the right in another 200 feet. The trails bear left and head north, with Bear Swamp to the left, then bear right and ascend steeply through a stand of laurel. At a T junction, reached at 4.4 miles, the two trails separate, with the Butler-Montville Trail turning right. (The Kinnelon-Boonton Trail, which turns left at the junction, leads in 400 feet to Tripod Rock.)

At 4.6 miles, the Butler-Montville Trail passes a white-on-blue-blazed side trail that leads right 300 feet to Lucy's Overlook, named for Lucy Meyer, who spearheaded efforts to preserve Pyramid Mountain. Soon, the Butler-Montville Trail joins the Yellow Trail, which comes in from the right. Both trails run jointly for 200 feet, and then the Yellow Trail leaves to the left. After a gradual ascent, the Butler-Montville Trail reaches the summit of Pyramid Mountain at 5.1 miles, with views to the east (towards Manhattan) and south. The trail now begins to descend. At 5.4 miles, the Red Trail begins to the right, while the Butler-Montville Trail turns left and continues to descend. Then, at 5.5 miles, the Butler-Montville Trail reaches a T junction under power lines. Here, the Kinnelon-Boonton Trail begins to the right, while the Butler-Montville Trail turns left and

Figure 10-16. View from Pyramid Mountain on the Butler-Montville Trail

continues to descend on a rocky footpath parallel to the power lines. At 5.6 miles, it turns left onto a woods road, and in another 150 feet, it passes the end of the Yellow Trail on the left. Continuing ahead, the Butler-Montville Trail crosses a wet area on puncheons, then crosses Stony Brook on a wooden bridge. At the east end of the bridge, the side trail to the Visitors Center continues ahead as the Butler-Montville Trail turns left onto a rocky footpath, which it follows to Boonton Avenue (County 511), reached at 5.8 miles. For the continuation of the trail on the east side of Boonton Avenue, see the Turkey Mountain section, below.

Butler Connecting Trail   *Length: 0.4 mile Blaze: blue on white*
The Butler Connecting Trail connects the Kinnelon-Boonton Trail with the Butler-Montville Trail, making possible a loop hike starting from the northern trailheads of these trails. The western trailhead of the Butler Connecting Trail is on the Kinnelon-Boonton Trail (white), 0.3 mile from its trailhead on Birch Road. The Butler Connecting Trail heads northwest, descending on a footpath through the woods to the dam/causeway at the north end of the Butler Reservoir. It turns left and crosses the dam to reach its terminus at the Butler-Montville Trail (blue).

Green Trail   *Length: 0.7 mile Blaze: green*
The Green Trail provides easy access from the north to the ridge overlooking the Taylortown Reservoir. Parking is available at the athletic field on Fayson Lakes Road, just north of its junction with Boonton Avenue (County 511). The trail begins at the northwest corner of the tennis courts. After climbing the ridge, the Green Trail ends at the Kinnelon-Boonton Trail (white), with Tripod Rock 0.7 mile to the left.

Kinnelon-Boonton Trail   *Length: 4.3 miles Blaze: white*
The Kinnelon-Boonton Trail extends north from the Pyramid Mountain Visitors Center on Boonton Avenue to Birch Road in Kinnelon. To reach the northern end of the trail, take Boonton Avenue (County 511) south from NJ 23 in Butler, and turn right in 0.2 mile onto Kakeout Road. Follow Kakeout Road for 0.7 mile (the road makes several turns) and turn left onto Birch Road, then continue along Birch Road to the end of the paved road. The trailhead is on the right side of the dirt extension of Birch Road. Parking for hikers is permitted along the dirt road, but hikers should park off the road and leave a note on the

Figure 10-17. Tripod Rock

dashboard indicating that they are using the trail. Public transportation is available via NJ Transit bus #194 to the Meadtown Shopping Center on NJ 23 in Butler.

To reach the southern end of the Kinnelon-Boonton Trail, follow the trail from the parking lot at the Visitors Center and turn left onto the Butler-Montville Trail (blue). In 0.2 mile, where the Butler-Montville Trail turns right and begins to climb the mountain, the Kinnelon-Boonton Trail continues ahead, following the power line, with abundant wildflowers along the route. (The southern trailhead of the Red Trail, which parallels the Kinnelon-Boonton Trail for the next 0.6 mile and offers a more pleasant route, away from the power line, is 0.1 mile along the Butler-Montville Trail.) At 0.4 mile from its start, the Kinnelon-Boonton Trail crosses Bear House Brook on a wooden bridge. It turns right and leaves the power line at 0.5 mile. Then, at 0.6 mile, the Red Trail ends to the right.

After paralleling a rock wall, the Kinnelon-Boonton Trail reaches Bear Rock at 0.8 mile. Here, the Kinnelon-Boonton Trail turns right to rejoin the Butler-Montville Trail. Both trails cross Bear House Brook on a wooden bridge and, in another 200 feet, reach a junction with the Yellow Trail, which leaves to the right. The trails continue heading north, with Bear Swamp to the left, until

they bear right and ascend steeply through a stand of laurel. At a T junction, reached at 1.1 miles, the trails separate, with the Butler-Montville Trail turning right. The Kinnelon-Boonton Trail turns left and reaches Tripod Rock at 1.2 miles. This unusual boulder, perched on three smaller stones, is believed by geologists to have been deposited here by glacial action, although some believe that it may be a Native American calendar site. After passing a small pond on the left at 1.3 miles, the Kinnelon-Boonton Trail reaches a junction with the Red-on-White Trail, which leaves to the left at 1.6 miles.

Continuing along the ridge, the Kinnelon-Boonton Trail reaches a junction, marked by a cairn, at 1.7 miles. Here, the Orange Trail leaves to the right. There are views to the east from open rocks about 100 feet along the Orange Trail. The Kinnelon-Boonton Trail now begins to descend, crossing a stream at 1.9 miles at the base of the descent. Just beyond, the Green Trail leaves to the right. The Kinnelon-Boonton Trail now climbs steeply up a hill, then descends gradually from the ridge, passing close to the backyards of homes along Reality Drive. It turns left and ascends along a stream until, at 2.4 miles, it turns left onto paved Reality Drive and immediately continues ahead onto Glen Rock Drive. After passing Lynnbrook Road on the left, the trail turns right onto Brentwood Drive, then again turns right onto Lakeview Drive. The trail follows Lakeview Drive for about 300 feet, then turns left and re-enters the woods at 2.7 miles.

After climbing a rise, the Kinnelon-Boonton Trail turns right onto a woods road that parallels the paved road. Reaching Fayson Lakes Road at 3.0 miles, the trail turns left and follows along the road for 250 feet, then turns right onto Toboggan Trail (a paved road, not a trail). At 3.2 miles, as the road curves to the right just beyond its intersection with West Crest Trail (another paved road), the Kinnelon-Boonton Trail turns left, leaving the paved road. It turns right onto a woods road and descends, soon approaching the shore of the Butler Reservoir. The trail continues over a dike of the reservoir, turns right, then bears left and reenters the woods, ascending gradually along an old woods road. At the crest of the hill, reached at 3.7 miles, the trail turns left, leaving the road, and begins to run along the side of a hill. The Butler Connecting Trail (blue on white), which leads in 0.4 mile to the Butler-Montville Trail, begins to the left at 4.2 miles. The Kinnelon-Boonton Trail continues ahead to end on the dirt extension of Birch Road, where parking is available, at 4.3 miles.

Orange Trail   *Length: 1.1 miles Blaze: orange*

The Orange Trail begins at a junction with the Yellow Trail, 0.2 mile from its southern terminus. From the trailhead, the Orange Trail heads northeast and descends gradually to reach the shore of Taylortown Reservoir at 0.3 mile. It continues along the shore of the reservoir, reaching a dramatic rock ledge overlooking the reservoir at 0.4 mile. After briefly detouring inland and passing cliffs to the left, the trail returns to the shore of the reservoir at 0.6 mile. At a rock ledge overlooking an island in the reservoir, the trail turns left and begins to ascend Pyramid Mountain, steeply in places. It reaches a viewpoint to the east, marked by a lone cedar tree, at 1.1 miles, and ends 100 feet beyond at a junction with the Kinnelon-Boonton Trail (white).

Red Trail   *Length: 0.5 mile Blaze: red*

The Red Trail parallels a section of the Kinnelon-Boonton Trail which runs along a power line, providing a more pleasant alternative route. Its southern trailhead is on the Butler-Montville Trail (blue), 0.1 mile north of its junction with the Kinnelon-Boonton Trail (white). In 200 feet, a short side trail, blazed with red circles, leads left to a viewpoint over the power line. The Red Trail now descends through the woods, just east of the power line. At 0.2 mile, it levels off and bears right, away from the power line, soon passing an interesting split boulder to the right. After crossing a stream on a split-log bridge, the Red Trail ends at 0.5 mile at a junction with the Kinnelon-Boonton Trail. Bear Rock is 0.2 mile to the right (north) along the Kinnelon-Boonton Trail.

Red-on-White Trail   *Length: 0.8 mile Blaze: red on white*

The Red-on-White Trail starts from the Kinnelon-Boonton Trail (white), 0.4 mile north of Tripod Rock. Meandering along with small ups and downs, the Red-on-White Trail passes a vernal pond to the right. It reaches the foot of Eagle Cliff and turns right at 0.3 mile, passing a glacial erratic to the left. In another 150 feet, with houses visible to the right, the trail turns left and ascends the ridge. At 0.5 mile, it goes by Whale Head Rock, a balanced boulder to the left, and it curves right to descend to a westerly overlook. Here, at 0.6 mile, it turns left and starts a steep, rocky descent through laurel. After crossing two streams on wooden bridges, the Red-on-White Trail ends at 0.8 mile, at a junction with the Butler-Montville Trail (blue).

Yellow Trail *Length: 1.0 mile Blaze: yellow*

The Yellow Trail provides an somewhat easier alternate route up Pyramid Mountain from the Visitors Center. To reach the Yellow Trail, take the trail from the parking area at the Visitors Center to the Butler-Montville Trail (blue), turn left, and cross the stream. The Yellow Trail begins to the right in another 300 feet. It heads north on a relatively level footpath, with large boulders above to the left, and a camp recreation area below to the right. At 0.3 mile, the Orange Trail leaves to the right. A short distance beyond, the Yellow Trail bears left and begins to climb rather steeply, reaching a viewpoint to the east at the crest of the rise. After descending slightly, the Yellow Trail turns right at a T junction, joining the Butler-Montville Trail, at 0.7 mile. The two trails run jointly for 200 feet, and then the Yellow Trail leaves to the left. The Yellow Trail now descends through a dense stand of laurel to end, at 1.0 mile, at a junction with the joint Kinnelon-Boonton and Butler-Montville trails (white/blue) just east of Bear Rock.

Turkey Mountain Trails

Turkey Mountain, east of Boonton Avenue, also has an extensive network of trails. The trails climb to several viewpoints from the summit of Turkey Mountain, run along an old limestone quarry, and lead to a scenic waterfall on North Valhalla Brook.

Butler-Montville Trail (Turkey Mountain Section)

Length: 1.5 miles Blaze: blue

To reach the Butler-Montville Trail from the Visitors Center, follow a short trail blazed with white diamonds, which begins at the northern end of the parking area and heads north, running parallel to and just west of Boonton Avenue. In about 500 feet, this trail ends at the Butler-Montville Trail. Turn right, climb to Boonton Avenue, and cross the road.

The Butler-Montville Trail begins to run under the power lines. It is level at first, but after 0.2 mile, it starts to climb, at first gently, then more steeply on a series of rock steps known as the "100 Steps." At 0.4 mile, the trail reaches the top of the power line cut, with good views to the west. A short distance beyond, it turns sharply right. (The Red Trail begins 50 feet further east along the power line cut.) The Butler-Montville Trail descends into the woods, soon reaching a T junction with a woods road. Here, the Waterfall Trail (green) begins to the left,

while the Butler-Montville Trail turns right and continues downhill. After leveling off and crossing a stream on a wooden bridge, the Butler-Montville Trail crosses the Yellow Trail at 0.9 mile. (To the right, the Yellow Trail leads back to the Visitors Center in 0.5 mile.) The Butler-Montville Trail now begins a gradual climb and, at 1.1 miles, reaches a junction with the Red Dot Trail, which leaves to the right. Here, the Butler-Montville Trail turns left to skirt a housing development. Just ahead, Lake Valhalla is visible through the trees to the left. The trail then turns left at a stone wall, passes through a stand of mountain laurel, and ends, 1.5 miles from the start, at a rock outcrop with westerly views.

Red Trail *Length: 0.9 mile Blaze: red*

The Red Trail begins 50 feet east of the Butler-Montville Trail (blue), near the top of the "100 Steps," along the power line cut. The trailhead is about 0.5 mile from the Visitors Center. The Red Trail descends for a short distance, then turns right and starts up a gentle slope. At 0.2 mile, an unmarked trail joins from the left. Here, the Red Trail turns right and soon begins a rolling series of ups and downs as it heads toward the summit of Turkey Mountain. After passing through a gap in a stone wall, it reaches a stand of cedar trees just below the summit of the mountain. A short distance beyond, at 0.5 mile, a T junction is reached. Here, the Yellow Trail leaves to the left, while the Red Trail turns right (south) and crosses a rock formation with seasonal views to the east. The Red Trail now descends steeply, with occasional glimpses of Lake Valhalla in the distance to the left. At 0.7 mile, at the base of the steep descent, the Red Trail turns right, joining the Waterfall Trail (green). The two trails cross a stream, pass under a power line, and turn left onto a woods road. A short distance beyond, the Waterfall Trail leaves to the right, while the Red Trail continues ahead to end at 0.9 mile at a junction with the Yellow Trail.

Red Dot Trail *Length: 0.7 mile Blaze: red dot*

The Red Dot Trail begins at a junction with the Yellow Trail, 0.2 mile east of Boonton Avenue. At first, it heads south along a narrow, flat, meandering path. At 0.2 mile, it turns left, crosses a stream in a wet area, and begins a gradual and often rocky ascent to end at a junction with the Butler-Montville Trail (blue) at 0.7 mile.

Waterfall Trail *Length: 1.5 miles Blaze: green*

The Waterfall Trail begins at a junction with the Butler-Montville Trail (blue)

Figure 10-18. Waterfall on North Valhalla Brook

just south of the power line cut, 0.5 mile east of Boonton Avenue. In 150 feet, it turns right, leaving the woods road, and soon reaches an overlook to the south over Lake Valhalla. Here, the trail turns sharply left. At 0.2 mile, the Waterfall Trail passes the ruins of one of several cabins that once dotted the top of Turkey Mountain. This particular cabin was never occupied, as the owner abandoned construction when the power lines came through. The Waterfall Trail now bears right and begins a steady descent.

At the base of the descent, at 0.4 mile, the Waterfall Trail turns left onto a woods road, joining the Red Trail. Just before the woods road begins a steep ascent, the two trails turn right, go under the power lines, and cross a stream. Here, the Red Trail leaves to the left and begins a steep climb of Turkey Mountain, while the Waterfall Trail continues straight ahead through a broad valley. At 0.9 mile, the trail turns left at a T junction with another woods road. An attractive waterfall on North Valhalla Brook is visible straight ahead. (The Yellow Trail is 40 feet to the right from the T junction.) After crossing a stream, the Waterfall Trail begins a steady climb of Turkey Mountain. The trail levels off on a shoulder of the mountain, descends slightly, and ends, 1.5 miles from the start, at a junction with the Yellow Trail.

Yellow Trail   *Length: 3.7 miles Blaze: yellow*
The Yellow Trail begins on the east side of Boonton Avenue, across from the

Visitors Center. It starts as a level, gravel-surfaced path. At 0.2 mile, the Red Dot Trail leaves to the right, and at 0.5 mile, the Yellow Trail crosses the Butler-Montville Trail (blue). Here, the gravel path ends and the trail begins a gradual descent. At 0.9 mile, the trail reaches a Y intersection where it turns left onto a woods road known as the "Horse Shoe Trail." The Yellow Trail crosses a small stream and climbs gently until it reaches a junction with the Red Trail, which leaves to the left at 1.2 miles. Just before the junction, it passes a ravine on the right—the remains of a quarry which operated in the last half of the nineteenth century. The rock quarried here was crushed and used to purify iron ore smelted in nearby Boonton. Although commonly referred to as limestone, the rock is actually an impure marble of Precambrian age.

The Yellow Trail now descends along the woods road, which curves to the right (south). At 1.4 miles, it turns sharply left, leaving the "Horse Shoe Trail," and heads north, passing Botts Pond, visible to the right in leafless seasons. The trail then goes under power lines (remains of quarrying operations are also visible here) and turns right. At 1.8 miles, it turns right at a T junction and reaches a bridge over North Valhalla Brook, just south of a scenic waterfall. (The Waterfall Trail (green) is 40 feet to the left from the T junction.) After crossing the bridge, the Yellow Trail joins a level woods road until, at 2.1 miles, it approaches paved Stony Brook Road. Here, the trail turns left, leaving the woods road, and begins to parallel the paved road to the right. After crossing a seasonal stream, the trail begins to parallel North Valhalla Brook to the left.

At 2.8 miles, the Yellow Trail bears right and reaches the intersection of Brook Valley Road and Stony Brook Road. Here, the trail crosses the brook on the highway bridge and immediately turns left onto a woods road. The trail skirts a swampy area to the left, then crosses a brook and begins to climb. At a junction with the northern end of the Waterfall Trail (green), 3.3 miles from the start, it leaves the woods road and turns right, beginning a gradual ascent of Turkey Mountain. It passes through a series of stone walls until, at 3.7 miles, it ends in a stand of cedar trees at a junction with the Red Trail.

SCHOOLEY'S MOUNTAIN COUNTY PARK

Schooley's Mountain County Park is the former site of Camp Washington, a YMCA camp from the 1920s to the 1950s. This 782-acre park is named after the Schooley family, who were landowners in the area in the late 1700s. Opened

in 1974, the park offers hiking, picnicking, boating, swimming, fishing, and winter activities. A two-mile section of the Patriots' Path (white) traverses the park from Fairview Avenue to Rock Road.

To reach Schooley's Mountain County Park from US 206 in Chester, take County 513 west for 5.1 miles. Beyond Long Valley, turn right on Camp Washington Road and follow it for 0.5 mile to the park information center. To reach the recreation facilities, continue to Springtown Road, turn right, and follow it to the park entrance, on the right. For more information, contact the Morris County Park Commission, 53 East Hanover Avenue, P.O. Box 1295, Morristown, NJ 07962-1295; (973) 326-7600; www.morrisparks.com.

TOURNE COUNTY PARK

Located in the townships of Denville, Boonton, and Mountain Lakes, Tourne County Park is the only remaining undeveloped fragment of the Great Boonton Tract, purchased by David Ogden, Colonial Attorney-General of New Jersey, in 1759. The 547-acre county park features an extensive network of trails, which follow both footpaths and woods roads through a dense deciduous forest. A highlight of the park is the view from the top of the Tourne (elevation 897 feet), which includes the New York City skyline on clear days. A fenced-in area is a sanctuary for wildflowers and other native plants, with several short nature trails. McCaffrey Lane, which serves as the main entrance to the park, dates back to 1767, when it was built by Samuel Ogden to haul iron ore from the mines in Hibernia to his ironworks in Boonton.

To reach Tourne County Park, take I-287 North to Exit 44 (Main Street, Boonton), and bear right onto Lathrop Avenue. Turn right at the stop sign onto Main Street, and follow Main Street for 1.1 miles until it bears sharply left. Continue ahead onto Hawkins Place, turn right onto Powerville Road, and make the next left onto McCaffrey Lane, which leads in 0.3 mile into the park. For more information, contact the Morris County Park Commission, 53 East Hanover Avenue, P.O. Box 1295, Morristown, NJ 07962-1295; (973) 326-7600; www.morrisparks.com.

DeCamp Trail   *Length: 1.3 miles Blaze: none*
Built by Clarence Addington DeCamp (1859-1948), who owned much of the land that is now preserved as Tourne County Park, the DeCamp Trail is a loop

trail that follows a gravel road to the top of the Tourne. From the second large parking area on McCaffrey Lane (coming from the east), walk across the road and follow a path up to the Red Trail, passing restrooms on the way. Turn right and follow the Red Trail for 300 feet, then turn left onto a gravel road, the route of the DeCamp Trail. The DeCamp Trail proceeds uphill on a winding route, gaining 300 feet in elevation in 0.6 mile. Near the top, it reaches a memorial to the September 11, 2001 World Trade Center tragedy. Just ahead, to the left, a grassy picnic area affords an expansive view to the south. The trail curves around the summit, passes a viewpoint to the northwest, and descends to end at 1.3 miles at the Red Trail. To return to the parking area, follow the Red Trail to the left for 0.1 mile, then turn right on the side trail that leads down to the parking area.

Red Trail   *Length: 3.3 miles Blaze: red*
The Red Trail loops around Tourne County Park, following attractive footpaths through heavily wooded areas for much of its route. It is described here in a counter-clockwise direction.

To reach the start of the Red Trail, park in the first large parking area on McCaffrey Lane (coming from the east) and proceed ahead along McCaffrey Lane for 0.1 mile. Just beyond a bridge over a stream, turn right at a small four-car parking area for the Wildflower Trail. Here, a triple red blaze marks the beginning of the Red Trail.

The trail proceeds through a gate in a fence which protects the wildflowers from damage by animals. In 100 feet, it curves sharply left and begins to parallel the paved road. Short side trails that leave to the right offer the opportunity to explore the adjacent wildflower gardens. At 0.1 mile, the Red Trail passes through a gate which marks the end of the wildflower area. Just beyond, it crosses the unblazed DeCamp Trail, a gravel road that leads to the top of the Tourne.

The Red Trail continues ahead on a gravel road. It passes the west end of the DeCamp Trail at 0.3 mile and reaches a parking area at 0.5 mile. Here, the Red Trail turns left, crosses the park entrance road, and reenters the woods on a footpath, now heading southwest through deep woods. At 0.8 mile, it turns right at a trail junction. After reaching the crest of the ridge at 1.3 miles, the trail descends to a T intersection, where it turns left and passes a pond to the right. Just beyond, the trail comes to two forks, bearing right at each.

Reaching its most southerly point at 1.7 miles, the Red Trail turns left at a sign pointing to the Tourne. It bears right at the next intersection, passing a

deep ravine to the left. At 2.0 miles, the trail crosses a gravel road and continues ahead on a woods road, with a large pond visible through the trees to the right. In 500 feet, it turns left at a bench and heads north on a footpath, passing a vernal pond to the left. After briefly joining an aqua-blazed trail, the Red Trail turns left at a T intersection at 2.6 miles and descends along a woods road. It passes through a stile (designed to prevent illegal use of the trail by off-road vehicles) at 3.0 miles. A short distance ahead, it bears right onto a gravel road. After bearing right again at the next fork, the Red Trail ends at McCaffrey Lane, opposite the parking area where the hike began, at 3.3 miles.

The Red Trail may be combined with the DeCamp Trail to make a 4.4-mile loop hike around the park.

ELEVEN

THE KITTATINNIES

Paralleling the 40-mile stretch of the Delaware River from Port Jervis to the Delaware Water Gap is the long, wooded ridge of the Kittatinnies, the Native American name for "Endless Mountain." The ridge continues on the Pennsylvania side of the Water Gap southwest to Wind Gap and beyond; northeast, the ridge continues into New York State as the Shawangunk Mountains. With elevations of 1,400 to 1,800 feet, the Kittatinnies offer panoramic views from High Point, Sunrise Mountain, and many other overlooks. In addition, approximately 43 miles of the New Jersey section of the Appalachian Trail run along the ridge.

Most of the ridge is publicly owned and is divided into four administrative areas: High Point State Park, Stokes State Forest, the Delaware Water Gap National Recreation Area, and Worthington State Forest. The land between the ridge and the Delaware River contains three wildlife management areas. Other wildlife management areas and public land are located in the Great Valley, east of the Kittatinny Ridge.

Geology

Topographically, the Kittatinnies are a continuation of the Shawangunk Mountains of New York State. Most of the crest of the ridge is composed of the Silurian-aged Shawangunk Formation, a geologic unit consisting of quartzite conglomerates and sandstones, which dip to the northwest. These layers are extremely resistant to erosion, in contrast to the older and less-resistant strata

that underlie the broad lowland area just east of the Kittatinny Ridge (Figure 4-4). This lowland belt—often referred to as the Great Valley— consists largely of folded Ordovician and Cambrian strata, worn to a near-level surface. Although few outcrops exist in the Great Valley, these folded rocks—which date back to the early Paleozoic era—may be seen in cuts along abandoned railroads that have been converted to rail trails.

Ecology

The Kittatinnies support a diverse array of flora and fauna, including a number of rare and endangered species. Forming a link between the central Appalachians and more northerly environments, the Kittatinnies are also a place where species with a decidedly northern character meld with more southern varieties: porcupines den in boulder fields used by copperheads, while shady hemlock groves grow near sun-parched cactus barrens.

Dry conditions prevail along much of the ridgetop, where shallow soils rest atop an impervious cap of conglomerate rock. As a result, only drought-resistant trees—such as oaks, hickories, pitch pines, and red maples—can survive here, and these trees tend to be stunted. Shade-intolerant red cedars mark rocky clearings, with old, heavy-trunked trees indicating an opening that has existed for many years. Cool ravines and north-facing slopes support canopy trees typical of more northerly forests, including maples, birches, and hemlocks. Grasses thrive along the ridgetop, and lichens embellish exposed rock surfaces. Low-growing shrubs, such as huckleberry and blueberry, flourish on the ridge's acidic soils, and mountain laurel thickets create a dense understory below canopy trees in many areas.

More than 260 species of birds have been recorded along the Kittatinny Ridge and its immediate environs. Perhaps most conspicuous is the turkey vulture—a large relative of the storks that can often be seen soaring effortlessly on thermal updrafts. Despite its large size and high visibility when airborne, this species is extremely secretive during nesting, raising its young in remote cave-like cavities. Each fall, thousands of migrating hawks exploit these same updrafts to aid their passage southward to their wintering grounds.

A diverse variety of mammals is also found in the Kittatinnies, but most species are not easily observed. White-tailed deer, eastern gray squirrels, and eastern chipmunks are the most visible mammals. Black bears are common and leave abundant signs in the form of scat piles and overturned rocks moved

during the bear's spirited search for ant larvae and other tasty morsels. At least one species, the Allegheny woodrat, was recently extirpated from the Kittatinnies, most likely due to a lethal parasitic roundworm carried by raccoons.

The Kittatinnies and its environs are also home to 14 species of snakes, eight kinds of turtles, and one lizard species. Two venomous snakes—the northern copperhead and the timber rattlesnake—are relatively numerous along the ridge but are rarely seen due to their secretive habits. Also found in the area is a harmless mimic of these species, the eastern hognose snake, which feigns death in a most impressive fashion when disturbed. Turtle species range in size from the diminutive bog turtle, an endangered species, to the imposing snapping turtle, a common inhabitant of wetlands and ponds. In upland forests, the eastern box turtle may be encountered following warm summer rains.

HIGH POINT STATE PARK

The 15,278-acre High Point State Park extends south ten miles from the New York state line. High Point has a natural landscape of unusual beauty onto which a designed landscape was placed. Recreational facilities are centered around the Lake Marcia and High Point Monument area, located north of NJ 23. As suggested by its name, the park includes the highest point within the state—1,803 feet. In 1930, a memorial modeled after the Bunker Hill Tower was erected on the highest point in New Jersey to honor the men of New Jersey who served in the nation's wars. In 2003, this 220-foot-high monument is closed for repairs; however, a viewing platform at the base of the monument affords good views of the surrounding countryside. The park includes the 1,500-acre Dryden Kuser Natural Area. The Sawmill camping area is located on Sawmill Lake, south of NJ 23, and group campsites are also available.

For more information, contact High Point State Park, 1480 State Route 23, Sussex, NJ 07461; (973) 875-4800; www.njparksandforests.org.

Figure 11-1. High Point Monument

History

For more than 150 years, High Point State Park has been a recreational area reflecting four phases in the region's leisure and vacation trends: summer hotels, gilded summer homes, the state park movement, and the work of the Civilian Conservation Corps (CCC). Each phase has left distinct historic and architectural imprints on the park property.

As early as 1855, the public used the Lake Marcia/High Point area for picnics and outings. By that time, the High Point area had been cleared for farming, but it was not suitable for agriculture and was poor in timber. In 1890, Charles St. John, a Port Jervis newspaper publisher, built the High Point Inn. Representative of the era of grand mountaintop hotels, it operated with great success until 1908, when a combination of hard economic times, the threat of forest fires, and St. John's health forced the inn into bankruptcy. Much of the estate was purchased in 1911 by John Fairfield Dryden, who intended to use the land as a nature preserve but did not live to do so. At the same time, the unaltered natural landscape was improved with the addition of carriage roads, paths, trails, rustic seats, and ornamental trees.

As the era of grand hotels waned, Dryden's son-in-law, Anthony Kuser—a New Jersey industrialist, philanthropist, and conservationist—converted the High Point Inn into a lavish summer residence. High Point's ultimate destiny as a state park reflects John Dryden's wish to use the property as a preserve.

In 1923, when the Kuser family donated the property to the state, High Point became a state park and so entered its third phase. Like Bear Mountain State Park and other pioneers in the state parks movement, High Point was within one to two hours of a major urban area. It provided recreational facilities that low- and middle-income residents could afford—in contrast with the national parks, which required considerable time and money to visit.

Soon after the park was created, the Olmsted Brothers, prominent landscape architects, were hired to design both a general development plan and specific features. The brothers were sons of Frederick Law Olmsted, who designed Central Park in New York City. Their design reflected the American romantic style of landscape architecture, with an emphasis on natural scenery, use of native raw materials, a lack of formal design, and curvilinear roads. During its first two decades, under the High Point Park Commission, the park flourished. The park was provided for as long as it remained a product of people with wealth, political connections, and vision. When they vanished, the

era of vast improvements vanished with them. Although not all of the improvements from that time have survived, High Point still has one of the finest assemblages of rustic park architecture in the northeast.

In 1933, High Point entered the last of its four historic eras with the establishment of a Civilian Conservation Corps camp. Men stationed at Camp Kuser worked under the direction of the National Park Service to expand and improve the park. Although the work the men did at High Point typifies CCC activities elsewhere, the plan they implemented was more ambitious than most others in New Jersey.

Several sets of master plans were drawn up between 1937 and 1941. The basic document that guided CCC efforts faithfully accepted the Olmsted Brothers' plan to spread activities across the park and relieve pressure on the Lake Marcia area. Extensive recreation facilities that were planned but never constructed included ballfields, tennis courts, a museum, an eastern perimeter park drive, and more picnicking and parking areas scattered throughout the park. The rustic architectural elements that the CCC added to High Point provide far more tangible evidence of their efforts than their conservation work. Unfortunately, many of their improvements—including a beach complex at Sawmill Lake, sections of boulder guardrail and curbing, a boardwalk around Lake Marcia, and the actual buildings of the camp—did not survive.

After 1945, the state's ambitious improvement plans for the park were abandoned. It was not until the late 1950s that the park received its next major slate of improvements, which involved upgrading or replacing deteriorating facilities at Lake Marcia. By the early 1960s, the state's primary concern was the acquisition and creation of new parks, and moneys were no longer funneled into expanding the facilities of existing parks. By the 1990s, the intense park development planned for High Point in the 1930s had fallen into environmental, planning, and aesthetic disfavor, as it became clear that non-native species crowd out native ones and altered landscapes are expensive to maintain.

Ecology

High Point State Park is renowned among naturalists for its Cedar Swamp. This large swamp of Atlantic white cedar trees is the farthest inland swamp of this type that is known to exist. Throughout the range of this species (from Maine to Florida), it thrives primarily in the flat lands bordering the coast. Only in New Jersey can a cedar swamp be found on an inland mountaintop. Early in

Colonial history, there were large stands of this highly valuable tree in the Hackensack Meadowlands, but these trees were killed in the early twentieth century when the Hackensack River was dammed to create the Oradell Reservoir, diverting fresh water from the Meadowlands and causing it to become salty. Today, in New Jersey, the Atlantic white cedar is found primarily in the Pinelands, where it forms remarkably dense, visually striking swamps. A small coastal stand of these trees exists in Cheesequake State Park. There are several other inland Atlantic white cedar swamps in New Jersey (one in Wawayanda State Park, another small swamp in nearby Abram S. Hewitt State Forest, and a more extensive swamp just over the New York border in Sterling Forest), but the Cedar Swamp in High Point State Park is the best known of all. A boardwalk that crosses the swamp—the route of the Shawangunk Ridge Trail—makes it possible for hikers to explore this unusual feature of the park.

Trails in High Point State Park

High Point State Park features twelve marked trails, including sections of the Appalachian and Shawangunk Ridge trails. The extensive network of trails makes it possible to create a number of loop hikes. Except for the Appalachian, Monument, and Shawangunk Ridge trails, all trails in High Point State Park are open to mountain bikes. Trails that are blazed with two colors have half of the dot in one color and the other half in another color.

During the winter, when conditions are suitable, snowmobiling and dogsledding are permitted on the Ayers, Parker, Fuller, Mashipacong, and Iris trails, all south of NJ 23. North of NJ 23, the trails and unplowed roads are open for snowshoeing and cross-country skiing, with a concessionaire providing groomed trails (fee charged) and ski rentals. For information about cross-country skiing at High Point, contact the concessionaire at (973) 702-1222.

Appalachian Trail (County 519 to Deckertown Turnpike)

Length: 8.3 miles Blaze: white

The Appalachian Trail (A.T.) traverses High Point State Park from north to south, passing many viewpoints along the way. It may be combined with the Iris Trail (which it intersects three times) or other trails to form loop hikes of varying lengths.

The Appalachian Trail, coming from the east, enters High Point State Park

at County 519 (where parking for day hikes is available), 0.6 mile south of the New Jersey-New York state line and about 3.5 miles north of NJ 23. After ascending on switchbacks, the trail emerges onto a field. It crosses the field, bears right, and climbs another switchback. At 0.5 mile, at the top of the switchback, the trail bears left and heads south along a relatively level footpath, soon passing through gaps in several old stone walls. After crossing an intermittent stream at the head of a ravine at 1.0 mile, the trail turns right at a large pile of rocks and begins to ascend. Just beyond, at 1.3 miles, a blue-blazed side trail to the left leads 0.1 mile to the High Point Shelter, a stone shelter with a wooden floor, built in 1936 by the Civilian Conservation Corps. Overnight camping is permitted here, and water is available from streams near the shelter (water should be purified prior to use).

Now heading west, the A.T. continues its climb of the Kittatinny Ridge. At 1.8 miles, after a steady ascent, it reaches a junction with the Monument Trail (red/green) at the crest of the ridge. (To the right, the Monument Trail (also the route of the Shawangunk Ridge Trail) leads in 0.5 mile to the High Point Monument; straight ahead, it leads to Lake Marcia.) The A.T. turns left at the junction and begins to head south along the ridge, reaching a wooden observation platform with a 360° view at 2.0 miles. The Great Valley is visible to the east, with Pochuck Mountain in the distance and Wawayanda Mountain on the horizon. Lake Marcia is in the foreground to the west, with the Pocono Mountains of Pennsylvania in the distance. The Delaware Water Gap may be seen to the southwest, and the High Point Monument dominates the ridge to the north.

The A.T. continues south along the ridge, passing through scrub oak and blueberry bushes. At 2.2 miles, it bears left and begins to descend. After crossing NJ 23 at 3.0 miles, the trail continues across the lawn of the park headquarters and reenters the woods south of the headquarters building. Parking for hikers is available at a separate parking area just to the south along NJ 23 (registration is required for overnight parking).

At 3.2 miles, after passing the western end of a short unmarked trail that connects the A.T. with the hikers' parking area, the A.T. reaches a junction marked by a four-foot-high white pipe to the left of the trail. Here, the Iris Trail (red on white) begins to the left, while the Mashipacong Trail (yellow on white) begins to the right. The A.T. continues ahead and climbs to regain the crest of the Kittatinny Ridge at 3.6 miles. It continues south along the ridge, passing the western terminus of the Blue Dot Trail, which descends to the Sawmill camping area on Sawmill Lake, at 3.9 miles. Just beyond, the A.T. reaches a west-facing

Figure 11-2. Mashipacong Shelter

viewpoint over Sawmill Lake.

The A.T. now bears left and descends to reach a low point between two ridges at 4.3 miles. It climbs to the eastern ridge, where it arrives at a west-facing viewpoint at 4.4 miles. The interior valley between the two ridges is visible below, with the Pocono Mountains in the distance to the southwest. The trail crosses to the opposite side of the ridge and continues south along the eastern ridge of Kittatinny Mountain, reaching a viewpoint from open rocks to the left at 5.4 miles. Lake Rutherford, the water supply for the Town of Sussex, may be seen to the northeast. Dutch Shoe Rock, another viewpoint to the east, is reached at 5.6 miles. Here, a blue-blazed side trail to the left leads 0.4 mile to the Rutherford Shelter, where overnight camping is permitted.

At 6.4 miles, the A.T. turns right onto a woods road, the route of the Iris Trail (red on white). The A.T. runs jointly with the Iris Trail for 350 feet. It then turns left, leaving the Iris Trail, and descends on a footpath, crossing a stream on logs at 6.8 miles. After climbing back to the ridge, it crosses a cleared strip of land—the route of a buried gas pipeline—at 7.2 miles. A short side trail to the left leads to a viewpoint over a farm landscape in the Wallkill Valley. Just beyond, the A.T. turns right, away from an old road that continues ahead onto private land.

After passing a trail register on a tree to the right of the trail, the A.T. reaches another intersection with the Iris Trail at 7.6 miles. It continues ahead and descends to cross Deckertown Turnpike, where parking for day hikes is available, at 8.3 miles. The Mashipacong Shelter is 0.2 mile south of this road

crossing. For a description of the A.T. south of Deckertown Turnpike, see the Stokes State Forest section of this chapter (pp. 291-94).

Ayers Trail   *Length: 0.9 mile Blaze: black*

This east–west woods road cuts through a mixed hardwood forest and an old farm site, established soon after the Civil War. The west end is on Park Ridge Road, where limited parking is available. Parking is also available 0.3 mile north of the eastern trailhead on Sawmill Road near the crossing of the Mashipacong Trail (yellow on white) and 0.4 mile south of the eastern trailhead at the Sawmill Lake parking area.

Blue Dot Trail   *Length: 0.4 mile Blaze: blue dot*

This short trail, one of the steepest in the park, connects the Sawmill camping area (where parking is available) with the Appalachian Trail. It begins in the camping area across from Campsite #15. At first, it climbs gradually through an oak-and-maple forest. At 0.2 mile, the grade steepens, and views of the pond and the surrounding countryside appear. The trail ends, 0.4 mile from the start, at a junction with the Appalachian Trail (white).

Fuller Trail   *Length: 0.8 mile Blaze: blue/red*

The Fuller Trail connects the Mashipacong Trail with the Life Trail. It begins on the west side of Sawmill Road at the crossing of the Mashipacong Trail (yellow on white), where parking is available. It runs next to a low boggy area for about 0.5 mile before reaching the midpoint of the Life Trail (brown). Turning right, it runs jointly with the Life Trail for another 0.3 mile before ending at a winter-use parking area on Park Ridge Road. The Fuller Trail may be combined with the Mashipacong Trail and a short section of Park Ridge Road to form a 2.3-mile loop hike.

Iris Trail   *Length: 4.3 miles Blaze: red on white*

The Iris Trail, a woods road, connects NJ 23 with Deckertown Turnpike. For its entire length, it roughly parallels the Appalachian Trail, intersecting with it three times. The Iris Trail can be combined with the Appalachian Trail to form loop hikes of 6.4 or 8.7 miles, starting from park headquarters on NJ 23.

   The Iris Trail begins at an intersection with the Appalachian Trail (A.T.) (white), 0.1 mile south of NJ 23. This intersection is marked by a four-foot-

NEW JERSEY WALK BOOK

high white pipe to the east of the trail. Here, the Mashipacong Trail (yellow on white) begins on the west side of the A.T. while the Iris Trail begins on the east side. The Iris Trail heads south, following a woods road through rolling country under a canopy of trees, and reaching Lake Rutherford at 1.5 miles. The trail continues along the west shore of the lake, with several rock outcrops along the lake shore offering attractive locations for rest stops. (Since it serves as a municipal water supply, swimming in the lake is not permitted.) Beyond the lake, the trail crosses a stream and, at 2.3 miles, it turns right and begins to follow a narrower woods road.

At 3.0 miles, the A.T. joins from the left. After running jointly with the Iris Trail for 350 feet, the A.T. leaves to the left, while the Iris Trail continues ahead on the woods road. The Iris Trail crosses the route of a gas pipeline at 3.3 miles, with views on both sides of the trail. It descends to cross a stream and climbs to again intersect the A.T. at 4.1 miles. The Iris Trail ends, 4.3 miles from its start, at Deckertown Turnpike, where parking is available.

Life Trail   *Length: 0.6 mile Blaze: brown*

This short horseshoe-shaped trail begins and ends on Park Ridge Road. Its western end is just east of the intersection of Park Ridge Road and Steeny Kill Road (about 0.7 mile west of Sawmill Road). Its eastern end is near the group camping area, where parking is available even in the winter. It reaches a junction with the Fuller Trail (blue/red) at its midpoint. The Life Trail is adjacent to a low, boggy area, with rich soil that supports a myriad of vegetation, including wildflowers, ferns, and fungi.

Mashipacong Trail   *Length: 2.8 miles Blaze: yellow on white*

The Mashipacong Trail begins at an intersection with the Appalachian Trail (white), 0.1 mile south of NJ 23. This intersection is marked by a four-foot-high white pipe to the east of the trail. Here, the Iris Trail (red on white) begins on the east side of the Appalachian Trail, while the Mashipacong Trail begins on the west side. After doubling back behind the park headquarters, the Mashipacong Trail turns left, crosses a service road leading to communications towers, and heads into the woods. The trail climbs slightly and then descends steadily to reach the intersection of Sawmill Road, Park Ridge Road, and a dirt road at 0.7 mile. Here, the Mashipacong Trail turns left onto the dirt road. At 1.2 miles, it turns right, leaving the road, and reenters the woods. For the next

Figure 11-3. Mashipacong Trail

half mile, the trail meanders back and forth between mature woods and over-grown fields. At 1.8 miles, the Mashipacong Trail turns left onto Sawmill Road. It runs jointly with the paved road for a short distance, then turns right onto a woods road. Here, the Fuller Trail (blue/red) begins to the right. The Mashipacong Trail ends, 2.8 miles from its start, at Park Ridge Road.

Monument Trail   *Length: 3.6 miles Blaze: red/green*

The Monument Trail is a loop trail which, for most of its length, passes through pristine backcountry unspoiled by the sounds of road traffic. It is described here in a counter-clockwise direction, beginning at the north end of the parking lot for the High Point Monument.

From the parking lot, the trail heads north into the woods, passing several rock outcrops, with views to the east. The trail continues northward along the ridge, descending, at 1.0 mile, to cross the outlet of Cedar Swamp on a wooden bridge. Just before the stream crossing (which is immediately south of the New Jersey-New York state line), the Shawangunk Ridge Trail (aqua) leaves to the

left. The Monument Trail now curves left and heads south through a level wooded area. At 1.6 miles, the Shawangunk Ridge Trail joins from the left, runs concurrently with the Monument Trail for 200 feet, then leaves to the right.

The Monument Trail continues through two rock outcrops with scraggly pitch pines and vistas to the northwest, and it descends to cross a wooden bridge over another stream at 2.4 miles. Just beyond, the Steeny Kill Trail (blue), which leads 0.7 mile to NJ 23 at Steeny Kill Lake, leaves to the right. The Monument Trail now climbs stone steps, levels off, and descends gradually. At 2.7 miles, it turns left onto the road that leads to the High Point Nature Center, crosses paved Kuser Road, and descends to Lake Marcia. It follows the northeast shore of Lake Marcia for about 300 feet, then turns left and climbs the hillside to cross a park road.

At 3.1 miles, the Monument Trail reaches the Appalachian Trail (white). Here, the Monument Trail turns left, while the Appalachian Trail is to the right and straight ahead. The Shawangunk Ridge Trail starts at this intersection and begins to run jointly with the Monument Trail (although this section of the Shawangunk Ridge Trail is not marked with aqua blazes). The Monument Trail now crosses another park road and climbs to the ridge, passing just west of the High Point Monument. It continues along the west side of the parking lot for the monument to reach the start of the trail at 3.6 miles.

Old Trail   *Length: 0.5 mile Blaze: brown/yellow*
The Old Trail, a woods road, connects the parking area at the Lake Marcia beach with NJ 23 at Sawmill Road. For its entire length, it runs alongside a stream, and it features a striking array of geologic formations. In the summer, the canopy of tall, old hardwood trees lends serenity and grandeur. At the southern end, the nearest available parking is at the winter-use parking area on Park Ridge Road, about 0.5 mile from the southern trailhead.

Parker Trail   *Length: 3.5 miles Blaze: blue*
The Parker Trail connects Park Ridge Road in High Point State Park with Grau Road in Stokes State Forest, passing the Steam Mill camping area on the way. Its northern trailhead is on Park Ridge Road, 0.3 mile west of its intersection with Sawmill Road. Parking is available 0.1 mile east of the trailhead. The Parker Trail heads south on a footpath, roughly paralleling the Big Flat Brook, which can be heard to the left in wet seasons. At 1.3 miles, the trail crosses Deckertown Turnpike. South of Deckertown Turnpike, the trail follows a woods

road, with stately hardwoods providing shade in the summer. The Howell Trail (gray) joins from the left at 2.3 miles and runs concurrently with the Parker Trail to Crigger Road. Both trails enter Stokes State Forest at 2.5 miles.

At 3.0 miles, the Parker Trail turns left onto Crigger Road. After passing the Steam Mill camping area (where parking is available), it turns right, reenters the woods, and once again begins to parallel the Big Flat Brook. It crosses Parker Brook at 3.4 miles and continues ahead to its terminus on Grau Road, 3.5 miles from the start.

Shawangunk Ridge Trail   *Length: 3.1 miles Blaze: aqua*

This southernmost section of the Shawangunk Ridge Trail (which extends north for 28 miles to a junction with the Long Path near Wurtsboro, N.Y.) follows several ridges of Kittatinny Mountain and crosses the unusual and ecologically significant Cedar Swamp.

The Shawangunk Ridge Trail begins at a junction with the Appalachian Trail (white) and the Monument Trail (red/green) near the northeast corner of Lake Marcia. Here, the Appalachian Trail heads east and south, while the Monument Trail comes in from the west and continues northward. The Shawangunk Ridge Trail proceeds north, following the Monument Trail, with which it is co-aligned for the next 1.5 miles. This section of the Shawangunk Ridge Trail is blazed only with the red/green blazes of the Monument Trail, not with the aqua blazes of the Shawangunk Ridge Trail.

The trail crosses a paved park road and climbs to the ridge, passing just west of the High Point Monument, which offers a 360° view. It proceeds along the west side of the parking lot for the monument, turns right and continues along the northern edge of the parking lot, then turns left at 0.5 mile and re-enters the woods between two boulders. Now heading north, the trail passes several rock outcrops, with views to the east. It continues northward along the ridge, then bears left and descends to the outlet of the Cedar Swamp. At 1.5 miles, just before this stream crossing (which is immediately south of the New Jersey-New York state line), the Shawangunk Ridge Trail turns left, leaving the Monument Trail, and begins to parallel the eastern edge of the Cedar Swamp on a woods road (from here on, the trail is blazed aqua).

At 1.9 miles, the Shawangunk Ridge Trail turns right and crosses the Cedar Swamp on a boardwalk. The swamp features cedar, rhododendron, and hemlock and represents the farthest inland occurrence of the Atlantic white

cedar—normally found only along the coastal plain (see pp. 281-82). After briefly following a woods road along the western edge of the swamp, the trail turns right, leaving the road, and climbs to reach a T intersection with the Monument Trail at 2.2 miles. The Shawangunk Ridge Trail turns left, runs concurrently with the Monument Trail for 200 feet, then turns right at the top of a rise, leaving the Monument Trail. It passes a westward view over the Delaware River and descends slightly, then continues north along the central ridge of Kittatinny Mountain.

The trail turns left at 2.7 miles and descends on an old woods road to cross a stream. It then climbs gradually and reaches the New Jersey-New York boundary (marked by a monument) at 3.1 miles. Here the trail leaves High Point State Park and crosses into New York State. For a description of the continuation of the Shawangunk Ridge Trail to the north, see the *Long Path Guide*, published by the Trail Conference.

Steeny Kill Trail   *Length: 0.7 mile Blaze: blue*
The Steeny Kill Trail connects NJ 23 at Steeny Kill Lake with the Monument Trail. The western trailhead is on NJ 23 just north of Steeny Kill Lake (parking is available at the Steeny Kill boat ramp just off NJ 23, south of the trailhead). The trail heads east along the northern shore of Steeny Kill Lake and ends at the Monument Trail (red/green).

STOKES STATE FOREST

Named in honor of Governor Edward Stokes, who donated the first 500 acres, this public area is managed for recreation and for timber, wildlife, and water conservation. Its 15,947 acres include some of the first land purchased for public use by the State of New Jersey.

The effects of human activities are everywhere. Lenni Lenape grew crops in the fertile areas and hunted in the forest-covered mountains. The English and Dutch farmed the area in the early 1700s. During the 1800s, the area was deforested through heavy harvesting of wood for lumber and for domestic and industrial fuel. Even into the twentieth century, many areas had no trees at all.

Like High Point, Stokes State Park was the site of Civilian Conservation Corps camps. During the 1930s, the young men in the CCC constructed Sunrise Mountain Road, developed the Lake Ocquittunk, Kittle Field, and Shotwell

areas, and built the park's extensive trail system. As part of their conservation efforts, they established evergreen plantations, which are evidence of early forest management in the area.

Camping is allowed at four locations in the park and at shelters along the Appalachian Trail, and hunting is permitted in certain areas of the park. For more information, contact Stokes State Forest, One Coursen Road, Branchville, NJ 07826; (973) 948-3820; www.njparksandforests.org.

Trails in Stokes State Forest

Stokes State Forest contains 24 marked trails, many of which follow old woods roads. (The Parker Trail, which connects Stokes State Forest with High Point State Park, is described in the High Point State Park section of this chapter, pp. 288-89). Most of these trails are quite short, although a 13-mile section of the Appalachian Trail traverses the park from north to south. Except for the Appalachian Trail and some trail sections adjacent to developed areas, the trails in this park—which pass through attractive evergreen and deciduous forests—are lightly used. Although some trails are isolated, others can be combined to form loop hikes of varying lengths. In the winter, when snow conditions permit, the Blue Mountain, Lackner, Coursen, Parker, Swenson, and Tinsley trails (all north of US 206) are designated for snowmobiles and dogsleds, while the trails in the area southwest of US 206 are set aside for snowshoeing and cross-country skiing.

Acropolis Trail *Length: 0.6 mile Blaze: gold/brown*
The Acropolis Trail connects US 206 with the Appalachian Trail. It begins on the southwest side of US 206, about 0.2 mile northwest of its junction with County 521, and 0.4 mile southeast of its junction with County 636 (Upper North Shore Road). Parking may be available at commercial establishments to the southeast along US 206. The trail proceeds rather steeply uphill, following a woods road. The Acropolis Trail crosses the Appalachian Trail (white) at 0.5 mile, and it ends a short distance beyond.

Appalachian Trail (Deckertown Turnpike to Brink Road)
Length: 12.7 miles Blaze: white
This section of the Appalachian Trail (A.T.) offers attractive hiking along the

Figure 11-4. Sunrise Mountain

Kittatinny Ridge. A highlight of the section is Sunrise Mountain, the second-highest point on the A.T. in New Jersey (1,653 feet), but there are many other panoramic viewpoints along the trail. Parking for day hikes is available at Deckertown Turnpike (the northern end of the section), at the summit of Sunrise Mountain (mile 3.5), on Sunrise Mountain Road just north of US 206 (mile 8.8), and (except in the winter) at the intersection of Brink Road and Woods Road, 0.2 mile west of the southern end of the section. Overnight parking is permitted only at the hikers' parking area on Sunrise Mountain Road near US 206, and registration with the park office is required for overnight parking. The A.T. can be combined with other trails to form loop hikes.

From Deckertown Turnpike, where parking is available (a water pump is also located here), the Appalachian Trail (A.T.) climbs to reach the Mashipacong Shelter, where overnight camping is permitted, at 0.2 mile. The A.T. leaves High Point State Park and enters Stokes State Forest at 0.7 mile. Then, at 0.9 mile, it turns left onto Swenson Road, a woods road. It follows the road for 225 feet, then turns right as the road curves to the left. The A.T. reenters the woods, ascending on a footpath. At 1.5 miles, the trail passes to the left of a rise and begins to descend through a mountain laurel thicket. After crossing the outlet of a swamp to the left of the trail at 1.9 miles, the trail crosses a stone wall and begins to climb rather steeply through birches. Soon, the trail starts to descend, crossing two more stone walls.

After crossing dirt Crigger Road at 2.8 miles, the A.T. begins a steady climb up Sunrise Mountain on a wide footpath. The Cartwright Trail (brown/red) leaves to the right at 3.2 miles. Then, at 3.5 miles, a path to the right leads to the southern end of the Sunrise Mountain parking area, and the A.T. climbs stone steps. At the top of the steps, a side trail leads left to a panoramic east-facing viewpoint over the Great Valley from a rock ledge.

At 3.6 miles, the A.T. reaches a pavilion with stone columns, built by the

Civilian Conservation Corps in 1937. Here, there are views both east and west, although the east-facing viewpoint just to the north offers a more pristine setting. The A.T. continues from the southeast corner of the pavilion and begins to descend. After a short level stretch at 4.1 miles, the trail climbs over a rise and descends to an area with low vegetation, with scrub oak and mountain laurel predominating.

The A.T. comes out onto a grassy clearing at 4.6 miles. Here, the Tinsley Trail (yellow) leaves to the right. The A.T. now begins a steady climb, leveling off amid a cluster of pines at 4.7 miles, where a short side trail to the right leads to a viewpoint from a rock ledge over the Pocono Mountains to the west. For the next mile, the A.T. follows a rather level footpath along the west side of the ridge, traversing a deciduous forest with an understory of mountain laurel and blueberry.

After passing a large vernal pool to the left at 5.6 miles, the A.T. crosses a wet area on puncheons. At 6.0 miles, it reaches a junction with the Stony Brook Trail (brown), which leaves to the right together with a short blue-blazed trail that leads in 0.1 mile to the Gren Anderson Shelter (overnight camping permitted). The A.T. crosses Stony Brook at 6.1 miles. After another level stretch, the trail begins to climb and, at 7.0 miles, it reaches a junction with the Tower Trail (dark green) at a west-facing viewpoint studded with pitch pines.

The A.T. continues to climb, reaching a large clearing with a picnic table at the base of the Culver Fire Tower (manned seasonally) at 7.1 miles. The A.T. bears right and continues on a footpath just south of the fire tower. At 7.2 miles, an unmarked side trail to the right leads to a west-facing viewpoint. The A.T. continues along the ridge, with Culver Lake visible through the trees to the left.

At 8.1 miles, after a brief descent, the A.T. reaches a west-facing viewpoint over Kittatinny Lake. The trail now bears right and begins a rather steep, rocky descent. It turns left on paved Sunrise Mountain Road at 8.6 miles, follows the road for 125 feet, then turns right and reenters the woods. An unmarked trail to the left at 8.8 miles leads to a hikers' parking area (accessed from Sunrise Mountain Road).

The A.T. reaches the intersection of County 636 (Upper North Shore Road) and US 206 at 9.1 miles. The trail turns left, crosses County 636, and follows US 206 for about 500 feet. It then turns right, crosses US 206, and begins to climb on a woods road. It passes under a power line at 9.6 miles, with views to the east over Culver Lake. Just beyond, the A.T. crosses a gravel road,

the route of the Acropolis Trail (gold/brown), and resumes a steady ascent, reaching a clearing at the crest of the ridge at 9.9 miles. Here, there are views to the east over US 206 and Culvers Gap below. The A.T. turns left and heads south along the Kittatinny Ridge on a relatively level footpath, reaching another east-facing viewpoint over Culver Lake and US 206 from a clearing at 10.3 miles.

After a gradual descent, the A.T. reaches an intersection with the Jacob's Ladder Trail (blue/gray), which leaves to the right at 11.0 miles. The A.T. now climbs briefly, then levels off and continues south along the ridge. It passes a large boulder field to the left of the trail at 12.1 miles and soon begins a gradual descent to dirt Brink Road, reached at 12.7 miles. The Brink Road Shelter, where overnight camping is permitted, is 0.2 mile to the right, and the intersection of Brink Road and Woods Road, where parking is available (except in winter), is just beyond. For a description of the A.T. south of Brink Road, see the Delaware Water Gap National Recreation Area section of this chapter (pp. 304-07).

Blue Mountain Trail   *Length: 1.4 miles Blaze: brown/green*
Following a relatively level woods road for its entire length, the Blue Mountain Trail connects the west end of Kittle Road with the Lake Ocquittunk camping area just south of Skellinger Road. It begins at a large parking area at the western terminus of Kittle Road and heads north, passing two old barns and crossing several old stone walls—remnants of the area's agricultural past. At 0.9 mile, the Blue Mountain Trail reaches a junction with the Silver Mine Trail (orange), which leaves to the right. The Blue Mountain Trail now begins a gentle descent, crossing several small streams on rocks and passing through a hemlock forest. It ends, 1.4 miles from the start, at the Lake Ocquittunk camping area, just south of Skellinger Road. Limited parking is available at the northern trailhead along the campground road.

Cartwright Trail   *Length: 1.3 miles Blaze: brown/red*
The Cartwright Trail connects the Swenson Trail with the Appalachian Trail, crossing Sunrise Mountain Road on the way. It begins on the Swenson Trail (red) just north of its crossing of a braided stream, 0.6 mile north of the Spring Cabin and 1.0 mile south of Crigger Road. The Cartwright Trail heads uphill, at first following a rocky path which resembles a streambed. The trail soon bears right onto drier ground and continues to climb. After bearing left and

crossing a stream at 0.2 mile, the trail levels off and gradually widens to a woods road, passing through a maple-hickory forest, with an understory of ferns.

The trail crosses paved Sunrise Mountain Road at 0.9 mile. East of the road, the trail narrows to a footpath and the grade steepens. At 1.1 miles, the trail comes out on an open slab of conglomerate rock studded with pitch pines, with views over the Pocono Mountains to the west. The grade now moderates. The Cartwright Trail ends at a junction with the Appalachian Trail (white) at 1.3 miles. Crigger Road is 0.4 mile to the north, and the pavilion at the summit of Sunrise Mountain (where parking is available) is 0.4 mile to the south.

Coursen Trail
Length: 1.4 miles Blaze: blue

The Coursen Trail connects the day-use area on Stony Lake with Sunrise Mountain Road, following a gentle grade for the entire distance. It begins at a signpost for the Station Trail at the center of the parking area at Stony Lake and heads east along a woods road, running at first jointly with the Station (light green), Stony Brook (brown), Swenson (red), and Tower (dark green) trails. The Swenson Trail leaves to the left in 300 feet, and one branch of the Station Trail departs to the left at 0.1 mile. At the next intersection, reached in another 375 feet, the Coursen Trail turns right and heads south on a woods road, crossing Stony Brook on a wooden footbridge at 0.4 mile. An unmaintained light-green-blazed trail which skirts the south side of Stony Lake and connects with the Lackner Trail (black) leaves to the right at 0.6 mile. The trail reaches the crest of a rise at 1.3 miles and descends slightly to its terminus on Sunrise Mountain Road, where limited parking is available on the right shoulder.

Criss Trail
Length: 2.3 miles Blaze: blue/green

The Criss Trail is a horseshoe-shaped loop, beginning and ending on Grau Road. It begins on Grau Road near Cabin 15 of the Lake Ocquittunk camping area and follows an old woods road parallel to Criss Brook. The Deep Root Trail (orange/yellow) leaves to the left at 0.4 mile, and the Criss Trail crosses DeGroat Road (passable for four-wheel-drive vehicles) at 1.4 miles. Now bending to the right and heading east, the Criss Trail reaches its terminus on Grau Road at 2.3 miles.

Deep Root Trail
Length: 1.3 miles Blaze: orange/yellow

Connecting DeGroat Road (passable for four-wheel-drive vehicles) with the

Criss Trail, the Deep Root Trail follows a grassy woods road along a low ridge. At 0.9 mile, it turns left and begins a steady descent, ending at 1.3 miles at the Criss Trail (blue/green). Grau Road is 0.5 mile to the right along the Criss Trail.

Howell Trail
Length: 2.3 miles Blaze: gray

The Howell Trail forms a loop, beginning and ending on Crigger Road. Its western trailhead is on Crigger Road, just north of the Steam Mill camping area, where parking is available. The Howell Trail heads north, running jointly with the Parker Trail (blue). At 0.7 mile, the Parker Trail continues ahead, while the Howell Trail turns right and heads east. It winds over small, gently sloping hills and curves south to end, 2.3 miles from its start, at Crigger Road, where parking is available. At 2.1 miles, an unmarked trail (an abandoned section of Crigger Road) leaves to the left and connects with the Appalachian Trail (white).

Jacob's Ladder Trail
Length: 0.4 mile Blaze: blue/gray

This short trail climbs steeply through mountain laurel, with an understory of blueberry, from the junction of Woods Road and Coss Road (where seasonal parking is available) to the Appalachian Trail (white) on the top of the ridge, where there is a view to the east of several lakes.

Lackner Trail
Length: 2.2 miles Blaze: black

The Lackner Trail connects Kittle Road, near Stony Lake, with the Stokes State Forest headquarters, on Coursen Road just north of US 206. For most of the way, it follows the slope of a low ridge, with blueberries and mountain laurel along the route.

The trail begins on Kittle Road, midway between the Kittle Field parking area and the day-use parking area at Stony Lake (each parking area is about 0.2 mile from the trailhead). It proceeds south along a woods road, with Stony Lake visible to the left at 0.2 mile. Just beyond, an unmaintained trail which goes around Stony Lake leaves to the left. At 0.8 mile, the Lead Mine Trail (blue/gray) leaves to the right. The Lackner Trail continues ahead, with the trail soon narrowing to a footpath. It crosses a dam that impounds a pond to the left of the trail at 1.8 miles. Just beyond, the trail turns sharply right on a wide road and heads west to its terminus on Coursen Road, 2.2 miles from its start. Parking is available in the park headquarters lot, 0.2 mile south along Coursen Road.

Lead Mine Trail   *Length: 0.6 mile Blaze: blue/gray*

The Lead Mine Trail connects Coursen Road, 0.5 mile north of park headquarters, with the Lackner Trail (black). It follows a woods road for its entire length and descends gently from Coursen Road to the Lackner Trail.

Rock Oak Trail   *Length: 1.5 miles Blaze: blue/yellow*

Traversing the northwestern corner of Stokes State Forest, the Rock Oak Trail connects Deckertown Turnpike with DeGroat Road. It follows a low ridge and passes through forests in various stages of succession. Along the lower portions of the trail, there are boulder fields and glacial till. Limited parking is available on Deckertown Turnpike.

Silver Mine Trail   *Length: 2.1 miles Blaze: orange*

Following an interesting and varied route, the Silver Mine Trail connects the Kittle Field parking area, just west of the intersection of Coursen Road with Kittle Road, with the Blue Mountain Trail. From the Kittle Field parking area, the trail heads north through a picnic area, crossing Stony Brook on a footbridge and continuing along a wide woods road parallel to the brook, which is to the left. At 0.4 mile, the trail bears right at a fork and climbs gently away from the brook. (The left fork is a woods road that continues along the brook, reaching the Blue Mountain Trail in 0.5 mile.) The Silver Mine Trail reaches another junction at 0.8 mile, with both forks of the trail blazed orange. The right fork leads in a short distance to the remains of a silver mine, active in the 1870s, after which the trail is named. The main trail takes the left fork.

At 1.6 miles, the trail passes an old concrete dam on the left. Here, the woods road ends and the trail continues ahead on a footpath. The trail descends, first steeply, then more gradually, with the footpath quite rocky in places. The Silver Mine Trail ends, 2.1 miles from its start, at a junction with the Blue Mountain Trail (brown/green). To the right, the Blue Mountain Trail leads 0.5 mile to the Lake Ocquittunk camping area, just south of Skellinger Road, where limited parking is available.

Spring Cabin Trail   *Length: 0.3 mile Blaze: blue*

This short trail connects the Tinsley and Swenson trails, following a gravel road for its entire length. It begins on the Tinsley Trail (yellow), 0.5 mile from that trail's western terminus on Skellinger Road, and heads east along the gated gravel road that provides vehicular access to the Spring Cabin. The Spring

Cabin Trail ends, 0.3 mile from its start, at a junction with the Swenson Trail (red), just past the Spring Cabin.

Station Trail   *Length: 0.9 mile Blaze: light green*

This short "lollipop"-loop trail begins at a signpost at the center of the day-use parking area on Stony Lake and heads east along a woods road, running at first jointly with the Coursen (blue), Stony Brook (brown), Swenson (red), and Tower (dark green) trails. The Swenson Trail leaves to the left in 300 feet. At 0.1 mile, a fork is reached. Here, the loop portion of the trail begins. Following the loop in a clockwise direction, the Station Trail bears left, leaving the other three trails, and heads north on a woods road, reaching a T intersection at 0.5 mile. Here, the Station Trail turns right, joining the Stony Brook Trail. In another 200 feet, the Tower Trail joins from the left. All three trails head south on a woods road that runs between a rocky embankment and spruce/pine forest on the right, and a wetland on the left. At 0.8 mile, the three trails turn sharply right as the Coursen Trail continues ahead. The start of the loop is reached at 0.9 mile, with the Stony Lake parking area 0.1 mile beyond.

Steam Mill Trail   *Length: 0.8 mile Blaze: blue*

The Steam Mill Trail connects Crigger Road, just east of the Steam Mill camping area, with Skellinger Road. It begins on Crigger Road, on the east side of the road bridge over the Big Flat Brook. Parking is available on the west side of the bridge, adjacent to the Steam Mill camping area, which is traversed by the Parker Trail (blue) (see pp. 288-89). At first, the Steam Mill Trail heads west through a hemlock grove, parallel to the Big Flat Brook. At 0.2 mile, it bears left, leaving the brook, and climbs gently through successional fields. It reaches the crest of the rise at 0.6 mile and descends gradually to its terminus on Skellinger Road. This section of the gravel road is closed to traffic. To the right, Skellinger Road leads in 0.3 mile to the New Jersey School of Conservation on Lake Wapalanne, where parking is available. To the left, it leads 0.7 mile back to Crigger Road, with the northern trailhead 0.2 mile west along the road.

Steffen Trail   *Length: 1.8 miles Blaze: black/gray*

Connecting Struble Road near US 206 with Coss Road, the Steffen Trail follows a gentle, wide route for its entire length. It begins on the east side of Struble Road, 700 feet south of its junction with US 206. Parking is available on

Struble Road, opposite the trailhead. The trail climbs gradually on a wide footpath (which has been groomed for cross-country skiing), first passing through a beautiful pine plantation, then emerging into a mature hardwood forest. At 0.7 mile, it joins a woods road that comes in from the left and continues to climb gently to the summit of the ridge, reached at 1.0 mile. It begins a gradual descent at 1.3 miles, and it ends, 1.8 miles from the start, on Coss Road. Seasonal parking is available at the intersection of Coss Road with Woods Road, 0.1 mile east of the southern trailhead.

Stoll Trail   *Length: 0.7 mile Blaze: light blue/gray*
This relatively level trail connects Dimon Road with Coss Road, 0.2 mile east of Struble Road. Beginning on the northeast side of Dimon Road (parking is available at the Rutgers/4H Camp, about 0.2 mile from the trailhead), it runs through a ravine, paralleling a brook. It gradually climbs out of the ravine and turns away from the brook, ending at Coss Road, 0.2 mile east of Struble Road, where limited parking is available.

Stony Brook Trail   *Length: 1.7 miles Blaze: brown*
The Stony Brook Trail connects the day-use area on Stony Lake with the Appalachian Trail near the Gren Anderson Shelter. It begins at a signpost for the Station Trail at the center of the parking area at Stony Lake and heads east along a woods road, running at first jointly with the Coursen (blue), Station (light green), Swenson (red), and Tower (dark green) trails. The Swenson Trail leaves to the left in 300 feet, and one branch of the Station Trail departs to the left at 0.1 mile. At the next intersection, reached in another 375 feet, the Coursen Trail leaves to the right. Here, the Stony Brook Trail (together with the Tower Trail and the other branch of the Station Trail) bears left and begins to run between a rocky embankment and spruce/pine forest on the left, and a wetland on the right.

At 0.5 mile, the Tower Trail turns off to the right and, in another 200 feet, the Station Trail leaves to the left. The Stony Brook Trail continues ahead, following an old woods road. It turns right at 0.8 mile, crosses two brooks, and begins a gradual climb, with Stony Brook on the right. The climb soon steepens.

After passing a cascade in the brook, the Stony Brook Trail crosses paved Sunrise Mountain Road at 1.4 miles. Then, at 1.6 miles, a short blue-blazed trail to the left leads to the Gren Anderson Shelter. The Stony Brook Trail

continues ahead to end, 1.7 miles from the start, at a junction with the Appalachian Trail (white).

Swenson Trail   *Length: 3.8 miles Blaze: red*

Named for a local subsistence farmer, the Swenson Trail connects the day-use area on Stony Lake with Crigger Road, following woods roads for most of the way. It begins at a signpost for the Station Trail in the center of the parking area at Stony Lake and heads east along a woods road, running at first jointly with the Coursen (blue), Station (light green), Stony Brook (brown), and Tower (dark green) trails. In 300 feet, the Swenson Trail turns left, leaving the other four trails, and heads north on a rocky woods road, climbing gradually. After reaching the crest of a rise at 0.3 mile, the trail descends briefly and levels off. At 1.0 mile, it crosses a stream on rocks, climbs briefly, and again levels off.

The Swenson Trail reaches a T intersection at 1.8 miles. Here, it turns left, joining the Tinsley Trail (yellow), which comes in from the right. Both trails descend steeply on a woods road for 500 feet. At 1.9 miles, the Swenson Trail turns right, leaving the woods road, and descends rather steeply on a rocky footpath, reaching the Spring Cabin in a clearing at 2.2 miles. The Swenson Trail goes around the right side of the cabin and reenters the woods beyond a wood shed, passing the eastern end of the Spring Cabin Trail (blue) to the left, and continuing along a level woods road.

After crossing several braids of a stream on rocks, the Swenson Trail reaches the western terminus of the Cartwright Trail (brown/red), which leaves to the right at 2.8 miles. The Swenson Trail continues ahead and descends to Crigger Road, where it ends at 3.8 miles. Parking is available near the trailhead.

The Swenson Trail may be combined with the Cartwright, Appalachian, and Tower trails to form an attractive ten-mile loop hike.

Tibbs Trail   *Length: 0.5 mile Blaze: blue/green*

The Tibbs Trail follows a woods road connecting the Shotwell camping area with Coursen Road. Beginning at the Shotwell camping area, where parking is available 0.1 mile from the trailhead, the trail crosses a brook on rocks at 0.1 mile. The trail then widens and passes a pond (which beavers created from a swamp) on the left. The Tibbs Trail ends at Coursen Road, midway between the park headquarters at US 206 and the Stony Lake day-use area. Limited parking is available at the Coursen Road trailhead.

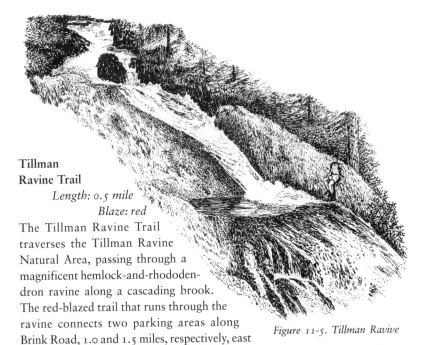

Tillman Ravine Trail

Length: 0.5 mile

Blaze: red

The Tillman Ravine Trail traverses the Tillman Ravine Natural Area, passing through a magnificent hemlock-and-rhododendron ravine along a cascading brook. The red-blazed trail that runs through the ravine connects two parking areas along Brink Road, 1.0 and 1.5 miles, respectively, east

Figure 11-5. Tillman Ravine

of Walpack Center. (This section of Brink Road is closed in the winter.) The trail crosses Tillman Brook five times on wooden bridges. An unmarked branch of the trail leads west, along the north side of the brook, to Mountain Road, just south of its intersection with Brink Road.

Tinsley Trail

Length: 2.0 miles Blaze: yellow

The Tinsley Trail traverses Stokes State Forest from west to east, connecting Skellinger Road with the Appalachian Trail, and following woods roads for its entire length. It begins on Skellinger Road, midway between the Lake Ocquittunk camping area and the New Jersey School of Conservation on Lake Wapalanne. Limited parking is available at the trailhead. The trail heads east, following a gated gravel road that provides vehicular access to the Spring Cabin. At 0.5 mile, the Tinsley Trail bears right, leaving the gravel road, and continues along a woods road, climbing gradually. (Straight ahead, the gravel road is blazed as the Spring Cabin Trail (blue) and leads to the cabin at a junction with the Swenson Trail (red) in 0.3 mile.)

At 1.0 mile, the grade steepens considerably. Just beyond, the Swenson Trail (red) joins from the left. The two trails run together for 500 feet, until the Swenson Trail leaves to the right at 1.1 miles. At 1.2 miles, the grade moderates, and the Tinsley Trail continues ahead on a grassy woods road. In the next half mile, a number of "kettle holes"—depressions created by the melting, at the end of the last ice age, of huge blocks of ice trapped in sand, gravel, and rock—are visible to the left of the trail. An unmarked trail that leaves to the left at 1.4 miles leads to several of these "kettle holes," some of which are filled with water.

The Tinsley Trail crosses paved Sunrise Mountain Road (where limited parking is available on the right shoulder of the road) at 1.9 miles. The trail continues ahead for another 0.1 mile to its terminus on the Appalachian Trail (white). The pavilion at Sunrise Mountain, where parking is available, is 1.0 mile to the left.

Tower Trail   *Length: 1.9 miles Blaze: dark green*

The Tower Trail connects the day-use area on Stony Lake with the Appalachian Trail near the Culver Fire Tower. It begins at a signpost for the Station Trail in the center of the parking area at Stony Lake and heads east along a woods road, running at first jointly with the Coursen (blue), Station (light green), Stony Brook (brown), and Swenson (red) trails. The Swenson Trail leaves to the left in 300 feet, and one branch of the Station Trail departs to the left at 0.1 mile. At the next intersection, reached in another 375 feet, the Coursen Trail leaves to the right. Here, the Tower Trail (together with the Stony Brook Trail and the other branch of the Station Trail) bears left and begins to run between a rocky embankment and spruce/pine forest on the left, and a wetland on the right.

At 0.5 mile, the Stony Brook and Station trails continue straight ahead as

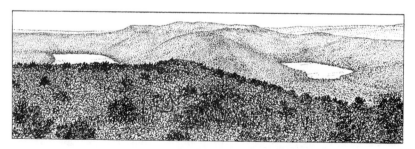

Figure 11-6. View from Culver Fire Tower

the Tower Trail turns off to the right to cross Stony Brook on rocks. At 0.7 mile, the Tower Trail begins a gradual climb up the Kittatinny Ridge. After crossing paved Sunrise Mountain Road at 1.4 miles, where limited parking is available, the climb steepens. The steepest part of the climb begins at 1.7 miles, where the trail starts to climb over rock ledges to its end at the Appalachian Trail (white), just north of the Culver Fire Tower.

DELAWARE WATER GAP
NATIONAL RECREATION AREA

Archeological evidence indicates that Native Americans came to the Delaware River Valley almost ten thousand years ago. Descendants of these early settlers participated in the Indian Wars of the eighteenth century. During the American Revolution, the valley was a vital communication link between New York and Philadelphia.

The first tourists came to the Gap around 1830 to marvel at its rocky crags, forested slopes, and winding river. When the railroad penetrated the Gap in 1855, the floodgates of tourism opened. The area soon acquired a body of legends and romance, as well as hotels and saloons. All kinds of natural features were given names—not a creek, crag, or vista escaped.

The idea of damming the Delaware River has danced in the heads of schemers for almost as long as industry has existed along the river. In 1868, powerful Trenton manufacturing interests defeated such a bill, but local supporters correctly predicted that someday a dam near the Water Gap would be proposed again. A devastating flood in 1955 convinced federal officials that the river should be dammed. Six major dams were proposed, but only one developed beyond paper. Beginning in 1956, plans were under way to construct a huge dam on Tocks Island that would span the valley, impounding a 28-mile-long lake for the purposes of flood control, electric generation, water supply, and, as an added benefit, recreation. In 1962, Congress authorized the construction of the Tocks Island Dam. In a frenzied attempt to prepare for the building of the reservoir, the Army Corps of Engineers condemned properties, evicted families, and razed thousands of homes and many historic structures. Eventually, the government purchased 55,161 acres from the Water Gap north almost to Port Jervis. The public attacked the project and its projected environmental consequences.

On September 1, 1965, President Lyndon B. Johnson signed into law the act authorizing establishment of the Delaware Water Gap National Recreation Area, with the dam and its man-made lake envisioned as its centerpiece. But opposition to the dam remained steadfast. Finally, after years of acrimonious debate, the Tocks Island Dam project was shelved by the Delaware River Basin Commission in 1975. It was not until 1992, however, that the proposed dam was officially de-authorized. Since water is an ever-important commodity and powerful lobbies exist that would like to be a part of a multi-billion-dollar construction project, it is conceivable that the project could be revived.

Parcels of private land are scattered throughout the recreation area. Please respect the rights of these landowners and do not trespass.

For more information, visit the Kittatinny Point Visitor Center, just off the last exit of I-80 in New Jersey, or contact the Delaware Water Gap National Recreation Area, Bushkill, PA 18324; (570) 588-2451; www.nps.gov/dewa.

Trails in the Delaware Water Gap National Recreation Area

The Appalachian Trail is the centerpiece of the trail system in the New Jersey section of the Delaware Water Gap National Recreation Area. Most of the other trails connect with and provide access to the Appalachian Trail, and some of them can be combined to form loop hikes. The park also offers an network of unmarked woods roads. The woods roads that surround Blue Mountain Lake (the remnants of a proposed vacation-home development that was thwarted by the creation of the park) are said to offer the best cross-country skiing in the state, given enough snow cover.

Appalachian Trail (Brink Road to Kaiser Road Trail)

Length: 16.2 miles Blaze: white

This section of the Appalachian Trail traverses the Kittatinny Ridge, with several side trails providing access and leading to points of interest. Parking is available at Brink Road at the northern end of the section (except in the winter), and cars may also be parked at Crater Lake (mile 4.9), at Blue Mountain Lake Road (mile 7.0), at Millbrook-Blairstown Road (mile 10.8), and at Camp Road (mile 14.3). In the southern portion of this section, the A.T. can be combined with the Rattlesnake Swamp Trail or with the Coppermines Trail and the Kaiser Road Trail to form loop hikes.

From Brink Road (seasonal parking for day hikes is available at the intersection of Woods Road and Brink Road, 0.2 mile west of the trail crossing of Brink Road), the A.T. begins a steady climb up Blue Mountain. After a brief descent, it reaches a cleared area at the crest of the ridge at 0.7 mile, with views to the west over the Delaware Valley and the Pocono Plateau in Pennsylvania. The A.T. descends through a wooded area to reach another west-facing viewpoint at 0.9 mile.

At 1.1 miles, the trail leaves Stokes State Forest and enters the Delaware Water Gap National Recreation Area (the boundary is marked by a sign). Just beyond, the A.T. turns left onto a dirt road, which it follows for 0.3 mile. At 1.4 miles, the trail turns left, leaving the dirt road, and descends on a rocky footpath, crossing a stream on rocks at 1.9 miles. The trail now begins to climb Rattlesnake Mountain, reaching its summit (1,492 feet) at 2.2 miles. There are expansive west-facing views from a rock outcrop that marks the summit.

The A.T. now descends, first rather steeply, then more gradually. At the base of the descent, it passes through a hemlock grove and reaches a blue-blazed side trail that leads left to a spring. Just beyond, at 2.6 miles, the trail crosses a stream on a wooden bridge. In another 200 feet, the trail turns left at a T intersection and resumes a steady climb. Near the top of the ascent, as the trail bears left at 3.1 miles, an unmarked side trail to the right leads to a west-facing viewpoint from slanted rock slabs, with pitch pines growing from cracks in the rocks.

After a relatively level stretch on a footpath along the ridge, the A.T. joins a gravel road that comes in from the left at 3.8 miles. This road was part of a vacation-home subdivision that was just getting started when the federal government acquired the land for the now-defunct Tocks Island Dam project. For the next 1.4 miles, the A.T. follows a series of gravel roads that were built for this intended development. The Buttermilk Falls Trail (blue) leaves to the right at 4.1 miles, and the Crater Lake Trail (orange) crosses at 4.9 miles. (To the left, this trail leads 0.3 mile to Crater Lake, where parking is available; to the right, it leads 0.5 mile to Hemlock Pond.)

At 5.2 miles, a side trail to the left leads 150 feet to a viewpoint overlooking Crater Lake—once a popular summer-home colony. In another 50 feet, the A.T. leaves the gravel road and turns right onto a footpath which leads to a west-facing viewpoint. The trail now loops back to the gravel road. Here, the Crater Lake Trail begins to the right. The A.T. crosses the road and soon begins steeply to descend the face of an escarpment. At the base of the escarpment, the trail

Figure 11-7. Appalachian Trail near Crater Lake

turns right and again crosses the Crater Lake Trail, which runs along a gravel road. After passing a swamp to the left of the Trail at 5.7 miles, the A.T. ascends steeply along a smooth rock face.

After crossing a dirt road, the A.T. reaches paved Blue Mountain Lake Road at 7.0 miles. The trail turns right, follows the paved road for 100 feet, then turns left onto a dirt road. Parking is available on either side of the trail crossing, although vehicular access is only from the west. After passing a water pump (a tested source of water) to the right, the A.T. continues south along the ridge on the relatively level dirt road. It passes several cleared areas—former homesites—to the left that offer views over Fairview Lake below.

When the dirt road ends, at 8.6 miles, the A.T. bears left and continues heading south on a footpath along the crest of the ridge. A red-on-white-blazed trail to the left leads down to Boy Scout Camp No-Be-Bo-Sco (private property) at 9.2 miles. Then, at 10.0 miles, a short side trail to the left leads to an expan-

sive east-facing viewpoint, with Sand Pond of Camp No-Be-Bo-Sco visible directly below. Just beyond, the A.T. reaches a clearing for a power line. It turns right, follows the power line across the ridge, with westward views over the Delaware Valley and Pocono Plateau, then bears left and reenters the woods.

After a steep descent at 10.3 miles, the A.T. bears left and then skirts a beaver pond to the right of the trail, crossing its outlet on a wooden bridge. It reaches paved Millbrook-Blairstown Road (NPS 602) at 10.8 miles, turns left and follows the road for about 500 feet. Parking is available at the trail crossing. The A.T. turns right, leaving the paved road, and continues south on a gravel road that leads to the Catfish Fire Tower.

The gravel road turns sharply right at 11.2 miles. In another 500 feet, the A.T. turns left, leaving the road, and climbs on a footpath through a rhododendron thicket. (The Rattlesnake Swamp Trail (orange) begins another 300 feet ahead along the dirt road.) At 11.5 miles, the A.T. turns left, rejoins the gravel road for 300 feet, then turns right and resumes its ascent on a footpath. Then, at 11.6 miles, the A.T. again turns right on the gravel road, and it reaches the Catfish Fire Tower (manned seasonally) at 11.9 miles.

After a long, level section, the A.T. comes out on an east-facing ledge, with panoramic views, at 12.9 miles. Here, the Rattlesnake Swamp Trail leaves to the right. At 13.9 miles, the A.T. begins to descend, and it crosses dirt Camp Road at the base of the descent at 14.3 miles. (To the right, Camp Road leads in 0.3 mile to the Mohican Outdoor Center of the Appalachian Mountain Club on Catfish Pond, where parking is available.) Just beyond, the A.T. crosses Yards Creek on a wooden bridge, and in another 100 feet, the Coppermines Trail (red) leaves to the right.

The A.T. now begins to climb, steeply in places. As the trail begins to level off on Raccoon Ridge at 14.9 miles, open areas to the left provide east-facing views. At 15.8 miles, the A.T. reaches a grassy area, with views to the left over the storage ponds for the Lower Yards Creek Reservoir. After a short descent, the A.T. reaches a junction with the Kaiser Road Trail, which leaves to the right at 16.2 miles. For a description of the continuation of the A.T. to the south, see the Worthington State Forest section of this chapter (pp. 314-15).

Buttermilk Falls Trail   *Length: 1.6 miles Blaze: blue*
The Buttermilk Falls Trail connects Buttermilk Falls—the highest waterfall in New Jersey—with the Appalachian Trail. To reach the trailhead, take County

615 to the village of Walpack Center. Proceed east through the village and continue along Brink Road. In 0.5 mile, turn right onto Mountain Road and follow it for 2.0 miles to the parking area for Buttermilk Falls, on the right (west) side of the road.

The trail starts on the east side of the road, opposite the parking area. It climbs to the left of the waterfall (actually, a series of cascades) on wooden steps and walkways. At 0.2 mile, the trail reaches a viewing platform at the top of the falls. It crosses the stream above the falls and steeply climbs through a ravine. The grade moderates at 0.3 mile, with the trail continuing to climb gradually. The unmarked Woods Road Trail crosses at 1.1 miles. The Buttermilk Falls Trail reaches a viewpoint to the west at 1.4 miles, and it ends, 1.6 miles from the start, at a junction with the Appalachian Trail (white).

Coppermines Trail

Length: 2.0 miles Blaze: red

The Coppermines Trail begins on the east side of Old Mine Road, across from the Coppermines parking area, 7.8 miles north of the Kittatinny Point Visitor Center. Just past the trailhead, a side trail to the left leads to the lower mine. The Coppermines Trail continues ahead on a grassy woods road, passing the ruins of a stone building to the left—the remnants of a mill that was built in the 1800s to process the copper ore. Although there is evidence that the Dutch explored the area for copper in the 1600s, and copper was mined here from the mid-1700s to the early 1900s, none of these mining ventures was commercially successful.

Beyond the mill ruins, the Coppermines Trail turns left and proceeds uphill. At 0.2 mile, a blue-blazed side trail that connects with the Kaiser Road Trail (blue) leaves to the right. At 0.3 mile, the barricaded entrance to the upper mine is to the right. The Coppermines Trail now heads into the heart of a hemlock gorge.

The hemlock grove through which the trail passes is a tragic illustration of the ravages of exotic insect pests. Until the mid 1990s, the mature hemlock forest in this ravine was among the finest examples of a New Jersey hemlock forest. As in the hemlock forests of New England, where the species reaches its best development, the dense canopies of the tree excluded most of light, and few herbs or shrubs, other than young hemlocks, could tolerate either the darkness or the thick forest floor of partially-decayed needles. In the 1920s, the hemlock woolly adelgid, an aphid-like insect that feeds on the sap of the hemlocks, was

accidentally introduced from Asia, and was initially observed in Virginia. Since then, the adelgid has spread from Georgia through Maine, into southern Canada, and west to Ohio, Michigan, and Wisconsin. It continues to spread at a rate of 10-15 miles per year. Infested trees usually die within four to 10 years after the insect arrives. These trees can be recognized by the dense woolly white encrustations on the bottoms of the needles, the sparse, open canopy of infected trees, and, of course, the presence of numerous dead trees in the grove. Most of New Jersey's hemlock forests are now infected by the adelgid. Scientists have been introducing a beetle which preys on the adelgid, in the hope of limiting its ability to kill trees. At present, it is too early to know whether this effort will be successful.

After crossing the brook on a wooden bridge, the trail begins to climb again. It ascends a switchback and then follows directly along the gorge, which features hemlocks, rhododendron, and a series of waterfalls. The trail leaves the gorge at 0.6 mile and continues to ascend moderately, paralleling a stream and passing through a hemlock glen for the next 0.2 mile. At 0.9 mile, another blue-blazed trail that connects with the Kaiser Road Trail leaves to the right. After crossing a seasonal brook, the Coppermines Trail steadily ascends the ridge, leveling off at 1.1 miles and passing rock ledges to the right and a boggy area at 1.3 miles. It then turns right and continues to ascend, reaching a height of land atop a knoll at 1.8 miles. After descending gradually, the Coppermines Trail ends, 2.0 miles from its start, at the Appalachian Trail (white).

Crater Lake Trail   *Length: 1.7 miles Blaze: orange*
The Crater Lake Trail loops around Crater Lake and continues to Hemlock Pond, intersecting the Appalachian Trail (A.T.) in three places. It can be combined with a short section of the A.T. to form a 1.5-mile loop hike. Parking is available at Crater Lake, which may be reached from Old Mine Road by following paved Blue Mountain Lake Road for 3.1 miles to its end and continuing on gravel Skyline Drive for another 2.4 miles.

From its trailhead on the A.T., 1.8 miles north (along the A.T.) of Blue Mountain Lake Road, the Crater Lake Trail heads southwest on a woods road. It loops around to cross the A.T. at 0.4 mile and continues along the south shore of Crater Lake, reaching a picnic area at the east end of the lake, where parking is available, at 0.9 mile. The Crater Lake Trail continues to follow the road around the north shore of the lake until, at 1.1 miles, it bears left, leaving

the main woods road, and heads uphill on a grassy woods road. At the crest of the ridge, at 1.2 miles, the Crater Lake Trail once again crosses the A.T. The Crater Lake Trail now descends on a rocky footpath. After crossing a woods road at 1.6 miles, it briefly joins another woods road, then continues to end at Hemlock Pond, 1.7 miles from the start.

Hamilton Ridge Trail *Length: 2.7 miles Blaze: blue*
An old public road, partially paved, that is now gated to exclude motorized traffic, the Hamilton Ridge Trail runs west of and parallel to Old Mine Road. It begins on the west side of Old Mine Road, 2.0 miles south of Millbrook Village and 0.1 mile south of the southern trailhead of the Van Campens Glen Trail (yellow). At 0.2 mile, the Pioneer Trail (orange) leaves to the left. The Hamilton Ridge Trail now begins a gradual ascent, passing the sites of former homes and overgrown fields. It crosses under a power line at 1.2 miles. The Pioneer Trail rejoins from the left at 1.5 miles, after which the grade moderates. At 2.3 miles, the Orchard Trail (orange) leaves to the right. The Hamilton Ridge Trail ends, 2.7 miles from the start, at Old Mine Road, 0.5 mile north of Millbrook Village. Parking is available at both ends of the trail.

Kaiser Road Trail *Length: 2.0 miles Blaze: blue*
The Kaiser Road Trail is a woods road that climbs the western side of the Kittatinny Ridge, running from Old Mine Road to the Appalachian Trail. It begins on the east side of Old Mine Road, 7.6 miles north of I-80, with parking available adjacent to the trailhead. At first, it climbs rather steeply, but the grade moderates at 0.5 mile. A blue-blazed side trail that connects to the Coppermines Trail (red) leaves to the right at 0.7 mile. Then, at 1.0 mile, another blue-blazed connecting trail to the Coppermines Trail leaves to the right. The Kaiser Road Trail now bends to the right and continues to ascend gradually, reaching the Appalachian Trail (white) at 2.0 miles. Formerly, the Kaiser Road Trail continued down the east side of the ridge; however, access to the eastern trailhead has been closed by the landowner, and the Kaiser Road Trail currently terminates at the Appalachian Trail.

Orchard Trail *Length: 0.6 mile Blaze: orange*
Following a wide path through overgrown fields, the Orchard Trail connects Millbrook Village with the Hamilton Ridge Trail. It starts opposite the Millbrook

Village parking area on Old Mine Road and heads uphill, passing an old home-site and spring at 0.2 mile. It ends at the Hamilton Ridge Trail at 0.6 mile. To the right, the Hamilton Ridge Trail (blue) leads back to Old Mine Road in 0.4 mile.

Pioneer Trail   *Length: 2.2 miles Blaze: orange*

Beginning and ending on the Hamilton Ridge Trail, the Pioneer Trail loops around to parallel the Delaware River. It can be combined with the Hamilton Ridge Trail to form a 3.9-mile loop hike.

The northern end of the Pioneer Trail is on the west side of the Hamilton Ridge Trail (blue), 1.2 miles from its northern terminus on Old Mine Road. The Pioneer Trail begins by heading south on a woods road. At 0.1 mile, it turns right onto a footpath and begins to descend. It turns left onto a woods road at 0.3 mile and descends more steeply along a ravine. At the base of the descent, at 0.7 mile, the trail turns right onto a footpath that follows along an overgrown field. Then, at 0.8 mile, the trail turns left and follows an old stone wall, reach-ing the top of cliffs that overlook the Delaware River at 1.0 mile.

The Pioneer Trail follows the crest of the bluff above the river for 0.2 mile and then bears left onto a woods road that veers away from the river, crossing under a power line at 1.5 miles. Following a level route, it passes an abandoned farmstead at 1.9 miles and ends, 2.2 miles from the start, on the Hamilton Ridge Trail, 0.2 mile from the southern terminus of that trail on Old Mine Road.

Rattlesnake Swamp Trail   *Length: 2.3 miles Blaze: orange*

The Rattlesnake Swamp Trail roughly parallels the Appalachian Trail for about two miles south of Millbrook-Blairstown Road (NPS 602) and can be com-bined with it to make a 4.5-mile loop hike. To reach the northern end of the Rattlesnake Swamp Trail, follow the Appalachian Trail (white) south from its crossing of Millbrook-Blairstown Road, where parking is available. After 0.4 mile, the Appalachian Trail turns left, leaving the gravel road that it has been following, and begins to climb on a footpath through a rhododendron thicket. Continue ahead on the gravel road, passing Rattlesnake Spring in 50 feet. The trailhead for the Rattlesnake Swamp Trail is 300 feet ahead, on the right side of the gravel road.

The trail proceeds ahead on a level footpath, with the Rattlesnake Swamp to the right. After several stream crossings, it reaches a side trail to the right at

1.9 miles. This side trail leads in 0.4 mile to the end of Camp Road at the Appalachian Mountain Club's Mohican Outdoor Center on Catfish Pond, where parking is available. The Rattlesnake Swamp Trail now heads east and climbs gradually to reach its terminus at the Appalachian Trail (white), 2.3 miles from the start.

Van Campens Glen Trail   *Length: 1.4 miles Blaze: yellow*
The Van Campens Glen Trail, which parallels Old Mine Road, goes through an attractive hemlock ravine. The southern trailhead is on Old Mine Road, 1.9 miles south of Millbrook Village. The trail enters a hemlock ravine and follows an undulating path through the ravine, passing a series of cascades on Van Campens Brook. After passing a large waterfall at 0.5 mile, the trail crosses the brook and begins to climb out of the ravine. At 0.9 mile, it crosses the dirt Cutoff Road (to the left, the dirt road leads 0.1 mile to a parking area on Old Mine Road.) The trail now widens to a woods road and ends, 1.4 miles from the start, at the Watergate Recreation Area parking area, 0.5 mile south of Millbrook Village. The woods road, now unmarked, continues ahead for 0.6 mile to Millbrook Village.

WORTHINGTON STATE FOREST

Located within the boundaries of the Delaware Water Gap National Recreation Area, but administered separately by the State of New Jersey, Worthington State Forest contains some of the most rugged terrain in the state. Comprising the southern part of the Kittatinny Ridge, the state forest extends approximately seven miles along the ridge and includes 6,233 acres.

Worthington was once called Buckwood Park, a private deer preserve of engineer Charles Campbell Worthington. His retirement home, Shawnee-on-Delaware, was later developed as a resort. Buckwood Park was first leased to the state as a game preserve in 1916, and was purchased from the Worthington estate in 1954. Among the forest's features is a glacial lake, Sunfish Pond, which was restored to the state after a long fight by conservationists defeated a planned pumped-storage utility project there.

At the southern end of the forest is the Dunnfield Creek Natural Area. The creek tumbles over a waterfall on its way from Mount Tammany to the Delaware River, and it is one of the few in the state to support native brook trout.

Overlooking this rocky stream are stands of hemlock, maple, and birch. Mountain laurel adds color to the area when in bloom.

For more information, contact Worthington State Forest, HC62, Box 2, Columbia, NJ 07832; (908) 841-9575; www.njparksandforests.org.

Ecology

The base of the western slope of the Kittatinny Ridge along Old Mine Road presents an interesting sight: dense thickets of Japanese barberry—often mixed with other exotic shrubs (such as wineberry, multiflora rose, and Japanese honeysuckle) and the exotic Japanese stilt grass—line the road for almost the entire length of the state forest. These thickets extend upslope, sometimes for several hundred feet, before being replaced by a more typical understory of native lowbush blueberries and huckleberries. These lower slopes had been cleared around homesteads, and probably were used for grazing cattle (the extremely rocky, thin soils would have precluded agriculture). Exotic plants established around the homesteads have spread out through the forests, crowding out the native species.

Up on the Kittatinny Ridge, these exotic species are rarely seen, although patches of stilt grass can be found along the Appalachian Trail—likely the result of seeds clinging to hikers' boots. The ridgetop forests are molded by the thin, nutrient-poor soils, the exposure to high winds and ice, and the recurrence of fire. Together, these factors produce open stands of chestnut oak, shadbush, pitch pine, and red maples—mostly small, twisted trees. Native sedges and rushes (relatives of the numerous species commonly found in wetlands) form a grass-like understory along much of the ridge.

Trails in Worthington State Forest

The trails in Worthington State Forest are among the most heavily used in the entire state, with the summit of Mount Tammany and Sunfish Pond being popular destinations. The Appalachian Trail runs through the center of the forest, and many other trails connect with it, making possible a variety of loop hikes. The unmarked Mount Tammany Fire Road, which runs along the east side of the Kittatinny Ridge, connecting the Blue Dot Trail with the Turquoise Trail, can also be used (in combination with other trails) to form a ten-mile loop hike to Sunfish Pond from the Dunnfield Creek parking area.

Appalachian Trail (Dunnfield Creek to Kaiser Road Trail)

Length: 6.9 miles Blaze: white

This section of the Appalachian Trail (A.T.) provides a popular route to Sunfish Pond and can be combined with the Dunnfield Creek Trail to form a loop hike. To reach the start of this section, take I-80 West to the "Rest Area" exit about a mile before the Delaware River bridge. Continue past the rest area and an underpass to the left, and turn right at a second parking area with a sign "Dunnfield Creek Natural Area."

The A.T. enters the woods at the rear of the parking area. At 0.1 mile, it turns left and crosses a wooden bridge over Dunnfield Creek. Then, in 150 feet, the A.T. turns right onto a woods road which parallels the creek. The trail continues through a gorge, with attractive cascades. At 0.4 mile, the Blue Dot Trail and the Dunnfield Creek Trail (green) leave to the right. Soon, the A.T. begins a gradual but steady ascent.

At 1.5 miles, a trail junction is reached. Here, the Beulahland Trail (yellow) leaves to the left, and the Holly Springs Trail (red) leaves to the right. An open area to the right of the trail at 2.2 miles provides a view over the Kittatinny Ridge, and a grassy woods road (which connects with the Douglas Trail) leaves to the left at 2.5 miles. At 3.1 miles, the A.T. reaches a wide woods road. To the left, this road is the route of the Douglas Trail (blue). The A.T. turns right and follows the road, passing the Backpacker Site, where overnight camping is allowed.

The A.T. reaches the southern end of Sunfish Pond at 3.7 miles. A monument just south of the pond notes that the Sunfish Pond Natural Area has been designated a registered national landmark. Here, the A.T. bears left and continues along the west side of the pond, while the Dunnfield Creek Trail (green) (which can be used as an alternate return route) leaves to the right, briefly following the Sunfish Pond Fire Road.

After crossing the outlet of Sunfish Pond at 4.0 miles, the A.T. continues through a rocky area, passing interesting rock sculptures—the work of enterprising hikers—to the right. It reaches the northern end of the pond at 4.4 miles. Just beyond, the Turquoise Trail leaves to the right. At 4.5 miles, the Garvey Springs Trail, which leads down to Old Mine Road, leaves to the left. The A.T. continues ahead on a relatively level footpath, crossing a stream near the Upper Yards Creek Reservoir at 5.4 miles.

A power line crosses the trail at 6.1 miles, with views on both sides of the ridge. Then, at 6.2 miles, the trail reaches another viewpoint, marked by a large

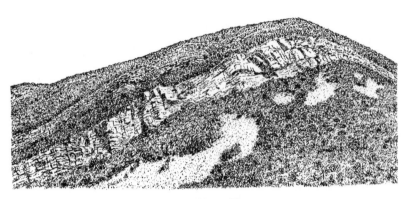

Figure 11-8. Mount Tammany

pile of rocks. The Lower Yards Creek Reservoir and storage ponds for the Yards Creek Pumped Storage Generating Station are visible to the right, and the Delaware River Valley may be seen to the left. A sign at 6.4 miles marks the boundary between Worthington State Forest and the Delaware Water Gap National Recreation Area. At 6.6 miles, a woods road joins from the right. The Kaiser Road Trail (blue), which leads down to Old Mine Road, leaves to the left at 6.9 miles.

For a description of the A.T. to the north, see the Delaware Water Gap National Recreation Area section of this chapter, pp. 304-07.

Beulahland Trail   *Length: 1.3 miles Blaze: yellow*
The Beulahland Trail connects Old Mine Road with the Appalachian Trail, providing alternate access for day trips to Sunfish Pond. It begins at the Farview parking area on Old Mine Road, 1.7 miles north of the Kittatinny Point Visitor Center of the Delaware Water Gap National Recreation Area, and steadily ascends the Kittatinny Ridge on a woods road. It ends at 1.3 miles at a junction with the Appalachian Trail (white). The Holly Springs Trail (red) begins directly ahead and descends the other side of the ridge, connecting to the Dunnfield Creek Trail (green).

Blue Dot Trail   *Length: 1.4 miles Blaze: blue dot on white*
The Blue Dot Trail provides an alternative, less steep access to the summit of

Mount Tammany. It is often combined with the Red Dot Trail and the Appalachian Trail to form a 3.1-mile loop hike up Mount Tammany.

To reach the start of the Blue Dot Trail, proceed north on the Appalachian Trail (white) from the Dunnfield Creek parking area on I-80. The Blue Dot Trail, together with the Dunnfield Creek Trail (green), begin to the right in 0.4 mile. At 0.2 mile, both trails cross the creek on a wooden footbridge. In another 300 feet, the Blue Dot Trail splits off to the right and begins a steady ascent of Mount Tammany. At 1.1 miles, it reaches the crest of the ridge. Here, the Blue Dot Trail turns right and heads south along the ridge, with views to the left over the Delaware River. To the left, the Mount Tammany Fire Road heads north along the ridge. The Blue Dot Trail ends, 1.4 miles from its start, at a junction with the Red Dot Trail, which continues ahead. At the trail junction, a path leads downhill to the left to a broad west-facing viewpoint over the Delaware Water Gap and Mount Minsi.

Douglas Trail   *Length: 1.7 miles Blaze: blue*

Named for the late U.S. Supreme Court Justice William O. Douglas, in recognition of his conservation efforts, the Douglas Trail begins on the east side of Old Mine Road, 3.9 miles north of I-80. The Douglas parking area is on the opposite side of the road.

The trail climbs gradually on a woods road through a mature maple forest. At 0.5 mile, the Rock Cores Trail (green on white) joins from the left, and both trails run jointly for 500 feet. After the Rock Cores Trail leaves to the right at 0.6 mile, the Douglas Trail narrows to a wide footpath and continues to climb on switchbacks. It ends, 1.7 miles from the start, at a junction with the Appalachian Trail (white). Sunfish Pond is 0.6 mile to the left. A backpacker camping site (for Appalachian Trail thru-hikers only) is located at the junction. No water is available, and ground fires are not permitted.

The Douglas Trail may be combined with the Appalachian Trail and the Garvey Springs Trail (orange) to make a 4.3-mile loop hike.

Dunnfield Creek Trail   *Length: 3.4 miles Blaze: green*

Following Dunnfield Creek for most of its route, the Dunnfield Creek Trail runs parallel to and east of the Appalachian Trail, and can be combined with it to form a 7.5-mile loop hike. The Dunnfield Creek Trail begins on the Appalachian Trail (white), 0.4 mile from the Dunnfield Creek parking area off I-80. At

first, it runs jointly with the Blue Dot Trail. Both trails cross Dunnfield Creek on a wooden footbridge at 0.2 mile. In another 300 feet, the Blue Dot Trail leaves to the right. The Dunnfield Creek Trail continues ahead on a woods road, paralleling the creek. After crossing three more bridges over the creek, the Dunnfield Creek Trail reaches an intersection with the Holly Springs Trail (red), which leaves to the left at 1.3 miles.

The Dunnfield Creek Trail continues ahead on a narrower and rockier footpath, still paralleling the creek, which it crosses several times on rocks. At 2.8 miles, in an open area, it bears left, leaving the creek, and begins to climb more steeply to the crest of the Kittatinny Ridge, which it reaches at 3.2 miles. It now descends, reaching the Sunfish Pond Fire Road near the south end of the pond at 3.4 miles. The Dunnfield Creek Trail turns left and follows the fire road a short distance to its terminus on the Appalachian Trail.

Garvey Springs Trail   *Length: 1.2 miles Blaze: orange*
Extending from Old Mine Road to the Appalachian Trail just north of Sunfish Pond, the Garvey Springs Trail provides the shortest route to Sunfish Pond. From its trailhead opposite the Douglas parking area on Old Mine Road, 3.9 miles north of I-80, the Garvey Springs Trail climbs gradually on a woods road. At 0.5 mile, it turns left and joins the Rock Cores Trail (green on white). After running concurrently with the Rock Cores Trail for 750 feet, the Garvey Springs Trail turns right onto a footpath and begins a steep, rocky ascent. After passing Garvey Springs at 1.1 miles, the trail descends slightly to end, 1.2 miles from its start, at a junction with the Appalachian Trail (white). Sunfish Pond is 0.1 mile to the right.

Holly Springs Trail   *Length: 0.4 mile Blaze: red*
An extension of the Beulahland Trail, the Holly Springs Trail connects the Appalachian Trail with the Dunnfield Creek Trail. It begins at the junction of the Beulahland Trail (yellow) with the Appalachian Trail (white), 1.5 miles north of the Dunnfield Creek parking area, and heads east along a grassy woods road, descending gradually. At 0.2 mile, it passes the Holly Springs. The trail ends, 0.4 mile from its start, at the Dunnfield Creek Trail (green).

The Appalachian, Holly Springs, and Dunnfield Creek trails may be combined to form a 3.6-mile "lollipop"-loop hike from the Dunnfield Creek parking area.

Red Dot Trail

Length: 1.3 miles Blaze: red dot on white
The Red Dot Trail provides the shortest, but steepest, route up Mount Tammany. It can be combined with the Blue Dot Trail to make a loop hike. Due to the steepness of this trail, most hikers prefer to climb to the summit on the Red Dot Trail and head down on the Blue Dot Trail.

The Red Dot Trail begins at the Dunnfield Creek parking area, just beyond a rest area off I-80, about one mile east of the Delaware River bridge. It climbs a set of steps and, at 0.1 mile, joins a branch of the trail that begins at the rest area. At 0.2 mile, a set of rock steps marks the beginning of a steeper ascent. After briefly following a woods road, the trail reaches a viewpoint over the

Figure 11-9. Rock steps on the Red Dot Trail

Delaware River and the Water Gap at 0.4 mile. Although broader views are available from higher points along the trail, this viewpoint provides the best views up and down the river.

The grade now moderates, but it steepens again at 0.7 mile, where the trail ascends on switchbacks and then climbs even more steeply over a talus slope. At 1.0 mile, another viewpoint appears on the right. Here, the trail turns left, and the grade again moderates. The Red Dot Trail ends, 1.3 miles from the start, at a junction with the Blue Dot Trail, which continues ahead. From the trail junction, a path leads downhill to the right to a broad viewpoint over the Water Gap and Mount Minsi.

Rock Cores Trail   *Length: 2.9 miles Blaze: green on white*
A self-guided nature trail (a brochure which describes the features of interest at 13 numbered signposts is available at the Worthington State Forest office), the Rock Cores Trail begins on the east side of Old Mine Road, 3.0 miles north of I-80. No parking is available at the trailhead, but cars may be parked at the Worthington State Forest office, 0.6 mile to the west along a paved road that

heads west from Old Mine Road just south of the trailhead.

From the trailhead, the Rock Cores Trail heads north, roughly parallel to Old Mine Road, ascending gradually on a wide path. At 0.7 mile, it turns left onto another woods road, the route of the Douglas Trail (blue), and both trails run jointly for 500 feet. The Rock Cores Trail turns right at 0.8 mile and continues to climb, leveling off at 1.0 mile. The Garvey Springs Trail (orange) joins from the left at 1.5 miles and leaves to the right in another 750 feet. Soon, the Rock Cores Trail begins to descend, passing the remains of rock cores drilled to test the rock in preparation for the construction of the proposed Tocks Island Dam (which was never built). Tocks Island is located in the Delaware River directly to the west. After crossing under a power line, the trail descends steeply to end, 2.9 miles from its start, at Old Mine Road, about five miles north of I-80. Parking is available 0.2 mile to the north along Old Mine Road.

Turquoise Trail   *Length: 1.3 miles Blaze: turquoise*
Connecting the Appalachian Trail with the Mount Tammany Fire Road, the Turquoise Trail is an important link that makes possible circular hikes around Sunfish Pond, as well as longer loop hikes from the Dunnfield Creek parking area. The Turquoise Trail begins on the east side of the Appalachian Trail (white) just beyond the northern end of Sunfish Pond, 4.4 miles from the Dunnfield Creek parking area. After passing an open area overlooking the pond at 0.1 mile, the trail continues along the pond's eastern shore. It climbs through mountain laurel and turns left onto the Sunfish Pond Fire Road at 0.3 mile. It turns right at 0.6 mile, leaving the road, and descends on a footpath to cross the headwaters of Dunnfield Creek in a rocky area at 0.8 mile. It now climbs to its terminus on the Mount Tammany Fire Road at 1.3 miles.

WILDLIFE MANAGEMENT AREAS

Flat Brook and its tributaries flow between the Kittatinny Ridge and the Delaware River. Along its banks are three wildlife management areas. Although these areas are primarily managed for wildlife and do not contain any marked trails, there are many acres to explore during non-hunting seasons. All three areas are covered on the NY-NJ Trail Conference Kittatinny Trails map set, or see the appropriate USGS topographic quadrangle maps mentioned below.

Hainesville Wildlife Management Area

The eastern edge of the Hainesville Wildlife Management Area nearly adjoins High Point State Park. It is one of the smaller, older wildlife management areas, and is managed for upland game hunting, with fields, hedgerows, and a pond which is fast becoming a swamp. Wild turkeys, deer, grouse, black ducks, mallards, and wood ducks are some of the species found within the area.

To reach the Hainesville Wildlife Management Area from Hainesville on US 206, proceed north for about 0.5 mile to Shaytown Road, continue east for about 0.5 mile, then go north on Cemetery Road 0.5 mile to a parking area at the entrance to the wildlife management area.

Since there are no marked trails, users of the area should obtain the Milford USGS topographic quadrangle map. For more information, contact the New Jersey Department of Environmental Protection (DEP), Division of Fish and Wildlife, 501 East State Street, P.O. Box 400, Trenton, NJ 08625; (609) 984-0547; www.njfishandwildlife.org.

Flatbrook Wildlife Management Area

Noted for its trout streams, the Flatbrook Wildlife Management Area contains 2,090 acres adjoining Stokes State Forest to its west. Birdwatching and winter cross-country skiing opportunities are also found here.

Parking is available on a road leading east from County 615 (Kuhn Road) just north of Peters Valley Craft Center on County 615 about 0.2 mile east of the intersection with County 640, and at the intersection of Flat Brook Road and the road leading south from Peters Valley Craft Center (continuing straight when County 615 takes a right turn).

Since there are no marked trails, users of the area should obtain the Culvers Gap USGS topographic quadrangle map. For more information, contact New Jersey DEP, Division of Fish and Wildlife, 501 East State Street, P.O. Box 400, Trenton, NJ 08625; (609) 984-0547; www.njfishandwildlife.org.

Walpack Wildlife Management Area

The 387-acre Walpack Wildlife Management area is a narrow strip extending for about two miles along County 615 north of Flatbrookville and is entirely contained within the Delaware Water Gap National Recreation Area. It offers fishing on Flat Brook and also has high ground along Pompey Ridge which overlooks the Delaware River. Parking is available.

Since there are no marked trails, users of the area should obtain the Flatbrookville and Lake Maskenozha USGS topographic quadrangle maps. For more information, contact New Jersey DEP, Division of Fish and Wildlife, 501 East State Street, P.O. Box 400, Trenton, NJ 08625; (609) 984-0547; www.njfishandwildlife.org.

THE GREAT VALLEY

Also known as the Kittatinny Valley, the Great Valley is a relatively flat expanse situated between the Kittatinny Mountains to the west and the Highlands to the east. The land is generally well-suited for agricultural uses, and much of it remains as farmland today. However, portions of the valley are now protected as parkland, and long sections of two abandoned railroads that pass through the valley have been converted to rail trails.

Kittatinny Valley State Park

Within the 3,349-acre Kittatinny Valley State Park, there are four lakes, extensive wetlands, and limestone ridges. The Aeroflex-Andover Airport, operated by the New Jersey Forest Fire Service, is located within the boundaries of the park. The park features two linear rail trails which are open to hiking, mountain biking, and horseback riding, as well as several miles of other marked trails. It also offers opportunities for picnicking, boating, fishing, birding, and cross-country skiing. Hunting is permitted in certain areas of the park.

Scattered through the park are numerous wetlands that are of considerable biological interest. They are open marshes, typically with a few scattered shrubs (including poison sumac, a relative of poison ivy). The limestone rock found in the area has created an alkaline soil in which only specially adapted species of plants can grow. However, many plants have adapted to this special type of soil, and these marshes are considered to be places of unusually high natural diversity. In addition, several rare species of amphibians and reptiles are found in these wetlands. Some of these wetlands have been invaded by purple loosestrife, an invasive exotic species, which can easily be seen as an expanse of purple spread across the marshes.

To reach the main portion of the park and the visitor center, take I-80 to Exit 25 and continue north on US 206 for about seven miles, passing through the Borough of Andover. Turn right onto Goodale Road, and follow it for 1.1

miles to the park entrance on the right. The visitor center is located 0.4 mile along the entrance road. For more information, contact Kittatinny Valley State Park, P.O. Box 621, Andover, NJ 07821-0621; (973) 786-6445; kittvlly@warwick.net; www.njparksandforests.org.

Rail Trails in Kittatinny Valley State Park

Northwestern New Jersey has a network of abandoned railroads, two of which have been converted into rail trails. These trails—the Paulinskill Valley Trail and the Sussex Branch Trail—are administered by Kittatinny Valley State Park.

Paulinskill Valley Trail   *Length: 27.4 miles Blaze: unmarked*

The Paulinskill Valley Trail follows the abandoned right-of-way of the western portion of the New York, Susquehanna & Western Railroad. Although open to all forms of non-motorized recreation, the right-of-way is not paved. Acquired by the state in October 1992, it parallels the Paulinskill River and borders working farms and lowland forests.

The western end of the trail is in Knowlton Township in Warren County, at Brugler Road near NJ 94, where parking is available. At 1.2 miles, the trail goes under the massive concrete Paulinskill Viaduct of the Lackawanna Cut-Off. Built in 1909 to provide the Lackawanna Railroad with an improved route through western New Jersey, the cut-off was abandoned in 1979, although there are plans to restore it as a route for rail passenger service from Scranton, Pennsylvania to Hoboken, New Jersey. The trail crosses Walnut Valley Road (County 655) in Vail at 3.8 miles and passes the Blairstown Airport (where a slight detour is made from the railbed to bypass the active runways) at 5.4 miles.

At 7.4 miles, the trail passes through Footbridge Park in Blairstown, adjacent to NJ 94. Parking is available here. Just beyond, the trail goes under NJ 94. The next 11.7 miles between Blairstown and Swartswood Station traverse hilly terrain; however, the grade of the rail trail remains nearly level. The trail crosses Spring Valley Road just north of NJ 94 in Marksboro, where parking is available, at 10.5 miles. At 11.2 miles, it crosses a truss bridge over the Paulinskill River. After crossing Paulinskill

*Figure 11-10.
Old milepost*

Figure 11-11. Paulinskill Valley Trail

Lake Road (County 614) at 16.8 miles, the trail begins to parallel scenic Paulinskill Lake, and it passes the site of the former Swartswood Station at 19.1 miles. Today, only the concrete base of the station remains. Just beyond, the trail crosses Newton-Swartswood Road (County 622), where parking is available.

The trail's easternmost section passes through the flatter and more developed portions of the Great Valley. It crosses County 519 at 22.2 miles, US 206 at 23.3 miles, and NJ 94 at 23.9 miles. Soon, it again begins to traverse a rural farm and forest landscape. After crossing a branch of the Paulinskill River on a 60-foot plate girder bridge at 25.0 miles, the trail reaches Warbasse Junction Road (County 663), where parking is available. Just beyond is Warbasse Junction, where the Paulinskill Valley Trail crosses the Sussex Branch Trail.

The Paulinskill Valley Trail crosses another branch of the Paulinskill River at 26.5 miles, and it reaches its terminus at Sparta Junction at 27.4 miles. East of here, the New York, Susquehanna and Western Railroad is an active rail line, and hikers should not proceed beyond this point.

For more information, contact Kittatinny Valley State Park, P.O. Box 621, Andover, NJ 07821; (973) 786-6445; kittvlly@warwick.net; www.njparksandforests.org; or the Paulinskill Valley Trail Committee, P.O. Box 175, Andover, NJ 07821-0175; (973) 684-4820; www.pvtc-kvsp.org. The committee publishes a trail map and leads organized hikes on the trail.

Sussex Branch Trail *Length: 18.7 miles Blaze: unmarked*
The Sussex Branch Trail follows the route of the abandoned Sussex Branch of the Erie-Lackawanna Railroad. This rail line originated as the Sussex Mine Railroad, built by Edward Cooper and Abram Hewitt to transport iron from the Andover mines to the Morris Canal beginning in 1851. By 1854, the line extended from Newton to Waterloo. Additional extensions brought the railroad to Branchville and Franklin, and established connections with other railroads. The Delaware, Lackawanna and Western Railroad acquired the Sussex Mine Railroad in 1881, and it soon carried agricultural produce and passengers as well as iron and zinc from local mines.

The Delaware, Lackawanna & Western merged with the Erie in 1960, but by that time both freight and passenger traffic on the Sussex Branch had greatly declined. Passenger service was discontinued in 1966, and the line was abandoned shortly thereafter. The state acquired the right-of-way between Netcong and Andover Junction in 1979 and between Andover Junction and Branchville in 1982. The rail trail traverses part of Kittatinny Valley State Park, farms, and forested lands, and passes by lakes and streams. In some sections, it is surrounded by commercial and residential development.

The southern terminus of the Sussex Branch Trail, where parking is available, is on Waterloo Road (County 604) in Allamuchy Mountain State Park, about one mile west of US 206 in Stanhope. The trail heads north, passing Jefferson Lake at 0.2 mile. It crosses the Highlands Trail (teal diamond) at 0.8 mile, with a waterfall below to the right. The Sussex Branch Trail reaches Cranberry Lake at 2.1 miles. Parking is available at 2.3 miles at the Cranberry Lake Park and Ride on the west side of US 206. At 3.3 miles, the trail reaches Whitehall Hill Road. Since the railbed to the north is poorly drained, the trail turns left and briefly joins Whitehall Hill Road, which parallels the railbed, regaining the railbed at 3.6 miles. The trail now runs along a high embankment, paralleling US 206, which is below to the right. At 4.3 miles, the embankment ends, and the trail continues north, parallel to but some distance away from US 206.

At 4.8 miles, the Sussex Branch Trail goes through a tunnel under the Pequest Fill of the Lackawanna Cut-Off. Built about 1910 to provide the Lackawanna Railroad with an improved route through western New Jersey, the cut-off was abandoned in 1979, although there are plans to restore it as a route for rail passenger service from Scranton, Pennsylvania to Hoboken, New Jersey. The trail now passes through the Borough of Andover, closely paralleling US 206. Parking is available at the Smith Street crossing at 5.3 miles. North of Andover, the rail trail crosses US 206 at 6.3 miles. A parking area is located on the east side of US 206 at the trail crossing. Beyond the road crossing, the trail heads north, away from US 206, and enters Kittatinny Valley State Park.

The Sussex Branch Trail crosses Goodale Road at 7.2 miles, with parking available at the adjacent Twin Lakes parking area of Kittatinny Valley State Park (just south of the trail crossing), which is connected to the Sussex Branch Trail by a short side trail. The trail parallels Goodale Road for the next 0.3 mile, and cars may also be parked at the park's Goodale Road parking area, across the road from the trail at 7.5 miles. After crossing Newton-Sparta Road (County 616) at 9.4 miles, the trail bends left to parallel the road.

The Sussex Branch Trail reaches Hicks Avenue (County 663) in Newton at 9.8 miles. The right-of-way through the Town of Newton is not state-owned, so hikers should detour by turning right and following Hicks Avenue north for one mile. Here, to the left, at a break in the guardrail, a trail leads for 300 feet to the Sussex Branch right-of-way. Hikers should turn right and continue north along the railbed. The trail crosses Warbasse Junction Road (County 663), where parking is available, at 13.2 miles and immediately reaches Warbasse Junction. Here, the Paulinskill Valley Trail crosses.

At 14.0 miles, the Sussex Branch Trail crosses NJ 94 near Lafayette Village, a shopping complex. It bends to the left and begins to head northwest, parallel to but some distance south of NJ 15. It crosses US 206 at 16.5 miles and continues heading northwest, now paralleling US 206. The rail trail passes beneath US 206 at 18.7 miles, and it ends just beyond.

Public transportation to the southern end of the trail is available on weekdays via the Hackettstown Line of NJ Transit. The trailhead on Waterloo Road is 1.5 miles from NJ Transit's Mt. Olive station, via Waterloo Valley Road, International Drive, and Continental Drive. About one mile of the roadwalk is along Continental Drive, which has been built on the right-of-way of the Sussex Branch south from Waterloo Road and offers a pedestrian walkway parallel to the road.

For more information, contact Kittatinny Valley State Park, P.O. Box 621, Andover, NJ 07821; (973) 786-6445; kittvlly@warwick.net; www.njparksandforests.org; or the Paulinskill Valley Trail Committee, P.O. Box 175, Andover, NJ 07821-0175; (973) 684-4820; www.pvtc-kvsp.org. The committee publishes a trail map and leads organized hikes on the trail. The southern section of the trail, from Waterloo Road to Cranberry Lake, which passes through Allamuchy Mountain State Park, is administered by Stephens State Park, 800 Willow Grove Street, Hackettstown, NJ 07840; (908) 852-3790; www.njparksandforests.org.

Swartswood State Park

This 2,250-acre park, named for the Swartout family who were killed in a Native American raid on the family farm in 1756, offers facilities for camping, swimming, boating, and fishing. In the fall, Swartswood Lake attracts a variety of migrating ducks. Hunting is permitted in designated areas. There are three marked trails totaling five miles, of which one is for equestrian use and cross-country skiing, with another accessible for the handicapped.

To reach Swartswood State Park, take NJ 94 or US 206 to Newton. From just north of the NJ 94/US 206 split in Newton, take County 519 north for 0.4 mile to County 622. Turn left on County 622 and follow it 4.3 miles to County 619. Turn left onto County 619. The main park entrance is to the right in 0.6 mile, but parking for the trails is at the Duck Pond Multi-Use Trail Area, on the left side of County 619 about 0.1 mile south of the park entrance. For more information, contact Swartswood State Park, East Shore Drive, Swartswood, NJ 07875; (973) 383-5230; www.njparksandforests.org.

Wallkill River National Wildlife Refuge

The 4,796-acre Wallkill River National Wildlife Refuge was established in 1990 to conserve the biological diversity of the Wallkill Valley by protecting and managing land, with a special emphasis on forest-dwelling and grassland birds, migrating waterfowl, wintering raptors, and endangered species. It contains three hiking trails, each of which is located in a different part of the refuge.

The level 2.5-mile Liberty Loop Trail, which traverses the northern portion of the refuge, follows the dikes of an abandoned sod farm around a wetland and grassland management area. It is co-aligned with the Appalachian Trail (white) for 1.5 miles. A portion of the trail utilizes the right-of-way of the

abandoned Lehigh and New England Railroad. Access to this trail is from a parking area on the south side of Oil City Road in Warwick, New York, about one mile west of Liberty Corners Road (known as Lake Wallkill Road in New Jersey), just north of the New Jersey–New York state line.

Beginning at the refuge headquarters on County 565, the Dagmar Dale Nature Trail traverses hilly terrain, passing through grasslands and hardwood forests on its way down to the Wallkill River. It consists of two loop trails, which may be combined to create a longer loop hike. The North Loop (blue) is 1.7 miles long, while the South Loop (yellow) is 1.0 mile long.

The 1.5-mile Wood Duck Nature Trail, a self-guided interpretive trail, follows the right-of-way of the Hanford Branch of the New York, Susquehanna and Western Railroad, abandoned in 1958, passing extensive wetlands along the way. The trailhead is on County 565, 0.1 mile east of NJ 23. In 2003, the trail dead-ends at the Wallkill River, and hikers must retrace their steps.

To reach the headquarters of the Wallkill River National Wildlife Refuge, take NJ 23 to County 565 (Glenwood Road). (This intersection is about three miles north of the junction of NJ 23 and NJ 94 in Hamburg.) Turn right and follow County 565 for 1.5 miles to the refuge headquarters, on the left side of the road. For more information, contact the Wallkill River National Wildlife Refuge, 1547 Route 565, Sussex, NJ 07461; (973) 702-7266; http://wallkillriver.fws.gov.

Whittingham Wildlife Management Area

The fact that there are no marked trails into the 1,930-acre Whittingham Wildlife Management Area should not deter anyone from enjoying a visit. The mowed paths along the edges and through the centers of former farm fields beckon hikers to savor a pastoral setting. Hedgerows and small stands of hardwoods separate the fields. Woods roads cutting through adjacent forests pass by limestone rocks, some looking like well-crafted stone walls.

Three types of forests are dominant in the area: North Jersey mixed oak, sugar maple mixed hardwood, and hemlock mixed hardwood. Visitors can find colorful wildflowers, abundant grasses, and humming insects in the summer. Wild turkey, pileated woodpecker, and ruffed grouse are year-round residents.

A 400-acre state-designated natural area contains a spring-fed swamp and the headwaters of the Pequest River. It can be reached via a one-mile hike along

a woods road and includes access to a pond. Hunting is permitted in season. During hunting season, hikers are advised to wear blaze orange or restrict their hikes to Sundays.

To reach Whittingham Wildlife Management Area, take I-80 to Exit 25 and proceed north on US 206 to Andover. Continue for 2.9 miles past the only traffic light in Andover and turn left onto County 619 (Springdale-Fredon Road). One parking area is on the left at 1.1 miles. To reach the second parking area, drive 0.3 mile past the first area and turn left at the junction, reaching the second area. Since there are no marked trails, users of the area should obtain the Newton West and Tranquility USGS topographic quadrangle maps. For more information, contact New Jersey DEP, Division of Fish and Wildlife, 501 East State Street, P.O. Box 400, Trenton, NJ 08625; (609) 984-0547; www.njfishandwildlife.org.

OTHER AREAS NEAR THE KITTATINNIES

Although they are geologically part of the Highlands, several state parks and wildlife management areas which offer many opportunities for hiking are situated in Sussex and Warren counties just east of the Kittatinnies. Because of their geographic proximity to the Kittatinnies, they are included in this chapter.

Allamuchy Mountain & Stephens State Parks

Embracing most of the Allamuchy Mountain upland between County 517 and the Musconetcong River, and bisected by I-80, Allamuchy Mountain and Stephens State Parks comprise 9,200 acres. Allamuchy Mountain State Park is undeveloped and offers hunting and fishing opportunities. Stephens State Park has camping, fishing, and picnic facilities and Waterloo Village, a restoration of Andover Forge, once a busy port along the Morris Canal. Earlier, it produced cannonballs for the colonists. The remnants of a limestone kiln may be seen adjacent to the park office. For more information, contact Stephens State Park, 800 Willow Grove Street, Hackettstown, NJ 07840; (908) 852-3790; www.njparksandforests.org.

Ecology

Allamuchy Mountain State Park presents blend of forest, northern marshlands, and overgrown fields—a mixture that supports an abundance of wild-

life. The forests are dominated by the oaks and hickories of the oak-hickory biome. Red oak, white oak, chestnut oak, and several kinds of hickories abound, but at least 20 other tree species can be found. The dense layer of low-growing blueberry and huckleberry shrubs may result from the low-intensity burning that was carried out here in the late 1800s. At the time, the forests in the area were managed for game (in particular, grouse and pheasant), and repeated burning of the forest undergrowth produced ideal conditions for these birds. Some parts of the forest have been heavily invaded by exotic species, particularly Japanese barberry, which forms impenetrable, thorny thickets. These are particularly obvious in the early spring, as this exotic shrub puts out leaves at least a month earlier than the native species. The fields along Deer Park Road are in various stages of succession back to forest. The acreage of these fields and their estimated age of abandonment are posted on signs, thus enabling the visitor to better understand the successional process.

Trails in Allamuchy Mountain & Stephens State Parks

Each of the three sections of Allamuchy Mountain and Stephens state parks has networks of hiking trails. The Allamuchy Natural Area around Deer Park Pond, south of I-80 and northwest of Waterloo Road (County 604), has several marked trails that can be combined to form a variety of loop hikes (see below). The developed area of Stephens State Park, east of Waterloo Road, about two miles north of Hackettstown, offers several marked loop trails that begin from the park office, as well as a section of the Highlands Trail. The portion of Allamuchy Mountain State Park north of I-80 has a section of the Sussex Branch Trail (see p. 324), a 4.4-mile section of the Highlands Trail (described below), and an extensive network of unmarked woods roads. Those who wish to explore this area off the marked trails should obtain the Tranquility and Stanhope topographic quadrangle maps. In addition, an 0.7-mile section of the Morris Canal towpath along Waterloo Road has been restored and is open to hikers. All trails in the park are open to bicyclists as well as hikers.

To reach the Allamuchy Natural Area, take I-80 to Exit 19, proceed south on County 517 for 2.1 miles, and turn left on Deer Park Road (there is a small brick house at the northeast corner of the intersection). The park boundary and the main parking area are reached after 0.7 mile on this dirt road. Two other parking areas are located farther along the road, at 1.0 and 1.5 miles,

respectively, from the park boundary.

A suggested 3.9-mile loop hike begins at the last parking area along the road. (In winter, the road may be closed beyond the second parking area; if so, park there and walk the remaining 0.5 mile along the road.) Walk around the gate and head straight into the forest on a white-blazed trail. (Do not follow the main dirt road, also blazed white, which turns right.) Continue ahead where a red-blazed trail leaves to the right in 200 feet. At 0.4 mile, turn right onto another red-blazed trail (this trail may not be blazed clearly at the junction) and follow it down to Deer Park Pond. After following the northwestern shore of the pond, the trail swings around, passes an old stone foundation, and reaches a small clearing just before a dense stand of evergreens at 1.2 miles.

Turn left here and head uphill on a trail that is soon marked with blue and white blazes. When the blue trail leaves to the right at 1.6 miles, bear left, now following the white trail. The trail crosses the outlet of a swamp and soon begins a gradual climb through rocky woods. After leveling off, the white trail bears left at a fork at 2.1 miles. The trail now begins to descend and crosses two stone walls. At 2.3 miles, just past the point where the trail turns left and begins to head south, turn right onto an unmarked footpath that passes through an opening in a fence and leads to a scenic overlook off I-80, with views of the Kittatinny Ridge and the Delaware Water Gap.

Return to the main trail and turn right. The trail heads southwest and begins to descend, passing a large overhanging boulder to the left. After a short climb, the trail goes through successional fields that are reverting to forest. Continue ahead on the white trail, which leads back to the parking area.

Highlands Trail (US 206 to Waterloo Road)

Length: 4.4 miles Blaze: teal diamond

To reach this section of the Highlands Trail, take I-80 to Exit 25 and proceed north on US 206 for 2.0 miles to Lackawanna Drive. Continue ahead on US 206 for another 0.1 mile and turn left onto Hi Glen Drive. At the T intersection, turn left onto Francis Terrace, which curves right and becomes Louis Drive. Just ahead, at an intersection with Norman Terrace, bear right as the road name changes to Drexel Drive. Cars may be parked at a wide turnaround in another 300 feet.

The Highlands Trail descends into the woods on the right side of the road, crossing a stone wall, paralleling it briefly, and crossing a stream on rocks. After passing a huge boulder to the right at 0.1 mile, the trail crosses another stone

Figure 11-12. Waterfall at the Sussex Branch Trail intersection

wall. At a third stone wall, reached at 0.3 mile, the trail bears left and climbs to a large rock outcrop. After a brief descent, the trail continues on a relatively level footpath, crossing several more stone walls.

At 1.1 miles, the trail emerges onto an open area on a hilltop, with a single large cedar tree. It bears right and begins to descend, soon passing through a large hemlock grove. The trail passes two mine pits to the right at 1.4 miles and descends to cross a stream on rocks at 1.6 miles. An attractive waterfall is a short distance downstream. Just beyond, the trail turns left onto the Sussex Branch Trail—the right-of-way of the abandoned Sussex Branch of the Erie-Lackawanna Railroad.

The Highlands Trail follows the Sussex Branch Trail for only 100 feet. It turns right and briefly follows a graded embankment—the route of the old Sussex Mine Railroad, built in 1851—then turns right again and begins to climb, passing some large glacial erratics. Near the crest of the hill, at 1.9 miles, it crosses a woods road. Soon, it goes across a rocky ravine and continues along undulating terrain. After a steady climb, it reaches a open, rocky area at 2.3 miles and begins to descend.

At 2.5 miles, the Highlands Trail turns left onto an old woods road. It follows the road for about 500 feet, then turns right and continues on a footpath. After crossing a dirt road in 250 feet, it crosses a stream on rocks. At 2.8 miles, it passes a wetland to the right, crosses a rocky area, and begins a steady climb. Reaching the top of the rise at 3.0 miles, it descends to cross a stream, then climbs again, passing through a large boulder field.

After a short level stretch, the Highlands Trail crosses a woods road at 3.3 miles and continues ahead on a wide footpath. It is joined by a white-blazed trail that comes in from the left on the woods road. At 3.5 miles, the white-blazed trail curves to the right as the Highlands Trail continues straight ahead, now beginning to descend.

The Highlands Trail reaches a panoramic viewpoint from an exposed rock outcrop at 3.6 miles. The Musconetcong River and an extensive area of wetlands are directly below, with the International Trade Center to the left, and the ridges of Pohatcong and Jenny Jump mountains to the right. The trail resumes from the uphill end of the viewpoint, bearing right and heading west along the southern edge of the ridge.

At 3.7 miles, the trail bears sharply left and descends steeply on a switchback. At the base of the descent, it turns right and proceeds south along the ridge on a relatively level footpath. After a short descent, it again bears sharply left onto a switchback at 4.1 miles. It turns right, crosses a stream on rocks, then continues to descend gradually, emerging in an open grassy area at 4.3 miles. The trail now bears left and follows a gravel road out to Waterloo Road (County 604), where limited parking is available, at 4.4 miles. This trailhead is 0.1 mile west of the entrance to Waterloo Village and 0.2 mile east of the I-80 overpass.

Hamburg Mountain Wildlife Management Area

This 2,774-acre tract is for those hikers who enjoy the challenge of bushwhacking or following unmarked woods roads and want to be away from crowds; however, Hamburg Mountain Wildlife Management Area is not the place to hike during hunting seasons. Elevations range from 700 to 1,495 feet. The mixed hardwood forest, with a blueberry understory, has pockets of hemlock, rhododendron, and laurel. Wetlands are found in the narrow valleys.

Access to Hamburg Mountain Wildlife Management Area is from the south because a ski area blocks access from the north. The main access point is the signed parking lot on the north side of NJ 23 about one mile east of County

517. A woods road begins at the northeast corner of the lot. A smaller parking area on the south side of NJ 23 just to the west (across a bridge), reached via a small opening in the guardrail, provides access to the Beaver Lake Rail Trail (see below). The Silver Lake fisherman's parking area may be reached by turning north onto Silver Grove Road at its western junction with NJ 23 and then turning left on Silver Lake Road.

On the east side of the wildlife management area, there is access from the Newark Watershed Conservation and Development Corporation (NWCDC) property on both sides of County 515 for five miles north of NJ 23. There are several small pull-off parking areas on both sides of the road. Permits are required to hike or park on NWCDC land. For more information or to obtain permits, contact NWCDC by mail at P.O. Box 319, Newfoundland, NJ 07435, or in person at their office, 223 Echo Lake Road, West Milford, NJ 07480; (973) 697-2850.

On the western side of the wildlife management area, Sand Lake Road leads east from County 517 north of Franklin. The wildlife management area begins where the paving ends. There is a small parking area here, from where a woods road leads off to the left. Further up Sand Lake Road, a larger parking area is on the right just before the road is gated where it enters the land of the Morford Conservation Corporation.

The Beaver Lake Rail Trail is south of NJ 23, across from the main tract. Part of the abandoned Hanford Branch of the New York, Susquehanna and Western Railroad, it runs for three miles from Beaver Lake Road to Ogdensburg through an upland forest. To maintain the rail grade, cuts were made into the limestone hillside. For most of its length, it parallels an active railroad line, separated by a small strip of trees. To reach the rail trail, either use the small parking area mentioned above and walk east to Beaver Lake Road, or park at the Ogdensburg Fire Station, cross County 517, and proceed east and then north. At the northern end, shortly before reaching Beaver Lake Road, the trail turns right at a point where there is a wooden bridge over a stream on the left (that leads to a private house) and it crosses the active railroad line (stop, look, and listen).

Since there are no marked trails in the Hamburg Mountain Wildlife Management Area, users of the area should obtain the Franklin, Hamburg, and Wawayanda USGS topographic quadrangle maps. For more information, contact New Jersey DEP, Division of Fish and Wildlife, 501 East State Street, P.O. Box 400, Trenton, NJ 08625; (609) 984-0547; www.njfishandwildlife.org.

Jenny Jump State Forest

This 2,014-acre forest rises like an emerald jewel from the surrounding farm-land, with overlooks along the ridge providing panoramic views over the fertile fields of the Great Valley. Established in 1931, Jenny Jump State Forest is located in Warren County, between Hope and Great Meadows. Situated about 12 miles southeast of the Delaware Water Gap, its elevations range from about 400 feet to 1,100 feet. Birders will enjoy both the trails in Jenny Jump State Forest and the roads that border the park. Common birds are the scarlet tanager, rose-breasted grosbeak, and a variety of warblers.

According to folklore, Jenny Jump Mountain derives its name from Jenny Lee, a young woman living with her aged father on the mountain. While in a remote area on the mountain, she was accosted by (depending on the account) either a spurned suitor or a Native American. After being chased to the edge of the cliff, she chose "death before dishonor" and jumped. In one account, how-ever, she lived to tell the tale. The authenticity of this pre-Revolutionary story is difficult to assess.

The state forest has a picnic area with sites for family-size groups. Near the forest headquarters, eight "camp shelters" can be rented year-round. The "shel-ters" are actually small enclosed cabins, each with a wood stove, an outdoor fire ring, and bunks for four people. Twenty-two campsites are available for tents or small camp trailers between April 1 and October 31. Some of the campsites are designated as "walk-in" sites.

To reach Jenny Jump State Forest, take I-80 to Exit 12 (Hope/Blairstown). Turn left and proceed south on County 521 for 1.1 miles to the old Moravian village of Hope. Turn left at the blinking light onto County 519 (Johnsonburg Road). Continue for 1.0 mile and turn right onto Shiloh Road. In 1.1 miles, turn right onto State Park Road and proceed to the park entrance, 1.0 mile on the left. For more information, contact Jenny Jump State Forest, P.O. Box 150, Hope, NJ 07844; (908) 459-4366; www.njparksandforests.org.

Geology

Jenny Jump State Forest is located at the very western edge of the Highlands, on the opposite side of the Great Valley from the Kittatinnies. Like almost all of the Highlands belt, the bedrock of Jenny Jump is composed of Precambrian granite gneiss. Many gneiss outcrops in Jenny Jump display well-preserved glacial stria-tions, and numerous erratic boulders are found along the trails.

The abundance of glacial boulders at Jenny Jump is the result of its proximity to the Ice Age terminal moraine located just to the south (see the color Geologic Map on the endpapers in the front of the book). This terminal moraine is a great heap of boulders and sand that marks the farthest advance of the Pleistocene glacial ice sheet. Areas adjacent to terminal moraines tend to have unusual concentrations of glacial erratics—far more than glaciated regions more distant from the glacier's terminus.

Trails in Jenny Jump State Forest

The trails in Jenny Jump State Forest provide panoramic views of the surrounding farms and woodlands. They offer a variety of hiking experiences, from eagle-view vistas over wide expanses of countryside to quiet strolls through low-lying areas. In addition to the trails described below, the 3.7-mile Mountain Lake Trail loops around an outlying section of the park, located to the southwest of the main park area. The Mountain Lake Trail is open to mountain bikes, but all other trails in the park are hiking-only.

An interesting 1.4-mile loop hike—which leads to the two best viewpoints—combines the Spring and Summit trails. A longer 2.5-mile loop hike can be created by combining the Summit and Swamp trails, along with a section of East Road—the paved road that leads to the campsites. Just past Campsite #21, a jagged glacial erratic on the north side of the road features a small evergreen tree growing out of the top of the boulder.

Figure 11-13. Causeway across Ghost Lake

Ghost Lake Trail

Length: 1.3 miles Blaze: turquoise
The Ghost Lake Trail connects Group Campsite B, at the end of East Road, with Ghost Lake. From the trailhead on East Road, where parking is available, it follows a level woods road jointly with the Summit Trail (yellow). At 0.2 mile, the Summit Trail leaves to the right, and the Ghost Lake Trail narrows to a footpath, soon passing sev-

eral interesting rock outcrops. After passing a jagged glacial erratic to the left at 0.5 mile, the trail begins to descend over rocks, steeply in places. It bears left and joins a woods road at 0.7 mile, continuing to descend more gradually.

At 0.9 mile, the trail approaches I-80, which can be seen ahead through the trees. Here, the trail bends sharply right and begins to head southwest. Just beyond, the trail passes a huge moss-covered overhanging boulder to the left of the trail. The trail continues to descend through an attractive ravine, with an understory of Christmas ferns. It ends, 1.3 miles from the start, at a grass-covered causeway that bisects Ghost Lake. To reach Shades of Death Road, where parking is available at a gravel car-top boat-launch turnout, cross the causeway and bear left at the fork in the road.

Orchard Trail
Length: 0.7 mile Blaze: white

The Orchard Trail offers a quiet walk through the woods, with some clear views of the Delaware Water Gap along the route. Starting at the Orchard Park picnic area, near the entrance to the park on State Park Road, the Orchard Trail runs along the northwest border of the park on a wide woods road, skirting farmland to the left. At 0.3 mile, the trail narrows to a footpath, and it ends, 0.7 mile from the start, on East Road. The trailheads of the Ghost Lake (turquoise) and Summit (yellow) trails are 0.2 mile to the left along East Road.

Spring Trail
Length: 0.8 mile Blaze: blue

Beginning at the far end of the second hikers' parking area, the Spring Trail runs along the south side of the base of the ridge. After skirting an open area to the left, it passes near the edge of a rocky ravine on the right, with views over the ravine. It then swings left and continues along the base of the ridge on a relatively level footpath. At 0.6 mile, after passing cliffs on the left, the trail turns left and climbs steeply to the ridge, where it crosses the Summit Trail (yellow). The Spring Trail now descends to end, 0.8 mile from the start, at a short gravel road that connects East Road with Campsite #18. East Road is to the right; the Swamp Trail (red), which can be used as an alternate return route, begins to the left at Campsite #18.

Summit Trail
Length: 1.5 miles Blaze: yellow

From the first hikers' parking area (across from a restroom building), the Summit Trail, running jointly with the Swamp Trail (red), climbs on a woods

Figure 11-14. View from the Summit Trail

road, passing two cabins and skirting Campsite #9. At 0.1 mile, the Swamp Trail leaves to the left. The Summit Trail continues to ascend, reaching, at 0.2 mile, a flat rock along the trail. Here, a side trail leads right to a panoramic viewpoint from a rock outcrop amid cedars, with farmlands of the Great Valley to the left, the Pinnacle directly ahead, and the Delaware Water Gap in the distance to the right. Glacial striations are clearly visible on the surface of the rock outcrop.

Just beyond this viewpoint, the Summit Trail turns left and soon levels off. At 0.4 mile, a side trail to the right leads to a south-facing viewpoint, which includes both forest and the fertile fields of the Great Valley. In another 100 feet, the Summit Trail passes two large glacial erratics in an open area. The one on the left is formed of limestone, which is very different from the underlying bedrock. Just beyond, the trail narrows to a footpath, with north-facing views through the trees on the left.

After a short descent, the Spring Trail (blue) crosses at 0.6 mile. The Summit Trail continues along the ridge, passing another viewpoint to the right, and then descending briefly. At the base of the descent, the trail bears right and continues along a relatively level footpath. At 0.9 mile, the trail passes a beech tree with many carved initials and climbs to a high point on the ridge. The trail now descends steadily, reaching a T intersection at 1.3 miles. Here, the Summit

Trail turns left, joining the Ghost Lake Trail (turquoise), which comes in from the right. Both trails continue along a woods road until the Summit Trail ends, 1.5 miles from its start, on East Road, near Group Campsite B, where parking is available.

Swamp Trail   *Length: 0.4 mile Blaze: red*
From the first hikers' parking area (across from a restroom building), the Swamp Trail, running jointly with the Summit Trail (yellow), climbs on a woods road, passing two cabins and skirting Campsite #9. At 0.1 mile, the Swamp Trail leaves to the left and continues along a relatively level woods road, passing a small swamp to the right and continuing through an attractive stand of evergreens. The trail ends at 0.4 mile at Campsite #18. Just ahead, along a gravel road, the Spring Trail (blue) begins to the right. Just beyond, the gravel road leads to the paved East Road.

Pequest Wildlife Management Area

Paralleling the Pequest River east of the intersection of US 46 and NJ 31, the approximately 4,000-acre Pequest Wildlife Management Area is managed for upland game hunting and trout fishing. It has three short marked hiking trails, two abandoned railbeds, and the Trout Hatchery and Natural Resource Education Center. From parking areas, farm roads and woods roads lead into the interior.

The three marked trails are located in the trout hatchery area. The Red Trail is an interpretive trail with numbered stops and connects with the Blue and Yellow trails. The Blue Trail begins just before the pond and goes through a glacial deposit of sand and gravel, fields, and mixed woodlands. The Yellow Trail begins at the pond, climbs through mature woods, and passes through old fields. Both the Blue and Yellow trails have views of the surrounding countryside. All three trails may be combined to form a 1.2-mile loop hike beginning and ending at the trout hatchery.

Abandoned routes of the Lehigh and Hudson River Railroad (L&HR) and the Delaware, Lackawanna and Western Railroad (DL&W) which run through the wildlife management area have not been formally converted to rail trails but are open to hikers. Constructed in 1881-82, the L&HR served the dairy industry and was an important link in rail freight transportation between Pennsylvania and New England.

Within the wildlife management area, a 4.1-mile segment of the Lehigh and Hudson River Railroad (L&HR) parallels US 46 and the Pequest River. Most of the ties have been removed, and the line now has a cinder surface. Along the right-of-way there are mile markers, signposts, piles of slag, remnants of an iron furnace, and a livestock underpass, which allowed livestock access to the river. There are four access points to the rail trail. The eastern end may be accessed at Pequest Road, 0.5 mile south of the intersection of Pequest Road with US 46. The trail may also be accessed via the trout hatchery entrance road, at the intersection of US 46 and Furnace Road, and at the northeast corner of the intersection of US 46 and NJ 31—the western end of the trail. Here, the L&HR passes under a concrete viaduct which once carried the main line of the DL&W—now a cinder-surfaced trail. A woods road connects the two railbeds further north.

To reach the Pequest Wildlife Management Area, proceed east on US 46 for 2.6 miles from the US 46/NJ 31 intersection. The entrance road to the trout hatchery and Natural Resource Education Center is on the right. Users of the Pequest Wildlife Management Area who wish to explore the area off trail should obtain the Washington USGS topographic quadrangle map. For more information, contact the Pequest Trout Hatchery and Natural Resource Education Center, 605 Pequest Road, Oxford, NJ 07863; (908) 637-4125; or the New Jersey DEP, Division of Fish and Wildlife, 501 East State Street, P.O. Box 400, Trenton, NJ 08625; (609) 984-0547; www.njfishandwildlife.org.

TWELVE

CENTRAL JERSEY

ew Jersey has always been a crossroads between New York City and Philadelphia. Even before the Europeans settled in the area, the Native Americans developed routes across the state, and these routes were later used by the settlers who established farms in the area. During the American Revolution, troops and supplies crossed the state many times as the Continental Army engaged in nearly 100 battles and skirmishes. In 1809, the completed Easton Turnpike began serving as an artery of commerce. Eleven years later, the Georgetown-Franklin Turnpike was completed. Soon, canals—and then railroads—became the preferred means of transportation and brought prosperity into an agricultural economy. The Camden and Amboy Railroad was completed between South Amboy and Bordentown in 1834.

Today, superhighways cross the state, but it is the county highways and local roads that ultimately lead residents and visitors to interesting places to hike. State, county, and municipal governments have set aside open space in order to protect water resources and wildlife habitat, ensure suburban and rural ambiance, and provide active and passive recreation. Hikers can avail themselves of a wide range of hiking opportunities—rail trails, towpaths, ravines, wooded hills, meadows, wetlands, and former fields. Small parks offer opportunities for fitness walking as well as wildlife observation. Wildlife management areas beckon the more adventuresome who enjoy prowling through woods, fields, and meadows (out of hunting season).

ASSUNPINK WILDLIFE MANAGEMENT AREA

Purchased under the Green Acres Program, the 5,746-acre Assunpink Wildlife Management Area includes man-made and natural lakes, wetlands, former farm fields, hedgerows, and mixed hardwood forests. The diverse habitats in the wildlife management area are home to a variety of wildlife, including deer, rabbits, squirrels, owls, and hawks. The three lakes are popular resting spots for migratory waterfowl. Woods roads and mowed strips provide access to uplands and open fields.

To reach the Assunpink Wildlife Management Area, take I-195 to Exit 11 (Imlaystown Road), and proceed north on Imlaystown Road to the second stop sign. Turn right onto Eldridge Road, and follow it to the headquarters of the wildlife management area. Since there are no marked trails in the Assunpink Wildlife Management Area, users of the area should obtain the Allentown and Roosevelt USGS topographic quadrangle maps. For more information, contact the New Jersey Department of Environmental Protection (DEP), Division of Fish and Wildlife, 501 East State Street, P.O. Box 400, Trenton, NJ 08625; (609) 984-0547; www.njfishandwildlife.org.

CAPOOLONG CREEK WILDLIFE MANAGEMENT AREA

Roughly paralleling Capoolong Creek, the Capoolong Creek Wildlife Management Area follows the right-of-way of the abandoned Pittstown Branch of the Lehigh Valley Railroad. The 3.7-mile rail trail follows the cinder railbed. Vegetation along the route includes hemlock, beech, and sycamore trees, honeysuckle, grapevines, and poison ivy.

To reach the Capoolong Creek Wildlife Management Area, take I-78 to Exit 15 (Clinton/Pittstown, NJ 173 East). At the end of the exit ramp, turn left onto County 513 South. To reach the southern end, continue for about four miles and turn left on Quakertown Road. The trail starts at the far end of the MCI Electric Company property, just after the road crosses a stream. Parking is available in Pittstown, a short distance to the north along County 513. To reach the northern end, follow County 513 South for 0.6 mile from Exit 15 and turn left (south) onto County 617 (Sydney Road). Continue for 1.4 miles, and turn left on Lower Landsdown Road. In 0.5 mile, turn right onto Landsdown

Road and cross the railroad tracks, where the trail starts.

From the southern end on Quakertown Road, the rail trail passes the abandoned Pittstown railroad station at 0.1 mile. At 0.8 mile, the trail reaches White Bridge Road. Here, the trail briefly disappears, and hikers must walk along the road. At 0.9 mile, the trail reappears and closely follows the creek. The trail crosses an iron bridge with ties at 1.3 miles, and it crosses Lower Kingstown Road at 1.7 miles. North of here, hikers walk along the road to rejoin the trail at 1.9 miles. After crossing a tie bridge over a drainage gully at 2.3 miles, the trail crosses two roads and ends at active railroad tracks at 3.7 miles. For more information, contact New Jersey DEP, Division of Fish and Wildlife, 501 East State Street, P.O. Box 400, Trenton, NJ 08625; (609) 984-0547; www.njfishandwildlife.org.

COLUMBIA TRAIL

The High Bridge Branch of the Central Railroad of New Jersey extended from the town of High Bridge, where it connected with the main line of the railroad, north to Hopatcong Junction, where it split into spurs that served iron mines at Hibernia, Mount Hope, Ogden, and other locations. Completed in 1876, it was once a key transportation link for the iron mines of the Highlands. Passenger service on the line ended in 1932, but freight service continued until 1975, when the section from Bartley south to High Bridge was abandoned. Subsequently, the right-of-way was purchased by the Columbia Gas Company, which installed an underground natural gas pipeline along the right-of-way. Freight service is still operated on the portion of the line north of Bartley.

From Bartley to High Bridge, the surface rights to the right-of-way have been acquired by Hunterdon and Morris counties, and it has been converted into a rail trail, known as the Columbia Trail. For much of its length, it parallels the South Branch of the Raritan River. The section from Long Valley to Ken Lockwood Gorge has been designated part of the Highlands Trail and is marked with teal diamond blazes.

To reach the northern end of the trail in Bartley, take I-80 to Exit 27A and proceed south on US 206 to Flanders. Turn right onto Flanders-Bartley Road (County 641) for 0.7 mile, then turn left and continue for 1.5 miles to the end of the active rail line. To reach Long Valley from I-80, take Exit 27A and continue south on US 206 for 8.0 miles. Turn right onto County 513 (formerly

designated as NJ 24) in Chester and follow it for 4.5 miles to Long Valley. To reach the southern end of the trail in High Bridge, take I-78 to Exit 17 (Clinton), continue north on NJ 31 for 1.9 miles, and turn right onto County 513. Public transportation is available to High Bridge via weekday commuter service on the NJ Transit Raritan Valley Line and entails a four-block walk from the station. Road access is also available at various other points along the trail.

For information about the Morris County section, contact the Morris County Park Commission, P.O. Box 1295, Morristown, NJ 07962; (973) 326-7600; www.morrisparks.com.

For information about the Hunterdon County section, contact the Hunterdon County Department of Parks and Recreation, P.O. Box 2900, Flemington, NJ 08822-2900; (908) 782-1158; www.co.hunterdon.nj.us.

Columbia Trail   *Length: 15.8 miles Blaze: unmarked*

From the northern trailhead in Bartley, the trail proceeds south, paralleling the South Branch of the Raritan River, which is to the right. At 0.5 mile, it crosses a bridge over Drake's Brook. After crossing North Four Bridges Road at 0.7 mile, it crosses the South Branch of the Raritan River at 1.0 mile. Naughright Road is crossed at 1.7 miles.

At 3.2 miles, the trail departs from the right-of-way and turns right onto a dirt road, then left onto Fairview Avenue. In 2003, there are plans to restore the right-of-way for the trail, but until these plans are effectuated, hikers must detour along the road. After crossing Schooley's Mountain Road in Long Valley at 3.9 miles, where the Highlands Trail (teal diamond) joins from the left, the trail regains the railbed, and it soon crosses a triple-track bridge over a stream.

The Columbia Trail crosses Middle Valley Road at 7.0 miles. Just beyond, it passes a collection of old cars from the 1950s to 1970s. Then, at 7.2 miles, the trail crosses the South Branch of the Raritan River on a 200-foot-long bridge. Reaching West Mill Road (County 513) at 7.9 miles, the trail turns right and detours along the road, as a commercial nursery has taken over the trail route. The trail turns left just before a fence, skirts the nursery, then turns right, regaining the railbed.

At 8.6 miles, the trail crosses Valley Brook Road near the intersection of Vernoy Road, where parking is available, and enters Hunterdon County. For the next 4.5 miles, the South Branch of the Raritan River, on the right, closely parallels the trail. Entering the small town of Califon at 10.3 miles, the trail crosses Main Street and then Academy Street (County 512), where the original

stone station still stands and now houses the museum of the Califon Historical Society (open on a very limited basis). Hoffman's Crossing Road is crossed at 12.1 miles.

At 13.1 miles, just north of the Ken Lockwood Gorge Wildlife Management Area, the Columbia Trail crosses the South Branch of the Raritan River on a 260-foot-long steel girder bridge, with the river about 80 feet below. At the south end of the bridge, the Highlands Trail leaves to the right. Now on the west side of the river, the Columbia Trail continues through a cut and then follows a narrow shelf above the river, lined with silver maples. It crosses a bridge over Cokesbury Road at 14.5 miles and passes by Boy Scout Camp Dill. After going through another cut, the trail continues above Lake Solitude, on the left, which was created by damming the river.

The Columbia Trail ends at Main Street in High Bridge, 15.8 miles from Bartley. Parking is available in the municipal parking lot across from the trailhead, and the NJ Transit High Bridge railroad station is 0.3 mile to the left.

DEER PATH PARK

The southern section of Deer Path Park in Readington Township offers picnic and pavilion facilities, along with ballfields and a one-mile fitness trail. The 236-acre Round Mountain section of the park, north of West Woodschurch Road, has a 1.5-mile self-guided nature trail and the 1.0-mile Peter Buell Trail, which branches off the nature trail, climbs over Round Mountain, and leads down to Foothill Road. To reach the park, take I-78 to Exit 17 (Clinton) and proceed south for 6.5 miles on NJ 31. Turn left onto West Woodschurch Road and continue for 0.7 mile to the park entrance, on the right. To access the trails, park in the lot for the soccer fields, go across the fields to a gate, and cross West Woodschurch Road to the trailhead. For more information, contact the Hunterdon County Department of Parks and Recreation, P.O. Box 2900, Flemington, NJ 08822-2900; (908) 782-1158; www.co.hunterdon.nj.us.

DELAWARE AND RARITAN CANAL STATE PARK

In the early part of the nineteenth century, people living in central New Jersey were isolated. The few roads that existed were at best difficult and at worst impassable. Rivers were not easily navigated, and railroads were in their in-

Figure 12-1. Delaware and Raritan Canal

fancy. A canal was seen as an effective means of transportation between Philadelphia and New York and a connection with the rest of the world. It took three years to build the 44-mile-long, 75-foot-wide, seven-foot-deep main canal and the 22-mile-long, 50-foot-wide, six-foot-deep feeder. Most of the workers were Irish immigrants, hired at very low pay to do the back-breaking work, mostly with hand tools.

Once completed, the Delaware and Raritan Canal became one of America's busiest navigational canals. Mule/horse- or steam-drawn tugs used it from 6 to 6 daily from early April until freeze. In 1871, its busiest year, total tonnage shipped surpassed the longer and more famous Erie Canal. With all the activity along the canal, it was necessary to impose a speed limit of four miles per hour to prevent damage to the canal banks.

To serve and be served by the canal boat operators, small commercial centers developed along the canal. The services offered were not limited to just stores. Canal boat operators, the majority of whom owned their own boats, could hire mules from barns at Bordentown, Griggstown, and New Brunswick. After the canal ceased operations, some of the towns remained, and they con-

tinued to offer services. In 1855, the Belvidere-Delaware Railroad was completed alongside the feeder canal. As railroads became a preferred mode of transportation, canals began to die. The D&R Canal ceased making a profit in 1892, although it continued to operate until 1933.

Once closed to navigation, both the main canal and the feeder were taken over by the State of New Jersey. After lock gates were removed and sluice gates installed, the canals became a source of water for farms, industry, and homes. As people began using the towpaths for walking, birding, and bicycling and the canals for canoeing, they realized they were valuable resources. In 1974, 67 miles of canal and a narrow strip of land on both banks became a state park. The abandoned Belvidere-Delaware Railroad right-of-way was added to the park in the 1980s. The towpath of the main canal is open to the public from Mulberry Street just north of Trenton to Landing Lane Bridge in New Brunswick, but there is a gap where the canal crosses US 1. The Belvidere-Delaware railbed, which does not allow horses, is the trail alongside the feeder canal.

Today, the canals offer hikers, birders, canoeists, anglers, equestrians, bicyclists, joggers, and picnickers the opportunity to enjoy the outdoors. There are more than 160 species of birds in the park, of which 90 are nesting. Turtles slide and frogs plop into the water at the first sound of danger. Wildflowers add color seasonally. Oak and maple trees form a canopy over the towpath in places. But regardless of what the vegetation along the towpath is, there seems to be an abundance of poison ivy.

The floodplain forest located between the canal and the Millstone River is an excellent example of the wetlands found along rivers in New Jersey, and much can be seen from the footpath without venturing down the poison-ivy-covered slope of the canal embankment. Unlike the trees in upland forests, the species in these forests can tolerate prolonged periods of flooding. Red and silver maples, boxelder (another species of maple), green ash, pin oak, and elms can grow to large size. Vines, including native grape vines and abundant poison ivy vines, are common in frequent openings in the canopy. Only a few shrubs—such as arrowwood viburnum and several kinds of shrubby dogwoods—can survive the flooding and damage from flowing water. Abundant sedges, rushes, and wetland grasses of many species form a dense herb layer on the forest floor.

A wide range of hikes is available, as there are small parking areas at nearly all road crossings providing access to the towpath. Users can easily keep track of how far they have gone, since mileposts on the main canal indicate mileage to Trenton and to New Brunswick. A four-mile loop hike is possible between

Kingston and Rocky Hill by following the canal towpath in one direction and an abandoned railbed in the other direction. An alternate route to the feeder canal is the Delaware Canal in Pennsylvania. More complete descriptions of selected sections on both canals are available in books listed in "Further Reading." For more information, contact Delaware and Raritan Canal State Park, 625 Canal Road, Somerset, NJ 08873; (732) 873-3050; www.njparksandforests.org.

DELAWARE CANAL STATE PARK

The 60-mile-long Delaware Canal towpath extends from Easton to Bristol and has been designated a National Recreation Trail. Once trod by mule teams pulling cargo boats along the canal—which provided an economical means of transporting coal from the Upper Lehigh Valley to Philadelphia—the towpath is used today by walkers, joggers, bicyclists, cross-country skiers, and bird watchers. Although the towpath is in Pennsylvania, it parallels the feeder canal of the Delaware and Raritan Canal for 30 miles, providing an alternate return route. The two trails, which are separated only by the Delaware River, are linked by six bridges. For more information, contact the Pennsylvania Department of Conservation and Natural Resources, Delaware Canal State Park, 11 Lodi Hill Road, Upper Black Eddy, PA 18972; (610) 982-5560; www.dcnr.state.pa.us.

FLEMINGTON GREENBELT

Hikers whose family members consider shopping a recreational activity have an alternative. Within walking distance of the outlet stores in Flemington are four small parks, none of which alone has enough trail mileage to keep a hiker busy. By combining the trails with roadwalks, the not-too-happy shopper can fill in what might otherwise be a boring time. The approximately 4.2-mile unmarked route is a loop and can be started at any point.

From Liberty Village, go north on Central Street and turn left onto Mine Street. Follow Mine Street past the main entrance to St. Magdalen Church and turn right on Shields Avenue, which becomes a country road. The Flemington water tower is on the right. Turn left on a footpath along the north end of a field, which leads to Mine Brook Park. Cross Mine Brook on a bridge, walk

right on the park trail, and cross Capner Street to enter the Morales Nature Preserve. Wide trails within the preserve are marked with signposts.

The trails begin just behind the kiosk with a trail map. Take the Main Trail as it wanders through the woods. After crossing the brook, walk up wooden steps and turn left on the Eagle Trail. Proceed uphill alongside the brook, entering an area with no understory. The edge of the path is delineated with rocks, so you can hike straight uphill or switchback up to a bench. Continue to the right on the Meditation Trail. Those who want a longer hike can take the left fork into the Uplands Reserve, part of the Hunterdon County park system. There, an old paved road leads to mowed paths along the edges of fields.

The Meditation Trail ends at the Main Trail, which should be followed back to the entrance. Turn left on Capner Street to walk along the Reading-Fleming Middle School perimeter fence to Tuccamirgan Park. Proceed on a trail to Bonnell Street. The rear entrance to the parking lot at St. Magdalen Church is across the street. To return to Liberty Village, either turn left, staying on Bonnell Street, turn right on Park Street, right on Central Street, and right on Mine Street, or walk through the church property to make a left on Mine Street.

HOFFMAN PARK

The former farm of Albert and Joyce Hoffman, who owned the Hoffman Beverage Company, this 354-acre county park includes hardwood forest, grasslands, and 32 ponds of various sizes, which offer good fishing. It is a favorite for birders, as several threatened and endangered species nest in the grassland habitat. The park has over three miles of trails, mostly old gravel or paved roads that meander through woods and past ponds. Access to the trails is via the rather steep Hairpin Lane that winds downhill from the parking area, but the trails themselves are nearly level. Bicycles are permitted on the trails.

To reach Hoffman Park, take I-78 West to Exit 11. Follow the circle to the left and cross over I-78, following the signs to Pattenburg. Turn left at the first traffic light, and bear right at a fork onto Baptist Church Road. Continue under a railroad overpass and turn left onto the park entrance road. For more information, contact the Hunterdon County Department of Parks and Recreation, P.O. Box 2900, Flemington, NJ 08822-2900; (908) 782-1158; www.co.hunterdon.nj.us.

HUNTERDON COUNTY ARBORETUM

Located in Clinton Township on NJ 31, six miles north of Flemington, the 105-acre Hunterdon County Arboretum is the headquarters of the Hunterdon County Department of Parks and Recreation. In 1953, George Bloomer established a commercial nursery on the site, and he sold the property to Hunterdon County in 1974 as a place for the public to observe and study natural science. A demonstration greenhouse was constructed, and display gardens were laid out for public enjoyment. A two-story gazebo, built in 1893, is the centerpiece of the gardens and is available for weddings. Several short trails, marked by orange squares—including a self-guided nature trail and the 1.1-mile Outer Loop Trail—wind through a network of ornamental trees and shrub plantations. The terrain is flat and suitable for easy walks. Educational programs are presented by park naturalists.

For more information, contact the Hunterdon County Department of Parks and Recreation, P.O. Box 2900, Flemington, NJ 08822-2900; (908) 782-1158; www.co.hunterdon.nj.us.

INSTITUTE WOODS

The 589-acre Institute Woods—a nature reserve of mature woodlands and fields—is part of the Institute for Advanced Study in Princeton, perhaps best known as the intellectual home of Albert Einstein. It features a network of about four miles of generally flat trails and cinder paths, providing a haven for walkers, birders, joggers, strolling scholars deep in thought, and scientists studying the Woods themselves. The Woods and the adjacent Rogers Refuge are considered one of the best places in New Jersey for observing the spring migration of warblers and other songbirds.

To reach the Woods, take NJ 27 to a left fork onto Mercer Road, just before its intersection with US 206 in Princeton. Turn left onto Olden Lane and drive to the end, where parking is available. The main cinder path starts from a point near the base of the turnaround at the end of the road. For more information, contact the Institute for Advanced Study, Einstein Drive, Princeton, NJ 08540; (609) 734-8000; www.ias.edu.

KEN LOCKWOOD GORGE

The 260-acre Ken Lockwood Wildlife Management Area is managed primarily for hunting and fishing. Towering hemlocks lining the steep walls of the Ken Lockwood Gorge provide shade and contribute to a sense of isolation. A 2.5-mile stretch of the South Branch of the Raritan River flows through the gorge, cascading over boulders, spilling over small waterfalls, and pouring into quiet pools. Fly fishermen test their skills in the stream, reported to be one of the best trout fishing streams in the region. Hikers can enjoy a stroll along the unpaved access road that parallels the river. For those not wishing to walk the whole distance, there are numerous pull-outs where cars may be parked.

A shuttle hike of 5.5 miles is possible if one car is left in the village of High Bridge and another vehicle driven to the north end of the gorge. After walking 2.5 miles along the road in the gorge, hikers can reach the other car in High Bridge via the Columbia Trail, which crosses the river on a high trestle.

Figure 12-2. Ken Lockwood Gorge

To reach Ken Lockwood Wildlife Management Area, take I-78 to Exit 17 and continue north on NJ 31 for 1.9 miles. Turn right onto County 513 and follow it as it zigzags through the village of High Bridge and past Voorhees State Park. After milepost 20, turn right onto County 512. After crossing the bridge, make an immediate right turn onto River Road and enter the gorge. Public transportation is available to High Bridge via weekday commuter service on the NJ Transit Raritan Valley Line. For more information, contact the New Jersey DEP, Division of Fish and Wildlife, 501 East State Street, P.O. Box 400, Trenton, NJ 08625; (609) 984-0547; www.njfishandwildlife.org.

LANDSDOWN TRAIL

Completed in 1881, the 1.8-mile Clinton Branch of the Lehigh Valley Railroad connected Clinton with the main line of the railroad at Landsdown. Operations on the line ended several decades ago, and the line was acquired by Hunterdon County in 1993 and converted to a multi-use rail trail. The trail, which extends from Lower Landsdown Road in Clinton Township to West Main Street in Clinton Borough, traverses open fields, forests, and wetlands.

To reach the southern end of the trail, where parking is available, take I-78 to Exit 15 and follow County 513 south. In 0.6 mile, turn left (south) onto County 617 (Sydney Road). Continue for 1.4 miles, and turn left onto Lower Landsdown Road. The parking area for the trail is on the left in 0.5 mile, just beyond the intersection of Landsdown Road. For more information, contact the Hunterdon County Department of Parks and Recreation, P.O. Box 2900, Flemington, NJ 08822-2900; (908) 782-1158; www.co.hunterdon.nj.us.

MERRILL CREEK RESERVOIR ENVIRONMENTAL PRESERVE

Located in Warren County, Merrill Creek Reservoir Environmental Preserve offers opportunities for year-round recreational activities on over 3,000 acres of open space. Owned by a consortium of seven electric utilities, the reservoir was built to provide stored water that can be released, when needed, into the Delaware River to ensure sufficient water flow for electric generating facilities along the river. Completed in 1988, it took six months to fill the 650-acre reservoir with over 16 billion gallons of water. Exhibits at the Visitors Center

display the wildlife found in the area and explain the operation of the reservoir and history of the area. Hunting is restricted to club members in designated areas.

To reach Merrill Creek Reservoir Environmental Preserve from the intersection of NJ 31 and NJ 57 in Washington, go west on NJ 57 for 6.5 miles and make a right turn onto Montana Road. Continue for two miles, bearing left at a Y junction. At 0.3 mile, turn left onto Merrill Creek Road. The Visitors Center is at the end of the right fork. For more information, contact the Merrill Creek Visitors Center, 34 Merrill Creek Road, Washington, NJ 07882; (908) 454-1213; www.merrillcreek.com.

Trails in Merrill Creek Reservoir Environmental Preserve

The 290-acre Merrill Creek Environmental Preserve is located on an arm that juts into Merrill Creek Reservoir. Seven trails within the preserve wind their way through a wide range of habitats. The easy-to-moderate grades and ample opportunities to view wildlife make the area ideal for families. Hikers pass through mixed hardwood forests, orchards, evergreen plantations, and fields, and travel along the lake shore, wetlands, and a stream.

Creek Trail *Length: 0.9 mile or 1.1 miles Blaze: orange*
Beginning at the intersection of the Shoreline (blue) and Timber (red) trails, the Creek Trail proceeds along spring-fed Merrill Creek. At 0.3 mile, it reaches a footbridge at the end of the Perimeter Trail (black) and follows close to Upper Merrill Creek. After intersecting with the Orchard Trail (green) at 0.4 mile, it reaches a junction at 0.7 mile. At this point, the hiker can either take the right branch to head directly to Merrill Creek Road at 0.9 mile, or take the left branch to proceed through wetlands along the way before reaching the road at 1.1 miles.

Eagle Trail *Length: 0.4 mile Blaze: unmarked*
This handicapped-accessible trail begins at the entrance drive. It passes through farm fields and an apple orchard to end at a wildlife observation blind.

Farmstead Trail *Length: 0.4 mile Blaze: yellow*
This old farm road connects the Shoreline Trail (blue) with the Timber (red)

and Eagle (unmarked) trails. It passes through a hardwood forest between two farm sites.

Orchard Trail　　　　　　　　　　　　*Length: 0.9 mile Blaze: green*
From the Visitors Center parking lot, the trail splits at 0.1 mile. The right fork rejoins the direct route at 0.2 mile and shortly crosses the Visitors Center Road to join the Eagle Trail (handicapped accessible). After passing the terminus of the Farmstead Trail (yellow) on the left, the two trails separate, with the Orchard Trail continuing straight ahead. The Orchard Trail passes through an abandoned orchard and ends at 0.9 mile at a junction with the Creek Trail (orange).

Perimeter Trail　　　　　　　　　　　　*Length: 3.8 miles Blaze: black*
Since the Perimeter Trail is a circular route, it can be started at three different points. Arbitrarily beginning at the boat trailer parking area and proceeding clockwise around the reservoir, at 0.5 mile the trail enters the woods and crosses the first of four earthen dams. After passing through fields, the trail splits, at 1.3 miles, to cross over the half-mile-long main dam. The route to the left crosses Lower Merrill Creek and Reservoir Road, and it is about a tenth of a mile longer.

After crossing the main dam, the Perimeter Trail goes through a stand of red pine trees. At 1.6 miles, the trail reaches the Overlook parking lot. An 0.2-mile side trail connects the parking lot and the observation deck. The Perimeter Trail reaches the third dam at 2.5 miles. After passing the Inlet/Outlet Tower at 2.6 miles, there are panoramic views of the countryside and the reservoir. The Perimeter Trail crosses the fourth dam at 3.0 miles. The remaining 0.8 mile of trail passes intermittently close to the reservoir before crossing a footbridge which leads to the hiking trails within the Environmental Preserve around the Visitors Center. The shortest path can be followed by turning left on the Creek Trail (orange) for 0.1 mile, then continuing on the Orchard Trail (green) for 0.9 mile back to the boat trailer parking lot. Care should be exercised at turns.

Shoreline Trail　　　　　　　　　　　　*Length: 1.7 miles Blaze: blue*
To reach the Shoreline Trail, take the gravel path on the side of the building that leads into the woods and bear left at a Y junction. Passing through a dense oak, tulip, and sassafras woods, the Shoreline Trail descends towards the reservoir. In 0.5 mile, it intersects an unmarked trail, then continues for another 0.2 mile,

passing several ruins on the right, to the Farmstead Trail (yellow) and more ruins. At 0.8 mile, the trail reaches a connection to the Timber Trail (red), with a lime kiln visible to the left. The trail passes close to the shore of the reservoir, including an area of flooded timber, in the final half mile. It ends at an intersection with the Timber (red) and Creek (orange) trails at 1.7 miles.

Timber Trail   *Length: 0.7 mile Blaze: red*
Leaving from the Visitors Center, the Timber Trail takes an interior route through the preserve, passing though pine plantations in various stages of succession. After crossing the Farmstead Trail (yellow) at 0.3 mile, it ends at the Creek (orange) and Shoreline (blue) trails at 0.7 mile.

MOUNTAIN LAKES NATURE PRESERVE

This 74-acre natural area located just outside downtown Princeton is a favorite for family walks, bird watching, and fishing. Originally part of King George III's land grant to William Penn, it was farmed until the late nineteenth century. In the 1880s, the Margerum family dammed two of the streams that flowed through the property, creating lakes that they used to harvest ice. The ice company closed in 1930, and when the property was threatened with development in the early 1980s, it was purchased by Princeton Township—in part through Green Acres funds—and is now preserved as open space.

A network of several miles of trails makes two main loops through the predominantly wooded preserve, with areas of wetlands. The parking lot is located on Mountain Avenue, just off US 206 in Princeton. For more information, contact Mountain Lakes Nature Preserve, P.O. Box 374, Princeton, NJ 08540; (609) 924-8720; www.princetontwp.org.

MUSCONETCONG RIVER RESERVATION

Rising in Lake Hopatcong in Morris County, the Musconetcong River flows 44 miles to the Delaware River. It is a trout stream, with forests buffeting large segments. In its lower reaches, the river slices through a deep limestone valley, shadowed by 1,000-foot ridges. Two sections of the river are protected as part of the Hunterdon County park system. The Musconetcong Gorge section and the Point Mountain section each offer the opportunity for hikers to combine an

easy stroll along the scenic river with a more strenuous route along the ridge. For more information, contact the Hunterdon County Department of Parks and Recreation, P.O. Box 2900, Flemington, NJ 08822-2900; (908) 782-1158; www.co.hunterdon.nj.us.

Musconetcong Gorge Section

Bisected by two creeks, the Musconetcong Gorge Section is a long, narrow 425-acre tract that slopes down to the Musconetcong River. Originally owned by the Warren Glen Paper Mill, located adjacent to the park, the tract was once used to harvest trees that were processed by the mill into paper products. The forest has since regrown, and the dense vegetation supports a variety of wildlife.

Two major trails extend through the park. A three-mile white-blazed trail heads northeast from the parking area and follows a rocky treadway along the side of the mountain, utilizing traces of old woods roads for part of its route. It descends towards the Musconetcong River along Pine Run, and continues by running southwest along an abandoned railroad grade to the paper mill at Scout Creek. For the first 1.4 miles, the white-blazed trail is co-aligned with the Highlands Trail (teal diamond). The 0.6-mile Nature Trail (orange) extends from the parking area to a junction with the white-blazed trail at Scout Creek, and features 12 numbered posts and an explanatory booklet. Two other trails—the unmarked Gasline Road and a red-blazed trail—connect the mountainside and railroad routes and can be used to form shorter loop hikes.

A suggested loop hike combines the white-blazed trail with the Nature Trail to form a 3.6-mile route. From the parking area, head northeast, following the white-blazed trail, which climbs over a slight rise and then descends, with views to the left through the trees over the Musconetcong River gorge. At 0.5 mile, the trail bears left onto a woods road. It crosses Scout Creek on rocks, then immediately bears right, leaving the woods road, and ascends steeply on switchbacks. The grade soon moderates, with the trail continuing to ascend along the side of the mountain. After passing several huge boulders to the left at 0.8 mile, the white trail reaches its highest point (920 feet) at 1.0 mile. A red-blazed trail which descends on switchbacks to the railroad grade (and can be used to shorten the hike) leaves to the left at 1.1 miles.

At 1.4 miles, the trail begins a steady descent from the ridge. It reaches Pine Run at 1.6 miles and turns left, following a rather steep path along the scenic

gorge of this rocky stream. After passing a small waterfall, the trail reaches an abandoned railroad grade—formerly a branch of the Lehigh Valley Railroad that served the paper mill—at 1.8 miles. It turns left and follows the level railbed parallel to the Musconetcong River, visible to the right downhill. Soon after passing a dam (built to channel the river into a canal to provide power for the mill) at 2.3 miles, the red-blazed trail ends to the left. Below the dam, the river is divided into a placid canal and a narrower channel in which the water follows its natural course over cascades and rapids.

At 2.9 miles, with the paper mill in view to the right, the railroad grade ends (the trestle that formerly connected the railbed with the paper mill has been removed). Here, the white-blazed trail turns left, and it ends, 3.0 miles from the start, at a junction with the Nature Trail (orange). Bear right and follow the Nature Trail, soon crossing Scout Creek on a wooden footbridge. The trail now bears right, uphill, then levels off, with a scenic view to the right over the stream below. At a fork, reached at 3.3 miles, bear left, then bear sharply left at the next junction (marked by signpost #2) and proceed uphill to return to the parking area.

To reach the Musconetcong Gorge section, take I-78 to Exit 7 (West Portal/Bloomsbury). Turn right at the bottom of the ramp and follow NJ 173 west for 1.3 miles. Where the road curves to the right, take the left fork (following the sign to Warren Glen/Riegelsville), and continue for 3.0 miles on County 639. At the stop sign, bear left onto County 519. Proceed for 0.3 mile, then turn left (continuing to follow County 519) and cross the bridge over the Musconetcong River. Continue for another 0.3 mile, passing the FiberMark paper mill to the left, and turn left onto unpaved Dennis Road. Proceed uphill for 0.1 mile to the parking area, which is on the left side of the road at a sharp hairpin turn to the right.

Point Mountain Section

The 745-acre Point Mountain section is approximately 15 miles upstream from the Gorge section in the northwest corner of the county. Its trails parallel the scenic Musconetcong River, traverse a mature forest, and follow mowed paths along cultivated fields. The 935-foot-high summit of Point Mountain offers sweeping views of small towns, fertile farmland, and the Musconetcong River valley.

Situated just south of the Pleistocene terminal moraine, Point Mountain is

Figure 12-3. Viewpoint on Point Mountain

an unglaciated area, devoid of glacial erratics, striations, rounded outcrops (*roches moutonées*), and other evidence of glaciation. By contrast, Jenny Jump Mountain—which is only ten miles away—is just north of the terminal moraine, and features abundant evidence of glaciation (see the color Geologic Map in the front endpapers of this book).

The many boulders found on the steep slopes of Point Mountain are more angular in shape than the partially rounded erratics of glaciated regions. Glacial erratics are usually a mix of rock types—some were carried from the north by the glacier, while others were formed of local rock types. By contrast, *all* of the boulders on Point Mountain are fragments of the local bedrock. Weathered by hundreds of thousands of years of rain and frost penetrating into cracks in the bedrock, the rock separated into angular fragments that eventually became the jumble of boulders now found on the slopes of Point Mountain.

There are three marked trails in the Point Mountain section. The 2.1-mile Riverwalk Trail (blue) is a relatively level loop trail that runs directly along the Musconetcong River for about half a mile. The 2.1-mile Ridge Trail (orange) climbs on a rocky footpath to the crest of Point Mountain, where there is a panoramic overlook over Warren County to the west, and loops back to meet the northern end of the Riverwalk Trail. The 0.1-mile Overlook Trail (yellow)

provides a short but steep route from Point Mountain Road to the overlook. Parking and trail access are available on Point Mountain Road, 0.4 mile south of NJ 57, and on Penwell Road, 0.5 mile east of NJ 57.

A suggested 4.1-mile loop hike, beginning at the Penwell Road parking area, combines the Ridge and Riverwalk trails. From the parking area, proceed south on the Ridge Trail (orange), which follows a wide mowed path to the left of cultivated fields, with views of Point Mountain ahead in the distance. At 0.3 mile, where the Ridge Trail turns left, continue ahead on the Riverwalk Trail (blue), which begins here. The Riverwalk Trail turns right at the end of the field, follows along its southern end, then turns left and descends on a footpath to the Musconetcong River. At 0.4 mile, it crosses a tributary stream and widens to a woods road.

At 0.6 mile, the Riverwalk Trail reaches a fork. Turn right, leaving the woods road, follow a footpath for 50 feet to the river, then turn left and proceed along the river. For the next 0.5 mile, the trail closely parallels the river, which features attractive cascades. After passing a huge sycamore tree, the trail crosses Point Mountain Road at 1.1 miles and heads slightly inland, following a footpath through wild rose thickets. At 1.4 miles, the trail bears left, away from the river, and begins to run through a deciduous forest. Then, at 1.6 miles, it bears sharply left and begins to head northeast, paralleling Musconetcong River Road, visible through the trees to the right.

The Riverwalk Trail recrosses Point Mountain Road at 2.0 miles, reaching a parking area on the east side of the road. Here, the trail turns right and begins to climb on a rocky footpath, reaching a trail junction in 250 feet. Continue ahead, uphill, now following the Ridge Trail (orange). At 2.2 miles, the climb steepens, and the trail continues to ascend on a rocky treadway, with some rock steps. After bearing sharply left in sight of a private home ahead, the trail reaches a panoramic viewpoint over the Musconetcong River valley from a rock outcrop to the left of the trail at 2.4 miles.

The Ridge Trail now briefly descends to a junction with the Overlook Trail (yellow), then climbs to regain the ridge. It continues along the ridge, with occasional views through the trees to the left. At 2.8 miles, it bears right and descends slightly, parallels an old stone wall for about 600 feet, then turns left and climbs back to the ridge. The trail begins a steady descent at 3.0 miles. After crossing a stream at 3.3 miles, it turns left and follows a woods road downhill. The trail emerges onto a field at 3.6 miles and follows a mowed path along its left side. At the end of the field, the Ridge Trail bears left and reaches a junction

with the Riverwalk Trail, which begins to the left at 3.8 miles. Turn right and follow along the right side of the fields to return to the Penwell Road parking area, completing the 4.1-mile hike.

To reach the Point Mountain section, take Exit 17 (Clinton) of I-78 and proceed north on NJ 31 for 8.0 miles to the traffic light at Asbury-Anderson Road (County 632). Turn right and follow County 632 for 4.0 miles to NJ 57, then turn right onto NJ 57. The next traffic light is Point Mountain Road. For the Point Mountain Road parking area, turn right onto Point Mountain Road and continue for 0.4 mile to a truss bridge over the Musconetcong River. The parking area is on the left, 300 feet beyond the bridge. For the Penwell Road parking area, continue on NJ 57 for 0.3 mile beyond Point Mountain Road and turn right onto Penwell Road (at a sign for "Penwell"). Proceed for 0.4 mile to a bridge over the Musconetcong River. About 500 feet beyond the bridge, turn right onto a gravel driveway just before a stone house (the small park sign at this location may be difficult to see) and continue for 0.1 mile to the parking area.

The Point Mountain section can also be reached from the north via I-80. Take Exit 26 (Budd Lake/Hackettstown) and proceed west on US 46 for 7.4 miles to Hackettstown. Turn left onto NJ 182/County 517 and follow it for 1.0 mile, then turn right onto NJ 57. Follow NJ 57 for 6.2 miles and turn left onto Penwell Road, or continue for another 0.3 mile beyond Penwell Road and turn left at the traffic light onto Point Mountain Road.

ROUND VALLEY

Located south of Lebanon in the northern portion of Hunterdon County, Cushetunk Mountain is a horseshoe-shaped ridge which encircles the Round Valley Reservoir. It consists of igneous rock, similar to the diabase of the Palisades of the Hudson, which has been exposed by the erosion of late Triassic strata that once overlaid it. This igneous rock abuts the Precambrian gneisses of the adjacent Highlands, which can be seen in outcrops along the Round Valley Reservoir. The Cushetunk ridge, never having been glaciated as were the Palisades, has more residual soil than the Palisades, with a second growth of hardwood covering most of its surface.

Round Valley Recreation Area

The Round Valley Reservoir was created in the 1960s. It is the deepest body of water in New Jersey. Surrounding the three-mile-long, two-mile-wide reservoir is a 1,288-acre multi-use recreation area, with hiking trails, picnic areas, and wilderness campsites (accessible only on foot, by bicycle, or by boat). There is a seasonal entrance fee. Boating, but not swimming, is permitted in the reservoir (although swimming is permitted in season at a beach on the west side of the reservoir). The wooded campsites, many of them near the water, are available by permit from April 1 to October 31. The recreation area is home to a variety of wildlife, with white-tailed deer being particularly abundant around the open areas near the reservoir dams.

To reach the Round Valley Recreation Area, take Exit 20A (Lebanon) from I-78 west. Continue ahead to US 22 and turn right. In 0.7 mile, take the jughandle turn, following the sign for the recreation area. Continue ahead for 1.4 miles, passing the boat launch area. After the road merges with County 629 (Lebanon-Stanton Road), turn left into the park. Public transportation is available to Lebanon via weekday commuter service on the NJ Transit Raritan Valley Line and entails a 2.4-mile walk from the Lebanon railroad station. From the train station, hikers should follow Railroad Avenue east to Cherry Street, then turn right onto Cherry Street. At the end of Cherry Street, turn left onto Lebanon-Stanton Road and follow it to the park entrance, on the left. For more information, contact the Round Valley Recreation Area, 1220 Lebanon-Stanton Road, Lebanon, NJ 08833; (908) 236-6355; www.njparksandforests.org.

Trails in the Round Valley Recreation Area

Round Valley Recreation Area has over 12 miles of trails, all of which (except for the hiking-only Pine Tree Trail) are multi-use trails, open to hikers, bikers, and equestrians. Two of the trails—the Pine Tree Trail and the Family Hiking and Biking Trail—are short loop trails that begin opposite the entrance to the south parking lot. The 8.3-mile Cushetunk Trail nearly encircles the reservoir. It was originally planned to form a complete loop around the reservoir, but the restricted areas at the dam have prevented that. Hikers must retrace their steps to return to the parking area, although the Lower Cushetunk Trail, which runs close to the shore of the reservoir for over three miles, can be used as an

alternate return route for part of the way. The Cushetunk and Lower Cushetunk trails can be combined to form "lollipop"-loop hikes of 9.6 or 12.3 miles.

Cushetunk Trail   *Length: 8.3 miles Blaze: red*
The Cushetunk Trail extends for most of the way around the Round Valley Reservoir, except for a restricted area at the northwest corner. It is occasionally marked with red-blazed plastic wands (mostly at junctions). In some areas, it is marked with yellow discs nailed to trees. For the most part, the trail is well-defined and easy to follow. The last 1.9 miles of the trail are closed from January 1 to August 1 to protect a sensitive environment.

From its start on the western side of the south parking lot, the Cushetunk Trail climbs a small rise which offers a panoramic view of the sparkling, deep-blue reservoir. Cushetunk Mountain is visible directly across the reservoir. After descending to the reservoir level, with another broad view across the water, the trail climbs a hill, then crosses under a power line. At 0.7 mile, the trail approaches Lebanon-Stanton Road. It turns left, roughly parallels the road for 0.2 mile, then bears left, away from the road. After a short climb, the trail goes through an opening in a chain-link fence and crosses a paved service road at 0.9 mile.

After climbing through woods and crossing under a power line at 1.3 miles, the trail begins to run between a chain-link fence on the left and the power line on the right. Soon, it begins a rather steep descent. At 1.5 miles, the trail turns left, leaving the power line, and continues along the chain-link fence, still descending steadily.

At 1.7 miles, the trail emerges onto a grassy strip between two chain-link fences, with Lebanon-Stanton Road to the right, and the grassy slope of the reservoir dam to the left. It crosses another paved service road and bears left, following a narrow dirt path parallel to the chain-link fence

Figure 12-4. Round Valley Reservoir

on the left. After crossing a stream, it climbs wooden steps up a rise. At the top, it curves to the left, then bears right, proceeding along a narrow wooded strip between two chain-link fences.

The trail passes through a gap in a chain-link fence at 1.8 miles and enters the property of the Round Valley Youth Center, where hikers are asked to stay on the trail. Soon, the trail begins a gradual climb, crossing an access road at 2.2 miles. With houses visible ahead, the trail curves to the left, passing a pavilion of the youth center. At a T intersection, reached at 2.4 miles, the trail turns left, and it soon turns right, with a picnic area of the youth center visible ahead. At a Y intersection, the trail bears right, continuing its gradual climb of the ridge.

At 2.8 miles, the Cushetunk Trail reaches its southern junction with the Lower Cushetunk Trail, which descends to the left. The Cushetunk Trail bears right and continues to climb the ridge of Cushetunk Mountain, with views of the reservoir through the trees to the left. Several log benches have been placed along the trail, affording hikers the opportunity for a brief rest. The crest of the ridge (820 feet) is reached at 3.2 miles. After a level stretch, the trail begins to descend gradually at 3.9 miles. It passes near a private home and crosses a gravel access road at 5.1 miles. To the left, the road leads to restrooms, water (available seasonally), a picnic pavilion, and the Lower Cushetunk Trail, which may be used as an alternate return route.

The Cushetunk Trail now climbs to regain the ridge of Cushetunk Mountain. It reaches the crest of the ridge at 5.4 miles but, after a short level stretch, it begins to descend, reaching a T intersection at 5.8 miles. To the left, a path leads down to the Lower Cushetunk Trail, but the Cushetunk Trail turns right and continues heading north along the base of the mountain, paralleling a low stone wall to the left.

At 6.4 miles, the Cushetunk Trail crosses another gravel road. To the left, the road leads to the northern end of the Lower Cushetunk Trail; to the right, it climbs over the crest of the ridge and descends into the Cushetunk Mountain Nature Preserve. North of this point, the Cushetunk Trail is closed from January 1 to August 1.

The Cushetunk Trail soon bears left and descends to approach the reservoir at 6.7 miles. It turns right and runs close to the reservoir for 0.5 mile, then again turns right and climbs very steeply to regain the crest of the ridge at 7.4 miles. Here, the Cushetunk Trail turns left and heads west along the ridge, with views through the trees on both sides of the ridge (the trail straight ahead at the junction descends into the Cushetunk Mountain Nature Preserve). At 8.0 miles,

the Cushetunk Trail arrives at a south-facing viewpoint over the reservoir, where benches have been placed. Now following a woods road, the trail descends gradually to end, 8.3 miles from its start, at a locked gate in a chain-link fence.

Lower Cushetunk Trail   *Length: 3.4 miles Blaze: unmarked*
A gravel road used to access the park's wilderness campsites, the Lower Cushetunk Trail begins at a junction with the Cushetunk Trail (red), 2.8 miles from the south parking lot at the entrance to the recreation area. The Lower Cushetunk Trail descends towards the reservoir and heads east, parallel to the shore of the reservoir. At 0.9 mile, it turns away from the reservoir and continues to parallel it at a higher elevation. After descending towards the reservoir, it passes a picnic pavilion and reaches a junction with a gravel access road at 2.2 miles. The Cushetunk Trail is a short distance to the right along this road. The Lower Cushetunk Trail continues ahead, parallel to the reservoir, reaching another gravel access road that connects with the Cushetunk Trail at 3.4 miles. The Lower Cushetunk Trail ends just ahead, at a restroom building.

Cushetunk Mountain Nature Preserve
Adjacent to Round Valley Recreation Area is the 380-acre Cushetunk Mountain Nature Preserve. Two short, unmarked trails from the parking lot connect to the crest of Cushetunk Mountain, where there are seasonal views of the nearby hills and valleys to the north and Round Valley Reservoir to the south. One trail, which leads directly from the parking area to the ridgetop, climbing 450 vertical feet in 0.5 mile, is closed from January 1 to August 1 to protect a sensitive environment. The other trail follows a wooden-pole power line to the east, parallel to the NJ Transit railroad tracks, which are just to the left. In 0.5 mile, at an intersection with steel-supported high-tension wires, the trail turns right, briefly follows under the high-tension wires, and turns right into the woods. It climbs Cushetunk Mountain, first gradually and then more steeply, arriving at the ridgetop at 1.2 miles. Both trails connect with the Cushetunk Trail in the Round Valley Recreation Area, described above.

To reach the Cushetunk Mountain Nature Preserve, take Exit 20A (Lebanon) from I-78 west. At the traffic light, turn left onto NJ 22 East. Follow NJ 22 for 2.3 miles and turn right onto Mountain Avenue. After 1.0 mile, turn right onto Railroad Avenue just before a one-lane bridge over the railroad tracks,

and follow Railroad Avenue for 0.8 mile to a T intersection. Turn left, cross the railroad tracks, and immediately turn left into the parking area for the preserve. Public transportation is available to Lebanon via weekday commuter service on the NJ Transit Raritan Valley Line and entails a 1.7-mile walk from the Lebanon railroad station. From the train station, hikers should follow Railroad Avenue east to Cherry Street, turn right onto Cherry Street, then turn left onto Old Mountain Road and follow it for 1.5 miles to the park entrance, on the right. For more information, contact the Hunterdon County Department of Parks and Recreation, P.O. Box 2900, Flemington, NJ 08822-2900; (908) 782-1158; www.co.hunterdon.nj.us.

RUTGERS UNIVERSITY

Rutgers University owns several natural areas near its New Brunswick campus that are open to the public and provide enjoyable opportunities for walking. Helyar Woods and Kilmer Woods are open to the public daily during daylight hours, while the Hutcheson Memorial Forest is open only for guided walks on selected Sundays. For more information and a schedule of guided walks, contact Rutgers University, Department of Ecology, Evolution, and Natural Resources, 14 College Farm Road, New Brunswick, NJ 08901; (732) 932-9631.

Helyar Woods

This 43-acre preserve, located adjacent to Weston's Mill Pond, offers several miles of trails that traverse an old-growth oak-hickory forest which has never been logged, a wetter sweetgum and maple forest, young forests recovering from prior clearing, and open fields. The Rutgers Display Gardens, adjacent to the preserve, offer walks through plantings of ornamental trees, shrubs, and flowers.

To reach the preserve from US 1, take the Ryder's Lane exit towards Milltown and proceed south for 0.2 mile to the first left turn. A sign for Rutgers University identifies the entrance. Follow the entrance road to the left, past the display gardens, towards the Log Cabin. Limited parking is available at the end of the road. For a trail and natural history guide, contact Rutgers University, Department of Ecology, Evolution, and Natural Resources, 14 College Farm Road, New Brunswick, NJ 08901; (732) 932-9631; or call the Rutgers Display Gardens at (732) 932-8451.

Hutcheson Memorial Forest

This forest is located in Somerset on Amwell Road (County 514), one mile east of East Millstone. Guided tours given by ecologists at the University are offered on selected Sundays, but the preserve is not otherwise open to the public.

Rutgers Ecological Preserve (Kilmer Woods)

Kilmer Woods is a 370-acre tract of woods and fields located on the Piscataway Campus of Rutgers University. The area was once part of the U.S. Army's Camp Kilmer, which included barracks, a mess hall, a prisoner-of-war camp, and bunkers for ammunition. All of these structures were removed when the Army vacated the area. Today, all that remains are some paved areas in the middle of the tract, and mounds of soil built to shield the troops from the ammunition stores. Several miles of trails wend through mature beech, maple, and oak forests and traverse fields in various stages of succession back to forest.

To reach Kilmer Woods from NJ 27 in Highland Park, proceed northwest on River Road (County 514), which intersects NJ 27 just north of the bridge over the Raritan River. In 0.7 mile, turn right onto Cedar Lane. Continue on Cedar Lane for 0.5 mile and turn left onto Road 1. Follow Road 1 for 0.4 mile and turn left onto Road 3. The parking area is 0.1 mile ahead, on the left side of the road, just before the road bends to the right.

SIX MILE RUN RESERVOIR SITE

Named for a stream that bisects the park, the 3,037-acre Six Mile Run tract in Franklin Township in Somerset County was acquired by the State of New Jersey in 1970 as a site for a future reservoir. However, alternate sites for the reservoir were identified in 1989, and the Six Mile Run tract is currently managed by the Division of Parks and Forestry for recreational uses. Over half of the land is leased for agricultural use, with the remainder consisting of open fields and forested lands.

Three trails traverse the site. The 3.8-mile Blue Trail, open to hikers, bikers, and equestrians, follows a winding route along the edges of fields and occasionally travels into the woods. The 1.5-mile hiking-only Red Trail traverses a variety of habitats, including open fields, young cedar groves, and upland forests. The 0.9-mile Yellow Trail, which passes through the lowland floodplain of

the Six Mile Run, is open to hikers and bikers. The Red and Blue trails may be combined to form a 5.3-mile loop, and shorter loop hikes are also possible.

For more information on the Six Mile Run Reservoir Site, contact Delaware and Raritan Canal State Park, 625 Canal Road, Somerset, NJ 08873; (732) 873-3050; www.njparksandforests.org.

SOURLAND MOUNTAIN

A ten-mile-wide-by-four-mile-long traprock ridge known as Sourland Mountain rises from the red sandstone plain and runs southwest of Somerville towards the Delaware River. This ridge was formed when geological forces turned a basaltic intrusion on end, and then softer layers of rock eroded away. Heavily forested with some rough, rocky terrain, the ridge is high enough to permit a view of Manhattan skyscrapers. It is quite evident when driving west from US 206 on County 514.

The exact origin of the name is not known. It might have been derived from the German word *sauerland*, meaning land that is not sweet. The land in the area is rocky and acidic. The name could also refer to the sorrel or red-brown color of the soil on the plains adjacent to the mountain. On some records, the name Sowerland is used.

Whatever the origin of the name, Sourland Mountain has remained largely undeveloped because the land has never been worth much agriculturally or commercially, and it is far from major thoroughfares. Its relative isolation has resulted in the area serving as a retreat for many people, including Charles Lindbergh, whose child was kidnapped there. However, its lack of development brought some people in the area to seek its preservation. Since 1989, the Sourland Regional Citizens Planning Council has pressed for its protection, which has proved to be difficult as the mountain is located in three counties—Hunterdon, Mercer, and Somerset.

Northern Stony Brook Greenway

Located along the ridge of Sourland Mountain, this 295-acre tract of privately owned land straddles the Hunterdon/Mercer county line. Northern Stony Brook Greenway is the headwaters for Stony Brook and is protected through easements by the Delaware and Raritan Greenway, Inc. This regional land conservancy is protecting and preserving land along the Delaware and Raritan Canal

and its tributary streams. A hike along the three miles of trails takes one through woodlands in varying stages of maturity, wetlands, and open meadows.

Begin at the yellow trail just to the left of the Greenway sign in the parking area. The yellow trail proceeds through a mature forest of northern red oak, shagbark

Figure 12-5. Box turtle

hickory, tulip, white ash, and walnut trees, with spice bush, viburnum, and sassafras as the understory. Bear left at the Y junction and follow the orange trail. After crossing two stone walls, the orange trail descends to a wetland. This heavily forested area has not been actively cut since the early 1920s.

The orange trail ends at a junction with the yellow trail. Continue on the yellow trail, passing a spring, where box and snapping turtles can sometimes be seen. Generally wandering in a southwesterly direction, the yellow trail encounters a former farm road and turns right. Leave the yellow trail at its junction with the blue trail and ascend, via the blue trail, through large boulders to the top of the hill. After reaching a meadow, the blue trail skirts a corner and enters a new-growth wooded area. After crossing stone walls, it reaches another former farm road and ends at a junction with the yellow trail. The parking area is straight ahead.

A right turn on the yellow trail heads southeast, crossing a large meadow on the left and an overgrown one on the right. In early spring, woodcocks may be seen in their mating flights. Turning southwest, the yellow trail passes the stone foundations of the original farm site along the former farm road. The trail bends left alongside another meadow carpeted with wildflowers in the spring and summer. The blue trail, which was the route followed earlier on the hike, is on the right. Stay on the yellow trail, retracing your route between the blue and the orange trails. Once past one end of the orange trail, en route to the parking area, one will pass through some wet areas and ascend a hill on a meandering course through a mature forest.

Figure 12-6. Wildflowers

To reach Northern Stony Brook Greenway,

take US 202/NJ 31 south from Flemington to the jughandle turn for Wertsville Road (County 602) east and proceed 3.3 miles to Rileyville Road (County 607). Turn right and, in just under two miles, turn right again on Mountain Road. The parking area is on the left, 0.6 mile from the intersection. For more information, contact the Delaware and Raritan Greenway, 1327 Canal Road, Princeton, NJ 08540; (609) 924-4646; www.delragreenway.org.

Sourland Mountain Nature Preserve

Formerly the site of a quarry for large boulders which were crushed to obtain railroad ballast, concrete aggregate, and surfacing for roadbeds, this 273-acre Hunterdon County Park is now covered by a second-growth oak forest. From the small parking area, the one-mile Service Road Trail, a woods road, follows a mostly level route into the boulder-strewn forest, passing a swamp along the way. The short South Loop Trail, which crosses a stream twice, can be used as an alternate route for part of the way on the return.

To reach the preserve, take US 202/NJ 31 south for five miles from the Flemington Circle to the jughandle turn for Wertsville Road (County 602) east and proceed 3.3 miles to Rileyville Road (County 607). Turn right and continue for 1.7 miles to the park entrance, which is on the left. For more information, contact the Hunterdon County Department of Parks and Recreation, P.O. Box 2900, Flemington, NJ 08822-2900; (908) 782-1158; www.co.hunterdon.nj.us.

Sourland Mountain Preserve

The largest of the three open spaces on Sourland Mountain is the 2,870-acre Sourland Mountain Preserve, a Somerset County park. The preserve contains nested loop and connecting trails through a mature hardwood forest of primarily oak, beech, and tulip trees. Volunteers from the Sourland Regional Citizens Planning Council, Boy Scout Troop 46, and the federal Youth Conservation Corps built the trails.

The Pondside Trail (circle) is an easy 0.5-mile loop trail over level to gently sloping terrain. Another easy trail, the Maple Flats Trail (triangle), loops 1.1 miles further into the preserve. Rising and descending moderately to the ridge, the Ridge Trail (rectangle) covers 3.3 miles. An unmarked connecting trail short-cuts a portion of the Ridge Trail.

In dry seasons, when posted as appropriate, mountain bikes and horses

can use the trails. The parking lot and trailhead are located on East Mountain Road, 0.6 mile south of NJ 514 (Amwell Road), off US 206 near Somerville. For more information, contact the Somerset County Park Commission, P.O. Box 5327, North Branch, NJ 08876; (908) 722-1200; www.park.co.somerset.nj.us.

SPRUCE RUN RECREATION AREA

Occupying a pair of peninsulas jutting into Spruce Run Reservoir, the 1,910-acre Spruce Run Recreation Area is typical of most of the day-use areas found in many of New Jersey's state parks and forests. A park office and visitor center await the visitor immediately upon entering the recreation area, a quick right off the entrance road. There is a seasonal parking fee for the beach area and bathhouse complex. Further down the peninsula is the overnight camping area, where campsites are available by permit from April 1 to October 31.

Like the Clinton Wildlife Management Area, which is adjacent to the recreation area and surrounds the rest of the reservoir, there are no marked trails, except for a segment of the Highlands Trail (teal diamond) (see p. 440). However, the hiker can ramble through the hardwood forest and explore the shoreline, with views to the south and west across the reservoir. Birders like the area, as the diverse habitat attracts a wide variety of migratory waterfowl.

Figure 12-7. Canada geese

To reach Spruce Run Recreation Area, take I-78 to Exit 17 (Clinton), and proceed north on NJ 31 for 3.0 miles to the traffic light at Van Syckels Road. Make a left at the light and continue for 1.4 miles to the recreation area entrance, on the left. For more information, contact Spruce Run Recreation Area, One Van Syckels Road, Clinton, NJ 08809-1053; (908) 638-8572.

Clinton Wildlife Management Area

This 1,115-acre wildlife management area surrounds most of Spruce Run Reservoir, with the exception of the day-use area of Spruce Run Recreation Area, which occupies two peninsulas jutting into the lake. Numerous woods roads and unmarked trails, which do not show on the High Bridge USGS topographic quadrangle map, crisscross the region, with some actively farmed areas.

The section of the management area on the north side of Van Syckels Road offers about two miles of woods roads that are mowed to allow access to the area, which makes for very easy hiking. The hiker will pass through varying terrain and a combination of hardwood forest (consisting primarily of oak and ash) and open fields. It is possible to walk some sections of the shoreline of the reservoir, especially when the water level is low; however, other sections are impassable. Birders know the reservoir for its migratory waterfowl.

To reach the Clinton Wildlife Management Area, take Exit 17 (Clinton) from I-78, and proceed north on NJ 31 for 3.0 miles to the traffic light at Van Syckels Road. Make a left at the light and continue for 1.4 miles, passing the entrance to the Spruce Run Recreation Area, on the left. Gravel parking areas for the wildlife management area are on either side of the road, about 0.5 mile beyond the entrance to Spruce Run, and the office of the Clinton Wildlife Management Area office is on the left, 1.4 miles beyond the Spruce Run entrance. For more information, contact the New Jersey DEP, Division of Fish and Wildlife, 501 East State Street, P.O. Box 400, Trenton, NJ 08625; (609) 984-0547; www.njfishandwildlife.org.

TEETERTOWN RAVINE NATURE PRESERVE

Named after John Teeter, the builder of a nearby mill complex (c. 1810), the 302-acre Teetertown Ravine Nature Preserve is one of the most significant natural areas in Hunterdon County. A narrow dirt road surrounded by dense woods leads into a ravine along a twisting stream, with its waters cascading

over rocks. The steep sides of the ravine, with its large boulders and rock outcroppings, contribute to the sense of solitude. Several varieties of ferns may be found under the mature tulip, black birch, maple, beech, and oak trees. Evidence of an iron forge has been found in the area. Within the preserve are areas that were quarried from 1896 to 1923. Teeter's house is now a private residence.

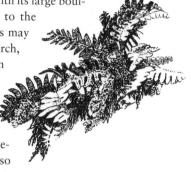

The Mountain Farm section of the preserve has two ponds and several fields. It also contains a stone farmhouse built in 1818, the home of the Lance family from the mid-

Figure 12-8. Ferns

1700s until 1926. The park visitor center offers educational nature films and contains exhibits on the history of the preserve. The preserve offers several miles of blazed trails, which are open to hiking, mountain biking, horseback riding, and cross-country skiing (except for the Blue Trail, which is for hiking only). Wilderness campsites are available on the Red Trail.

To reach Teetertown Ravine Nature Preserve, take I-78 to Exit 17 and continue north on NJ 31 for 1.9 miles. Turn right onto County 513, and continue north on County 513 for 6.8 miles to Sliker Road. Turn left onto Sliker Road and continue for 1.5 miles, then turn right onto Pleasant Valley Road. The park entrance is on the right in 0.6 mile. For more information, contact the Hunterdon County Department of Parks and Recreation, P.O. Box 2900, Flemington, NJ 08822-2900; (908) 782-1158; www.co.hunterdon.nj.us.

UNION FURNACE NATURE PRESERVE

Perched on a hillside overlooking Spruce Run Reservoir, this 97-acre Hunterdon County Park is named for the ironworks that flourished nearby from 1742 to 1781 (the actual site of the furnace was flooded by the reservoir). It contains a hardwood forest of oak, ash, and maple. An 0.9-mile section of the Highlands Trail (teal diamond) passes through the preserve. Beginning on the north side of Van Syckels Road, opposite the parking area, the trail ascends the embankment of an old mill race and follows it for 0.1 mile, climbs to the top of a hill, then descends to emerge on Serpentine Drive, which can be followed for 0.3 mile

back to Van Syckels Road. The remaining trails consist of overgrown woods roads that are not easily navigated due to the dense vegetation and hilly terrain.

To reach Union Furnace Nature Preserve, take I-78 West to Exit 17 (Clinton) and proceed north on NJ 31 for 3.0 miles to the traffic light at Van Syckels Road. Make a left at the light, cross a bridge over a stream, and park in the gravel parking area on the left. The trailhead is on the opposite side of the road. For more information, contact the Hunterdon County Department of Parks and Recreation, P.O. Box 2900, Flemington, NJ 08822-2900; (908) 782-1158; www.co.hunterdon.nj.us.

VOORHEES STATE PARK

Situated in the rolling hills of Hunterdon County, Voorhees State Park was the home of Foster M. Voorhees, a former governor of New Jersey. In 1929, he donated his 325-acre farm "Hill Acres" to become a state park. During the Great Depression, the Civilian Conservation Corps (CCC) developed the park's picnic sites, parking areas, roads, and trails. Today, it encompasses over 600 acres, with year-round camping facilities, an observatory, and five trails that meander along varying terrain through a mixed hardwood forest. Some of the trails are multi-use. A 1.7-mile section of the Highlands Trail (teal diamond) (which includes an 0.5-mile roadwalk) traverses the park.

To reach Voorhees State Park, take I-78 West to Exit 17 (Clinton), go north on NJ 31 for 1.9 miles, then turn right on County 513, and proceed for 1.2 miles to High Bridge. Continue north on County 513 for another two miles to the park entrance on the left. Public transportation is available to High Bridge via weekday commuter service on the NJ Transit Raritan Valley Line and entails a two-mile roadwalk to the park. For more information, contact Voorhees State Park, 251 County Route 513, Glen Gardner, NJ 08826; (908) 638-6969; www.njparksandforests.org.

WASHINGTON CROSSING STATE PARK

Established in 1912, Washington Crossing State Park is the site where the Continental Army landed after crossing the Delaware River on Christmas night 1776. Originally the park contained 100 acres, but it has grown to 900 acres, of which 500 acres were purchased through the Green Acres program. A por-

tion of the park is a 140-acre natural area which contains fields in various stages of secondary succession and a mixed hardwood forest. With 13 miles of hiking trails, there are plenty of places to walk in the park. In winter, when conditions are favorable, these trails may be used for cross-country skiing or snowshoeing. Other facilities in the park are a visitor center, interpretive center, Ferry House, open-air theater, picnic grove, and group campsites.

To reach the park, take NJ 29 north from Trenton to County 546. A right turn onto County 546 leads to the park entrance and visitor center. A left turn onto County 546 and then a right turn onto River Road leads to parking lots near the approximate site of the crossing. There is a seasonal entrance fee. For more information, contact Washington Crossing State Park, 355 Washington Crossing/Penn Road, Titusville, NJ 08560; (609) 737-0623; www.njparksandforests.org.

WOODFIELD RESERVATION

This 100-acre reservation near Princeton is owned by Princeton Township. Approximately half of the reservation was made available for public use by Mrs. John P. Poe in 1964 and subsequently acquired by the township. It is a mix of dry hardwood forest and wetland, with an understory of shrubs, ferns, and wildflowers. The woods are home to a wide range of birds, including migrant songbirds. The two unmarked hiking trails cross small streams to reach Council Rock, which overlooks a boulder basin, and Tent Rock, a large boulder. These boulders are the result of weathering and erosion, and were not deposited by glaciers (which did not extend this far south).

To reach Woodfield Reservation from the junction of US 206 and NJ 27 in Princeton, go south on US 206 and turn right at the traffic light at Elm Street. At 0.6 mile, the name changes to The Great Road. Bear right at the Y junction onto Old Great Road. The parking area, with a trail map, is across from the Tenacre Foundation. A gravel drive leads to the parking area. For more information, contact Princeton Township, 400 Witherspoon Street, Princeton, NJ 08540; (609) 921-7077; www.princetontwp.org.

THIRTEEN

THE JERSEY SHORE

ummertime at the Jersey Shore evokes images of Atlantic City, hordes of summer sunbathers, and traffic crawling on the Garden State Parkway. When those crowds diminish, however, walkers have a chance to enjoy brisk autumn, winter, and spring treks along miles of empty beaches. Geologically, the Jersey Shore is part of the outer portion of the Atlantic Coastal Plain, a physiographic region that forms 45% of the land mass of the state. But behind these sandy shores, teeming marshes and patches of forest offer other delightful strolls over rolling hills, past wildflowers, and through bird-filled meadows. County and state parks offer glimpses into the past—the American Revolution, early industry, or a businessman's country estate. Since New Jersey is on the flyway for both spring and fall bird migrations, there are many places to observe these annual events.

The Jersey Shore is not just resorts thriving on sandy beaches. It is also associated with lighthouses, historic villages, and wildlife migrations. It is because of New Jersey's long association with the sea that, in 1988, Congress established the New Jersey Coastal Heritage Trail Route. The National Park Service, the State of New Jersey, and many organizations are working together to provide for public appreciation, education, understanding, and enjoyment of natural and cultural sites along the coast. The Coastal Heritage Trail is divided into five regions, linked by the common heritage of life on the Jersey Shore and the Raritan and Delaware bays. Five themes—maritime history, coastal habitats, wildlife migration, historic settlements, and relaxation and inspira-

tion—focus on the various aspects of coastal life. Although the New Jersey Coastal Heritage Trail is designed for vehicular touring, it connects areas of interest to hikers. The trail is identified by the New Jersey Coastal Heritage Trail logo. For more information, contact New Jersey Coastal Heritage Trail Route, National Park Service, 389 Fortescue Road, P.O. Box 568, Newport, NJ 08345-0568; (856) 447-0103; www.nps.gov/neje.

Ecology

Along the sandy barrier of islands and spits that separates the mainland of New Jersey from the ocean, a group of plant communities shaped by salt-laden winds and waters may be found. On a walk along the beach, one can see the pioneer plants that are capable of withstanding shifting and storm-deposited sands, salty winds, and a nearly complete lack of soil-borne nutrients. Dune grass is the most prominent and important of these plants. It can grow through more than three feet of deposited sand and send out runners in all directions to stabilize newly formed dunes, creating an environment that allows other plants to survive. Other species within this pioneer zone include sea rocket, seaside goldenrod, and dusty miller. These plants have thick succulent leaves and dense layers of hairs that protect them from dessication and salt.

Behind the primary dunes, the vegetation becomes more diverse, as a number of shrub species—including bayberry, beach plum, poison ivy, and sumac—join the grasses and forbs of the dune crest and form often impenetrable thickets. The salt-laden winds prune the bushes and keep the vegetation from emerging from behind the protection of the dune crest. As the distance from the ocean increases, the vegetation becomes more forest-like. Sassafras, holly, black cherry, serviceberry, and red cedar are prominent; in some places (notably in the Sandy Hook unit of the Gateway National Recreation Area), the hollies are hundreds of years old and exceptionally large and beautiful.

The water between the lee side of the barrier formations and the mainland was historically the site of extensive salt marshes. Although large sections of marsh have been destroyed to create marinas and deepwater channels for boats, substantial areas of marsh remain and can be viewed from nature trails in parks along the coast. Along the junction between upland and marsh, the only two species of woody plants that are tolerant of salt water—marsh elder and groundsel bush—are often intermixed with tall, coarse grasses, including common reed, *Phragmites australis*. Beyond this junction is the high marsh, identifiable

by the slicked-down salt meadow grass (until recently, widely harvested and used as salt hay) and the dark green black grass (actually a rush). Several other species of grasses, sedges, and forbs are also found here. This portion of the marsh is flooded only during the higher tides that occur at the full and new moons ("spring" tides). Extending beyond the high marsh to the water's edge is the low marsh, flooded twice every day, and composed almost entirely of one species—salt marsh cordgrass. The uniformity of the vegetation belies the diversity of invertebrates which thrive in the sediments and of birds which thrive on the invertebrates.

ALLAIRE STATE PARK

The 3,063-acre Allaire State Park is located on the New Jersey coastal plain. One-third of the park lies south of the Manasquan River and is on the northern fringe of the Pinelands, thus supporting a pine forest community. Birders will find spring migrating warblers and other songbirds as well as a variety of breeding birds, such as owls, warblers, vireos, and indigo buntings.

Allaire State Park is named for James P. Allaire who, in 1822, purchased an iron furnace that dated from the 1790s. The furnace produced castings and pig iron for his foundry in New York and pots for the retail market. Under Allaire's guidance, the site became a self-contained community. As many as 500 people lived there during the years that the village prospered. With the discovery of high grade iron ore in Pennsylvania, the village declined as an industrial community, and the furnaces were extinguished in 1848.

Figure 13-1. Allaire Village

Arthur Brisbane, a Hearst newspaperman, purchased the property in 1907. In 1941, his estate deeded 800 acres, including the village, to the State of New Jersey. Since then, Allaire has more than tripled in size with acquisitions of land under the Green Acres program.

Through the combined efforts of the State of New Jersey and Allaire Village, Inc., most of the original working buildings from the historic village have been restored. Allaire Village, Inc., a not-for-profit organization, assists the state in preserving, maintaining, and operating the village. Open to the public daily, except Mondays and Tuesdays, in the summer, and on weekends in the spring and fall, this living museum has costumed interpreters who demonstrate crafts and recount history. For more information about the historic village, contact Allaire Village, Inc., P.O. Box 220, Allaire, NJ 07727; (732) 938-2253; www.allairevillage.org.

The park offers nearly 20 miles of marked trails. Three hiking-only trails begin from Allaire Village or from the nearby Nature Center. The Green Trail is a 2.5-mile loop trail that begins at the village. The 0.5-mile Floodplain Trail (yellow) leads from the village down to the Manasquan River. The 1.0-mile Nature Trail is a loop trail that begins at the Nature Center. Several multi-use trails for hikers, bicyclists, and equestrians start at a parking area on Hospital Road, including the 4.6-mile Orange Trail, which forms a loop, the 3.1-mile Blue Trail, and the 2.3-mile White Trail. Another four-mile multi-use trail, also blazed orange, is in the northern section of the park.

Other park uses include canoeing and fishing along the Manasquan River, hunting, and a narrow-gauge steam train. Family and group campsites, as well as rustic cabins, are also available. The park is open year-round, with a parking fee charged from Memorial Day to Labor Day.

To reach Allaire State Park, take the Garden State Parkway to Exit 98 and proceed west on County 524 for two miles to the park entrance. For more information, contact Allaire State Park, P.O. Box 220, Farmingdale, NJ 07727; (732) 938-2371; www.njparksandforests.com.

CATTUS ISLAND COUNTY PARK

This 500-acre Ocean County park, north of Toms River, was funded in part by New Jersey's Green Acres program. Seventy percent of the park consists of salt marshes, with some lowland and upland forests and a stand of the once-

common Atlantic white cedar. John Cattus, a New York importer in 1895, purchased the land for weekend vacations. Central to the park is the Cooper Environmental Center, where visitors may see natural science exhibits and live animals, register for a variety of nature programs, or obtain a trail map and wander on their own.

Six miles of marked trails and four miles of dirt fire roads wander through the wetland and wooded areas. The marked trails are for hiking only. Several trails are accessible

Figure 13-2. Cattus Island

to the handicapped. Sections of boardwalk thread through the marshes, allowing walkers a close look at the complex life in the otherwise inaccessible wetland habitat. Trees to look for are maple, gum, magnolia, holly, and white cedar. The trailhead for the White Trail, known as the Causeway, is at the park entrance, and leads out to Page's Point. An observation deck offers a view of the osprey platforms as well as shorebirds and Atlantic Flyway migratory birds. The preserve is referred to as an "island" because the area is surrounded by salt marshes. As a result, there are mainland and island trails, identified on the map/brochures.

The Red Trail, leaving from the paved path at the Visitor Center, proceeds on a boardwalk through a hardwood swamp typical of those throughout southern Jersey. Red maples, sweet-bay magnolias, black gums, and an occasional pitch pine grow above a dense understory of many kinds of shrubs (including the native highbush blueberry). The hardwood forest gives way to thin bands of Atlantic white cedar and *Phragmites* marsh before reaching a viewpoint over the extensive salt marshes. Other trails take the visitor through Pinelands vegetation on small "islands" of upland within the marsh.

In an effort to control mosquitos, ditches were dug through the salt marshes many decades ago. The parallel, linear ditches constructed in the 1930s and 1940s are visible from the visitor center. "Spoil" piles—formed of the excavated material—are found alongside the ditches and provide a location for high marsh and non-wetland species to grow. From the viewpoint on the Red Trail,

though, the curving ditches of an improved method of mosquito management (called "open water marsh management") may be seen. This approach uses a digging machine that spreads the spoil out in a thin layer over the marsh, so that the marsh retains its normal character. It also involves the digging of deeper pools connected to the ditches, which permit fish to travel into the pools during high tides and then eat the mosquito larvae.

Cattus Island Park is open daily, dawn to dusk, and the Environmental Center is open from 8:00 a.m. to 4:30 p.m. A ramp makes the center and its wildlife view deck accessible to the handicapped. There is no parking fee.

To reach Cattus Island Park, take the Garden State Parkway to Exit 82 (Route 37, Seaside) and continue east on NJ 37 for six miles. Use the jughandle to turn north onto Fisher Boulevard, and proceed for two miles to Cattus Island Boulevard, which leads to the park entrance. For more information, contact Cattus Island Park, 1170 Cattus Island Boulevard, Toms River, NJ 08753; (732) 270-6960; www.co.ocean.nj.us/parks/cattus.html.

CHEESEQUAKE STATE PARK

Located in Middlesex County in a developed region on the western end of Raritan Bay, the 1,291-acre Cheesequake State Park is a botanical preserve comprised mostly of salt marsh, pine barrens, and mixed oak forest. An Interpretive Center, which offers informative exhibits, is open all year. A beach, playground, and picnic area with parking are located one mile from the park entrance. Brochures with maps of the park are available at the office (at the park entrance) or at the Interpretive Center.

To reach Cheesequake State Park, take the Garden State Parkway to Exit 120. Turn right at the end of the ramp and continue to the first traffic light. Turn right at the light onto Morristown Road, then turn right again at the next traffic light onto Gordon Road. Follow Gordon Road as it turns sharply left and continue ahead into the park. To reach the trails, proceed for 0.1 mile beyond the toll booth (a parking fee is charged from Memorial Day to Labor Day) to a trailhead parking area on the left side of the road. For more information, contact Cheesequake State Park, 300 Gordon Road, Matawan, NJ 07747; (732) 566-2161; www.njparksandforests.org.

Trails in Cheesequake State Park

Cheesequake State Park has four marked loop trails, for hiking only, that start at the Interpretive Center parking area, a short distance from the park entrance. In addition, a 2.7-mile white-blazed multi-use trail is open to hikers, bicyclists, and cross-country skiers.

Blue Trail *Length: 1.9 miles Blaze: blue*

The Blue Trail crosses a salt marsh on a long boardwalk, runs along Perrine Pond, and returns to the start along several roads. Beginning at the trailhead parking area, the Blue Trail follows the route of the Green Trail for 0.3 mile (see description of Green Trail, below). At 0.3 mile, after climbing a set of wooden steps, the Blue Trail turns right and begins to head west. After twice dipping down to cross wet areas on short boardwalks, the Blue Trail, at 0.5 mile, crosses a long boardwalk over a salt marsh. It climbs wooden stairs at the end of the boardwalk and continues through a hardwood forest. After going through a stand of white pine, the trail turns right onto the sandy Perrine Road at 0.8 mile, then immediately bears left at a fork.

Soon, the trail begins to pass between Perrine Pond, on the left, and a salt marsh, on the right. Perrine Pond was the site of clay mining in the late 1800s and early 1900s. At 1.0 mile, near the end of the pond, a former park landfill on the right is being restored. At a T intersection, reached at 1.1 miles, the trail turns right onto a gravel road. The Red and Green trails cross at 1.3 miles (to the right, the Red Trail can be used as an alternate return route to avoid some of the roadwalking). Then, at 1.5 miles, after passing a gate, the Blue Trail turns left onto Museum Road. The Red and Green trails join from the right at 1.7 miles, and all three trails continue, past a turnoff to the Interpretive Center, back to the parking area where the hike began.

Green Trail *Length: 2.9 miles Blaze:green*

The longest and most varied of the park's trails, the Green Trail leads through a designated Natural Area, with pitch pines, a hardwood forest, a freshwater marsh, and an Atlantic white cedar swamp.

From the large trail map at the end of the trailhead parking area, the Green Trail follows a joint route with the Red, Yellow, and Blue trails. In 100 feet, the

returning loop of the Yellow Trail joins from the right. The four trails continue ahead, descending a boardwalk with wooden steps. At the next intersection, the Yellow Trail continues straight ahead, while the Green, Red, and Blue trails turn left, following a narrower path. The three trails cross a wooden bridge and head uphill to the park's Interpretive Center.

The trails continue through a hardwood forest, soon reaching a seasonal viewpoint over a salt marsh to the right of the trail. After descending to cross a wooden boardwalk, the trails climb a set of wooden steps. At the top of the steps, at 0.3 mile, the Blue Trail leaves to the right, while the Green and Red trails bear left, then turn right at the next T intersection. The two trails now pass through an area with some pitch pines, the species typical of the southern New Jersey Pinelands. They then descend wooden steps to cross a bridge over a ravine. At 0.6 mile, the trails cross a sandy road known as Perrine Road, the route of the Blue Trail.

Just beyond the road, a T intersection is reached. Here, the Red Trail leaves to the left, while the Green Trail turns right. After descending rather steeply and skirting a stand of tall *Phragmites* (common reed), the trail climbs a small rise and goes down wooden steps to cross a freshwater marsh on a long boardwalk. At 0.9 mile, near the end of the boardwalk, benches are provided where the boardwalk has been built around several large red maple trees, providing the hiker with the opportunity to contemplate this tranquil setting. At the end of the marsh, the trail climbs wooden steps and bears right. Soon, it descends to cross another boardwalk which passes through an Atlantic white cedar swamp, with the thick needles of the cedars forming a dense canopy overhead. A layer of clay beneath the surface traps the water and prevents it from draining off.

At the end of the cedar swamp, the Green Trail continues ahead through deciduous woods, crosses a boardwalk over a wet area, and climbs over a rise. At 1.1 miles, the trail crosses the sandy Museum Road. (To the right, this road leads in

Figure 13-3. Phragmites

0.5 mile to the remains of an old steamboat landing on Cheesequake Creek, once used by local farmers to bring their produce for shipment to market.) Just beyond, it passes several huge white pine trees—estimated to be over 150 years old—to the right. One of these pines was toppled in a storm in the fall of 2003. The trail now bears left to climb over exposed tree roots, ascends wooden steps, and bears left at the top of the rise. It descends gradually, turns right to cross a ravine on a wooden bridge at 1.4 miles, and continues ahead on a level path.

At 1.7 miles, after descending on an eroded path through a shallow ravine, the Green Trail bears right, as an unmarked trail joins from the left. Just beyond, a depressed area is visible to the left of the trail. This is all that remains of a park museum, built in the 1950s but never used. The building—after which Museum Road is named—was demolished soon after it was constructed.

At the next T intersection, the Green Trail turns right. It skirts a marshy area to the left, then—just beyond a huge oak tree to the left of the trail—turns left, proceeds across a densely vegetated low area on a muddy path and boardwalk, and crosses a stream. After passing another swampy area to the left, the trail reaches a boardwalk with an observation platform at 2.1 miles. The dead trees in a pond to the left were killed by siltation from development outside the park that has settled into this low area. The trail continues over several more stretches of boardwalk and then reenters a hardwood forest. It climbs through a ravine, levels off, and finally emerges on paved Perrine Road at 2.4 miles.

The Green Trail turns left and follows the road past the entrance to Gordon Field, a group camping area (restrooms are located here). About 150 feet beyond the field, the Green Trail turns right at a wooden arch and—now again running jointly with the Red Trail—follows a footpath into the woods. The joint trails skirt to the left of the field, then bear left and descend to Museum Road, reached at 2.7 miles. The trails turn right on this road and—now joined by the Blue Trail—follow it, past a turnoff to the Interpretive Center, back to the parking area where the hike began.

Red Trail   *Length: 1.3 miles Blaze: red*
The Red Trail is a shortened version of the Green Trail, suitable for easier hikes. Beginning at the trailhead parking area, the Red Trail follows the route of the Green Trail for 0.6 mile (see description of Green Trail, above). After crossing Perrine Road at 0.6 mile, it turns left, leaving the Green Trail, and follows a level path through hardwood forests. It crosses Museum Road at 0.8 mile and continues through an area of mixed hardwoods and pitch pines. At 0.9 mile, it

turns right onto Perrine Road for 125 feet, then turns left, leaving the road and rejoining the Green Trail. The joint trails skirt to the left of Gordon Field, then bear left and descend to Museum Road, reached at 1.1 miles. The trails turn right on this road and—now joined by the Blue Trail—follow it, past a turnoff to the Interpretive Center, back to the parking area where the hike began.

Yellow Trail

Length: 0.7 mile Blaze: yellow

The Yellow Trail is a short loop trail, marked with signposts that identify a number of interesting natural features along the trail. It runs along a salt marsh and parallels Hooks Creek Lake, where swimming is permitted in the summer.

From the large trail map at the end of the trailhead parking area, the Yellow Trail follows a joint route with the Green, Red, and Blue trails. In 100 feet, the returning loop of the Yellow Trail joins from the right. The four trails continue ahead, descending a boardwalk with wooden steps.

At the next intersection, the Green, Red, and Blue trails turn left, while the Yellow Trail continues straight ahead, passing wild azalea bushes, which bloom in the spring. It soon begins to parallel a salt marsh to the left, curving to the right to follow the edge of the marsh.

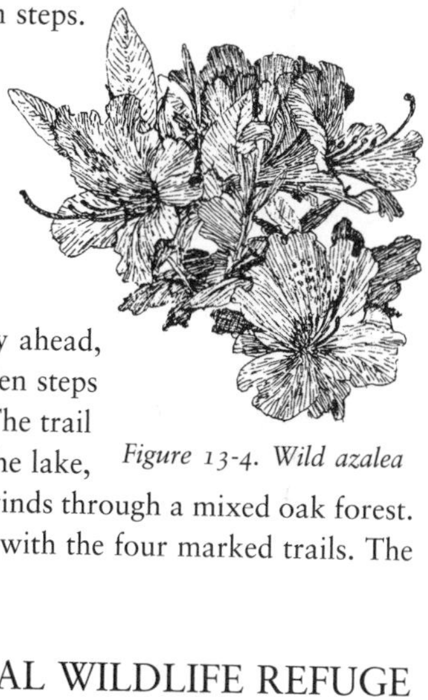

At 0.3 mile, with the lake visible directly ahead, the Yellow Trail turns right and climbs wooden steps to a viewpoint over the lake and the marsh. The trail continues to parallel the lake. At the end of the lake,

Figure 13-4. Wild azalea

reached at 0.4 mile, the trail turns right and winds through a mixed oak forest. It ends, 0.7 mile from the start, at a junction with the four marked trails. The parking area is 100 feet to the left.

EDWIN B. FORSYTHE NATIONAL WILDLIFE REFUGE

The Edwin B. Forsythe National Wildlife Refuge, comprising 50,000 acres of tidal wetlands and shallow bay habitat, is managed to protect migratory birds. The Brigantine and Barnegat divisions were originally two distinct refuges, established in 1939 and 1967, respectively. In 1984, they were combined and renamed to honor the late conservationist congressman from New Jersey.

The refuge's location on one of the Atlantic Flyway's most active paths makes it an important link in the network of national wildlife refuges. Ninety percent of Forsythe Refuge is tidal salt meadow and marsh, interspersed with shallow coves and bays.

More than 6,000 acres are designated wilderness areas, including Holgate and Little Beach, two of the few remaining undeveloped barrier beaches in New Jersey. They protect nesting and feeding habitat for the endangered piping plover, black skimmer, and least tern. To minimize disturbance to these birds and their habitat, public access is limited. Holgate is closed to public use during nesting season, April 1 until September 1. During all other times, the beachfront is open, although the dunes are always off limits. Little Beach is closed all year except by special-use permit for research or education.

About 3,000 acres are woodlands dominated by pitch pine, white oak, and white cedar. Fields amidst the woods provide habitat diversity. A wide variety of upland wildlife species frequent these areas.

The Brigantine Division includes an eight-mile self-guiding Wildlife Drive, three short foot trails (0.2, 0.5, and 1.0 mile), observation towers, and the refuge headquarters. Migratory birds and other wildlife may be photographed and observed from the Wildlife Drive, a one-way loop road on dikes constructed over bay water. The best wildlife viewing is in the spring and fall. The Barnegat Division is all salt marsh. Seasonal waterfowl and deer hunting, fishing, and crabbing are permitted in designated areas of both divisions of the refuge.

Figure 13-5. Rock shell

The refuge is open year-round during daylight hours. Wildlife Drive brochures, maps, guides, and bird lists are available at headquarters. An entrance fee is charged year-round.

To reach the Brigantine Division, take the Garden State Parkway to Exit 48, and proceed south for six miles on US 9 to Oceanville. At the traffic light, where a sign indicates the refuge entrance to the left, turn left onto Great Creek Road. Follow Great Creek Road for one mile to the refuge entrance, headquarters, and parking. For the Holgate Division, take NJ 72 east to the town of Ship Bottom on Long Beach Island, turn right, and continue south for eight miles to the dead end, where

there is parking and access to the beach edge (open only from September 1 until April 1). There are no public facilities at the Barnegat Division.

For more information, contact the Edwin B. Forsythe National Wildlife Refuge, Great Creek Road, P.O. Box 72, Oceanville, NJ 08231; (609) 652-1665; http://forsythe.fws.gov.

HARTSHORNE WOODS PARK

A unit of the Monmouth County park system, Hartshorne Woods Park is named after Richard Hartshorne (pronounced "hart's horn"), the first European settler in the area, who purchased the land from the Native Americans. About two-thirds of the present 736 acres were acquired by the county in 1974. The Rocky Point section, which had been the site of the Highlands Army Air Defense Command since 1940, was declared surplus property by the Department of Defense in 1979 and acquired by the county as an addition to the park. The area was restored and opened to the public in the early 1990s.

The park rises from sea level at the Shrewsbury and Navesink rivers to 274 feet above sea level. Located along an otherwise flat coastal plain, Hartshorne Woods sits astride a line of low but steep-sided hills. These hills mark the edge of a *cuesta*—a geomorphic landscape feature formed from sandstone layers that are slightly tilted. These layers, composed of quartz and other particles, were cemented together by iron oxides, and were thus more resistant to erosion than the unconsolidated sediments which once overlayed them. The forest is more similar to New Jersey's northern highlands than to the rest of Monmouth County. The hills support forests of oak, hickory, and tulip trees, with an understory of American holly and mountain laurel.

To reach the Buttermilk Valley parking area of Hartshorne Woods Park, take the Garden State Parkway to Exit 117. Bear left beyond the toll booths and continue on NJ 36 for 11.0 miles. After passing through Atlantic Highlands, turn right at the exit for Red Bank/Scenic Road, then turn right at the stop sign onto Navesink Avenue. Continue for 0.3 mile to the Buttermilk Valley parking area, on the left side of the road. (Do *not* turn right at the intersection of Memorial Drive and Navesink Avenue in Atlantic Highlands.) Public transportation to the intersection of NJ 36 and Navesink Avenue in Highlands is available via NJ Transit bus #834, which connects with NJ Transit North Jersey Coast Line trains at Red Bank. Direct bus service to Highlands from the Port

Authority Bus Terminal in New York City is provided by the Academy Line, (201) 420-7000; www.academybus.com.

To reach the Rocky Point parking area, continue on NJ 36 for 12.3 miles from Exit 117 of the Parkway. Just before the Highlands-Sea Bright bridge, turn right onto Portland Avenue, and follow Portland Avenue for 0.8 mile to the parking area (which is directly ahead when the road makes a very sharp right turn).

For more information, contact the Monmouth County Park System, 805 Newman Springs Road, Lincroft, NJ 07738-1695; (732)842-3000; www.monmouthcountyparks.com.

Trails in Hartshorne Woods Park

Hartshorne Woods Park contains over ten miles of trails. All but two short trails—the Candlestick and Kings Hollow trails, both of which start at the Buttermilk Valley parking area—are multi-use trails, open to walkers, runners, bicyclists, and equestrians. The trails are heavily used by bicyclists and joggers. Park regulations provide that bicyclists must yield to all other trail users; however, many trails open to bicycles are narrow, winding, "single-track" routes. Thus, hikers should be alert for approaching bicycles. Hikers must yield to equestrians.

The trails in the park are not blazed, although they have been classified into three categories, based on difficulty. Signposts at trail junctions use colored symbols to designate these three classes of trails—"easy" trails are designated by green circles, "moderate" trails by blue squares, and "challenging" trails by black diamonds. These designations are geared primarily towards bicyclists. Thus, while trails designated with black diamonds are stated to be "challenging . . . with obstructions and steep grades," most hikers will find these trails to be of no more than moderate difficulty.

Candlestick Trail   *Length: 1.3 miles (including both legs of loop) Blaze: none*
This hook-shaped hiking-only trail—with two alternative, parallel routes in the central section—leads from the Buttermilk Valley parking area to the top of a ridge. It begins at a "Foot Traffic Only" sign near the large trail map. In 250 feet, at a signpost, it turns left, as the Kings Hollow Trail continues ahead. After a rather steep climb through dense mountain laurel, the trail reaches a junction

at 0.3 mile. The alternative route leaves to the right, but an arrow indicates that hikers should continue ahead on the more easterly route. The trail now levels off. At 0.7 mile, the alternative route rejoins from the right (note the 1875 survey monument to the left). The Candlestick Trail bears left and continues to its end at a limited overlook, with the views largely obscured by trees, at 1.0 mile. The alternative western route, which may be used for the return to the parking area, is 0.1 mile shorter than the eastern route. The round-trip to the overlook and back is 1.9 miles.

Cuesta Ridge Trail   *Length: 1.6 miles Blaze: none*
The Cuesta Ridge Trail is a gravel road that follows the ridge of the *cuesta* that runs through Hartshorne Woods. To reach the Cuesta Ridge Trail from the Buttermilk Valley trailhead, follow the Laurel Ridge Trail for 0.4 mile to its intersection with the Grand Tour Trail. The Cuesta Ridge Trail begins here, continuing ahead on the gravel road. In 0.3 mile, the Grand Tour Trail again crosses. The Cuesta Ridge Trail continues along the ridge on a relatively level route. Then, at 1.4 miles, a side trail that connects to the western end of the Rocky Point Trail leaves to the right. The Cuesta Ridge Trail ends, 1.6 miles from its start, at a paved service road. The Rocky Point parking area is 0.1 mile to the left.

Grand Tour Trail   *Length: 3.4 miles Blaze: none*
The Grand Tour Trail is a figure-eight loop that can be divided into two smaller loops. It is accessible both from the Buttermilk Valley parking area on the west side of the park and from the Rocky Point parking area on the park's east side. Although rated by the park as "challenging" and marked at signposts with black diamonds, the trail—which traverses the remote Monmouth Hills section of the park—is of no more than moderate difficulty for average hikers. It is described below starting from the Buttermilk Valley trailhead.

From the Buttermilk Valley trailhead, follow the Laurel Ridge Trail for 0.4 mile to its intersection with a narrow gravel road, where the Grand Tour Trail crosses. To follow the Grand Tour Trail in a clockwise direction, turn left (north) on the narrow gravel road. Soon, the trail bears right at a split-rail fence and ascends gradually on a winding, eroded footpath through mountain laurel thickets. At 0.2 mile, it crosses a crushed-stone service road. Near the top of the hill, it approaches this road, but bears left, away from it. Then, at 0.4 mile, it again crosses the road. The elevation at this junction, 268 feet above sea level, is

the highest on the trail. Just to the left – at the southwest corner of the fence that surrounds a water tower—is the highest point in Monmouth County, 274 feet above sea level.

The Grand Tour Trail now descends on a gravel road, soon crossing the Cuesta Ridge Trail, which follows a wider gravel road (there is no signpost at this intersection). It continues to descend gradually (with one rather steep section) until it reaches, at 1.0 mile, a short connecting trail (which is the center of the figure-eight loop). To hike only the western loop, turn right, continuing to follow the gravel road, then turn right again at the next junction. To continue along the longer loop (described here), proceed straight ahead as the trail narrows to a footpath and enters the remote Monmouth Hills section of the park.

The winding trail passes through stands of holly, goes under a power line, and continues through an area with tangled vines. At 1.7 miles, it reaches a junction marked by a signpost. Here, a connecting trail which leads towards the Rocky Point parking area leaves to the left. The Grand Tour Trail continues straight ahead, following signs to the "trailhead." Then, at 1.9 miles, after passing through another area with holly trees and tangled vines, the trail reaches another junction marked with a signpost. Here, the trail turns right (to the left, the gravel road leads in a short distance to the paved Grand Tour Road) and soon again crosses under the power line.

At 2.2 miles, the trail arrives at a junction, marked by a signpost. Straight ahead is the short connecting trail that is the center of the "figure-eight." To continue on the longer loop, turn left and follow the trail past several huge trees, then continue to ascend on a winding path to the crest of a hill. The trail now begins to descend, passing a wooden cabin on the left, and reaches another intersection at 2.7 miles. This is the lowest point on the trail, 40 feet above sea level. Here, the trail turns right on a gravel road, passing houses to the left. Soon, the gravel road curves to the right, while the Grand Tour Trail continues straight ahead on a footpath, passing through mountain laurel thickets.

Figure 13-6. Holly

To the left of the trail, at 3.0 miles,

a tulip tree appears to be growing out of a horizontal log. The most likely explanation of this unusual feature is that the tree was blown over when young, but its roots remained intact and an upward-pointing branch continued growing as the new trunk. About 300 feet beyond, the trail passes a split-log fence to the right, and it climbs to reach a junction with the Laurel Ridge Trail at 3.2 miles. The Grand Tour Trail turns right and runs jointly with the Laurel Ridge Trail, returning to the trailhead at 3.4 miles.

The Grand Tour Trail may be combined with the Laurel Ridge Trail to make a 5.7-mile loop hike from the Buttermilk Valley parking area.

Kings Hollow Trail *Length: 0.6 mile Blaze: none*
This short loop trail, for hikers only, begins at a "Foot Traffic Only" sign near the large trail map at the Buttermilk Valley parking area. In 250 feet, at a signpost, the Candlestick Trail leaves to the left. The Kings Hollow Trail continues ahead, reaching a fork at 0.1 mile, where an arrow on a signpost indicates that the hiker should bear left to follow the loop in a clockwise direction. The trail loops through a wooded area, returning to the start of the loop at 0.6 mile.

Laurel Ridge Trail *Length: 2.5 miles Blaze: none*
The Laurel Ridge Trail, rated by the park as "moderate" (blue square), starts at a large trail map adjacent to the Buttermilk Valley parking area. It begins by heading left on a wide gravel road that proceeds north, parallel to Navesink Avenue. The road soon curves to the right and ascends gradually through an oak-maple forest, with some mountain laurel. Reaching the crest of the hill, it descends to a junction, marked by signposts, at 0.4 mile. Here, the road ahead is designated the Cuesta Ridge Trail, and the Grand Tour Trail crosses. The Laurel Ridge Trail turns right onto a narrower gravel road, joining the Grand Tour Trail. Both trails run concurrently until, at 0.6 mile, the Grand Tour Trail leaves to the left. The Laurel Ridge Trail continues ahead along the side of a hill, with views through the trees of the ridge to the east. It proceeds through mountain laurel thickets, then passes holly trees and tangled vines.

At 1.0 mile, the trail curves sharply to the right and begins to ascend, now heading northward. Leveling off on the crest of the ridge at 1.2 miles, it reaches a junction (marked by a signpost) where an 0.2-mile side trail to the left leads to the Claypit Creek Overlook. When there are no leaves on the trees, Claypit Creek, the Navesink River, the Oceanic Bridge, and the Rumson Peninsula are visible to the southeast. The Laurel Ridge Trail now begins to descend, first on

a broad switchback, then through mountain laurel thickets, reaching a Y intersection at 2.0 miles, with paved Hartshorne Road directly ahead. Here, the trail bears right and heads north. After descending rather steeply, it returns to the trail sign at the Buttermilk Valley parking area on Navesink Road at 2.5 miles, completing the loop.

Rocky Point Trail

Length: 2.2 miles Blaze: none

Although rated by the park as "challenging" and marked at signposts with black diamonds, the Rocky Point Trail—which loops around the Rocky Point peninsula and passes fortifications dating back to World War II—is of no more than moderate difficulty for average hikers. The trailhead is on a paved park service road, about 100 feet east of the entrance to the Rocky Point parking area.

The Rocky Point Trail begins by descending on a winding path through stands of holly to cross a bridge over a stream. It continues through dense vegetation, approaching the Shrewsbury River at 0.5 mile. Here, to the left of the trail, many trees have been downed by the strong winds from the ocean. Just beyond, a short side trail to the left leads to a viewpoint over the river, with homes on the Sea Bright peninsula visible across the river.

After a short climb, the remains of two concrete Coast Watch Stations may be seen to the right. The trail continues ahead, parallel to the river below to the left, reaching a paved service road at 0.7 mile. To the left, the road leads in about 250 feet to a grassy area with picnic tables overlooking the confluence of the Shrewsbury and Navesink rivers. (To the right, the road leads back to the parking area.)

The Rocky Point Trail now climbs a rise. At the top, some interesting ivy-covered trees may be seen to the right. The trail descends past a dense stand of holly to reach another paved service road at 1.0 mile. To the left, this road leads downhill a short distance to the Blackfish Cove fishing pier, with broad views over Navesink River (there are also picnic tables and a privy here). The Rocky Point Trail turns right, follows the service road for 50 feet, then turns left and reenters the woods.

The trail crosses a footbridge over a small stream, climbs gradually, and levels off. Then, at 1.5 miles, it ascends quite steeply on a switchback. At the top of the climb (marked by a huge fallen tree on the left), an unmarked side trail to the left leads in 500 feet to a viewpoint over the Navesink River, with the view partially obscured by the trees.

The Rocky Point Trail now begins a gradual descent, passing through dense stands of mountain laurel. At 2.0 miles, it crosses another paved service road (to the left, this road leads to an abandoned Army bunker; to the right, it leads back to the parking area). The trail now climbs to cross a small bridge, descends briefly, then continues to climb past remnants of an old chain-link fence. After ascending on switchbacks, the Rocky Point Trail ends at a paved service road, marked by two concrete pillars to the left, at 2.2 miles. Across the road, a connecting trail (marked with a black diamond) leads downhill 0.2 mile to the Grand Tour Trail. To return to the Rocky Point parking area, turn right on the service road, follow it for 0.2 mile, then bear right at the fork.

HENRY HUDSON TRAIL

The nine-mile paved Henry Hudson Trail, open to hikers, bicyclists, and equestrians, follows the right-of-way of the abandoned Highlands Branch of the Central Railroad of New Jersey from the Aberdeen/Keyport boundary to Avenue D in Atlantic Highlands. The western section of the trail features an elevated railbed and bridge crossings that provide views of stream corridors, tidal wetlands, and the Raritan Bay. The eastern section (east of Atlantic Avenue in Middletown) closely parallels NJ 36. Parking is available at the western end of the trail (at the intersection of Gerard Avenue/Clark Street and Lloyd Road/Broadway, at the Aberdeen/Keyport boundary), on Spruce Street in Union Beach, in McMahon Park (off Atlantic Avenue) in North Middletown, and at the Henry Hudson Trail Activity Center on NJ 36 in Leonardo (just west of the trail's eastern terminus at Avenue D).

Figure 13-7. Bridge near Raritan Bay

Public transportation to the trail is available via NJ Transit's North Jersey Coast Line to the Matawan-Aberdeen station, which is about one mile from the western end of the trail. NJ Transit bus #834, which connects the Red Bank railroad station with Highlands, stops at the intersection of NJ 36 and Leonard Avenue in Leonardo, 0.5 mile west of the trail's eastern terminus. Direct bus service to Atlantic Highlands from the Port Authority Bus Terminal in New York City is provided by the Academy Line, (201) 420-7000; www.academybus.com.

In 2003, work is underway on a 12-mile extension of the Henry Hudson Trail from the Matawan-Aberdeen railroad station south to Main Street (County 537) in Freehold Borough, following the abandoned Freehold Branch of the Central Railroad of New Jersey. It is anticipated that portions of this extension will open in the summer of 2004.

For more information, contact the Monmouth County Park System, 805 Newman Springs Road, Lincroft, NJ 07738-1695; (732) 842-4000; www.monmouthcountyparks.com.

HOLMDEL PARK

In 1962, the Monmouth County park system acquired this 347-acre property which includes the living-history Longstreet Farm, an arboretum, two trout-stocked ponds, and several picnic areas. The park has about six miles of trails, including a boardwalk over a marsh. The trails—most of which are in the northern end of the park and can be most easily accessed from Parking Lots #2 and #3—may be combined to form loop hikes of varying lengths.

A suggested three-mile loop hike begins at Parking Lot #2. From the western end of the parking lot, head uphill towards the woods on a broad gravel path, with a playground to the left and restrooms on the right. At a signpost for the Beech Glen Trail, turn left onto this trail, which follows an attractive stream and passes through a beech grove. In 0.5 mile, the Beech Glen Trail ends at the gravel Cross Country Trail. Turn left and follow this trail, which runs parallel to the park service road, to Parking Lot #3. Here, the trail turns left to skirt the parking lot. Just beyond the parking lot, where the trail again briefly parallels the road, turn right, cross the road, and turn left onto the return loop of the Cross Country Trail. The trail parallels the road, then curves sharply right, soon leaving the road, and heads downhill along a grassy field.

At 1.6 miles, turn right and cross a wooden bridge over a stream. At the next junction, turn left onto the High Point Trail. The High Point Trail parallels the stream, then turns right and begins to climb, reaching a junction with the Marsh Trail at 1.8 miles. The Marsh Trail, most of which follows a boardwalk, proceeds through a freshwater marsh, passes the park's Program Building and Activity Center, and connects with the Ridge Walk Trail at 2.3 miles. In 2003, however, much of the trail is flooded, except during dry periods, so hikers are advised to continue ahead on the High Point Trail.

At the next junction, reached at 2.0 miles, turn left onto the Ridge Walk Trail. After descending gradually to cross a bridge over a stream at 2.3 miles (just before the bridge, the Marsh Trail joins from the left), the Ridge Walk Trail ascends through a hemlock grove. At the next junction, turn right. Bear left at the next Y junction, and turn left when the trail reaches the park service road. Follow the trail as it crosses the road and leads back to Parking Area #2, where the hike began.

To reach Holmdel Park, take the Garden State Parkway to Exit 114 and proceed west on Red Hill Road to Everett Road. Turn right on Everett Road and continue to Roberts Road. Turn left on Roberts Road, follow it to Longstreet Road, and turn right. The park entrance is just ahead on the left. For more information, contact the Monmouth County Park System, 805 Newman Springs Road, Lincroft, NJ 07738-1695; (732) 842-3000; www.monmouthcountyparks.com.

HUBER WOODS PARK

In 1974, the children of Hans and Catherine Huber, a manufacturer of pigments used in dry inks, donated 118 acres of woodlands to the Monmouth County Park System. The park was enlarged to 258 acres by subsequent donations, including the Huber family home, built in 1927, which has been transformed into an environmental center.

Although the six miles of multi-use trails are open to hikers, bicyclists, equestrians, and cross-country skiers (in season), bicyclists generally prefer the nearby Hartshorne Woods Park. The trails lead through stands of tulip trees, oak-hickory forest, and meadows and can be combined to form loop hikes of varying lengths. The park also offers an equestrian program which includes people with physical and mental disabilities.

A suggested 3.7-mile "figure-eight" loop hike begins at the trailhead kiosk at the eastern end of the parking area. From the kiosk, bear left and follow a footpath through a meadow. At a trail junction at the end of the meadow, turn right and follow a footpath through wild rose thickets and tangled vines, then continue through second-growth woodlands, descending gradually on a winding footpath. At the next trail junction, reached at 0.3 mile and marked by a signpost, bear right and continue on a footpath through dense laurel thickets.

At 0.6 mile, another junction is reached, with the trailhead of the Claypit Run Trail to the right. Turn left here, following the Valley View Trail, which briefly descends on an eroded path through evergreens and then continues through thick laurel. At 0.9 mile, continue ahead where a side trail leaves to the right at an unmarked signpost. Just beyond, turn right at a T intersection, proceed for 100 feet to a Y intersection, then bear right and continue through a wooded area. After a moderate climb, a T intersection, marked by a signpost, is reached at 1.2 miles. Turn right and continue on a relatively level trail.

The trail crosses dirt Brown's Dock Road diagonally to the left at 1.4 miles. Just beyond, bear right and loop around a meadow overgrown with cedar and dogwood trees. Continue about halfway around the meadow, then proceed ahead on a wide path as an unmarked trail joins from the left. At the next trail junction, reached in 125 feet, turn right and proceed for 100 feet to another junction. Turn right at this junction onto the Many Log Run, rated by the park as "challenging" (black diamond). Soon, the trail begins to descend through thick laurels on an eroded footpath. At the base of the descent, the trail curves to the left and starts a gentle climb.

After proceeding through thick laurels, the trail reaches a fork at 2.1 miles. Bear right here, and continue ahead in 75 feet, as a trail joins from the left at a signpost. The trail makes a short, steep climb, then levels off. Continue ahead where an unmarked trail crosses at a blacked-out signpost. At 2.3 miles, with McClees Road visible ahead through the trees, the trail bears left and continues on an undulating, winding footpath.

A wide, unmarked path leads to the right at 2.9 miles. Just beyond is a junction marked by a signpost and a map. Turn left here, now following the Meadow Ramble Trail, marked with a blue square on the park map and on the signpost. In 400 feet, the trail emerges onto a meadow overgrown with cedar trees. Follow along the left side of the meadow. At a junction marked by a signpost at the northern end of the meadow, bear right, following the blue square marker, and continue along the northern edge of the meadow.

At the northeast corner of the meadow, a house is visible ahead. Here, at 3.1 miles, turn left at the signpost, following the blue square marker, and proceed for 400 feet to a T intersection. Turn right at this intersection, still following the blue square markers. Then, at the next intersection, reached in 150 feet, continue ahead. At the following signpost, bear right at the fork, following the sign to the "trailhead."

After again crossing Brown's Dock Road at 3.4 miles, continue ahead, parallel to the road, as another trail joins from the left at a signpost. At the next trail junction, with a meadow and the parking area visible to the right, turn right and follow the trail through the meadow to the trailhead where the hike began.

To reach Huber Woods Park, take the Garden State Parkway south to Exit 109. Turn left at the traffic light beyond the toll booths onto Newman Springs Road (County Route 520). Immediately beyond the Parkway overpass, turn right onto a jughandle ramp, and continue ahead for 0.5 mile on Half Mile Road. At the end of this road, turn right at the traffic light onto West Front Street. Continue on West Front Street for 0.8 mile, then turn left onto Hubbard Avenue and continue for 0.6 mile to Navesink River Road. Turn right onto Navesink River Road and follow it for 3.2 miles to Brown's Dock Road (a gravel road). Turn left and follow Brown's Dock Road for 0.3 mile to the park environmental center, on the right.

For more information on Huber Woods Park, contact the Environmental Education Center at (732) 872-2670, or the Monmouth County Park System, 805 Newman Springs Road, Lincroft, NJ 07738-1695; (732) 842-4000; www.monmouthcountyparks.com.

ISLAND BEACH STATE PARK

An undeveloped stretch of barrier beach and salt marsh on the north side of Barnegat Inlet, this 3,001-acre strip of unspoiled dune land has an almost impenetrable barrier of brier, holly, bayberry, and other shrubs between the fore dunes and the bay. Little grows above the height of the dunes, which shelter the vegetation from killing salt spray.

The 13 miles of trails include the beach for horseback riding, a paved bicycle path, and a canoe trail in Barnegat Bay. A recommended walk is the central paved road extending through the eight-mile length of the park, ending

at a parking area. From there, 1.5 miles of beach lead to Barnegat Inlet, the passage to Barnegat Bay, and the tip of the park. Across Barnegat Inlet is Barnegat Lighthouse (172 feet), whose spiral staircase leads to views of the bay and the ocean. The lighthouse is open May through October.

To reach Island Beach State Park, take the Garden State Parkway to Exit 82. Follow NJ 37 East to NJ 35 South, and continue for two miles to the park entrance. An entrance fee is charged daily year-round.

To reach the Barnegat Lighthouse, take the Parkway to Exit 63, and proceed east on NJ 72 across Barnegat Bay to Long Beach Island and the town of Ship Bottom. Turn left (north) and continue for 8.5 miles to the north end of Long Beach Island. For more information, contact Island Beach State Park, P.O. Box 37, Seaside Park, NJ 08752; (732) 793-0506; www.njparksandforests.org.

*Figure 13-8.
Barnegat Lighthouse*

MANASQUAN RESERVOIR

Located in Howell Township, this park—which encompasses 1,204 acres of land and water—surrounds the four-billion-gallon Manasquan Reservoir, completed in 1990. The reservoir is open for fishing year-round, and boating is permitted from March to November (subject to a daily or seasonal launch fee). Boating and fishing access is from the Joseph C. Irwin Recreation Area Visitor Center on Windeler Road. Near the visitor center is a floating dock and launch area which is accessible to the handicapped. A boat rental and tackle/bait shop is on the lower level of the visitor center. Boat tours of the reservoir are offered on weekend afternoons from May to October.

The Manasquan Reservoir Environmental Center, on Georgia Tavern Road, offers exhibits and programs related to wetlands ecology and wildlife and habitat protection, with emphasis on the importance of water resources. The center is open daily, except holidays, from 10:00 a.m. to 5:00 p.m.

A five-mile perimeter gravel trail provides hikers, bicyclists, and equestri-

ans with a scenic route around the reservoir. This wide trail proceeds through young woods, wetlands, and grassy fields that border the reservoir, and it crosses dikes over several arms of the reservoir. The trail offers many opportunities to view waterfowl, including several endangered species.

To reach the Manasquan Reservoir, take I-195 to Exit 28B. Proceed north on US 9 and turn right at the first traffic light onto Georgia Tavern Road. The environmental center is on the right in 0.7 mile. For the visitor center, continue on Georgia Tavern Road for 0.4 mile, turn right onto Windeler Road, and proceed for 1.6 miles to the park entrance, on the left.

For more information, call the visitor center at (732) 919-0996 or the environmental center at (732) 751-9453, or contact the Monmouth County Park System, 805 Newman Springs Road, Lincroft, NJ 07738-1695; (732) 842-4000; www.monmouthcountyparks.com.

MONMOUTH BATTLEFIELD STATE PARK

The 2,366-acre Monmouth Battlefield State Park is the site of one of the longest battles fought during the Revolutionary War. Tramping through the gently rolling terrain of the former battlefield, hikers can almost hear the guns firing and the cries of the wounded as they sounded on that bloody June day during the Battle of Monmouth. The park has four miles of marked paths and a many miles of unmarked ones. Some of the trails are multi-use, open to hikers, bicyclists, and equestrians. The visitor center, open on weekend afternoons, contains battle displays and a gift shop. On the fourth weekend in June, Revolutionary War encampments and battles are reenacted. A portion of the park is leased to a family which operates a "pick-your-own" orchard.

The Battle of Monmouth took place on June 28, 1778, as an effort to stop the British army retreat from Philadelphia to New York. George Washington sent 5,000 troops under General Charles Lee into Freehold to attack the rear guard of the British Army. General Lee encountered a stronger force than he had anticipated, and he retreated, leaving units stranded in the field. After encountering Lee, Washington sent him to the rear and took over full command. Americans reformed their lines as British and Hessian soldiers counterattacked. In the overwhelming heat of the afternoon, all fighting ceased except for an artillery duel. Gradually, the Americans gained control. It was during this artillery battle that Mary Hays, known as "Molly Pitcher," carried water for

the soldiers to quench their thirst and to cool the cannons. When her husband was fatally wounded by enemy fire, she took his position loading the cannon. The British continued their withdrawal, leaving the area after dark.

Who won at Monmouth is open to debate. Although the Americans succeeded in holding the blood-soaked terrain, the British wagon train reached Sandy Hook safely. But never again would the British Army engage George Washington and the main American Army. The training that Baron Friedrich von Steuben gave at Valley Forge had made the Continental Army the equal of the British regulars.

To reach Monmouth Battlefield State Park, take the Garden State Parkway to Exit 123 and proceed south on US 9 for 15 miles to NJ

Figure 13-9. Monmouth Battlefield State Park

Business 33. Turn right and follow NJ Business 33 West for 1.5 miles to the park entrance, on the right. For more information, contact Monmouth Battlefield State Park, 347 Freehold-Englishtown Road, Manapalan, NJ 07726; (732) 462-9616; www.njparksandforests.com.

PORICY PARK

This 250-acre park has a four-mile trail system that leads past a freshwater marsh, a hardwood forest, a pond, wet meadows, and fields. The fossil bed at Poricy Brook is what makes Poricy Park different from other nature preserves and historic sites. Not only can visitors dig for fossils, but they may also take them home. The fossils are approximately 72 million years old; most are shellfish. The park asks that visitors sift the sand and gravel in the stream bed and

refrain from digging directly into the banks, which causes erosion. As the park frequently schedules programs at the fossil beds, it is advisable to call ahead.

Although the Township of Middletown owns the land and buildings, funding for the programs, professional staff, furnishings, and equipment are provided by the Poricy Park Citizens Committee. The site includes a restored Colonial house and barn dating to 1767.

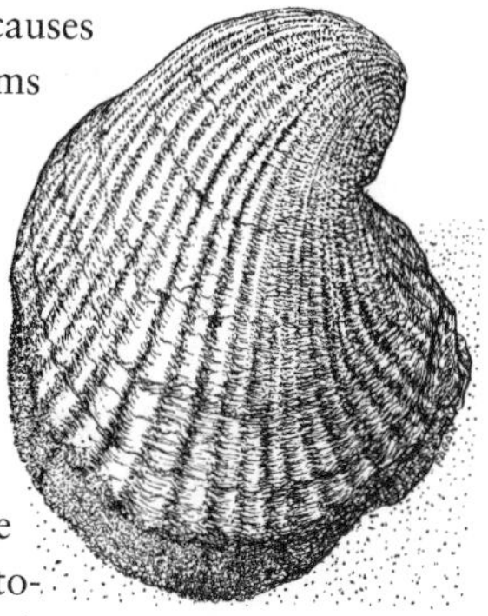

To reach Poricy Park, take the Garden State Parkway to Exit 114 and follow Red Hill Road towards Middletown. In 0.8 mile, turn right on Balm Hollow/Oak Hill Road and continue for two miles to the park entrance on the right, immediately before the second set of railroad tracks. For more information, contact Poricy Park, P.O. Box 36, Middletown, NJ 07748; (732) 842-5966; www.poricypark.com.

Figure 13-10.
Oyster fossil

SANDY HOOK

Sandy Hook is a unit of Gateway National Recreation Area, created by Congress in 1972 to provide parkland around New York Harbor—the gateway through which millions of immigrants entered the New World. The park includes six miles of ocean beaches, the waters of Sandy Hook Bay, salt marshes, dunes, hiking trails, shorebird habitat, historic Fort Hancock, and the Sandy Hook Lighthouse. There is a parking fee from Memorial Day to Labor Day.

This 6.5-mile-long sand spit boasts a rich history and varied habitats. Monstrous storms have wreaked havoc to Sandy Hook, ripping large parts of the spit away and sometimes creating islands that are later washed away. As a result, beaches have drastically changed in size and shape.

Sandy Hook Lighthouse, built in 1764, is the oldest lighthouse in the United States. Today, it lies 1.5 miles south of Sandy Hook's growing tip, the result of over two centuries of littoral drift. On the 200th anniversary of its first lighting, the Sandy Hook Lighthouse was declared a National Historic Landmark. Guided tours of this now-automated lighthouse are offered on weekend afternoons from April to November.

Fort Hancock, at the northern end of Sandy Hook, was built in 1895 to

protect New York Harbor as part of the coastal defense system. A camouflaged concrete wall hid guns that could fire on unsuspecting ships. In the 1950s, Nike missiles replaced the guns, which could disappear in the ramparts. The post was closed in 1974. The remote and deserted coastline was also used as a proving ground for military weapons between 1870 and 1919. Fort Hancock Museum and History House are open on weekends throughout the year, with extended hours during July and August.

Vegetation typical of barrier beaches thrives here: bayberry, beach plum, wild cherry, prickly pear, and poison ivy. A 60-acre stand of American holly, some of which is over 300 years old, is accessible through guided tours. Sandy Hook is on the principal migratory flyway and, as a result, is an excellent place to watch for hawks, migratory shorebirds, and monarch butterflies.

The beaches attract hordes of sunbathers during the summer. However, the off-season visitor can use those same beaches for flying kites, walking, and fishing. During spring and summer, several sections of beach are closed to

protect nesting shorebirds. A 5.5-mile-long paved multi-use trail, open to hikers, joggers, and bicyclists, extends from the toll booths at the southern end of the park to Fort Hancock on the northern end, running between the main park road and the ocean for most of the way.

The Spermaceti Cove Visitor Center offers ranger-led historical and natural interpretive programs. The Visitor Center is a former U.S. Life-Saving Station and features history and nature exhibits. From the Visitor Center, the one-mile Old Dune Trail meanders north through heather and bayberry to a portion of the holly forest. A natural history guide to the trail is available at the Visitor Center. Along the trail is a freshwater pond that harbors marsh hawks, turtles, and frogs. The trail eventually leads to a beach, then loops back toward Spermaceti Cove, completing its circuit.

Figure 13-11. Sandy Hook Lighthouse

The Fisherman's Trail starts at the Area K lot, at the northern end of the park, and leads 1.5 miles to the tip of Sandy Hook at the ocean shore. An observation deck, reached at 0.5 mile, offers a view of the Manhattan skyline.

To reach Sandy Hook, take the Garden State Parkway to Exit 117, and continue on NJ 36 East for 13.5 miles, following signs to the Gateway National Recreation Area. Public transportation to Highlands is available via NJ Transit bus #834, which connects with NJ Transit North Jersey Coast Line trains at Red Bank. Direct bus service to Highlands from the Port Authority Bus Terminal in New York City is provided by the Academy Line, (201) 420-7000; www.academybus.com. On weekends during the summer, direct ferry service from East 34th Street and Pier 11 in Manhattan to Sandy Hook is provided by SeaStreak America, Inc., 1-800-BOATRIDE; www.seastreak.com. For more information about the Sandy Hook unit of the Gateway National Recreation Area, contact Superintendent, Sandy Hook Unit, Gateway NRA, P.O. Box 530, Fort Hancock, NJ 07732; (732) 872-5970.

TURKEY SWAMP

Located in Freehold Township, Turkey Swamp Park and Turkey Swamp Wildlife Management Area are on the northern edge of the Pinelands. Part of the Monmouth County Park System, the 1,168-acre Turkey Swamp Park offers a variety of outdoor recreation activities. In addition to a campground, picnic facilities, and a 17-acre lake that offers boating and fishing opportunities (boat rentals are available), there are four miles of marked trails. Ranging in length from 0.5 mile to 1.7 miles, these mostly level pathways cut through forests of pitch pine and oak. Adjacent to the county park, Turkey Swamp Wildlife Management Area includes 2,457 acres of upland pine oak, woodlands, lowlands, and swampy areas.

To reach Turkey Swamp Park, take I-195 to Exit 22, and proceed north on Jackson Mills Road to Georgia Road. Turn left on Georgia Road and continue for 1.7 miles to the park entrance. For more information, contact the Monmouth County Park System, 805 Newman Springs Road, Lincroft, NJ 07738-1695; (732) 842-4000; www.monmouthcountyparks.com, or the New Jersey Department of Environmental Protection, Division of Fish and Wildlife, 501 East State Street, P.O. Box 400, Trenton, NJ 08625; (609) 984-0547; www.njfishandwildlife.org.

FOURTEEN

THE PINELANDS

ascinating and strange, the New Jersey Pinelands is a unique area with its own wild beauty. A block of wilderness close to the urban areas of New York and Philadelphia, the region is a broad expanse of relatively level land covering approximately one million acres. Roughly 80 miles long and 30 miles wide, it lies on the coastal plain and extends into nine counties in southern New Jersey. The region is entirely unglaciated, with few hills and no rock outcroppings.

A person flying over this area or driving its long straight highways is likely to think of the Pinelands (also known as the Pine Barrens) as wasteland. Pine forests, sometimes scorched or scrubby, cover vast sandy stretches with little sign of habitation, crops, or livestock. But this remarkable physiographic and biologic province is far from being botanically barren. Despite the monotonous landscape of twisted pines, the region boasts a large diversity of plants, many of them unusual and unique to this area, and an equally large diversity of wildlife.

This wild and primitive region claimed the attention of early naturalists and became especially well known for unusual plants. To botanists, the Pinelands is a natural wilderness that has recovered from intensive clear-cutting by lumbermen and charcoal burners in the 1700s and 1800s, when the region was a center for bog-iron mining, furnaces, and forges. A number of areas in the Pinelands have become major botanical meccas, and many have historical value as well. In addition, the region is a critically important source of pure ground water for both the human and the ecological communities of south Jersey. The combination of natural and human history, and the importance of the Pinelands as a water source, demanded that the ecological integrity of the region be pre-

served, and the Pinelands is now one of the most stringently managed regions in the entire United States.

Underlying the whole region beneath the mats of vegetation and layers of sand are great aquifers. This tremendous water reserve, estimated at more than seventeen trillion gallons, influenced Joseph Wharton (industrialist and founder of the Wharton School of Finance and Commerce at the University of Pennsylvania) to acquire nearly 100,000 acres in the late 1800s. Wharton estimated that the water from his holdings would furnish Philadelphia and surrounding areas with up to 300 million gallons daily. In 1905, however, New Jersey passed a law that gave the state control of the export of its waters, and Wharton could not carry out his plan. Subsequent laws have replaced the 1905 law, but the state retains control over its waters, and a 1981 law specifically restricts removal of water from the Pinelands.

The trend has been for slow, but continuous, development which has eaten away at the edge of the Pinelands. Uncontrolled development could have a negative effect not only on the surface environment, but also on the quality and yield of the aquifer beneath the Pinelands. The disturbance that would be caused by new industry, housing developments, and highways is incalculable.

Fortunately, legislation has recognized the value of the Pinelands and has attempted to control development of the area. In 1978, the federal government established the Pinelands National Reserve, the first such designation in the United States, and called for the State of New Jersey to adopt a comprehensive plan for the region. In 1979, New Jersey adopted the Pinelands Protection Act, which specified a framework for the plan. The Pinelands are divided into seven management areas, each accommodating a particular class of land use: Preservation Area, Protection Area, Agricultural Production Area, Rural Development Area, Regional Growth Area, Pinelands Towns, and Military and Federal Installations.

The two largest management areas are the Preservation Area and the Protection Area. The Preservation Area, covering about 370,000 acres in the heart of the Pinelands, preserves a large, contiguous tract of land in its natural state and allows only compatible agricultural, horticultural, and recreational uses. The Protection Area, covering about 790,000 acres extending through much of the state east and south of the Preservation Area, preserves the essential character of the existing Pinelands environment, while accommodating needed development in an orderly way. Preserved open space in the Pinelands includes state forests and parks, county parks, wildlife management areas, natural ar-

eas, and wild river areas, all of which are managed in accordance with the uses for each area.

One of the management zones, the Agricultural Production Area, is specifically designed to protect and promote the native berry agriculture that characterizes the region as much as its pitch pines. Commercial blueberry production in the Pinelands is based on the highbush blueberry (rather than the lowbush species harvested in Maine). This species, native to the Pinelands wetlands, was first domesticated at Whitesbog (in Pemberton) by Elizabeth White, who sought out the best-tasting berries from plants in the nearby swamps and bred them to produce a harvestable and highly desirable crop. Highbush blueberries now account for most of the blueberries marketed in the United States, and the New Jersey Pinelands ranks second in production of blueberries nationally.

Figure 14-1. Highbush blueberry

Cranberry agriculture is also important in the Pinelands, with commercial cranberry bogs prominently visible along the roads that cross the area. Like blueberries, cranberries are native to the Pinelands wetlands, but they are now cultivated in wetlands artificially constructed for their production. Since the cranberry industry is dependent on the abundant supply of pure water available in the Pinelands, cranberry production has helped to maintain the quality of the water in the region. New Jersey is the third largest producer of cranberries in the nation, and all of New Jersey's cranberries are grown in the Pinelands.

Other statutes regulating the Pinelands continue to be introduced in the state legislature. The Pinelands Protection Act and the Pinelands Commission created by the act have accomplished a notable feat in both controlling development and channeling it into the peripheral parts of the region. However, development pressures continue to be strong, and the region faces continuous threats from burgeoning populations.

Human activities in the Pinelands are generally in keeping with the area's natural aspect and condition. Forest management practices—such as selective harvesting of timber in special plots, experimental planting, and controlled

burning to combat wildfire and maintain the dominance of the fire-dependent pines—have little effect on the Pinelands as a whole. The culture of cranberries and blueberries contributes to the appeal of the area, which has been used for berry growing for almost 100 years.

Hikers, canoeists, campers, hunters, fishermen, birders, nature students, history buffs, and solitude seekers can find opportunities to pursue their interests. Some sites offer opportunities to glimpse life in the Pinelands, visit nature centers, or walk along bogs. Other places are for sportsmen and, as such, are managed for hunting or fishing. The wildlife management areas (WMAs) often have multiple access points, such as the numerous sand roads which lead off of paved country roads. With no main entry point, the diamond-shaped WMA signs posted along the roads are the easiest way to find the areas.

A bewildering web of sand roads interlaces the thousands of acres of forests and cedar swamps of the Pinelands. Every now and then along these roads, ghost towns appear, sometimes with one or two structures, and sometimes with a remnant of non-native vegetation—vague reminders of a flourishing past. Few of these routes are marked, but to the hiker who knows how to use a map and compass, there are many opportunities for exploration, ranging from a few hours to many days. The miles of marked trails are few in comparison with the miles of sand roads, and include the Batona Trail, short nature walks in the state parks, state forests, and wildlife management areas, and trail networks in Belleplain State Forest and Wells Mills County Park. The Batona Trail is the longest hiking trail, running 49.5 miles through Brendan T. Byrne, Wharton, and Bass River state forests.

With many rivers in the area, it is not surprising that there are ample opportunities for canoeing. The principal streams are several branches of Rancocas Creek, the Great Egg Harbor, Toms, and Metedeconk rivers, Westecunck, Oyster, and Cedar creeks, and the Mullica River and its tributaries (Wading, Bass, and Batsto rivers, and Nescochague and Landing creeks). The Oswego River and Tulpehocken Creek flow into the Wading River. The popular canoe routes are on the bigger streams, with stretches of the Oswego, Wading, Batsto, and Mullica rivers being most frequently used. A number of campsites are available to canoeists and hikers on the major streams and hiking trails.

History

The first white people to enter the Pinelands of southern New Jersey undoubtedly followed the trails of the Lenni Lenape that led to the shell fisheries on the coast. The peculiar wildness of the region, empty of human life, must have impressed these early explorers, accustomed to the massive deciduous forests and the grass meadows of the uplands, and the river valleys and coastal marshes where an occasional Native American village could be found. Although these trails through the pines represented a long day's journey, there is no evidence of any permanent Native American camp or village within the area. The Native Americans apparently held the deep Pinelands in a certain awe and avoided them as much as possible.

From the earliest Colonial period, the people of New Jersey have used the region for whatever profitable ventures it afforded. First to move in were the loggers, who clear-cut the forests. Pine and cedar lumber moved steadily to shipyards and nearby towns for years before, during, and after the Revolution. A tree favored by loggers was the Atlantic white cedar, whose logs were especially valued for their straightness (essential for ship masts) and resistance to decay. Hollowed-out cedar logs were used to construct urban water systems; these "pipes" are still in use in parts of Philadelphia. Large dead cedar trees, embedded in the peat of the wetlands, were excavated and used to make shingles ("shakes") for the exterior of houses. Prior to the Revolution, many logs were exported to Britain to construct the ships of the British Navy.

Roads to the coastal communities followed the loggers and charcoal burners, and hostelries were established at a number of places along the sand roads. Bog iron was discovered in the Pinelands, and forges and furnaces were built on the major streams and their tributaries. The iron industry in the Pinelands boomed during the late 1700s and early 1800s, supplying much of the ammunition, wagon wheels, and other iron products for both the Revolutionary War and the War of 1812. The network of sand roads that now provide ample opportunities for hiking mostly dates back to this period.

Iron proved a fairly profitable venture for a generation or so, but the bog iron works were forced to rely on iron ore of uncertain quality and charcoal of limited availability for fueling their forges. Shortly after the mid-nineteenth century, the Jersey iron industry practically disappeared, overwhelmed by competition from Pennsylvania furnaces, with their superior ore and coal fuel.

Glassmaking, using the fine silica sands of certain areas, followed the iron era and flourished for a time. A few large glassworks still exist on the southern

edge of the Pinelands, around Glassboro. Paper mills were built on several of the streams, with salt hay used for fiber, but they, too, were short-lived. The ruins of a paper mill and its community can be seen at Harrisville.

The gathering and drying of sphagnum moss for sale to nurseries and for packing and insulating is an industry that has disappeared in many sections. In former days, local inhabitants augmented the family income by gathering laurel, mistletoe, arbutus, and medicinal herbs for sale in Philadelphia and other cities. In a few localities, as in the vicinity of Tabernacle and Indian Mills, considerable truck farming still exists.

By the start of the twentieth century, extensive acreage of cut-over white cedar swamps had been cleared for cranberry growing, while large tracts of drier ground were used for blueberry production, continuing to the present day. Cranberrying has expanded to some extent. Construction of dikes allowed blueberry fields to be converted to cranberry bogs. These two industries are the only substantial and profitable ones active in the Pinelands.

Aside from the berry growing, the Pinelands have been put to little productive or consumptive use. Both individuals and land promoters made many attempts to settle the area with homes and farms. Most were complete failures, resulting in property abandonment, tax sales, removal of names from assessment lists, selling and reselling, subdividing, and a general confusion of ownership. Clear titles were often difficult to obtain. The land appeared worthless to many hopeful owners, and the attempt to populate the uninhabited Pinelands slowed to a halt. In recent years, retirement villages have been built, increasing the population, and providing jobs which help the local economy.

Where the ironworks once stood, nature has practically obliterated all traces of once-busy communities. Ghost towns dot the Pinelands, most just an open grassy area set within the forest, and a few with the remains of a structure or two as a vague reminder of the places where people once lived and worked. A number of the ponds that were built to power sawmills and gristmills and to furnish water for other purposes still remain. The shores of these ponds, such as the ones at Harrisville and Martha, provide fertile grounds for Pinelands flora. Likewise, abandoned cranberry bogs and old clearings have become ideal propagation grounds for the characteristic growth of the Pinelands.

Ecology

The Pinelands represent the primary northern limit of the oak-pine forest biome,

which stretches from southern New Jersey to northern Florida. (Isolated patches of oak-pine forests can also be found on Cape Cod and Long Island.) Throughout this region, on the flat expanses of Coastal Plain soil, forests of pine trees, oaks, and mixtures of oaks and pines thrive. The pines—mostly loblolly pine, slash pine, and shortleaf pine—are extensively planted and harvested for paper and lumber. In the Pinelands of New Jersey, by contrast, the forest is composed primarily of pitch pines—a species also prominent on rocky outcrops along ridgetops in the northern part of the state.

A unique region of exceptional biological value, the characteristics of the New Jersey Pinelands are quite distinct from those of the pine-oak forests found in the southern states. The Pinelands is home to over 850 species of plants, of which about 380 are found only in this habitat. These plants, in turn, support some 13,000 species of animals, including several rare and endangered species, such as Pine Barrens tree frogs and pine snakes. Its landscapes present a striking contrast to those of northern New Jersey, as widely spaced pitch pines—sometimes mixed with canopy oaks—emerge from a dense shrub layer of scrubby oaks and other low-growing shrubs over nearly perfectly level land. A network of unpaved roads and tracks, which offers abundant opportunities for hikers, exposes the coarse white sand which underlies the region and accounts for the unique plant communities.

The unusual vegetation of the Pinelands is supported by the extreme qualities of the soils found in the area. Derived from coarse beach sand deposited on an ancient shoreline about 22 million years ago, the soils create a challenging environment for plants, as they contain very few plant nutrients, have very little ability to retain moisture, and are very acidic. Only those plants which have adapted themselves to such extreme and harsh conditions can grow here.

The upland forests are, for the most part, dominated by pitch pine. Not only

Figure 14-2. Pitch pine

is this remarkable plant tolerant of the acidic, nutrient-poor, dry soil, but it possesses numerous adaptations that enable it to survive the frequent fires which are an essential part of the ecology of the region. Hikers who walk through recently-burned areas (apparent from the charring of the tree trunks) will note the tufts of new needles that emerge from the tree trunks. This trait, which makes the trees resemble bottle brushes, is an adaptation found only in fire-scarred trees. Other adaptations characteristic of the pitch pine are the thick bark that insulates the tree and the abundant, vigorous sprouts that emerge from the base of severely burned trees. The pitch pine's hardiness—its ability to thrive in difficult environments that most other species shun—is demonstrated by its appearance in northern New Jersey, on the rocky outcrops of the ridgetops. There, conditions similar to the Pinelands—thin, acidic soils with very little ability to hold moisture—eliminate most other trees and allow the hardy pitch pine to prevail.

Pitch pines are actually dependent on fire for reproduction. On many trees—especially those in the eastern Pinelands and in the Pine Plains—the cones remain on the trees, sealed shut, until a fire releases the seeds by melting the resinous "glue" that holds them closed. In the absence of fire, the pine-dominated forests are slowly overtaken by the less fire-tolerant oaks. Indeed, the forested areas along the western edge of the region—where fire has been more vigorously suppressed because of adjacent human settlement—are mixtures of oak and pine, or even entirely composed of oaks (white, black, and chestnut). Only in the eastern Pinelands, where fires have been allowed to take their natural course, are the forests dominated by pitch pines. Seeds falling to the forest floor also need bare soil, devoid of thick litter and the shading of shrubs, in order to germinate and grow—conditions that are ideally provided by a good fire.

In the eastern Pinelands, several tracts of dwarf trees, referred to as the "Pine Plains," are particularly worth a visit. In these areas, on higher ground than the surrounding normal-sized forest, the trees are generally no more than six-to-eight feet high—indeed, one can look out over the canopy of the forest and see the horizon. Mixed with these dwarf trees—which are genetically distinct from the normal-sized plants growing nearby—are blackjack and scrub oaks and lowbush blueberries; together, the plants form an impenetrable thicket. In clearings and along the sides of the sand roads, two northern species—bearberry and broom crowberry—form low-growing mats. Crowberry is a rare species in New Jersey, represented by only the few small populations found

in this part of the Pinelands. The tiny, needle-like leaves of this plant are characteristic of plants growing in particularly harsh environments (such as Arctic tundra). It is believed that the higher frequency of fire in these exposed regions accounts for the unusual vegetation.

The frequency of fire has decreased dramatically since World War II, when modern fire-fighting equipment—and a belief that all fires should be suppressed—were introduced. Now, although the importance of fire for maintaining the Pinelands is recognized, it is hard to allow fires to burn because of the presence of houses throughout the region. Controlled burning is practiced in some areas to reduce the chances of a major crown fire. Small ditches are often seen in the woods; these are dug when fires are started, to prevent the fire from spreading. The largest fire in recent years was the 20,000-acre fire in 1995, which extended to both sides of County 539, near the Greenwood Forest Wildlife Management Area. The patterns of recovery from fire can easily be seen from the sand roads that traverse the area.

Beneath the trees in Pinelands forests, several layers of shrubs are commonly found. Scrub oak—a type of oak that grows as a multi-stemmed shrub—can form head-high thickets. Its small leaves and coarsely branched stems give it a distinctive appearance. Below these taller shrubs, a layer of lowbush blueberries and huckleberries covers the ground (and provides tasty snacks in the middle of the summer). The leathery, shiny evergreen leaves of the wintergreen—a low growing sub-shrub—hug the ground, gracing the forest floor with small bell-shaped flowers in the spring and edible leaves year-round. Exposed sandy areas, resulting from frequent openings in the shrub layer, are coated with a layer of lichens and mosses, reminiscent of the boreal forests far to the north. One of the most common lichens, British soldier (named for the red uniforms of the British soldiers during the Revolutionary War), can be identified by its bright red spore capsules atop short, light-green stems.

The coarse sandy soils cannot retain moisture for plant roots at the surface because it rapidly percolates downward. However, the thick beds of sand often found only a short distance below the surface hold a large amount of water. This groundwater aquifer—one of the largest in the world—supports extensive wetlands. A dip in elevation that is barely apparent to the hiker, if noticeable at all, allows the water table to reach the land surface. Over 25% of the Pinelands is classified as wetland. The old sand roads often skirt the edges of the wetlands; thus, their plant communities may easily be observed by hikers without having to get their feet wet.

There are four main types of wetland easily viewed from the sand roads and trails. Pine lowlands wetlands are saturated but not flooded. In these areas, the pitch pines (which can tolerate wet conditions as well as extremely dry conditions) are small and distantly spaced, and the ground is covered with an extremely dense growth of many species of shrubs. Some of these shrubs—including sheep laurel, inkberry, and leatherleaf—are evergreens, thus facilitating the identification of this type of wetland in the winter. In late spring, the pine lowlands are peppered with tall flowering spikes of turkeybeard. Wetter, flooded wetlands bordering the streams include red maple swamps and, most conspicuously, Atlantic white-cedar swamps. The closely-packed, tall cedars cast a dense shadow, creating a dark, peaceful, and strikingly beautiful environment. The ground surface is often coated with a spongy carpet of peat mosses in which highly specialized and unusual herbaceous plants grow. Carnivorous plants—including sundews, pitcher plants, and bladderworts—are commonly found along the sunlit edges of the swamps or in openings created by windthrown trees. Red maple swamps, usually located adjacent to cedar swamps, have canopies that let in much light, allowing a luxuriant growth of shrubs in the understory. This type of swamp has become more prevalent in the last century as a result of unsound logging practices that destroyed many cedar swamps in the Pinelands. Trails may also skirt the edges of open marshes in which low-growing grasses and sedges are found. Despite their drab appearance, these marshes are home to a large number of rare and endangered plant species, including the globally-endangered bog asphodel, several rare types of grasses and sedges, and a variety of orchids.

Cranberry bogs, built on former pine swamps and cedar bogs, are prominent throughout the central portion of the Pinelands. At harvest time (mid-October), the bogs are flooded, and the cranberries form a bright red layer floating on the surface of the water. Where the bogs have been abandoned, a variety of plant communities, from marshes to young red maple swamps, can be found.

Wildlife is abundant in the Pinelands—sometimes, too abundant. Deer have become superabundant here, as elsewhere in the state. Their extensive browsing on Atlantic white cedar during the winter often prevents this species from growing back when a stand is disturbed by fire or logging. Many other kinds of mammals are found in the Pinelands, including gray fox, skunk, raccoon, rabbit, beaver, opossum, muskrat, otter, mink, weasel, a variety of mice and voles, shrews, and bats. Eighteen species of snakes—including the pine

snake and the timber rattlesnake, both endangered species—are found. The rattlers often choose to spend the winter in cavities beneath the roots of cedars, deep in the swamps. The amphibia (frogs and salamanders) include several rare species, notably the Pine Barrens tree frog and the carpenter frog.

BASS RIVER STATE FOREST

Acquired by the State of New Jersey in 1905, Bass River State Forest was the first state forest in New Jersey. It encompasses 26,537 acres to the southeast of Wharton State Forest. The forest headquarters is at Lake Absegami, a 67-acre lake created in the 1920s, where there are camping areas, a beach, cabins, shelters, lean-tos, a nature center, and a short nature trail that traverses a cedar swamp.

Five loop trails vary in length from 1.0 to 3.3 miles, and the Batona Trail traverses the forest. With map and compass, it is possible to hike any number of circular routes over the sand roads in the area. A circular hike of about ten miles to Munion Field and back leads through typical Pinelands forests, with stands of oak and cedar as well as pine, and passes through private lands where timber has been heavily harvested.

Figure 14-3. Sand road in Bass River State Forest

From northern New Jersey, take Exit 52 (New Gretna) of the Garden State Parkway and turn right onto County 654 (East Green Street), following the signs to Bass River State Forest. Bear right at the stop sign onto Stage Road. The state forest headquarters is about a mile on the left. From southern New Jersey, take Exit 50 (New Gretna, US 9) of the Garden State Parkway to New Gretna and turn left onto County 679. After 1.5 miles, bear right onto County 654.

At the junction with Stage Road, bear right and follow the signs to the park headquarters. For more information, contact Bass River State Forest, P.O. Box 118, New Gretna, NJ 08224; (609) 296-1114; www.njparksandforests.org.

BATONA TRAIL

Extending 49.5 miles through the heart of the Pinelands, the Batona Trail (pink) is the longest blazed hiking trail in southern New Jersey. It starts from Bass River State Forest and goes through Wharton State Forest and Brendan T. Byrne State Forest to Ong's Hat on Buddtown Road, 1.5 miles northwest of Four Mile Circle. The trail was established in 1961 by the Batona (Back to Nature) Hiking Club of Philadelphia, and it is still maintained by that group. To pierce the genuine wilderness of the area, the Batona Trail avoids the sand roads as much as possible. About 20 percent of the treadway is soft sand, which makes for slower-than-expected progress in parts of this mostly level trail.

Good starting points for trips on the trail are the Brendan T. Byrne State Forest headquarters and the Batsto Visitor Center. Permits, trail maps, and information may be obtained there, as well as at the Atsion Ranger Station and the Bass River Forest Office. A permit is required to camp along the trail in the state forests. There are three campsites in an 18-mile stretch along the northern half of the trail. Paved roads cross the trail in a number of places, making possible a variety of trips. A New Jersey DEP map for the Batona Trail is available. For more information about the Batona Trail, contact either Wharton State Forest, Batsto Village, 4110 Nesco Road, Hammonton, NJ 08037; (609) 561-0024, or Brendan Byrne State Forest, P.O. Box 215, New Lisbon, NJ 08064; (609) 726-1191; www.njparksandforests.org.

Batona Trail   *Length: 49.5 miles Blaze: pink*
The Batona Trail begins near the junction of Coal Road and Stage Road, near Lake Absegami, in the Bass River State Forest. It parallels Stage Road before turning north to cross Martha Road and Oswego Road. It loops around to return to Martha Road going west, which it follows to Martha Bridge at 6.7 miles, entering Wharton State Forest en route. It reaches County 679 at 8.0 miles and Evans Bridge on County 563 at 8.7 miles.

From the Evans Bridge parking area, which is also a take-out for canoe

trips on the Wading River, the Batona Trail runs generally west, and at 9.2 miles reaches Batsto Village, the restored iron town where the headquarters of Wharton State Forest is located. Camping is possible at nearby Buttonwood Hill, which is not directly on the trail, but is accessible by car. From Batsto, the trail proceeds north, generally following the Batsto River and playing tag with Goodwater Road (a sand road) that also parallels the eastern bank of the stream. The trail passes Quaker Bridge 6.1 miles from Batsto, at a point where several sand roads converge to cross the river. From here, the trail follows a sand road for 0.1 mile, then veers northeast through the woods. At 7.1 miles from Batsto, an 0.2-mile spur heads north along the river to the Lower Forge Camp. This camp is also used on canoe trips on the Batsto River, and is not accessible by car.

Twelve miles from Batsto, the Batona Trail crosses railroad tracks to reach the Carranza Memorial, on Carranza Road, 0.2 mile west of the trail crossing. It is a monument to the Mexican pilot Emilio Carranza, whose plane crashed here in 1928 while he was returning to Mexico City after a goodwill flight to New York. Half a mile to the north is the Batona Camp, which can be crowded and noisy, since it is accessible by paved and sand roads. Leaving the camp, the trail turns eastward on the south side of Skit Branch and then crosses Skit Branch Stream about a mile farther on. The trail goes up and down over several hummocks, then reaches the fire tower on Apple Pie Hill, which is the highest point on the trail and provides a view over the Pinelands.

For the next six miles, the trail continues on a northeasterly course, generally on sand roads, crossing several paved roads before reaching NJ 72 and Brendan T. Byrne State Forest. The Batona Trail turns northwest through the forest, generally paralleling NJ 72, past Pakim Pond and the site of the Lebanon Glass Works. The trail comes within 0.1 mile of forest headquarters, about 27 miles from Batsto. A mile later, Deep Hollow Pond is reached on the way to the trail's northernmost point at Carpenter Spring. The trail turns southwesterly, passing through oak-pine forests. The Batona Trail ends at Ong's Hat on Buddtown Road (NJ 72), 40.3 miles from Batsto and 49.5 miles from the terminus at Stage Road in the Bass River State Forest.

BELLEPLAIN STATE FOREST

Located in the southern Pinelands, Belleplain State Forest contains over 20,000

acres of lowland hardwood swamps, former agricultural areas, stands of cedar, plantations of evergreens, and marshes. Established in 1928, the state forest is used for public recreation, timber production, wildlife management, and water conservation. In the 1930s, three Civilian Conservation Corps camps were established on the property. In addition to constructing the nature center and the maintenance buildings, the corps created much of the road system, bridges, and dams and improved vast tracts of fields and forest through silvicultural techniques. Hunting, trapping, and fishing are permitted within the forest, subject to New Jersey's fish and game laws. Wildlife includes deer, grouse, squirrel, rabbit, raccoon, fox, and various waterfowl.

Motorized routes, multi-use trails, and the abandoned railroad bed of the former Pennsylvania-Reading Seashore Lines criss-cross the state forest. The East Creek Trail extends for 6.5 miles around Lake Nummy, named in honor of the chief of the Kechemeches, the last to rule in the Cape May area. The Pickle Pond Trail is about a mile long. The forest also has two nature trails that are accessible to people with disabilities and approximately ten miles of additional marked paths.

To reach Belleplain State Forest, take Exit 17 (Woodbine/Sea Isle City) of the Garden State Parkway. Bear right, then turn right onto US 9 for 0.6 mile. After a left turn onto County 550, go 6.3 miles to Woodbine, where County 550 makes a left and then a right. From here, it is 1.4 miles to the state forest, with the entrance road on the left. Once inside the state forest, turn right at the first intersection to reach Lake Nummy and the nature center. For more information, contact Belleplain State Forest, County Route 550, P.O. Box 450, Woodbine, NJ 08270; (609) 861-2404; www.njparksandforests.org.

BRENDAN T. BYRNE STATE FOREST

Brendan T. Byrne State Forest (formerly known as Lebanon State Forest)—New Jersey's second-largest state forest—covers over 34,000 acres in the northern Pinelands. It encompasses the site of the Lebanon Glass Works that, between 1851 and 1867, was a thriving manufacturer of window glass and bottles. When the wood supply was exhausted, the industry collapsed, and the small town it supported was abandoned. The state began acquiring the property in 1908. Over the years, as the acreage expanded, so did the recreation opportunities. Today, the forest offers opportunities to hike, camp, bicycle, bird, horse-

back ride, and picnic. A handicapped-accessible trail is near Pakim Pond.

There is no shortage of cedar swamps in Brendan T. Byrne State Forest, and a portion of the state forest is designated the Cedar Swamp Natural Area. Tall Atlantic white cedar crowd together with dense vegetation at their base— orchids, sundews, pitcher plants, and curly grass ferns. A portion of the Batona Trail (pink) goes through this area. Along the gravel road, it is accessible to the handicapped.

Within Brendan T. Byrne State Forest is Whitesbog Village, an historic site open to the public. Here, at the turn of the twentieth century, J.J. White established a large cranberry plantation. Although also known as the place that cultivated the first successful blueberry crops, there is birding at Whitesbog, with over 200 species of birds. A chain of sand roads connects the 3,000 acres of bogs, fields, wetlands, and forests. The state leases portions of the state forest to commercial growers. Hunting is allowed, so users of the area should take precautions in the fall or visit the area on Sundays, when hunting is not permitted. An annual festival is held in June, with Pinelands bluegrass music, ecological tours, and blueberry and cranberry foods.

The headquarters of Brendan T. Byrne State Forest is a starting point for hikes that use the Batona Trail (pink). Directly across the road from the office, a blue-blazed trail leads 0.1 mile to a junction with the Batona Trail. In order not to miss the turn on the return trip, hikers should walk a few steps, turn, and then note what the intersection looks like. A right turn at the trail junction leads four miles northwest to the terminus of the Batona Trail at Ong's Hat on Buddtown Road and passes stands of pine, oak, and cedar. A left turn at the intersection leads, in about three miles, to

Figure 14-4. Tundra swans wintering in pond at Whitesbog

Pakim Pond, with pic-

nic tables, camping facilities, and guided nature walks. There is a cedar swamp just on the other side of the dam. The 2.7-mile handicapped-accessible Cranberry Trail (red) also connects the park office with Pakim Pond and can be used as an alternate return route. Pakim Pond can be used as a starting point for hikes on the Batona Trail, and it is the start of the 8.5-mile Mount Misery Trail (white), a loop trail. Both the Cranberry Trail and the Mount Misery Trail are open to mountain bikes.

To reach the headquarters of Brendan T. Byrne State Forest, take the Garden State Parkway to Exit 88 (NJ 70 West). Follow NJ 70 West for about 25 miles to the entrance road to Brendan T. Byrne State Forest, marked by a sign just past a blinking yellow light at Lebanon Lakes and Presidential Lakes. Turn left and follow the park entrance road for 0.7 mile to the park headquarters, on the right side of the road.

To reach Whitesbog Village, take the Garden State Parkway to Exit 88 (NJ 70 West). Follow NJ 70 West and turn right onto County 530. In one mile, turn onto the paved portion of Whitesbog Road and follow the road a short distance to Whitesbog Village. For the best birding opportunities, turn right at the stop sign and stay to the right as you go through the town until you reach a large reservoir on the left and cranberry bogs on the right. Visitors to Brendan T. Byrne State Forest who wish to use the sand roads should obtain the Browns Mills, Chatsworth, Whiting, and Woodmansie USGS topographic quadrangle maps or the New Jersey DEP Brendan T. Byrne State Forest map. For more information, contact Brendan T. Byrne State Forest, P.O. Box 215, New Lisbon, NJ 08064; (609) 726-1191; www.njparksandforests.org.

COLLIERS MILLS WILDLIFE MANAGEMENT AREA

Covering more than 12,000 acres, the Colliers Mills Wildlife Management Area is comprised of pitch pine and scrub oak forests, white cedar swamps, fields, and lakes. A main sand road leads past lakes, through the heart of the area, and exits on the other side. Other sand roads interlace the area, including some which restrict vehicles. The size of the wildlife management area invites exploration and solitude; however, in some areas, heavy greenbrier undergrowth prevents bushwhacking.

Colliers Mills Wildlife Management Area is a good place to hear the Pine Barrens tree frogs in the late spring and summer. Rabbits, squirrels, foxes,

grouse, deer, mallards, black ducks, wood ducks, teals, and quail are the principal wildlife residents. Hunters heavily use the area in the fall hunting season, so hikers should take appropriate precautions.

To reach Colliers Mills Wildlife Management Area, take Exit 16A (Six Flags) of I-195 and turn right onto County 537. Continue for 3.4 miles and turn left onto Hawkin Road. The office is on the left, with a main sand road leading into the area just beyond. Visitors to the area should obtain the Casswood and Lakehurst USGS topographic quadrangle maps. For more information, contact the New Jersey Department of Environmental Protection (DEP), Division of Fish and Wildlife, 501 East State Street, P.O. Box 400, Trenton, NJ 08625; (609) 984-0547; www.njfishandwildlife.org.

DOUBLE TROUBLE STATE PARK

Unfortunately, there is only speculation about how Double Trouble State Park was named. But it is not just an intriguing name that should draw visitors. Located a few miles south of Toms River, the 7,336-acre park is a captivating blend of natural and cultural history. Productive cranberry bogs, a sawmill, a 1.5-mile hiking trail, and a restored village are on what once was a thriving nineteenth century lumbering operation. Along the upper reaches of Cedar Creek is a typical white cedar swamp. The restored Double Trouble Village contains 14 historic structures, including a sawmill, pickers' cottages, a cranberry sorting and packing house, a general

Figure 14-5. A picker's cottage in Double Trouble State Park

419

store, and a one-room schoolhouse built in 1890.

To reach Double Trouble State Park, take the Garden State Parkway to Exit 77, and proceed west on Pinewald-Keswick Road for 0.5 mile to the park entrance, which is on the left. For more information, contact Double Trouble State Park, P.O. Box 175, Bayville, NJ 08721; (732) 341-6662; www.njparksandforests.org.

GREENWOOD FOREST WILDLIFE MANAGEMENT AREA

The Greenwood Forest Wildlife Management Area stretches for miles along County 539 in Ocean County. The 28,000 acres contain forests of pitch pine and scrub oak in uplands areas and white cedar swamps in the lowlands. Its fields are managed for wildlife, with hedgerows and plantings of wildlife food and cover crops. In 2003, blackened trees are reminders of the April 1995 fire which swept through the Pinelands.

Sand roads lead into the vast interior. For those not wishing to venture too far, there is a boardwalk at Webb's Mill Bog Cedar Swamp for observation of native plants and animals. Sundew, St. Johnswort, cranberry, curly-grass fern, orchids, dwarf huckleberry, and leatherleaf grow on sphagnum moss hummocks. At slightly higher elevations, pine, clammy azalea, sheep laurel, inkberry, and swamp magnolias surround the bog. Upland vegetation includes golden heather, sand myrtle, bearberry, scrub oak, and bayberry. The boardwalk is also an ideal place for viewing reptiles and amphibians. During late spring evenings, a chorus of Pine Barrens tree frogs may be heard.

To reach Greenwood Forest Wildlife Management Area, turn north at the intersection of NJ 72 and County 539. Sand roads leave from both sides of the road into the interior. To reach the boardwalk at Webb's Mill Branch, drive 6.5 miles from the intersection of NJ 72 and County 539 and park by the bridge, where the boardwalk is visible. Hikers wishing to explore the area should obtain the Keswick Grove, Whiting, Woodmansie, and Brookville USGS topographic quadrangle maps. For more information, contact New Jersey DEP, Division of Fish and Wildlife, 501 East State Street, P.O. Box 400, Trenton, NJ 08625; (609) 984-0547; www.njfishandwildlife.org.

MANCHESTER WILDLIFE MANAGEMENT AREA

Located in Ocean County, the Manchester Wildlife Management Area contains 3,085 acres, which include white cedar swamps. The uplands of pitch pine and scrub oak provide habitat for deer, turkey, rabbit, and quail. Even though the area is rimmed with private homes, once away on the sand roads, there is only a hint or two of human intrusion. In spring and summer, the beauty of bog flowers and the fragrance of sun-warmed pines and cedars is apparent. Autumn brings a colorful palette, while winter offers a stark, and sometimes snow-streaked landscape.

To reach the Manchester Wildlife Management Area, take NJ 70 to the junction with either Beckertown Road or County 539 and turn north. Sand roads lead off the paved roads into the interior. Private properties line the edges of the paved roads, so hikers should take care not to trespass. Hikers wishing to use the area should obtain the Cassville, Keswick Grove, and Whiting USGS topographic quadrangle maps. For more information, contact New Jersey DEP, Division of Fish and Wildlife, 501 East State Street, P.O. Box 400, Trenton, NJ 08625; (609) 984-0547; www.njfishandwildlife.org.

PENN STATE FOREST

A prime attraction of the 3,366-acre Penn State Forest is Oswego Lake, whose water, because of the iron and the cedar in the Pinelands, is the color of tea. Stretching out northeast from the lake, the forest is interlaced with sand roads that can be hiked in many combinations. In the center of the forest is Bear Swamp Hill, where there is parking and the foundation of a fire tower that was knocked down in an airplane crash in 1971.

In Penn State Forest, as in other sections in the Pinelands, activity by military aircraft is quite noticeable. Fort Dix, McGuire Air Force Base, and Lakehurst Naval Air Station form a huge presence in the northern part of the Pinelands. About four miles east of Oswego Lake is the U.S. Navy Target Area at Warren Grove, and it is common in the Pinelands to see fighters and bombers practice here. The area around the target installation, just west of County 539, is one of the best places to see the Pine Plains, the unusual pygmy forests in which full-grown trees are no more than six-to-eight feet tall.

To reach Penn State Forest, take County 563 and turn east onto

Chatsworth-New Gretna Road for 3.2 miles to Oswego Lake. This intersection is 1.4 miles north of the junction with County 679. The parking area is on the right, just over the bridge. Visitors to Penn State Forest should obtain the Oswego and Woodmansie USGS topographic quadrangle maps or the New Jersey DEP Penn State Forest map. Penn State Forest is administered by Bass River State Forest. For more information, contact Bass River State Forest, P.O. Box 118, New Gretna, NJ 08224; (609) 296-1114; www.njparksandforests.org.

RANCOCAS STATE PARK

Located on the western edge of the Pinelands, the 1,252-acre Rancocas State Park is a mix of extensive lowlands, upland forest, overgrown fields, and freshwater streams and marshes. The New Jersey Audubon Society operates the Rancocas Nature Center, which is housed in a 130-year-old farm house. The center and 120 acres are leased from the State of New Jersey.

Mowed trails cross the fields, providing opportunities to view a variety of plants, some of which were introduced by early European settlers. Self-guided nature trails inform visitors about Inner Coastal Plain vegetation. Wildlife in the area includes house wrens, chickadees, tree swallows, a variety of ducks, beaver, red fox, white-tailed deer, gray and red squirrels, raccoons, and an occasional great horned owl.

To reach Rancocas State Park, take Exit 44A from I-295, and go east on Rancocas Road for 1.5 miles to the Rancocas Nature Center entrance on the right-hand side of the road. For more information about the nature center, contact Rancocas Nature Center, 794 Rancocas Road, Mt. Holly, NJ 08060; (609) 261-2495; www.njaudubon.org/centers/rancocas. For information about the state park, contact Brendan T. Byrne

Figure 14-6. Red fox

State Forest, P.O. Box 215, New Lisbon, NJ 08318; (609) 726-1191; www.njparksandforests.org.

STAFFORD FORGE WILDLIFE MANAGEMENT AREA

Easily reached via the Garden State Parkway, the 15,905-acre Stafford Forge Wildlife Management Area is used by hikers, birders, hunters, and fishermen. Access is via sand roads, some of which go the length of the wildlife management area. Dense underbrush and pitch pines make bushwhacking through some of the terrain extremely difficult. Both birds and birders alike find the series of four ponds along dammed Westecunk Creek attractive. Sand roads go along both sides of the southernmost and largest pond. It is possible to cross the dikes between the ponds on foot. There are numerous sand roads leading away from the ponds.

Wildlife found in the area includes deer, rabbit, quail, tundra swan, purple martin, and wood duck. Hunters frequent the area in the fall, so hikers should take precautions during that season or visit the area on Sundays, when hunting is prohibited.

To reach Stafford Forge Wildlife Management Area, take Exit 58 (Tuckerton/Warren Grove) of the Garden State Parkway and turn right onto County 539. Proceed 0.3 mile and turn right onto County 606 (Forge Road). The southernmost of the ponds is at 1.3 miles along the left side of Forge Road. Hikers wishing to use the area should obtain the West Creek and Oswego Lake USGS topographic quadrangle maps. For more information, contact New Jersey DEP, Division of Fish and Wildlife, 501 East State Street, P.O. Box 400, Trenton, NJ 08625; (609) 984-0547; www.njfishandwildlife.org.

WELLS MILLS COUNTY PARK

The land in what is now Wells Mills County Park has had a productive past. The abundance of Atlantic white cedar on the property prompted James Wells, in the latter part of the eighteenth century, to build a sawmill and dam Oyster Creek for water power. Cedar is a strong, rot-resistant wood, a characteristic that the ship and boat industry sought. Shipments of lumber milled at the site reached ports along the Atlantic coast. The mill passed through several owners and was eventually purchased by Christopher Estlow and his sons. It was Tilden Estlow, a grandson, who added moss gathering, shingle making, lumbering, and clay gathering to the site's products. The clay was hauled to a Trenton factory where it was made into pottery and china. The site was purchased for

private recreational purposes in 1936 and eventually, in the late 1970s, became public open space.

The 910-acre park—the largest park in the Ocean County park system—offers a nature center, observation deck, canoe rental, and fishing on the mill pond. Fifteen miles of marked trails lead visitors through pine-oak forests, Atlantic white cedar swamps, freshwater bogs, and maple gum swamps. The 8.4-mile Penns Hill Trail (white) circles the park, and several short trails are designated for tree identification, nature study, and the visually impaired. Mountain bikes are permitted only on a 3.2-mile yellow-blazed trail designated for that use. A portion of three co-aligned trails leads briefly into an adjacent Boy Scout camp, and users are asked to stay on the trail. A trail map is available at the information kiosk and the visitors center.

From northern New Jersey, take Exit 67 of the Garden State Parkway and go west on County 554 for about five miles to NJ 72. Stay on NJ 72 West briefly and make the next right turn onto County 532. The park entrance is on the right in 3.8 miles. From southern New Jersey, take Exit 69 of the Garden State Parkway, proceed west on County 532, and continue for 2.5 miles to the park entrance on the left. For more information, contact Wells Mills County Park, Box 905, Wells Mills Road, Waretown, NJ 08758; (609) 971-3085; www.co.ocean.nj.us/parks/wellsmills.html.

WHARTON STATE FOREST

Located in the heart of the Pinelands, Wharton State Forest is well known as a canoeist's paradise, with narrow, twisting streams gently flowing through the cedar, pine, and oak forests. For those who prefer to explore drier routes, there is a network of 500 miles of sand roads and trails in the 120,000-acre tract. The central part of the forest is farther from a paved road than any other place in New Jersey. The state forest is the largest tract of public land administered by the State of New Jersey.

What is now Wharton State Forest once played an important role in the industrial development of the United States. Bog ore and the ready supply of trees and water resulted in the building of iron furnaces and sawmills. Between 1766 and 1876, the business and property were sold many times. The last owner was Joseph Wharton who, before he died in 1909, purchased nearly 100,000 acres of land, established a cranberry industry, and experimented with

scientific methods of forest management. He also hoped to use the large aquifer of the Pinelands to supply Philadelphia and adjacent areas with pure water, but his plan was thwarted by the enactment of legislation that prohibited the export of New Jersey's waters to other states. In 1954-55, the state purchased the forest as recreation and watershed lands. Aside from the facilities at Batsto and Atsion, the property has remained undeveloped. Within the state forest are Batsto and Oswego River natural areas, and Batsto Village, a National Historic Site.

A principal community of the iron days, Batsto Village was established in 1766, a few miles from the salt reaches of the lower Mullica River. Some of the original buildings still remain, and the state has restored them, re-creating a nineteenth-century Pinelands village. These restored buildings include the man-

sion, several workers' cottages, the general store and post office, a sawmill, a gristmill, and a number of farm buildings. Some of these buildings are open to the public.

Batsto Village is located on County 542 at the southern edge of Wharton State Forest. The visitor center has maps and books for sale, including

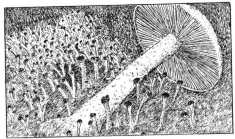

Figure 14-7. British soldier lichen with mushroom

books on the history of Batsto and the other iron towns in the area. Several nature trails offer the opportunity to observe pitcher plants, sphagnum moss, and British soldiers (a lichen with a red head). Nearby, the Batona Trail (pink) can be combined with sand roads for a variety of hikes.

A 12-mile circular hike from Batsto Village begins by following village trails up the east side of Batsto Lake. The red, blue, and white trails offer views of the lake. The lake becomes shallower toward the north, more filled with grasses and trees, grading off at the sides into cedar swamp. Many cedar stumps rise above the surface at the north end of the lake. Most likely, these are remnants of Atlantic white cedar trees that were flooded when the Batsto Lake dam was constructed over 200 years ago. The path runs along the shore of the lake, following a fire-cut and a sand road. After skirting the lake for its full length of about a mile, the path meets the Batona Trail (pink), which comes from the south, having crossed Washington Pike near the fire tower a few hundred yards

northeast of Batsto. The circular route continues on the Batona Trail (pink) for about six miles to a convergence of four sand roads into a single sand road that crosses the Batsto River on Quaker Bridge. This spot was the site of a tavern on the stage route from Philadelphia to Tuckerton. The route proceeds across the bridge and turns left on the first sand road on the west side of the Batsto River. It heads back south to Batsto Village.

Another hike from Batsto is to Atsion, about ten miles northwest. Atsion is the site of another Pinelands iron town, with a manor house and several other buildings still standing, though none of the historic buildings (except for the general store, which now serves as the park office) are open to the public. Several routes over sand roads connect Atsion and Batsto, including the section of the Batona Trail between Batsto and Quaker Bridge, and the Mullica River Trail (yellow), which closely parallels the Mullica River and provides access to the Mullica River Wilderness Campsite. Atsion has an office, a campground, and cabins at Atsion Lake, and can be reached by car from US 206. The area between Atsion and Batsto is on the Atsion USGS topographic quadrangle map.

Hiking is also possible in the southeast area of Wharton State Forest, around Evans Bridge on County 563. West of Evans Bridge, sand roads lead several miles to Washington, the site of a former Pinelands town, where a stone ruin stands in the middle of the woods. Southeast of Evans Bridge are the ruins of Harrisville on the Oswego River, where a paper mill once stood, and a little farther upriver is the site of Martha, an iron town of which almost no traces remain. A great diversity of plants characteristic of the Pinelands wetlands live near the ponds at Harrisville and Martha.

There are many access points to Wharton State Forest. To reach Batsto, follow the signs from Exit 52 of the Garden State Parkway. Access to Evans Bridge is via County 563, where there is parking at Evans Bridge, or from County 679, where there is room for several cars to park along the road at Harrisville. Hikers wishing to use the area should obtain the Atsion, Chatsworth, Greenbank, Hammonton, Indian Mills, Jenkins, or Medford Lakes USGS topographic quadrangle maps. The New Jersey DEP Wharton State Forest map is available at the park office. For more information, contact Wharton State Forest, Batsto Village, 4110 Nesco Road, Hammonton, NJ 08037; (609) 561-0024; www.njparksandforests.org.

FIFTEEN

LONG DISTANCE TRAILS

Most trails that cannot be walked comfortably from end to end in one day are considered long distance trails. These trails, typically spanning multiple chapters within this book, can be completed by hiking one section at a time or by backpacking. Hikers need to plan for transportation at the end point. Alternately, hikers can cover a segment of the trail out to a point and then hike back to the starting point the same way they came or on a different trail, if one is available.

The New York metropolitan area boasts two premier long distance trails—the Appalachian Trail and the Long Path. The Long Path Trail System includes the Shawangunk Ridge Trail, which connects the Appalachian Trail at High Point State Park in New Jersey with the Long Path in the Shawangunks.

Another important long distance trail that traverses both New Jersey and New York is the Highlands Trail. As of 2003, about 120 miles of the Highlands Trail are open and blazed. Eventually, it will extend from Storm King Mountain on the Hudson River to the Delaware River.

Long distance trails that are contained within a single region are described in the relevant chapter of this book. The Batona Trail and the Long Path are examples of this type of long distance trail. (For a history of the Long Path and a brief description of its route in New York, see the *New York Walk Book*, chapter 19, "Long Distance Trails." For a more detailed description of the route of the Long Path, see the *Long Path Guide*, published by the Trail Conference.)

APPALACHIAN NATIONAL SCENIC TRAIL

The Appalachian Trail, known by hikers as the A.T., extends from Springer Mountain in Georgia to Mount Katahdin in Maine, a distance of about 2,160 miles. In the New Jersey-New York area, it runs from the Delaware Water Gap to Connecticut. In general, it follows the spine of the Appalachian Mountains and seemingly goes over every mountain along the way.

Benton MacKaye, a regional planner, first proposed the trail in the *Journal of the American Institute of Architects* in 1921, in an article entitled "An Appalachian Trail, a Project in Regional Planning." He foresaw the large concentration of an urban population along the east coast and their need to retreat to nature for spiritual renewal.

The first section of the Appalachian Trail was built by volunteers from the New York-New Jersey Trail Conference in 1922-23, from the Bear Mountain Bridge to the Ramapo River south of Arden in Bear Mountain-Harriman State Parks. The following year, they completed the section from Arden to Greenwood Lake. The entire trail from Georgia to Maine was completed in 1937; however, much of it was on private land and subject to interruptions as landowners changed. In 1968, Congress passed the National Trails System Act, which designated the Appalachian Trail and the Pacific Crest Trail as the first official National Scenic Trails. As of 2003, there are eight National Scenic Trails and 15 National Historic Trails. Additional provisions of the Act included assigning responsibility for the National Scenic Trails to the National Park Service and the U.S. Forest Service, acquiring rights-of-way for the trail where it is outside federal or state lands, and protecting the trails from incompatible uses—specifically, limiting the Appalachian Trail to primarily foot traffic. Funding for land purchases first became available in amendments to the Act in 1978. In 1982, New Jersey became the first state to acquire a complete corridor on protected lands.

Figure 15-1. Appalachian Trail blaze

In 1984, the U.S. Department of the Interior signed an agreement with the Appalachian Trail Conference (formed in 1925) to manage the trail and the newly purchased corridor. The Appalachian Trail Conference delegates its re-

sponsibilities to trail clubs along the length of the trail. In this area, the New York-New Jersey Trail Conference has responsibility for the 162 miles in New York and New Jersey. This cooperative agreement among national, state, and local governments and volunteers serves as a model for efficient use of resources in an era of declining budgets. In 2003, only 13 miles of the entire A.T., from Maine to Georgia, remain unprotected.

Every year, several hundred people *thru-hike* the Appalachian Trail—that is, they hike it continuously from end to end—generally taking from five to seven months to complete it. Many other people complete the trail over several years or decades, doing it a section at a time.

The *Appalachian Trail Guide to New York-New Jersey* and similar guides for other states describe the trail in great detail, with comments about trail features every few tenths of a mile. These guides are revised every three to five years. The *Appalachian Trail Data Book*, published by the Appalachian Trail Conference, is revised yearly and covers the whole trail in less than a hundred pages. It lists only major features along the trail, such as road crossings, shelters, rivers, and mountain tops. The trail is uniformly marked with a 2" × 6" white-painted, vertical blaze. Most major road crossings are well marked, and the basic trail route appears even on most commercial road maps, although not always accurately.

New York-New Jersey State Line to High Point State Park

From its crossing of the New York-New Jersey state line, just west of Greenwood Lake, the Appalachian Trail heads northwest, roughly paralleling the state line to High Point State Park. At first, it weaves its way through the Highlands, briefly crossing Abram S. Hewitt State Forest and then traversing Wawayanda State Park, where it climbs to a panoramic west-facing viewpoint. After crossing the Pochuck Marsh on a series of boardwalks and a suspension bridge, it climbs Pochuck Mountain and then descends to begin a traverse of the Great Valley, passing through a varied landscape of farms, forests, and wetlands. Except where it traverses preexisting state park land, this section of the trail follows a narrow corridor acquired by the State of New Jersey to protect the route of the A.T. through New Jersey.

The section of the A.T. from Warwick Turnpike to NJ 94, which traverses Wawayanda State Park, is described in chapter 8, "Bearfort Ridge and Wawayanda," pp. 170-71. The A.T. section from NJ 94 to County 517, which

includes the Pochuck suspension bridge and boardwalk, is described below. For a detailed description of the remainder of this section, see the *Appalachian Trail Guide to New York-New Jersey.*

NJ 94 to County 517 *Length: 2.3 miles Blaze: white*

The eastern end of this section is on NJ 94, 0.6 mile north of its intersection with Maple Grange Road. Cars may be parked in a designated parking area on the east side of NJ 94. The trail heads west, crossing a cow pasture on puncheons. At 0.2 mile, hikers climb over stiles to cross the active New York, Susque-hanna and Western Railroad. The trail continues through forests and fields until, at 0.7 mile, it turns left to cross a wooden bridge over Wawayanda Creek.

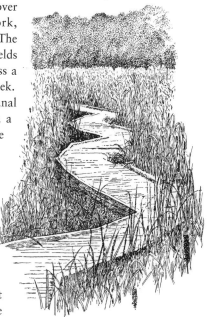

At 0.9 mile, the trail reaches Canal Road, where there is a parking area a short distance to the south along the road. The trail turns right and crosses a bridge over a stream (the former route of the canal). It then turns left, follows a woods road for 25 feet, and turns right onto a footpath. The trail climbs a knoll, reaching its crest at 1.2 miles, then descends to reach the Pochuck Marsh at 1.4 miles. The trail crosses this wide marsh on a series of boardwalks built on thin pilings bored deep into the swampy ground. The boardwalks were designed to permit the passage of water even during periodic floods.

Figure 15-2. Pochuck Marsh boardwalk

The construction of these boardwalks and the suspension bridge over Pochuck Creek was one of the most complicated and expensive projects in the history of the entire A.T., and it took over seven years to complete. The work was largely accomplished by volunteers of the New York-New Jersey Trail Conference, in partnership with the Appalachian Trail Conference and the State of New Jersey.

After proceeding across an 850-foot-long section of boardwalk, the trail crosses a 146-foot-long suspension bridge over Pochuck Creek, completed in 1996. The walkway is 14 feet above the creek—five feet above the 100-year flood level—and the bridge was designed to permit it to withstand floods that send logs and debris down the creek. On the western side of the bridge, the trail traverses two more stretches of boardwalk—one 1,100 feet long, and the other 2,000 feet long—with a short stretch of dry land in between. Just beyond the end of the last boardwalk, at 2.3 miles, the trail reaches County 517. Parking is available along the shoulder on the east side of the road, just south of the trail crossing.

The Kittatinny Ridge

From High Point State Park south to the Delaware Water Gap, where it crosses into Pennsylvania, the A.T. follows the ridge of the Kittatinny Mountains. There are some climbs and descents, but for the most part, this 43-mile stretch of the A.T. follows a relatively level path along the ridgetop, with many viewpoints on both sides of the ridge. The Kittatinny Ridge, which is entirely protected as parkland, it is subdivided into four parks for administrative purposes. The route of the A.T. along the ridge is described in detail in chapter 11, "The Kittatinnies," with a separate section for each of the four parks which the trail passes through. The section from County 519 to Deckertown Turnpike, which traverses High Point State Park, is described on pp. 282-85. The section from Deckertown Turnpike to Brink Road, which goes through Stokes State Forest, is described on pp. 291-94. A description of the A.T. through the Delaware Water Gap National Recreation Area, from Brink Road to the Kaiser Road Trail, may be found on pp. 304-07. The southernmost section of the A.T. in New Jersey, which traverses Worthington State Forest and extends from the Kaiser Road Trail to the Dunnfield Creek parking area along I-80, is described on pp. 314-15.

HIGHLANDS TRAIL

The Highlands Trail highlights the natural beauty of the New Jersey and the New York Highlands region, and draws the public's attention to this endangered resource. It is a cooperative effort of the New York-New Jersey Trail

Conference, conservation organizations, state and local governments, and local businesses. When completed, it will extend over 150 miles from Storm King Mountain on the Hudson River in New York south to Phillipsburg, New Jersey, on the Delaware River. The route will connect major scenic attractions in both states. Ultimately, a network of trails, including alternate routes and multi-use paths, is envisioned.

The Highlands Trail is a combination of co-alignment on established trails, new trails, and road walking. The co-aligned route bears both blazes. Highlands Trail logos at critical points. Hikers must pay attention at intersections and turns, as the Highlands Trail often leaves one trail to join another. See individual trail descriptions for more details of the co-aligned trails.

Portions of the Highlands Trail traverse the Pequannock Watershed, where hiking is by permit only. For more information, or to obtain a hiking permit, contact the NWCDC, by mail at P.O. Box 319, Newfoundland, NJ 07435; or in person at their office at 223 Echo Lake Road, West Milford, NJ 07480; (973) 697-2850.

Since camping is not generally permitted along the Highlands Trail, thru-hikers should plan to stay in bed-and-breakfast facilities. Additional information about the Highlands Trail and accommodations along the trail, and a trail guide, may be obtained from the New York-New Jersey Trail Conference, 156 Ramapo Valley Road, Mahwah, NJ 07430; (201) 512-9348; www.nynjtc.org/trails.

Greenwood Lake Turnpike to Otter Hole

Length: 13.1 miles Blaze: teal diamond
For most of this section, the Highlands Trail is co-aligned with other trails that are described in detail in other chapters of this book. Reference should be made to these trail descriptions for more information on the route of the Highlands Trail.

From the intersection of Greenwood Lake Turnpike (County 511) and East Shore Road, where parking is available, the Highlands Trail heads south along the Hewitt-Butler Trail (blue). At 0.9 mile, the Hewitt-Butler Trail turns right, and the Highlands Trail continues ahead, now following the Horse Pond Mountain Trail (white). The Horse Pond Mountain Trail ends at 3.0 miles. Here, the Highlands Trail turns left and follows the Stonetown Circular Trail (red triangle on white) for 5.3 miles over Board, Bear, and Windbeam mountains. Limited parking is available at 3.6 miles at the end of Lake Riconda Road.

At 8.3 miles, the Stonetown Circular Trail crosses Stonetown Road, where limited parking is available. In 2003, from here to just below Wyanokie High Point, the proposed route of the Highlands Trail has not been completed. Hikers should turn left onto Stonetown Road, follow it for 0.2 mile, turn right onto West Brook Road for 0.5 mile, then turn left onto Snake Den Road and follow it for 0.6 mile to a large parking area for the Weis Ecology Center. Here, at 9.6 miles, the Otter Hole Trail (green) begins. Hikers should continue on this trail, which proceeds ahead along Snake Den Road, for 0.4 mile, then turn left onto the Hewitt-Butler Trail (blue).

In 0.6 mile, the Hewitt-Butler Trail reaches a junction with the Wyanokie Circular Trail (red on white). Here, 10.6 miles from Greenwood Lake Turnpike, the teal diamond blazes of the Highlands Trail resume and continue ahead along the Hewitt-Butler Trail for another 2.5 miles. The Highlands Trail follows the Hewitt-Butler Trail over Carris Hill and down to Posts Brook. At 13.1 miles, the Highlands Trail turns right, leaving the Hewitt-Butler Trail and continuing along the Otter Hole Trail (green). The Otter Hole—an attractive area of pools and cascades on Posts Brook—is a short distance ahead along the Hewitt-Butler Trail, which leads in 0.1 mile to Glenwild Avenue, where parking is available.

Otter Hole to Echo Lake Road *Length: 6.1 miles Blaze: teal diamond*
To reach this section of the Highlands Trail, follow the Hewitt-Butler Trail north for 0.1 mile from the parking area on Glenwild Road at the Bloomingdale/West Milford boundary, crossing Posts Brook at the Otter Hole. Just beyond the brook crossing, an intersection with the Highlands Trail is reached. Proceeding west, the Highlands Trail follows the Otter Hole Trail (green) for 0.4 mile and then turns left onto the Wyanokie Crest Trail (yellow), which climbs to two viewpoints on Buck Mountain.

At 0.9 mile, after following the Wyanokie Crest Trail for 0.5 mile, the Highlands Trail turns left, leaving the Wyanokie Crest Trail. It now follows its own route, marked only with teal diamond blazes. The Highlands Trail descends to reach Otter Hole Road at 1.3 miles. It turns right and follows Otter Hole Road for 0.2 mile, crossing the outlet stream connecting two lakes. At 1.5 miles, it turns left onto Crescent Road, then turns right at a T junction and follows Newton Terrace to Algonquin Way. At the end of the road, 2.0 miles from the beginning of the section, the Highlands Trail reenters the woods, briefly following a woods road.

The Highlands Trail soon turns left, leaving the woods road, and begins a gradual climb. Over the next 0.5 mile, the trail crosses and joins several woods roads. At 2.7 miles, the trail crosses a wide woods road and narrows to a footpath. It now descends, crossing a woods road at 3.0 miles. After crossing the outlet of a wetland, the trail reaches a rock outcrop with a seasonal view at 3.2 miles and begins a steep descent. It crosses a dirt road at 3.3 miles, entering the Pequannock Watershed (where hiking is by permit only), and continues through a pine forest. The Highlands Trail crosses Macopin Road diagonally to the right at 3.9 miles and continues ahead through another pine forest. After passing the ruins of an old hotel to the right at 4.5 miles, the trail descends to Echo Lake.

At 4.8 miles, the Highlands Trail reaches the shore of Echo Lake. Here, it turns left and begins to follow the Echo Lake East Trail (white) south along the lakeshore. Reaching Echo Lake Road at 5.8 miles, the Highlands Trail turns right and follows the road for 0.3 mile to the office of the Newark Watershed Conservation and Development Corporation, 1.1 miles north of NJ 23. Parking is available at the office.

Echo Lake Road to Clinton Road   *Length: 7.1 miles Blaze: teal diamond*

This entire section traverses the Pequannock Watershed, where hiking is by permit only. The eastern end of the section is at the office of the Newark Watershed Conservation and Development Corporation on Echo Lake Road, 1.1 miles north of NJ 23. Parking is available at the office. The trail heads west and descends to the Echo Lake dam, which it crosses. It then turns right and proceeds north along the western shore of the lake. Reaching the northwestern tip of the lake at 1.9 miles, the trail bears left and begins to ascend Kanouse Mountain. At 2.2 miles, it turns right and follows dirt Kanouse Road for 500 feet, then turns left and descends through hemlocks, with an understory of mountain laurel. Now leveling off, the trail crosses Gould Road at 3.2 miles, a power line at 3.8 miles, and Union Valley Road at 4.0 miles.

From Union Valley Road, the trail heads west and soon begins a

Figure 15-3. Mountain laurel

steep climb. It reaches a large rock outcrop, with east-facing views over Union Valley and Kanouse Mountain, at 4.8 miles. Here, the Highlands Trail turns right onto the Hanks East Trail (white) for 250 feet, then turns left and crosses the ridge to reach the Hanks West Trail (blue/white) at 5.0 miles. The Highlands Trail turns left and follows the Hanks West Trail for 100 feet, then turns right and steeply ascends the ridge of Bearfort Mountain to reach the Bearfort Fire Tower (manned seasonally) at 5.3 miles. The Highlands Trail turns right at a cement pillar just south of the tower. In another 50 feet, it turns left onto the Fire Tower West Trail (yellow), which it follows for 0.8 mile along the ridge of Bearfort Mountain. Then, at 6.1 miles, it turns right onto the Twin Brooks Trail (white), which it follows for 1.0 mile to parking area P4 on the east side of Clinton Road, 4.5 miles north of NJ 23.

Clinton Road to NJ 23 *Length: 6.6 miles Blaze: teal diamond*
This entire section traverses the Pequannock Watershed, where hiking is by permit only. The eastern end of the section is at parking area P4, on the east side of Clinton Road, 4.5 miles north of NJ 23. From the parking area, the Highlands Trail proceeds south on Clinton Road for 400 feet, crossing a bridge over Mossmans Brook. The Highlands Trail now turns right and joins the Clinton West Trail (white), which it follows for 3.8 miles. At 3.9 miles (0.9 mile south of the dam that separates Buckabear Pond from the Clinton Reservoir), the Highlands Trail turns right and begins to head west, crossing an area with many stone walls. At 4.2 miles, the trail crosses an old farm road between stone walls. It turns right onto Lud Day Road at 4.6 miles, briefly follows the road, then turns left and begins to ascend, with a pine forest to the left. Reaching the crest of the rise at 4.8 miles, the trail begins to descend. At the base of the descent, at 5.0 miles, it turns left, joins a woods road for 150 feet, then turns right onto a footpath. Now continuing to descend, the trail goes through a hemlock grove at 5.4 miles and soon reaches Dunker Pond. It turns left to parallel the narrow, rocky gorge of the outlet stream that drains the pond, then turns right and crosses the stream. It turns right onto a woods road, climbs to the crest of a rise, then descends to reach Canistear Road at 6.6 miles. Here, the trail turns left and proceeds through a one-lane stone underpass beneath the tracks of the New York, Susquehanna and Western Railroad to reach a parking area on the east side of the road, just north of NJ 23.

NJ 23 to Weldon Road   *Length: 11.4 miles Blaze: teal diamond*

To reach this section of the Highlands Trail from I-287, take Exit 52 and proceed west on NJ 23 towards Butler. The northern end of this section is at the intersection of NJ 23 and Canistear Road, 13.1 miles west of I-287, where parking is available. To reach the southern end of the section, continue west on NJ 23 for another 1.5 miles to Holland Mountain Road (reached shortly after NJ 23 becomes a non-divided highway). Turn left and follow Holland Mountain Road south for 3.7 miles to Ridge Road. Turn left onto Ridge Road for only 0.2 mile, then turn right onto Russia Road. Follow Russia Road for 1.4 miles and turn right onto Weldon Road. The southern end of the section is at the picnic parking area for Mahlon Dickerson Reservation, 1.9 miles south of Russia Road, on the right side of the road. (The southern end of this section can also be reached from I-80 and NJ 15; see directions in the next section, below.)

This section of the Highlands Trail is remarkably free from visible intrusions of civilization. From the parking area on Canistear Road just north of NJ 23, the Highlands Trail crosses to the south side of NJ 23, turns left, and heads east along the road shoulder. At 0.3 mile, immediately after NJ 23 crosses a bridge over the Pequannock River, the trail turns right, leaving the road, and enters the woods on a footpath. For the next 4.7 miles, the trail traverses the Pequannock Watershed, where hiking is by permit only.

The trail heads steadily uphill through an open deciduous forest until it gains the crest of the ridge at 0.7 mile. It levels off and follows the ridge, crossing two stone walls. After a short climb, it reaches a rock ledge—with views through the trees to the left over the Oak Ridge Reservoir—at 1.8 miles. The trail descends steadily from the ridge, reaching a woods road at 2.3 miles. It turns right, follows the road for 250 feet, then turns right, leaving the road. The trail soon begins to climb Green Pond Ridge, steeply in places, crossing several woods roads on the way. There are limited views from the rocky summit, reached at 2.7 miles.

Now descending, the trail traverses a mixed pine-and-deciduous forest and crosses several woods roads. At the base of the descent, at 3.1 miles, the trail turns left onto a woods road, crosses a stream, then turns right and climbs another hill. From the top of the hill, it descends gradually, reaching paved Holland Mountain Road at 3.8 miles.

The Highlands Trail turns right, follows the road for 150 feet, then turns left and reenters the woods. It soon turns right onto a narrow dirt road, which

it follows for 0.2 mile. Watch carefully for a double blaze, marking the point where the trail turns left, leaving the dirt road. The trail descends to cross a stream and turns left onto a graded path, which it follows across a second stream. Just beyond the second stream crossing, the trail turns right, leaving the graded path, and climbs through the woods to cross paved Rock Lodge Road at 4.6 miles.

The trail now ascends gradually on a footpath. After passing two large glacial erratics to the right at 4.8 miles, the trail reaches the crest of the rise and begins to descend. It turns left onto a woods road and again reaches Rock Lodge Road at 5.0 miles, leaving the Pequannock Watershed. The trail now turns right and follows the paved road to an intersection at 5.2 miles. Here, the trail bears left, continuing to follow Rock Lodge Road, as Fall Drive continues straight ahead. At 5.3 miles, the paved road ends at a turnaround.

The Highlands Trail continues ahead, now following a woods road (the extension of Rock Lodge Road). The trail continues along the unpaved road, which may be rutted and muddy in places, for the next 1.2 miles. In the summer of 2003, this section of the trail was poorly blazed, and some blazes on the right side of the road were blacked out. At intersections, follow the main road that proceeds straight ahead.

At 6.5 miles—after the road begins to descend, and before reaching a large wetland—the Highlands Trail turns left, leaving Rock Lodge Road, and enters property of the New Jersey Audubon Society. For the next 1.3 miles, the trail is sometimes blazed with the "bird symbol" blazes of the Audubon Society. The trail briefly follows a woods road, then continues on a footpath that gradually widens to a woods road. It passes an interesting rock ledge to the right at 6.9 miles and descends, soon beginning to parallel scenic Ryker Lake, visible through the trees to the right. Side trails to the right lead to points along the lake shore. At the far end of the lake, at 7.3 miles, the trail bears left, leaving the woods road. Just ahead, it turns left at a T intersection and descends to a Y intersection, where it bears right.

The Highlands Trail reaches a wide woods road at 7.8 miles. Take care to follow the teal diamond blazes (which cross the road and continue ahead through the woods), as the "bird symbol" Audubon Society blazes turn left onto the woods road. Just beyond, the Highlands Trail crosses Russia Brook on rocks. This crossing may be difficult at times of high water, but there is an old bridge well downstream to the left. Just beyond, at 7.9 miles, the trail crosses paved Ridge Road and then goes under a power line.

The trail now begins to traverse the property of the Missionary Society of St. Paul the Apostle (Paulist Fathers). It gradually climbs a hill, then descends rather steeply to a col, where it turns right and briefly follows a faint woods road. Leaving the road to the left, it steeply climbs a second hill, then descends to reach a woods road at 9.1 miles. It turns right onto the woods road and almost immediately bears left at a Y intersection onto another woods road. After crossing a stream, the trail bears right at a fork at 9.3 miles, continuing to ascend on a woods road. Then, at 9.6 miles, the Highlands Trail turns left, leaving the woods road. After a brief but steep descent over rock ledges, the trail reaches Sparta Mountain Road, where limited parking is available, at 10.0 miles.

The trail crosses the road, entering Mahlon Dickerson Reservation, and turns left to join the Pine Swamp Loop Trail (white). It follows the Pine Swamp Loop Trail for 1.2 miles, then turns left and proceeds for 0.2 mile to the picnic parking area, reached at 11.4 miles.

Weldon Road to NJ 15 *Length: 4.3 miles Blaze: teal diamond*
There are three points of access to this section of the Highlands Trail, all of which may be reached from Weldon Road. To reach this section from I-80, take Exit 34B, proceed north on NJ 15 for 5.0 miles to the Weldon Road (Milton/Oak Ridge) exit, and follow Weldon Road north. Winona Trail (an unpaved road), which leads left to the southern end of the section, is on the left, 2.3 miles north of NJ 15 (no parking is available). The Saffin Pond parking area, from where an 0.3-mile side trail (blazed with small black diamonds on teal diamonds) leads to the Highlands Trail, is on the right side of the road, 3.0 miles north of NJ 15. The picnic parking area at the northern end of the section is 4.3 miles north of NJ 15, on the left side of the road.

The northern 2.9 miles of this section (from the picnic parking area to the junction with the 0.3-mile side trail leading to the Saffin Pond parking area) is described in the Mahlon Dickerson Reservation section of chapter 10, "Morris County," pp. 253-54. From this junction, the Highlands Trail bears left and follows along the southern end of Saffin Pond. At the southwest corner of the pond, it turns left onto the railbed of the abandoned Ogden Mine Railroad. The Highlands Trail turns right and leaves the railbed at 3.3 miles (from the picnic parking area), immediately crossing Weldon Road. After passing a gate, the trail turns right onto a woods road. At 3.8 miles, it crosses a power line right-of-way, where it bears left to re-enter the woods. After approaching NJ

15, the trail turns away from it, recrosses under the power line, and reaches Winona Trail (an unpaved road) at 4.3 miles. In 2003, there is a gap in the Highlands Trail west of here. To the left, Winona Trail may be followed back to Weldon Road.

NJ 15 to US 46   *Blaze: teal diamond*

In 2003, only isolated sections of the Highlands Trail have been completed between NJ 15 and US 46. A 3.7-mile section extends from NJ 181, about three miles south of Sparta, to Bear Pond. Another 2.0-mile section parallels the massive "Cut-Off" of the Delaware, Lackawanna and Western Railroad from Lake Drive to Mansfield Drive in Byram Township. A 4.4-mile section of the Highlands Trail from US 206 to Waterloo Road, which traverses Allamuchy Mountain State Park, is described in chapter 11, "The Kittatinnies," pp. 330-32.

The 4.2-mile section from Waterloo Road, 0.6 mile east of the I-80 overpass, to the intersection of Waterloo Road and Waterloo Valley Road has not been completed as of fall 2003. This section of the Highlands Trail will follow the towpath of the Morris Canal, which is being restored by the Canal Society of New Jersey. As of fall 2003, only an 0.7-mile segment of this section of the Highlands Trail is open and blazed.

Figure 15-4. Limestone kiln

From the intersection of Waterloo Road and Waterloo Valley Road, the Highlands Trail follows Waterloo Valley Road for 0.1 mile, then turns right into Stephens State Park. It follows the gated park road for 0.4 mile to the park office, passing the stone ruins of an historic limestone kiln to the left of the office. A 2.4-mile blazed section of the Highlands Trail begins here. The Highlands Trail heads south through a picnic area to parallel the Musconetcong River for about 0.5 mile. It bears left at a fork, climbs a hill, and descends to cross unpaved Mine Hill Road at 1.3 miles. Here, the trail enters the property of the Hackettstown Municipal Utilities Authority. After crossing another dirt road and passing under a power line, the

trail continues through a stand of straight, evenly-spaced evergreens and descends to cross a stream at 1.9 miles. The trail climbs on an old woods road, turns left, then turns right and descends to reach US 46 at 2.4 miles. A shopping center, where parking may be available, is 0.3 mile to the east along US 46, at its intersection with Naughright Road (2.7 miles east of the intersection of Willow Grove Road and US 46 in Hackettstown).

In 2003, there is a long gap in the Highlands Trail between US 46 and Long Valley. For more detailed information about the various sections of the Highlands Trail from NJ 15 to US 46, consult the trail guide to the Highlands Trail, available from the New York-New Jersey Trail Conference.

Long Valley to Van Syckels Road   *Length: 15.5 miles Blaze: teal diamond*
From Schooley's Mountain Road (County 517) in Long Valley, the Highlands Trail proceeds south for 9.0 miles on the Columbia Trail (for a description of this trail, see chapter 12, "Central Jersey," pp. 343-45). After crossing the South Branch of the Raritan River on a former railroad trestle in Ken Lockwood Gorge, the Highlands Trail turns right, leaving the Columbia Trail, and ascends the west side of the gorge on switchbacks. After briefly joining a woods road at 9.4 miles, the trail turns left onto a dirt road, which it follows to County 513 at 9.8 miles. The Highlands Trail turns left and follows County 513 to the entrance to Voorhees State Park, where parking is available. Here, at 10.4 miles, the trail turns right and continues along the park entrance road. It turns left, leaving the park road, at 10.9 miles, crosses a wooden bridge, and continues on the Brookside Trail. After crossing under a power line at 11.9 miles, the trail reaches Observatory Road, where parking is available, at 12.1 miles.

The Highlands Trail turns right, follows Observatory Road for 0.3 mile, then turns sharply left onto Buffalo Hollow Road. At 13.1 miles, the trail turns left onto NJ 31. Then, at 13.3 miles, it turns right onto Van Syckels Road. It follows Van Syckels Road for 0.1 mile to the entrance to Union Furnace Nature Preserve, where parking is available. Here, the trail turns right, ascends the embankment of an old mill race, climbs to the top of a hill, then descends to emerge on Serpentine Drive at 14.3 miles. The Highlands Trail follows Serpentine Drive down to Van Syckels Road, reached at 14.6 miles. It briefly turns right onto Van Syckels Road, then turns left and enters the Spruce Run Recreation Area. After crossing a park road near a boat launch area at 15.1 miles, the trail loops back to again reach Van Syckels Road at 15.5 miles.

Figure 15-5. Delaware Water Gap

Van Syckels Road to Delaware River   *Blaze: teal diamond*

In 2003, only two isolated sections of the trail have been completed beyond Van Syckels Road. A 1.4-mile section follows woods roads north from Van Syckels Road to Black Brook Road (which can be followed north to Polktown Road). Another 1.4-mile section of the trail has been blazed through the Musconetcong Gorge section of the Musconetcong River Reservation (see chapter 12, "Central Jersey," p. 356). For more detailed information about this portion of the Highlands Trail, consult the trail guide to the Highlands Trail, available from the New York-New Jersey Trail Conference.

LIBERTY-WATER GAP TRAIL

The Liberty-Water Gap Trail will, when completed, extend from Liberty State Park in Jersey City across five New Jersey counties to the Delaware Water Gap. For most of its route, it will follow four major trails that are described elsewhere in this book—the Lenape Trail, the Patriots' Path, the Sussex Branch Trail, and the Paulinskill Valley Trail. As of 2003, none of the trail has been marked on the ground. For more information, call (212) 360-3327, or visit the trail's web site, www.libertygap.org.

FURTHER READING

Backcountry Ethics

Hampton, Bruce, David Cole, and National Outdoor Leadership School Staff. *NOLS Soft Paths : How to Enjoy the Wilderness without Harming It.* 3rd ed. Mechanicsburg, PA: Stackpole Books, 2003.

Harmon, Will. *Leave No Trace: Minimum Impact Outdoor Recreation: The Official Manual of the American Hiking Society.* Helena, MT: Falcon, 1997.

Hodgson, Michael. *The Basic Essentials of Minimizing Impact on the Wilderness.* Guilford, CT: Globe Pequot Press, 1998.

Waterman, Laura, and Guy Waterman. *Backwoods Ethics: Environmental Issues for Hikers and Campers.* 2nd ed. Woodstock, VT: Countryman Press, 1993.

Waterman, Laura, and Guy Waterman. *Wilderness Ethics: Preserving the Spirit of Wildness.* 2nd ed. Woodstock, VT: Countryman Press, 2000.

Flora and Fauna

Barbour, Anita, and Spider Barbour. *Wild Flora of the Northeast.* New York: Overlook Press, 1991.

Boyd, Howard P. *A Field Guide to the Pine Barrens of New Jersey: Its Flora, Fauna, Ecology, and Historic Sites.* Medford, NJ: Plexus Publishing, 1991.

Boyle, William J. *A Guide to Bird Finding in New Jersey.* Rev. ed. New Brunswick, NJ: Rutgers University Press, 2002.

Cobb, Boughton. *A Field Guide to Ferns and Their Related Families: Northeastern and Central North America.* Boston: Houghton Mifflin, 1984.

Conant, Roger. *A Field Guide to Reptiles and Amphibians: Eastern and Central North America.* 3rd ed. Boston: Houghton Mifflin, 1999.

Eastman, John, and Amelia Hansen. *The Book of Forest and Thicket: Trees, Shrubs, and Wildflowers of Eastern North America.* Harrisburg, PA: Stackpole Books, 1992.

Eastman, John, and Amelia Hansen. *The Book of Swamp and Bog: Trees, Shrubs, and Wildflowers of Eastern Freshwater Wetlands.* Harrisburg, PA: Stackpole Books, 1994.

Fadala, Sam. *Basic Projects in Wildlife Watching: Learn More About Wild Birds and Animals through Your Own First-Hand Experience*. Harrisburg, PA: Stackpole Books, 1989.

Forrest, Louise Richardson, and Denise Casey. *Field Guide to Tracking Animals in Snow*. Harrisburg, PA: Stackpole Books, 1988.

Held, Patricia Contreras. *A Field Guide to New Jersey Nature Centers*. New Brunswick, NJ: Rutgers University Press, 1988.

Krieger, Louis C. *The Mushroom Handbook*. New York: Dover Publications, 1967.

Miller, Dorcas S. *Berry Finder: A Guide to Native Plants with Fleshy Fruits for Eastern North America*. Berkeley, CA: Nature Study Guild, 1986.

Murie, Olaus Johan. *A Field Guide to Animal Tracks*. 2nd ed. Boston: Houghton Mifflin, 1982.

Peterson, Roger Tory. *A Field Guide to the Birds: A Completely New Guide to All the Birds of Eastern and Central North America*. 4th ed. Boston: Houghton Mifflin, 1998.

Petrides, George A., and Janet Wehr. *A Field Guide to Eastern Trees: Eastern United States and Canada, Including the Midwest*. 2nd ed. Boston: Houghton Mifflin, 1998.

Pettigrew, Laurie. *New Jersey Wildlife Viewing Guide*. Helena, MT: Falcon, 1998.

Robichaud, Beryl, and Karl Anderson. *Plant Communities of New Jersey: A Study in Landscape Diversity*. New Brunswick, NJ: Rutgers University Press, 1994.

Sibley, David A. *The Sibley Guide to Birds*. New York: Knopf, 2000.

Sibley, David A. *The Sibley Field Guide to Birds of Eastern North America*. New York: Knopf, 2003.

Stanne, Stephen P., Roger G. Panetta, and Brian E. Forist. *The Hudson: An Illustrated Guide to the Living River*. New Brunswick, NJ: Rutgers University Press, 1996.

Sutton, Ann, and Myron Sutton. *Eastern Forests*. New York: Knopf, 1985.

Tekiela, Stan. *Birds of New Jersey: A Field Guide*. Cambridge, MN: Adventure Publications, 2000.

Tiner, Ralph W. *In Search of Swampland: A Wetland Sourcebook and Field Guide*. New Brunswick, NJ: Rutgers University Press, 1998.

Food

Angier, Bradford. *Field Guide to Edible Wild Plants*. Harrisburg, PA: Stackpole Books, 1974.

Conners, Tim, and Christine Conners. *Lipsmackin' Backpackin': Lightweight, Trail-Tested Recipes for Backcountry Trips*. Helena, MT: Three Forks, 2000.

Conners, Tim, and Christine Conners. *Lipsmackin' Vegetarian Backpackin'*. Guilford, CT: Three Forks, 2004.

Fleming, June. *The Well-Fed Backpacker*. 3rd ed. New York: Vintage Books, 1986.

Gray, Melissa, and Buck Tilton. *Cooking the One-Burner Way: Gourmet Cuisine for the Backcountry Chef*. 2nd ed. Guilford, CT: Globe Pequot Press, 2000.

Jacobson, Cliff. *Basic Essentials: Cooking in the Outdoors*. 2nd ed. Old Saybrook, CT: Globe Pequot Press, 1999.

McHugh, Gretchen. *The Hungry Hiker's Book of Good Cooking*. New York: Knopf, 1982.

Pearson, Claudia, ed. *NOLS Cookery*. 4th ed. Mechanicsburg, PA: Stackpole Books, 1997.

Prater, Yvonne, and Ruth Mendenhall. *Gorp, Glop and Glue Stew: Favorite Foods from 165 Outdoor Experts*. Seattle, WA: The Mountaineers, 1982.

Geology

American Association of Petroleum Geologists. "Geological Highway Map of the Northeastern Region." Tulsa, OK: American Association of Petroleum Geologists, 1995.

Bates, Robert Latimer, and Julia A. Jackson, eds. *Dictionary of Geological Terms*. 3rd ed. Garden City, NY: Anchor Press/Doubleday, 1984.

Chew, V. Collins. *Underfoot: A Geologic Guide to the Appalachian Trail*. 2nd ed. Harpers Ferry, WV: Appalachian Trail Conference, 1993.

McPhee, John. *In Suspect Terrain*. New York: Farrar, Straus and Giroux, 1984.

Raymo, Chet, and Maureen E. Raymo. *Written in Stone: A Geological History of the Northeastern United States*. 2nd ed. Hensonville, NY: Black Dome Press, 2001.

Widmer, Kemble. *The Geology and Geography of New Jersey*. Princeton, NJ: Van Nostrand, 1964.

Wolfe, Peter Edward. *The Geology and Landscapes of New Jersey*. New York: Crane, Russak, 1977.

Wyckoff, Jerome. *Reading the Earth: Landforms in the Making*. Mahwah, NJ: Adastra West, 1999.

Health and Safety

Allen, Dan H. *Don't Die on the Mountain*. 2nd ed. New London, NH: Diapensia Press, 1998.

Auerbach, Paul S., Christine Gralapp, and Alexandrine Bartlett. *Medicine for the Outdoors: The Essential Guide to Emergency Medical Procedures and First Aid*. 4th ed. New York: Lyons Press, 2003.

Bane, Michael. *Trail Safe: Averting Threatening Human Behavior in the Outdoors*. Berkeley, CA: Wilderness Press, 2000.

Forgey, William W. *Basic Essentials: Wilderness First Aid*. 2nd ed. Old Saybrook, CT: Globe Pequot Press, 2000.

Forgey, William W. *Wilderness Medicine: Beyond First Aid*. 5th ed. Guilford, CT: Globe Pequot Press, 1999.

Rosen, Albert P. *Health Hints for Hikers*. New York: New York-New Jersey Trail Conference, 1994.

Wilkerson, James A. *Medicine for Mountaineering and Other Wilderness Activities*. 5th ed. Seattle, WA: The Mountaineers, 2001.

Hiking and Camping

The Ten Essentials for Travel in the Outdoors. Seattle, WA: The Mountaineers, 1993.

Angier, Bradford. *How to Stay Alive in the Woods: A Complete Guide to Food, Shelter, and Self-Preservation—Anywhere*. 2nd ed. New York: Black Dog & Leventhal, 2001.

Berger, Karen. *Everyday Wisdom: 1001 Expert Tips for Hikers*. Seattle, WA: The Mountaineers, 1997.

Berger, Karen. *Hiking and Backpacking: A Complete Guide*. Rev. ed. New York: W.W. Norton, 2002.

Berger, Karen. *More Everyday Wisdom*. Seattle, WA: The Mountaineers, 2002.

Churchill, James E. *Basic Essentials: Survival*. 2nd ed. Old Saybrook, CT: Globe Pequot Press, 1999.

Evans, Jeremy. *Camping and Survival*. New York: Crestwood House, 1992.

Fletcher, Colin, and C.L. Rawlins. *The Complete Walker IV.* 4th ed. New York: Knopf, 2002.

Frazine, Richard Keith. *The Barefoot Hiker: A Book About Bare Feet.* Berkeley, CA: Ten Speed Press, 1993.

Getchell, Annie, Dave Getchell, Jon Eaton, and Joanne Allen. *The Essential Outdoor Gear Manual: Equipment Care, Repair, and Selection.* 2nd ed. Camden, ME: Ragged Mountain Press, 2000.

Goll, John, and Harry Roberts. *The Camper's Pocket Handbook: A Backcountry Traveler's Companion.* 2nd ed. Old Saybrook, CT: Globe Pequot Press, 1998.

Hollomon, Kurt D., Greg Eiden, and Cat Arnes. *On Foot: A Journal for Walkers, Hikers and Trekkers.* San Francisco: Chronicle Books, 1999.

Howe, Steve. *Making Camp: The Complete Guide for Hikers, Mountain Bikers, Paddlers and Skiers.* Seattle, WA: The Mountaineers, 1997.

Jacobson, Cliff. *The Basic Essentials of Trailside Shelters and Emergency Shelters.* Merrillville, IN: ICS Books, 1992.

Jacobson, Cliff. *Basic Essentials: Camping.* 2nd ed. Guilford, CT: Globe Pequot Press, 1999.

Logue, Victoria. *Backpacking: Essential Skills to Advanced Techniques.* Birmingham, AL: Menasha Ridge Press, 2000.

Meyer, Kathleen. *How to Shit in the Woods: An Environmentally Sound Approach to a Lost Art.* 2nd ed. Berkeley, CA: Ten Speed Press, 1994.

Moser, David S., and Jerry Schad, eds. *Wilderness Basics: The Complete Handbook for Hikers and Backpackers.* Seattle, WA: The Mountaineers, 1993.

Roberts, Harry, and Adrienne Hall. *Basic Essentials: Backpacking.* 2nd ed. Old Saybrook, CT: Globe Pequot Press, 1999.

Ross, Cindy, and Todd Gladfelter. *A Hiker's Companion: 12,000 Miles of Trail-Tested Wisdom.* Seattle, WA: The Mountaineers, 1993.

Seaborg, Eric, and Ellen Dudley. *Hiking and Backpacking.* Champaign, IL: Human Kinetics, 1994.

Sumner, Louise Lindgren. *Sew and Repair Your Outdoor Gear.* Seattle, WA: The Mountaineers, 1988.

Townsend, Chris. *The Backpacker's Handbook.* 2nd ed. Camden, ME: Ragged Mountain Press, 1997.

Wood, Robert S. *Dayhiker: Walking for Fitness, Fun, and Adventure.* Berkeley, CA: Ten Speed Press, 1991.

Hiking and Camping – Children

Cary, Alice. *Parents' Guide to Hiking and Camping: A Trailside Guide.* New York: W.W. Norton, 1997.

Euser, Barbara J. *Take 'Em Along: Sharing the Wilderness with Your Children.* Evergreen, CO: Cordillera Press, 1987.

Foster, Lynne, and Martha Weston. *Take a Hike!: The Sierra Club Kid's Guide to Hiking and Backpacking.* Boston: Little, Brown, 1991.

Silverman, Goldie. *Backpacking with Babies and Small Children: A Guide to Taking the Kids Along on Day Hikes, Overnighters, and Long Trail Trips.* 3rd ed. Berkeley, CA: Wilderness Press, 1998.

Sisson, Edith A. *Nature with Children of All Ages: Activities and Adventures for Exploring, Learning and Enjoying the World around Us.* Englewood Cliffs, NJ: Prentice-Hall, 1982.

Hiking and Camping – Map and Compass

Barnes, Scottie, Cliff Jacobson, and James E. Churchill. *The Ultimate Guide to Wilderness Navigation: How to Use Global Positioning Systems; How to Find Your Way with Map and Compass; How to Survive in the Backcountry.* Guilford, CT: Globe Pequot Press, 2002.

Burns, Bob, and Mike Burns. *Wilderness Navigation: Finding Your Way Using Maps, Compass, Altimeter, and GPS.* Seattle, WA: The Mountaineers, 1999.

Fleming, June. *Staying Found: The Complete Map and Compass Handbook.* 3rd ed. Seattle, WA: The Mountaineers, 2001.

Jacobson, Cliff. *Basic Essentials: Map and Compass.* 2nd ed. Old Saybrook, CT: Globe Pequot Press, 1999.

Kjellström, Björn. *Be Expert with Map and Compass: The Complete Orienteering Handbook.* 2nd ed. New York: Collier, 1994.

Randall, Glenn. *The Outward Bound Map and Compass Handbook.* 2nd ed. New York: Lyons Press, 1998.

Hiking and Camping – Winter

Conover, Garrett, and Alexandra Conover. *A Snow Walker's Companion: Winter Trail Skills from the Far North.* Camden, ME: Ragged Mountain Press, 1995.

Dunn, John M. *Winterwise: A Backpacker's Guide.* 2nd ed. Lake George, NY: Adirondack Mountain Club, 1996.

Gorman, Stephen. *Winter Camping*. 2nd ed. Boston: Appalachian Mountain Club, 1999.

Prater, Gene, and Dave Felkley. *Snowshoeing*. 5th ed. Seattle, WA: The Mountaineers, 2002.

Weiss, Hal. *Secrets of Warmth: For Comfort or Survival*. 2nd ed. Seattle, WA: The Mountaineers, 1998.

History

Albert, Richard C. *Damming the Delaware: The Rise and Fall of Tocks Island Dam*. University Park, PA: Pennsylvania State University Press, 1987.

Binnewies, Robert O. *Palisades: 100,000 Acres in 100 Years*. New York: Fordham University Press, 2001.

Carmer, Carl. *The Hudson*. 50th Anniversary ed. New York: Fordham University Press, 1989.

Cavanaugh, Cam. *Saving the Great Swamp: The People, the Power Brokers, and an Urban Wilderness*. Frenchtown, NJ: Columbia Publishing Company, 1978.

Cohen, David S. *The Ramapo Mountain People*. New Brunswick, NJ: Rutgers University Press, 1989.

Cottrell, Alden T. *The Story of Ringwood Manor*. 8th ed. Trenton, NJ: New Jersey Department of Conservation and Economic Development, 1969.

Garvey, Edward B. *Appalachian Hiker II*. Rev. ed. Oakton, VA: Appalachian Books, 1978.

Mack, Arthur C. *The Palisades of the Hudson: Their Formation, Tradition, Romance, Historical Associations, Natural Wonders and Preservation*. New York: Walking News, 1909, reprinted 1982.

McPhee, John. *The Pine Barrens*. New York: Farrar, Strauss and Giroux, 1978.

Ransom, James M. *Vanishing Ironworks of the Ramapos*. New Brunswick, NJ: Rutgers University Press, 1966.

Serrao, John. *The Wild Palisades of the Hudson*. Westwood, NJ: Lind Publications, 1986.

Thomas, Lester S. *The Pine Barrens of New Jersey*. Trenton, NJ: Department of Environmental Protection, 1985.

Wilson, Harold F. *The Story of the Jersey Shore*. Princeton, NJ: Van Nostrand, 1964.

Trail Guides

Chazin, Daniel D. *Appalachian Trail Data Book, 2004.* 26th ed. Harpers Ferry, WV: Appalachian Trail Conference, 2003.

Dann, Kevin T. *30 Walks in New Jersey.* Rev. and Expanded ed. New Brunswick, NJ: Rutgers University Press, 1992.

Della Penna, Craig P. *24 Great Rail-Trails of New Jersey.* Amherst, MA: New England Cartographics, 1999.

Lenik, Edward J. *Iron Mine Trails.* New York: New York-New Jersey Trail Conference, 1996.

New York-New Jersey Trail Conference. *Day Walker: 32 Hikes in the New York Metropolitan Area.* 2nd ed. New York: New York-New Jersey Trail Conference, 2001.

New York-New Jersey Trail Conference. *New York Walk Book.* 7th ed. Mahwah, NJ: New York-New Jersey Trail Conference, 2001.

New York-New Jersey Trail Conference. *The Long Path Guide.* 5th ed. Mahwah, NJ: New York-New Jersey Trail Conference, 2002.

New York-New Jersey Trail Conference. *Appalachian Trail Guide to New York-New Jersey.* 15th ed. Harpers Ferry, WV: Appalachian Trail Conference, 2002.

Robinson, Patricia. *Wonderwalks: The Trails of New Jersey Audubon.* Medford, NJ: Plexus Publishing, 2003.

Rosenfeld, Lucy D., and Marina Harrison. *A Guide to Green New Jersey: Nature Walks in the Garden State.* New Brunswick, NJ: Rutgers University Press, 2003.

Scherer, Glenn. *Nature Walks in New Jersey: AMC Guide to the Best Trails from the Highlands to Cape May.* 2nd ed. Boston: Appalachian Mountain Club, 2003.

Scofield, Bruce, Stella J. Green, and H. Neil Zimmerman. *50 Hikes in New Jersey: Walks, Hikes, and Backpacking Trips from the Kittatinnies into Cape May.* 2nd ed. Woodstock, VT: Backcountry Publications, 1997.

Scofield, Bruce. *Circuit Hikes in Northern New Jersey.* 5th ed. Mahwah, NJ: New York-New Jersey Trail Conference, 2003.

Zatz, Arline, and Joel Zatz. *Best Hikes with Children in New Jersey.* Seattle, WA: The Mountaineers, 1992.

INDEX

Page numbers in **bold** refer to trail descriptions.
Page numbers in *italics* refer to illustrations.

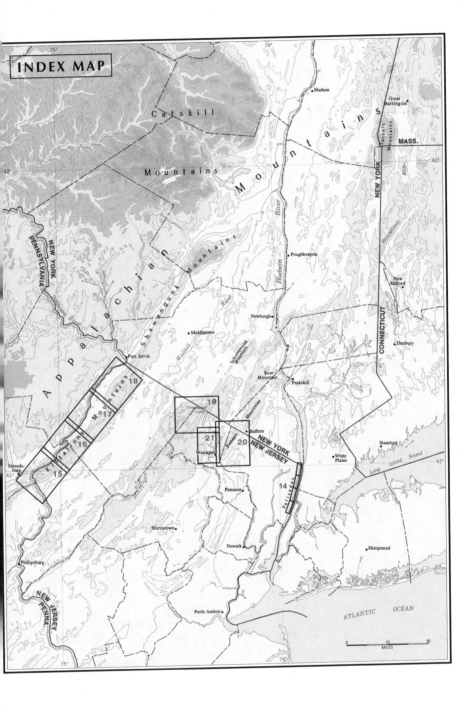

INDEX MAP

LEGEND

───────── Marked Trail

(B) Blue (BL) Black (BR) Brown (G) Green

(W) White (Y) Yellow (R) Red (O) Orange

─ ─ ─ ─ ─ Unmarked Trail or Woods Road

━━ ─ ─ ━━ State Boundary

━━ ─ ━━ County Boundary

═══════ Highway

━━━━━━━ Main Road

─────── Secondary Road

P　Parking

KO　Keep Out

★　Viewpoint

S　Shelter

◉　Tower

⚒　Mine

✕　Quarry or Pit

•　Spring or Well

⩫　Marsh

•*1423*　Spot Height in Feet
(contours every 100 feet, except in the Catskills)

+―+―+―+ Railroad

+ + + + Abandoned Railroad

─ · ─── ·── Powerline

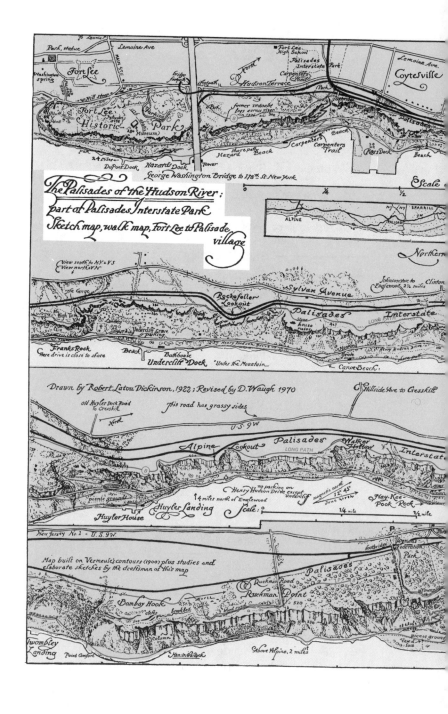

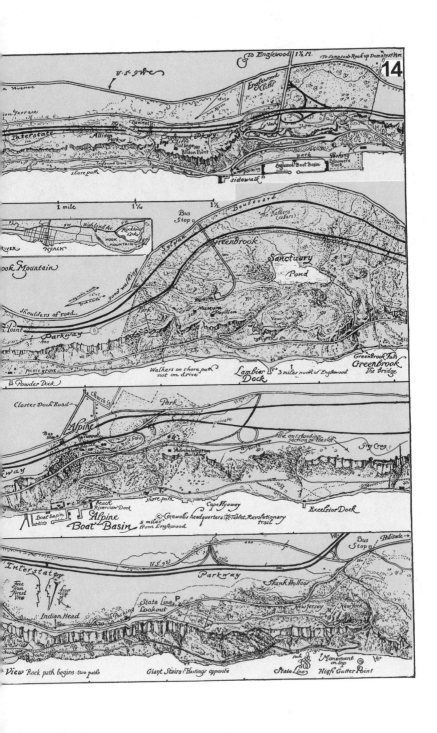

To Englewood 1¾ M.   To Sunnyside Rock up Dyckes ... Ave

U. S. 9 W

Englewood Cliffs

Allison Park   Englewood Pkwy.
Interstate   Cottage   path   Parking   Bloomers Dock
Tunnel   Allison Point   Dock
shore path   parking   Englewood Boat Basin
sidewalk

1 mile   1¼   1½   Boulevard   The Nellers (cedars)
Bus Stop   Greenbrook
Highland Av.   Rockland Lake   Sylvan
RIVER   NYACK   HOOK MOUNTAIN   Sanctuary   Pond
... Mountain   pond walk up
magnetic north   true north   Museum   Pavilion
shoulders of road
... Point   Parkway   in park   Greenbrook fish
Picnic grove   Walkers on shore path   Greenbrook
Powder Dock   not on drive   Lambier   3 miles north of Englewood   The bridge
Dock

Closter Dock Road   Church St.   Park   private
Alpine   Tunnel   Administration   The outstanding section of the cliff   Grey Crag
Bus Stop   Building   North
...way
Beach   shore path   Cape Flyaway   Excelsior Dock
Boat basin   Riverview Dock   Cornwallis headquarters, Tablet. Revolutionary
Alpine   5 miles   trail
Boat Basin   from Englewood

Palisade
Bus Stop
Interstate   U. S. 9 W   Parkway   Skunk Hollow   New York
View from Forest View   State Line   New Jersey
Indian Head   Lookout   Parking   State Line   Monument on top
View Rock path begins two p...   Giant Stairs: Hastings opposite   State Line   High Gutter Point

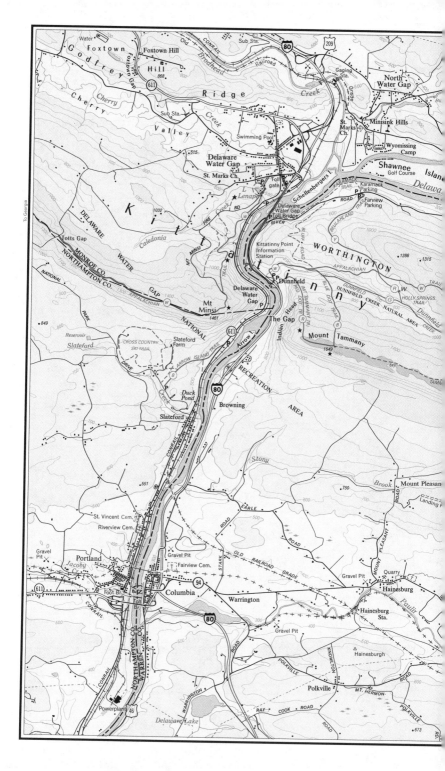

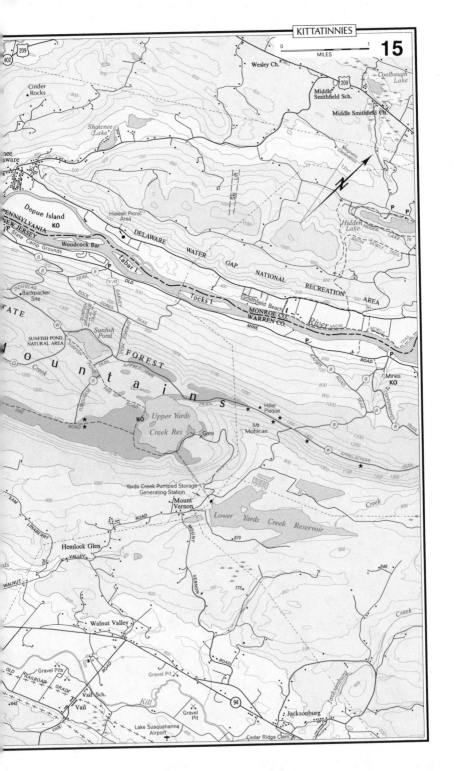

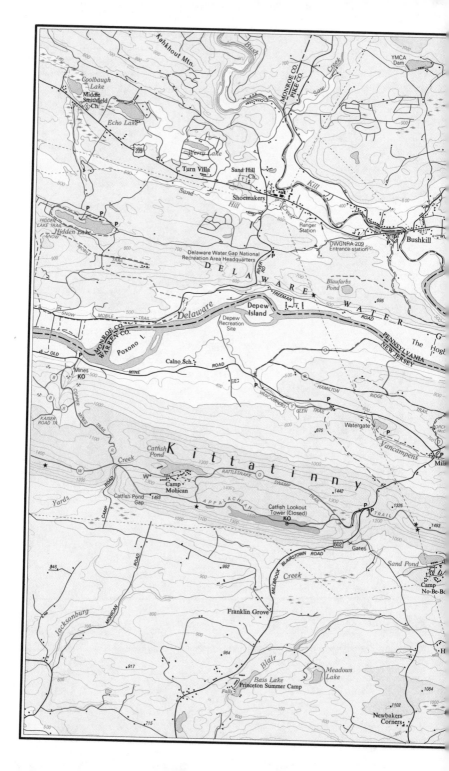

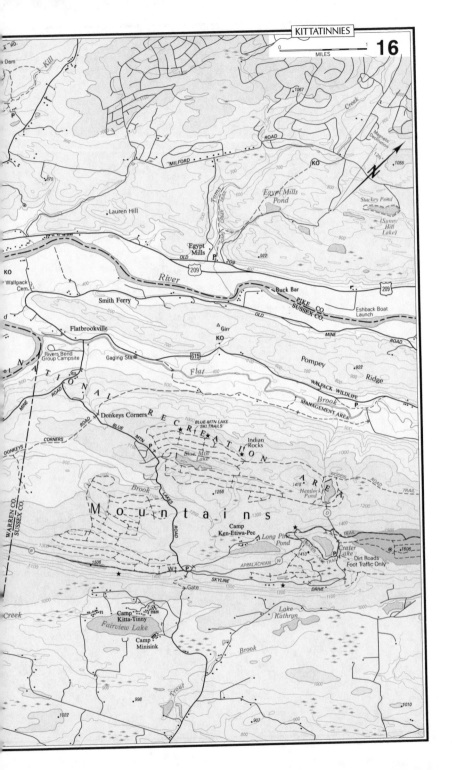

MILES

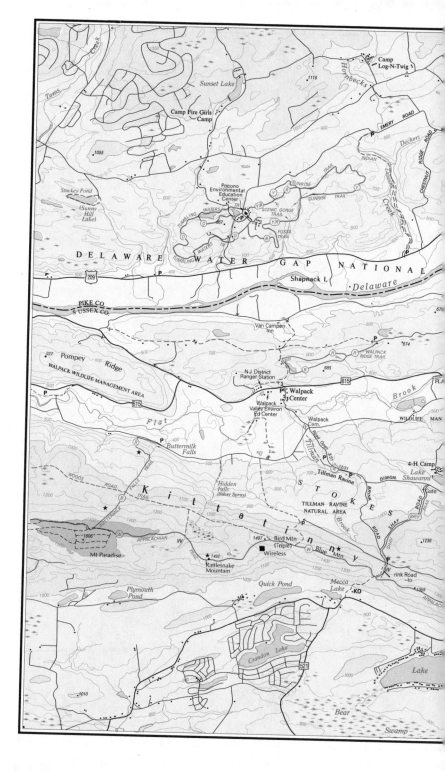

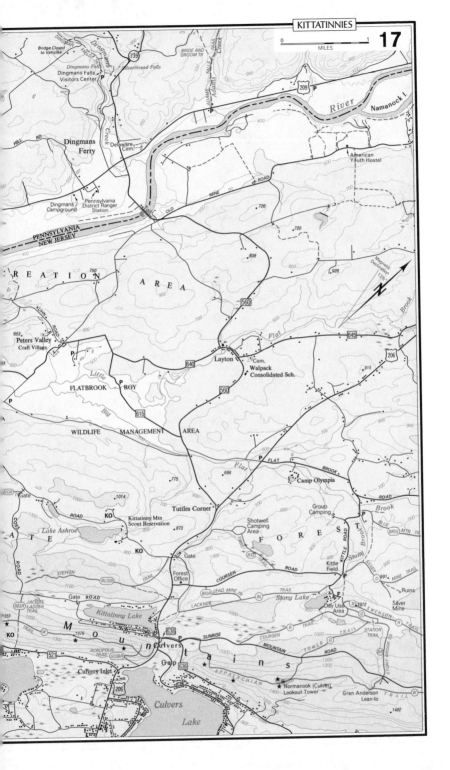

0   MILES   1

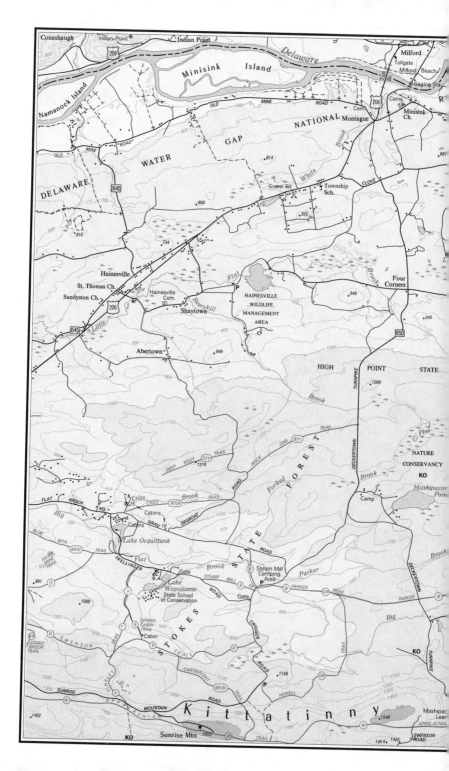

0
MILES

AREA

Quicks I.

Mashipacong Island

H.Y.
6
209

Delaware
Valley
High School

1095

690

84

GAR

PIKE CO.
SUSSEX CO.

River

PENNSYLVANIA
NEW JERSEY

521

Rock View
House

Decker Cem.

714

717

750

751

ROAD

iday Lakes

Mill

732

Brook

REINHARDT

CLOVE
653

PRESERVE

Clove
School

ROAD

Rock Quarry

Church
School

(NATURAL

LANDS TRUST)

1007

ROAD

STEENY

KILL

1200

PARK

JOHN D KUSER

NATURAL AREA

Brook

ROAD

STATE

23

STEENY

KILL

1336

RIDGE

P

Gate

MASHIPACONG

FULLER
TRAIL

LIFE
TRAIL

Steeny Kill
Lake

Nature
Center

Gate

MONUMENT

TRAIL

SHAWANGUNK
RIDGE
TRAIL

AYERS

B

BL

TRAIL

B

P

Gate

Y

Group
Camping
Area

P

Lodge

High
Point

1903

B

RIG

RIG

P O I N T

Gate

Sawmill
Camping
Area

ROAD

Lake Marcia

BRV

TRAIL

OLD

APPALACHIAN

TRAIL

B

Brook

P

BLUE DOT
TRAIL

Sawmill
Lake

B

AT&T
Tower

Gate

Park
Office

W

TRAIL

High Point
Lean-to

Williams Corners

W

ROAD

P

ROAD

P

1622

R

TRAIL

KO

519

GH

P

P

lat

Dutch Shoe
Rock

1519

APPALACHIAN

W

TRAIL

IRIS

Rutherford
Lean-to

Lake
Rutherford
KO

MOUNTAIN

Creek

Magnetic
Declination
12°

P

TRAIL

1423

W

647

BRINK

ROAD

Clove

519

23

Colesville

M o u n t a i n s

To Maine

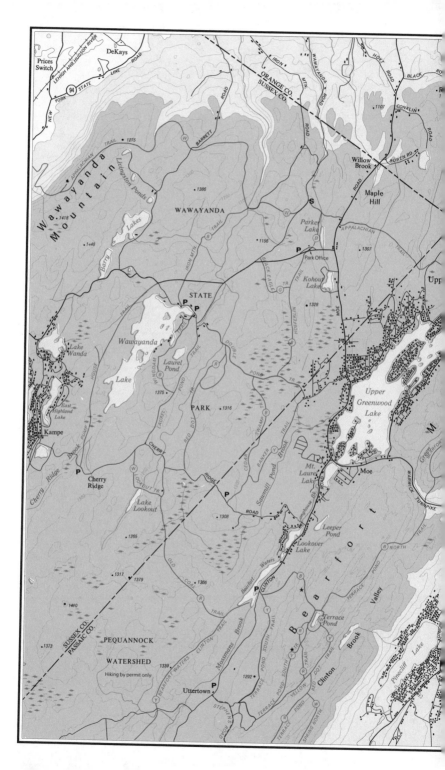

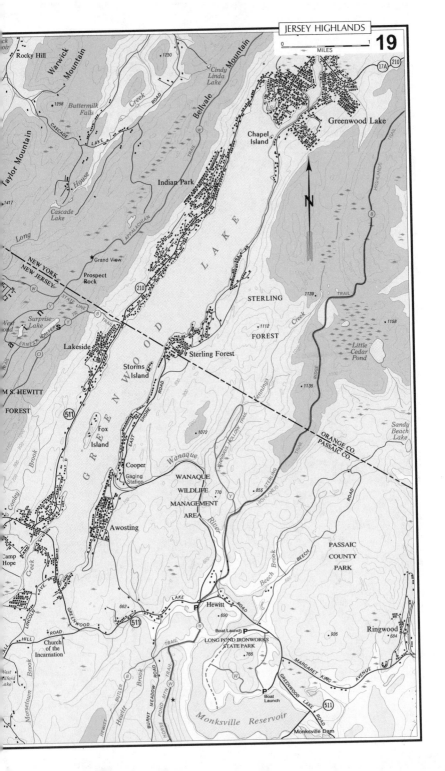

0   MILES   1

17A 210

Rocky Hill

Warwick Mountain

•1230

Cindy Linda Lake

Greenwood Lake

•1258

Buttermilk Falls

Bellvale Mountain

Chapel Island

Taylor Mountain

Indian Park

N

•1417

Cascade Lake

APPALACHIAN TRAIL

Cascade Lake

Grand View

NEW YORK
NEW JERSEY

Prospect Rock

210

STERLING

•1139

HIGHLANDS TRAIL

Surprise Lake

West
ond

STATE LINE TR.

ERNEST WALTER

Lakeside

FOREST

•1112

Little Cedar Pond

•1158

Sterling Forest

Storms Island

G
R
E
E
N
W
O
O
D

L
A
K
E

•1135

Sandy Beach Lake

M.S. HEWITT

FOREST

511

Fox Island

EAST SHORE ROAD

•1072

Hannings

JENNINGS HOLLOW TRAIL

ORANGE CO.
PASSAIC CO.

Cooper

Wanaque

Gaging Station

WANAQUE

•855

STERLING

Cooley

Brook

WILDLIFE

770

MANAGEMENT

HIGHLANDS TRAIL

AREA

BEECH

ROAD

PASSAIC

Awosting

River

COUNTY

PARK

Camp Hope

Creek

Beech Brook

•926

Ringwood

LINCOLN

LAKE

662

Hewitt

•690

•684

GREENWOOD

511

HILL

Boat Launch

P

LONG POND IRONWORKS
STATE PARK

MARGARET KING

Church of the Incarnation

TRAIL

•766

AVENUE

West
ilford
ake

Morsetown

HEWITT

BUTLER

Brook

BURNT MEADOW ROAD

HORSE POND MTN. TRAIL

Boat Launch
P

GREENWOOD
LAKE
ROAD

511

Monksville Reservoir

Monksville Dam

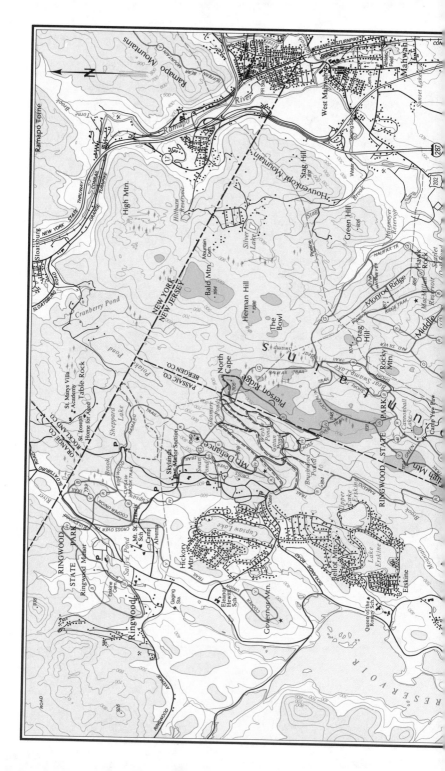

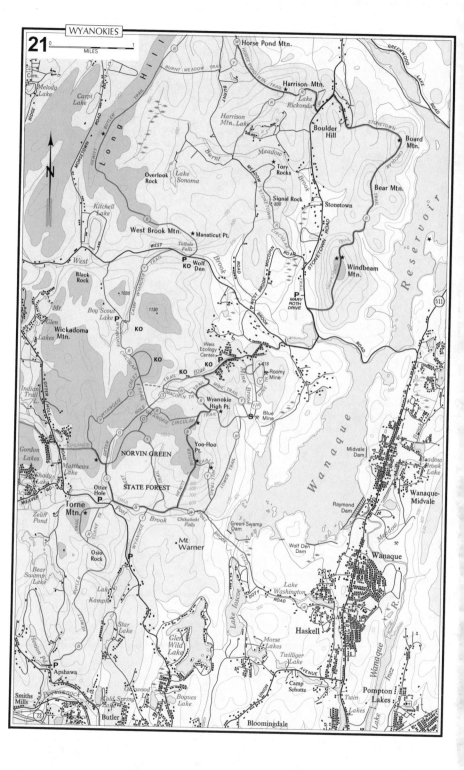

NEW YORK-NEW JERSEY TRAIL CONFERENCE 1920

We invite you to join

the organization of hikers, environmentalists, and volunteers whose tireless efforts produced this edition of the *New Jersey Walk Book*.

Since our founding in 1920, the **New York-New Jersey Trail Conference's** mission has been to provide the public with the opportunity to directly experience nature and, by doing so, help preserve the region's environmental integrity. The Conference's three-pronged approach— protection, stewardship, and education—is achieved largely through the efforts of volunteers.

Join now and as a member:

■ You will receive the *Trail Walker*, a bi-monthly source of news, information, and events concerning area trails and hiking. The *Trail Walker* lists hikes throughout the New York-New Jersey region by many of our 88 member hiking clubs.

■ You are entitled to purchase our authoritative maps and books at *significant discounts*. Our highly accurate trail maps, printed on durable Tyvek, and our informative guidebooks enable you to hike with assurance in the New York-New Jersey metropolitan region.

■ In addition, you are entitled to discounts of 10% (and sometimes more!) at most local outdoor stores and many mountain inns and lodges.

■ Most importantly, you will become part of a community of volunteer activists with similar passions and dreams.

Your membership helps give us the clout to protect and maintain more trails. As a member of the **New York-New Jersey Trail Conference,** you will be helping to ensure that public access to nature will continue to expand.

NEW YORK-NEW JERSEY TRAIL CONFERENCE

156 Ramapo Valley Road ❖ Mahwah, NJ 07430 ❖ (201) 512-9348
www.nynjtc.org info@nynjtc.org

Other Hiking Books Available From the Trail Conference!

Authoritative Hiking Maps and Books
by the Volunteers Who Maintain the Trails

CIRCUIT HIKES IN NORTHERN NEW JERSEY

Fifth Edition (2003) Bruce Scofield
Revised and expanded, the author describes 25 hikes in the New Jersey Highlands that can be walked without the need for a car shuttle or significant retracing of steps.
sc. 176 pgs., 4¾ x 6¾, B&W photos and maps.

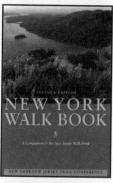

NEW YORK WALK BOOK

Seventh Edition (2001) Edited by Daniel Chazin
Illustrations by Jack Fagan and Robert L. Dickinson
"Indispensable reference to trails in New York State from Long Island to Albany. The hikers' "Bible" since 1923." *The New York Times*, 10/26/2001. Significant additions and revisions to sections on geology, Catskills, Sterling Forest, Shawangunk Ridge and Schunemunk Mountain, as well as new sketches.
sc. 474 pgs., 5⅜ x 8⅛, B&W illus., full color maps.

DAY WALKER:
32 hikes in the New York Metro Area

Second Edition (2002)
A collection of 32 walks in the New York metropolitan area for new and experienced hikers. The *Day Walker* presents a sample of walks within 60 miles of the George Washington Bridge, of varying levels of difficulty and most accessible by public transport.
sc. 301 pgs., 5⅜ x 8 ⅛, B&W photos and maps.

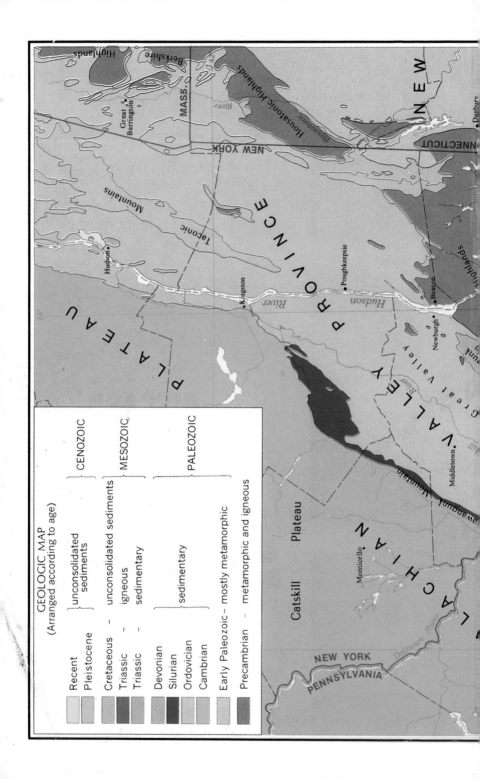

GEOLOGIC MAP
(Arranged according to age)

Recent — unconsolidated sediments — CENOZOIC
Pleistocene

Cretaceous — unconsolidated sediments
Triassic — igneous — MESOZOIC
Triassic — sedimentary

Devonian
Silurian — sedimentary
Ordovician
Cambrian — PALEOZOIC

Early Paleozoic – mostly metamorphic

Precambrian – metamorphic and igneous